Sub-creating Arda:
World-building in J.R.R. Tolkien's Work, its
Precursors and its Legacies

Sub-creating Arda:
World-building in J.R.R. Tolkien's Work, its Precursors and its Legacies

edited by
Dimitra Fimi & Thomas Honegger

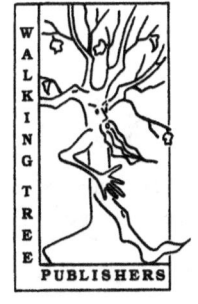

2019

Cormarë Series No. 40

Series Editors:
Peter Buchs • Thomas Honegger • Andrew Moglestue • Johanna Schön • Doreen Triebel

Series Editor responsible for this volume: Thomas Honegger

Library of Congress Cataloguing-in-Publication Data

Dimitra Fimi & Thomas Honegger (eds.):
Sub-creating Arda: World-building in J.R.R. Tolkien's Work, its Precursors and its Legacies
ISBN 978-3-905703-40-5

Subject headings:
Tolkien, J.R.R. (John Ronald Reuel), 1892-1973
World-building
Sub-creation
Fantasy
Interdisciplinary Perspectives
Middle-earth
The Lord of the Rings
The Hobbit
The Silmarillion

Cormarë Series No. 40

First published 2019

© Walking Tree Publishers, Zurich and Jena, 2019

All rights reserved. No portion of this book may be reproduced, by any process or technique, without the express written consent of the publisher

Set in Adobe Garamond Pro and Shannon by Walking Tree Publishers

Cover by Jay Johnstone (copyright by the artist, published by permission of the artist)

Board of Advisors

Academic Advisors

Douglas A. Anderson (independent scholar)

Patrick Curry (independent scholar)

Michael D.C. Drout (Wheaton College)

Vincent Ferré (Université de Paris-Est Créteil UPEC)

Dimitra Fimi (University of Glasgow)

Verlyn Flieger (University of Maryland)

Thomas Fornet-Ponse (Rheinische Friedrich-Wilhelms-Universität Bonn)

Christopher Garbowski (University of Lublin, Poland)

Mark T. Hooker (Indiana University)

Andrew James Johnston (Freie Universität Berlin)

Rainer Nagel (Johannes Gutenberg-Universität Mainz)

Helmut W. Pesch (independent scholar)

Tom Shippey (University of Winchester)

Allan Turner (Friedrich-Schiller-Universität Jena)

Frank Weinreich (independent scholar)

General Readers

Johan Boots

Jean Chausse

Friedhelm Schneidewind

Isaac Juan Tomas

Patrick Van den hole

Johan Vanhecke (Letterenhuis, Antwerp)

Acknowledgments

Many thanks to all those who worked with us to make this volume possible – most prominently, of course, the contributors, but also my co-editor Dimitra Fimi, who proved herself a sagacious, patient and resourceful collaborator on whom I could always rely when tackling the various challenges posed by this project.

A great 'thank you' also to Larissa Zoller and Sophia Mehlhausen who were in charge of the layouting and proofreading of the text, respectively. The stunning cover is the work of Jay Johnstone, whose pictures took the audience by storm when first exhibited at the 2012 Tolkien conference at Loughborough University. He has, since then, continued his artistic exploration of Tolkien's world and the cover is one of his most recent works. Also I want to thank my colleagues at Walking Tree Publishers, Andrew Moglestue, Peter Buchs, and Johanna Schön, who did a great job with the quality management of the layout, the proofing, and who made sure that all the numerous administrative tasks involved in producing a book were taken care of efficiently and responsibly.

Jena, November 2018
Thomas Honegger, Series Editor

Contents

Dimitra Fimi & Thomas Honegger
Introduction — i

Mark J.P. Wolf
Concerning the "Sub" in "Subcreation": The Act of Creating Under — 1

Allan Turner
One Pair of Eyes: Focalisation and Worldbuilding — 17

Massimiliano Izzo
Worldbuilding and Mythopoeia
in Tolkien and post-Tolkienian Fantasy Literature — 31

Péter Kristóf Makai
Beyond Fantastic Self-indulgence: Aesthetic Limits to World-building — 57

N. Trevor Brierly
Worldbuilding Design Patterns in the Works of J.R.R. Tolkien — 93

John Garth
Ilu's Music: The Creation of Tolkien's Creation Myth — 117

Gergely Nagy
On No Magic in Tolkien:
Resisting the Representational Criteria of Realism — 153

Renée Vink
Tolkien the Tinkerer: World-building versus Storytelling — 177

Jonathan Nauman
Composition as Exploration:
Fictional Development in J.R.R. Tolkien's *The Lord of the Rings* — 199

Anahit Behrooz
Temporal Topographies: Mapping the Geological
and Anthropological Effects of Time in J.R.R. Tolkien's Legendarium — 217

Robin Markus Auer
Sundering Seas and Watchers in the Water:
Water as a Subversive Element in Middle-earth — 237

Michaela Hausmann
Lyrics on Lost Lands: Constructing Lost Places
through Poetry in J.R.R. Tolkien's *The Lord of the Rings* — 261

Hamish Williams
Mountain People in Middle-earth: Ecology and the Primitive — 285

Timo Lothmann, Arndt Heilmann, Sven Hintzen
Then Smaug Spoke:
On Constructing the Fantastic via Dialogue in Tolkien's Story Cosmos — 313

Maureen F. Mann
Artefacts and Immersion
in the Worldbuilding of Tolkien and the Brontës — 335

Bradford Lee Eden
Sub-creation by any Other Name:
The Artist and God in the Early Twentieth Century — 359

Kristine Larsen
A Mythology for Poland:
Andrzej Sapkowski's *Witcher* Fantasy Series as a Tolkienian Subcreation — 371

Andrew Higgins
More than Narrative: The Role of Paratexts in the World-building
of Austin Tappan Wright, J.R.R. Tolkien, and Ursula K. Le Guin — 395

Tom Shippey
The Faërie World of Michael Swanwick — 415

Łukasz Neubauer
Absence of gods vs. Absence of God:
The Spiritual Landscapes of J.R.R. Tolkien's
Middle-earth and George R.R. Martin's Westeros — 431

Introduction

Literary sub-creation and world-building are, in many ways, nothing new in the practice of writing fiction, and fantasy literature in particular. Already in the 19th century, George MacDonald was theorizing the creative processes we now call sub-creation and world-building in his essay 'The Fantastic Imagination':

> The natural world has its laws, and no man must interfere with them in the way of presentment any more than in the way of use; but they themselves may suggest laws of other kinds, and man may, if he pleases, invent a little world of his own, with its own laws; for there is that in him which delights in calling up new forms – which is the nearest, perhaps, he can come to creation. […] His world once invented, the highest law that comes next into play is, that there shall be harmony between the laws by which the new world has begun to exist; and in the process of his creation, the inventor must hold by those laws. The moment he forgets one of them, he makes the story, by its own postulates, incredible. (314-15)

MacDonald's essay already prefigures Tolkien's understanding of sub-creation in quasi-theological terms in his seminal essay 'On Fairy-stories'. Tolkien talks about creating a 'Secondary World' (a term that is now standard in literary criticism and theory on fantasy literature) as a natural artistic imitation of God's demiurgic act in creating our Primary World (*TOFS* 64-6). But MacDonald also points to the cornerstones of world-building: an invented world needs 'laws' which should exist in 'harmony' – again, very much prefiguring Tolkien's key point about the need of 'inner consistency of reality' in Secondary Worlds (59-60).

But both sub-creation and world-building, whether seen as distinct but complementary, or as roughly synonymous concepts, are certainly the focus of a new interest in academic scholarship. The turning point was Mark J.P. Wolf's 2012 monograph *Building Imaginary Worlds: The Theory and History of Subcreation*, which argued for a shift of focus from narrative as the default centre of academic attention, to the many (often paratextual) elements of world-building as worthy of studying in their own right. Wolf provided a solid framework for the analysis of imaginary worlds centred on 'secondary world infrastructures' apart from narrative, namely maps, timelines, genealogies, nature, culture, language, mythology, and philosophy (Wolf 154-97). Of course, these categories are not meant to be taken as rigidly prescriptive, but as a kind of 'grammar' for secondary worlds, admitting exceptions to the rules. Wolf's contribution also brought together texts from different periods and genres, united by world-building practices: from early modern utopias and travellers' tales, to fantasy and science fiction, all the way to transmedial franchise focusing on superheroes or intergalactic empires.

This volume has taken up this shift towards literary sub-creation and world-building as worthy subjects of academic discourse. Locating Tolkien's work as a paradigmatic example of these processes, it seeks to illuminate hitherto neglected aspects of his sub-creation, but also to open up the debate of theorizing world-building and sub-creation, and exploring other writer's world-building via a Tolkienian lens. The essays in this volume are a clear sign of the growing popularity of sub-creation and worldbuilding as a subject of scholarly examination in the academic discourses across the humanities and beyond. Accordingly, the Call for Papers and our inquiries with experts in the field yielded more than thirty proposals, out of which we selected, in co-operation with members of the Board of Advisors, a score of papers that fall into three large categories. The first five deal with theoretical aspects of literary world-building, while the nine contributions in the second section focus on Tolkien's work. The final six essays, then, open up the discussion towards other authors.

The pride of place for the opening paper goes, for good reasons, to Mark J.P. Wolf's theoretical exploration of the concept of sub-creation. In follow-up essay to his influential monograph, he discusses the possibilities and limits of inventing new worlds by means of manipulating or changing the different aspects of a world ('realms') and tries to answer the question of how distant a sub-created world can be from a real one. He thus provides the general theoretical framework for many of the essays in the subsequent sections that also deal with this topic but with focus on the works of specific authors. Allan Turner's essay approaches the question of how an author creates a world through language differently. Turner looks at the crucial role of focalisation in a literary text and compares Tolkien's use of this technique in world-building to that of Sir Walter Scott's in two of his historical novels – according to the motto 'the past is a foreign country' (or better 'foreign world'). Massimiliano Izzo, then, investigates the qualitative differences between the related yet not identical concepts of mythopoetic sub-creation and the more technical world-building. The latter differs from the narrative-centred sub-creation especially when it focuses on the details of Secondary World economics, politics, or logistics. Tolkien, Izzo argues, succeeded in creating a balance between these two elements in his The Lord of the Rings, whereas other authors often erred by putting too much emphasis on either of the two aspects. The essay by Péter Kristóf Makai explores a similar topic by undertaking a critical evaluation of the widespread contemporary emphasis on world-building, which happens often at the expense of the more traditional narrative techniques such as improving the plausibility of a protagonist's actions or the careful construction of the story arc – to the detriment of the entire work. Lastly, N. Trevor Brierly adapts the concept of 'design pattern' from architecture and software engineering and provides a discussion of and an overview of such 'design patterns' in Tolkien's works and their use in his world-building.

The second section opens with John Garth's in-depth investigation of hitherto largely unsubstantiated speculations as to early influences and inspirational sources for Tolkien's 'The Music of the Ainur'. His essay reads a bit like a literary-historical 'whodunnit' with Garth as the brilliant sleuth presenting the evidence bit by bit and, in the end, proposing a new potential chronology for Tolkien's creation myth. While Garth focuses on one relatively short period of Tolkien's work, Gergely Nagy takes a wider view and discusses Tolkien's non-use of magic in the continuous development of his secondary world. He argues that the increasing avoidance of magic led to a greater stress on the mythopoetic aspect, which constitutes Tolkien's own answer to the challenge of the ideology of realism.

Both Garth's and Nagy's papers have the early and, in Nagy's case, also the middle stages of creation at the centre of their attention. This is complemented by the contributions by Renée Vink and Jonathan Nauman, respectively, that take up the question of the relationship between 'storytelling' and 'world-building' specifically in the middle and the later phases of Tolkien's work. Nauman's paper looks closely at the interaction between character development and world-building during the writing of *The Lord of the Rings*, whereas Vink's discussion of the creative process also takes the creative phases before and especially after Tolkien's opus magnum into consideration. The evidence, Vink concludes, points in the direction of a greater preoccupation with questions of world-building towards the end of Tolkien's life.

The following four papers all select one specific aspect of world-building and discuss its connection to and implications for a larger context. Anahit Behrooz analyses the status and function of maps. She demonstrates that they do not merely function as representational tools capturing and fixating the landscape, but that they also represent the passage of time and are thus connected with broader questions surrounding change and loss. A similarly 'connecting' function is argued for the element of water, which is the subject of Robin Auer's contribution. He discusses the obvious and less obvious occurrences of water in Tolkien's works and shows how the liquid element is essential to the unfolding of the story of Middle-earth and pervades the different stages of development.

Tolkien's work is characterised by what Tom Shippey once called 'Beowulfian depth', which is created by means of digressions and allusions to stories and events outside the narrative proper. Poems about 'lost places' such as Valinor or Beleriand, as Michaela Hausmann argues, fulfil a similar function and add depth to world-building. The paper by Hamish Williams links the mountains as a very concrete habitat of various peoples with their characterisation as ethnic groups. He presents the ethno-topographic theories that have determined the perception of peoples since antiquity, traces their lasting influence into the first half of the twentieth century and their use as elements for world-building. Finally, Timo Lothmann, Arndt Heilmann and Sven Hintzen use corpus-analytical tools and a cognitive approach for an exemplary analysis of the dialogic interaction between Bilbo and Smaug and the potential world-building function of dialogues. Their use of linguistic methodology complements, to some extent the more general approach presented by Allan Turner in his paper on focalisation.

The third section gathers all those papers that look at the concrete world-building and sub-creation in authors other than Tolkien or compare them to the Professor's approach. Maureen Mann opens the series with an investigation into the prolonged and multi-dimensional world-building of the Brontë siblings. She compares this little-known aspect of the Brontës's creativity with Tolkien's creation of an immersive imaginary world, highlighting thus similarities and differences. Mann's in-depth exploration of 19th century world-building is followed by Bradford Lee Eden's more generalizing overview of the relationship between God and the artist in the works and thoughts of a number of late nineteen- and early twenty-century writers and philosophers, many of whom were contemporaries of Tolkien's or are known to have influenced him one way or another. Eden's essay thus provides a helpful sketch of the wider intellectual and philosophical framework within which Tolkien's own ideas on world-building developed and may inspire future research into the topics sketched.

Kristine Larsen's contribution, then, stands at the head of the group of papers that discuss post-Tolkien world-building. She takes a closer look at Andrzej Sapkowski's *Witcher* fantasy series as an example of a contemporary work that produced a detailed and self-contained secondary world and an (almost) successful sub-created mythology for Poland. Andrew Higgins takes paratextual elements such as maps, genealogies, and invented languages from the works of Austin Tappan Wright, J.R.R. Tolkien, and Ursula K. Le Guin in order to explore and compare their functions in their respective world-building projects. The enigmatic list of sprites and supernatural beings in *The Denham Tracts* that has been identified as the possible source for the word 'hobbit' is also one of the inspirations for Michael Swanwick's novels. Tom Shippey provides a knowledgeable introduction to Swanwick's very idiosyncratic take on traditional folklore in general and to faërie in particular and pays homage to the world-building talent of this often-neglected author. The volume concludes with Lukasz Neubauer's comparative exploration of the spiritual-religious landscapes of Tolkien and Martin respectively – two authors who share a Catholic background yet put their knowledge to very different use. We are all quite curious to see how Martin's Secondary World is going to escape the apocalyptic winter-ending that threatens the Known World, and it is likely that this won't be due to the intercession of any of the numerous gods and goddesses. Tolkien's Middle-earth, by contrast, will finally participate in the biblical apocalypse and thus exist 'until the dragon comes' (BMC 34).

Glasgow & Jena, November 2018
Dimitra Fimi & Thomas Honegger

Abbreviations

BMC   TOLKIEN, J.R.R. 'Beowulf: The Monsters and the Critics.' *The Monsters and the Critics and Other Essays*. Ed. Christopher Tolkien. London: HarperCollins, 1997. 5-48.

TOFS TOLKIEN, J.R.R. *Tolkien On Fairy-stories*. Ed. Verlyn Flieger and Douglas A. Anderson. London: HarperCollins, 2008.

Bibliography

MACDONALD, George. *A Dish of Orts: Chiefly Papers on the Imagination, and on Shakespeare*. London: Low, 1893.

WOLF, Mark J. *Building Imaginary Worlds. The Theory and History of Subcreation*. New York: Routledge, 2012.

Mark J.P. Wolf

Concerning the "Sub" in "Subcreation": The Act of Creating Under

Abstract

Subcreation is the term Tolkien used to differentiate the creations of human beings to the *ex nihilio* creation of God. Because we exist within God's creation, we can only "create under" (or subcreate) the restrictions which it places on us and our imaginations. Whatever we do not invent in a subcreated world uses defaults from the real world; but how far can human beings subcreate a world? How many world defaults can be changed, and just how far can a subcreated world be from the real world? This essay explores and attempts to answer exactly these questions.

Introducion

As a Roman Catholic philologist who was increasingly aware of the philosophical implications of his writing and world-building, J. R. R. Tolkien made the distinction early on between the kind of creation that human authors and world-builders do, and God's *ex nihilo* (from nothing) creation. Human beings, created in the image of God, also have a desire to create, but such creative activity differs in both degree and kind from *ex nihilo* creative power, since it uses the existing concepts and ideas found in our world (the "Primary World") and recombines them in the building of an imaginary (or "secondary") world; thus, human creation is "creating under" or in Tolkien's term, "subcreating", within God's Creation. A secondary world, then relies on the Primary World for its raw materials, as well as for whatever elements and features make it able to be understood by, and related to, an audience. And because invention in a secondary world resets Primary World defaults, a secondary world relies on Primary World defaults for anything that is not specifically replaced or reinvented within the secondary world.

So secondary worlds, then, can be seen as versions of the Primary World in which things have been added, subtracted, or changed, and the more changes that are made, the more invention occurs, the more "secondary" the world becomes. When enough is changed, we have what appears to be a new world, different from our own, an imaginary world. This, of course, raises the question, just how different can a secondary world be from the Primary World? To what degree can subcreating be done? If one were to try to subcreate a world with as *little* reliance on Primary World defaults as possible, how far could one go, and what might such a world be like? While designing an imaginary world, couldn't one simply keep locating Primary World defaults and changing them, until no such defaults remain?

To begin the exploration of the extreme reaches of subcreative possibility, we could begin with the various levels of invention which I have written about elsewhere, the *nominal, cultural, natural,* and *ontological*.[1] Invention which changes the *nominal* realm merely gives new names to existing things; taken to an extreme, this is essentially the making of a new language, which renames existing things. Although it has the potential to cast a new light on the things it names, by emphasizing certain aspects about them or relating them to each in new ways through linguistic similarities, the level of actual invention is somewhat shallow compared to the other levels.

Invention which changes the *cultural* realm deals with all things made by humans (or other creatures), and in which new objects, artifacts, technologies, customs, institutions, ideas, and so forth appear. Much subcreation falls within this realm, and is what allows a secondary world depicted in audiovisual media to have a distinct appearance and style, including costumes, art, architecture, food, technology, and so forth, and distinct sounds as well (like the hum of lightsabers in the Star Wars galaxy, or the sound of the transporter beam in the Star Trek galaxy). Invented terms can also indicate new cultural concepts, such as J. R. R. Tolkien's "mathom" or Philip K. Dick's "kipple".[2] Since a wide range of cultural designs and artifacts can be found in the Primary World, there is a great latitude

---

1 See Wolf (2012: 35-37).
2 Tolkien wrote, "anything that Hobbits had no immediate use for, but were unwilling to throw away, they called a *mathom*." (*LotR* 5); while Dick (1990: 57) wrote, "Kipple is useless objects, like junk mail or match folders after you use the last match or gum wrappers or yesterday's homeopape. When nobody's around, kipple reproduces itself."

for invention, especially when one considers that even in the Primary World, such things need not be practical or necessary in order to exist.

Beyond the *cultural* realm, invention in the *natural* realm changes nature itself, and includes new land masses, planets, plants and animals, entire ecosystems, and other aspects of the natural world itself which are changed or invented by an author. Invention in the natural realm will often still rely on designs or conventions found in the Primary World; for example, a unicorn is an invented animal, but its appearance is like that of a horse, except for its single horn. New plants and animals are usually based on combined features of existing plants and animals, so as to give them plausible zoological or biological explanations. On a larger scale, inventions may include new planetary forms, such as the worlds of Larry Niven's *Ringworld* series or Terry Pratchett's *Discworld* series, which have planets shaped like rings and discs, respectively. Although elements of the natural world are changed at this level, the resulting inventions are still usually designed so that their existence might be considered plausible with the universe we know.

The next level, the *ontological* realm, determines the parameters of a world's existence, that is, the materiality and laws of physics, space, time, and so forth that constitute the world, and which can differ from the universe of the Primary World. For example, the worlds of Edwin Abbott's *Flatland* (1884) and A. K. Dewdney's *The Planiverse* (1984) are both set in universes with only two spatial dimensions, which automatically make them quite different from the universe of three spatial dimensions in which we live. Such worlds, though very different from our own, are still often connected in some way to the Primary World, whether through portals, communication technologies, or other devices or conventions; and much of their content is similar, though often by analogy. Alan Lightman's *Einstein's Dreams* also features vignettes of universes in which time and space behave differently, reflecting philosophically on each one, and together they are connected to our world as a series of dreams that Einstein has while working on his theories. Some common science fiction conventions, including faster-than-light travel, other dimensions, time travel, and wormholes used for interstellar travel, usually imply laws of physics that are different than those currently understood, though the full consequences of such differences are sometimes not carried out in the design of the worlds that use them. Because the consequences of ontological changes are so vast and all-encompassing, relatively few worlds are subcreated at this depth to the degree they could be; many choose to simply use conventions as accepted solutions for problems like space travel over long distances.

Changes on the natural and even ontological levels are possible due to the way familiar concepts can be recombined. Tolkien noted that the separation of adjectives and nouns made this possible in literature:

> When we can take green from grass, blue from heaven, and red from blood, we have already an enchanter's power – upon one plane; and the desire to wield that power in the world external to our minds awakes. It does not follow that we shall use that power well upon any plane. We may put a deadly green on a man's face and produce a horror; we may make the rare and terrible blue moon to shine; or we may cause woods to spring with silver leaves and rams to wear fleeces of gold, and put hot fire into the belly of the cold worm. But in such 'fantasy', as it is called, new form is made … Man becomes a sub-creator.[3]

Authors subcreating in the ontological realm can go even farther than combining colors with objects, using the concept of color itself to create new colors that do not exist in the Primary World; such as "jale" and "ulfire" (due to the blue sun in David Lindsay's *A Voyage to Arcturus* (1920)), "rej" in Philip K. Dick's *Galactic Pot-Healer* (1969), or "octarine", the "color of magic" in Terry Pratchett's *Discworld* universe. Some colors may not be given a name; as Raymond King Cummings writes in *The Girl in the Golden Atom* (1922), "Her lips were full and of a color for which in English there is no name. It would have been red doubtless by sunlight in the world above, but here in this silver light of phosphorescence, the color red, as we see it, was impossible."[4] Naturally, all of these new colors occur in novels rather than audiovisual media, since they would otherwise have to actually be visualized. Other worlds that have different laws of physics are also best left to nonvisual media, such as the world of Greg Egan's *The Clockwork Rocket* (2011) where light has no universal speed. On the other hand, some films visually depict such things like travel through other dimensions, as in *Doctor Strange* (2016), while some video game worlds let players experience alternative physical laws, like the negative gravity in some

---

3 *TOFS* 41-42.
4 Cummings, 'The City of Arite.' Chapter XIX of *The Girl in the Golden Atom* (1922).

of the "universes" in *Gravitar* (1982), the non-Euclidean wraparound space of *Asteroids* (1979), or the user-generated spatial connections of *Portal* (2007).

But all of these worlds, different as they may be, are still worlds in which stories are set. In worlds where many of the Primary World defaults have been changed, even at the natural and ontological levels, there are still a number of connections and similarities to the Primary World that a secondary world must retain, in order to be a successful vehicle for stories which engage audiences and remain a place to which they can still relate in some manner.

Secondary Worlds and Storytelling

As more and more Primary World defaults are changed in the realms just described above, the resulting secondary worlds grow ever-farther away from the Primary World in similarity, leading one to ask what the minimum requirements are for a world, if it is still to contain compelling stories which are relatable to audiences. These elements are reducible to four elements necessary for relatability: structures and experiences which are analogous to those of the Primary World; plausible cause-and-effect relationships; a moral dimension to choices, behavior, and outcomes; and emotional realism.

The first of these four elements lays the ground work for the other three. In order for a narrative to be relatable, it must be analogous to Primary World experiences, so that audiences have some way to map the narrative onto their own experiences. We can relate to characters like Luke Skywalker or Frodo Baggins because we can find similarities in their experiences to our own, even though their worlds differ greatly from ours. Even nonanthropomorphic characters and the stories told about them can become engaging and relatable, if enough analogous connections exist; for example, the lives of the rabbits in Richard Adams's *Watership Down* (1972), or all the animals in Beatrix Potter stories. One could even tell stories about diaphanous gasbag creatures that live in the atmospheric layers of Jupiter; coming-of-age stories about younger gasbags leaving their parents, stories of courtship and reproduction, conflicts of warring groups competing with each other for resources or territory, and stories of sacrifice and loss as lives end. Physically, such creatures and their environment are far from anything like human beings on Earth, yet socially and emotionally, there may be enough analogous experience to keep an audience engaged, though bringing out the similarities that create the analogies may be difficult. Thus, many such fantastic stories rely on conventions and narrative tropes to make themselves relatable, sometimes resulting in stories that are too well-known and overdone. We might refer to these basic requirements for such analogies as *space, time,* and *character*; in other words, *someone* who is *somewhere* doing *something*. Or, more particularly, *beings* living in an *environment* using *resources*, from which some kind of narrative goal or conflict can develop. For these to develop, we need the second element, plausible cause-and-effect relationships.

Causality, connecting actions and their consequences in predictable, repeatable ways, allows characters to exhibit teleological behavior and work toward goals; one has to have some sense of what consequences one's actions will have if one is to plan to accomplish anything. These connections should also be plausible, at least within the world's own ontological rules and laws of physics, even if they are different from those of the Primary World; we might accept that a space station's superlaser can cause a planet to completely explode (as opposed to merely burning a hole through it, as one might more reasonably expect), but we are not likely, even in the most outlandish science fiction story, to accept a hand-held gun that is able to destroy a whole galaxy with one shot.[5] Cause-and-effect relationships presume physical laws of some kind, and spatial and temporal dimensions in which actions occur and cause reactions and other kinds of consequences. Again, these can be quite different than those of the Primary World, but they are conceptually similar. A.K. Dewdney's Planiverse has only two spatial dimensions, which change the nature of wave dissipation through space; sound, light, and gravity diminish less over distances because they are spreading within a two-dimensional space instead of a three-dimensional space.[6] The concept of wave dissipation, however, remains the same, and the same mathematics are applied to both the Primary World and the secondary world of the Planiverse; and as a re-

---

5 The superlaser reference is, of course, referring to the Death Star space stations of the Star Wars galaxy. Since the diameter of the superlaser beam appears to be smaller than a city, at least, one would expect it to drill a hole through a planet-sized body; yet the planets it strikes explode as if made entirely of flammable materials.
6 See Dewdney (2001: 110).

sult, predictable behaviors, and casuality, remain. Of course, causality often cannot entirely explain the actions of sentient beings, and characters can be so different that they are not understood by the audience or other human characters in the secondary world. A good example of this is the sentient ocean in Stanisław Lem's *Solaris* (1961), which the story's scientists know is intelligent even though they are unable to find a way to communicate with it, even by the novel's end.

A predictable set of plausible cause-and-effect relationships not only means that characters can plan ahead, guessing the outcomes of their actions, but that characters can choose actions with either more desirable or less desirable outcomes, or even outcomes which hurt other characters. Thus we come to the third element, a moral dimension to choices, behavior, and outcomes. Without a sense of right and wrong, characters' actions would have no meaning, and stories would have no purpose. Scottish author George MacDonald recognized this in 'The Fantastic Imagination', the Introduction to *The Light Princess and other Fairy Tales* (1893: 424-25), where he examined how laws are used to form an internally-consistent imaginary world, and the role of moral laws within one as well:

> The natural world has its laws, and no man must interfere with them in the way of presentment any more than in the way of use; but they themselves may suggest laws of other kinds, and man may, if he pleases, invent a little world of his own, with its own laws; for there is that in him which delights in calling up new forms – which is the nearest, perhaps, he can come to creation. When such forms are new embodiments of old truths, we call them products of the Imagination; when they are mere inventions, however lovely, I should call them the work of Fancy; in either case, Law has been diligently at work.
>
> His world once invented, the highest law that comes next into play is, that there shall be harmony between the laws by which the new world has begun to exist; and in the process of his creation, the inventor must hold by those laws. The moment he forgets one of them, he makes the story, by its own postulates, incredible. To be able to live a moment in an imagined world, we must see the laws of its existence obeyed. Those broken, we fall out of it. The imagination in us, whose exercise is essential to the most temporary submission to the imagination of another, immediately, with the disappearance of Law, ceases to act. [...] A man's inventions may be stupid or clever, but if he does not hold by the laws of them, or if he makes one law jar with another, he contradicts himself as an inventor, he is no artist. He does not rightly

consort his instruments, or he tunes them in different keys… Obeying law, the maker works like his creator; not obeying law, he is such a fool as heaps a pile of stones and calls it a church.

In the moral world it is different: there a man may clothe in new forms, and for this employ his imagination freely, but he must invent nothing. He may not, for any purpose, turn its laws upside down. He must not meddle with the relations of live souls. The laws of the spirit man must hold, alike in this world and in any world he may invent. It were no offence to suppose a world in which everything repelled instead of attracted the things around it; it would be wicked to write a tale representing a man it called good as always doing bad things, or a man it called bad as always doing good things: the notion itself is absolutely lawless. In physical things a man may invent; in moral things he must obey – and take their laws with him into his invented world as well.

Wicked though it may be, it is possible "to write a tale representing a man it called good as always doing bad things, or a man it called bad as always doing good things"; but even in such a story, there is still a sense of right and wrong, even if the characters' notions of them disagree with right and wrong as understood by the audience. Characters can have a faulty moral compass or act lawlessly, but the notions of right and wrong still exist in the secondary world, and are even what make such things possible. It means that what characters do matters. Likewise, outcomes are also valued as good or bad, and affect the meaning of the story, character arcs, and how the audience responds to the story.

Finally, emotional realism is built on all the other elements, and determines to what degree the emotions felt by the characters will be shared by the audience who identify with them. Emotions may have different or new forms of expression, or even be suppressed (as with *Star Trek*'s Vulcans), but they must be present to seem degree in character interactions, to evoke empathy or sympathy. A character's actions and reactions must be solidly based on his or her emotional makeup; the more we know about the character, the more nuanced their emotional states need to be. If we do not feel that the character is acting as we would act in a similar situation, identification may become lessened or even lost; instead, we may even grow angry that the character is making choices which seem foolish or stupid, and thus consider the character, and perhaps even the story, unrealistic – or at least badly written. While many other implausible elements are accepted – some perhaps grudgingly, simply because the audience likes the characters or the world – a lack of emotional realism will leave an audience cold and without an emotional connection to the world or its action.

Most imaginary worlds exist because they are the settings in which the author's stories are told, so a story's success or failure often means success or failure for the world as well. In many cases, the world is only there to support the story, and world-building is a background activity, allowing storytelling to remain in the foreground of the audience's experience. At times, however, world-building may overtake storytelling. In worlds designed primarily for entertainment (like James Cameron's Pandora in *Avatar* (2009)), for satirical purposes (like Samuel Butler's *Erewhon*), for the purpose of scientific speculation (like A. K. Dewdney's Planiverse), or for thought experiments of a philosophical nature (like those of Alan Lightman's *Einstein's Dreams* (1992)) or a political or social nature (like Thomas More's *Utopia*), exposition regarding the peculiarities of a secondary world can completely overtake narrative, reducing it to little more than a frame story. In many video games, narrative also becomes a way of providing a context for the games' action, and is relatively thin and simple, compared to the richly-detailed three-dimensional worlds where many games now take place.

So what if a world-builder is not all that concerned about whether a story works emotionally, or whether it works at all? Or even if there is any story at all? Video games, for example, can give a player a detailed, immersive sandbox-style world to wander around in, with little or no preplanned narrative; and as long as the world is interesting, this won't even bother many players. Even when a pre-planned story is available, a player may ignore it just to wander around the world, as in *Grand Theft Auto V* (2013), where players can forego the game's missions to simply roam about the world, stealing cars and other vehicles, getting into police chases, and generally creating their own narrative material as they interact with the world. Of course, this then becomes a replacement narrative of sorts; but one can also just wander around as an observer, with little or no concern for the absence of a storyline.

Secondary Worlds Beyond Storytelling

Once we eliminate the requirements for narrative as described above, we are free to replace even more world defaults, subcreating even further away from the Primary World template. We may have stories which no longer are as engaging, with characters like the sentient ocean of Solaris, whom we cannot understand or relate to; and perhaps even the cause-and-effect relationships are abstracted to such a degree that they are bewildering. Or perhaps there is really no story or narrative structure at all, just information about a world.

Without a narrative, a work depicting a world can be structured as a collection of smaller texts, like an encyclopedia or an atlas, or even something more experimental, like Luigi Serafini's *Codex Seraphinianus* (1981), a profusely-illustrated 360-page book written in an untranslated made-up language that is designed to look like a scientific treatise describing the flora, fauna, inventions, and civilizations of an unnamed imaginary world. With an unreadable text, one can only browse and speculate, and the book's many strange and whimsical images do not entirely come together to suggest a complete and consistent world on their own, which appears to be part of the author's design, since speculation plays such a large part of the experience of the book.

At this point in the journey into deeper and deeper subcreating, the nature of the world defaults being changed also begins to change. Most of the changes described in the previous section involve the material, physical aspects of the world, and sometimes additional concepts, but leave much of the Primary World's *conceptual* realm intact. We may see a wide variety of vehicles and weapons in science fiction, but the conceptual categories of *vehicles* and *weapons* remains the same, and helps the audience relate to the world. Even in the *Codex Seraphinianus*, conceptual categories from the Primary World (such as *plant, animal, food, clothing,* and *shelter*) still remain in use, and give many of the book's images the little relatability that they have. In order to subcreate even further away from the Primary World, the changed defaults, then, must move from the physical and perceptual realm into the conceptual realm; and the *Codex* does this in some places, by providing objects which appear to blur the boundaries of conceptual categories; creatures that appear to be part plant, part animal, and part vehicle (with wheels growing out of them), and other objects with no apparent use or Primary World analogs. Events are also depicted which have no clear purpose, and which mix beings, machines, and raw materials together in ways that make them difficult to categorize. This is a good part of the book's creativity; the images, which are forced to stand on their own due to the unintelligible text, seem like they are often deliberately designed to cross conceptual boundaries and try to present things which are as startlingly inexplicable as possible. Yet, many drawings hint at or contain recognizable bits and pieces from the Primary World – an eyeball here, part of an alligator head there, droplets of liquid transforming into something else – enough for the book to still be engaging visually, regardless of the viewer's own cultural background.

Our next step, then, would be to try to subcreate a world like that of the *Codex*, but one in which we remove even those little details that come from the Primary World, as well as any conceptual categories that indicate purpose, function, and use, or even such binary oppositions as *animate* versus *inanimate*. We could eliminate all written text, and make all the imagery appearing entirely abstract (at least from a human point of view), even though it would be, at the same time, completely representative of the world being depicted. But would such a book or film made up of such imagery even be identifiable as a world? We get brief glimpses of such places in films like *2001: A Space Odyssey* (1968) and *Doctor Strange* (2016) when their main characters fly through interdimensional portals, and are surrounding by patterns of light and colorful, moving abstractions representing other worlds beyond what we know. The weirdness and unexplainedness of these places is exactly what the filmmaker wants, to disorient the audience as much as possible and show something which is not understandable. But these are relatively brief glimpses, and we still have a main character passing through who is a human, and the alien intelligences contacting the human characters in both films give them recognizable things to work with; in *2001*, David Bowman finds himself in a strange bedroom with Louis XVI décor and renaissance sculptures and paintings, while Doctor Strange lands and walks on a planetary surface while Dormammu, ruler of the "Dark Dimension", appears to him as an anthropomorphic face and converses with him in English. A world without such connections, without recognizable objects or narrative material, completely unfamiliar and abstract (to us) would be hard to maintain longer than a glimpse, and would we even be able to recognize it as a world?

Hitting the Glass Ceiling of Subcreative Possibilities

At this point, it becomes increasingly difficult to identify and continue changing the remaining Primary World defaults, either because we do not know what to change them to, or because we are not even fully aware of them all, having taken them for granted as the only possible way something can be. It is sometimes said that mathematics must be the same in all parts of the universe, which makes it a possible bridge to alien cultures, being something we would share in common with them.[7] Some theorists even go so far as to say that mathematics would have to be the same in *any universe*, regardless of how different that universe is from our own; but this says more about our ability to conceptualize than it does about math. Just because we cannot conceptualize or imagine something does not mean that it cannot exist; it would rather arrogant to suggest that the universe must be limited to containing only those things which human beings are able to detect and understand.

If we are depicting an imaginary world, then we still have default concepts such as *beings* (or in authorial terms, characters) who exist within a *time* and *space*. We could drop the idea of characters, imagining an empty universe devoid of any sentient beings, similar to the early universe before life existed within it. But the notions of *space* and *time* do seem to be particularly hard to do without; we can reduce space to two or even one dimensions, but even lines and points are always depicted as having some visible form, instead of the infinitesimally small and featureless mathematical objects that they are supposed to be. Likewise, we can imagine different types of time, or configurations of variations of time, running at different speeds, or backwards, but there is always some idea of time involved (even frozen time), just as depictions of points and lines al-

---

7 See, for example, Martin Rees, 'Mathematics: the only true universal language.'

ways take up some amount of actual space, instead of being infinitesimally small. What it would be like to have *no* space or *no* time is unimaginable to beings like us familiar only with spatiotemporal existence.

Theologically speaking, as the Creator of the universe and of the space and time that make it up, God is not subject to space and time, and exists outside their bounds.[8] Angels, devils (which are fallen angels), departed souls, Heaven, and Hell likewise exist outside the spatiotemporal universe we live in, existing in what we sometimes refer to as the Eternal. Yet we cannot help imagining even these things as existing within spatiotemporal dimensions; the Eternal is imagined as time that just keeps on continuing, and Heaven and Hell as places which angels or devils are depicted occupying in crowds, along with the souls of the departed. They are, for the most part depicted as extensions of the only existence we know, but in extreme degrees and durations.

Although we can posit these things and imagine being outside of time and space, exactly what that means or what it would be like is beyond our grasp, limited as we are to our current spatiotemporal existence. Try as we might, we can only imagine such things by way of analogy, reflecting our experience in the Primary World. Even if we can recognize the concepts of *time* and *space* and *matter* and *energy* (the last two of which are really two forms of the same thing, as Einstein showed) as defaults that are not necessary to Creation (that is to say, God could create a universe without them), we cannot imagine what the alternatives might be. Not only can we not create *ex nihilo* the way God can, then, but we are limited to create within – or "under" – the current universe in which we live, and our own creations will always necessarily reflect those limitations to some extent. (At least while we are still here on earth; if the subcreative urge in human beings is one way in which we are created in the image of God, as Tolkien supposed, then perhaps we will be given new subcreative abilities in the afterlife, something which Tolkien suggests by way of analogy in his short story 'Leaf by Niggle' (1945), which ends with Niggle finding the unfinished painting he was working on complete and no longer just an image but an actual world.)

---

8 Religious belief is not necessary for speculations as to what is "outside" the universe we know; for example, the Many-Worlds Interpretation of Quantum Theory, a form of which was first posited by Hugh Everett in 1957, suggests myriads of parallel universes with alternate histories and futures.

Currently, however, we are inevitably limited in how far we are able to subcreate a secondary world. Far from lamenting our limitations, though, we should be more appreciative of just how amazingly far we *can go*; most worlds still fall short of what can be done, and we have just begun in earnest to scratch the surface of possible worlds and their construction. Of course, some secondary worlds will always be closer to the Primary World in their design, and not all worlds need to be subcreated into the ontological realm in order to convey their ideas or stories. But it is good to know the possibilities are there.

The subcreational act of world-building involves not only making choices between options but also being aware of what options are available, and sometimes the latter can be more difficult than the former. Awareness of defaults, and how they can be changed, necessarily precedes advancements of any kind, be they technological, cultural, or social ones. A healthy subcreative urge can also keep us aware of the possibilities available to us in the Primary World, for its own reshaping, and keep us from falling prey to fatalism and despair; and that alone makes for a better world.

About the Author

MARK J.P. WOLF is a Professor in the Communication Department at Concordia University Wisconsin. He has a Ph.D. (1995) in Critical Studies from the School of Cinematic Arts at the University of Southern California. His books include *Building Imaginary Worlds: The Theory and History of Subcreation* (2012), *Revisiting Imaginary Worlds: A Subcreation Studies Anthology* (2017), *The Routledge Companion to Imaginary Worlds* (2017), eleven books on video games, four other media studies books, and two unpublished novels for which his agent is looking for a publisher. He lives in Wisconsin with his wife Diane and his sons Michael, Christian, and Francis.

Bibliography

CUMMINGS, Raymond King. 'The City of Arite.' Chapter XIX of *The Girl in the Golden Atom* (1922).

DEWDNEY, A. K. *The Planiverse: Computer Contact with a Two-Dimensional World.* New York: Copernicus, 2001.

Dick, Philip K. *Do Androids Dream of Electric Sheep*. (Originally published in 1968), New York: Ballantine Books, 1990.

MacDonald, George. 'The Fantastic Imagination.' In *The Light Princess and other Fairy Tales* (1893). Reprinted in *The Heart of George MacDonald*. Edited by Rolland Hein. Vancouver: Regent College Publishing, 1994.

Rees, Martin. 'Mathematics: the only true universal language.' *New Scientist*, February 11, 2009, available at https://www.newscientist.com/article/mg20126951-800-mathematics-the-only-true-universal-language/.

Tolkien, J.R.R., "On Fairy-stories", reprinted in Verlyn Flieger and Douglas A. Anderson (eds.), *Tolkien On Fairy-stories*, London: HarperCollins.

Tolkien J.R.R. *The Lord of the Rings*. Paperback one-volume edition. Boston and New York: Houghton Mifflin, 1994.

Wolf, Mark J.P. *Building Imaginary Worlds: The Theory and History of Subcreation*. New York: Routledge, 2012.

Allan Turner

One Pair of Eyes: Focalisation and Worldbuilding

Abstract

World-building is often thought of as belonging exclusively to the elaboration of science fiction and fantasy. However, many cognitive linguists see it as the necessary basis for communication through language; every interaction relies on building a mental representation of a personal world or modifying it through dialogue. The conceptualisation of a situation which is not accessible through our own eyes is made possible by the human capability of projection, that is visualising things from a different angle, such as through the eyes of another person. That is why focalisation is such an important narrative technique to help the reader become immersed in fictional events taking place in an unfamilar setting. A different historical period can be almost as unfamiliar as a different world. In this paper I will compare the use of focalisation in Tolkien's world-building with that of Sir Walter Scott's historical novels *Waverley* and *Rob Roy*.

This article is about literary worldbuilding, with the emphasis on the adjective 'literary'. Of course anybody can make up an imaginary world in private, but then they are under no obligation to consider how they will present their world to others within a clear and cogent narrative framework expressed through language. The present study will investigate one technique used in a literary genre, typically a novel, although it might also be a narrative poem, to open up a world unfamiliar to the reader: focalisation, through which the world may be explored through the eyes of a participant in the narrative. I propose to compare the use of focalisation in the worldbuilding of Tolkien with that of Sir Walter Scott's historical novels *Waverley* and *Rob Roy*.

From the point of view of conventional literary criticism it might seem unusual to make a direct comparison across genres in this way, since the historical novel, which represents past events in the real world, and the fantasy novel, which involves beings or powers not observable in our known world, were routinely considered to have a completely different ontological status. However, with more research being devoted to the phenomenon of imaginary worlds, the opinion has been growing that within the sphere of fiction the distinction between the realistic and the imaginary may be scalar rather than absolute. Mark J. P. Wolf has proposed that there are "degrees of subcreation", since there can be wide variations in secondary worlds (that is, any fictional world that is not entirely congruent with the Primary World as we know it), in terms of their relationship and accessiblity to the Primary World in time, space and human experience (25-29). He cites the example of Tolstoy's *War and Peace*, which, although it is built around historical events, nevertheless features invented characters and their equally invented estates.

The categories proposed by Wolf seem to offer a powerful tool for understanding what exactly imaginary worlds are and how they can be created. However, they remain on a very general level, particularly since they cover a number of different media including film and video games, so that their usefulness for the investigation of purely literary worldbuilding needs to be established through case studies based on concrete examples. One such study is that by Dimitra Fimi which compares three examples of medievalism, by Tolkien, Thomas Chatterton and Umberto Eco. Each of these texts involves a representation or reimagining of aspects of the Middle Ages which in spite of, or rather because of, the manifest attempts to create a sense of historical reality, for example by "forged" documents, actually distances the action from the Primary World so that in each case an imaginary world is brought into being with a greater or lesser degree of inner consistency and separateness from the reader's own experience. Her conclusion, as reflected in the title of her article, is that medievalism in itself can be considered a kind of subcreation.

The two novels by Scott that will be considered here can certainly not be classified as medievalism unless that term is to be extended to cover the representation of *any* pre-modern culture. Indeed, many of the events and characters had been experienced by some elderly people, such as Alexander Stewart of Invernahyle, who recounted them to Scott in his youth, and the historical documents that he introduced in the Magnum edition to underline the historicity of his narratives were unquestionably real. However, Scottish society had changed so much since 1745, both in the Highlands and in the Lowlands, that he was necessarily striving to recreate a culture with which his contemporaries had lost direct contact, so there is a parallel at least to that extent to Chatterton and Eco. The following comparison with Tolkien on the micro-level of focalisation will examine the phenomenon from a different direction.

In addition to this, I will attempt to link the macro-level arguments of Wolf with a more detailed linguistics-based theory to give them a grounding which at present may be largely implicit. Linguists tend to wonder: How does language work?, and in particular: What makes communication through language possible? Similarly we may ask ourselves how it can make sense to talk about the "character" even of such a fascinating invention in the realistic novel tradition as Jane Austen's Emma Woodhouse, given that Emma does not exist and never has existed; she consists only of black marks on white paper.[1]

There have been a number of theoretical approaches that have attempted to explain the link between word and idea in terms of human cognitive experience. One that is particularly useful for the present purpose is *Text World Theory* by Joanna Gavins, which takes into account not only everyday registers but also literary texts, and indeed has the advantage of linking well with literary theories like the narratology of Gérard Genette. Gavins explains that for the cognitive linguist, worldbuilding is not restricted to imaginative literature, but rather it is what we do every time we communicate through language. Making or receiving utterances involves creating mental representations of human experience in a number of different ways. Each time we conceptualise a situation, we build something like a small world embodying that time, that place, those participants, and so on.

An example of a short text making a simple text world is: "Can we come in?" The request presupposes an enclosure of some kind with an entrance, with at least two people outside ('we') and at least one inside, who has the authority to give or withhold permission. Note that the meaning is derived not just from the words themselves, which individually have little definable semantic content, but from the interaction of this form of words with our knowledge of the world and the situations that may arise in it.

---

[1] Film adaptations of novels are of course a totally different phenomenon, which anyway could not exist without a reading of the written text.

This assumed knowledge of the world suggests that we do not have to build up our world from scratch every time. Instead we acquire a repertoire of frequent situations that have their own 'scripts', that is to say standard patterns of discourse where similar kinds of utterance regularly occur. A typical script of this kind is the restaurant, where we have internalised a standard sequence of events (requesting a table, looking at the menu, ordering, paying the bill, etc.) and the forms of words used to facilitate it. Whether or not the responses come in the expected form can tell us something about the internal text worlds of the other participant(s) in the discourse, or what we perceive as their "character".

These limited text worlds, that is to say the mental representations that we create for ourselves, can be extended by negotiation with other participants in the discourse. Gavins gives an example from her own experience of such a successful negotiation of an unexpected turn in a familiar script, where she goes into a sandwich shop in Madison, Wisconsin and tries to order a sandwich from the list displayed (her comments after the first and second turns are omitted here):

> S1: I'll have a chicken sandwich please.
> S2: Sure. What kind of cheese?
> S1: No, a chicken sandwich.
> S2: Sure. What kind of cheese?
> S1: I don't want cheese.
> S2: It's included.
> S1: You mean I have to have cheese?
> S2: No, you don't have to have it, but you're paying for it.
> S1: But I can have a sandwich without cheese?
> S2: I guess.
> S1: OK, I'll just have chicken on its own, then.
> S2: No cheese?
> S1: No cheese.
> (19-20)

The different cultural backgrounds of the British participant (S1) and the American one (S2) means that they start off with slightly varying mental representations of the situation. In particular S1 does not realise that, since Wisconsin is the dairy state of America, a large amount of cheese is eaten there, so that it is a standard ingredient in sandwiches; therefore S2's initial response makes her feel that something has gone wrong with the script. S2 on the other hand does not realise that cheese is not a usual ingredient of chicken sandwiches in some other places, and also finds it strange that someone should not want something that they are paying for. However, both speakers apply the Gricean cooperative principle and negotiate their way to an understanding, through the achievement of which they both slightly expand their own text world. This outlines one important function of dialogue in narratives which present an unfamiliar world to the reader.[2]

Another important feature of our mental representational ability is seen in the first example, "Can we come in?" The verb *come* normally expresses motion towards the speaker, e.g. "Come here", and is contrasted with *go*, which would suggest movement away from the present position. However, "Can we go in" would signify something different and can only be imagined as addressed to the speaker's companion(s) outside the enclosure. What has happened is that the speaker has cooperatively expressed the situation from the point of view of the other participant. This human ability to see through someone else's eyes, known as projection, is the means by which we can become absorbed in stories. Projection also allows us to react to the responses in fictional scripts just as we would do in the real world, creating an empathy with characters like Emma Woodhouse, who do not exist outside the minds of readers. It explains the importance of focalisation (sometimes known in English as 'point of view') as a novelistic technique which enables us to explore the text world through the eyes of one or more of its characters. We are, as it were, inside the story.

Note that focalisation is not to be confused with narrative voice. In *The Hobbit* there is a sometimes intrusive narrative voice that presents and comments on the plot from outside as it unfolds, but all the events as they happen are seen as through the eyes of Bilbo, and we follow the feelings aroused in him by them – he is the focaliser. Nothing is directly experienced where he is not present, so that other events have to be told to him afterwards for our benefit, such as the dwarves' escape from the goblins in the Misty Mountains.

---

2 The misunderstandings and explanations in this dialogue also underpin a point made by Wolf in Chapter 1, implicitly in his frequent use of the word *default* in relation to the known facts of the Primary World, and explicitly in his citation of Marie-Laure Ryan's "principle of minimal departure" (55): we assume that the world depicted in a work of fiction functions in a way that conforms to our own experience until something is presented to the contrary. Gavins makes it clear that this is not a purely literary phenomenon; in fact the whole of human discourse is a "dynamic cognitive process" dependent upon the exploitation and expansion of experiential knowledge (24).

Focalisation in *The Lord of the Rings* is more complex, where the intrusive narrative voice has been largely eliminated. At first we perceive events almost entirely through Frodo, just like a second Bilbo, but from Book IV on the focalisation shifts increasingly to Sam as Frodo becomes more and more fixated on his struggle with the Ring and Sam has to take the initiative. However, there are many chapters in which the Fellowship is scattered and neither of these main focalisers is present. In some situations the focalisation is passed to the other hobbits, in particular to Pippin in Minas Tirith or Merry with the Rohirrim, including the striking passage in V/3 as the Rohirrim ride down from the mountains to Dunharrow and Merry feels "borne down by the insupportable weight of Middle-earth" (791). Otherwise the focalisation is much weaker, as in the chase of Aragorn, Legolas and Gimli through Rohan after the Orcs, much of which is not seen from the particular point of view of any of the characters involved, but only in a generalised way through the eyes of all three, if at all. Thus the impression that the narrative is hobbit-centred, as implied by the conceit of the Red Book of Westmarch, is strengthened by the literary (and cognitive) technique of focalisation.

Tom Shippey in *The Road to Middle-earth* (81) points out that Bilbo (and by extension Frodo and the other hobbits) helps to mediate the archaic, heroic world to a modern reader who is uneasy with the idea of heroism. That is a very important point, but it is only one of the more refined aspects of the mediating function of hobbits. On a more general level, the hobbit focalisers take the role of inexperienced strangers in a big wide, unknown world. To put it in cognitive terms, their repertoire of scripts within the fictional text world is very restricted, and it is only as they expand their mental representations that readers have the opportunity to expand their own conceptions of Middle-earth.

A similar narrative technique can be seen in Scott's historical novels. *Waverley*, commonly regarded as the first successful historical novel in English, was published in 1814 but begun several years earlier. *Rob Roy*, which is vaguely similar in subject matter but set in an earlier period of Scottish history, followed in 1817. Both novels take place against the background of two armed rebellions by Scottish Highlanders against the Hanoverian government of Britain in favour of the Catholic House of Stuart, the former kings of Scotland, the last of whom,

James II of England and VII of Scotland, had been deposed in 1688 to guarantee a Protestant succession. The uprisings led by his son in 1715 and his grandson, Bonnie Prince Charlie, in 1745 could be seen as the last flare-up of the conflict between Catholics and Protestants like that which had dominated Germany in the 17th century. The suppression of the second of these rebellions led to the systematic eradication by the British government of the archaic clan structure that had survived in the Highlands and was unique in western Europe.

In his youth Scott had talked to survivors of the 1745 uprising and drew on these first-hand experiences to present what was probably an idealised view of a past age. According to Shippey he was like William Morris and Tolkien in feeling "the perilous charm of the archaic world of the North" (80). The historical events of *Waverley* took place only 60 years before he began writing it (hence its subtitle, *'Tis Sixty Years Since*, which the narrator repeats on several occasions to remind readers of the time difference), but the huge change in social structures had made the old Highland culture seem like a lost world, a fantasy which just happened to be real. In this novel, though, the past as a foreign country applies in more than one sense, since although Scott was writing for his fellow-Scots who were becoming unfamiliar with parts of their national past, he also felt an ambition to mediate Scottish history and culture to his substantial English readership, for many of whom Scotland was still strange and remote, even after a century of political union.[3]

Edward Waverley is a young Englishman who has grown up with little parental supervision and has spent a lot of his time reading romances, so that he has hardly any direct experience of the world. When his uncle, who is a Stuart sympathiser, decides that he should join the army as a career, he is sent to join his regiment in Scotland, with a recommendation to visit a friend of his uncle not far away from the army headquarters. On this visit he first experiences the culture of the Lowland Scots, with its significant linguistic and social differences, but also with a political difference, since it is here

---

3 In the General Preface of 1829 he states: "I felt that something might be attempted for my own country, of the same kind with that which Miss Edgeworth so fortunately achieved for Ireland – something which might introduce her natives to those of the sister kingdom, in a more favourable light than they had been placed hitherto, and tend to procure sympathy for their virtues and indulgence for their foibles" (*Waverley*, 352f.).

that he first becomes aware of the Scottish resentment of Hanoverian rule from England. Not only that, but through a chance event – his host's cattle are stolen by raiders from the Highlands – he comes into contact with a Highland chieftain, Fergus Mac-Ivor, through whom he not only experiences Highland culture but also finds himself becoming involved in the rebellion on the side of Charles Stuart.

The novel is focalised strongly through the character of Edward Waverley, similar to Bilbo Baggins in *The Hobbit*. It also has a similarly intrusive narrator, much more in the style of earlier authors like Fielding. Just as we have seen that Tolkien avoided that fault in *The Lord of the Rings*, so Scott had learnt to avoid it in *Rob Roy* by making that novel a first person, homodiegetic narrative, so that nothing intrudes between the focalisation of the hero Francis Osbaldistone, also a young, inexperienced Englishman caught up in Scottish affairs, and the reader. Both of these characters actually experience *two* new cultures: that of the Lowland Scots, in their way of life much closer to the English, and the more exotic, traditional and feudal society of the Highlanders. Georg Lukács claims that Scott's heroes are deliberately made ordinary and neutral because their main function is not to enact their own passions but "to bring the extremes whose struggle fills the novel, whose clash expresses artistically a great crisis in society, into contact with one another" (36). It might also be argued that this same neutrality enables them to act all the more effectively as focalisers, as conduits to convey the discovery of place and custom to the reader.

Scott uses the inexperienced Waverley as a focaliser in just the same way as Tolkien uses Bilbo, as the representative of the normality of the reader who has to negotiate his way through new places and situations, thus revealing them to the reader at the same time. In cognitive terms, Waverley starts off with his familiar presuppositions but finds he has to change and expand his mental representations on the pattern of Gavins's cheese sandwich example, as in the following passage in which he slowly works out in conversation with his host's daughter who exactly Fergus Mac-Ivor is and how he can help to restore the Baron's stolen cattle:

> The Baron having also retired to give some necessary directions, Waverley seized the opportunity to ask, whether this Fergus, with the unpronounceable name, were the chief thief-taker of the district?
>
> "Thief-taker!" answered Rose, laughing; "he is a gentleman of great honour and consequence; the chieftain of an independent branch of a powerful Highland clan, and is much respected, both for his own power, and that of his *kith*, *kin*, and *allies*."
>
> "And what has he to do with the thieves then? Is he a magistrate, or in the commission of peace?"
>
> "The commission of war rather, if there be such a thing," said Rose; "for he is a very unquiet neighbour to his *un-friends*, and keeps a greater *following* on foot than many that have thrice his estate. As to his connection with the thieves, that I cannot well explain; but the boldest of them will never steal a hoof from any one that pays *black-mail* to Vich Ian Vohr." (70)

Waverley's first guess is that Mac-Ivor must be a man who earns a living by catching thieves, a concept that must have been familiar to him from his background in the English countryside. When Rose points out his error, he then makes a second assumption, an officer of the law, again taken from completely the wrong cultural context. It will not fit in with his pre-existing conceptual categories that someone can be a gentleman and at the same time collect "black-mail", or to use the modern term, protection money. It is not surprising that Rose laughs, since false cultural assumptions of this kind often appear comical, at least to an outsider. This laughter is important also because it allows the reader, who is experiencing this through Waverley's eyes and is probably also still struggling to understand, to laugh off his or her own incomprehension too. It is worth noting that Scott helpfully italicises some words as a visual clue that they belong to a culture different from that of the reader and might therefore be misunderstood, even as Rose offers further potential for confusion by referring to Mac-Ivor by his Gaelic title, Vich Ian Vohr.

One equivalent of such a misunderstanding in *The Hobbit* is deliberately played for comedy:

> "If you must know more, his name is Beorn. He is very strong, and he is a skin-changer."
>
> "What! a furrier, a man that calls rabbits conies, when he doesn't turn their skins into squirrels?" asked Bilbo.

> "Good gracious heavens, no, no, NO, NO!" said Gandalf. "Don't be a fool Mr Baggins if you can help it [...] He is a skin-changer. He changes his skin: sometimes he is a huge black bear, sometimes he is a great strong black-haired man with huge arms and a great beard." (146-47)

Bilbo's supposition might have been reasonable in the Shire, or even more so in the reader's 1937 England, but he needs to build a new mental representation that will be valid in Wilderland.

Literary worldbuilding also makes implicit use of the scripts that were mentioned above as patterns for verbal interactions. Although there are no restaurants in an archaic world, nevertheless there are banquets, which also create the expectation of a certain sequence of events – food, entertainment, social interaction – but also allow for novel situations which may have to be negotiated, like a more complex version of buying a chicken sandwich without the cheese.[4]

The most significant banquet in *The Lord of the Rings* is the one that takes place in the house of Elrond at the beginning of Book II, where Frodo acts as the focaliser. Through the "many meetings" he (together with the reader) extends his text world by seeing familiar persons in a new context, and therefore gains a first glimpse of their importance in a wider history than has been evident so far. The courteous behaviour of his neighbour in picking up his scattered cushions leads to an extended conversation with Glóin, which opens up new perspectives of prosperity, but also disquiet, at Erebor, as well as connecting at a deeper narrative level with the history of Bilbo and his acquisition of the Ring. The banquet is completed by an entertainment with poetry and music, where Frodo is reunited with Bilbo, through which he comes to understand something of the power of elvish art, but also gains further evidence of the evil of the Ring through its momentary effect both on Bilbo and on himself.

A further example of negotiating a meal script appears when Frodo and Sam are entertained by Faramir at Henneth Annûn. There is a comic exchange when the hobbit servant Sam misunderstands the purpose of the bowl of water of-

---

[4] I am grateful to Thomas Honegger for suggesting to me the significance of different treatments of the banquet script by different authors, and to Dimitra Fimi for reminding me of the Henneth Annûn episode.

fered to him to rinse his hands and solves the problem by using it to wash his head. The Gondorian waiting on him tentatively misinterprets this as a Shire custom, and is partially corrected by Sam, who has not understood the full significance of the question. Shortly afterwards, Frodo is made to think critically about the manners of the Shire when he is introduced to the Gondorian custom of facing west before the meal.

Scott makes use of a similar script, since Waverley as focaliser experiences not one banquet but two. The first takes place in the Lowlands, and is used by the author to recreate a sense of Lowland customs from a recent but nevertheless vanished past cut off from the English reader both in time and space. It is at this small dinner that he is first introduced to Balmawhapple, who will turn out to be his antagonist. His (and our) understanding of the banquet script is extended as he finds himself faced with a degree of ceremony that he is not used to, involving the ritualised drinking of large amounts of alcohol, and we follow his thoughts as he tries to negotiate this without causing offence. However, his efforts fail because the others have drunk more than he has, and an incident occurs which will cause difficulties for him in the future.

The second banquet takes place as a vivid introduction for both the hero and the reader to the completely different culture of the Highlands. Through Waverley's eyes we experience a much more extensive account of a feudal feast in the communal hall of a great chieftain who relies on such lavish entertainment to guarantee the loyalty of his followers. As a ritual preparation a surly old woman comes to wash his feet, which is not a part of the script that is familiar to him, so he has to decide how to repond appropriately. Fortunately he reaches the correct decision by giving her a generous tip. There follows a detailed description of the proceedings seen from the point of view of his position near the head of the table, where in a hall full of retainers of all social classes, the behaviour lower down is depicted in a way that the reader, through Waverley's eyes (and ears), is likely to find excessive and even primitive:

> Lower down stood immense clumsy joints of mutton and beef, which, but for the absence of pork, resembled the rude festivity of the banquet of Penelope's suitors. But the central dish was a yearling lamb, called "a hog in harst", roasted whole. It was set upon its legs, with a bunch of parsley in its mouth, and was

probably exhibited in that form to gratify the pride of the cook, who piqued himself more on the plenty than the elegance of his master's table. The sides of this poor animal were fiercely attacked by the clans-men, some with dirks, others with the knives which were usually in the same sheath with the dagger, so that it was soon rendered a mangled and rueful spectacle. (96)

However, in spite of the emphasis on its unfamiliarity, the meal is seen to follow a set of conventions that prevent it from deteriorating as disastrously as the convivial evening in the Lowlands.

The focalisation makes use of a kind of indirect free speech which subtly underlines the extent to which the feast is alien to Waverley's experience and sense of decorum:

> The bagpipers, three in number, screamed during the whole time of dinner, a tremendous war-tune; and the echoing of the vaulted roof, and clang of the Celtic tongue, produced such a Babel of noises, that Waverley dreaded his ears would never recover it. (96-97)

The horror that English people claim to feel towards bagpipes is well known, so clearly this is presented as Waverley's subjective impressions; a Scot would be highly unlikely to think of the sound of bagpipes as "screaming" or of the Gaelic language as a "clang". The focaliser here mediates the scene not so much to the experience as to the prejudices of the English readers.

It is hoped that these few examples will have gone at least a part of the way to demonstrating that focalisation is an important literary technique in the creation of a credible world that is unfamiliar, but can nevertheless be mediated for the reader by using the viewpoint of a character whose nucleus of experience is not so different from the reader's own. In doing this, the author chooses situations which correspond to the archetypal ones in which human beings negotiate an extended mental representation of the world around them. Because of the distancing effect of time and change, the historical novel depends to some extent on worldbuilding, just as in fantasy and science fiction, with which it is more commonly associated. If there were not a considerable overlap between the historical novel and the Tolkienian immersion fantasy, it would not have been so easy for Tolkien to indulge in the joke of presenting *The Hobbit* and *The Lord of the Rings* as histories, complete with the tongue-in-cheek paratextual commentaries which were pioneered more than 200 years earlier by Scott.[5]

About the Author

ALLAN TURNER is interested particularly in stylistic and linguistic aspects of Tolkien. He has master's degrees in both medieval studies and general linguistics, and gained a Ph.D. in translation studies with a dissertation on the translations of names in *The Lord of the Rings*. He has taught at universities both in Germany and in the UK; before his retirement he was Lecturer in English at the Friedrich-Schiller-Universität Jena. He has attended DTG Seminars regularly since 2005.

Bibliography

FIMI, Dimitra. 'The Past as an Imaginary World: The Case of Medievalism.' *Revisiting Imaginary Worlds: A Subcreation Studies Anthology*. Ed. Mark J. P. Wolf. New York and Abingdon: Routledge, 2017. 46-65.

GAVINS, Joanna. *Text World Theory: An Introduction*. Edinburgh: Edinburgh University Press, 2007.

LUKÁCS, Georg. *The Historical Novel*. Harmondsworth: Penguin, 1981.

SCOTT, Walter. *Waverley*. Ed. Claire Lamont. Oxford: Oxford University Press, 1986.

SHIPPEY, Tom. *The Road to Middle-earth*. Third edition. London: HarperCollins, 2005.

TOLKIEN, J.R.R. *The Hobbit*. London: HarperCollins, 1998.

— *The Lord of the Rings*. 50th anniversary edition. London: HarperCollins, 2005.

WOLF, Mark J.P. *Building Imaginary Worlds: The Theory and History of Subcreation*. New York and Abingdon: Routledge, 2012.

---

5 Fimi comments that, because it is patently fictitious, the paratextual framing of both Tolkien and Eco ironically undermines the sense of historical veracity at the same time as it appears to strengthen it on the surface level. Note that Scott's paratexts are ironical only when they are concerned with the putative author, since the Waverley novels were originally published anonymously. Any historical documentation is meant to be taken at its face value.

Massimiliano Izzo

Worldbuilding and Mythopoeia in Tolkien and post-Tolkienian Fantasy Literature

Abstract

In his book *Imaginary Worlds. The Theory and History of Sub-creation*, Mark J.P. Wolf treats the terms "worldbuilding" and "sub-creation" as synonyms. The term sub-creation was first used by J.R.R. Tolkien in his seminal essay 'On fairy-stories', in relation with mythopoeia, or myth-making. Tolkien describes sub-creation as "an aspect of mythology" and as an art connected to the Elvish Enchantment, the capability to make a secondary world with an inner consistency of reality. However, mythopoetic sub-creation is often at odds, if not even in conflict, with extensive and detailed worldbuilding, especially when the latter focuses on mundane aspects such as economics, politics, and logistics. In *The Lord of the Rings*, Tolkien was careful to maintain a balance between the mythological dimension and the encyclopaedic impulse of worldbuilding. Most fantasy authors who followed in Tolkien's footsteps have failed to achieve a comparable level of balance. They either use detailed worldbuilding as the foundation of their work (e.g. Robert Jordan, George R.R. Martin, Brandon Sanderson, etc.) or discard it altogether, seeing it as a constraint on imagination. These authors focus rather on myth-making (e.g. Peter S. Beagle, Neil Gaiman, Catherynne M. Valente, etc.). This paper analyses the nature of the dichotomy between mythopoeia and worldbuilding, and proposes possible ways to overcome this opposition with the aim of producing literary works that possess both.

Worldbuilding, the construction of imaginary worlds, has acquired a preeminent role in contemporary fantasy literature, probably more than in any other literary genre. Nowadays, a majority of fantasy novels comes not only with a map, but fully equipped with details on history, politics, economics, heraldry, cultures, warfare logistics, and complex magical systems. J.R.R. Tolkien's *The Lord of the Rings*, first published in three volumes in 1954-55, represents the ur-example of high fantasy novel set in an extensively developed secondary world. Even if fantasy novels with maps[1] and timelines had been published before – such as *The Worm Ouroboros* (1922) and *Mistress of Mistresses* (1935) by E.R. Eddison – Tolkien's opus was unprecedented

---

1 For a detailed account on maps in fantasy literature see Ekman 14-68.

in its breadth and scope, with extensive chronicles spanning over two ages of his world, annals and lineages of four kingdoms and peoples, and long dissertations on language and calendars. Tolkien was not only a practitioner of the genre, but a theorist and apologist as well. He wrote a manifesto of sorts – the essay 'On Fairy-stories', originally presented as a lecture in honour of Andrew Lang at the University of St. Andrews in 1939 – to defend the legitimacy of fantasy. In this essay he coined the term *sub-creation*, which describes the fantasist's creative process as subordinate to the existence and experience of the Primary World.

In the last decade worldbuilding has gained interest as a subject of study among scholars. In 2012 Mark J.P. Wolf published *Building Imaginary Worlds: the Theory and History of Subcreation*, the first book-length comprehensive study on worldbuidling across multiple media, with an emphasis on literature and gaming. Not surprisingly, both Tolkien's secondary world and 'On Fairy-stories' are discussed at length (Wolf 22-25; 130-34; 202-05). At the beginning of his book, Wolf draws a parallel between the concepts of worldbuilding and sub-creation, to the point that the latter appears in the title rather than the former, and the sub-creator is equated with the builder of imaginary world: "Thus, a 'subcreator' is a specific kind of author, one who very deliberately builds an imaginary world, and does so for reasons beyond that of merely providing a backdrop for a story" (Wolf 23). Afterwards, Wolf states that "secondary worlds that are geographically distinct from the Primary World" and "those that are used for stories whose action occurs mainly within a secondary world" are "the ones that contain the most subcreation" (Wolf 28) and that these will be the subject of his study. Throughout the book he proceeds to examine various imaginary worlds, with a particular focus on trans-medial worlds such as the world of Oz, the Star Wars and Star Trek universes, and the Myst franchise world. Obviously, popular contemporary fantasy worlds such as Randland from Robert Jordan's *The Wheel of Time*, Roshar and the entire Cosmere universe from Brandon Sanderson's *The Stormlight Archive*, and Westeros from George R.R. Martin's *A Song of Ice and Fire* would perfectly fit Wolf's definition of worlds containing "the most sub-creation". However, I am not convinced that Tolkien was discussing this type of imaginary worlds when he first introduced the concept of sub-creation. I think that this approach of considering worldbuilding and sub-creation as two equivalent concepts that proceed alongside each other is misleading and overlooks some fundamental differences between the two. The main thesis I will defend in this paper is that the two concepts – even if complementary to some extent – do not really proceed hand in hand, but rather they often find themselves at odds with. I will argue this along two lines: first, discussing the origin of the term sub-creation and explaining how it was applied by Tolkien in his own work; and second, I will offer evidence as to how the evolution of Tolkien-influenced modern fantasy validates the difference between the two concepts. For the latter, I will focus almost exclusively on those fantasy authors who avowedly recognised Tolkien and his work as an inspiration and an influence.

The concept of sub-creation – and the cognate term sub-creator – first appears in the section 'Origins' of the aforementioned essay 'On Fairy-stories', where the origins of fairy and folk tales are considered. It must be noted that fairy tales are a type of narrative with little or no worldbuilding as currently understood. They are usually set "long ago in a place far away" and this is as much as we know in most cases. In 'Origins', Tolkien defines sub-creation as the faculty of the human mind ("endowed with the powers of abstraction and generalisation") to produce, through the use of language, images and concepts not present in the Primary World. He offers the use of the adjective as the best example of the sub-creative power of language:

> When we can take green from grass, blue from heaven, and red from blood, we have already an enchanter's power – upon one plane; and the desire to wield that power in the world external to our minds awakes. It does not follow that we shall use that power well upon any plane. We may put a deadly green upon a man's face and produce a horror; we may make the rare and terrible blue moon to shine; or we may cause woods to spring with silver leaves and rams to wear fleeces of gold, and put hot fire into the belly of the cold worm. But in such 'fantasy', as it is called, new form is made; Faërie begins; Man becomes a sub-creator. (*TOFS* 41)

Tolkien goes on to state that "This aspect of *mythology* – sub-creation – (…) is, I think, too little considered" (*TOFS* 42). Sub-creation is therefore considered by Tolkien as an aspect of mythology, and moreover more present in the so-called "lower mythology" – referring to legends, fairy tales, and folk tales, usually transmitted orally – rather than in the "higher", the written body of works relating the accounts of divine or supernatural beings (*TOFS* 42). Even if in the section 'Fantasy' of 'On Fairy-stories' the concept of sub-creation is broadened to encompass the act of inventing secondary worlds, the chief image used by Tolkien – the "green sun" – remains still purely linguistic. To make a green sun believable in the Primary World, Tolkien states that some kind of elvish craft is required (*TOFS* 61) rather than the tools of a scientist or an engineer: a skill that preserves the enchantment, the sense of wonder that is the key to gaining a glimpse of Faërie.

Now, a few observations must be made here. In the first draft of the essay, published in the expanded edition curated by Verlyn Flieger and Douglas Anderson under the name 'Manuscript A', Tolkien explicitly states that "mythology is language and language is mythology. The mind, and the tongue, and the tale are coeval" (*TOFS* 181). Only the second sentence was carried on – in a slightly edited form – in the published essay. However the equivalence of language and mythology remained. Given that sub-creation – or at least the type of sub-creation described above – is grounded on language, it follows that it must be grounded on mythology as well. Mark Atherton calls this (sub)creative use of language, and of the adjective in particular, "mythical grammar" (Atherton 46-47). But there is more. When Tolkien gave his lecture at St. Andrews, he had been working on his mythology and related writings for almost 25 years since he originally composed the poem 'The Voyage of Éarendel the Evening Star' in September 1914. In this period he had developed his own approach to myth-making that was inextricably linked to language and the sub-creation of fantastic elements. The sub-creator, for Tolkien, was a maker of myths. Tolkien borrowed from the Ancient Greek the term 'mythopoeia' to better emphasise how the sub-creative process works with mythological sources to produce new myths. He also used the term as a title for a poem with strong Christian undertones where he defends the value of myth and the right of Man to produce new myths through sub-creation, in the image of God's creation.

In order to analyse sub-creation as myth-making, however, a proper definition for mythology is required. A mythology is usually defined as a collection of myths. Now, as we have seen above, it can be inferred from the *Letters* (such as the famous Letter 131 to Milton Waldman) that Tolkien does use the word "myth" in a broad context encompassing higher myths, legends, fairy tales, and folk-tales. This definition essentially puts all of his literary output – the whole legendarium as well as the short works unrelated to it (*Smith of Wootton Major*, *Farmer Giles of Ham*, and *Roverandom*) and poems like *The Fall of Arthur* and 'The New Lay of the Völsungs' – under the umbrella of myth. In this broader view, myth can be defined as a narrative, characterised by an aura of truth and timelessness, that explains "why the world is as it is", whose goal is to provide meaning to the world, a unified picture of it (Hiley 839-40). Recently, myth has also been envisioned "as a process that allows different societies to express their worldviews, beliefs, fears, and anxieties, not by attempting a scientific 'explanation' or using empirical methods, but by telling a story" (Fimi 58). The view of myth as a process takes into account its fluid, self-transforming and ever-evolving nature (Attebery 31-32). The two definitions above place myth in dialectic opposition with 'science', as the latter is currently understood. Natural science often adopts analytical reasoning to explain phenomena, and adopts a reductionist approach to solve – with success – many of the problems it faces. Whereas myth strives to provide a coherent meaning through a linguistic narrative, the scientific interpretation of the world is achieved through a variety of disciplines (physics, chemistry, biology, ...) each of them with its own field of applicability. In mythical narratives belief cannot be obtained through rational communication as in science. Hence, the language used by successful mythical narratives aims to evoke a sense of wonder that elicits belief in the audience. The capability to provoke this 'secondary belief' in the reader is what Tolkien considers akin to Elvish Enchantment. To achieve this goal, mythical language tends to be more elusive, poetic, and less literal than ordinary language; it leaves a lot unexplained and mysterious, without resorting to detailed knowledge-based explanations. This consideration can be extended to other scholarly evidence-based disciplines – sometimes included in a broader definition of 'sciences' – such as history, economics and politics. This contradistinction between myth and science will be useful when I pit the mythopoeic approach against the approach of worldbuilding adopted in most contemporary high fantasy literature, as well as in video and tabletop games. Myth and science can be seen as 'competitive' methods to explain the world. In the last four centuries, the sciences have acted as demythologisers, providing evidence-based explanation for, or falsifying, the accounts of ancient myth. Tolkien, however, did not share the belief that myths are lies, and he devoted the poem 'Mythopoeia' to defend his position. In the letter to Milton Waldman he stated that "legends and myths are largely made of 'truths' and indeed present aspects of it that can only be received in this mode" (*Letters* 147). This firm conviction, together with the desire to go back to the original meaning of terms with mythical significance, is the foundation of Tolkien's sub-creative approach.

Tolkien's sub-creation: Worldbuilding and mythopoeia

> Fantasy is an arena – I believe the primary arena – in which competing claims about myth can be contested and different relationships with myth tried out. The reasons have to do with the development of our modern understanding of myth, on the one hand, and the invention of the fantasy genre, on the other – and with the fact that these are not two different stories but two aspects of the same historical narrative. (Attebery 16)

According to Brian Attebery, the scholarly study of myth and the emergence of modern fantasy literature in the second half of the Nineteenth century are two intertwined processes: the same people were involved in both endeavours. Tolkien's work was built on the shoulders of these fore-fathers: the brothers Grimm, Elias Lönnrot, George MacDonald (an author whom, in his later years, Tolkien came to despise), William Morris, and Andrew Lang himself. William Morris was also one of the first to build a fully developed independent secondary world as a setting for his romances *The Wood Beyond the World* and *The Well at the World's End*. However, Tolkien was the first to use worldbuilding and myth-making as the cornerstone of his narratives. His work popularised the use of these techniques in fantasy literature as well as in other genres and media.

At the heart of Tolkien's method for myth-making are two concepts: (1) sub-creation, seen as an integral component of mythology, and (2) the idea of the Cauldron of Story as discussed in 'On Fairy-stories' (*TOFS* 44-47). These two elements feed one on another, as newly sub-created elements end up in the Cauldron to be used in further iterations of the sub-creative process. The Cauldron (or Pot) represents the figurative place from where all the stories composed by humankind emerge: in it various "bits" or ingredients simmer and blend to produce new stories: historical figures and events, elements from higher and lower mythologies, and ultimately all the narratives, written and oral[2], produced in the past. At a more basic level the Pot contains powerful mythical archetypes and words or terms infused with mythical force. Tolkien's imagination sprang from these elements while focused on solving the philological puzzles they often represented. Tolkien constructed his secondary world, sub-creating from fragments of Primary World mythologies, mostly from the few existing bits of Old English, Norse and Germanic mythologies that presented philological puzzles in medieval and later English – and, in a broader context, European[3] – literature. These fragments had "deep and ancient roots", and they gave the illusion of a pre-existing whole, a lost mythology or asterisk-reality, as termed by Tom Shippey in his *The Road to Middle-earth* (27-31). This procedure of invention through reconstruction was on the one hand inherently philological and grounded in language, in "bits and pieces", fragments of language resonating mythological power. On the other hand, it was also a sort of mythical and mystical quest, as Tolkien claimed at various times: "I had the sense of recording what was already 'there' somewhere: not of 'inventing'" (*Letters* 145). This sense of sub-creation as recollection is stressed by an in-world reference: the Quenya term *olor* that refers to dreams, but not the dream of sleep for Men. Rather, it refers to the vivid contents of the Eldar's mind, as well as to their imagination (*UT* 512; Cook 8-10). This is associated with the term *olo-s*, glossed as "phantasy, vision" (*UT* 513), that is, a construction of the mind that the Eldar could make visible or sensible by Art (so without the objective of deceiving or acquiring power). Here the equivalence between imagination and recollection is reinforced and held true for the Eldar at least, if not for Men. Hinting – albeit ambiguously – that for the Elves, the sub-creators par excellence among the incarnates, imaginations and recollection are described by the same word implies that history and myth are ultimately made of the same stuff, and that myth – and mythopoeic fantasy as a type of myth – contains elements of truth. The concepts of "vivid dreams" and of real history becoming more mythical moving backwards in time rather than the opposite lies at the heart of the unfinished novel 'The Notion Club Papers', and one can only

---

2 Within this category falls the memorate, "a firsthand account of an experience [...] that links the teller to a traditional belief or legend" (Atteberry 53).
3 The influence of Celtic and Finnish mythology on Tolkien has been extensively examined, among others, by Verlyn Flieger and Dimitra Fimi. Even Middle Eastern myths had an influence on the legendarium: as it has been shown by John Garth in his paper 'Ilu's music: the creation of Tolkien's creation myth' presented ad the German Tolkien Society Seminar 2017, in Augsburg.

speculate how much of Tolkien's beliefs and methods are expressed by Ramer, Jeremy and the other members of the Notion Club (*SD* 227-29).

Regardless of his beliefs in the Primary World, in Tolkien's secondary world(s) history and myth are the same. Tolkien wrote his major novels – *The Hobbit* and, in particular, *The Lord of the Rings* – against the backdrop of his independently conceived and, as we have seen before, long established body of mythologies, the legendarium. Among the most effectively sub-created scenes in the two books are the descriptions of events from past ages and times, when narrated or referred to in the main narrative. These sub-creative pieces of Tolkien's writing have the best qualities of fairy tales: to "open a door to Other Time, and for a moment maybe to be outside Time altogether" (*TOFS* 48). This is the effect produced, for instance, by the account of the various peoples of the Elves in the chapter 'Flies and Spiders' of *The Hobbit* (*H* 154) and by the short tale of Beren and Luthien as narrated to the hobbits by Aragorn at Weathertop in the chapter 'A Knife in the Dark' (*LotR* 193-94). I will now examine the latter as a prime example of the craft of Tolkien as sub-creator within his masterpiece. The whole piece, condensed in just 450 words, has an aura of timelessness produced by the introductory rhetorical expression "when the world was young". Here the mythical grammar proper of mythological sub-creation creates the "time abyss" (Clute and Grant 946-47) between the events narrated by Aragorn and the age where the adventures of Frodo and his friends unfold. A second time abyss exists between the age of the hobbits in *The Lord of the Rings*, and the "mundane" age where we, the readers, are situated. To this effect of temporal displacement an effect of spatial displacement is added as well: all the locations introduced in the narration had never been named before in the book. Some of them are referred to only in the Elven tongues (mostly in Sindarin), but are also given evocative appellatives in English that produce a sub-creative effect: "the Hidden Kingdom", "a glade beside the enchanted river Esgalduin", "the Sundering Seas", "the confines of this world". The characters too are the stock of fairy tales, in a larger-than-life context: the "Great Enemy" (whose almost casual introduction redefines the figure of Sauron and the main narrative of *The Lord of the Rings* in a broader context), the "Elves of the West", the "fathers of Men", the "Wolf that came from the gates of Angband". In addition, these few lines bear some concepts of great mythical power, themes that are recurrent in the tradition of folk and fairy-tales: the overthrow of a great Evil, the loss to an immortal race of their most beloved daughter, the lineage of a more ancient, nobler (and immortal) race transmitted to mortal Men. Tolkien uses the kind of temporal displacement here illustrated, in multiple occasions throughout the novel, to create mythical depth and open the doors that lead to Faërie. His sub-creative art is stronger in passages such as this and the narration of Elrond on the origin of the Ring during the Council (*LotR* 242-43), but there are other examples throughout *The Lord of the Rings*. The narrative of the book consists of multiple displacements in time, from the ordinary time in the Shire to the 'other' mythical Time of ageless places such as Rivendell, Lothlórien, and Fangorn, but also of the lands of 'legendary people' such as the Rohirrim and the Númenóreans. The illusion of displacement in time is produced linguistically, which sets the tone for each of the episodes and displaces one from the other: all appear to happen in a mythical or legendary past, compared with the prosaic setting of the 'pseudo-Victorian/Edwardian' Shire. The return to the 'present' time and 'ordinary' place as the four hobbit go back to the Shire at the end of the novel is described variously as the fading of a dream by Merry and as "falling asleep again" by Frodo (*LotR* 997). These examples show how mythological sub-creation is used in *The Lord of Rings*, but Tolkien demonstrates his theory by applying it to other contexts: in his fairy-tales *Roverandom* and *Smith of Wootton Major*. In the former while describing all the dangerous creatures that inhabit the Moon (*TPR* 29-30), and in the latter especially when describing the excursions and the encounters of Smith in Faery (*TPR* 258-60). Other powerful examples can be found in the unfinished "scientifiction" thriller 'The Notion Club Papers', when Ramer relates various fragments from his "vivid dreams" (*SD* 194, 198-99).

The mythological sub-creation I have illustrated was extensively used by Tolkien in all his works, and it mostly coexisted with a more encyclopaedic and 'scientific' worldbuilding. This became more prominent in *The Lord of the Rings* and in the later rewritings of the 'Silmarillion'. Tolkien was extremely careful in multiple aspects of his worldbuilding, from history and geography to genealogy and astronomy. According to Michael Salter, Tolkien's approach to fantastic worldbuilding fits in the tradition of the 'New Romance', a fin-de-siècle Anglo-American literary mode that tried to reconcile reason and enchantment without disdaining modern science and rationality (Salter 20). In *The Lord of the Rings* the encyclopaedic and 'scientific' worldbuilding is brought to the fore mostly in the Appendices, but it often emerges in the narrative. This produces some demythologising effects: Orcs and Trolls, for instance, once systematised as corruptions of the Enemy, become less the stuff of fairy-tales than they were in *The Hobbit* and more akin to a degenerate life form. This process becomes even more pronounced in the final rewritings of the 'Silmarillion' where Tolkien felt the urge to modify some long established mythological concepts to make its secondary world more believable to modern readers (see 'Myths Transformed', *MR* 370-94). He very soon realised that the power of some of these concepts (the most evident being the Two Trees of Valinor) would have been lost irredeemably, and that the whole legendarium might not have survived such a transformation unscathed. This inability to harmonise the old mythical themes with a more scientifically acceptable cosmology might have been one of the reasons why he was never able to conclude the 'Silmarillion'. The tension between mythopoeia and worldbuilding in Tolkien's work explored here became even more marked in the works of the authors that came after him and who drew inspiration from his work.

Fantasy after Tolkien

It took the literary and publishing world at least two decades to absorb the import of *The Lord of the Rings*. In this sense, 1977 can be rightly considered the game-changing year, thanks to the efforts and marketing strategies of editors Lester and Judy-Lynn Del Rey at Ballantine Books. The commercial success of Terry Brooks's *The Sword of Shannara* and Stephen Donaldson's *Lord Foul's Bane* – together with the long awaited publication of *The Silmarillion* – demonstrated the viability of high fantasy as a commercial genre. These books codified the genre for over a decade afterwards, and denoted a change in worldbuilding strategies. Rather than using Tolkien's mythopoeic approach of re-construction from fragments, more and more writers were drawn into using the whole that he sub-created as a template, and proceeded to fill the gaps and systematise it. Terry Brooks, for instance, always admitted his admiration for *The Lord of the Rings* and the influence it exerted on him, but he stressed that did not share Tolkien's "interest in cultural studies". Therefore, he omitted from his own novel "the poetry and songs, the digressions on the ways and habits of types of characters, and the appendices of language and backstory that characterised and informed Tolkien's work" (Brooks, *Sometimes the Magic Works* 188). Brooks discarded altogether Tolkien's mythopoeic approach; however the influence of Tolkien on him was so strong that he ended up using Middle-earth as a template for the Four Lands and *The Lord of the Rings* as a blueprint for *The Sword of Shannara*. It is interesting, in this respect, to compare the long narrative background given by the wizard Allanon to the main character Shea in the second chapter of *The Sword of Shannara* with the similar conversation between Gandalf and Frodo in the analogous chapter of *The Fellowship of the Ring*, 'The Shadow of the Past'. Here we can see already what can be called the encyclopaedic impulse of the cataloguer taking over the narrative. Allanon offers Shea a detailed explanation – it takes most of the chapter, and almost 2,500 words – on the origin of the Four Lands and of the various races which inhabit them, the two Wars of the Races, and the rise of Brona the Dark Lord (Brooks, *The Sword of Shannara* 21-32; ch. 2). This passage is significantly longer than the corresponding one in 'The Shadow of the Past', the narrative presented referred in direct discourse, devoid of the mythical grammar and poetic language used by Tolkien. That was not the strategy used by Tolkien: Gandalf offers Frodo only glimpses of the past and the War of the Last Alliance, and Tolkien omits most of the narration from the text, leaving more things unsaid than explained.[4] In Tolkien there was an economy of worldbuilding information download[5] in the text that is not found in Brooks. The shadow of Tolkien is also discernible in *Lord Foul's Bane*'s worldbuilding, but Stephen Donaldson still offers us some glimpses of mythical poetry. The story of the King and the Queen is a finely crafted fairy-tale story encased in the main narrative (Donaldson 75-76; ch. 6), even though the way it is narrated as a coda to a poem bears many similarities with Aragorn's tale of Beren and Luthien.[6] However, sub-creative myth-making is mostly sidelined in the rest of the novel. The main innovation of the novel

---

4 He relates a detailed account of the finding of the ring by Smeagol-Gollum, but the story is related in a mundane rather than mythical tone.
5 The term "information download" in a text is here used in the sense provided by Farah Mendlesohn in *Rhetorics of Fantasy* (Mendlesohn 33; 40-41).
6 The story even involves a character named Berek Halfhand, all too reminiscent of Beren the One-handed.

is the protagonist Thomas Covenant's tormented psychology and his attitude towards the Land, the secondary world he finds himself in and that does not quite believe to be real.

This worldbuilding practice proved so successful that in the following years numerous writers took the easier road, and, rather than sub-create their own fantasies from the Primary World myths, felt drawn into using Tolkien's own world and narrative as a template for their imaginary stories. As a result, they failed to tap into what Tolkien referred to as the "reservoir of power" that lies behind Faërie (*TOFS* 270), and their novels lacked this mythological quality while keeping the adventure story traits and epic scope of *The Lord of the Rings*. Successful authors such as David Eddings and Dennis L. McKiernan reused to varying extents the building blocks of Tolkien's secondary world. At almost the same time a new factor, which was to become another great influence for worldbuilding, came into play. *Dungeons & Dragons* (*D&D*), the table-top role-playing game (RPG), was invented by E. Gary Gygax in 1974 drawing inspiration from various fantasy and horror authors, who were duly acknowledged in the famous 'Appendix N' of the *Advanced D&D Dungeon Master's Guide* in 1977. By the beginning of the eighties many shared worlds had been built as settings for *D&D* or similar RPGs, notable examples being Midkemia, developed by a group of students at the University of California, and the *Dragonlance* world conceived by Laura and Tracy Hickman. In the first half of the 1980s, authors started to publish works set in such worlds: Raymond E. Feist's *Magician* came out in 1982, while Margaret Weis and Tracy Hickman's *Dragons of Autumn Twilight* was published in 1984. Both books garnered great commercial success and were followed by a slew of sequels. These worlds still retain many trappings from Tolkien's worldbuilding (see for instance the parallel similarities of the elven kingdoms of Elvandar and Qualinesti with Lothlorien) but they are now filtered through a system of rules to make them playable. The closure of the feedback loop between fantasy literature and RPGs had profound consequences on worldbuilding, more so than on other aspects of the narrative. In games, the main objective of building a secondary world is not artistic, but aimed at controlling the game and the options available to players in order to make it enjoyable, fair, reliable, and reproducible. This requires, among other things, providing extensive details of multiple aspects of the world. These aspects may not be needed to move forward a narrative in a novel, but once they have been developed (for gaming purposes, at least initially), they are used in the book to put more 'flesh' on the world, in a sense to make it more realistic. This aspect becomes almost inescapable when we study the worldbuilding strategies of authors from the middle 1980s to the present: a great majority of them have been RPG or Multi-massive online RPG (MMORPG) players or even game masters,[7] and that makes a huge difference compared with the approaches available to authors of the previous decades such as E.R. Eddison, J.R.R. Tolkien, and Lloyd Alexander.

This ubiquitous reuse of Tolkien's tropes in fantasy worldbuilding without drawing inspiration from his original sources, and the success thereof, produced a reaction around the middle of the 1980s. This is best exemplified by Canadian author Gavriel Guy Kay, who explains the origin of his *Fionavar Tapestry* high fantasy trilogy as a conscious reaction to the flood of commercial fantasy:

> Well, Fionovar [*sic*] was planned as a trilogy because it was a self-conscious, self-aware attempt to make a statement. In retrospect it's amusing. But back then I was "shocked and appalled" at the barbarians in the temple – the post-Tolkien trivialization of fantasy that I saw happening. And the serious writers of fantasy – the people I respected – were it seemed to me turning away from epic fantasy to other kinds of smaller scale work. Urban fantasy was born around that time – people like Megan Lindholm, Charles de Lint. Small, precise, nicely done books. But they were almost a kind of abandoning of the field of the epic scale to the hacks. And it ticked me off a bit. It seemed to me a premature abandonment. I really felt that the elements of high fantasy – the elements that Tolkien had taken from myth and legend – not the elements he invented, the elements he took from primary sources – were still there to be taken and worked with. And they could be recombined in different ways – you could work with those same core elements and come to a different destination. (Schellenberg and Switzer)

Kay did his best to boil his stew from the Pot, but the secondary world that he concocted appears to me even less consistent than those conceived by many of the so-called 'barbarians', such as Brooks or McKiernan. Kay lifted various concepts from a variety of mythologies – Arthur and Lancelot from the Round Table stories, a few deities from Norse and Celtic myths, and cultures remi-

---

7 Some notable worlds which started as RPGs settings are: R. Scott Bakker's Earwa, Steven Erikson and Ian Esslemont's Malaz World, and Elizabeth Moon's *The Deed of Paksenarrion*'s world. Other authors who played RPGs in their formative years include George R.R. Martin, China Mieville, Brandon Sanderson, Scott Lynch, Joe Abercrombie.

niscent of the Native Americans and Chinese – and put them in a world still heavily indebted to Tolkien's legendarium (now mostly *The Silmarillion*, which he helped to edit) and a story reminiscent of Joy Chant's *Red Moon and Black Mountain*, achieving as a result a jarring of poorly amalgamated sources. As an additional difficulty, the protagonists of the series come from Earth (they are five students of the University of Toronto) and the secondary world, Fionavar, is supposed to be the original and most important of all worlds. However, the effect is that Fionavar's simplicity and the flatness of its inhabitants are just highlighted by the contrast with the complexities of the Primary World. *The Fionavar Tapestry* achieved a modest commercial success, but it proved unable to inspire other writers in bringing back to the core of high fantasy novels the myth-making and sub-creative approach theorised and used by Tolkien. Most of the writers of this period who were interested in going back to the Cauldron of Story and the sub-creative power of language – authors like Patricia A. McKillip, Charles de Lint, Peter S. Beagle, Ursula K. Le Guin and others – turned their backs on high fantasy, focusing on a variety of other sub-genres from science fiction romance to small scale fantasy novels far from the grandiose scope of *The Lord of the Rings* and its slew of imitators. As a consequence, these writers moved away from detailed and extensive worldbuiding and went to explore the numinous possibilities of magic in more familiar and rustic environments (consider for instance McKillip's *The Changeling Sea*, Le Guin's *Tehanu*, or Ellen Kushner's *Thomas the Rhymer*), in contemporary urban settings (such as Ottawa in de Lint's *Moonheart*), or in loosely described imaginary worlds rich in sub-created invention (such as in Tanith Lee's *Tales from the Flat Earth* series or in Diana Wynne-Jones's *Howl's Moving Castle*).

At the end of the eighties, the commodified high fantasy series – mostly still retaining the format of trilogies – whose worldbuilding still retained most of the trappings and binary oppositions that constituted the basis of Tolkien's secondary world (good/evil, dark/light, hero/villain, material/spiritual) began to show fatigue. Readers who had fallen into the genre at the beginning of the eighties had grown up in the meantime and were now demanding more 'realistic' fantasy, and more careful worldbuilding. Tad William's *Memory, Thorn, and Sorrow*, represented an early tentative attempt to broaden the scope of the world, adding detail at the level of political machinations and the number of factions and cultures depicted in the secondary world. At the same time, while still moving in a Tolkienesque trajectory, he tried to deconstruct some of the formulae of the established narrative, such as the return of an ancient Evil from the past, here recast as a kind of deranged tragic hero. In the following two decades worldbuilding in high fantasy evolved along two lines: (1) increase in detail, and (2) deconstruction of (allegedly) established tropes. More often than not, these two aspects proceeded alongside one another, and the overall effect was a further demythologisation of the secondary worlds. The trailblazer in this scenario was Robert Jordan; the success of *The Wheel of Time* brought new life to the high fantasy genre and opened the gates for the multi-volume series of doorstoppers that would expand the scope of worldbuilding at an unprecedented level. *The Eye of the World*, the first book in the series, starts by adopting many of the defaults of Tolkien's world and narrative, but Jordan devotes a good deal of his novels to describing the various cultures and factions in his world, putting in the narrative far more worldbuilding detail than anybody before him. While these do not necessarily help in moving the story forward – a multiplication of storylines and side-quests sidestep the main confrontation between the protagonist and the Dark Lord – they help to make the world more complex that many of his predecessors'. The background narrations are once again long-winded and detailed, in the tradition of Brooks and Eddings, and even if Jordan tries to imitate Tolkien's poetic language from time to time, the result is more historic than mythic. Jordan, as the most of worldbuilders who came after him, does not accept Tolkien's theory that going back in time history will become more mythical; rather, the opposite happens.[8] Even figures who might seem inspired by Primary World legends, such as the king Artur Paendrag (an obvious reference to Arthur Pendragon), are developed as purely historical figures within the secondary world without trying to use the mythical motifs that were at the root of their Primary World sources of inspiration. The legendary characters of the series, such as the evil Forsaken or the immortal heroes like Paendrag or Birgitte the archer, come to appear quite mundane when they interact with the protagonists of the series. Consider this comment by Birgitte

---

[8] The theory for which mythology arises from real history and deities originate from men whose stature has been magnified by the lens of Time is called euhemerism, after the Greek mythographer Euhemerus (4th century BC). In relation to the Norse mythology it has been adopted in the 12th-13th century by Snorri Sturluson in the *Ynglinga Saga* and the prologue to *Edda* and by Saxo Grammaticus in *Gesta Danorum* (Simek 75-76).

on circus master Valan Luca, when disguised as a performer in *The Fires of Heaven*: "He has nice legs, but I have never liked tall men. Add a pretty face, and they are always insufferable" (Jordan 524; ch.36). Hardly the language you would expect from Galadriel when commenting on the graces of Aragorn or Boromir. Detailed explanations of the magical system (which is referred to as One Power, rather than magic, but acts as such) are also provided throughout the novels. Finally, Jordan's worldbuilding, even in its multi-faceted complexity, is entirely subordinate to the story and not an independent endeavour of years if not decades, as was Tolkien's. The consequence is that any element of worldbuilding has its raison d'être in the framework of the final battle between the protagonist Rand Al'Thor and the Dark One. The characteristics of Jordan's worldbuilding here outlined can be applied to many subsequent high fantasy writers, from Brandon Sanderson,[9] to Steven Erikson, to R. Scott Bakker. The worldbuilding approach is more and more 'scientific', reliable rules govern magical systems, and the invented creatures and races are 'naturalised'. None of these authors construct a mythical past: when there are myths or legends, they arise through a collective loss of memory from original historical events. Thus the Parshendi become the mythical Voidbringers in *The Stormlight Archive*, or the Tiste Andii's divinity Mother Dark is revealed to have originally been a Tiste herself in *Malazan Book of the Fallen*. George R. R. Martin's *A Song of Ice and Fire* expands even more the complexities of the world, but preserves some characteristics of Tolkienesque high fantasy and old school sword'n'sorcery in the tradition of R.E. Howard. Magic in Westeros remains a mysterious and dangerous art, and it is mostly a tool in the hands of a very few individuals. That said, even for Martin, excessive details produce demythologisation: his dragons, however mighty, are more like powerful steeds than the primordial embodiment of evil represented by Smaug or (even more) Glaurung.[10]

The other path followed in the last twenty years – even if its seeds can be traced in Tolkien himself, considering the 'Narn i Chîn Húrin', especially

---

9 On the subordination of worldbuilding to the story in Branderson's *The Stormlight Archive*, see Givens.
10 We are provided a good deal of anatomical and physiological details about Martin's dragons, such as that their bones are rich in iron, they can only eat cooked meat, and that they possess only four limbs (two legs and two wings) because, "Now, there are no actual dragons, to be sure. But there are bats, and there are birds, and once upon a time there were pterodactyls. Those are the models to use when designing a dragon. No beast in nature has four legs AND wings" (Martin).

the converse of Húrin with Morgoth (*UT* 66-68) – can be defined a "deconstructive" approach in the sense that it tries to dismantle from within some of the assumed tropes and metaphysical conventions of the fantasy literature that *The Lord of the Rings* popularised. This deconstructionist approach goes further than merely taking a disenchanted look into history. The lines between good and evil, hero and villain are blurred, so that the worlds become in most if not all aspects morally grey and teleologically bleak. If there are divinities, or supernatural beings, they usually range from being amoral to utterly immoral and lack any salvific qualities. Most of these narratives subscribe a materialistic worldview: the demythologisation of the world entails the lack of a spiritual dimension, with no possibility of salvation, damnation, or redemption. Hence, evil manifests itself purely on a physical basis: physical abuse, mutilation, and sexual violence are used extensively and explicitly, often to shock the reader, and provide a tool to identify the 'wicked' characters. The most popular among the 'deconstructive' sub-currents of fantasy is 'Grimdark', which boasts authors such as R. Scott Bakker, Joe Abercrombie, and Mark Lawrence. The level of worldbuilding detail varies: R. Scott Bakker's Eärwa (first introduced in *The Darkness that Comes Before*) is one of the most complex and detailed secondary worlds developed after Tolkien's, with over four thousand years of human history, and more of previous non-human civilisation, described minutely. Abercrombie's narratives – such as *The First Law* trilogy – are more character-oriented, and only the key historical events are reported throughout the story. In both cases, the inspiration is drawn from history and related disciplines rather than myth. In Abercrombie's work, there is no aura of enchantment surrounding the immortal characters, such as Bayaz and the other mages, whose behaviour is practical and down to earth, driven by materialistic urges to accumulate power and control for power's sake. The Nomen, Bakker's immortal race, are materialistic deconstructions of Tolkien's Elves, deranged and decayed beyond any possibility of recovery. In a distant past they were mortal, and even if noble or beautiful, they were more the stuff of history than of myth, as the ruins of their majestic civilisation demonstrate. In Grimdark worlds, the monsters have been naturalised and stripped too of their primeval mythical powers: Sranc, Bashrag, and Wracu – Bakker's equivalent of Orcs, Trolls, and Dragons – are the product of advanced science used by an ancient alien race, while in Abercrombie's world there are the Shanka, humanoids produced by Kanedias the Master Maker using clay, metal, and leftover flesh. In both cases their origin is purely material, and seem to some extent bring to the ultimate conclusion the hypotheses that Tolkien explored regarding the origins of his own Orcs (*MR* 409-22). Magic is systematised to a great extent in Bakker's world, while it is more blurred in Abercrombie's: in both cases it is mostly used as a destructive weapon and never possesses the artistic and enchanting qualities described by Tolkien.

As we have seen from this survey, the main two trends of worldbuilding in fantasy have sidelined the mythopoeic approach that was at the basis of Tolkien's theory of sub-creation. This has clearly survived in other currents of fantasy that, as described before, had already flourished in the 1980s. Some genre authors kept on working with material and themes from fairy and folk tales, either setting their stories in small-scale and unmapped secondary worlds (such as Patricia McKillip in *The Book of Atrix Wolfe*, *Ombria in Shadow*, and *In the Forests of Serre*), or, to some extent, the Primary World with an access to the Otherworld (Peter Beagle's *Tamsin*, Neil Gaiman's *Stardust*, or Juliet Marillier's *Wildwood Dancing*), while in some cases the placeless and timeless quality of fairy-stories is preserved (Grace Lin's *Where the Mountain meets the Moon*, for instance). Other authors have dabbled and experimented to a greater extent with literary currents, especially postmodernism and magical realism, to bring new life to ancient myths. Within this current, the term "mythpunk" has been coined by Catherynne Valente to describe her work and those of fellow writers such as C.S.E. Cooney, Amal El-Mohtar, and Theodora Goss. All the mythopoeic authors share some common strategies of worldbuilding. They do not provide a map of their world, and often their world (or the Faërie part of it) resists any such mapping: the borders are not clearly defined, places shift locations. Faërie remains a perilous realm, as Tolkien postulated in his essay, but the danger is more in losing one's self (or soul), rather than physical peril. Magic has a subtle quality, and it is more directly related to the sub-creative possibilities offered by language. One, or more, of the fairy-tale's functions posited by Tolkien are satisfied: recovery, escape, and consolation. More than that, they are still "faërie tales" according to Tolkien's definition, as they are concerned with humans who are offered some access to the world of Faërie and the wonders therein. The writers from this second category tend to be more appreciated by critics and are often recipients of literary awards such as the Nebula, the World Fantasy, or the Mythopoeic Award. However, with few notable exceptions – Neil Gaiman stands out – they are usually outsold by writers of worldbuilding-reliant high fantasy. The lack of commercial success and recognition among readers may be a factor behind the criticism that more literary and mythopoeic-oriented writers have aimed at worldbuilding for the role it has played in disenchanting fantasy literature.

Critiques of Worldbuilding

The incompatibility – or strain – between worldbuilding and mythopoiesis has been observed by various critics in the recent years. The first comes from M. John Harrison, author of the *Viriconium* quartet, who famously dubbed worldbuilding "the clomped foot of nerdism" in an essay published on his personal weblog (Harrison, 'Very Afraid'). That essay was actually a continuation of a previous short piece, entitled 'What It Might Be Like to Live in Viriconium.' Here, as we can see, his critique is more aimed at post-Tolkienian worlbuilding, rather that at Tolkien's sub-creation itself:

> The commercial fantasy that has replaced them [*the "classical" modern fantasies (curator's note)*] is often based on a mistaken attempt to literalise someone else's metaphor, or realise someone else's rhetorical imagery. For instance, the moment you begin to ask (or rather to answer) questions like, "Yes, but what did Sauron look like?"; or, "Just how might an Orc regiment organise itself?"; the moment you concern yourself with the economic geography of pseudo-feudal societies, with the real way to use swords, with the politics of courts, you have diluted the poetic power of Tolkien's images. You have brought them under control. You have tamed, colonised and put your own cultural mark on them. Literalisation is important to both writers and readers of commercial fantasy. The apparent depth of the great fantasy inscapes – their appearance of being a whole world – is exhilarating: but that very depth creates anxiety. The revisionist wants to learn to operate in the inscape: this relieves anxiety and reasserts a sense of control over "Tolkien's World."

> Given this, another trajectory (reflecting, of course, another invitation to consume) immediately presents itself: the relationship between fantasy and games – medieval re-enactment societies, role-play, and computer games. Games are centred on control. "Re-enactment" is essentially revision, which is essentially reassertion of control, or domestication. (Harrison, 'What It Might Be Like to Live in Viriconium')

Harrison's main concern regarding worldbuilding is related to the impulse of the author to control the secondary worlds, a sentiment that curiously mirrors a central theme of Tolkien's legendarium: that sub-creators may desire to become masters of their little worlds, leading to rebellion against the only Creator and consequent effort to tyrannise the Primary World itself. Harrison does not share Tolkien's Catholic faith and his motivations are different. However the concern is the same, with ethical implications in the real world. For the purpose of this paper, it is sufficient to stress that Harrison sees excessive worldbuilding as an agent that destroys the poetic of the secondary world. In Tolkien's case this poetic is a mythical one. Hence, if we accept Harrison's argument, it follows that worldbuilding acts as an opposing force to mythopoeia: the more you supply of the first the more you tame and dilute the latter, weakening its mythical power.

Similar concerns, but from authors more actively engaged in reusing Tolkien's mythopoeic method, have been raised in two recent lectures in honour of Tolkien at Pembroke College in Oxford. The first one was from Lev Grossman, literary critic of the *Time* magazine and author of the *Magicians* trilogy, who pointed out the increasing mundanity of imaginary worlds in fantasy:

> And you write about these worlds differently. You do not treat them as fantastic, you write them in the same way that you would write about the mundane world, using the ordinary tools and conventions of realism. Narnia has no economy that I am aware of, but more and more fantasy worlds do, and not only that. They have ecology and geology. […]. Magic has rules now. (Grossman 20:24-21:02)

An even more radical rebuttal against worldbuilding was pronounced by Terri Windling, an author and editor firmly rooted in the mythopoeic side:

> If we could map Narnia, or Middle-earth, or Prydain, or the great Earthsea Archipelago so that every detail is defined, every alleyway known, […] it would no longer be fantasy, for the mystery would be gone and, when the mystery is dead, fantasy is dead. (Windling 6:29-6:58)

Most of these critiques, together with Gavriel Guy Kay's remarks quoted in the previous section, as honestly felt as they are, betray some kind of literary contempt towards (most of) contemporary high fantasy, seen as commercial and facile. However they also reveal the need for a new generation of authors able to tap again into the sources that Tolkien used (or to similar ones), the reservoir of power from which Faërie draws sustenance.

Conclusions or, is there a way back?

This paper aimed to show evidence of a fundamental difference between mythopoeia and worldbuilding. The first employs a language rich with mythical resonance, to evoke a sense of wonder in the reader, tantalise him/her with glimpses of "unattainable vistas" (*Letters* 333), and provide access to – or at least a glance of – the land of Faërie, the realm of imagination. The second leverages a variety of 'scientific' (including human sciences) disciplines to construct imaginary worlds that obey strict and reliable rules, the way the Primary World – as contemporarily understood – does. Mythopoeic worlds eschew this additional layer of detail that explains away all the mysteries, and still can create the illusion of depth just by hinting at what lies in the background of the narrative. Obviously in practice there is no clear-cut difference, but after Tolkien high fantasy has relied more and more on worldbuilding and less on mythopoeia. However, the opposition between worldbuilding and myth-making does not necessarily correlate with an opposition between high fantasy and 'low' fantasy. There exist many definitions of high fantasy, but I think the best has been provided by Fletcher Vredenburgh:

> Epic high fantasy needn't be epic in length. What matters is the story: creation – or at least the world – is at stake, the outcome will be settled between the forces of good and evil, and the tale is told from multiple viewpoints. (Vredenburgh)

Many works with strong mythopoeic themes – such as Alexander's *The Chronicles of Prydain*, Joy Chant's *Red Moon and Black Mountain*, Patricia A. McKillip's *The Riddle-master* – fit the definition of high fantasy provided above. Even if we consider the constraint that high fantasy must be (mostly) set in a wholly independent secondary world, as in the definition originally formulated by Kenneth Zahorski and Robert Boyer (Ekman 27; Wolfe 52), all the works above would still qualify.

Fragmentation is an unavoidable consequence of an established genre; however, one wonders whether the sundered paths of mythopoeia and worldbuilding can come back together in the future. Looking at the past 40 years this would not seem easy, as there are only a handful of works that tried to bring back a mythopoeic approach to high fantasy,[11] and the majority were not successful, either artistically or commercially. However most of the criticisms come from 'myth-makers' regarding the loss of numinous magic and mystery in the contemporary high fantasy worlds. High fantasy writers accept the current status quo and it is unlikely that they will go back and try to adopt Tolkien's mythopoeic approach, which is fraught with perils and pitfalls. I would argue that, rather than tending their little garden, it is up to mythopoeic writers to 'reach out', and write stories that can satisfy both desires: to provide a glimpse of Faërie as well as an immersive experience in a massive story. It is still possible to build large-scale imaginary worlds starting with the tools they already master, language and mythology, while keeping most of the worldbuilding efforts outside the text,[12] as it is what is left unexplained that mostly resonates in the imagination of the reader. This is not an easy endeavour but in it lies, I think, the road that brings back together the sundered paths of mythopoeia and worldbuilding.

Acknowledgements

Special thanks to Giovanni Carmine Costabile and Claudio Antonio Testi for providing feedback on the paper's subject. Very special thanks to Davide Chiarella for proofreading and discussion on contemporary fantasy literature, and to Milo Thurston and Bethan Jenkins for providing precious revisions and suggestions to the final draft.

---

11 A few works striving to balance mythopoeia and worldbuilding, with varying degrees of success, are the already mentioned *The Riddle-master* trilogy (1976-79) by Patricia A. McKillip, Charles de Lint's *The Riddle of the Wren* (1984), *A Gathering of Heroes* (1987) by Paul Edwin Zimmer, and *Abengoni: First Calling* (2014) by Charles Saunders.
12 Worldbuilding should remain an independent activity and impact as little as possible on the narrative (see the comparison between Tolkien and Sanderson in Givens).

About the Author

MASSIMILIANO IZZO was born and raised in Genoa, Italy, and currently lives in Oxford. He is a passionate reader of high fantasy, speculative fiction, and all sorts of mythological stuff. His previous contributions to Tolkien studies – 'Recurrent Patterns of the Fall in Tolkien's legendarium' and 'In Search of the Wandering Fire: Otherworldly Imagery in "The Song of Ælfwine"' – were presented at the 2016 and 2017 Tolkien Seminars in Leeds and have been published in the conference proceedings.

Abbreviations

H	TOLKIEN, J.R.R. *The Hobbit*. London: HarperCollins, 1995.
Letters	TOLKIEN, J.R.R. *The Letters of J.R.R. Tolkien*. Ed. Humphrey Carpenter, with the assistance of Christopher Tolkien. London: George Allen & Unwin: Boston: Houghton Mifflin, 1981.
LotR	TOLKIEN, J.R.R. *The Lord of the Rings*. 50th anniversary edition. London: HarperCollins, 2005.
MR	TOLKIEN, J.R.R. *Morgoth's Ring*. (The History of Middle-earth 10). Edited by Christopher Tolkien. London: HarperCollins, 1993.
SD	TOLKIEN, J.R.R. *Sauron Defeated*. (The History of Middle-earth 9). Edited by Christopher Tolkien. London: HarperCollins, 1992
TOFS	TOLKIEN, J.R.R. *Tolkien On Fairy-stories*. Expanded edition, with commentary and notes. Ed. Verlyn Flieger & Douglas A. Anderson. London: HarperCollins, 2008.
TPR	TOLKIEN, J.R.R. *Tales from the Perilous Realm*. London: HarperCollins, 2009.
UT	TOLKIEN, J.R.R. *Unfinished Tales of Númenor and Middle-earth*. Edited by Christopher Tolkien. London: HarperCollins, 2010.

Bibliography

ATHERTON, Mark. *There and Back Again: J.R.R. Tolkien and the Origins of the Hobbit*. London: IB Tauris, 2014.

ATTEBERY, Brian. *Stories about Stories: Fantasy and the Remaking of Myth*. electronic ed. New York: Oxford University Press, 2014.

BROOKS, Terry. *The Sword of Shannara*. [1977]. 5th ed. London: Orbit, 2006.

Sometimes the Magic Works. London: Simon & Schuster UK, 2003.

CLUTE, John and John GRANT (eds.). *The Encyclopedia of Fantasy*. London: Orbit, 1997.

COOK, Simon J. 'Fantasy Incarnate: Of Elves and Men.' *Journal of Tolkien Research* 3 (2016): Iss. 1, Article 1. <http://scholar.valpo.edu/journaloftolkienresearch/vol3/iss1/1>

DONALDSON, Stephen. *The Chronicles of Thomas Covenant, the Unbeliever*. London: HarperCollins, 1996.

EKMAN, Stefan. *Here Be Dragons: Exploring Fantasy Maps and Settings*. Middletown: Wesleyan University Press, 2013.

FIMI, Dimitra. 'Tolkien and the Fantasy Tradition.' *Critical Insights: The Fantastic*. Ed. Claire Whitehead. Hackensack: Salem Press, 2012. 40-60.

GIVENS, Nathaniel. 'Failing Tolkien: The Fall of High Fantasy.' *Difficult Run*. 19 August 2014 <http://difficultrun.nathanielgivens.com/2014/08/19/failing-tolkien-the-fall-of-high-fantasy/>

GROSSMAN, Lev. 'Fear and Loathing in Aslan's Land.' *Tolkien Lecture on Fantasy Literature*. 13 May 2015 <https://youtu.be/EcIWgPvx41c>

HARRISON, M. John. 'Very Afraid.' 27 January 2007 <http://web.archive.org/web/20080410181840/http://uzwi.wordpress.com/2007/01/27/very-afraid/>

―― 'What It Might Be Like to Live in Viriconium.' 15 October 2001 <https://www2.warwick.ac.uk/fac/arts/english/currentstudents/undergraduate/modules/en361fantastika/bibliography/2.7harrison_mj._2001what_might_it_be_like_to_live_in_viriconium.pdf>

HILEY, Margaret. 'Stolen Language, Cosmic Models: Myth and Mythology in Tolkien.' *MFS Modern Fiction Studies* 50.4 (2004): 838-60.

JORDAN, Robert. *The Fires of Heaven*. [1993]. London: Orbit, 2014.

MARTIN, George R.R. 'Dany and the Dragons.' *Not a Blog*. 8 July 2013 <https://grrm.livejournal.com/327410.html?thread=17902322#t17902322>

MENDLESOHN, Farah. *Rhetorics of Fantasy*. Middletown: Wesleyan University Press, 2008.

SALTER, Michael. *As If: Modern Enchantment and the Literary Prehistory of Virtual Reality*. electronic ed. New York: Oxford University Press, 2012.

SCHELLENBERG, James and David M. SWITZER. 'Interview with Guy Gabriel Kay.' *Challenging Destiny*. 6 November 2000 <https://www.challengingdestiny.com/interviews/kay.htm>

SHIPPEY, Tom. *The Road to Middle-earth*. Revised and expanded electronic edition. Boston: Houghton Mifflin Harcourt, 2014.

SIMEK, Rudolph. *Dictionary of Northern Mythology*. Cambridge: D.S. Brewer, 1993.

TOLKIEN, J.R.R. *The Hobbit*. London: HarperCollins, 1995.

The Letters of J.R.R. Tolkien. Edited by Humphrey Carpenter, with the assistance of Christopher Tolkien. London: George Allen & Unwin, 1981.

The Lord of the Rings. 50th anniversary ed. London: HarperCollins, 2005.

Morgoth's Ring. (The History of Middle-earth 10). Edited by Christopher Tolkien. London: HarperCollins, 1993.

Sauron Defeated. (The History of Middle-earth 9). Edited by Christopher Tolkien. London: HarperCollins, 1992.

Tales from the Perilous Realm. London: HarperCollins, 2009.

Tolkien On Fairy-stories. Edited by Verlyn Flieger and Douglas A. Anderson. London: HarperCollins, 2008.

Unfinished Tales of Númenor and Middle-earth. Edited by Christopher Tolkien. London: HarperCollins, 2010.

VREDENBURGH, Fletcher. 'Red Moon and Black Mountain by Joy Chant.' *Black Gate*. 10 November 2015 <https://www.blackgate.com/2015/11/10/red-moon-and-black-mountain-by-joy-chant/>

WINDLING, Terri. 'Reflections on Fantasy Literature in the Post-Tolkien Era.' *Tolkien Lecture on Fantasy Literature*. 26 May 2016 <https://youtu.be/SXh6oms0Kqg>

WOLF, Mark J. *Building Imaginary Worlds. The Theory and History of Subcreation*. electronic ed. New York: Routledge, 2014.

WOLFE, Gary K. *Critical Terms for Science Fiction and Fantasy. A Glossary and Guide to Scholarship*. Westport: Greenwood Press, 1986.

Péter Kristóf Makai

Beyond Fantastic Self-indulgence: Aesthetic Limits to World-building

Abstract

Contemporary fantasy and science-fiction construct original story-worlds to distance them from the primary world of the reader. This cognitive estrangement is supposed to perform a critical function, serving as a way to comment upon the social, economic and cultural relations of the author's primary world. This paper offers a cognitively infused criticism of the emphasis laid on world-building in today's SF/F fiction. In the contemporary media landscape, the proliferation of world-building fiction is largely due to the desperate need for the limitless expansion of successful intellectual property franchises. Rather than the plausibility of character actions and story arcs, these intellectual properties depend on the plausibility of the world for their success. Contrasting M. John Harrison's *Viriconium* universe and Jeff VanderMeer's *The Southern Reach Trilogy* with the aesthetics of world-building fiction, I employ a historico-critical approach to explore the limits of inner consistency in speculative writing and the (im)possibility of these story-worlds.

Off the top of your head, do you know when Paul Atreides landed on Arrakis? Or when the Battle of the Five Armies took place? Or when the United Federation of Planets was formed? You must have quite a nerd brain if you have just mentally rattled off 10191 AG, TA 2941 and AD 2161 without googling. But the fact that we *can* know the exact date of these fictional historical events is revealing. This encyclopedisation is symptomatic of the degree to which commercially successful fictional universes have passed from being the backdrops of epic adventures to fully formed worlds, complete with historical timelines, copyrighted material cultures and hundreds of thousands of fans who demand pitch-perfect accuracy in these minor details for every new addition, every sequel and prequel. In fact, it could be said that fans no longer consume the stories and spectacles of individual media products, but rather, the inner consistency of fictional universes.

And the word 'universe' is a telling one. Without wanting to be unduly constrictive in my definition of the term, I would argue that *world-building fiction* always looks beyond the individual media product. It thinks in universes, rather than works. World-building fiction is *ab ovo* a transfictional and transmedia phenomenon, spanning literature, films, radio, TV, comic books, analogue and digital games, virtual worlds, real-life encounters in fandom, material collections and more. Even though the world of *Game of Thrones* is heavily rooted in George R.R. Martin's *A Song of Ice and Fire* series, aspects of the world change and gaps in the world get filled in by TV series, computer games, fan fiction and replica shop items. Increasingly, we have to think of works such as Star Wars, Star Trek, Battlestar Galactica, the world of Azeroth, Tamriel or Hyrule, or the haunting landscapes of H.P. Lovecraft as narrative universes in their own right, with a recognisable cast of characters and props that can serve as themes for entertainment in vastly different media.

For all their believability, there is a tendency in today's worlds of speculative fiction (SF/F) to hew closer towards a greater realism than is strictly necessary to tell the tale the author devised. In the contemporary media landscape, this reality effect is not an artistic requirement but a commercial one. As story-worlds grow, so do the opportunities for marketing. The recent ballooning of 'lore' in commercial intellectual property 'story bibles' (which is the industry term for the document that tallies the characters, plots, history and material culture of a given story-world, used as a reference work for scriptwriting teams) and the Disneyisation of fandom (whereby consumers of cultural products become 'guests' or inhabitants of a story-world, who 'make the magic come alive', to evoke Disney discourse; see Smoodin) are telling examples of a digimodernist (Kirby) culture, in which the virtual reality of story franchises is their unique selling point. Rather than the plausibility of character actions and story arcs, these intellectual properties depend on the plausibility of the setting for their success.

In this paper, I examine the contemporary emphasis laid on 'realistic' world-building in SF/F fiction writing. I define world-building as the aesthetic practice of imbuing the story-world of a literary piece (especially works of speculative fiction) with a semblance of believable completeness by inventing a faux-history, detailed geography, mythology, social history, economy and fantastic infrastructure that keeps the societies of the fictional world alive and ticking. Now, world-building, like narrativity, is a scalar concept. It can be minimal or totalitarian, it can be done gracefully and almost invisibly, it can thoughtfully impact a story or it can get out of hand where writers trot out every insignificant detail they came up with. As all narratives require some world-building, I am not denouncing it as unnecessary, but I wish to offer a cognitively infused critique of elevating world-building into an art form of its own, removed from the concerns of mediality and narrative, where the story functions as a vehicle for the presentation of the world itself. To do so, I enlist the help of post-classical narratology and empirical studies of reading. I also draw from James C. Scott's critique of authoritative modernism on real-world utopianism (Scott). My main interest here lies in the aesthetic possibilities inherent in the fictional realm beyond the borders of realism. I focus on M. John Harrison's criticisms of world-building, his *Viriconium* cycle of stories and Jeff VanderMeer's *The Southern Reach Trilogy* to show how weird fictional domains counterbalance the dominance of world-building, where the desires for the "inner consistency of reality" (*TOFS* 59), fantasy and enchantment result in carbon-copied fantastic worlds based on the aesthetics of JRR Tolkien's *On Fairy-Stories*. I do this in an effort to highlight problems with catering to the desire of knowability and coherence that suffuse most world-building exercises functioning as fiction.

In my effort to highlight some disquieting tendencies in the current eagerness to embrace world-building as the *raison d'être* of speculative fiction, my arguments will necessarily touch upon the poetic (and sometimes downright vatic) question: 'What is literature *for*?' I profess to have no preference with regard to the manifold uses of literature. In a vulgar receptionist view, it is what people get out of it. Writing about the *Uses of Literature* in 2008, Rita Felski describes four of its intended effects, each a powerful emotional term in its own right: *recognition, enchantment, knowledge* and *shock*.

The one which interests us most as scholars of fantastic fiction, enchantment, describes the power of the novel to make us feel 'at home' with the storyworld. Although not conversant with Tolkien's mythopoetic work, Felski nonetheless describes two strategies of heightened attention to texts, one being "micro, paying fastidious attention to the luminous aesthetic detail; the other is macro, involving an all-embracing sense of being swept up into another world. The first requires a literary education in the protocols of close reading; the second epitomizes the seductive pull of popular entertainment" (53-54). The subject of this issue, the practice of world-building, is a form of "narrative architecture" (Jenkins 2004) that caters to the reader's sense of wonder and desire for "worldness" (Klastrup 2009) that produces enchantment on the triple-decker and omnibus scale.

To be fair to Felski, she is a natural ally to many Tolkien critics who had to fight an uphill battle against equating enchantment with the detrimental effects of escapism. She argues that

> enchantment matters because one reason that people turn to works of art is [...] to be pulled into an altered state of consciousness. [... It] is richer and more multi-faceted than literary theory has allowed [...]. Indeed, enchantment may turn out to be an exceptionally fruitful idiom for rethinking the tenets of literary theory. (Felski 76)

However, in fantastic and speculative fiction where world-building has become institutionalised, the knowability of the world is fetishised.

Strangely, the encyclopedic appeal of the mythopoetic imagination did not become a dominant organising force of world-building in the immediate aftermath of Tolkien's reinvigoration of the fantasy genre. (Although it has to be said that science fiction's love story with encyclopedias originates in earlier times, at least going back to the Encyclopedia Galactica of Isaac Asimov, evoking the Enlightenment project of collecting all knowledge.) Instead, readers had to wait until the 1970s and 80s to see the rapid burgeoning of fantastic worlds, which coincided with the rise of information technology, the home computer revolution, the emergence of the pen-and-paper role-playing game (Peterson) and the formation of late capitalism (Jameson). At the exact moment graph paper and the computer became a medium, encyclopedic vehicles for telling stories, the storyworlds of 'ordinary' novels became more spatialised and encyclopedic. Writing about Ballard's speculative fiction, Jameson actually suggests that enchantment can be found in "the affect released by the minute, and not unenthusiastic, exploration of this whole new world of spatiality, and the sharp pang of the death of the modern that accompanies it" (155). It is the degree to which this minuteness, this simulationist aspect of enchantment rules speculative fiction that I turn my attention to.

The enjoyment of literature never owes its allegiance to just one form of engagement. It will have to be aesthetic, escapist, political, moral, but most of all, memorable and tellable in order to make an impact and have staying power. In the evolutionary approach I find the most insightful, literature latches onto the human instinct and refined art to tell stories as tools for adaptive problem-solving (Boyd). Taking a simplified Darwinian look, one would be content to merely say that literature, and world-building literature in particular, is an exercise in adapting to the changing needs of societies to hold their advances up to the light of defamiliarization. Yet, there are many poetic powers invented worlds are invested with. So a naïve adaptationist view is never enough.

For a child, such as I was when I first began reading fiction, and speculative fiction at that, the discovery of another world, the world of the imagination, speaks to the wonder of possibility, of what could have been, and what could be, still. For the genre connoisseur, the mapping of a possible world could satisfy the desire to see past histories, motifs and alternative communities come alive. Or it might be a reassurance that their moral compass is straight, that even though our own world might not be the best place to live in, there is hope for change. Or it might be a delightful power-fantasy of humankind to actively shape the world to our needs, despite conflict. For the artist, a highly subjective engram of felt experience, organised in dense code, symbols to be unpacked. For the revolutionary, a politically conscious reflection upon society. For the miniaturist in all of us, the delight of an understandable microcosm that seems to work without being real, by the virtue of being fiction. There are no limits to the enjoyment and uses of world-building fiction, but I hope I might show that some styles of presenting the world are critically crude, pretentious, or self-serving, while others are commendable for the depth, precision and economy of their world-building.

Granted, all narratives take place in a world. In fact, positing a fictional world is a precondition for a narrative to be told. According to David Herman, a narrative is always situated in a storyworld where something unusual occurs that is relevant to human or human-like agents (*worldmaking/world-disruption*). But the focus, even in an alien world, is never just on the world itself, but on a human protagonist, on how they experience and act in that disrupted world (adapted from Herman xvi). Mark J.P. Wolf also argues that no storyworld is wholly divorced from our own primary world, that there are "degrees of secondariness" (25-28), as the reader has to ground the fantastical and otherworldly elements of the storyworld in the human sensorium, and extending the imagination with reference to the felt reality of the primary world.

Most often, in oral storytelling, the storyworld is a real setting, the here-and-now of the real world on Earth that you and I inhabit. After all, the art of storytelling is a cultural adaptation to evolutionary problems humankind has faced (Boyd), coding information and truth-claims in forms that can be passed down verbally or physically rather than genetically. But our ability to decouple what is being said from present reality, the ease with which we project our minds into the unseen worlds of 'What if?' also equipped us with an unprecedented flexibility to shape our own worlds by coming up with alternative societies that function better than present ones (Wolf 84-95). Explicitly fictional worlds first proliferated in the Age of Exploration, when travellers often made up fantastic societies to please their readers, but once the world-making genie was out of the bottle, there would be no end to the creativity of authors to entertain by describing worlds people may never visit.

Today, world-building is a commercial art form, designed not just to elicit wonder or to inspire the imagination, but to create recognisable intellectual properties. Producers can draw on these intellectual properties to deliver transmedia products with a stable, loyal base of superconsumers. As the foreword to *Eighth Day Genesis*, a world-building how-to manual says:

> The depth of your world is important ... even essential. Worlds should be able to be touched, smelled, seen, and heard. Each of these things is vital *to creating reality*. The smallest details can illuminate volumes. It is surprising what details wi[ll] bring forth entire feelings, associations, and images. (Klein 2, emphasis added)

This goes way beyond creating a setting for a story. As a world gets more detailed, consumers will increasingly become more attached to *something* within the fictional universe, forming emotional bonds with characters and objects that take on a semblance of reality, which can be used as markers of the fauxthenticity of fictional worlds, and not just in licenced products, but in fannish cultures as well (Hills).

We should not look at these designed opportunities for transmedia storytelling as purely calculated and overly exploitative. Fans are neither mindless consumers, nor are they totally dependent on authorial meaning-making to take pleasure in the world-play of convergent media platforms. Yet, as Dan Hassler-Forest articulates in an interview with Henry Jenkins,

> we've seen how transmedia franchising and world-building has really surged [...], to the point where fantastic fiction seems to dominate the media industries [...]. For fans of these genres, it's great in a way, because there is such a wealth of material being developed and produced in popular fantasy, and most of it caters directly to fans' sensibilities and desires. At the same time, I also think this is ultimately bad for fan culture, because all this stuff is being produced by media conglomerates working in a very competitive environment, and the sheer amount of material seems to impact fans' ability to participate creatively in any meaningful way. (Hassler-Forest, 'Science Fiction World Building')

Another issue is that I still struggle with seeing world-making as an independent art form, as constructed storyworlds are never articulated on their own, but as backdrops for historically situated, "qualified media" (Elleström 19). World-building manuals such as *Eighth Day Genesis* suggest otherwise, but the instructions they give are seldom media-specific, even though different media require and allow different degrees of detailedness to be presented to the media consumer, and have to be fitted to the conventions of storytelling and experiential design in order to create a satisfying end product.

Note that Sabrina Klein in *Eighth Day Genesis* draws attention to the qualitative aspects of fictionality, the multisensory, VR-esque desire to deliver simulated experiences, which is but one facet of our enjoyment of literature. This is storytelling in the experience economy, the new era in which intangible, virtual goods are produced using digital and emotional labour. Worlds based on SF/F literature are particularly prone to commercialisation and virtualisation because they can easily transcend ontological boundaries and present expectation-violating concepts that are memorable and only minimally counterintuitive to our folk notions of objects and world-systems (Porubanova-Norquist et al., Porubanova et al.).

In B. Joseph Pine II and James H. Gilmore's influential tract *The Experience Economy*, they discuss how retail environments should be constructed. They argue that the most sellable experiences are always themed and storied, and they provide important clues as to what will provide the most user engagement.

> They *must* alter a guest's sense of reality [...] by affecting the experience of space, time, and matter, [... and] integrate space, time, and matter into a cohesive, realistic whole. [...] Therein lies the power of storytelling and other narratives as a vehicle to script themes, [which] are strengthened by creating multiple places within a place [to] fit the character of the enterprise staging the experience. (Pine II and Gilmore, emphasis in original)

If this sounds very much like world-building, it is for a very good reason. The paradigmatic model of the experience economy is the Disney-style theme park, the first expression of a commercial interest in making story-driven, analogue virtual worlds for guests to experience and shop in, and a wildly successful one at that. Digital virtual worlds, such as those of computer games and massively multiplayer online environments (MMOs) resemble theme parks in that they are similarly suffused with stories in which the paying customer becomes the protagonist (Makai, 'From Neomedievalism'). Players in MMOs and off-line games may make purchases within games to enjoy the fast track to success and dress their in-game character in custom, personalised vestments. This model of in-game purchases are known as microtransactions in the games industry, and it is becoming ubiquitous in AAA titles. Both kinds of entertainment venues are known for their remarkable attention to detail, the unfamiliarity and exotic nature of their presented worlds, and the believability they inspire in the patrons that interact with the landscape. In other words, their worldness.

In the realm of games, Lisbeth Klastrup defines *worldness* as a "meaning-producing system" which is comprised of

> the complex interplay between a) the aesthetics of the gameworld as both an actualised explorable and mentally imagined universe; b) the experiences and means of expression the world as a game system and tool allows and affords; c) the social interaction in and about the world, that the unique characteristics of a world, its 'worldness' emerges, that which makes it different from all worlds of the same genre, both gamewise and socially. (Klastrup)

But, just as fruitfully, we could say that all fictional worlds with significant world-building could function as explorable and mentally imagined universes through cross- and transmedia representations or simulation, capable of producing aesthetic experiences and means of expression through social interactions within and about the world. For the players of *Everquest*, in Kastrup's example, that storyworld is palpably different in its heroic derring-do from, say, the mix of epic boss battles and the light-hearted quests of *World of Warcraft*, or the traditionally unpolished graphics, complex storylines and downright British humour of my own favourite MMO world, Jagex's *RuneScape*.

Pulling the focus of the lens a little wider, I would argue that there is a qualitative difference in how speculative genres treat their worlds, compared to stories rooted deeply in the primary world. While most literary fiction, high- and middlebrow realistic fiction stick to the believable, unchallengeably mundane primary world, other genres have thrived on mixing the stuff of legends and technological advancements with the world of the ordinary, and that very choice defined, determined their relationship with the story-worlds they create. Postmodern, genre-mixing works, of course, offer gateways into created worlds, but in those cases, the impenetrability or the unfamiliarity of language, the experimentation with representational codes get in the way of the aesthetic immersion of readers. The narrative worlds such as those presented in J.G. Ballard's *High-Rise* or Greg Bear's *Slant* present the storyworld as consciously and effortlessly built, allowing the reader's self-reflexion upon the ambitions of modernity to construct a radically anthropocentric and industrial life-world (Mateos-Aparicio). These, and other works of the same kind are designed to work against the natural instincts of the readers to confer reality status upon the fictional worlds they create.

Of all literary genres today, fantasy and science-fiction remained closest to the first instances of commercial, printed fiction, the genre of the Early Modern utopia, which constructed imagined story-worlds in a direct discursive relationship with power structures of the era they were conceived in (Jameson 22-56). This nascent genre of fiction was predicated upon a readerly expectation of adventurous reportage, internal coherence, a degree of vraisemblance to contemporary or past political entities, and a socio-critical awareness masquerading as ethnographical desire (Levitas; Vieira; Cottrell-Smith). Utopias were the crucibles in which the first fictional universes were forged.

However, the mass desire for world-building in the twentieth century emerged in the wake of cataclysmic destruction, in a century particularly predisposed to escape the horrors of industrial-scale carnage. Tolkien's Arda has been thoroughly infused by outrage at (if not wholly written in reaction to) the death toll of the two World Wars (Croft; Garth). Dungeons and Dragons, the seminal role-playing game with the largest campaign settings of any RPG to date were created by wargaming enthusiasts at the tail-end of the Vietnam war, roughly around the time video games were first devised, with an early focus on simulating war-like conflict (MacDougall; Mead; Peterson). So, from a historical perspective, world-building fiction is inextricably interwoven with modern violence, the taming of this violence, and escape from it.

At a certain point, though, world-building fiction seems not to so much heal those traumas, but to erase them. There is a fine line to walk between an adaptive engagement with fictional worlds, paracosmic play and what Eli Somer calls "maladaptive daydreaming", and transmedia storytelling facilitates (or hijacks) this immersion with commercially available material and immaterial props (and just as expected, trauma victims are much more prone to become maladaptive daydreamers; Somer, Tsoulis-Reay). Fan cultures today operate "both in opposition to and in collaboration with new forms of corporate power" and the media industry utilises "fantastic capitalism" to render fans' immaterial labour into word-of-mouth advertising and commercially exploitable intellectual property (Hassler-Forest, *Science Fiction*).

World-building as an overriding aesthetic for commercial fiction is unquestionably the product of the post-war yearning for a safe haven from the ravages of warfare. And yet, it finds its greatest expression in the contemporary world, in an age when computer simulation has become the handmaiden of fantasy. Novels (and to a lesser extent, comic books) are only the cheapest form(s) for getting the word out on interesting worlds that grip the imagination, which, if they find commercial success, are extended into more costly media franchises, encompassing films, TV, and/or computer games (Wolf 245-67).

Eighth Day Genesis is a fair example of the degree to which the *architecture* and *infrastructure* of SF/F worlds must be designed to fit genre expectations. Just by browsing through its table of contents, it gives pointers as to how the writer should conceive the geography and evolution of the world (67-98), its creatures (99-114), domesticated animals (115-26), cities (127-32), religiosity (133-44), magic systems (145-50), material culture (159-76), technology (177-92), historical timeline (193-200), government (215-32), legal system (251-68), and the world's consistency (293-301), among other topics. Even if any given novel for a particular setting might not require some, or even most of the aspects covered in *Eighth Day Genesis*, creators are encouraged to make these worlds easier on the imagination by thinking as much as possible about the interplay between the various natural and social interactions, and the implications thereof, to make them compelling and more impervious to the fans' nitpicking. It is as if the willing suspension of disbelief is less taken for granted and more hoped-for, just in case the creators slip up, which they invariably do.

In his *Travels in Hyperreality*, Umberto Eco addresses the allure of neomedievalism by calling it a result of our desire to reconstruct (and thereby efface) the past: "since we want to come back to the real roots, we are looking for 'reliable Middle Ages,' not for romance and fantasy, though frequently [...] we indulge in a sort of escapism *à la* Tolkien" (Eco 65). Setting aside the false diagnosis of Tolkien's fiction as escapist (and here I would stress again, that most world-building in fiction is functional and is therefore not inherently detrimental), Eco is savvy to the extent to which the Middle Ages have become a Rorschach test for cultural worldviews, having explored different aspects of the period in *The Name of The Rose* and *Baudolino*, to name just two of his works. The strong thematic, self-reflexive focus of these novels, their conscious incoherence, numerous anachronisms and their insistence at being works of "historiographic metafiction" (Hutcheon) are in stark aesthetic contrast with the simulationist drive of much world-building fiction. Somewhat crudely, Eco refers to the sword-and-sorcery genre as the epitome of a romantic medievalism, where "one is asked to celebrate [a] virile, brute force, the glories of a new Aryanism. It is a shaggy medievalism, and the shaggier its heroes, the more profoundly ideological its superficial naïveté" (Eco 69). Even so, sword-and-sorcery is less interested in the detailed construction of their fictional world's infrastructure than fleshing out traditional masculinities and advancing the plot of the story. Dimitra Fimi insightfully points out that Eco is miles away from the aesthetics of total detail, arguing that postmodern authors write about the Middle Ages "in order to interrogate, elucidate, or even mock our relationship with the past" (Fimi 56), whereas world-building fiction of the sort I outlined at the beginning of the article tend to eschew self-reflexivity and foster a more enthusiastic engagement, effacing the medium in favour of rapturous immersion.

On the other hand, I contend that even as world-building fiction advertises itself as a source of enchantment, it is strongly implicated in one of Felski's other functions of literature, knowledge (77-104). Fiction promotes a (social and object-related) epistemology "more akin to *connaître* than *savoir*, 'seeing as' rather than 'seeing that,' learning by habituation and acquaintance rather than by instruction" (93). Accepting this as a starting point in making sense of how world-building fiction 'sees', I argue that world-building proceeds according to a logic of "authoritarian high modernism", as James C. Scott (87) calls the tendency of modern states to impose total schemata of life on their presumably autonomous citizens. Scott connects this totalitarian desire with the war-torn history of the 20th century, which has "required unprecedented steps toward the total mobilization of the society and the economy" (97). In *Seeing Like a State*, Scott argues that the motivation for totalising governmentality is rooted in "a supreme self-confidence about continued linear progress, the development of scientific and technical knowledge, the expansion of production, the rational design of social order, the growing satisfaction of human needs, and, not least, an increasing control over nature" (89). Although Scott does not waste a single word on literature or fictional art of any kind, this view of civilization, the built environment and the proposed trajectory of human life finds ample support in the aesthetics of world-building fiction, offline computer games and table-top RPGs. Continued linear progress is the essence of the journey narrative, which is the underlying structure of most world-building fiction. It is also inherent in the gathering of experience points in wargaming and RPGs that amount to a steady rise on the discrete and hierarchical scale of development by "levelling up", described as "stratified progression" by Jon Peterson (341-58). The rational desire for an ordered social life is part and parcel of any decent world-building fiction, especially because said social order must be presented to the reader with a world-defining conflict in mind that drives the narrative. "There are few things that impact on the world of a speculative fiction story more than the governments that rule that world," Graham Storrs contends in *Eighth Day Genesis*, espousing the notion that government "interacts with all aspects of our lives" (Storr 233, 240). Even though he discusses the limits of government in the fairy-tale medievalism of standard fantasy settings, he still maintains a rather modern, authoritarian view of the relationship between a government and its subjects.

World-building fiction also mirrors high modernist governmentality because of the latter's self-consciously autopoietic nature: "At its most radical, high modernism imagined wiping the slate utterly clean and beginning from zero" (Scott 94), literally offering the blank page of the writer to the urban planner and the forest manager, giving them the power to author a nature better suited to human desires. Scott recognises this drive towards writerly authorship in how "social engineers consciously set out to design and maintain a more perfect social order" (92) by emphasising that they were endowed with a sense of "responsibility for the great works of nation building and social transformation" (96). As Scott describes the many modernist projects of ill-fated social engineering projects, we come to realise that the bureaucratic intelligentsia, the planners and engineers are building worlds, and reading fantastic and speculative fiction caters to the same governmentality in which well-thought-out worlds are accessible for the reader's exploration.

Scott calls this aesthetic "the miniaturization of perfection" (257), and draws attention to the many model cities and Potemkin villages which were, in effect, not just planned but *authored* cities. The fact that they were such failures (and why most people flee these cities and districts as fast as they can) indicates that authorial perfection and rational mastery of the environment is antithetic to the messiness of ordinary life. But the desire to improve on the life of a country and its people in the name of social order is a universal struggle in history, so Scott identifies the canals these thwarted desires were channelled into. He singles out the entertainment industry, which excels in catering to would-be planners and perfectionists. These media products offer "a small, relatively self-contained, utopian space where high-modernist aspirations might more nearly be realized. The limiting case, where control is maximized but impact on the external world is minimized, is in the museum or the theme park" (257).

Theme parks have appeared before in our discussion as the precursors to and logical culminations of the experience economy. But they are also catalysts and templates for the post-WWII turn towards utopian pasts and futures.

Disneyland, with its Fantasyland and Tomorrowland, was opened the same year the last volume of *The Lord of the Rings* trilogy was published in the UK. Other theme parks, such as Busch Gardens (1959) and Six Flags Over Texas (1961) soon followed, while in the domain of fiction, 'hard' SF and high fantasy coincided with the emergence and development of high modernity in architecture and urban planning. May they manifest in self-enclosed Cinderella worlds or Cities of Tomorrow, model terrain wargaming rematches of WWII battles, sprawling left-justified fantasy maps or galactic empires famed for their encyclopedias, utopias have shrunk in size to swell in ambition. No longer tasked with changing the physical world and providing prototypes for better living, Lilliputian secondary worlds soared high for the delight of those who visited them. Dystopias are invaluable critical responses to authoritarian high modernism, as they provide logical thought experiments that extrapolate the progress and decay of society based on (distortions of) high modernist ideals (Booker 1994). But dystopias are much more frequently interested in the complicity of the (liberal humanist) subject in the functioning of dystopias or their individual escapes from dystopic states rather than their democratic transformation (Stacy). Despite their promise of critical insights and revolutionary change, dystopias are deeply embedded in neoliberal culture and increasingly produced by teams of creators for a wide range of audiences, which affects how the storyworld prefers itself to be read and what that implies for their consumers. By destroying a libertarian dystopia, people could still be drawn further into the logic of commercial world-building (Pérez-Latorre and Oliva).

And when it comes to built worlds, size does matter. Despite the scale of the worlds depicted, the "visual aesthetic of miniaturization seems significant as well. Just as the architectural drawing, the model, and the map are ways of dealing with a larger reality […], the miniaturization of high-modernist development offers a visually complete example of what the future looks like" (258). Indeed, maps of continents or star systems, elaborate timelines, family trees, architectural illustrations are all favoured paratexts in SF/F fiction, designed to generate a reality effect in the reader, a sense of history, geology and cosmology of the fictional world. Even though Scott's examples of authoritative high modernism – like Brasília, a town authored by Lúcio Costa, forced villagization in Tanzania under Julius Nyerere, and Ludwik Lejzer Zamenhof's conlang,

Esperanto – all come from the real world, it becomes painful to see how central the rational construction of modernist capitals are to the aesthetics of science fiction, and 'forced villagization' is as apt a metaphor for much fantastic fiction as I can find, where people speak tongues created by a secret vice.

However, Scott witheringly observes that

> the planned city, the planned village, and the planned language [are] likely to be thin cities, villages, and languages. They […] cannot reasonably plan for anything more than a few schematic aspects of the inexhaustibly complex activities that characterize 'thick' cities and villages. (Scott 261)

Of course, fictional towns hardly need to be anthropologically thick, as they only need to provide reality until the heroes of the novel pass through it. But in world-building fiction, writers are admonished, "the cities you write about need to feel real" (Spendlove 127), otherwise "it will not be believable, and […] will seem drab and odd," so the best course of action, they advise, is to "treat them as [characters] when you write about them" (129-30). This means thinking about everything, from systems of trade and industry, monumental public buildings, systems of writing, sewage systems, waste disposal, the quality of roads and the locations of marketplaces. Yet, this infrastructural view is most often not essential for a convincing and emotionally moving story, even in fantasy worlds. The authorial desire to realise a fully living, breathing world on paper or screen will inevitably result in slip-ups and cutting corners in production. After all, all simulations necessarily leave out something from the source material of the simulation, and fictional worlds are no different. Even in real life, as the case of planned communities show: "the greater the pretence of and insistence on an officially decreed micro-order, the greater the volume of nonconforming practices necessary to sustain that fiction" (Scott 261). Indeed, Scott's insight that the order authoritative modernist projects promote *are* fictions is almost Hayden Whitean in its justified conflation of the world and the work, of historical and fictional narrative. World-building narratives are totalising discourses in the sense that they aspire to an inner consistency of reality by showcasing the author's ability to construct a whole universe.

The desire to experience a world without inconsistencies (Festinger) is a natural human urge, especially given the fact that our own real world does not resolve into neat motivations and rounded characters, with a plot that has a beginning, a middle, and an end. That we nonetheless impose these requirements on the everyday stories we construct testifies to the power of story structure, something we have devised and refined over millennia to best suit our evolved minds' capabilities. Whether it is academic achievement and minority identity (Sherman et al.), failing to climb Mount Everest (Burke, Sparkes, and Allen-Collinson), or religious deconversion (Wright et al.), we want to maintain a positive, stable identity even when changes in our worldview or achievements would posit us as someone different. People who fail to climb Everest or to lead their lives as born-again atheists have to fit their previous life narratives in new forms in order to account for the emotional, rational, and moral distance between the lives they were planning to lead and the discoveries they have faced along the way.

At the same time, these narratives of change follow persistent patterns of storytelling that prioritise socioenvironmental changes that pose adaptive problems for the protagonist who gets to solve this problem (Austin; Gottschall; Swirski). Heavily world-built narratives extend the sociocultural environments of the protagonists not necessarily to paint the landscape of action that impinges on their decision-making process, but to flesh out further narrative possibilities (the 'series potential', so to speak) and to emphasise the exotic otherness of the worlds the SF/F protagonists inhabit, often to the detriment of the story they are writing.

Frankly, criticism of world-building to this tune is hardly unknown in the world of speculative fiction. Authors who rail against the Tolkienian grain of a fully developed, world-like realm of story include Michael Moorcock, who focuses on stylistic matters ('Epic Pooh', revised version), M. John Harrison ('very afraid'), or Lincoln Michel ('Against Worldbuilding', 'More Notes on Worldbuilding'). Even Charlie Jane Anders, who acknowledges the important differences between so-so and stellar worldbuilding, criticises the "seven deadly sins of world-building" that detract from the general narrative thrust of the story. Meanwhile, Kate Elliot argues that world-building is not required for worlds in which the power structures of the fantastic story-world are expected to be similar to historical distributions of power, reflecting a systemic racist, colonialist, sexist bias, but story-worlds in which the social strata of the protagonists are markedly different from those of the (former) *status quo* on Earth benefit from a thoughtful (re)construction of progressive and alternative segmentations of power.

As a critic of worldbuilding, M. John Harrison's thoughts are perhaps the most articulate and most scathing. 2017 marks the ten-year anniversary of his essay on why he is "very afraid" of world-builders (Harrison, 'very afraid'), because they put "the great clomping foot of nerdism" to use as they "*exhaustively* survey a place that isn't there" (emphasis added). His criticism begins by separating ordinary writers and worldbuilders based on "assumptions about language, representation & the construction of 'the' world," namely by suggesting that writers wilfully accept that their fiction is make-believe, made up and otherwise artificially wrought, rife with inconsistencies and unexplored avenues. Meanwhile, worldbuilders "literalise the urge to invent" by attempting to "rationalise the fiction [with] exhaustive grounding, or by making it 'logical in its own terms', so that it becomes less an act of imagination," than an excuse for making things up. The author of *A Secret Vice* would no doubt cringe here, as his essay is an apologia *par excellence* for "legitimis[ing] an otherwise questionable activity" in Harrison's opinion.

He then proceeds to argue that worldbuilding is less a working method than an *ideology* for a particular type of authorial creation, and this is where he hits closest to home for many of us taking delight in meticulously invented worlds. But his warning is worth examining in greater detail, because it contains an important shift in the authorship of the storyworld from a logocentric, conservative one to a stance more congenial to reader-response criticism. He writes that worldbuilding "centralises the author, who hands down her mechanical toy to a complaisant audience [...] as a little god. And it flatters everyone further into the illusions of anthropocentric demiurgy." In other words, by feigning worldness through the obsessive attention to detail, readers are required to supply less of their own imagination to the work and are invited to behold the glory of the created world of the author. What Harrison might have overlooked in this essay, however, is the potential for fictional worlds to be dissociated from individual authors and become collaborative franchises, alternative universes of different (am)*auteurs* (as is the case with the endless torrents of fanfiction or the 'Abramsverse' installments of Star Trek). Nonetheless, once constructed and released, the world retains its primacy, beyond the power of individual authors, sustained by the imaginations of its everyday consumers and creators, the 'readers'.

Harrison takes a refreshingly Iserian view of literature, emphasising its ludic quality and the importance of interpretation, of gap-filling: "Reading was always 'active'; the text itself always demanded the reader's interaction […]. There was always a game being played, between writers and readers […], who knew they were gaming a system." In this perspective, there is more than a hint of the *Textspiel* (Iser). Harrison contrasts this with the supposed contemporary requirements genre readers make of speculative fiction, where they want to have an immersive literary experience, "a kind of non-writing which claims to be rather than to simulate," which I think would be clearer expressed if I rephrased it as "claim to simulate rather than represent," to be more mimetic rather than diegetic. In my own exploration of Tolkien's 'On Fairy-stories' and the power of fantastic fiction to create virtual reality by engaging the readers' imagination (Makai, 'Faërian Cyberdrama'), I have argued that something similar occurs in most reading experiences, albeit I use the word 'simulation' in the cognitive sense.

In my view, well-supported by empirical studies of reading and theories of fiction (Goldman; Holland; Oatley; Van Dantzig and Pecher; Zwaan and Pecher), there is a significant degree of mental simulation in all reading/imagining activities, so both M. John Harrison's writers and worldbuilders benefit from this basic human capability, but immersive texts (such as those in explicitly world-built SF/F) create more props for the imagination than is relevant for the processing of the event. It is not simply the case that the prose is adorned in these works, but rather, that language becomes a tool for illusion instead of illumination. It changes from a visible code to an invisible encoding. The fiction Harrison declaims, the one that 'claims to be' saturates the imagination with detail, and makes literature a transparent medium (Ryan), in which the mental simulation is made effortless and imperceptible by the very virtue of giving every imaginable verbal prop to the reader.

What Harrison calls a literature that claims 'to simulate' presents a clear layer of abstraction upon the constructed world: the artifice is clear for all to see, the text is palpably gappy and visible throughout the experience of reading – even as the prose leaves plenty of material to be mentally simulated, making the text more writerly, to use the old Derridean phrase. There is no game, as Harrison envisages it, in the world-built text, because verisimilitude and description trumps the collaborative imagination of the reader. I get the distinct sensation that Harrison suggests these setting-heavy fantasies and SF works are essentially world porn. They are not unlike the HD nature documentaries of the BBC and National Geographic that capture the world as it fades from view forever, with a tacked-on voice-over narration that imposes a soothing, yet melancholy storyline that aestheticises anthropogenic climate destruction.

Harrison himself admits the political nature of his argument, and contextualises it in the contemporary media landscape:

> prior to any act of reading, we already live in a fantasy world constructed by [...] media, politics and the built or prosthetic environment [...]. As a result the world we live in is already a 'secondary creation'. It is already invented. Epic fantasies, gaming & second lives [...] seem to me to be a smallish contributory subset of it. (Harrison, 'very afraid')

And not simply complicit in the exploitation of the imagination, these fictional media worlds have also contributed to *The Disneyisation of Society*, as Alan Bryman puts it.

Large media franchises thrive on large transmedia worlds because of the economical changes that ushered in the late capitalist or digimodernist (Kirby) era of virtualised worlds and the consumption of virtual goods, all of which crucially depend on grand *fictional* narratives for the continued engagement of the consumer base with these products. Once compact and self-contained, these stories turn into vast, sprawling worlds, culminating in the literally endless "content" of Massively Multiplayer On-line game worlds, which, Harrison argues, allows "the massively managed and flattered contemporary self to ignore the steady destruction of the actual world on which it depends" (Harrison, 'very afraid') and thereby defuse the conservationist, world-building agency of humankind.

His own masterpiece, the Viriconium cycle of stories, collected in *Viriconium* is a fine example of the spirit Harrison would later articulate in his admonitions against world-building. As Neil Gaiman explains in the foreword, this is a science fiction story that shades into fantasy as technological warfare has destroyed Earth, where old forms of warfare mingle with new as the remaining energy weapons of advanced civilisations fall in the hands of knights, swordsmen and magicians. But, more importantly, the mind-numbing amount of detail that makes Tolkien's major works inaccessible to non-genre readers is thankfully missing. So is the oversimulation of the world: "as you will discover, [there is] no consistency to Viriconium. Each time we return to it, it has changed, or we have. The nature of reality shifts and changes. The Viriconium stories are palimpsests, and other stories and other cities can be seen beneath the surface" (Gaiman in Harrison, xii). Then again, the name of the main city around which the heroic, sword-and-sorcery(-and-raygun) plot is organised, Viriconium itself is borrowed from a Roman settlement near Wroxeter, Viriconium Cornoviorum. And it is an unmappable city in an unmappable world, "two cities in one, in which nothing is consistent, tale to tale, save a scattering of place-names, although I am never certain that the names describe the same place from story to story" (xi-xii). John Coulthart, a cover designer who criticised most of the dust jacket covers the Viriconium stories received in a thoughtful blog post, advised that illustrators should bear in mind that "Viriconium stands for all the cities that have ever been, and with its avenues, *rues* and *strasses* often seems to be a composite of them all. [...] Its fixture in time is indeterminate [...] while the streets and quarters never remain anchored enough for any kind of map to be drawn" (Coulthart). Unmappability and compositeness appear to be essential for any artist who mentions the Viriconium cycle, and the lack of consistency, the lack of easy description remains in opposition to the coherence demanded by the aesthetics of world-building.

In hindsight, Harrison is programmatic in its denunciation of world-building. *The Pastel City* begins with the following description of Viriconium: Of the seventeen fictional realms that exist on the face of the Earth after the fall of civilization, "all but one are unimportant to this narrative, and there is little need to speak of them save to say that none of them lasted for less than a millennium, none for more than ten" (Harrison, *Viriconium* 3). An immediate focus, paring down the world to its essentials, Harrison wastes no time with names, timelines, genealogies or any material at all that would confer reality status upon the world. The plausibility of historylessness is warranted by the lack of written annals and the loss of linguistic knowledge, so central to Tolkien and Tolkienesque fantasy, as the last empire to fall "left its name written in the stars, but no one who came later could read it" (3).

Namelessness is intimately fused with indeterminacy. Lord tegeus-Cromis, who considers himself to be more of a poet than a knight, wields "his plain long sword, which, contrary to the fashion of the time, had no name" (7). This is Harrison sidestepping the pitfalls of Chrysaors, Nagelrings, Balmungs and Grams and their ilk which clutter the readers' mind in much of fantasy which mistakes the effusion of names for well-constructed mythology. Opting to foreclose the barrage of names and their integration into a vision of mythological mastery is to renounce the possibility of creating a *fac simile* mythos that plagues derivative world-building fiction. Nominalism and a modern encyclopedic attitude towards knowledge is explicitly denied by the equally nameless, deceptively omniscient narrator: Cromis "was more possessed by the essential qualities of things than by their names; concerned with the reality of Reality, rather than with the names men gave it" (7). It is an aesthetic that construes the entire world of Viriconium from a radically detached perspective, constituted by the paradoxical perceptions of individual characters. Viriconium is rebuilt in each focalising characters' mind, as if they, somehow, lived in subtly different worlds on the same planet.

As Cromis embarks on a perilous journey across the devastated countryside to protect his queen with the help of his brother-in-arms, Grif, his companion notes: "The landscape is so static [...] that Time is drawn out, and runs at a strange, slow speed" (44). It's as if these large swathes of land they pass through are characterised by their featurelessness. Which is not to say that Harrison is incapable or unwilling to engage in world-building at all, as his description of one of the travellers' stops proves:

> After seven days of that, and a further fortnight of travel in the grim mountains at the southern end of the Rannoch, he was glad to see the arable lands around Lendalfoot and catch a glimpse at last of the grey sea breaking on the dark volcanic beaches of Girvan Bay. Lendalfoot was a fishing town built of

pale fawn stone, a cluster of one-roomed cottages and long drying sheds, their edges weathered, blurred by accumulations of moss and lichen. Here and there rose the tall white houses of local dignitaries. In the summer, fine pink sand blown off the shifting dunes of Girvan Bay filled its steep, winding streets; the fishwives argued bare-armed in the sun; and creaking carts carried the catch up the Great South Road into Soubridge. (69)

Here, to my mind, is a fine example of world-building that could easily find its home in any fantasy series: placid, pastoral, defined, determined, idyllic and illustrated but not too expository. There is a liveliness to the scene that captures the reader's imagination without overloading it. Yet, this is only a flash of convention that is counterpointed with the indeterminacy of Dunmore's suburbs: "Something in the resigned, defeated landscape (or was it simply waiting to be born? Who can tell at which end of Time these places have their existence?) called out to his senses, demanded his attention and understanding" (68). There are patches of land that seem to be places in the world of Viriconium, and in much the same way as the cognitive mapping of the landscape demands the reader's attention by foiling their understanding, scenery in *Viriconium* is often divorced from the characters' ordinary sense of reality, defamiliarising the backdrops of epic adventure by their unreadability and indeterminacy.

Even the initial description of the Pastel City is closer to an artist's bird's-eye view, painted with broad, evocative strokes rather than meticulous, horse-hair brushes:

> The Pastel City. Five thousand Northmen march the length of Proton Circuit, their faces flushed with triumph. A tavern in the Artists' Quarter: spilt wine, sawdust, vomit. A line of refugees. The Pastel Towers, scarred in the final battle, when the last ship of the Queen's Flight detonated the power-source of the last remaining energy cannon in the empire, in a vain attempt to repeat Benedict Paucemanly's relief of the siege of Mingulay. (77)

So much history and geopolitics is crammed into this passage that most of world-building infodumps pale in comparison. The stylistic choices imply a heavily subjective, impressionistic view of a culture and the city, leaving more room for the reader to supply their own set of meanings to the description. The world-building the author treats us to is metonymic, vignette-like, flickering, rather than authoritarian. Sadly, the size and gracious prose of the Viriconium cycle deserves several separate papers to fully untangle its relationship to the history of world-building, but perhaps these examples reveal some of the depths of unreadability that is an essential feature of the half-constructed world of Viriconium. As tegeus-Cromis confesses, "It is important to my nature [...] that it remain a mystery to me" (108). His poem, recited in the epilogue aptly characterises the intended effect of Viriconium upon its readers: "The narrative of this place: other than the smashed arris of the ridge there are only sad winds and silences" (107). We, too, enjoy Viriconium for its poetic language and its melancholy lament of a passing cultural certitude of knowability.

As evidenced by the phenomenal success of long-stretching and/or dense fantasy series heavy on world-building, such as Terry Pratchett's Discworld novels, G.R.R. Martin's *A Song of Ice and Fire* cycle, or Jim Butcher's *The Dresden Files* and in SF, Asimov's Robot-Foundation-Empire universe, or Frank Herbert's Dune universe (among others), readers of speculative fiction have a much larger attention span and craving for detail than readers of other genres. Trained on intricately wrought fictional worlds, they retain minute trivia and navigate the arcane political, historical terrains and kinship relationships with ease. One key to this cognitive skill is the deployment of event memory, distinct from episodic memory, which distils the plethora of recurring, theme-like fictional events into neat, vivid snapshots that involve 1) the self and/or the other without necessarily having a first-hand experience, 2) a mental construction of a scene 3) that might entail a single event or the synthesis of several events collapsed into a cognitive template (Rubin and Umanath). Another factor is our ability to separate fictional worlds into discreet categories and separate our knowledge about them. Children have a keen understanding that there are different fictional worlds (Weisberg and Bloom) and are capable of distinguishing between reality and fantasy reliably at a relatively early age (5-7 years), not to mention that they can be sceptical of the fictional worlds they encounter (Woolley and Ghossainy). They are also capable of distinguishing between likely and unlikely cross-overs between fictional worlds (Skolnick and Bloom). This distinction between different fictional universes uses different brain areas and elicit different responses than distinguishing between reality and fiction (Yang and Xue), suggesting that much of fictional world-building occurs on the semantic level without reality-testing. We are also much more lenient towards strange and incongruous events when fictional worlds are crossed and characters behave inconsistently as opposed to the erroneous facts we read in fiction about the real world (Filik and Leuthold).

Yet another principle that readers learn in childhood is to draw inferences from real-world contexts and to generalise event structures in fictional contexts (Walker, Ganea, and Gopnik). As they hear more and more stories, children learn to create causal structures of events from tales. They also assume that everything not described explicitly to work according to the laws of the fictional world will probably behave similarly to their real-world counterparts. This goes by many names, such as "the principle of minimal departure" in narratology (Ryan), "reality principle" in psychology (Walton), and "gap-filling" in literary theory (Iser). Taken together, these scholars argue that readers actively participate in the meaning-making process by defaulting to their naive theories about how the primary world works. Readers also learn facts about the real world from fictional works, and they may also accept inaccurate or downright false information from stories, which have an impact on their problem-solving in the domain the false information pertains to (Butler, Dennis and Marsh). Ironically, the more time people spend with a particular text or the more often they reread one, the more susceptible they become to adopting false beliefs about that world, even in fiction (Eslick, Fazio and Marsh).

Now, all of this paints a certain picture of credulity, of our disarming facility and willingness to take fictional information for granted. Furthermore, it appears that although we are good at distinguishing fictional worlds from reality, and we can separate fictional knowledge from different worlds into their own metarepresentations, as we source-tag them, the fictional status seems to be only important for most readers as an information about the decision-making process on whether we should act upon the information we receive (Holland, 36-37, 47-58, and in passim), and when we decide it is no longer real, we can enjoy the ride.

Most devastating of all to any hope of finding limits to what we can imagine is the fact that fiction is free of any laws of physics that might constrain the creative powers of language. The real-world human ability of "mental time travel", that is, imagining the future and the past, are literalised in science fiction (Suddendorf, Addis and Corballis; de Bourcier). Fictional consistency is an art in itself, as Tolkien and other writers have long realised.

Seemingly, there is no limit to what we can believe about fictional worlds. Nonetheless, imaginative limits to world-building do exist. In recent years, a newly-founded Nordic school of unnatural narratology has focused on the anti-mimetic qualities of storyworlds. Fascinated by the many ways authors violate our preconceived notions of what is possible in the diegetic realms of fiction, these scholars explore what readers do when they can no longer operate the basic cognitive functions they use to interpret more mimetic (i.e. realistic) narratives. Jan Alber distinguishes between two kinds of impossibility or unnaturality: violations of physical possibility space and violations of logical possibility spaces (Alber). There is a great difference between a fictional city that is floating in the clouds (as is the case with the Star Wars Universe's Cloud City) and the nestedness of fictional worlds in a story that violates the accepted rules of ontology (as in Philip K. Dick's *The Three Stigmata of Palmer Eldritch* or *Ubik*) or causality (such as the film *Predestination*). People are much more willing to accept physically impossible storyworlds than ontologically or causally impossible storyworlds, because the former only require them to suspend their judgements about physical possibilities not immediately perceptible to the characters, whereas the latter questions very basic childhood experiences about the consequences of actions and event sequencing, which are foundational to the narrative understanding of the world. We are much stricter or narrow-minded as to what can cause what as opposed to what the world can be built upon (Foy).

Like most speculative fiction, the 'new weird' genre is dedicated to bringing original, thought-provoking concepts to life by presenting fictional worlds in which nothing is as it seems. Although it is a sub-genre of speculative fiction, Jeff VanderMeer's *Southern Reach Trilogy* (composed of *Annihilation*, *Authority* and *Acceptance*) is celebrated for its inventiveness of making the primary world (in this case, Southern Florida) seem like an alien world. He does so by taking a government expedition into the jungles of Florida in search of a mysterious lifeform that warped the environment to make a new *Umwelt* for mysterious creatures. The characters have to face the fact that their scientific methods prove inadequate to fully describe and thereby capture the *genius loci* of Area X.

The point of the expeditions, organised by the novel's shadowy government corporation, the Southern Reach, is to ascertain the nature of the invasive species and strange happenings in the locale only known as Area X. However, the inquisitive desire to know is repeatedly thwarted by the seemingly sentient Area X, bringing madness to all who come into contact with the territory. Area X functions as a full-on antagonist – a land that has to be, but cannot be known. At least, not by humans.

With the elision of the names of the expedition crew, who are only referred to by their occupations (such as the biologist, the surveyor, etc.), Area X becomes an equal participant on whom the readers' attention is focussed. In a way, this is a dream of world-builders: a story in which the setting becomes a character. However, by the beginning of the novel, there have been numerous expeditions to come and survey Area X, none of which came back with definitive conclusions about this land, and the ability of Area X to stump the biggest minds of the storyworld only serves to wrestle away the power of its would-be surveyors.

The current expedition we come to accompany as readers are designated as the 12th Expedition, but we later come to realise that there have been numerous 11th expeditions, and that the expeditions explore an ever-changing Area X, as expeditions come back with conflicting and contradictory reports. Furthermore, members of the expeditions seldom arrive as the people they have left. If this description sounds mysterious, it is because Area X changes people and the world around them. Like the author, expedition members arrive as potential world-builders, but in the unknowable terrain, they themselves are reconstituted by the inconsistent internal logic of the world they wish to describe. The world has the power to rewrite humans.

By way of an example, there is a concave structure within Area X that consists of a cavernous, downward spiral, almost like a spiral staircase, that bores deep into the earth. The narrator of the Twelfth Expedition, however, constantly speaks of the architectural object as a tower. The biologist also speaks of this "tower" in biological terms that suggests a certain sentience: "We had no sense of its purpose" (*Annihilation* 8), "the tower was *breathing*" (41, emphasis in the original), "the tower steps kept revealing themselves" (47), "something below us is writing" (51). The tower exerts a curious influence upon all who visit it. Guests can no longer think of it in terms of its actual architectural structure, but rather, as a cognitive impression that some alien presence has imposed upon them. Hence, a hole in the ground can become a tower, by directly rewiring the cognition of story-world characters in a way that is fully inconsistent with what I call their intuitive, *folk architectural notions* (in analogy with *folk biology* and *folk psychology*).

Area X has a porous boundary, always expanding and colonising the realm of the storyworld, the territory of realism. The border is a perilous territory the Southern Reach experiments on to figure out how it works. Assuredly, the scientific method and cognitively-ruled techniques of seeking knowledge will prove to be unfruitful. In one of the experiments Southern Reach devised, the personnel of the institute herded two thousand rabbits into the border from the outside. The rabbits were "squirming atop one another as they formed sloppy rabbit pyramids in their efforts not to be pushed into the border" and then vanished inside the borders (VanderMeer, *Authority* 56). Within the diegetic world, when the video footage of the experiment is brought in for analysis, the government servicemen found "a microsecond of transition in which a half or quarter of a rabbit might appear on the screen," which charted a "moment between there and not-there. In one still, this translated into staring at the hindquarters of about four dozen jostling rabbits, mostly in mid-leap, disembodied from their heads and torsos" (56). But after the rabbits disappeared, later expeditions cannot find a trace of any lagomorphic activity in Area X.

The world no longer follows the world-building logic of realism, and veers into the territory of the uncanny. This impossible storyworld might be following its own rules, but we will not be able to describe them. Playing with the expectations of the genre reader raised on coherent and detailed storyworlds, VanderMeer abandons the logic of internally consistent world-building in favour of a technique that retains the awe of the traveller into the realm of the unknown. In effect, Area X is woven from the same material than Faërie, the Perilous Realm. As Tolkien wrote, "Faërie cannot be caught in a net of words; for it is one of its qualities to be indescribable, though not imperceptible. It has many ingredients, but analysis will not necessarily discover the secret of the whole" (*TOFS* 114). In this respect, worlds like M. John Harrison's Viriconium and VanderMeer's Area X are more faithful to Tolkien's original conception of the story-world of fairy-stories than the über-consistency of *The Lord of the Rings* or much of carefully invented world-built fantasies.

The contemporary exhortations of speculative fiction teachers to create meticulously coherent worlds, rich in trivia and doodads, work against the aesthetic ethos of the novel (founded on the principle of social mind-reading) and inculcate a particularly statist, geopolitical view of worlds in the reader. World-building teaches you how to "see like a state" (Scott). World-building is the high modernist planner's wet dream: you get to design everything from gravity to flora, fauna, infrastructure, people, customs, towns, kingdoms, intergalactic relations, and everything works according to the grand plan, the plot of the book. Of course, one of the great reliefs of writing a book is that everything needs to go only as 'wrong' as the plot requires for the hero to emerge from it victorious. But in world-building fiction, the case is not so much that the hero saves the world. Instead, the world saves the hero, and when the world is saved, the writer is saved, because their commercial fates are interlinked.

Nothing resists the machinations of the world-builder, who is aided and abetted by the legions of fans who require ever more details and consistency, dooming the writer to be crushed by the weight of internal logic. From Harry Potter fans' outcry over publishing *Harry Potter and the Cursed Child* as a script (Vincent), to the establishment of the Wizarding World of Harry Potter in Orlando with the express purpose of making a fictional world a reality (Godwin, 'Theme Park'); from fannish insertion of the creative self as an ethnographer of fictional worlds (Gunnels and Cole) to media tourism that functions as an extension to fictional world-building (Norris; Waysdorf and Reijnders), all the way to Secret Cinema's in-depth recreation of movie scenes in real-world locations (Atkinson and Kennedy), we are coming to see how the encyclopedic nature and the inner consistency of reality becomes an imperative and a driving logic for the creation of new fictional universes. Scale-accurate miniatures with intricately detailed paintwork and the stories fans create with them approach a level of unprecedented, *trompe l'oeil* photorealism (Godwin, 'Mimetic Fandom').

Admittedly an extreme (and enviable) case is one of Robert Wardhaugh, a London, Ontario resident who has been playing the same Dungeons and Dragons campaign for over 35 years. His story spans several campaign settings that are made realistic with over 20000 miniature figurines and dozens of model terrains (Great Big Story). But despite its amazingly admirable over-elaboration, Wardhaugh's pastime is just a logical culmination of the totalising aesthetic of world-building.

Even so, this piece was not written to destroy speculative and fantastic fiction for its insistence on bringing their readers the pleasures of 'world play', so to speak. Our willingness to create paracosms, utopias of the mind are as universal as fiction itself. In a cognitive, evolutionary view, our ability to create counterfactual, fictional worlds is one of our defining features. Alternative pasts compete for our memories. We construe the future as we tell stories about it. And yet, our yearning for detail and verisimilitude detract and deviate from the sublime virtue of fiction to gather strength from it to change the world. We must fill in the gaps with the powers of the creative mind always seeking new, real worlds to construct.

About the Author

Péter Kristóf Makai wrote his PhD about autism fiction in contemporary British and American novels, has been working as a freelance literary translator, and is currently a Postdoctoral Research Fellow at Linnaeus University's Centre for Intermedial and Multimodal Studies. As a games studies scholar, he has contributed to Wiley-Blackwell's *A Companion to J.R.R. Tolkien* and *Tolkien Studies,* and has also published on issues in sci-fi and the fantastic in several international journals and edited volumes.

Abbreviations

TOFS   TOLKIEN, J.R.R. *Tolkien On Fairy-stories*. Ed. Verlyn Flieger and Douglas A. Anderson. London: HarperCollins, 2008.

Bibliography

ALBER, Jan. 'Impossible Storyworlds – and What to Do with Them.' *StoryWorlds: A Journal of Narrative Studies* 1 (2009): 79-96.

ANDERS, Charlie Jane. '7 Deadly Sins of Worldbuilding.' *io9*, Aug 2, 2013. https://io9.gizmodo.com/7-deadly-sins-of-worldbuilding-998817537

ATKINSON, Sarah and W. KENNEDY. 'From Conflict to Revolution: The secret aesthetic, narrative spatialisation and audience experience in immersive cinema design.' *Participations* 13.1 (2016): 252-79. <http://www.participations.org/Volume%2013/Issue%201/S1/7.pdf>

AUSTIN, Michael. *Useful Fictions: Evolution, Anxiety, and the Origins of Literature*. Lincoln NE and London: University of Nebraska Press, 2010.

BALLARD, J. G. *High-Rise*. London: Jonathan Cape, 1975.

BEAR, Greg. *Slant*. New York: Tor Books, 1997.

BLIZZARD ENTERTAINMENT. *World of Warcraft*. On-line World, 2004ff.

BOOKER, M. Keith. *The Dystopian Impulse in Modern Literature: Fiction as Social Criticism*. Westport CT: Praeger, 1994.

BOYD, Brian. *On the Origin of Stories: Evolution, Cognition, and Fiction*. Cambridge MA and London: Belknap-Harvard, 2009.

BRYMAN, Alan. *The Disneyization of Society*. London: Sage Publications, 2004.

BURKE, Shauna M., Andrew C. SPARKES, and Jacquelyne ALLEN-COLLINSON. 'High Altitude Climbers as Ethnomethodologists Making Sense of Cognitive Dissonance: Ethnographic Insights from an Attempt to Scale Mt Everest.' *The Sport Psychologist* 22.3 (2008): 336-55.

BUTLER, Andrew C., Nancy A. DENNIS, and Elizabeth J. MARSH. 'Inferring Facts From Fiction: Reading Correct and Incorrect Information Affects Memory for Related Information.' *Memory* 20.5 (2012): 487-98. <doi: 10.1080/09658211.2012.682067>

COTTRELL-SMITH, Cheryl. 'The Island Utopia and the Chronotope: Temporal Distortion in Utopian Fiction of the Renaissance.' *Bristol Journal of English*

Studies 1 (Summer 2012). <http://englishjournal.blogs.ilrt.org/files/2012/07/The-Island-Utopia-and-the-Chronotope-Cheryl-Cottrell-Smith.pdf>

COULTHART, John. 'Covering Viriconium.' {*feuilleton*}. <http://www.johncoulthart.com/feuilleton/2012/06/11/covering-viriconium/>

CROFT, Janet Brennan. *War and the Works of J.R.R. Tolkien*. Westport CT: Praeger, 2004.

DAYBREAK GAME COMPANY. *Everquest*. San Diego CA: Sony Online Entertainment, 1999. On-line World.

DE BOURCIER, Simon. 'Impossible Objects, Thought Experiments, and the Logic of Fictional Worlds.' *GLITS-e: A Journal of Criticism* 2:2011-12. <https://www.gold.ac.uk/glits-e/glits-e-2011-2012/impossible-objects-thought-experiments-and-the-l/>

DICK, Philip K. *The Three Stigmata of Palmer Eldritch*. London: Gollancz, 2003.

Ubik. London: Gollancz, 2004.

ECO, Umberto. *Baudolino*. London: Secker and Warburg, 2002.

The Name of the Rose. New York: Harcourt, 1983.

Travels in Hyperreality. Trans. William Weaver. San Diego CA: Harcourt Brace and Company, 1986.

ELLESTRÖM, Lars. *Media Transformation: The Transfer of Media Characteristics Among Media*. Basingstoke: Palgrave Macmillan, 2014.

ELLIOT, Kate. 'The Status Quo Does Not Need World-Building.' *I Make Up Worlds*. <http://www.imakeupworlds.com/index.php/2013/09/the-status-quo-does-not-need-world-building/>.

ESLICK, Andrea N., Lisa K. FAZIO, and Elizabeth J. MARSH. 'Ironic Effects of Drawing Attention to Story Errors.' *Memory* 19.2 (2011): 184-91. <doi:10.1080/09658211.2010.543908>

FESTINGER, Leon. *A Theory of Cognitive Dissonance*. Stanford CA: Stanford University Press, 1957.

FILIK, Ruth and Harmuth LEUTHOLD. 'The Role of Character-based Knowledge in Online Narrative Comprehension: Evidence from Eye Movements and ERPs.' *Brain Research* 1506 (2013): 94-104.

FIMI, Dimitra. 'The Past as an Imaginary World: The Case of Medievalism.' *Revisiting Imaginary Worlds: A Subcreation Studies Anthology*. Ed. Mark J.P. Wolf. New York: Routledge, 2017. 46-65.

Foy, Jeffrey E. and Richard J. Gerrig. 'Flying to Neverland: How Readers Tacitly Judge Norms during Comprehension.' *Memory & Cognition* 42.8 (2014), 1250-59. <doi: 10.3758/s13421-014-0436-8>

Garth, John. *Tolkien and the Great War: The Threshold of Middle-Earth*. London: HarperCollins, 2003.

Godwin, Victoria. 'Mimetic Fandom and one-sixth-scale Action Figures.' *Transformative Works and Cultures* 20 (2015). <http://journal.transformativeworks.org/index.php/twc/article/view/686/550>

'Theme Park as Interface to the Wizarding (Story) World of Harry Potter.' *Transformative Works and Cultures* 25 (2017). <http://journal.transformativeworks.org/index.php/twc/article/view/1078/871>

Goldman, Alvin I. *Simulating Minds: The Philosophy, Psychology, and Neuroscience of Mindreading*. Oxford: Oxford University Press, 2006.

Gottschall, Jonathan. *Literature, Science, and a New Humanities*. New York: Palgrave Macmillan, 2008.

Gunnels, Jen and Carrie J. Cole. 'Culturally Mapping Universes: Fan Production as Ethnographic Fragments.' *Transformative Works and Cultures* 7 (2011). <http://journal.transformativeworks.org/index.php/twc/article/view/241/220>

Great Big Story. 'The Neverending Game of Dungeons and Dragons.' <https://www.greatbigstory.com/stories/the-never-ending-game-of-dungeons-dragons>

Harrison, M. John. *Viriconium*. Foreword by Neil Gaiman. New York: Spectra, 2005.

'very afraid.' Archived from *Uncle Zip's Window*. <http://web.archive.org/web/20080410181840/http://uzwi.wordpress.com/2007/01/27/very-afraid/>

Hassler-Forest, Dan. 'Science Fiction World Building in a Capitalist Society: An Interview with Dan Hassler-Forest (Part One).' Interview by Henry Jenkins, Sept. 2016. http://henryjenkins.org/blog/2016/09/science-fiction-world-building-in-a-capitalist-society-an-interview-with-dan-hassler-forest-part-one.html

Science Fiction, Fantasy and Politics: Transmedia World-building Beyond Capitalism. London: Rowman & Littlefield, 2016.

Herman, David. *Basic Elements of Narrative*. Oxford: Wiley-Blackwell, 2009.

Hills, Matt. 2014. 'From Dalek Half Balls to Daft Punk Helmets: Mimetic Fandom and the Crafting of Replicas.' *Transformative Works and Cultures* 16. <http://journal.transformativeworks.org/index.php/twc/article/view/531/448>

Holland, Norman N. *Literature and the Brain*. Gainesville FL: PsyArt Foundation, 2009.

HUTCHEON, Linda. 'Historiographic Metafiction: 'The Pastime of Past time'.' *A Poetics of Postmodernism: History, Theory, Fiction.* New York: Routledge, 1988. 105-23.

ISER, Wolfgang. *The Act of Reading: A Theory of Aesthetic Response.* Baltimore: Johns Hopkins University Press, 1978.

JAGEX GAMES STUDIO. *RuneScape.* 2001ff. On-line World.

JAMESON, Fredric. *Archaeologies of the Future: The Desire Called Utopia and Other Science Fictions.* New York: Verso, 2005.

JENKINS, Henry. 'Game Design as Narrative Architecture.' 2004. <http://homes.lmc.gatech.edu/~bogost/courses/spring07/lcc3710/readings/jenkins_game-design.pdf>

KIRBY, Alan. *Digimodernism: How New Technologies Dismantle the Postmodern and Reconfigure Our Culture.* London: Continuum, 2009.

KLASTRUP, Lisbeth. 'The Worldness of EverQuest – Exploring a 21st Century Fiction.' *Game Studies* 9.1 (2009). <http://gamestudies.org/0901/articles/klastrup>

KLEIN, Sabrina (ed.). *Eighth Day Genesis: A Worldbuilding Codex for Writers and Creatives.* Dayton OH: Alliteration Ink, 2012.

LEVITAS, Ruth. *Utopia as Method: The Imaginary Reconstruction of Society.* Basingstoke and New York: Palgrave Macmillan, 2013.

MACDOUGALL, Robert. 'Fantasy Vietnam.' Archived from personal webpage. <https://web.archive.org/web/20160818162017/http://www.robmacdougall.org/blog/2009/05/fantasy-vietnam/>

MAKAI, Péter Kristóf. 'Faërian Cyberdrama: When Fantasy Becomes Virtual Reality.' *Tolkien Studies* 7 (2010): 35-53.

'From Neomedievalism to Retrofuturism: A Virtual Addition to the Genealogy of the Pleasure Ground.' *Time and Temporality in Theme Parks.* Ed. Filippo Carla-Uhink, Florian Freitag, Sabrina Mittermeier, and Ariane Schwarz. Hannover: Wehrhahn Verlag, 2017. 201-22.

MATEOS-APARICIO, Angel. 'Impenetrable Edifices: The Building as Metaphor of Postmodern Social Structure in J.G. Ballard and Greg Bear.' Repository of the Universidad de Castilla-La Mancha. <https://ruidera.uclm.es/xmlui/handle/10578/2343>

MEAD, Corey. *War Play: Video Games and the Future of Armed Conflict.* Boston MA: Houghton Mifflin Harcourt, 2013.

Michel, Lincoln. 'Against Worldbuilding: Why 'worldbuilding' is the most overrated and overused concept in fiction.' *ElectricLiterature*, Apr 6 2017. <https://electricliterature.com/against-worldbuilding-700e4861c26b>

'More Thoughts about Worldbuilding and Food: How we should or shouldn't imagine imagine new worlds.' *ElectricLiterature*, May 12 2017. <https://electricliterature.com/more-thoughts-about-worldbuilding-and-food-d8d53789bd3e>

Moorcock, Michael. 'Epic Pooh.' *Revolution Science Fiction* 2002 [1978]. <http://www.revolutionsf.com/article.php?id=953>.

Norris, Craig. 'Japanese Media Tourism as World-building: Akihabara's Electric Town and Ikebukuro's Maiden Road.' *Participations* 13.1 (2016): 656-81. <http://www.participations.org/Volume%2013/Issue%201/S3/10.pdf>

Oatley, Keith. *Such Stuff as Dreams: The Psychology of Fiction*. Oxford: Wiley-Blackwell, 2011.

Pérez-Latorre, Óliver and Mercè Oliva. 'Video Games, Dystopia, and Neoliberalism: The Case of BioShock Infinite.' *Games and Culture*. 10.1177/1555412017727226.

Peterson, Jon. *Playing at the World: A History of Simulating Wars, People, and Fantastic Adventures: From Chess to Role-Playing Games*. San Diego CA: Unreason Press, 2012.

Pine II, Joseph and James Gilmore. *The Experience Economy*. Boston MA: Harvard Business School Press, 1999.

Porubanova, Michaela, Daniel Joel Shaw, Ryan McKay and Dimitris Xygalatas. 'Memory for Expectation-Violating Concepts: The Effects of Agents and Cultural Familiarity.' *PloS One* 9.4 (2014): e90684 <https://doi.org/10.1371/journal.pone.0090684>

Porubanova-Norquist, Michaela, Daniel Joel Shaw and Dimitris Xygalatas. 'Minimal-Counterintuitiveness Revisited: Effects of cultural and ontological violations on concept memorability.' *Journal for the Cognitive Science of Religion* 1.2 (2013): 181-92. <doi:10.1558/jcsr.v1i2.181>

Predestination. Written and dir. Michael and Peter Spierig, 2014. Prod. Screen Australia. Distrib. Pinnacle Films, Stage 6 Films.

Rubin, David C. and Sharda Umanath. 'Event Memory: A Theory of Memory for Laboratory, Autobiographical, and Fictional Events.' *Psychological Review* 122.1 (2015): 1-23. <doi: 10.1037/a0037907>.

Ryan, Marie-Laure. 'Fiction, Non-factuals, and the Principle of Minimal Departure.' *Poetics* 9 (1980): 403-22.

Narrative as Virtual Reality. Baltimore: Johns Hopkins University Press, 1997.

SCOTT, James C. *Seeing Like a State: How Certain Schemes to Improve the Human Condition Have Failed*. New Haven and London: Yale University Press, 1999.

SHERMAN, David K., Kimberly A. HARTSON, Kevin R. BINNING, Valerie PURDIE-VAUGHNS, Julio GARCIA, Suzanne TABORSKY-BARBA, Sarah TOMASSETTI, A. David NUSSBAUM, and Geoffrey L. COHEN. 'Deflecting the Trajectory and Changing the Narrative: How self-affirmation affects academic performance and motivation under identity threat.' *Journal of Personality and Social Psychology* 104.4 (2013): 591-618.

SKOLNICK, Deena and Paul BLOOM. 'What does Batman think about SpongeBob? Children's Understanding of the Fantasy/Fantasy Distinction.' *Cognition* 101.1 (2006): B9-18. <https://doi.org/10.1016/j.cognition.2005.10.001>.

SMOODIN, Eric Loren (ed.). *Disney Discourse: Producing the Magic Kingdom*. Los Angeles CA: American Film Institute, 1994.

SOMER, Eli. 'Maladaptive Daydreaming: A Qualitative Inquiry.' *Journal of Contemporary Psychotherapy* 32.2-3 (2002): 197-212.

SPENDLOVE, Janine K. 'Crafting Urban Landscapes.' *Eighth Day Genesis: A Worldbuilding Codex for Writers and Creatives*. Ed. Sabrina Klein. Dayton OH: Alliteration Ink, 2012. 127-32.

STACY, Ivan. 'Complicity in Dystopia: Failures of Witnessing in China Miéville's *The City and the City* and Kazuo Ishiguro's *Never Let Me Go*.' *Partial Answers: Journal of Literature and the History of Ideas* 13.2 (2015): 225-50. 10.1353/pan.2015.0021.

STORRS, Graham. 'The Effects of Forming a Government.' *Eighth Day Genesis: A Worldbuilding Codex for Writers and Creatives*. Ed. Sabrina Klein. Dayton OH: Alliteration Ink, 2012. 233-50.

SUDDENDORF, Thomas, Donna Rose ADDIS, and Michael C. CORBALLIS. 'Mental Time Travel and the Shaping of the Human Mind.' *Philos Trans R Soc Lond B Biol Sci* 364.1521 (2009): 1317-24. <doi:10.1098/rstb.2008.0301>.

SWIRSKI, Peter. *Of Literature and Knowledge: Explorations in Narrative Thought Experiments, Evolution, and Game Theory*. New York: Routledge, 2007.

TOLKIEN, J.R.R. *Tolkien On Fairy-stories*. Ed. Verlyn Flieger and Douglas A. Anderson. London: HarperCollins, 2008.

TSOULIS-REAY, Alexa. 'What It's Like When Your Daydreams Are Just As Real As Life.' *The Cut* (12 Oct 2016). <https://www.thecut.com/2016/10/what-its-like-to-be-a-maladaptive-daydreamer.html>

VAN DANTZIG, Saskia and Diane PECHER. 'Spatial Attention Is Driven by Mental Simulations.' *Frontiers in Psychology* 2.40 (2011): 1-2. <doi: 10.3389/fpsyg.2011.00040>.

VanderMeer, Jeff. *Annihilation*. New York: Farrar, Straus and Giroux, 2014.

Authority. New York: Farrar, Straus and Giroux, 2014.

Acceptance. New York: Farrar, Straus and Giroux, 2014.

Vieira, Fátima. 'The Concept of Utopia.' *The Cambridge Companion to Utopian Literature*. Ed. Gregory Claeys. Cambridge: Cambridge University Press, 2010. 3-27. Cambridge Collections Online.

Vincent, Alice. "Rowling, you owe your fans a BOOK!': Harry Potter fans outraged that *Cursed Child* script is, in fact, a script.' *The Telegraph* (4 August 2016). <http://www.telegraph.co.uk/theatre/what-to-see/rowling-you-owe-your-fans-a-book-harry-potter-fans-outraged-that/>

Walker, Caren M., Patricia A. Ganea, and Alison Gopnik. 'Learning to Learn from Stories: Children's Developing Sensitivity to the Causal Structure of Fictional Worlds.' *Child Development* 86.1 (2015): 310-18. <doi: 10.1111/cdev.12287>.

Walton, Kendall. *Mimesis as Make-Believe: On the Foundations of the Representational Arts*. Cambridge MA: Harvard University Press, 1990.

Waysdorf, Abby and Stijn Reijnders. 'The Role of Imagination in the Film Tourist Experience: The Case of *Game of Thrones*.' *Participations* 14.1 (2017): 170-91. <http://www.participations.org/Volume%2014/Issue%201/10.pdf>.

Weisberg, Deena Skolnick and Paul Bloom. 'Young Children Separate Multiple Pretend Worlds.' *Developmental Science*, 12 (2009): 699-705. <doi: 10.1111/j.1467-7687.2009.00819.x>.

Wolf, Mark J.P. *Building Imaginary Worlds: The Theory and History of Subcreation*. New York and London: Routledge, 2012.

Woolley, Jacqueline D. and Maliki E. Ghossainy. 'Revisiting the Fantasy-Reality Distinction: Children as Naïve Skeptics.' *Child Development* 84 (2013): 1496–1510. <doi: 10.1111/cdev.12081>.

Wright, Bradley R. E., Dina Giovanelli, Emily G. Dolan, and Mark Evan Edwards. 'Explaining Deconversion from Christianity: A Study of Online Narratives.' *Journal of Religion & Society* 13 (2011): 1-17.

Yang, Jie and Jin Xue. 'Reality/Fiction Distinction and Fiction/Fiction Distinction during Sentence Comprehension.' *Universal Journal of Psychology* 3.6 (2015): 165-75. <doi:10.13189/ujp.2015.030603>.

Zwaan, Rolf A. and Diane Pecher. 'Revisiting Mental Simulation in Language Comprehension: Six Replication Attempts.' *PLoS One* 7 (2012): e51382. <doi:10.1371/journal.pone.0051382>.

N. Trevor Brierly

Worldbuilding Design Patterns in the Works of J.R.R. Tolkien

Abstract

A 'design pattern' is a formalized description of a common problem in a field of endeavor, accompanied by a recommendation towards a solution. Design patterns are widely used in architecture and software engineering, and there is growing interest in discovering and identifying design patterns in other fields of creative endeavor. The art of worldbuilding could benefit from the discovery and identification of design patterns and a design pattern language. Such a pattern language would be useful guidance to authors, game designers, enthusiasts and others who are involved in the design of secondary worlds.

Design patterns are discovered or identified by a combination of the observation of common problems and successful solutions in the Primary World, introspection and experimentation. Examining the work of successful creators of secondary worlds may uncover design patterns applicable to worldbuilding. This essay will examine worldbuilding by J.R.R. Tolkien, the problems and solutions he found and how they can be formulated into design patterns and contribute towards a pattern language for world-building. An Appendix includes a collection of 25 design patterns for worldbuilding, as discerned in the works of Tolkien.

A 'design pattern' is a formalized description of a common problem in a field of endeavor, accompanied by a recommendation towards a solution. The term 'design pattern' was introduced in the architecture classic *A Pattern Language: Towns, Buildings, Construction*, published in 1977 by Christopher Alexander and others. Alexander and his colleagues were interested in discovering and codifying architectural elements that result in a building, neighborhood or town having 'life' or 'spirit' and being a pleasant and enriching place to live and work in (Alexander 1977, ix). They developed a system of design patterns (a 'design pattern language') which described ways of designing buildings and urban areas to achieve that purpose.

An example of an architecture design pattern for building a community is the 'sidewalk café'. Alexander et al describe this design pattern:

> The street cafe provides a unique setting, special to cities: a place where people can sit lazily, legitimately, be on view, and watch the world go by [...] Encourage local cafes to spring up in each neighborhood. Make them intimate places, with several rooms, open to a busy path, where people can sit with coffee or a drink and watch the world go by. Build the front of the cafe so that a set of tables stretch out of the cafe, right into the street. (Alexander 1977, 437, 439)

Another example of a design pattern in architecture, this time for home design, is 'Light on Two Sides of Every Room'. This pattern notes that people will gravitate towards rooms which have light on two sides, and avoid rooms which are only lit from one side. If a builder wishes to have 'successful' rooms in a house this pattern would need to be kept in mind, with rooms being designed with light from two sides (Alexander 1977, 747).

Other fields of endeavor have developed design pattern languages. Software engineering has developed a pattern language over the past 35 years which describes recommended approaches to solving common problems while designing computer software. There is growing interest in discovering and identifying design patterns in other fields of creative endeavor besides architecture and software design. The art of worldbuilding, of designing new secondary worlds, could benefit from the discovery and identification of common problems and good solutions and the formulation of design patterns and a pattern language. Such a pattern language could be useful guidance to authors, game designers, enthusiasts (worldbuilding as another 'secret vice'?) and others who are involved in the design and construction of secondary worlds that need to be believable and have the illusion of depth.

Design patterns are discovered or identified by observation of common problems and successful solutions in the Primary World and by introspection and experimentation. Examining the work of successful creators of secondary worlds may uncover design patterns applicable to worldbuilding. J.R.R. Tolkien is one of the most successful literary worldbuilders of all time. This essay will examine his approach to worldbuilding, to discern the problems and solutions he found, and formulate them into design patterns to contribute towards a pattern language for that art.

What is the purpose of Design Patterns?

A design pattern is more than just a 'technique' or 'trope' or even a 'best practice'. Design patterns are ultimately about solving problems that occur during design. They don't give precise instructions, but describe an approach that has been shown to result in an effective solution. Metsker described design patterns as "a way to capture and convey the wisdom of a craft" (Metsker 2). Alexander (1979, x) wrote that "each pattern describes a problem which occurs over and over again in our environment and then describes the core of the solution to that problem in such a way that you can use this solution a million times over, without ever doing it the same way twice."

A design pattern is also a way of pursuing a purpose. Alexander and his colleagues believed that the architecture design patterns they discovered could lead to the creation of towns and buildings which would be enjoyable and spiritually nourishing to live in, that would have "life" and "spirit" (Alexander 1979, x). Worldbuilding design patterns working together as a design pattern language have a similar goal: the creation of worlds that will have consistency, completeness and effective invention, that will be enjoyable to visit and inhabit and that will evoke the sense of awe and wonder that is at the heart of all successful sub-creation.

Why Design Patterns?

There are benefits from identifying and describing design patterns in an area of endeavour. The first is 'codification' – there is value to recording and describing the characteristics of a design pattern in a standard and concise format. Some patterns will seem to be 'common sense' or obvious, but will be new to others and thus deserve notation. Experienced world designers will likely be aware of some of the design patterns described below, but may also find something new.

The second benefit is 'completeness'. The process of discerning design patterns aspires to completeness, to identify all possible design patterns. This is impossible, since there will always be new patterns to discover. But a design pattern language that is in the continual process of expanding and identifying new patterns may be of use to worldbuilders.

Thirdly, design patterns provide a 'common language' for use by worldbuilders. It is difficult to talk about things which are unnamed, or if different names are used. Commonly known names for ideas and best practices makes it easier to refer to them and discuss them. Design patterns together form a design pattern language to provide practitioners with a common set of terms to discuss design ideas.

Finally, there is value to identifying those specific design patterns used by Tolkien. Those who study his work may find it useful to understand his approach to worldbuilding. By examining the ideas he found important, the problems and solutions that he found, a better understanding of Tolkien's craft is possible.

Invention, Completeness and Consistency

If design patterns are about solving problems, what are the primary problems faced by worldbuilders? Wolf in his *Building Imaginary Worlds* describes the three aspects that a world will need to have if it is to be believable and interesting: invention, completeness and consistency (33).

Invention according to Wolf (34) is "the degree to which default assumptions based on the Primary World have been changed, regarding such things as geography, history, language, physics, biology, culture, custom, and so on." Worldbuilders are in the business of deception, of creating an illusion so compelling that the audience gladly relinquishes disbelief and attention for the privilege of experiencing that illusion. Worldbuilders create that compelling illusion through careful invention, by considering the best ways to change the aspects of a secondary world. A design pattern language can provide guidance towards successful invention.

Tolkien comments extensively on sub-creation and fairy-tales in his essay 'On Fairy-stories', and much of it applies to worldbuilding as a form of sub-creation. Tolkien spoke of the importance of having "the inner consistency of reality", but he also spoke of "strangeness and wonder" (*TOFS* 59-60). These two phrases describe the two (sometimes mutually exclusive) goals of the worldbuilder. A created fantasy world must be similar enough to the Primary World to be believable and consistent, but must also evoke awe and wonder, or no longer be fantastical. Wolf (37) notes that "in order for a world to be taken seriously, audiences have to be able to relate to a world and its inhabitants, comparing their situations to similar ones in the Primary World."

A continuum can be imagined between the completely Alien and the completely Mundane, between perfect strangeness and perfect familiarity. The audience cannot connect with the completely Alien world, it is too strange. Completely Alien worlds are very rare, since it takes considerable effort for the worldbuilder to completely step outside of everything that is familiar.

The completely Mundane at the other extreme is certainly a legitimate mode to work in (in fact most literature is to be found at this end), but it is no longer a fantasy world at that point, but a variant of the Primary World. Between these two extremes is a 'zone of wonder' where fantasy worlds exist, with some combination of familiarity and strangeness, of comfort and wonder. (See Appendix B for a diagram of the 'Zone of Wonder'.)

Consistency is "the degree to which world details are plausible, feasible and without contradiction" (Wolf 43). It either follows the laws of (Primary World) Nature, or has its own internally consistent laws. Everything has explanations that make sense within the created world. There are no anachronisms and elements that 'don't belong'. Consistency requires close attention to detail coupled with a mastery of the existing intricacies of the secondary world. Setting 'bibles', continuity databases and other resources can assist with these goals.

The level of believability required often depends on the audience. The more experience of the world an audience has, the more is required from the worldbuilder. Tolkien and Lewis were widely knowledgeable and part of the reason their created worlds are so compelling is their use of that knowledge. For example, Tolkien's linguistic expertise enables him to develop a completely believable language system for Middle-earth.

Completeness is defined by Wolf (38) as "the degree to which the world contains explanations and details covering all the various aspects of its characters' experiences, as well as background details which together suggest a feasible, practical world." Wolf (39) notes that completeness is impossible, but that an "illusion of completeness" can be created by the addition of carefully thought-out detail. Completeness contributes to the sense that a created world appears to have more to it than immediately appears to the audience, that there is more 'offstage'. Design patterns used to bring this about are related to the human tendency to extrapolate from what is known to what is unknown. We map our understanding and expectations of the Primary World onto created worlds. If a historical event is mentioned or described, or ruins are found, or old songs are sung, then the audience can believe that there is a fuller history and background to a world, of which that event, ruin or song is only a part.

Completeness involves including detail in what the audience sees, particularly details that are not necessary for the story that are mentioned in passing. C.S. Lewis, another master worldbuilder, speaks of the "perception of Reality" in his *An Experiment in Criticism*: it is "the art of bringing something close to us, making it palpable and vivid, by sharply observed or sharply imagined detail" (Lewis 57). In a compelling created world, there can be the sense that detail is 'fractal'. At every level the audience is zoomed into or out to, an equal density and distribution of detail will be perceived.

These three elements of worldbuilding as identified by Wolf are interrelated and contribute to a sense of 'depth'. Shippey notes that the concept of 'depth' was extremely important to Tolkien and describes it as "a sense that the author knew more than he was telling, that behind his immediate story there was a coherent, consistent, deeply fascinating world about which he had no time (then) to speak" (Shippey 229). Depth is the most important prerequisite for the quality of "conceptual immersion", which Wolf (377) describes as the potential of a world to allow an audience to be "surrounded or engulfed" by it. Wolf (49) also identifies the concept of "absorption" which is similar to "immersion" but includes the active participation of the audience, of their imagination and senses to "absorb" and interact with the world. Depth, immersion and absorption are among the aims of successful worldbuilding and a rich and comprehensive system of worldbuilding design patterns can provide guidance towards these goals.

Conclusion

Humans have always imagined other worlds. Only recently have we given much thought to how they are created, or how they could be better designed. The number of secondary worlds has exploded in recent years, and they have become big business. Audiences are highly demanding, very discerning and very engaged with their favorite worlds. The study of worldbuilding as an art form is just getting started. Worldbuilding design patterns may be useful to worldbuilders who want to build better and more compelling places for the enjoyment of audiences, and for students of worldbuilding who want to understand the art better.

Appendix A includes 25 design patterns discerned from Tolkien's works, primarily *The Lord of the Rings* and *The Silmarillion*. This is can only be an incomplete list, there are certainly others. Design pattern languages are collaborative efforts, so those in the audience of this essay are encouraged to seek to discern others. Each pattern is described, along with one or more examples from Tolkien's works that demonstrate the pattern. Examples from the Primary World may also be included. Suggestions for using the design pattern in worldbuilding are offered in most cases.

Appendix A: An (Incomplete) Catalog of Worldbuilding Design Patterns Discerned in Tolkien's Works

Culture Design Patterns

Creation Story

Most cultures have one or more creation stories that are foundational to that culture. They describe the origin of the culture, the nature of the divine and sacred and establish values important to the culture. Primary World examples include Genesis 1-2 (Hebrew), the *Enuma Elish* (Babylonian), *Rig Veda* (Hindu) and many more. Tolkien provides a creation story for Middle-earth in the 'Valaquenta' in *The Silmarillion*. Middle-earth is created by the One God, Eru or Ilúvatar, but much of the creation work is actually done by the Valar, divine beings who take an active role in Middle-earth. Creation itself takes place through music, but is marred by the discord of Melkor, one of the Valar who rebels against Ilúvatar. Elves are created and awake first, and then Men and Dwarves.

Worldbuilders can add depth to a culture by inventing creation stories which would serve a foundational role. They will describe the origin of the culture and the divine being(s) revered by the culture and their interaction. The way the creation took place might demonstrate values, attributes and customs important to the culture. An interesting experiment would be to begin with a creation story and imagine the culture that might arise from that story.

Earlier Peoples

When the Rohirrim ride to the aid of Gondor in Book V of the *Lord of the Rings* they encounter the Woses, the "Wild Men of the Wood", who are believed to be "[r]emnants of an older time […] living few and secretly, wild and wary as the beasts" and "woodcrafty beyond compare" (*RK*, V, v, 105-09). They are the original inhabitants of the land, first to cross the Anduin. But they have been pushed out of their land and persecuted, by Orcs but also by other men.

One of the conditions of their help to the Rohirrim is that they "not hunt them like beasts any more". *Unfinished Tales* provides more information about them:

> They were a secretive people, suspicious of other kinds of Men by whom they had been harried and persecuted as long as they could remember, and they had wandered west seeking a land where they could be hidden and have peace. (*UT* 383)

The Woses, or "Drúedain" in Sindarin, are perhaps meant to be analogues of the Native Americans or Australian Aborigines, but may also be roughly analogous to the Tuatha De Danaan. According to Irish mythology this once-powerful people were persecuted by peoples that came after them. To survive they became secretive and hid in the hills. They became known later as the Daoine Sídhe, or the Faerie Folk.

A worldbuilder could add depth to a secondary world by considering the original inhabitants of an area. Are they still there? What was their culture like? Are they in reduced circumstances? How has their culture changed? What do the dominant inhabitants think of them? Are they regarded as dangerous? quaint? mysterious?

Ethnic Groups Have Subgroups

Ethnic groups are often composed of, or include, subgroups which share many traits, but are distinct in some ways. Tolkien's hobbits come in three varieties, or "breeds" as Tolkien refers to them: Stoors, Harfoots and Fallohides. They are physically different, have cultural distinctions, and each variety has an affinity for one of the other major races of Free Peoples (*FR*, Prologue, 12). Over time the Elves differentiate into various groups depending upon whether they have been to Valinor or not and whether they returned or not, among other things.

Worldbuilders can add depth to a culture by considering the existence of subcultures within it. What traits do they share or not share with the main culture? Why are they different? What is the relationship between the subcultures and the larger culture, or between subcultures?

Imitation of Other Cultures

There are numerous examples of this in Tolkien's works, but perhaps the most important is the Elvish culture. Some cultures of Middle-earth view the Elvish culture as superior and seek to imitate it. The Elves are generally generous with their knowledge (*RK*, Appendix A, 315, *S* 149). The languages of Men and Dwarves use Elvish letters, such as the Tengwar of Fëanor, and the Cirth (*RK*, Appendix E, 395). The calendar used by Dúnedain and the Shirefolk was of Eldarin origin (*RK*, Appendix D, 385). The languages of Men and other peoples included many Elvish words and features, particularly the language of the Númenoreans, who were close to the Elves (*RK*, Appendix F, 406-07). The Elves even teach the trees (Ents) to talk (*TT*, III, iv, 71).

Worldbuilders can add depth to a culture by considering which cultures it tends to imitate, and which ones imitate it. Does it imitate an 'older, wiser' culture, one that has been around longer? Does it imitate a 'younger, more vibrant' culture that has just come into the picture? Is the imitativeness found across the entire culture, or just in certain classes or subcultures? Are certain kinds of traits (art and style, industry, religion, scholarship) copied over others?

Literate Cultures in Contrast to Oral Cultures

Literacy or the lack of it tends to have a profound effect upon cultures which make more than incidental use of it. Tolkien was familiar with both oral and literate cultures in his language and literature studies. He portrays the Rohirrim as an oral culture, as opposed to the literate culture of the Gondorians. Aragorn describes the Rohirrim:

> They are proud and wilful, but they are true-hearted, generous in thought and deed; bold but not cruel; wise but unlearned, writing no books but singing many songs, after the manner of the children of Men before the Dark Years. (*TT*, III, ii, 33)

Memory plays a greater role in oral cultures, and their literature tends to be structured so that it is easier to memorize and recite. Wisdom and knowledge is stored in orally conveyed proverbs, sayings and songs instead of books. There are no written contracts, so someone's word is their bond. Oral cultures are fundamentally different from literate ones, and those of us who are in literate cultures may find it challenging to understand oral cultures. Walter J. Ong wrote extensively on this subject and his works describing and discussing orality and literacy are recommended for worldbuilders interested in exploring this area.

Worldbuilders can add depth to the cultures of their secondary world by considering whether cultures are oral, literate or somewhere in between. What effect does their literacy status have upon their culture? How does it affect how they are viewed by other cultures?

Migration of People

Migration is very common in human history. Tolkien's history of Middle-earth also includes numerous migrations by its peoples. Migrations take place when peoples move to an area that provides more opportunity. Some of the many migrations of the Rohirrim seem to be for this reason (*RK*, Appendix A, 344-45). After many migrations the Hobbits move into the area that would become the Shire (*RK*, Appendix A, 366-67). Migrations also take place when people are fleeing something dangerous, in at least one case the hobbits are fleeing Orcs and Nazgûl (c. 1300 Third Age) (*RK*, Appendix B, 366).

Worldbuilders can add depth to a culture by considering what migrations have taken place by the people in that culture. Where have they come from? Why did they leave? Were they forced out by war or plague, etc., or were they moving to 'greener pastures'? Was it a peaceful migration, or the result of war or conquest? What hardships or other events may have taken place during the migration? Did it take place slowly or all at once? Did they remove or displace other peoples already living on the land? What is the significance of the migrations in the culture?

Unique Literary Forms

Cultures often develop unique poetic forms and literary styles. Primary World examples include *haikai* and *tanka* (Japan), the *sonnet* (Europe) and the *ghazal* (Arabia). Tolkien's elves have several unique forms, one of which is the *ann-thennath*. We have only 1 example of the ann-thennath form, and it is translated into English ('Song of Beren and Lúthien' *FR*, I, xi, 203-05). It is a complex form, characterized by an iambic trimeter metre with an *abac babc* rhyme scheme, with the c-lines having feminine endings and the a- and b-lines having masculine endings (Wynne 113).

Poetry is characterized by pattern and repetition. There are many ways that repetition can occur. The most common in the Western culture in the real world is "syllabic" in which the last syllables of each line rhyme. But there are other forms, such as alliteration, in which the initial sounds are similar. A good example of alliterative poetry in Tolkien's work is the 'Lament for Théoden' (*RK*, V, iii, 76-77). There are also forms of poetry in which the repetition is of ideas. Hebrew poetry employs 'parallelism', in which the same idea is expressed twice (or more) in separate lines, but in different words.

Worldbuilders can add depth to a culture by creating unique poetic forms for that culture. Poetic forms can vary by metre, rhyme scheme, form of repetition, word choice, style and other elements. How does the poetic form reflect the culture? What role does the poetic form play in the culture? Who uses that form? Is it primarily used by the elite, or by the common folk, or by some other group? Is it an oral form or a written form? Is it set to music, or recited? Is it considered sacred, or secular? Is it considered a difficult form to create, requiring skill and education, or a simple form usable by the common folk?

Detail Design Patterns

Tolkien was a master of the use of detail, and much of the depth perceived in his works comes from the details that he presents. Middle-earth is vividly and beautifully described throughout his works, and it is largely in the details that this vividness and beauty is conveyed. An example of attention to detail in Lord of the Rings is the description of the Balrog the Fellowship faces in Moria. The audience is given a lot of information about this creature:

> What it was could not be seen: it was like a great shadow, in the middle of which was a dark form, of man-shape maybe, or greater; and a power and terror seemed to be in it and to go before it [...] Then with a rush it leaped across the fissure. The flames roared up to greet it, and wreathed about it; and a black smoke swirled in the air. Its streaming mane kindled, and blazed behind it. In its right hand was a blade like a stabbing tongue of fire; in its left it held a whip of many thongs [...] the shadow about it reached out like two vast wings

[...] Fire came from its nostrils [...] suddenly it drew itself up to a great height, and its wings were spread from wall to wall. (*FR*, II, v, 343-45)

In the description of the Balrog the audience is given vivid details about its appearance – a large winged creature, a mixture of shadow and flame. There is information about its capabilities – it is capable of great leaps and of wielding terrible weapons. The audience is also given some clues as to how we are meant to react to it: with 'terror'.

Tolkien does not give the audience all these details at once, but rather they are spread over the entire encounter, which takes over 500 words to describe. Too much detail can overwhelm the audience, Tolkien gives us a lot of information, but it is spread out skillfully to heighten the impact.

A worldbuilder can add depth to a world through careful use of detail. There are many kinds of details that can add verisimilitude if they are developed and expanded. Below are patterns for using detail in worldbuilding.

Historical References

Tom Shippey (299) writes:

> One quality which that work [*Lord of the Rings*] has in abundance is the Beowulfian 'impression of depth', created just as in the old epic by songs and digressions like Aragorn's lay of Tinúviel, Sam Gamgee's allusions to the Silmaril and the Iron Crown, Elrond's account of Celebrimbor and dozens more.

References to historical events give the impression of depth over time. The audience senses that there is more to the secondary world than is immediately visible, that it has a history just as the Primary World does. It also increases engagement as the audience is often interested in learning more about historical events.

Minor Characters

Tolkien will sometimes give names and other details of characters which have little to do with the plot. For example, the day after Bilbo leaves the Shire, Frodo evicts a young hobbit named Sancho Proudfoot who has been excavating his pantry looking for gold. The audience is told that Sancho is "old Odo Proudfoot's grandson" (*FR* 48). This extra detail goes a long way to establishing the sense that there is a large and complexly interrelated society in which the hobbit characters exist. Family trees are a technique which Tolkien uses to introduce and organize minor characters which have little or no relevance for the story, but show the depth of family relationships to the main characters.

Natural Details

The audience of *The Lord of the Rings* is frequently given information about the weather and the phase of the moon at locations along the travels of the Fellowship. The plant-life is also often described. Some of these plants exist in the Primary World, which gives the visitor a connection with the familiar. But also mentioned and described are plants that do not exist in our world, such as the *mallorn* trees and *simbelmynë* flower, which remind the visitor that Middle-earth is both familiar and alien to us. Wildlife is also described, though less often. Together these details help give the sense of Middle-earth as a world whose physical systems are as complex and rich as those of our Primary World, and indeed is our own world, though in a distant fictional past.

Historical Design Patterns

Divide History into Periods

Tolkien divides the history of Middle-earth into 'ages'. Each of these ages ends with a conclusive battle against evil, against either Morgoth or his servant Sauron. The events of *The Silmarillion* take place largely in the First Age which ends with a battle that overthrows Morgoth. The Second Age ends with the overthrow of Sauron, though he is not completely destroyed. The events of *The Lord of the Rings*, the destruction of the One Ring and the final overthrow of Sauron mark the end of the Third Age. Dividing long periods of history into 'ages' or periods is one way that historians begin to analyze and describe history.

A worldbuilder could add depth to the history of a culture in a secondary world by breaking that history into 'smaller pieces'. There are many ways that periods of a history can be marked. Periods can be sections of time that share common characteristics. The 'Mediaeval Age' (i.e. the Middle Ages) is a Primary World example, it was a long and relatively static period in Western civilization. Periods can also delineate times of rapid change, such as the 'Victorian Era'. Periods are sometimes associated with a century ('Twentieth Century') or decade ('The Roaring Twenties'), but sometimes correspond to actual events. For example, the 'Cold War' period can be marked as 1945-1991 (though some argue for different start dates), that is, the end of World War 2 through the fall of the Berlin Wall. Sometimes specific events, such as the birth of a famous person (Jesus Christ), founding of a city (Rome) or a war (American Civil War) will mark the beginning or end of a period. Particularly common, especially in ancient civilizations, is to divide their history by their rulers. The 3500+ years of Egyptian history are divided into some 30+ dynasties, which helps Egyptologists to keep track of it all. What ages or periods exist in the history of a culture in the secondary world? What characterizes each of the periods, and what events, etc. mark the end of each period? Is the system of periods assigned by the inhabitants of the culture themselves, or by someone else? How do other cultures in the secondary world think about the history of that culture?

Rise and Fall of Empires

The region of Eriador is a part of Middle-earth that has become largely an empty wasteland, except for a few places such as the Shire, Bree and Rivendell. Its population was once much greater. It was the kingdom of Arnor, one of the two great Númenorean realms in Middle-earth. The other Númenorean realm was Gondor, which thrived. But Arnor suffered a long series of misfortunes, beginning with a division into three parts which struggled with each other, and followed by a long struggle with the evil realm of Angmar to the North and then great plagues. The three kingdoms of Arnor eventually disintegrated, leaving scattered peoples, many of whom dwindled away completely or were destroyed by invasions of Orcs and other evil creatures. There are parallels with the fall of the western Roman Empire, which left many smaller, weaker, disconnected states amidst great areas of wasteland.

A worldbuilder could add depth to the cultures in a secondary world by considering how empires rise but also how they fall. What happens to an area that was once a mighty realm or empire but has succumbed to misfortune? What kinds of misfortune have brought it to this point? What do the remaining inhabitants have to face now that the central power is gone? How do they survive? How much influence does the imperial culture still have over the survivors?

Ruins

Ruins, old buildings that are no longer in regular use and are falling apart, can be used to give a sense that an area has been populated for a long time, that it is no longer populated, or that it was once populated by a different people. There are multiple examples of ruins in *The Lord of the Rings*, particularly in Books 1 and 2, where the Fellowship is passing through the region of Eriador. Amon Sûl, or Weathertop, where Aragorn and the hobbits encounter the Nazgûl, is perhaps the most familiar example. It was a tower built by Elendil and in 1409 TA the tower was destroyed by an army of Rhudaur dominated by Angmar. When Aragorn and the hobbits are there, it is described as "a wide ring of ancient stone-work, now crumbling or covered with age-long grass" (*FK*, I, xi, 198). It would have been more than 3000 years old at that time, and destroyed nearly 1600 years beforehand.

A worldbuilder could add depth to a secondary world by considering whether the presence of ruins would add evidence of previous inhabitation. Are there areas that were once populated, but are no longer? Or were populated by a previous culture? Or have been populated for so long that some buildings are no longer in use? If there are ruins, are they unknown, or well known? Are they considered mysterious, or just a pile of rubble? What do they indicate about the history of the area? What kinds of things or creatures might be found in them?

Language Design Patterns

Languages Change Over Time: Sound Changes

Languages change over time, often according to rules that can be discerned by linguists and philologists. Perhaps the most famous of these rules is Grimm's Law which describes changes taking place in the Germanic branch of the Indo-European languages. Tolkien describes the sound changes that Sindarin has undergone (*RK*, Appendix E, 393).

Worldbuilders can add depth to language systems by considering how the sounds in a language change over time. Sound changes tend to follow rules.

Languages Change Over Time: Variant Forms

Languages change over time, and one of the results is they tend to develop variant forms, such as dialects. Variant forms may be mutually intelligible, though often with some difficulty, but eventually may become separate languages. Variants tend to develop in situations of isolation. For example, populations that originally spoke the same language but are isolated geographically will tend to develop variants as each area's language changes separately. Isolation need not be geographical, some dialects form within class, ethnic or religious lines.

Tolkien notes that the process of creating variants was beginning to take place with Westron (Common Speech) but that he lessened the differences while 'translating' the Red Book into English. He writes:

> The Common Speech, as the language of the Hobbits and their narratives, has inevitably been turned into modern English. In the process the difference between the varieties observable in the use of the Westron has been lessened. Some attempt has been made to represent these varieties by variations in the kind of English used; but the divergence between the pronunciation and idiom of the Shire and the Westron tongue in the mouths of the Elves or of the high men of Gondor was greater than has been shown in this book. Hobbits indeed spoke for the most part a rustic dialect, whereas in Gondor and Rohan a more antique language was used, more formal and more terse. (*RK*, Appendix E, 411)

Worldbuilders can add depth to language systems by considering how formation of variants may be taking place within languages. What kinds of isolation are present, and how could these lead to variant forms of the language? How do speakers of one variety of the language consider speakers of other varieties? Are any varieties considered 'inferior' or 'superior' to others? Which variants have writing systems, and which are more colloquial? How does language vary across classes? ethnic groups and subgroups? religions? Do speakers know more than one variant at that same time, such as at home and also at school or in society?

Languages Develop or Borrow Scripts

Many of the peoples of Middle-earth adapted writing systems devised by the Elves, such as the Tengwar of Fëanor, and the Cirth, for their own languages. As cultures become literate they will need a script to represent their language. Some cultures invent their own writing system, but it is also common to adapt one already in use. A Primary World example is the Latin alphabet, which is used by more than 60 languages, from Icelandic to Vietnamese.

Worldbuilders can add depth to the language system of a secondary world by considering the writing systems in use. Not every language will need its own script. A language that is in the process of becoming literate may adopt and adapt a script from another culture. Cultures acquiring literacy may borrow a script from an older, more sophisticated, or dominant culture, and adapt it if needed.

Languages Have a 'Sound'

The human vocal system is capable of producing more than 100 sounds or phonemes, but individual languages will only use a subset of these. Within this subset, some will be used more than others, giving that language a distinct and unique 'sound'. For example, a quick analysis of Quenya as found in *Ai! laurië lantar lassi súrinen* (*FR*, II, viii, 394) reveals a very frequent usage of 'l' (32 times), 'n' (29 times), 'r' (36 times), and rare usage of 'c', 'b' and 'h' (3, 2 and 3 times respectively). This selection of certain sounds over others is only one of the factors that go into the distinctive 'sound' of a language, such as combinations of sounds, accenting, word length, syllable choice, etc.

Worldbuilders can add depth to the language system of a secondary world by considering that each language will have its own 'sound'. Which of the sounds produced by the human vocal system is used by each language? Which sounds and combinations of sound, etc. are preferred over others?

Languages Have Different Basic Structures

As a linguist and philologist Tolkien would have known well that languages have different basic structures. His invented languages reflect a diversity in these basic structures. The Elvish language Quenya uses a structure of inflected verbs and affixes, like many Indo-European languages. Khuzdûl, the Dwarvish language, uses a triconsonantal root system which has been described by Tolkien as similar to Hebrew (Vink 123-24). Tolkien described the Entish language as "agglomerative" (*RK*, Appendix F, 409) which may be similar to agglutinative languages like Finnish, Turkish and Hungarian "in which complex words are formed by stringing together morphemes, each with a single grammatical or semantic meaning" (Wikipedia 'Agglutination').

Worldbuilders can add depth to the system of languages in a secondary world by varying the basic structure of those languages. Some research into Primary World languages will give a sense of the many possibilities available for basic structuring principles, and some inspiration for creating new structures.

Vehicular Language (Lingua Franca)

A 'lingua franca' or 'vehicular language' is a language which becomes used to facilitate communication between people who do not have the same native language. It will be the second, etc. language for many of these people, but may also be a first language ('vernacular') for other people. 'Westron' or 'Common Speech' is an example of a vehicular language in Tolkien's work. It began as the vernacular language of the Númenoreans, who journeyed from their home island of Númenor and interacted with peoples on the mainland of Middle-earth. The Númenorean language became mixed with that of those peoples and developed into Common, which served as a vehicular language for many peoples. It was widely spoken and eventually became the native language of many of the peoples of Middle-earth.

Worldbuilders can add depth to a secondary world by considering whether any of the languages on that world are in a position to serve as a vehicular language for an area, or whether a vehicular language might come to be used in a region. A vehicular language is often the language of dominant cultures, such as that of the Westron of the Númenoreans. They can also be the language of conquerors and empires. A Primary World example is English, which due to being the native language of the British Empire, has become a vehicular language for many peoples who dwell in areas once part of the British Empire. But vehicular languages can develop for other reasons as well. Swahili developed more peacefully as a vehicular language in East Africa through trade relations, though it was later promoted as such by British and German colonial powers. Vehicular languages can come to be used anywhere where peoples with different vernacular languages need to interact. In these situations a number of things can occur, such as development of pidgins and creoles. But sometimes a vehicular language is used instead.

Naming Design Patterns

Avoid Primary World Names (anti-pattern)

Tolkien largely avoids a common naming practice by worldbuilders which has many pitfalls. That is to use Primary World names, or names that sound similar to Primary World names. These should generally be avoided, suggests Lin Carter (Carter 192-212). He quotes an essay by H.P. Lovecraft on Robert E. Howard's names in the *Conan* series:

> The only flaw in this stuff is R.E.H.'s incurable tendency to devise names too closely resembling actual names of ancient history – names which, for us, have a very different set of associations. In many cases he does this designedly – on the theory that familiar names descended from the fabulous realms he describes – but such a design is invalidated by the fact that we clearly know the etymology of many of the historic terms, hence cannot accept the pedigree he suggests. (Carter 195)

Primary World names break the 'impression of depth' by bringing in Primary World associations that may not be appropriate. If a worldbuilder is attempting to create a world which is not directly connected to the Primary World, then the use of Primary World names breaks that sense of disassociation. Middle-earth is our own world in a 'distant imagined past', but Tolkien comes up with names which are not from the Primary World. There are some apparent exceptions to this, particularly with hobbit names, but these are explained as translations from the hobbitish languages, or from Westron (Common Speech) into names more familiar to the audience.

Don't Use Apostrophes in Names Unless Really Necessary (anti-pattern)

Tolkien almost entirely avoids one naming mistake that many worldbuilders make, which is to use apostrophes in names where they are not necessary. Apostrophes used to make a name seem more exotic are unnecessary, overused, and bring up questions on pronunciation. Many audience members find them annoying (Allen, Fogarty, Williams).

However, apostrophes do have legitimate uses in representing the transliteration of languages. Languages such as Hawai'ian and Arabic have a sound called a 'glottal stop' which does not exist in Latin and Germanic languages and for which there is no letter. This is often represented by an apostrophe. Apostrophes may also be used to break up pairs of letters that should not be pronounced together. For example, the two parts of the name 'Muad'dib' should be pronounced separately instead of run together. In Irish and Scottish the apostrophe is traditional. (http://en.wikipedia.org/wiki/Apostrophe#Use_in_transliteration)

Multiple Names for the Same Thing

Tolkien loved coming up with names and epithets, and he often gives more than one to characters and even objects. Aragorn for example declares himself to the Riders of Rohan: "Aragorn son of Arathorn, and am called Elessar, the Elfstone, Dúnadan, the heir of Isildur Elendil's son of Gondor" (*TT*, III, ii, 36). He was also known as Estel as a young man. Gandalf in particular has names from the many places he visits. The Ring itself has many names and epithets:

'Isildur's Bane', the 'One Ring', the 'Ruling Ring', the 'Great Ring of Sauron', the 'Great Ring of the Enemy' and others.

Worldbuilders can add depth to people, places and things in secondary worlds by considering whether they may have multiple names and epithets. They may have names in more than one language like Gandalf, or multiple names and epithets that reflect roles or statuses, such as Aragorn's status as 'heir of Isildur'. Changes may result in new names or additional epithets. Aragorn gives Narsil, the Sword-that-was-broken, a new name, Andúril, when it is reforged. Sméagol undergoes a drastic change after stealing the Ring and becomes known as Gollum.

Use Primary World Sources for Naming Inspiration

While using Primary World names may not be a good idea, many good names resonate with Primary World languages. One example from Tolkien is 'Sauron' whose name includes the Greek root 'saur-' for 'lizard', 'reptile' or 'snake'. Similarly, the name 'Mordor' gains some of its sinister sound from its similarity to 'murder', 'mortal', 'mortality'. We are not meant to understand that these names originated in Greek roots, etc. in Middle-earth, but rather that certain combinations of sounds have associations. Tolkien was a master at finding these associations and coming up with names which use them without sounding like Primary World names. Worldbuilders can use Primary World words, roots, languages, etc. to inspire new names.

Appendix B: The Zone of Wonder

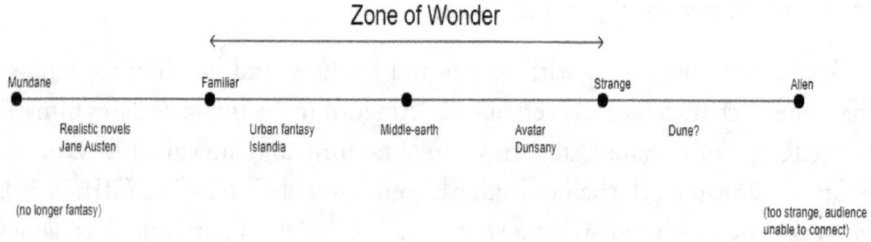

About the Author

N. Trevor Brierly works as a software engineer in Northern Virginia, USA. He has a BA in English from George Mason University and an MLIS from University of Texas-Austin, and is working on a degree in Tolkien Studies from Signum University. He is also working on a book of meditations for people who are recovering from spiritual abuse and a monograph on "Islandia", by Austin Tappan Wright.

Abbreviations

FR   Tolkien, J.R.R. *The Fellowship of the King.* 2nd ed. Boston: Houghton Mifflin Company, 1993.

RK   Tolkien, J.R.R. *The Return of the King.* 2nd ed. Boston: Houghton Mifflin Company, 1993.

S   Tolkien, J.R.R. *The Silmarillion.* London: George Allen & Unwin, 1977.

TOFS Tolkien, J.R.R. *Tolkien On Fairy-stories.* Expanded edition, with commentary and notes. Ed. Verlyn Flieger & Douglas A. Anderson. London: HarperCollins, 2008.

TT   Tolkien, J.R.R. *The Two Towers.* 2nd ed. Boston: Houghton Mifflin Company, 1993.

UT   Tolkien, J.R.R. *Unfinished Tales of Númenor and Middle-earth.* Ed. Christopher Tolkien. Boston: Houghton Mifflin Company, 1980.

Bibliography

Alexander, Christopher, Sara Ishikawa, and Murray Silverstein. *A Pattern Language.* New York: Oxford University Press, 1977.

Alexander, Christopher. *The Timeless Way of Building.* New York: Oxford University Press, 1979.

Allen, Moira. 'What's in a Name?' 26 December 2014. http://www.writing-world.com/sf/name.shtml

Carter, Lin. *A Look Behind the Lord of the Rings.* New York: Ballantine Books, 1969.

Fogarty, Mignon. 'Apostrophes in Science Fiction and Fantasy Names.' 26 December 2014 <http://www.quickanddirtytips.com/education/grammar/apostrophes-in-science-fiction-and-fantasy-names>

HART, Trevor. 'Tolkien, Creation and Creativity.' *Tree of Tales Tolkien, Literature, and Theology*. Ed. Trevor Hart and Ivan Khovacs. Waco, TX: Baylor University Press, 2007. 39-53.

LEWIS, C. S. *An Experiment in Criticism*. Cambridge, UK: Cambridge University Press, 1961.

LEEMING, David and Margaret. *A Dictionary of Creation Myths*. New York: Oxford University Press, 1994.

METSKER, Steven John. *Design Patterns in C#*. Boston, MA: Addison-Wesley, 2004.

ONG, Walter J. *Orality and Literacy*. 2nd ed. New York: Routledge, 2002.

TOLKIEN, J.R.R. *The Fellowship of the King*. 2nd ed. Boston: Houghton Mifflin Company, 1993.

The Return of the King. 2nd ed. Boston: Houghton Mifflin Company, 1993.

The Silmarillion. 2nd ed. Ed. Christopher Tolkien. Boston: Houghton Mifflin Company, 2001.

Tolkien On Fairy-stories. Ed. Verlyn Flieger and Douglas C. Anderson. London: HarperCollinsPublishers, 2008.

The Two Towers. 2nd ed. Boston: Houghton Mifflin Company, 1993.

Unfinished Tales of Númenor and Middle-earth. Ed. Christopher Tolkien. Boston: Houghton Mifflin Company, 1980.

SHIPPEY, Tom. *The Road to Middle-earth*. Boston: Houghton Mifflin Company, 2003.

VINK, Renée. "'Jewish' Dwarves: Tolkien and Anti-Semitic Stereotyping.' *Tolkien Studies* 10 (2013): 123-145

WILLIAMS, Imogen Russell. 'What's in a name? A lot, when it comes to fantasy.' 26 December 2014, <http://www.theguardian.com/books/booksblog/2010/mar/16/fantasy-character-names>

WOLF, Mark J.P. *Building Imaginary Worlds*. Routledge, 2012.

WYNNE, Patrick, and Carl F. HOSTETTER. 'Three Elvish Verse Modes: Ann-thennath, Minlamad thent /estent, and Linnod.' *Tolkien's Legendarium Essays of The History of Middle-earth*. Ed. Verlyn Flieger and Carl Hostetter. Westport, CT: Greenwood Press, 2000. 113-139.

John Garth

Ilu's Music:
The Creation of Tolkien's Creation Myth[1]

Abstract

This paper investigates the sources of inspiration for Tolkien's creation myth. Through a reappraisal of published evidence, it tentatively suggests that he may have composed *The Music of the Ainur* in 1917, rather than in Oxford after the end of the First World War. Through an examination of context and correspondence, it argues that *The Music of the Ainur* is a consolatory myth in response to the war, written partly for the only other survivor of Tolkien's T.C.B.S circle of friends, Christopher Wiseman. It brings evidence that an analogous story of a heavenly music and revolt, discovered by Peter Gilliver, is indeed the source for Tolkien's myth; and it considers the implications for Tolkien's themes.

On 27 February 1917, a junior officer in the British army reached the end of his convalescence at home and faced a military medical board. From July to October 1916, he had been in charge of communications for an army battalion during the Battle of the Somme. Since late October he had been recovering from the trench fever he had caught in the trenches, and also fresh grief over the deaths of friends there. Fortunately for J.R.R. Tolkien's sanity, and fortunately for us, he had been able to turn this time to good account. He had begun the mythology which he came to call *The Book of Lost Tales*.

When Sam Gamgee looks into the Mere of Dead Faces in *The Lord of the Rings*, he sees the phantom after-images of ancient battle as if through "some window, glazed with grimy glass" (*LotR* 627). Examining the whens and whys of Tolkien's creative life can sometimes be like that too. Rub carefully at the grime, and some new insight may reward you through the

---

1 This is a substantially enlarged version of the talk by the same title first presented at at the German Tolkien Society's Tolkien Seminar on Literary Worldbuilding, at Augsburg University, 28 October 2017. I would like to express my thanks to Carl F. Hostetter, Jennifer Raimundo, Robin Darwall-Smith and various audiences who have given me encouragement and food for thought. I am especially grateful to Peter Gilliver for the insight which first animated my inquiry.

half-cleared glass. Sometimes, however, it pays to keep on rubbing away at that same spot. The accumulated obscurity of long years can take a lot of shifting, but much more than phantoms may lie beneath.

Timeline

Tolkien recalled that *The Fall of Gondolin*, the first 'Lost Tale', "was written 'out of my head', during sickleave in 1917."[2] Of the several partially contradictory statements about the date, this is the one best supported by contemporary evidence neglected in previous investigations, including my own *Tolkien and the Great War*. There I gave undue weight to two other recollections: that the story was written "in hospital and on leave after surviving the Battle of the Somme in 1916" and that it was composed in "1916-17".[3] The evidence actually points to early 1917.

Tolkien convalesced at Great Haywood in Staffordshire with Edith Tolkien from December into January. His friend Christopher Luke Wiseman, returning several poems Tolkien had sent him from hospital in Birmingham in late 1916, told him on 18 January 1917, "You ought to start the epic." To a letter from Tolkien after his 27 February meeting with the military medical board, Wiseman responded, "As to the burning question of epics, I am delighted to have touched you off."[4]

What Wiseman had heard is unclear. Perhaps Tolkien counted the beginning of the "epic" as *The Cottage of Lost Play*, written by 12 February, the date Edith wrote on her fair copy of this opening frame-story. Perhaps he meant *The Fall of Gondolin* itself. Together with Wiseman's comments, a reminiscence from Tolkien that *The Fall of Gondolin* was written "in hospital and on leave" suggests that at least some was written in Furness Auxiliary Hospital in Harrogate, from 27 February; some perhaps too while convalescing nearby at 95 Valley Drive from 28 March to 18 April.[5]

---

2 *Letters*, no. 257, to Christopher Bretherton, 16 July 1964.
3 *Letters*, no. 165, to Houghton Mifflin Co., 30 June 1955; no. 297, drafts for a letter to 'Mr Rang', August 1967. Tolkien also said *The Fall of Gondolin* was written "during sick-leave at the end of 1916" (*Letters*, no. 163, to W. H. Auden, 7 June 1955).
4 Christopher Wiseman to Tolkien, 18 January and 4 March 1917.
5 *Letters*, no. 165, to Houghton Mifflin Co., 30 June 1955.

On 19 April 1917, Tolkien was finally ordered to proceed for duty; but thank goodness, not in the trenches. Sent to guard the east coast near the Yorkshire town of Withernsea, Tolkien was still actually far from full recovery. He continued working on his *Book of Lost Tales* during recurrent stretches in hospital until the end of the Great War in November 1918. Indeed, a reappraisal of published evidence suggests that he may have created more of his mythology during that period than previously realised; and that it included his creation myth, *The Music of the Ainur*. If so, it would radically alter the accepted timeline, according to which Tolkien wrote no more than four or five of the 'Lost Tales' during the war, and all the rest in Oxford after the Armistice.

The case is complex and demands further investigation of Tolkien's nigglings with his invented languages and names, so I will only allude to it here as a possibility. Indeed, it must be stressed that there may be unpublished evidence against it. At any rate, the further arguments in this paper do not depend on it, but if it is correct they are certainly illuminated by it.

Looking back in 1964, Tolkien recalled that he wrote his "cosmogonical myth, 'The Music of the Ainur'" while on the staff of the *Oxford English Dictionary* from late 1918, straight after the First World War.[6] Manuscript evidence suggests it was only after *The Music of the Ainur* that he wrote most of *The Book of Lost Tales* – notably, everything set in Valinor. Tolkien's writings about his invented languages, now published in the journal *Parma Eldalamberon*, suggest *The Music of the Ainur* predated Tolkien's Gnomish Lexicon – or at least its main, ink layer, which carries a dateline of Withernsea, 1917.[7] In short, the contemporary date on the Gnomish Lexicon, and the comparative evidence of Tolkien's nigglings, may outweigh Tolkien's recollection nearly fifty years later.

Such a revised timeline would make sense of a different recollection, where he says that besides the *Tale of Tinúviel* (also 1917) he "wrote a lot else in hospitals before the end of the First Great War."[8] One of his talents was to turn boredom and mental ferment into outpourings of creativity. He had a huge opportunity between leaving the Somme and the Armistice – about 35 weeks in hospital

---

6 *Letters*, no. 257, to Christopher Bretherton, 16 July 1964.
7 *Parma Eldalamberon* 11: 3-4.
8 *Letters*, no 163, to W H Auden, 7 June 1955.

and 19 weeks on leave. By contrast the window of opportunity in post-war Oxford was brief and crowded. Other evidence shows that Tolkien virtually ceased work on *The Book of Lost Tales* in the summer of 1919.[9] To write most of the tales in six or seven months, alongside a day job and a busy family life, seems a very tall order.

Somme echoes

If *The Music of the Ainur* was indeed written in early 1917 it would make abundant sense in terms of Tolkien's creative ambitions. The "cosmogonical myth" establishes the theory of the legendarium, providing the moral and thematic underpinnings that would survive and evolve throughout his life. A succession of versions up to the 1950s remained remarkably consistent.

It would also make sense if *The Music of the Ainur* was contemporary with the *Fall of Gondolin*. They form a diptych of theory and practice, problem and outcome, with two falls: the cosmic and the earthly, the mythic and the epic, each with the satanic figure of Melko as instigator. In both tales, Tolkien sought to exorcise the nightmare of war, with passages of terror, fire and mechanical slaughter in *The Fall of Gondolin*, and in *The Music of the Ainur* a catalogue of evils that match what Tolkien had lived through or witnessed on the Somme: "pain and misery […] cruelty, and ravening, and darkness, loathly mire and all putrescence of thought or thing, foul mists and violent flame, cold without mercy […] and death without hope" (*LT I* 55).

The Music of the Ainur is also an attempt to grapple with the riddle of why God would permit such deaths.

Two of his closest friends had been killed on the Somme battlefield in 1916 – Robert Quilter Gilson in July and Geoffrey Bache Smith in December, members of the Tea Club and Barrovian Society (T.C.B.S.), the circle of former schoolfriends which deserves to be called Tolkien's first 'fellowship'. Christopher

---

9 In June 1919, Tolkien was asked to compile the glossary for Kenneth Sisam's *Fourteenth Century Verse and Prose*. A huge undertaking, it seems likely to have swallowed most of his free time until early 1922 (Gilliver, Marshall & Weiner 35-36; further information from Peter Gilliver). There is also uncorroborated evidence from Humphrey Carpenter that assigns one of the very latest changes in the 'Lost Tales' nomenclature (Thingol as the name for Tinúviel's father) to c. June 1919 (*LT II* 69).

Wiseman, fortunate to be a naval officer far from the Somme, had heard of Smith's death from his father, who had written to him, "I am truly distressed at this news, not indeed for him or his fate, but for you who I know loved him so deeply: & I can hardly see to write for the mist which will cover my eyes as I think of your grief when you read what I have to tell you." Frederick Luke Wiseman, a leading figure in the Methodist Church, had advised that though "the tidings of grief […] is come on you through this orgy of unreason" (the war), "Somehow God is in it: at any rate over it"; and he prayed that his son would "have the grace to bear this trouble with fortitude and trustfulness."[10]

Christopher Wiseman could not bring himself to offer any such consolation to Tolkien in his bleak letter passing on the news of Smith's death: "I can't say very much about it now. I humbly pray Almighty God I may be accounted worthy of him."[11] Tolkien wrote back, apparently before Christmas, but nearly four more weeks passed before Wiseman replied with an apology, assuring him that

> since December 24th 1916 I have written four separate and distinct letters to you, that this is the fifth, & that even this is not like to fare better than its predecessors. I don't know why I have so suddenly grown fastidious about letters […] But now I cannot bring myself to send them. I commence a letter in one mood & finish it in another. I work off a hysterical fit on this pad, & on re-reading it feel convinced that I haven't said a true word from beginning to end of the effusion. So I delay it, tear it up, & start afresh. But that gets me no forrarder, for I only describe a fresh & more transient mood, & two days later the whole thing appears hyperbolical.

Fit to burst with seesawing thoughts and emotions, Wiseman had been unable to express them. Now, sending his fervent hope that Tolkien's illness would keep him safe in England, he finally shared his bewildered grief over the deaths of their friends:

> The whole thing is so ineffably mysterious. To have seen two of God's giants pass before our eyes, to have lived and laughed with them, to have learnt of them, to have found them something like ourselves, and to see them go back again into the mist whence they came out. My dear John Ronald, I don't know what to make of it. Do you? You must have seen death before now, and have made up your mind about it. But the hideous incongruity of the whole business appals me. What was a man created for but to create and to

---

10 Frederick Luke Wiseman to Christopher Wiseman, 13 December 1916 (courtesy of the Wiseman family).
11 Christopher Wiseman to Tolkien, 16 December 1916 (Tolkien family papers).

work? And why is a man made sensitive and nervous if it is to die in agony? And how can this life be a pilgrimage, if here in mortality we are [not] to do immortal work which is afterwards to be tested by fire whether it be of gold, iron, wood, straw, stubble?

Here Christopher Wiseman refers to a passage from the First Epistle to the Corinthians, in which St Paul says that the afterlife will assay the true value of all that we achieved in life.[12] Wiseman's point is that Smith and Gilson achieved almost none of their true promise, and through no fault of their own. "It is all so unaccountable, & unbelievable," he writes.[13]

The death of Smith, a poet, seems to have almost silenced the poet in Tolkien – in the first eight months of 1917 his only verse was an elegy for Smith and Gilson. But if *The Music of the Ainur* is indeed now restored to its proper time and place, it demonstrates that the philosopher was not silenced.

Music and creation

What follows will demonstrate that Tolkien is still half a stranger to us, with inspirations and motivations we still only half understand. The sources of his inspiration were not confined to the literatures we primarily associate with him: Germanic or Celtic legend, Middle English romance, 19th-century adventure yarns, fairy-stories. And the Tolkien we will meet here is not a "bandersnatch" (in C.S. Lewis's words) immune to influence from others or from contemporary events, but a creative artist responding directly to the immediacies of his own experience, and working almost collaboratively with a close audience.[14]

---

12 1 Cor 3: 12–13 (*King James Version*): "Now if any man build upon this foundation [i.e. the foundation of Christ] gold, silver, precious stones, wood, hay, stubble; Every man's work shall be made manifest: for the day shall declare it, because it shall be revealed by fire; and the fire shall try every man's work of what sort it is."
13 Christopher Wiseman to Tolkien, 18 January 1917 (Tolkien family papers). I am grateful to Dr Michael Ward for elucidating this passage, and for suggesting that Wiseman inadvertently omitted a vital 'not' from the sentence about life as a pilgrimage. Tolkien's response to Wiseman's 16 December letter does not survive.
14 "No one ever influenced Tolkien – you might as well try to influence a bandersnatch. We [the Inklings] listened to his work, but could affect it only by encouragement. He has only two reactions to criticism: either he begins the whole work over again from the beginning or else takes no notice at all." C.S. Lewis to Charles Moorman, 15 May 1959 in Lewis 1049.

Tolkien scholarship has established some likely sources for aspects of Tolkien's Creation myth, but all fall well short of the full picture. For the revolt of the angels led by Melko, an obvious forerunner is John Milton's *Paradise Lost*, the 17th-century epic. There are compelling parallels too with the Old English *Genesis*, which some scholars have suggested Milton knew – and which Tolkien certainly did. Yet the Old English *Genesis* presents Satan via the tropes of heroic literature, and the Satan of *Paradise Lost* seems so heroic that William Blake, in his *The Marriage of Heaven and Hell*, famously declared Milton was "of the Devil's party". Tolkien neither makes Melko heroic nor invites us to weigh up the justice of his cause.

A key question has been why Tolkien chose music as the medium for Creation – choral music, but wordless. His Creation myth in its earliest versions has no match for St John's statement that in the beginning was the Word – no divine cry of *Eä*, "Let these things be!" as in late versions.[15] As the creative principle of a world made specifically to house invented languages, music seems a strange choice.

It is particularly striking that it comes from a man deeply conscious of his own inadequacy in music. "I love music, but have no aptitude for it," he said. Having failed to learn the violin himself, he thought anyone who could play a stringed instrument "a wizard worthy of deep respect[.]"[16]

But amid these comments from much later, there is one that points to a partial answer to the question of why Tolkien the mythmaker chose music as the medium for Creation. "Such music as was in me," he said, "was submerged (until I married a musician), or transformed into linguistic terms."[17]

He and Edith Bratt had married just before he was sent to the Somme. Surely it was during his convalescence the following winter of 1916-17, when he and Edith lived together for the first time, that "such music as was in" him rose towards the surface. She could sing, and in the evenings she would play her piano.

---

15 John 1:1. The cry *Eä*, also used as the name for the created universe, first emerged as an emendation to the last version of what Tolkien by then called *Ainulindalë*, written between 1948 and 1951 (*MR* 7, 31).
16 *Letters*, no. 142, to Robert Murray, SJ, 2 December 1953.
17 *Letters*, no. 260, to Carey Blyton, 16 August 1964.

Tolkien's writing was often just as performative. He had been writing poetry since 1914 at least with Edith or the T.C.B.S. in mind. Now, Tolkien was no doubt writing his stories partly for Edith – who twice painstakingly wrote out fair copies of his heavily emended first drafts – and for his dearest surviving friend, Wiseman.

For Christopher Wiseman, music was a keystone of life and thought. A later memorial essay on his father celebrates the Wiseman family's love "of the activity of music, the drama of the contrasts of organ, orchestra, chorus, singer; brass against strings, trumpet against voice, hands and toes, great tones sustained in clashes[.]" To be a Wiseman, he wrote, meant loving music "because you could not help yourself, because musical instruments sometimes produced noises that made you catch your breath, because there were tunes that filled you with exaltation or perhaps with an unearthly sadness[.]"[18] There seems no reason to doubt that even in his youth Wiseman was capable of such eloquence on his favourite topic. On Tolkien, it must surely have cast its spell.

The Music of the Ainur is foreshadowed in something Wiseman, in 1916, had told Tolkien about his Elves:

> The completed work is vanity; the process of the working is everlasting. Why these creatures live to you is because you are still creating them. [...] Just as the fugue is nothing on the page; it is only vital as it works its way out.[19]

The fugue was a musical form dear to Wiseman, whose memoirs speak of "counterpoints that went on and on miraculously" and of "musical patterns that wound themselves in and out through surprising vicissitudes until they resolved themselves at the end like a fairy-tale[.]"[20]

In a fugue, several voices or parts pursue the same theme but in a stepped or staggered progression. Typically, one vocal part introduces the theme; another enters a few bars later but from the beginning of the theme; and then a further voice joins in a few bars further on, but again from the beginning of the theme. Schoolchildren practise a simple form of this, the round, with *Frère Jacques*, *London's Burning*, or *Row, Row, Row Your Boat*. There is scope for independent

---

18 Christopher Wiseman, untitled chapter in Burnett et al. 35.
19 Christopher Wiseman to Tolkien, 14 March 1916 (Tolkien family papers).
20 Christopher Wiseman in Burnett et al. 35.

elaboration of the theme by any of the voices. Instruments may join the voices or take their place altogether. But the real beauty of the form lies in the way that what might seem a recipe for clashing, chaotic dissonance can instead produce startlingly unexpected harmonies.

The fugue seems precisely the form Tolkien imagined for the Music of the Ainur, from the very first version of the tale. Here the single voice of God (Ilu or Ilúvatar) introduces each theme, which is then taken up by the angels or gods (Ainur) – each pursuing that theme, each elaborating upon it in individual ways.[21] It produces an effect more than the sum of its parts:

> mighty melodies changing and interchanging, mingling and dissolving amid the thunder of harmonies greater than the roar of the great seas, till the places of the dwelling of Ilúvatar and the regions of the Ainur were filled to overflowing with music, and the echo of music, and the echo of the echoes of music which flowed even into the dark and empty spaces far off. (*LT I* 53)

The music fills the heavenly arena but also, superabundantly, overspills into the void.

By making fugal music the mode of divine creation, Tolkien executes a major departure from Judaeo-Christian traditions. Ilu does not sing to himself; the Ainur do not sing only for Ilu nor for themselves. Together the Creator and his angels shape the world that will be. God is the fountainhead of creative inspiration, and only his divine power can give actuality to this new-shaped world, yet he is not the sole author of Creation: the angels are his collaborators.

So the heavenly music of Tolkien's cosmogonic myth is both personal and collaborative; it is guided by a lead musician yet individually and communally elaborative. It fuses diverse talents, "the harpists, and the lutanists, the flautists and pipers, the organs and the countless choirs" (*LT I* 53). Likewise Wiseman's writings marvel over the paradox that music, a medium that evokes such personal and private responses, is "written by and for performers, […] played and sung with others and to others[.]"[22]

---

21 For simplicity in this literary discussion, I use the better known plural form *Ainur* even though the pencil draft has *Ainu*. However, I use *Ilu* for God the Creator (alongside *Ilúvatar*), because it will prove pertinent to the discussion of Tolkien's sources.
22 Christopher Wiseman in Burnett et al. 45.

Taken together, Tolkien's *Music of the Ainur* and Wiseman's reflections on music demonstrate the profound truth in comments in February 1916 from G.B. Smith to Tolkien about the T.C.B.S. fellowship of friends that also included Rob Gilson.

> You need never reproach yourself that you have taken up too much time and discourse. We believe in your work, we others, and recognise with pleasure our own finger in it. Christopher declares that he and Rob and I write your poems, and it is not altogether untrue, though not wholly true either.[23]

It is surely no coincidence that in *The Music of the Ainur* Tolkien pursued an idea so close to Wiseman's heart, in a story about creation which is collaborative to the core.

However much Tolkien may have reproached himself for taking up his three friends' time with his ideas, he too had believed they were collaborators. He believed "the T.C.B.S. had been granted some spark of fire – certainly as a body if not singly – that was destined to kindle a new light, or, what is the same thing, rekindle an old light in the world[.]"[24]

Immediately after the death of Gilson, he had been plunged into doubt; for how could God have meant them to do anything as a body if that body was going to be savagely dismembered by war? Yet his cosmogonic myth, written less than a year after Gilson's death, echoes the idea of the "spark of fire" granted by God. It is the very key that turns the Music into an act of world-building, as Ilúvatar tells the Ainur: "'One thing only have I added, the fire that giveth Life and Reality' – and behold, the Secret Fire burnt at the heart of the world" (*LT I* 55). It is an affirmation of the idea of illumination through imagination and creativity that Tolkien had shared with his three dearest friends.

Fugue, fate and free will

The fugal model in *The Music of the Ainur* does more than simply celebrate collaborative art; it enshrines free will at the heart of the creative process. In Tolkien's model, God's creation of an angelic order with free will is a prerequi-

---

23 G.B. Smith to Tolkien, 9 February 1916 (Tolkien family papers).
24 *Letters*, no. 5, to G.B. Smith, 12 August 1916.

site for wider Creation. Without those other free wills, implicitly, all Creation might be nothing more than solipsism on God's part: however vast, just a hall of mirrors and a vanity. To employ God-given talent in elaborating God's themes is a virtuous exercise of free will of the kind Tolkien and the T.C.B.S. surely had in mind.

However, it is the very pith of free will that it may act against God's will. In the fugal Music, this takes the form of an attempt to establish a theme other than God's. Melko, the Ainu who has "fared most often alone into the dark places and voids[,]" brings to the Music "matters of his own vain imagining" (*LT I* 53). The attempt to find inspiration either in nothingness or in division from divinity, or both, is vain in two senses – fruitless and self-regarding.

Collaboration is no guarantee of creative virtue; it too can be perverted to other ends. Melko rallies less powerful Ainur to join his revolt. They disrupt the larger harmony, and the Music breaks into confusion. The world-shaping goes awry, and Creation is infused with the evils described by Ilúvatar in terms so reminiscent of the sufferings Tolkien had witnessed at the Somme.

Here in *The Music of the Ainur*, Tolkien begins to address what Christopher Wiseman had described as the "ineffably mysterious" destruction of such rich promise as Gilson and Smith had represented, its "hideous incongruity". The tale begins to answer Wiseman's questions: "why is a man made sensitive and nervous if it is to die in agony? And how can this life be a pilgrimage, if here in mortality we are [not] to do immortal work […]."

Its fugal model suggests through myth exactly how (in Wiseman's father's words on the death of Smith) "Somehow God is in it: at any rate over it." An omnipotent, benevolent and wise Creator finds himself in a divine paradox. He could simply stop folly and malevolence at root, yet to do so would be to uproot the free will necessary to true Creation as distinct from mere self-propagation. But Tolkien's cosmogonic myth also offers a solution to the divine paradox. Ilúvatar trusts free will itself to overcome the evil which free will necessarily permits.

This is seen first within the heavenly music. After Melko has disrupted the music inspired by one divine theme, Ilu introduces a further theme for the faithful Ainur to descant upon; and the process is repeated; but when he introduces a third theme to which the Ainur attune themselves once again, the clashing discords begin to be resolved into a greater harmony, so that "ever, as it essayed to clash most fearsomely[,]" Melko's discord finds itself "in some manner supplementing or harmonising with its rival" (*LT I* 54). By participating in the Music – even if only in a bid to disrupt it – Melko is part of the collaborative act of Creation. Thinking he has found inspiration in the void, Melko merely deludes himself, because all inspiration comes ultimately from Ilu or the Secret Fire. Melko is unable to do anything completely outside the range of divine order.

As above, so below: as in the heavenly music, so in the unfolding history of the world. The world is not just a space but a process; in the words of Tolkien's much later version, not just "habitation" but also "history".[25] Within Creation, discords will be resolved. Within Creation, the collaborative and elaborative role is extended to others of God's creatures: Elves and Men, together known as the Children of Ilúvatar because they are his creation solely. But Ilúvatar has imbued Men, too, with free will. They are able to elaborate in their own way upon the themes introduced into the world. As the pencil draft puts it:

> And he devised that they should have free will and the power of fashioning and designing beyond the original music of the Ainu, that by reason of their operations all things shall in shape and deed be fulfilled, and the world that comes of the music of the Ainu be completed unto the last and smallest.[26]

Despite the worst intentions and outcomes, despite the evils and sufferings within the created world, the discord will somehow enhance Creation. With it, the story of our world will be a better, braver and more beautiful one. Again, the metaphor underlying this redemptive model is the fugue. The *Lost Tales* and all the later narratives that Tolkien set in the world of his legendarium match Wiseman's description of "patterns that wound themselves in and out through surprising vicissitudes until they resolved themselves at the end like a fairy-tale[.]"

---

25 The words *habitation* and *history* were introduced prominently and methodically in *Ainulindalë* C, written between 1948 and 1951 (*MR* 7, 11-14 passim, 16).

26 In the ink fair copy of the *Music* this is called "a free virtue"; it is unclear whether it is distinct from free will or the same thing. I do not enter here into the debate over whether or not Elves have free will, for which see my brief comment in *Tolkien and the Great War* 275 and Verlyn Flieger's extensive counter-argument in 'The Music and the Task: Fate and Free Will in Middle-earth.'

Possible precedents

Was there, however, any *literary* model for Tolkien's heavenly music – one which could have offered Tolkien a narrative shape for Wiseman's ideas about the fugue?

There are indeed mythic forerunners that link Creation and divine song. In Hesiod's *Theogony*, the Muses sing to Zeus on Olympus about the beginnings of the world. In the *Book of Job* the period of creation is when "when the morning stars sang together, and all the sons of God shouted for joy[.]"[27] The analogue closest to Tolkien's heart is the *Kalevala*, the cycle of Finnish legends, part of which he had tried adapting in 1914 in the *Story of Kullervo*, the stepping stone to Middle-earth. In the *Kalevala*, song is the medium of creative power within the world, and it is the medium of the magic-battles fought there.

No doubt all of these precedents, Hesiod, *Job*, *Kalevala*, were in Tolkien's mind when he wrote *The Music of the Ainur* – and also the revolt of Satan in *Paradise Lost* and the Old English *Genesis*. But in none of them is music the actual medium of creation.

What else is missing? Tolkien's cosmogonic myth tells how God presents his angels with three great themes of music on which they elaborate. But one rebel angel breaks the harmony by straying from God's original themes. Others join in his discord, so the Music becomes a battle between opposing principles of order and chaos, beauty and ugliness, divine inspiration and self-regard. None of this is in any of the examples we have seen.

It is all present, however, in another, almost unnoticed model for this Creation myth.

A chord struck

I wish I had made the discovery myself. But it took a particular person with a very particular set of interests to do so. This insight comes from one of Tolkien's latter-day successors at the *Oxford English Dictionary*, Peter Gilliver. Rather

---

27 Job 38:7, cited by Gilliver, 'Making the Music'; Scarf 140; Styers 121; among others.

beautifully, it struck him as he took part in a choral performance in Oxford in 2006.[28] Peter launched the exploration with a talk on the topic at the Tolkien Society's *Return of the Ring* conference in 2012, but I hope here to be able to steer it within sight of a firm landing.

The choir was singing Benjamin Britten's *The Company of Heaven*, in which the singing is interspersed with spoken readings. One runs like this:

> When all the sons of God shouted for joy, Lucifer would not take part, but sang his own song. This song of Lucifer's was a dwelling on his own beauty, an instressing of his own inscape, and like a performance on the organ and instrument of his own being; it was a sounding, as they say, of his own trumpet and a hymn in his own praise. Moreover it became an incantation: others were drawn in; it became a concert of voices, a concerting of selfpraise, an enchantment, a magic, by which they were dizzied, dazzled and bewitched. They would not listen to the note which summoned each to his own place and distributed them here and there in the liturgy of the sacrifice; they gathered rather closer and closer home under Lucifer's lead and drowned it, raising a countermusic and countertemple and altar, a counterpoint of dissonance and not of harmony.

In Peter, the reading had found just the right person to spot the similarities to Tolkien's Creation myth. He and his colleagues Edmund Weiner and Jeremy Marshall published their book about Tolkien's work at the *OED*, *The Ring of Words*, the same year.

On hearing the reading during *The Company of Heaven*, Peter recalled,

> the similarities were so striking to me […] that I began to wonder whether, rather than composing the *Music of the Ainur* as a completely novel conception, Tolkien had rather made a reworking – greatly extended and elaborated, certainly – of another writer's already substantially developed image: a method he had certainly adopted in some of his earliest creative writing, such as his adaptation of the Finnish legend of Kullervo. (Gilliver, 'Making Music')

Peter recognised

> almost all of the key images of the opening paragraphs of Tolkien's text: the call to the angels (= Ainur) to sing to/for God (= Ilúvatar), the desire of Lucifer (= Melko) to sing something of his own devising, the seduction of others into singing with him, and the resulting "counterpoint of dissonance" in which Lucifer and his band seek to drown the "note" of God. (Gilliver, 'Making Music')

---

28 Peter Gilliver, 'Making the Music.' He was performing with the Oxford University Press Choir on 18 November 2006 in Mansfield College chapel.

Britten's *The Company of Heaven*, written for broadcast by the BBC in 1937, cannot have been known to Tolkien when he wrote the *Music of the Ainur*. But the peculiar phrase "an instressing of his own inscape" is pure Gerard Manley Hopkins, the 19th-century Catholic visionary poet. Peter found that the text in *The Company of Heaven* had come from from a note by Hopkins written about 1881.[29] The note was not published until 1937 either, but Peter sleuthed out several routes by which Hopkins's unpublished ideas might have reached Tolkien, via Oxford Catholic circles.[30]

Peter ended his paper to the 2012 Tolkien Society conference by suggesting "one other intriguing possibility". In his note, Hopkins had drawn on two other Creation narratives – "Babylonian and Welsh texts". Had Tolkien, instead of adapting Hopkins, actually used one of these as his source for *The Music of the Ainur*? About the Welsh text, I agree with Peter that it is plainly a dead end as far as this 'Lost Tale' is concerned (if not, maybe, for later versions).[31]

But the "Babylonian" one is a different matter entirely. This is a fragmentary cuneiform tablet from Mesopotamia which Hopkins had seen in translation in

---

29 See Devlin 200-01.
30 Most promising is Father Joseph Rickaby, a high-profile figure in Oxford Catholicism, whose meditative 1907 book *Waters That Go Softly* had included a passage highly reminiscent of Hopkins's note and quite probably inspired by it. Rickaby, who had known Hopkins, may have put these ideas into wider circulation in the small and close-knit Catholic community in Oxford when Tolkien was an undergraduate there. Peter also considered that Henry Bradley, Tolkien's boss at the *Oxford English Dictionary*, might have known Hopkins' note through his friend Robert Bridges, who edited the first collection of Hopkins's poetry for Oxford University Press, published in 1918. But if *The Music of the Ainur* was indeed written in 1917, this conjecture will have to be ruled out.
31 The Welsh text, *The Iolo Manuscripts*, was compiled by antiquarian Edward Williams under his bardic name, Iolo Morganwg, and published in 1848. Tolkien's copy, now at the Bodleian Library (VC156), was acquired in 1922, later than *The Music of the Ainur*. But one passage it is suggestive of the divine cry of *Eä* which Tolkien introduced in emendations to the last version of *Ainulindalë* (1948-51, *MR* 7, 31), where *Eä* is both the divine *fiat* ('Let these things be!') and the name of the created world ('That which is'). Originating in an MS in Raglan Castle library, *The Iolo Manuscripts* claims to be a record of oral traditions but turns out to have been a forgery. It states: "GOD, in vocalising his Name, said /|\, and, with the Word, all worlds and animations sprang co-instantaneously to being and life from their non-existence; shouting, in extacy [sic] of joy, /|\, and thus repeating the name of the Deity. Still and small was that melodiously sounding voice (i. e. the Divine utterance) which will never be equalled again until GOD shall renovate every pre-existence from the mortality entailed on it by sin, by re-vocalising that name, from the primary utterance of which emanated all lays and melodies, whether of the voice or of stringed instruments; and also all the joys, extacies [sic], beings, vitalities, felicities, origins, and, descents appertaining to existence and animation" (Williams (Iolo Morganwg), 424). I am grateful to Yoko Hemmi and Catherine McIlwaine for checking for annotations on this page of Tolkien's copy, which they judge to be in another's hand (perhaps the previous owner's) and which appear neither characteristic of Tolkien nor pertinent to the above quotations from *The Iolo Manuscripts* and *Ainulindalë*.

the journal *Records of the Past* in 1876, under the title *The Revolt in Heaven*.[32] Hopkins had drawn much of his cosmogonic narrative directly from the translation. The similarities between *The Music of the Ainur* and *The Revolt in Heaven* are even more compelling than those with the Hopkins passage.

> The Divine Being spoke three times, the commencement of a Psalm.
> The god of holy songs, Lord of religion and worship
> seated a thousand singers and musicians: and established a choral band
> who to his hymn were to respond in multitudes. [...]
> (Talbot, *Records of the Past* 127)

Tolkien's Creator is likewise a God of holy songs, and it is through song that he creates his holy retinue. These are referred to as "gods", but they parallel the angels of Judaeo-Christian tradition. The Creator teaches them music, and gives them holy themes to sing or play on "the voices of their instruments". The most specific and remarkable common feature is how Tolkien's Creator begins three times a new theme for his choirs and orchestras to take up.

> With a loud cry of contempt they broke up his holy song
> Spoiling, confusing, confounding, his hymn of praise.
> (Talbot, *Records of the Past* 127)

In Tolkien's text the divinely ordained song is likewise disrupted and spoilt by a rebel minority.

> The god of the bright crown with a wish to summon his adherents
> sounded a trumpet blast which would wake the dead,
> which to those rebel angels prohibited return,
> he stopped their service [...] (Talbot, *Records of the Past* 127)

The 1876 translator explains that "the god of the bright crown" is another epithet for the Creator. The "trumpet blast" which ends the rebellion echoes, surely, in Tolkien's memorable "one unfathomed chord, deeper then the firmament, more glorious than the sun, and piercing as the light of Ilúvatar's glance" (*LT I* 54) with which the Music and discord are suddenly brought to a halt.

This is the final point of close similarity, and from here the accounts diverge. But it is not the end of the investigation.

---

32 Devlin 352. Talbot 123-28.

Ilu's music

We do not have to go very far before encountering an even more telling congruence between the *Music of the Ainur* and the translation work on this particular cuneiform tablet – the clincher, I believe, in the debate over its influence on Tolkien.

Records of the Past, which Hopkins saw, was a journal for popular consumption. But its article *The Revolt in Heaven* was only a summary of a longer piece by that title in the 1876 *Transactions of the Society of Biblical Archaeology*.[33] This fuller version has additional commentary and linguistic notes, plus the original cuneiform text and a transliteration of the language – Akkadian (sometimes known as Assyrian). It was by Henry Fox Talbot, famous as the man who pioneered photography in Britain, but also an enthusiastic amateur philologist, who in his old age was a busy contributor to efforts to understand Assyrian cuneiform.

Actually Talbot's translation should sound a strong cautionary note to anyone who engages in source criticism, who looks for literary influences and finds apparent similarities. As Eleanor Robson, Professor of Ancient Near Eastern History at University College London, has commented, "His translations were always superseded, often very quickly, by others in his field" (Robson 208). In an analysis of Talbot's work on another cuneiform tablet, she concludes that he "entangled etymological and cultural similarity to produce a text that fulfilled readers' thirst for biblical parallels" (Robson 213). The translation seen by Hopkins, and evidently by Tolkien too, was wholly wrong, and a rival 1876 translation by Assyriologist George Smith is the one that led the way forward. The cuneiform fragment turns out to be part of the Seventh Tablet of the *Seven Tablets of Creation*, an epic also known as *Enuma Elish*. What Talbot had thought a myth about creation through music was actually part of a litany of names of honour given to Marduk, the god of Babylon.[34] There is no heavenly choir,

---

33 Cf. Talbot, 'The Revolt in Heaven: from a Chaldean tablet.' *Transactions of the Society of Biblical Archaeology*. Vol. 4 (1876). 349-62.
34 George Smith thought the tablet (K.8522 in the British Museum register) was about "the story of man's original innocence" in which "the Deity [...] delivers a long address to the newly created being [...] pointing out the glory of his state" (Smith 15). This, too, was wrong, as was known by 1902 (see King xxvii, 97). But in detail Smith's translation was much more accurate. What Talbot interpreted as "The god of life divine three times spoke the commencement of a psalm[,]" Smith (82) translated as "The god Ziku (Noble life) quickly called; Director of purity[.]" A recent translation gives "Tutu-Ziku they called him thirdly, the establisher of purification" (Lambert 124); cf. Dalley 268.

no music and no discord; no divine trumpet blast nor casting out of rebels. In these early days of decipherment, Talbot had misconstrued many words, seen something that reminded him of the story of Genesis, and imagined the music and all the rest of it.

Who knows whether Tolkien knew Talbot's error. Even if he did know, there is little reason to think it would have deterred him from using the story for his cosmogonic myth. If he used the 'translation', it was not to authenticate *The Music of the Ainur*, but to give it poetic shape. It might be observed, in any case, that if Tolkien derived such beauty from error, there was poetic justice in it: his myth embodies the very process of redemptive creation which it celebrates.

But the obvious question to ask is, if Talbot could get it so wrong why not Peter Gilliver, and why not me? Firstly, the hunt for analogues for *The Music of the Ainur* has turned up nothing remotely as close as this. Secondly, there is further evidence which I think clinches the case.

It has to do with Elvish. The answer to the question of a shaping influence on Tolkien's cosmogonic myth has been lying concealed within the name *Ilúvatar* (first published in the 1977 *Silmarillion*) and in its precursor *Ilu* (first published in 1983 in *The Book of Lost Tales*, *LT I* 61). Here is the beginning of Talbot's translation and transliteration (Talbot, *Transactions* 353-54):

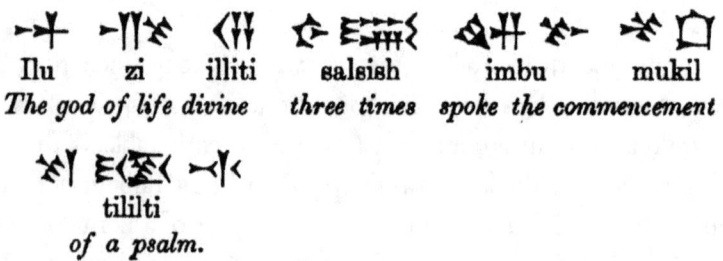

The Akkadian word *ilu* is related to Hebrew *El* and *Elohim* as well as Arabic *Allah* (al-'ilāh).

Talbot (*Transactions* 360) gives further thoughts on a title (as he understood it) for the leader of the Revolt: "*Zalmat kakkadu* (crowned head), usually signifies 'a king'. [...] In some texts it replaces *malku sha kiprati* 'king of the nations'."

Now this is interesting too, because Tolkien's 1915 Qenya Lexicon had provided the word *malko* 'Lord, Sir', and said it derived from an earlier *malkŭ*.[35] With a little help from Hebrew *melekh* (a cognate of the Akkadian *malku*), that seems to have led to the name Melko for the Satan figure Tolkien invented in the winter of 1916-17.

In his 1876 paper, Talbot, excited to see biblical parallels in Babylonian cosmogony, equates the Akkadian 'crowned head' to Satan: "In the present passage I think the phrase means 'a serpent', not generically, but that particular serpent which was fabled to wear a Crown upon its head, and was for that reason called the Basilisk, from Βασιλισκος [Basiliskos] 'a little king'. In some medieval pictures I think that the Tempter Serpent wears a Crown [...]" (Talbot, *Transactions* 360). The Melko of the Fall of Gondolin is a throned tyrant (*LT II* 169), but from the summer of 1917 and the *Tale of Tinúviel* onwards, his distinctive mark is his Iron Crown.

Tolkien would also have had access to dictionaries of Akkadian and Sumerian, its (unrelated) predecessor in Mesopotamia. One, the 1875 *Assyrian Grammar and Reading Book* by A.H. Sayce, shows that the same cuneiform sign for *ilu* 'god' was used for other words meaning 'sky', 'high', and for *sa* 'star' (Sayce 2).[36]

4.	an, ana ...	➤-Y	sakū, samū, ilu, Anu,	*high, sky, god, the god Anu*
	anna, annab...	,,	sakū, samū, ilu, Anu,	*high, sky, god, the god Anu*
	dimir, dingir...	,,	ilu	*god*
	sa	,,	cacabu	*star*
	essa	,,	ilutu sa sibri ...	*divinity of corn*
	an	,,	supultu	*depth*

There are striking parallels with Tolkien's divine names in the period when he was writing *The Music of the Ainur*. On the meaning of Qenya *Ilu* he vacillated: did it mean God or 'heaven'?[37] But Qenya *Sá* is "Fire, especially in temples, etc. A mystic name identified with Holy Ghost" and is what Tolkien meant in

---

35 *Parma Eldalamberon* 12: 62, s.v. MĻKĻ.
36 The first column shows words in the older, non-Semitic Sumerian language; the third shows words in the later, Semitic Akkadian. I use the modern language names Sumerian and Akkadian where the original books confusingly give "Akkadian" and "Assyrian" respectively.
37 With *Ilu* = God in the pencil *Music*, contrast *Ilu* "ether, the slender airs among the stars" in the Qenya Lexicon (*Parma Eldalamberon* 12: 42). The *Name-list to The Fall of Gondolin* has the Gnomish equivalent *Ilon* "sky" emended to a name for Ilúvatar (*Parma Eldalamberon* 15: 27).

the tale by "the fire that giveth Life and Reality", the "Secret Fire" set to burn "at the heart of the world".[38]

Noting the Akkadian *Anu*, a god's name and a generic word meaning 'god', we turn a few pages in the same cuneiform syllabary to find Sumerian *en*, Akkadian *enu* 'lord', also sharing a cuneiform sign with Sumerian *enu* 'sky' (Sayce 10).

96. en	⊢𝕀	belu, enu	...	...	*lord, lord*
	,,	adi ...	...	...	*up to*
enu	,,	samü	...	...	*sky*

In the Qenya Lexicon and the name-lists to the *Fall of Gondolin*, the proper name of Ilu or Ilúvatar is *En* or *Enu*.[39] The name was early abandoned, but the shape persisted, especially the *-u* ending, so common in Akkadian but almost exclusively reserved in Tolkien's Qenya for the names of primal, divine or demonic beings. One such is *Ainu*.[40] Another is the name that in the 1950s Tolkien ultimately chose for God, *Eru* "the One".[41]

Despite various denials of influence by Tolkien on specific points (generally relating to the much later *The Lord of the Rings*), there is abundant evidence that in practice real-world parallels did sometimes play a part in his inventions (linguistic and otherwise). Several pitfalls should be avoided when considering congruences between Tolkien's inventions and real-world elements. One is to take a single similarity, or any highly dispersed scattering of similarities, as evidence for any conscious and deliberate parallel. In a corpus as vast as Tolkien's, coincidental matches are bound to occur. Another pitfall is to think Tolkien sought at any time to produce an extensive, over-arching and systematic 'code' which can be solved by reference to the real world, unlocking his legendarium

---

38 Qenya Lexicon, *Parma Eldalamberon* 12: 81. s.v. SAHA; *LT I* 53, 55. Tolkien later said the Secret Fire was the Holy Spirit (cf. Kilby 59).
39 Qenya Lexicon, *Parma Eldalamberon* 12: 35; *Official Name List*, *Parma Eldalamberon* 13: 103; Name-list to The Fall of Gondolin, *Parma Eldalamberon* 15: 23.
40 It seems noteworthy that Tolkien's word for angel/god, *Ainu*, is so similar to Qenya/Assyrian *Enu* and to Assyrian *Anu*. His Qenya Lexicon derives *Ainu* from a root AYA 'honour, revere' (*Parma Eldalamberon* 12: 34) but queries the origin of the name *Enu* (35). The accompanying Qenya Phonology suggests the sound *aj* could undergo 'simplification' as *e* (*Parma Eldalamberon* 12: 11-13). Did Tolkien want *Ainu* (both singular and plural in his first draft of the *Music*) to be associated with *Enu*, as the Ainu(r) constitute the very thought of Enu?
41 See note on later echoes of Akkadian in Tolkien's legendarium.

like a magic key. That would have been anathema to him in his linguistic inventions as much as in his narratives, which he strenuously sought to distinguish from allegory. We should be aware, too, that Tolkien's habit of creative niggling meant that any correspondences might soon fall by the wayside.[42]

However, none of this is to deny that Tolkien did, in limited but richly significant ways, consciously mould his material to conform to real-world influences. Where a cluster of congruences occurs in a contemporaneous part of his corpus, we may be right to suspect that it means something. The important thing is to establish what, if anything. But before that, we need to establish whether Tolkien would have recognised the matches himself, whether he would have known they existed.

Lost worlds

Why would such works of Assyriology have reached Tolkien? We have the answer from the horse's mouth. "Naturally, as one interested in antiquity and notably in the history of languages and 'writing'," he once wrote, "I knew and had read a good deal about Mesopotamia."[43] His use of Assyrian sources for his mystic names has a parallel in his invention (by 1919) of the Rúmilian script, the visual forms of which are clearly modelled on Devanagari, used in Sanskrit scriptures. For his earliest divine names and his earliest writing system, he turned to the most ancient available real-world models.

The project of Assyriology was also inspired by, and ran in parallel with, the Indo-European philological project to which Tolkien was committed. Part of that project was the disinterment of 'lost tales', which is exactly what Talbot was attempting to do in the 1876 *Revolt in Heaven*. The biggest inspiration of Talbot's era had been the discovery by George Smith at Nineveh in 1872 of the tablets from the Epic of Gilgamesh referring to a Great Flood – an older tale than the story of Noah but obviously related to it somehow.

---

42 It is clear that even in the pencil draft of the *Music*, he did not want to present a hulking, obvious parallel with Akkadian: he did not use *malku* but *Melko*. In the ink fair copy he changed *Ilu* to *Ilúvatar*, concealing the Akkadian within an echo of Allfather, Old Norse *Alföðr*.
43 *Letters*, no. 297, drafts for a letter to 'Mr Rang', August 1967. Tolkien makes the statement while denying any connection between the biblical Erech and the place of that name in Gondor of *The Lord of the Rings*.

Assyriology was an essential part of the philological side of undergraduate courses in Bible studies, like the one taken by a man Tolkien called "one of the most delightful Christian men I have met"[44] – Christopher Wiseman's father, Frederick Luke Wiseman. Fred Wiseman excelled in his studies at Didsbury College from 1879; becoming assistant tutor in Biblical Languages there from 1882, "he seemed now to have found his life's work" (Greeves 3). Only the fact that he was put in charge of Birmingham's main Methodist meeting hall in 1887 had forced him to shelve his linguistic work.[45]

In an unpublished memoir, Christopher Wiseman recalls his father's "vast library" in which "as I grew older I discovered that there were grammars of other Semitic languages as Assyrian" – what we now call Akkadian. Christopher tried to learn it but was defeated and made a hobby of Egyptian hieroglyphics instead.[46] Tolkien may have been able to find books on Akkadian at the Birmingham Oratory, which was very much a place of learning; at Birmingham's very substantial central library; and, of course, at Oxford. But I would bet my boots that it was at the Wiseman family home at 12 Greenfield Crescent, Edgbaston, during his intense teenage friendship with Christopher Wiseman, that Tolkien encountered the *Assyrian Grammar and Reading Book* carrying the entries *ilu*, *en*, *enu*, and *sa*. It was one of only two such grammars available in English in the 1870s. I would not be surprised, either, if Tolkien was introduced to Talbot's *Revolt in Heaven* translation by Wiseman's father. Fred Wiseman was a man of deep faith, his passion was music, and the college where he had studied and taught Biblical Languages held a copy of the very volume in which *The Revolt in Heaven* was published.[47]

---

44 *Letters*, no. 306, to Michael Tolkien, 1967-68.
45 *Letters*, no. 306, to Michael Tolkien, 1967-68; Wiseman 89; Greeves 3. According to Greeves, "The Chief Rabbi once said of Mr. Wiseman that if he had had time to concentrate on the study of Hebrew he would be been his best scholar and independent authority." Didsbury College, near Manchester, was the oldest theological college established by Methodists.
46 Christopher Wiseman, unpublished memoir, courtesy of Susan Wood / Jonathan Wiseman. Tolkien celebrates Christopher Wiseman's Egyptological passions by nicknaming him *Sekhet* in his rugby poem *The Battle of the Eastern Field* (*King Edward's School Chronicle*, March 1911, 22-27). Tolkien himself acquired the 1896 edition of Budge's *An Egyptian Reading Book for Beginners* (cf. *TOFS* 99).
47 F. L. Wiseman's tutor for Biblical Languages at Didsbury College, Prof. John Dury Geden, is listed among the subscribers in *Transactions of the Society of Biblical Archaeology*, vol. 4 (406). Though Geden stayed on the staff until his death at the college in March 1886, he retired from actual teaching due to ill-health in 1883 and does not appear to have been replaced; so Wiseman's role as assistant tutor in Biblical Languages from 1882 was probably effectively a senior one. See French; Wiseman 92.

The 19th-century discoveries in Mesopotamia and Egypt, at Troy and Mycenae, had a literary impact on Tolkien, too. They inspired the entire genre of 'Lost World' fiction, beginning with Henry Rider Haggard's 1885 *King Solomon's Mines*, a Tolkien favourite. The big idea of Lost World fiction was that somewhere off the map ancient civilisations like those of Mesopotamia might still be thriving.

Allan Quatermain, Haggard's 1887 sequel to *King Solomon's Mines*, shows how Mesopotamia had resonated in the opposite way, too. Lost worlds uncovered by archaeology stood as a reminder of the transience of civilisations. Contemplating the ruins of an East African city, the hero muses:

> Gone! quite gone! the way that everything must go. Like the nobles and the ladies who lived within their gates, these cities have had their day, and now they are as Babylon and Nineveh, and as London and Paris will one day be. Nothing may endure. That is the inexorable law. [...] In this ruined and forgotten place the moralist may behold a symbol of the universal destiny. (Haggard, *Allan Quatermain* 20)

The same trope is seen in Rudyard Kipling's 1897 poem *Recessional*, with a different set of ancient cities to represent impermanence: "Lo, all our pomp of yesterday / is one with Nineveh and Tyre!" Tolkien had this idea of transience – and the same historic precedents as Haggard – very much in mind when he wrote *The Fall of Gondolin*. The tale ends with a reference to Troy and Rome – longer-established classical examples of fallen glory – but also Babylon and Nineveh (names he emended to their Gnomish forms, as given here):

> Glory dwelt in that city of Gondolin of the Seven Names, and its ruin was the most dread of all the sacks of cities upon the face of Earth. Nor Bablon, nor Ninwi, nor the towers of Trui, nor all the many takings of Rûm that is greatest among Men, saw such terror as fell that day [...]. (*LT II* 196; cf. also 203)

Such comparisons were entirely apt in the face of the disaster of Tolkien's own civilisation, the Great War. The crumbled ruins of Babylon and Nineveh offered an analogy for a lost pre-1914 world that already seemed impossibly remote, as well as a warning that the disaster could become total. Even as

Tolkien wrote, Mesopotamia was the scene of war between two latter-day empires, the British and the Ottoman, either of which might fall.[48]

Signpost to Babel

But the parallel that brings us back to Tolkien's Creation myth, and what I believe may have been his chief original rationale for using Mesopotamian divine names, is the Fall of Babel, Babylon's legendary predecessor in the Old Testament.

There is evidence that Tolkien was interested in Babel, too, in the period when he was writing *The Music of the Ainur*. It lies in the name he chose in *The Fall of Gondolin* for the father of the hero Tuor – *Peleg*.

In Gnomish it means 'axe'; there is also a Qenya equivalent, *Pelek* or *pelekko*, supposed to derive from an older form *pelekku*.[49] There can be no doubt whatsoever that Tolkien, as a classicist, knew the synonymous Greek *pelekeus*. As a philologist he doubtless also knew that *pelekeus* and its Sanskrit cognate *parasu*, having no known origin in their own Indo-European language family, were believed to be *Wanderwörter* (wandering or migratory words) that had spread along trade routes from the Near East – from Akkadian *pilakku* and Sumerian *balag*, both meaning 'axe'.[50] Knowing all this, why would Tolkien choose Gnomish and Qenya words that were so similar? I have previously argued that this is one of several instances where he wanted to suggest a fictional Elvish origin of certain historically attested but etymologically problematic words.[51] But the name Peleg for Tuor's father has a different, or additional, significance.

There is also a Peleg in the Book of Genesis – he is the father of Reu, a name that would have interested John Ronald Reuel Tolkien for obvious

---

48 G.B. Smith's brother Roger was there, as Tolkien knew (by letter from Ruth Smith, 16 November 1916). He was killed on 25 January 1917, and Wiseman informed Tolkien in the same 4 March letter which applauds him for starting the 'epic'.
49 *Official Name List, Parma Eldalamberon* 13: 103; Qenya Lexicon, *Parma Eldalamberon* 12: 73.
50 There has been much debate more recently over whether the Mesopotamian words actually meant 'spindle' rather than 'axe'. For a typical contemporary example see Schrader 55. See further Mallory and Adams 243; and Buck 561.
51 See Garth 98.

reasons. Bolstered by certain autobiographical aspects in the coming-of-age and coming-to-responsibility story of Tuor, a set of parallels takes shape:[52]

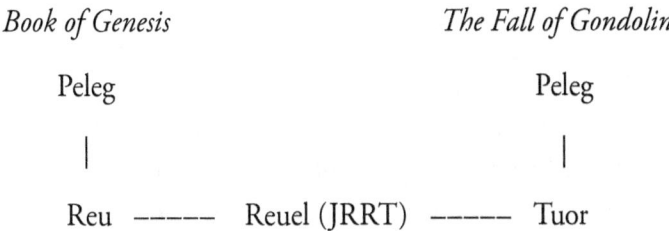

Tolkien was a man who delighted in crosswords, in visual and verbal patterns, in puns, in doublings or triplings of meaning. If he had not wanted to communicate stories, he might have written *Finnegans Wake*. The biblical Peleg and Reu were the near forefathers of Abraham, so there may be a redemptive symbolism in Tolkien's use of the name Peleg for patriarch in the line that produces Tuor and his son Eärendel. But of all those in *Genesis*' Abrahamic line, Peleg has a unique significance.

Hebrew *Peleg* is commonly translated 'division', and *Genesis* says Reu's father was so called because "in his days was the earth divided."[53] That phrase had been taken by Bede and other medieval commentators to refer to the story of the fall of the Tower of Babel, which is told just a few verses further on in the Book of Genesis, with the division of the earth into different nations speaking different languages.[54] After the Great Flood, when still "the whole earth was of one language, and of one speech[,]" the descendants of Noah had decided to build "a city and a tower, whose top may reach unto heaven[.]"

---

52 On Tuor as analogue for Tolkien, see Garth 216.
53 For this and closely related words, see Brown, Driver and Briggs (eds.), *A Hebrew and English Lexicon of the Old Testament* provides verbal senses 'distinguish', 'split, divide', or 'be separated, distinct', as well as the substantive senses 'cleft, channel, canal'. I should note, incidentally, that Hebrew *Peleg* does not appear to be related to Akkadian *pilakku*; a modern dictionary connects it instead with Akkadian *palgu* 'canal' and *puluggu* or *pulungu* 'district' (see Klein 508). I am grateful to Carl F. Hostetter for locating these items.
54 Isidore of Seville's *Etymologies* places Peleg's birth in the same year that "the tower is built (and in this time occurred the division of languages, and the people were dispersed through the whole earth because of the building of the tower)" (Barney et al. 130). On the name, he states: "Peleg means 'division', and his father imposed such a name on him because he was born when the earth was divided by its languages" (Barney et al. 163). See also Bede, *On Genesis* (Kendall 222-23 n68). Bede adds (224) that Scripture called him Peleg, 'division', as a mark of his piety in *preserving* the original world-speech, Hebrew, in this time of the confounding of tongues.

For their hubris and arrogance, God destroyed the tower, and "did there confound the language of all the earth[,]" so there was no longer a single world language. The people were scattered "abroad upon the face of all the earth" (Genesis 11: 1-9).

However, in these 'Lost Tales' writings a suggestive pattern is indeed apparent. Tolkien's choice of the name Peleg for the father of Tuor tells us that in *The Fall of Gondolin* – which now seems to have been written in the same months as the Creation myth – we are in an ancient era of an already fallen world, splintered into nations and languages.

This signpost to Babel offers the most satisfying answer to the question of why Tolkien used Akkadian for the divine names *Ilu*, *En*, *Enu*, *Sá*, and *Melko* in the *Music of the Ainur* and associated writings. In these earliest conceptions, I think he wanted to imply that Akkadian, the tongue of Babylon, inherited these names from the unitary world-speech that had existed before the fall that divided it into a multitude of languages. I think he wanted to imply that the divine names might indeed derive from the language of heaven itself.[55]

Language and legend

For the people of Babel the fall of their tower was bad news. For a world divided into mutually uncomprehending nations, it was a disaster – or at least that is the gist of *Genesis*. But in the long run at least the fall of Babel gave philologists a reason to exist. "O felix peccatum Babel!" Tolkien (*E&W* 194) once exclaimed: O happy (or fortunate) sin of Babel! Though the senti-

---

55 In Tolkien's 'Lost Tales' conceptions, the Valar (those Ainur who descend into the world) speak their own language, which the Elves had also used as a "secret tongue" of lore besides their own languages, Qenya and Gnomish (*LT I* 48, 51-52). In later conceptions embodied in the *Lhammas*, the mid-1930s essay on languages, all languages descend from Valarin (*LR* 168ff.) The final conception, seen in the 1959-60 essay Quendi and Eldar, was similar to the earliest, with Valarin a distinct language known only to the wisest Elves, from which only a few words and names entered the Elvish languages (*WJ* 397ff.). The idea that all the world's languages descended from one true original persisted into the era of comparative philology, which has failed, however, to show persuasive connections between the various language families now known to have existed in late human prehistory. Up to Tolkien's invention of the fictional Elvish tongues (examples of what are now known as 'artlangs'), the craft of language invention was primarily concerned with finding a 'cure for Babel' by providing one auxiliary language that could become universal. See Fimi and Higgins in *Secret Vice*, xlii-xliii; Okrent 26.

ment was expressed in 1955, there can be no doubt that it captures Tolkien's lifelong feeling about the beauties and fascinations of languages and their evolution – the inspiration behind his own invented languages with their intertwining histories. Though it applies to language, not history, the 1955 statement also curiously matches the underlying logic of his cosmogonic myth: disaster produces something that would not otherwise have existed; something wonderful.

The fictional history or legendarium which Tolkien created was founded on its languages. "It was just as the 1914 War burst on me that I made the discovery that 'legends' depend on the language to which they belong; but a living language depends equally on the 'legends' which it conveys by tradition," he wrote in 1956. "So though [...] I began with language, I found myself involved in inventing 'legends' of the same 'taste'. The early work was mostly done in camps and hospitals between 1915 and 1918 [...]."[56] Pinpointing the period of *The Fall of Gondolin* and (as it now seems) *The Music of the Ainur*, Tolkien states that even then he had worked from a clear consciousness of this interdependency of language and legend.[57]

In 1967, asked by journalists Charlotte and Denis Plimmer how language invention could have led to the creation of Middle-earth, he stated the founding principle of his mythology in different terms: "a language requires a suitable *habitation*, and a *history* in which it can develop"[58] [my emphases]. The words *habitation* and *history* were carefully chosen, with the Music of the Ainur in mind. Tolkien had used *history* even in the first, pencil draft of the Creation myth, and retained it through all subsequent versions.[59] But *habitation* emerged abruptly and with notable repetition in the 1940s versions, culminating in the words of the elven narrator, "it is not my part at this time to instruct thee in the *history* of the Earth. And now behold! here is the *habitation* of the Children of

---

56 *Letters*, no. 180, draft to 'Mr Thompson', 14 January 1956.
57 Tolkien had indeed expressed the same conviction about the interdependency of story and language in November 1914, telling fellow students "there is something kindred in the imagination of the speakers of Indo-European languages" that was not akin to what Finno-Ugric imaginations had produced in the Finnish *Kalevala* (Tolkien, *On the 'Kalevala' or Land of Heroes*, in *Kullervo* 68).
58 *Letters*, no. 294, to Charlotte and Denis Plimmer, 8 February 1967.
59 "And even as Ilu was speaking to Ulmo[,] the Ainu beheld how the great history which Ilu had propounded to them [...]" (*LT I* 60).

Ilúvatar established at the last [...]."⁶⁰ The world is repeatedly called a *habitation* for Elves and Men, where their *history* can unfold. After writing this version, Tolkien had cogitated deeply on interrelated Quenya words – *Ambar* (or *Imbar*) 'the Habitation' and *Umbar* 'history, fate, doom' – which embody in their close kinship the intertwining of the two in Ilúvatar's Creation.⁶¹ No doubt they were intended to be the very words translated in the Creation myth by English habitation and history. No doubt, too, all this was in Tolkien's mind when he told the Plimmers he had created Middle-earth as "habitation" and "history" in which his languages could develop.

So Tolkien, at this much later stage, was quite conscious of a parallel between the unfolding history in his legendarium – the pattern laid out in the Music of the Ainur – and the evolution of its languages. Such parallels, perhaps, actively interested him only in old age, as he turned increasingly away from actual making to thinking about what he had already made. But it seems plausible that in his letter to the Plimmers he was merely disinterring a parallel that he had long ago planted in *The Music of the Ainur* by the naming of Ilu and in *The Fall of Gondolin* by the naming of Peleg – both signposts to Babel. Explicitly, his Creation myth would tell the story of the origin of the world and promise resolution for the vicissitudes of history. Implicitly, through its Akkadian names, it would imply a matching story about the origin of language and the outcome of language change.

There is no Tower of Babel in Tolkien's legendarium, but the whole invented history is about why the languages of Elves and Men divide into multitudes. The

---

60 *Ainulindalë* version C, *MR* 16 (my emphases). Cf. also "And as they looked and wondered this World began to unfold its *history*, and it seemed to them that it lived and grew. [...] And they saw with amazement the coming of the Children of Ilúvatar, and the *habitation* that was prepared for them [...]" (*MR* 11). The choice of words is careful and deliberate, as with every revision Tolkien made to this myth – the only *Lost Tale* not to have been scrapped and begun again from scratch in the mid-1920s (*LR* 155).

61 *Imbar*, 'Commentary' on 'Athrabeth Finrod ah Andreth' (*MR* 337); *Ambar*, 'Quendi and Eldar' (*WJ* 402) – both 1959-60. A note from the late 1950s or early 1960s derives both *ambar* 'world' and *umbar* 'fate' from a Primitive Eldarin (Elvish) base √MBAR and elaborates: "The decision, the fixing of the place [Ambar], was thought of as proceeding from *Eru* and so was part of his *Umbar*. *Umbar*, so used, might be said to be 'the history of *Ambar*', so far as it was already accomplished, and its future so far as already arranged and defined" (*Eldarin Roots and Stems*, in *Parma Eldalamberon* 17: 163). A further note from 1968 or later (close to the period of the Plimmer letter) again defines *ambar* as "the great habitation" and says "the full implication of this word cannot be understood without reference to Eldarin views and ideas concerning 'fate' and 'free will'" (*Fate and Free Will*, in *Tolkien Studies* 6: 183).

unfolding drama of world events is matched by the unfolding and diversification of languages. The consolations for the evils instilled in history by Melko are matched by the beauties of language deriving from the *felix peccatum*, the happy sin, of Babel.

Note: Later echoes of Akkadian in Tolkien's legendarium

Eru, the late and well-known equivalent of the obscure *Enu* that appears as a name for Ilúvatar in the earliest *Lost Tales* notes, is just one of a complex of names in Tolkien's invented languages that echo Akkadian and dance between the meanings 'God' and 'world'. In the mid-1930s cosmological essay *Ambarkanta*, *ilu* means 'the world' (*SM* 241). It appears with that meaning, too, in the 1937 time-travel story *The Lost Road*, in interlinear texts of cataclysm (*LR* 63, 72). These texts were the precursors of the interlinear fragments in the 1945-46 time-travel story *The Notion Club Papers* where *eru* first emerges as the name of Ilúvatar in the newly invented Adunaic, the language of Atlantean Númenor. In the Quenya versions of these same 1945-46 fragments, *eru* then appears as an emendation to Quenya *ilu* 'world' (*SD* 247-49, 310-13). By 1951 *Eru* appears as the Quenya name of Ilúvatar and the new word *Eä* had been devised as the name for the world or universe, and as Ilúvatar's *fiat* creating it (*MR* 7, 31).

Visually, the interlinear fragments of *The Lost Road* recall any number of contemporary discussions of ancient texts; but they would seem to acquire a special resonance if we accept that Tolkien knew those published in *Transactions of the Society of Biblical Archaeology*, such as Talbot's *Revolt in Heaven*. This is doubly true of those in *The Notion Club Papers* (*SD* 247):

Kadō	*zigūrun*	*zabathān*	*unakkha* ...	*ēruhinim*	*dubdam*	*ugru-dalad*
and so	?	humbled	he-came	?	fell	?shadow under

The resemblance lies not only in the interlinear arrangement, the ellipses marking missing words, and the queries marking uninterpretable items, but also in the Adunaic itself – a language styled phonologically and morphologically on Semitic languages and strikingly similar to Akkadian.

Adunaic *zigûr* 'wizard', also a name for Sauron, has a dual form *zigūrăt* which can hardly have been coined without thought of the English *ziggurat*, a word for the temple towers of Mesopotamia which is derived from the Akkadian verb meaning 'to build high'. Building such a temple is part of Sauron's strategy to destroy Númenor (*SD* 347).

Predating the invention of Adunaic but also worthy of note is *Istar* (*LR* 15) in *The Fall of Númenor* (1936-37), the earliest-coined name for the last queen of Númenor (whom Tolkien much later renamed *Tar-Míriel*, containing Quenya *mírë*, 'jewel'). In 1924 Tolkien had written with interest about the idea that English *star* is a "migratory word" that ultimately comes "some 4,000 years ago from Accadian *istar*, Venus."[62]

It may be pertinent that shortly before the development of Adunaic, in an essay developing the concepts behind the evolving legend of Númenor, Tolkien wrote that "Men awoke in Mesopotamia" (replaced in a rewritten version by "in the midst of the Great Middle Earth (Europe and Asia)").[63] At any rate, such points as these suggest we should sift Tolkien's words carefully when he writes, in 1967, that "no connexions in my mind or intention between Mesopotamia and the Númenóreans or their predecessors can be deduced" from the Gondorian place-name *Erech*.[64] That may be strictly true of *Erech* itself, but can hardly be true of the other evidence here. I would suggest that there was indeed a conscious connection between Mesopotamia and Númenor, at least up to the mid-1940s; and that it probably hinged on these shared features: both were primal, high civilisations associated with hubris, a Great Flood and the downfall of a totemic tower.

---

62 'Philology: General Works' 40. In *The Notion Club Papers* Michael Ramer dreams of another world called *Tekel-Ishtar*, described as "a land of crystals" and then renamed *Tekel-Mirim* (*SD* 207, 222 n67).
63 Sketch I and II (*SD* 410, 398).
64 *Letters*, no. 297, draft to 'Mr Rang', August 1967.

About the Author

JOHN GARTH is author of the acclaimed biographical *Tolkien and the Great War*, winner of the Mythopoeic Award for Scholarship 2004, and was Fellow in Humanistic Studies for 2015-16 at the Black Mountain Institute, University of Las Vegas, Nevada. As well as journalism, other writings include the definitive study of Tolkien's undergraduate life, *Tolkien at Exeter College*, nominated for the same award in 2015, and the chapter on the Inklings for Catherine McIlwaine's book accompanying the 2018 Bodleian Libraries exhibition, *Tolkien: Maker of Middle-earth*. See also John's homepage at: http://www.johngarth.co.uk/

Abbreviations

E&W   TOLKIEN, John Ronald Reuel. *English and Welsh*. In *Angles and Britons: O'Donnell Lectures*. University of Wales Press, 1963. Reprinted in *The Monsters and the Critics*. Ed. Christopher Tolkien. First published 1983. Paperback edition. London: HarperCollins, 1997. 162-97.

Kullervo   TOLKIEN, John Ronald Reuel. *The Story of Kullervo*. Ed. Verlyn Flieger. London: HarperCollis, 2015.

Letters   TOLKIEN, John Ronald Reuel. *The Letters of J.R.R. Tolkien*. Ed. Humphrey Carenter, with the assistance of Christopher Tolkien. London: George Allen & Unwin, 1981. Reprinted Boston: Houghton Mifflin, 2000.

LotR   TOLKIEN, John Ronald Reuel. *The Lord of the Rings*. First published 1954/55. 50th Anniversary one-volume edition. Boston and New York: Houghton Mifflin Company, 2004.

LR   TOLKIEN, John Ronald Reuel. *The Lost Road and Other Writings*. The History of Middle-earth 5. Ed. Christopher Tolkien. First published 1987. London: Grafton, 1992.

LT I   TOLKIEN, John Ronald Reuel. *The Book of Lost Tales 1*. The History of Middle-earth 1. Ed. Christopher Tolkien. First published 1983. London: HarperCollins, 1994.

LT II   TOLKIEN, John Ronald Reuel. *The Book of Lost Tales 2*. The History of Middle-earth 2. Ed. Christopher Tolkien. First published 1984. London: Grafton, 1992.

MR   TOLKIEN, John Ronald Reuel. *Morgoth's Ring*. The History of Middle-earth 10. Ed. Christopher Tolkien. First published 1993. London: HarperCollins, 1994.

SD TOLKIEN, John Ronald Reuel. *Sauron Defeated*. The History of Middle-earth 9. Ed. Christopher Tolkien. First published 1992. London: HarperCollins, 1993.

SM TOLKIEN, John Ronald Reuel. *The Shaping of Middle-Earth*. The History of Middle-earth 4. Ed. Christopher Tolkien. First published 1986. London: HarperCollins, 1993.

TOFS TOLKIEN, John Ronald Reuel. *Tolkien On Fairy-stories*. Expanded edition, with commentaries and notes. Ed. Verlyn Flieger and Douglas A. Anderson. London: HarperCollins, 2008.

WJ TOLKIEN, John Ronald Reuel. *The War of the Jewels*. The History of Middle-earth 11. Ed. Christopher Tolkien. First published 1994. London: HarperCollins, 1995.

Bibliography

BARNEY, Stephen A., W.J. LEWIS, J.A. BEACH, Oliver BERGHOF, with the collaboration of Muriel HALL (eds. and trans.). *The Etymologies of Isidore of Seville*. Cambridge: Cambridge University Press, 2006.

BROWN, Francis, B.B. DRIVER and Charles A. BRIGGS (eds.). *A Hebrew and English Lexicon of the Old Testament*. Oxford: Clarendon Press, 1906.

BUCK, Carl Darling. *A Dictionary of Selected Synonyms in the Principal Indo-European Languages*. Chicago: University of Chicago Press, 1949; paperback edition, 1988.

BURNETT, Richard George, et al. *Frederick Luke Wiseman: A Commemorative Record*. London: Epworth Press, 1954.

BRITTEN, Benjamin. *The Company of Heaven (1937): Cantata for speaker(s), soprano solo, tenor solo, chorus (SATB), timpani, organ and strings, with words selected by R. Ellis Roberts*. London: Faber Music, 1990.

DALLEY, Stephanie (trans.). *Myths from Mesopotamia: Creation, The Flood, Gilgamesh, and Others*. Oxford: Oxford University Press, 1989. Revised edition 2000.

DEVLIN, C. (ed.). *The Sermons and Devotional Writings of Gerard Manley Hopkins*. London: Oxford University Press, for the Society of Jesus, 1959.

FIMI, Dimitra and Andrew HIGGINS. 'Introduction.' In J.R.R. Tolkien. *A Secret Vice. Tolkien on Invented Languages*. Edited by Dimitra Fimi and Andrew Higgins. London: HarperCollins, xi-lxv.

FLIEGER, Verlyn. 'The Music and the Task: Fate and Free Will in Middle-earth.' *Green Suns and Faërie*. Kent OH: Kent State University Press, 2012. 14-40.

FRENCH, A.J. 'Geden, John Dury (1822-1886), Wesleyan Methodist minister.' Revised by Tim Macquiban. *Oxford Dictionary of National Biography*.

GARTH, John. 2003. *Tolkien and the Great War: The Threshold of Middle-earth*. London: HarperCollins.

GILLIVER, Peter. 'Making the Music: a possible source for the Ainulindalë.' (unpublished paper).

GREEVES, Edward. 'The New President of the Conference. The Rev. Fred L Wiseman. The Man and his Work.' *The Methodist Recorder*, 18 July 1912. 3.

HAGGARD, Henry Rider. *Allan Quatermain*. London: Longmans, Green, 1887.

KENDALL, Calvin B. (trans.). *Bede: On Genesis*. Liverpool: Liverpool University Press, 2008.

KING, Leonard W. *The Seven Tablets of Creation. Vol. 1: English Translations, etc.* London: Luzac, 1902.

KLEIN, Ernst. *A Comprehensive Etymological Dictionary of the Hebrew Language*. Jerusalem: Carta, 1987.

LAMBERT, Wilfred G. *Babylonian Creation Myths*. Mesopotamian Civilization 16. Winonan Lake IN: Eisenbrauns, 2013.

LEWIS, C.S. *Collected Letters, Vol. 3: Narnia, Cambridge and Joy 1950-1963*. London: HarperCollins, 2006.

MALLORY, J.P. and D.Q. ADAMS. *The Oxford Introduction to Proto-Indo-European and the Proto-Indo-European World*. Oxford: Oxford University Press, 2006.

OKRENT, Arika. *In the Land of Invented Languages: A Celebration of Linguistic Creativity*. New York: Spiegel & Grau, 2009.

ROBSON, Eleanor. 'Bel and the Dragons: Deciphering Cuneiform after Decipherment.' *William Henry Fox Talbot: Beyond Photography*. Ed. Mirjam Brusius, Katrina Dean, and Chitra Ramalingam. New Haven CT: Yale University Press, 2013. 193-218.

SAYCE, A.H. *An Elementary Grammar, with Full Syllabary and Progressive Reading Book, of the Assyrian Language in the Cuneiform Type*. London: Samuel Bagster, 1875.

SCARF, Christopher. *The Ideal of Kingship in the Writings of Charles Williams, C.S. Lewis and J.R.R. Tolkien*. Cambridge: James Clarke, 2013.

SCHRADER, Otto. *Reallexikon der indogermanischen Altertumskunde*. Strassburg, Trübner, 1901.

SMITH, George. *The Chaldean Account of Genesis*. London: Sampson Low, Marston, Searle and Rivington, 1876.

STYERS, Norman. 'The Creation of the World, Middle-earth, and Narnia.' *C.S. Lewis and the Inklings: Discovering the Hidden Truth*. Ed. Salwa Khoddam, Mark R. Hall, with Jason Fisher. Newcastle-upon-Tyne: Cambridge Scholars, 2012. 116-33.

TALBOT, Henry Fox. 'The Revolt in Heaven.' *Records of the Past, being English Translations of the Assyrian and Egyptian Monuments. Vol. VII: Assyrian Texts*. London: Samuel Bagster and Sons for the Society of Biblical Archaeology, 1876. 123-28.

'The Revolt in Heaven: from a Chaldean tablet.' *Transactions of the Society of Biblical Archaeology. Vol. 4*. London: Longmans, Green, Reader, and Dyer, 1876. 349-62.

TOLKIEN, John Ronald Reuel. *The Book of Lost Tales 1*. The History of Middle-earth 1. Ed. Christopher Tolkien. First published 1983. London: HarperCollins, 1994.

The Book of Lost Tales 2. The History of Middle-earth 2. Ed. Christopher Tolkien. First published 1984. London: Grafton, 1992.

English and Welsh. In *Angles and Britons: O'Donnell Lectures*. University of Wales Press, 1963. Reprinted in *The Monsters and the Critics*. Ed. Christopher Tolkien. First published 1983. Paperback edition. London: HarperCollins, 1997. 162-97.

The Letters of J.R.R. Tolkien. Ed. Humphrey Carpenter, with the assistance of Christopher Tolkien. London: George Allen & Unwin, 1981. Reprinted Boston: Houghton Mifflin, 2000.

The Lord of the Rings. First published 1954/55. 50th Anniversary one-volume edition. Boston and New York: Houghton Mifflin Company, 2004.

The Lost Road and Other Writings. The History of Middle-earth 5. Ed. Christopher Tolkien. First published 1987. London: Grafton, 1992.

The Monsters and the Critics and Other Essays. Ed. Christopher Tolkien. First published 1983. Paperback edition. London: HarperCollins, 1997.

Morgoth's Ring. The History of Middle-earth 10. Ed. Christopher Tolkien. First published 1993. London: HarperCollins, 1994.

'Philology: General Works.' *The Year's Work in English Studies* 5 (1924). Ed. F.S. Boas and C.H. Herford. London: Oxford Universit Press, 1926. 26-65.

Sauron Defeated. The History of Middle-earth 9. Ed. Christopher Tolkien. First published 1992. London: HarperCollins, 1993.

The Shaping of Middle-Earth. The History of Middle-earth 4. Ed. Christopher Tolkien. First published 1986. London: HarperCollins, 1993.

The Story of Kullervo. Ed. Verlyn Flieger. London: HarperCollis, 2015.

Tolkien On Fairy-stories. Expanded edition, with commentaries and notes. Ed. Verlyn Flieger and Douglas A. Anderson. London: HarperCollins, 2008.

The War of the Jewels. The History of Middle-earth 11. Ed. Christopher Tolkien. First published 1994. London: HarperCollins, 1995.

WILLIAMS, Edward (Iolo Morganwg). *Iolo Manuscripts: A Selection of Ancient Welsh Texts*. Llandovery: William Rees for the Welsh MSS Society, 1848.

WISEMAN, Frederick Luke. 'Didsbury College Sixty Years Ago.' *Didsbury College Centenary 1842–1942*. Ed. W. Bardsley Brash and Charles J. Wright. London: Epworth Press, 1942. 89-95.

Gergely Nagy

On No Magic in Tolkien: Resisting the Representational Criteria of Realism

Abstract

Although in theoretical and generic criticism of 'fantasy', magic has always been a very prominent term, in both J.R.R. Tolkien's Middle-earth and his own theoretical work relatively little is made of it. While developing his *legendarium*, Tolkien gradually got rid of most of his earlier 'magical' ideas and transformed them into manifestations of the theological hierarchy of Middle-earth in the literary texts and the fascination of art in 'On Fairy-Stories'. Tolkien's finished Middle-earth texts and the 1977 *Silmarillion* therefore contain no magic at all in traditional cultural historical sense. This is an aspect of Tolkien's specific brand of systematic mythopoetic practice as opposed to the ideologically charged representational criteria of realism: an opposition to the ideology of realism is something that makes the literary fantastic, certainly Tolkien's variety of it, possible.

It is very convenient to see things in either/or distinctions, but as Frank Herbert says, "the beginning is the time for taking the most delicate care that the balances are correct" (Herbert 3) – it would be too easy to say there certainly is magic in Tolkien, and it would be equally too easy to say there certainly is not. Magic is itself an either/or thing: it either works or it doesn't, in which case you are doing something wrong. Critics always feel the need to qualify their statements about this kind of magic in Tolkien: they say that there is 'very little' or 'relatively few occurrences' of it, but ever since I read *The Silmarillion*, I have believed there is actually none at all. Going through the *History of Middle-earth* later made me qualify my conviction too: *there used to be, but by the time Tolkien got to write his most complete and most popular works, it dwindled and disappeared* – like the fairies, or elves that he wanted to write about originally. But then there is another sort, which critics often also see as an either/or phenomenon: the tale is either *marvellous*, in which case there is magic (of a fairly undefined kind), or *uncanny*, in which case there is not; there is either magic, in which case the tale is fantasy, or there is technology, in which case it is science fiction. Happily these divisions are not any more the unchallenged standard in the criticism of the fantastic, and in any case the argument was called into question both by Tolkien, for whom technology *is a kind of magic*, and by Arthur C. Clarke, who claimed that "any sufficiently advanced technology is indistinguishable from magic" (Clarke 21). This (fairly undefined) 'critical magic' derives from another either/or: either there is something in the tale that we do not believe possible, and is not explained by technology, or not. So when saying "there is no magic in Tolkien", one needs to take that Herbertian delicate care for the balances, and reflect (somewhat trivially) that it all depends.

The question to ask is rather "what sort of magic *is* or *isn't* there in Tolkien?" There are concepts of magic that are certainly there, at least at the beginning, and others that are not; and towards the end, there is less and less of any sort, and this is inextricably bound up with history, cultural and textual, with the evolving of Middle-earth and its framework, and also with texts, their genres and moods. Some Victorian fairy tale magic is undeniably present in *The Book of Lost Tales* and even in the verse 'Lay of Leithian'; the very common 'fantasy magic', the *Dragons of the Something Something* kind that some theorists apparently expect from 'fantasy' seems to me not to be there at all. And the magic that Tolkien himself talks about in 'On Fairy-stories' is certainly there, but it is very different from either of these. Which is why one needs to take care for the balance, but even more importantly for the definitions: there are *several magics* that critics talk about, and these are not very well differentiated.

The first kind of either/or magic is the cultural historical or anthropological understanding: the coercion of the 'supernatural' (itself a function of what any given cultural period understands as 'natural') by means of ritual actions, objects, or words, which, if performed correctly, unfailingly give results. Tolkien's own usage in 'On Fairy-stories', *enchantment*, has a philological connection to this, since the word comes ultimately from Latin *incantare*, "to cast under a spell, to bewitch" (*TOFS* 112), formed from *cantare*, 'to sing' (which Tolkien would have been very conscious of). This kind of magic has a long history, going back to antiquity and quite certainly beyond, with a lot of interesting developments in the Middle Ages (which, again, Tolkien would have been very aware of). 'Natural magic' and the interference of Christianity aside, there is still a lot in the "common tradition of magic", as Richard Kieckhefer calls it (Kieckhefer 56-57): part of this is the traditional magic of the Germanic tribes, which survives for example in the Anglo-Saxon charms or the fact that in the Norse pantheon, Odin is explicitly the god of magic, runes and hidden knowledge (see Kieckhefer 43-55). This is the kind that survives most in fairy-tales, in the most unreflected form: no one ever questions how magicians or witches perform their magic, whether it is 'natural', 'supernatural', or 'demonic'. One of the greatest problems of medieval theoreticians of magic was whether all magic is demonic or not (Kieckhefer 182-86) – they came to the conclusion that "many types of magic might be natural [but] virtually all types might be demonic" (Kieckhefer 184), and that conveniently solved the question, since it rerouted it into religion and theology. But there is no Thomas Aquinas in fairy-tales, and therefore their magic remains non-theological and even non-religious (even when there is something like a 'default religion' in the tale itself, like in medieval romance). It is also this kind of simple either/or spellwork in much fantasy literature, without any attempt at explaining the background. *Harry Potter* works perfectly well without once asking the question "what sort of power is drawn on in all this performance?" But for Tolkien the source of power is always a relevant question, a question of background, which he cannot leave unsolved. And so he solved it, I believe, by getting rid of this kind of magic altogether.

But when critics of the fantastic expect magic in a fantasy text, this is not what they mean. Things in the story are either explainable in everyday scientific terms or not: if not, *that* is 'magic'. Ultimately this leads to sometimes declaring the fantastic to go back to the *Iliad*: since there are no gods, it could not *really* have been Aphrodite who saved Paris in Book 3. But for the Greeks, the gods were part of nature, and in this sense not 'supernatural' at all. 'Magic' in this sense is not a question of ritual or performance, not even of story or events: it is a question of background, the basic presuppositions about the world of the fiction, and assumptions about the real world. If the two sets of assumptions do not match, the subtle differences of fictional worlds from the 'real' one all just register as this: as 'magic'. In *Strategies of Fantasy*, Brian Attebery argued that what the critics of the fantastic, from Todorov on, somewhat uncritically apply to fantastic texts are in fact the criteria of *realism*. It is not only that we read with a contemporary understanding of what *can* happen in the world and what *cannot*, but also that we read with the interiorized criteria of *how* the world is to be described and written about. Attebery, therefore, examines elements of narrative like character, story, or time, and shows how 'fantastic' texts' usage of these differ from what we have learnt to expect in good solid down-to-earth realist novels. But he also shows how it is also the question of *language* in the fantastic: all these narratological concepts are abstractions, and they are always manifested in actual texts. The fantastic, as Attebery treats it, is basically a *different narrative language* from that of realism: and that is what seems to confuse critics to identify 'magic' as its definitive ingredient. But the criteria of realism are also frustrated in fantastic works because these construct a *radically fictitious* secondary world – a world that is fundamentally *different* from what critics like to call 'consensus reality'. When Tolkien, in 'On Fairy-story', insists that a fairy-story's world, Faërie, cannot be connected with the primary world by means of some spatial or temporal machinery (*TOFS* 33-34) or even by that of dreams (*TOFS* 35), it is this he advocates in embryonic form. A fictional world that is explicitly and radically different from the real one obviously cannot be written about in 'mimetic' terms and language. But the interesting thing is that *within* these radically fictitious worlds, fantastic texts (some of Tolkien's own, for instance) actually preserve much of the realistic logic, and often proceed exactly by the criteria of 'realistic description', if not those of character or plot. For one thing, they keep the *novel* as their (at least nominal) genre of reference.

We can more or less say that Tolkien himself excised 'cultural historical magic' from his world, and that 'theoretical magic' is sought in his works largely because he himself used the term, and because of the still somewhat prevalent, partly ideological assumption that anything that is not 'realist' must be 'magical'. These two lacks of magic are what I would like to explore in this paper: how Tolkien progressively got rid of the ritualistic magical descriptions that appeared as late as the 'Lay of Leithian', and how his type of 'fantastic' writing in fact goes against the realist ideology that supposes 'magic' to be there whenever something is 'too fictional'. The first line of enquiry is, one could say, philological, since it involves texts, their details and language. The second one is theoretical, for it is based on Tolkien's own and others' theoretical considerations of what constitutes 'magic' in 20th-century narrative. I think we would all be better off if the question of magic in Tolkien was resolved in these two areas; we could then concentrate on how Tolkien handles the concept of power (which largely came to stand in for early magic) and how his work integrates into (even stands at the beginning of) a particular type of 20th-century narrative that is not explicitly realistic, but not explicitly and post-modernly theoretical either.

Tolkien is usually seen to draw most of his inspiration, at least at the beginning, from medieval works; but there is more to it than this. Richard C. West has explored in depth how the *Kalevala*, with its shamanistic magic songs, "set the rocket off in story" (*Letters* 214, no. 163; see West), and Dimitra Fimi has shown how the Victorian and Edwardian fairy tradition was also influential in Tolkien's early writings (Fimi 28-61). It is therefore not surprising to find fairy magic all over the place in the *Book of Lost Tales*, which would not qualify as a fairy-story anyway by Tolkien's later standards, since it uses both the machinery of the dream and that of spatial travel, and is anyway clearly connected to the primary world. The connecting character of Eriol and later Ælfwine ties the fairy isle not just to the primary world, but a very explicit locality, England; and the fairies, if not diminutive, are definitely closer to Victorian fairies than to Tolkien's own later elves. Even the *Qenya Lexicon* shows, as Fimi argues, that Tolkien "not only 'liked' [flower-fairies], but also considered them part of his nascent mythology" (Fimi 34). The very device of the Cottage of Lost Play, with "old tales, old songs, and elfin music" (*LT I* 9) is fairy-tale-like, even connected to children, and so are the countless references to magic isles, seas, cars, conches, and so on.[1] But as early as the *Lost Tales*, Tolkien also associated magical 'functions' with his Valar and elves. Palúrien (Yavanna) is called "mother of magic", and several of the Valar are said to have their own magic.[2] The Valar as a group are said to have their magic too (*LT I* 137, 200, 236; cf. *SME* 16). When there is any actual magic done, it is often associated with *songs* (perhaps a nod to the *Kalevala*): even Ilúvatar "sang into being the Ainur first" (*LT I* 49), and it is by "songs of utmost enchantment" (*LT I* 104) that Palúrien starts growth in Middle-earth. To revive the Trees, Lórien sings "most wistful songs of magic and enchantment" and Vána "old golden songs" (*LT I* 199). Yavanna attempts this with "songs of unfading growth and a song of resurrec-

---

[1] See in particular *LT I* 9, 10, 198 (Ulmo's "magic car"), 238, 240, 242 ("magic conches").
[2] *LT I* 76; Aulë: *LT I* 132, 206, 208; Ulmo: *LT I* 68, 242, *LT II* 5 (as "ancient mariner"); Palúrien: *LT I* 76, 113, 206, 207, 213; Lórien: *LT I* 199; Kémi: *LT I* 236; Oromë: *LT I* 239; Vána: *LT I* 199.

tion after death and withering" (*LT I* 205). Much of Lúthien's magic is also done by songs (as it still is in *The Silmarillion*). Enchantment and spell seem to be hardly separable from these, and there are countless examples of the Valar performing some kind of spell. Ulmo even connects his to "the great word that Ilúvatar said to me" (*LT I* 241). There are spells that bind stones together,[3] and Melko is said to cast "the spell of bottomless dread […] upon his slaves".[4] There is Thû the Wizard, whom Melko taught "much black magic" (*LT I* 266). The Silmarils are said to have "a fierce and holy magic" (*LT II* 33), the dragon can cast a "binding spell" (*LT II* 87), and the "magics" of Gwendeling (Melian) the fay are well-known (becoming an alliterative formula in the alliterative Húrin: "the magic mazes of Melian the Queen"[5]). But most often these 'magics' are just a matter of course, reported without any concern to *how* they work.

There are, however, some few occasions when it *is* said how they work. Common with these is that they all occur relatively early in Tolkien's writings, and then subsequently diminish or are excised altogether. A good example for this is the Valar's creation of the Two Trees: the 'Tale of the Coming of the Valar' has them dig "two great pits" (*LT I* 71) and do elaborate physical preparations, then Palúrien waves "spells about these two places, deep enchantments of life and growth and putting forth of leaves, blessing and yielding of fruit" (*LT I* 71). In a note, Christopher Tolkien remarks that "the preparations of the Valar […] with all the detail of physical 'magic', were afterwards abandoned" (*LT I* 92); and in the 'Sketch of the Mythology', the Trees are indeed said merely to "grow under [Yavanna's] songs" (*SME* 12; cf. commentary, *SME* 49, 50), and the 'Qenta' even says the Trees were "planted" (*SME* 97). Both versions of the 'Annals of Valinor' simply state that the Valar "brought into being" the Trees (*SME* 312; *LR* 123[6]). The version in *The Silmarillion* arose in the 'Quenta Silmarillion' (*LR* 229), and only preserved the element of song. The making of the Silmarils is another case: where the *Lost Tales* version describes a complicated process (*LT I* 138) and the commentary again adds that all this was "abandoned" (*LT I* 151), later accounts simply call the Silmarils "magic" or

---

3 Tevildo: *LT I* 28, 29; Thû: *LB* 303, *SME* 134.
4 *LT I* 272, 274, 276; *LT II* 78, 159, 161: "so that he seemed ever nigh them".
5 *LB* 12; even in the Old English translation of the 'Annals of Valinor': 'Vala-gealdrum begól' (*SME* 343).
6 The Old English version of the earlier 'Annals' uses the verb "awehtan" (*SME* 335) and "gescópon 7 onwehtan" (*SME* 340).

"holy", fashioned with "spells of the Gods and Gnomes" (*LT II* 33). "Thrice-enchanted" occurs twice in the poems of the 1920s (*LB* 162, the 'Flight of the Noldoli' fragment; *LB* 254, Leithian Canto VI.1642) and surfaces again in the later 'Annals of Valinor' as "thrice-renowned" (*LR* 125). Even the introduction of the early 'Annals of Beleriand' calls them "magic gems" (*SME* 352), but by the 'Quenta Silmarillion', even Fëanor's "subtle magic" ('Qenta', *SME* 106) is modified to "subtle skill" (*LR* 249, which is the wording of *The Silmarillion*). Sometimes a magical ritual pops up in an already established story, like Beleg's "whetting spell" in the alliterative *Húrin* (LB 51-2, 'Húrin' 2.1203-1223): "an entirely new element," says Christopher Tolkien, "and without a trace later", but "in style reminiscent of Lúthien's 'lengthening spell'" (*LB* 63).

Lúthien's 'lengthening spell' is perhaps the most detailed account of actual cultural historical magic in all of Tolkien's works. This has distinct ingredients with detailed instructions: the "clearest water of the stream below," for example, "must be drawn at midnight in a silver bowl, and brought to my hand with no word spoken" (*LT II* 17) – like in a medieval manual of magic, the instructions are detailed and clear, suggesting that the spell works only if they are followed to the letter. There are other ingredients, and then, alone, "singing a very magical song", Tinúviel mixes the substances and sings "another song [with] the names of all the tallest and longest things upon Earth" (*LT II* 17). Much of this survives into the verse 'Lay of Leithian' (*LB* 245-47), with a long list of the longest things; but in the 'Sketch', she simply "escapes" without any magic mentioned (*SME* 27, cf. 'Qenta', *SME* 132), and in *The Silmarillion* she only "put[s] forth her arts of enchantment" (*S* 172). However, by the time of writing the poems, Tolkien had already built up quite a lot of background about his fictional world. Some late revisions for the poems, in Christopher Tolkien's opinion, show how he was trying to downsize magic in them, even dispensing with the word altogether.[7] Tolkien also got rid of the primary connection of Eriol/Ælfwine, although in the 1930s the concept was still strong enough for him to start translating Annals to Old English where he used the word "gealdrum" (dat.pl. of 'gealdor') for Melian's magic (*SME* 343). Tolkien's early creative period is important in 'magical' terms at least partly because he wrote in rather different genres: 'tales', poems, annals, condensed sketches of

---

7 See n. to 'Leithian' Canto XIII.3969, *LB* 360 and n. to the second version of Canto III.131, *LB* 422.

the mythology – kinds of text that make very clear that realistic criteria cannot possibly apply.

This is what changed radically with *The Hobbit*. However unwillingly and unforeseen, here Tolkien embarked on a quite different project when he undertook to present his tale in the form of a children's book, a form of the novel. It was not in any way a *realistic* novel, as children's books very rarely are, and it still had remnants of the fairy-tale magic in the figure of Gandalf, the Dwarves and the Elves too. Gandalf's ineffectiveness against the wolves ("wizard though he was": *Hobbit* 95) is often commented on, while of the Wood-elves it is said that "their magic was strong" (*Hobbit* 154; the Elvenking even boasts about his "magic doors", *Hobbit* 158), and Beorn is said to be "under no enchantment but his own" (*Hobbit* 108). Perhaps the Dwarves have closest associations with magic, as already in the *Lost Tales*.[8] They put "a great many spells" (*Hobbit* 41) over the Trolls' gold, are credited with inventing the Moon-letters (*Hobbit* 50), and even they cannot do anything against "the magic that had shut" (*Hobbit* 192) the side-door into the Mountain (not even with "fragments of broken spells of opening", *Hobbit* 190-91). The inside of the Mountain and the treasure tempts even Bilbo with the "dragon-spell" (*Hobbit* 206)[9], and the Arkenstone's "enchantment" draws his arms towards it (*Hobbit* 217). And there is the "magic ring" (*Hobbit* 80) too which Bilbo can hardly believe he found by accident: an object that works automatically, irrespective of who is using it, to produce a well-defined effect: make its wearer invisible. Again, magic seems much more an inherent power made use of by those who have it, and not a codified, manualised technique. It comes closest to that, ironically, in the ring (such as it is in *The Hobbit*), and when 'spells' are mentioned, but there is nothing like Lúthien's "lengthening spell". Perhaps the most sinister detail is the "Necromancer", a "black sorcerer" about whom even Bilbo had heard (*Hobbit* 129; see Rateliff 81-84). This is an interesting use: necromancy is definitely a term for medieval magic, one that originally meant telling the future by conjuring and asking the dead, but also demons, until "the conjuring of demons came to be known as necromancy; this was the ordinary meaning of the term in later medieval

---

8 Seen primarily in the figure of Mîm (*LT II* 113-14, 224), which survived into the 'Sketch' (*SME* 36) and the 'Qenta' (*SME* 158-9). See Rateliff 54-55.
9 Cf. Mîm's spells on the gold in *LT II* 226, 227, 230, 242, and Christopher Tolkien's commentary at *LT II* 247.

Europe" (Kieckhefer 152-53). You would think there is magic in a fictional world that has a 'Necromancer'. But we do not know what he does, only that the "great council of the white wizards, masters of lore and good magic" drove him out of Mirkwood (*Hobbit* 270).

By this time, the overarching story that later became the 'Silmarillion' and its background had already been written. Tolkien has worked through stories (early ones like 'Kullervo' and the 'Lost Tales') to systematically build up his secondary world (complete with detailed languages), and that secondary world had less and less to do with the primary one, until finally the whole Eriol/Ælfwine frame fell away. Stories like 'The Fall of Númenor' rose and were integrated, and *The Hobbit* had a more or less already 'constructed' world to find its place in. This world was, however, different from that of the 'Lost Tales' and even the longer poems, the only previous texts of some length. The world of *The Hobbit* is, for lack of a better word, *Northern*: the use of dwarf-names from the 'Dvergatal' (Völuspa), the Norse concept of the dragon guarding the treasure (also in *Beowulf*), the Germanic feud that the dwarves take up against Smaug, the shape-changing Beorn and the forest of Mirkwood all infuse the story with a Northernness that some critics (C.S. Lewis, for one) recognised and which Tolkien himself used later, when he worked out properly the fiction of translation in *The Lord of the Rings*. But that device, even when it maintains a very flimsy connection to the primary world, also serves to distance the text from it. By the time of *The Lord of the Rings* (certainly the revised edition), the only explicit connection Tolkien left between Middle-earth and the primary world was the fiction of the translator/editor. And even that is a mere practicality, mirroring the textual activities of figures within the fiction.

It says a lot about this process that the very starting premise of *The Lord of the Rings* is a bit of eliminated magic from *The Hobbit*: providing an explanation for the either/or 'magic' ring that Bilbo found. For it turns out the Ring does not work irrespective of its user: it does matter who uses it, and its power is certainly not simply that of invisibility. Tolkien steadily shifts the focus from the effects of hidden knowledge (which could come out as 'magic') to knowledge itself, its various sources and uses; and to power, in its various manifestations. In explaining to Frodo, Gandalf says Rings of Power are "magic rings as you call them" (*FR* I.ii.45), and this exemplifies the approach of *The Lord of the Rings* perfectly: Tolkien seems to say magic is a matter not of knowledge but of ignorance. People who know little (about the world, history, other people) will see some things as magic. This is evident in the reactions to Lórien: while Boromir just calls it "perilous" (*FR* II.vi.329), others like Éomer accuse Aragorn and his companions of being "net-weavers and sorcerers" (*TT* III.ii.422) if they have Galadriel's favour. Wormtongue claims "webs of deceit were ever woven" (*TT* III.vi.502) there; and only Faramir admits simply that he does not know much about it: "long now it has lain beyond the knowledge of Men" (*TT* IV.v.651-52). But Wormtongue's accusation is just an inversion: in a much-quoted passage, Galadriel remarks about her Mirror that "this is what [hobbits] would call magic, I believe; though I do not understand clearly what they mean; and they seem to use the same word of the deceits of the Enemy" (*FR* II.vii.353). Early critics again often felt the need to remark on Gandalf's ineffectuality as a 'wizard': he tries to open the gates of Moria by 'spells' (and varies his delivery and formula when they do not work: *FR* II.iv.299), shuts the door against the Orcs with a "shutting-spell" and when the Balrog comes, a "word of Command" (*FR* II.v.319), and is not very successful at either. Other characters are said to use 'spells' too, more or less metaphorically: Old Man Willow, Tom Bombadil, the Barrow-wight. Saruman's voice is described as an "enchantment" and the hearers fall "under the spell" (*TT* III.x.564). It is also a "spell that knit [the Witch-king's] unseen sinews to his will" (*RK* V.vi.826).

Again, some of this undoubtedly seems like cultural historical magic: a word is spoken, and the gates of Moria open; Gandalf says something and his staff begins to glow; Galadriel breathes on the water and the Mirror shows images. But even in these instances, the reader has been warned: Gandalf and Galadriel had been consistently described as 'different', and even though the reader has no clear idea about what the source of their power is, it is clear that what they do is no simple ritual and command. Is Sauron's "let[ting] a great part of his own former power pass into" (*FR* I.ii.50) the Ring an instance of the magical motif that Tolkien mentions in 'On Fairy-stories' as 'The Monkey's Heart' (*TOFS* 37-38)? Are Galadriel's Mirror or the *palantíri* 'magical'? Tom Shippey has pointed out how both can be related to the original meaning of *speculatio*, "looking in a *speculum* – a mirror, a glass, a crystal ball" (Shippey,

'Another Road' 380), but also to being deceived and coming to the wrong conclusion: the dangers of another meaning of 'speculation' (382). Is this an instance of magic?

What happens in *The Lord of the Rings* is that Tolkien sets his story in a fictional world that has a very clearcut hierarchy of power, not just military, political or historical, but theological. The theological hierarchy of Middle-earth had more or less been there in the sketches of the mythologies and 'lost tales', while *The Hobbit*, at least at its writing, was a tangent: it did not necessitate much reference to that hierarchy. *The Lord of the Rings* did, but Tolkien deliberately withheld this reference: his much-quoted letter says it is a "fundamentally religious and Catholic work; unconsciously so at first, but consciously in the revision. That is why I have not put in, or have cut out practically all references to anything like 'religion,' to cults or practices, in the imaginary world" (*Letters* 172, no. 142). The discourse he wanted to avoid is, surprisingly, that of religion: but since magic and religion have always had quite blurry boundaries (see Kieckhefer 8-17), the less explicit the religious discourse, the hazier and therefore more 'magical' the doubtful elements will seem. The only more or less clear references to the theological structure of Middle-earth in *The Lord of the Rings* are Gandalf's "naked I was *sent back*" (*TT* III.v.491; italics mine) and "Olórin I was in my youth in the West that is forgotten" (*TT* IV.v.655); Faramir's "that which is beyond Elvenhome and will ever be" (*TT* IV.v.661); and the cry of Faramir's men at the sight of the Mûmak: "May the Valar turn him aside!" (*TT* IV.iv.646). The reader (and apparently most people in Middle-earth) simply does not know about the theological structure of the fictional world (as Frodo does not know about Rings of Power) – and so in ignorance interprets (as most Men in Middle-earth) these instances as 'magic'. And as long as there is no context, they may well be.

But once one reads *The Silmarillion*, one knows they are not, and sees the pattern too: how Tolkien systematically made his secondary world more and more discrete, distinct, disconnected from the primary world, constructed and consolidated its theological structure, and so supplied a context for the stand-alone stories that completely reinterpret them. But of course, it was not an unknown context for *Tolkien*, and this undoubtedly formed part of why he so desperately wanted to publish *The Silmarillion* together with *The Lord of the Rings*: it is not just the 'story context' that he wanted to supply. He had been working and reworking the group of texts that are referred to as the 'Silmarillion' corpus, and he kept doing it after *The Lord of the Rings* was finally published. When after his death, *The Silmarillion* became his first posthumously published work, readers could get a glimpse of that context, and that glimpse alone was enough to validate the conclusion that there is no cultural historical magic in Tolkien at all. But readers had to wait for the whole *History of Middle-earth* series to be able to see the *process*, to appreciate the subtle workings of Tolkien's fictional world and his endless reworkings of the texts. *The Hobbit* and *The Lord of the Rings*, however, introduced two aspects into the creative history that Tolkien was not very used to: the genre of the novel, and fixity (cf. Fimi 119-20). "The transition from myth to history, from writing a mythology to writing a 'pseudo-historical' or fantasy novel, made Middle-earth more 'realistic'", as Fimi suggests (Fimi 189). Tolkien could never finish *The Silmarillion* because he never discovered how he could possibly put it in even remotely novelistic form – "what he could not finish was the post-*Lord of the Rings* 'Silmarillion'" (Fimi 194). This had the very important effect on the theological/magical: even *The Lord of the Rings* was stretching the genre for a lot of critics, and the theology of Middle-earth would simply have exploded the form. Tolkien's compulsive rewritings were also checked by the fact that *The Hobbit* and *The Lord of the Rings*, being published, were supposed to be fixed, and the rest was supposed to be coherent with them. Tolkien could not even bear this, and tinkered even with the fixed texts (and then even incorporated the fact that he changed *The Hobbit* into the story as an illustration for the Ring's effect on Bilbo). Both these factors contributed to his getting lost in the conceptual and other details of the 'Silmarillion' corpus, clarifying and refining points but not changing the story or the conceptual framework. The theological structure of Middle-earth had taken shape and consolidated even before *The Hobbit*; it went through further changes of story but relatively little of concept during the writing of *The Lord of the Rings*, which meant that there was literally *no room for magic* in it.

The theological hierarchy of Middle-earth, as evolved in the early 'Silmarillion' writings, in fact goes a long way to explain away every bit of what looks like magic in Tolkien. In these texts, Tolkien evolved a world much to his liking: one similar to the medieval world model insofar as there is a metaphysical centre to it, the creator Ilúvatar. Everything else is his work: the Valar, the Ainur, the

Maiar, the Children of Ilúvatar, Elves and Men, the children of Aulë, Dwarves, and the totally unforeseen hobbits too. Ilúvatar functions in Middle-earth much as God functioned in the medieval world: the guarantee that each and every bit of his created world *has a meaning*. Following Yuri Lotman's typology of cultures (see Lotman), I will call this a *pansemiotic world model*, one where everything is a sign, and ultimately refers back to the Creator. Just like in the medieval 'great chain of being', everyone has their place in descending order, and with these places come knowledge and innate power. Ilúvatar is the totality of meaning, knowledge, and power. The Ainur each "comprehended only that part of the mind of Ilúvatar from which [they] came" (S 15) and are asked to interpret the themes of music expounded to them "each with his own thoughts and devices, if he will" (S 15). The Valar are then given power over Arda, the physical world, about which they know much more than anyone else; within Arda, the Children and adopted children of Ilúvatar are also arranged in a hierarchy. The Elves have primacy, and Dwarves have special skills and knowledge from Aulë; Men and hobbits are down towards the bottom. This structure, Fimi says, was already in place in the early writings (Fimi 48, 141-44), but is eventually put in a historical perspective: by the time of *The Hobbit* and *The Lord of the Rings*, the end of the Third Age, the Elves had mostly left, Men are losing their ancient knowledge, and the Valar are all but forgotten. This contributes to that often remarked-on quality of depth in Tolkien too: because it creates the overwhelming and pervasive sense of something lost, of knowledge to be unearthed, and of ignorance. But it is there, and that is made clear too: Théoden recognises the Ents from old stories when he sees one; the tales of Ioreth about the King's healing hands or the virtues of athelas prove true; Gandalf finds Isildur's long-forgotten manuscript in Minas Tirith. Knowledge is lost but can be recovered; power is veiled but can still be used: Gandalf and Aragorn occasionally rise to an image of majesty and power, Galadriel is revealed to all of the Fellowship as clearly very powerful, and of course there is Sauron, a massive and threatening locus of power.

In this world there is and can be no cultural historical magic. Gandalf's 'magic' is things he does by his 'angelic' power: Gandalf is a Maia, rather high up in the hierarchy compared to everyone else (except for Sauron and to some extent, the Balrog). Sauron does not perform demonic magic as his *Hobbit* nickname 'the Necromancer' suggests: he is a Maia too, in the terminology of the medieval theologians, himself a demon, and no one does any magic to coerce Sauron to do anything. Galadriel is a Noldorin elf, one of the last on Middle-earth: she does things by her innate power. Elrond is half-elven, a son of Earendil, while Aragorn is the heir to the other line of Earendil's children, to Elros and the Númenóreans. The reader can be excused if he or she does not see or understand this: most people in Middle-earth do not either. Maybe it is not surprising that Sam takes Galadriel's acts as 'magic'. Wormtongue even calls her a "Sorceress" (*TT* III.vi.502), and even Boromir, who as a Gondorian could be expected to know better, is also wary of Galadriel. She herself only says that she does not clearly see the distinction: after all, 'magic' is the word that some "seem to use [...] of the deceits of the Enemy" (*FR* II.vii.353). But all this is in fact a function of the character's place in the theological hierarchy. They influence the world with their innate power, not by some other power harnessed through ritual, object or incantation. We can find any number of parallels in primary world literature and religion: Zeus doesn't 'do magic', he is a god. God doesn't create the world by a 'word of power': his word is powerful because He is God. Jesus doesn't raise Lazarus by saying it, but by being Jesus. Even the apostles don't heal people by magic, but by the power granted to them by Jesus. And even though early Christians did have problems arguing this (Kieckhefer 33-36), it all depends on the kind of world we are talking about. In a way, early Christians had to argue exactly the same thing: that in a pansemiotic world, where their God is the ultimate metaphysical centre and the guarantee of meaning and power, He grants them power to do what they do. A late antique pagan or early Anglo-Saxon might have had his doubts, especially seeing the highly ritualized liturgy of the Christian church, their dogma of transubstantiation (even though it was codified later), and so on. But for a medieval theologian, and so for Tolkien, well-versed in both medieval culture and Christian theology, this would have been easy enough to accept. I think Tolkien is even playing a philological joke here, giving another clue that what might seem magic in the rather implicitly pansemiotic world of *The Lord of the Rings* are actually manifestations of theological power: this is the very word 'spell' used for example for some of Gandalf's 'magic'. Even though this word is commonly used for magical incantations or commands (even in fantasy where there certainly is magic), Tolkien subverts its meaning by Gandalf's status, which he points out in a letter: "I wd. venture to say that he was an *incarnate* 'angel'," he explains to Robert Murray, SJ, "an emissary from the Lords of the West, sent to Middle-earth" (*Letters* 202, no. 156), and with this, immediately brings into play some Old English meanings. Clark Hall's *Concise Anglo-Saxon Dictionary* defines 'spell' as meaning "narrative, history, story, fable; speech, discourse, homily; message, news, statement, observation" (Clark Hall 315; cf. Wormtongue calling Gandalf *Láthspell*, *TT* III.vi.502), and lists compounds such as *spellboc* 'book of sermons', *spellboda* 'messenger' (the original meaning of the Greek word 'angelos'), and of course there is *godspel* 'gospel, glad tidings' (158), the exact translation of Greek *evangelion*. When Tolkien uses 'spell' for Gandalf's 'magic', he plays on this meaning: these acts are Gandalf's way of manifesting his power, of bearing and communicating the 'glad tidings', that the power of Ilúvatar is there and it endures. There is no Christ in Middle-earth to bring tidings of, so the good news is that there is at least a god who wields, guarantees and delegates power.

But there was another factor in this process that also came into play roughly after *The Hobbit* and before *The Lord of the Rings*: this was 'On Fairy-stories', where Tolkien systematically expounded his views on the writing of the kind of stories he liked to write – part of which was his views on 'magic'. Here he talked about "Faërie" as the subject of fairy-stories, which for him, as he explained, meant a historically layered, more or less traditional *fiction*: "a parallel reality tangential in time and space to the ordinary world" (*TOFS* 85), as editors Flieger and Anderson comment. As mentioned earlier, he maintained that this fiction should be unconnected to the primary world: so unconnected, in fact, that he called it a "Secondary World" (*TOFS* 52, 64). To (sub-)create such a fiction, the author needs a kind of "elvish craft" (*TOFS* 63) which Tolkien calls, instead of Magic, Enchantment (*TOFS* 64). He says that the 'magic' of Faërie is "of a peculiar mood and power, at the furthest pole from the vulgar devices of the laborious, scientific, magician" (*TOFS* 32-33). Magic 'proper' "produces, or pretends to produce, an alteration in the Primary World. It does not matter by whom it is said to be practiced, fay or mortal [...]; it is not an art but a technique; its desire is *power* in this world, domination of things and wills" (*TOFS* 64). Tolkien's use of *enchantment* I have already commented upon: his word choice underscores even philologically his argument that the primary medium of fairy-stories is literature, language, since it comes ultimately from

Latin *incantare*, a use of language to bewitch. He even comments on *spell*, underscoring my point that he uses this word too with an eye to its origin: "spell means both a story told, and a formula of power over living men" (*TOFS* 48). But in 'On Fairy-stories', Tolkien's use of "magic" (or "enchantment", even "glamour": *TOFS* 29) is somewhat off the mark for the either/or magic that we are now after. He uses it as a metaphor for the *effect* of fairy-stories: this kind of enchantment, he argues, is necessary for the creation of a successful Secondary World. It is the Art, the "elvish craft" that lends the fiction "the inner consistency of reality" (*TOFS* 59), so that within that world, its story "is 'true': it accords with the laws of that world" – it produces "literary belief" (*TOFS* 52). It thus appears that in this essay Tolkien merely touches upon the theme of magic, and mentions 'magic as technique' only in passing, and not very favourably, as something he is not really interested in. How would it appear in his work if he barely just mentions it in his theoretical manifesto?

But in his letters, mostly after *The Lord of the Rings*, he does treat magic in a bit more detail, and even introduces distinctions: his well-known differentiation between 'magia' and 'goeteia' (notice his uses of Greek terms). Despite how much is sometimes made of these in criticism,[10] even the evidence of the letters bear out my contention that there is no either/or, automatic, cultural historical magic in Tolkien. The most important quote is "a difference in the use of 'magic' in this story is that it is not to be come by by 'lore' or spells; but is in an *inherent power* not possessed or attainable by Men as such" (*Letters* 200, no. 155; italics mine). Both *magia* and *goeteia* Tolkien sees as manifestations of one's 'inherent power': the position in the theological hierarchy that assigns that power. It is never a question of just 'knowledge', knowing the right formula or incantation. This should by itself be enough to close the argument for ever. The explanations that the letters affix to these aspects ('magic' as Art, 'goetic' as the Machine) match the shorter remarks that we have seen in 'On Fairy-stories': there he wrote that "An essential power of Faërie is thus the power of making immediately effective by the will the visions of 'fantasy'" (*TOFS* 42) and that magic "produces, or pretends to produce, an alteration in the Primary World" (*TOFS* 64). In the letters, he says that the "basic motive for *magia* [...]

---

10 See especially Bachmann and, in the same volume, Shippey ('New Learning') for a discussion of these and related terms.

is immediacy: [...] reduction [...] to a minimum (or vanishing point) of the gap between the idea or desire and the result or effect" (*Letters* 200, no. 155). In the famous Milton Waldman letter he is more careful and accurate: by 'magic', he means "all use of external plans or devices (apparatus) instead of development of the inherent inner powers or talents – or even the use of these talents with the corrupted motive of dominating" (*Letters* 145-46, no. 131). Again, he simply refers to 'inherent inner powers' instead of any either/or magic, and declares that "Neither [magia or goeteia] is, in this tale, good or bad (per se), but only by motive or purpose or use" (*Letters* 199, no. 155). Indeed, he even explains some of the instances that seem *like* magic in *The Lord of the Rings*: "Their *magia* the Elves and Gandalf use (sparingly): a *magia*, producing real results (like fire in a wet faggot) for specific beneficent purposes" (*Letters* 200, no. 155), and remarks that in Eregion, "Elves came their nearest to falling to 'magic' and machinery. With the aid of Sauron's lore they made *Rings of Power* [...] [which] enhanced the natural powers of a possessor – thus approaching 'magic'" (*Letters* 152, no. 131). It thus seems that Tolkien's own arguments in 'On Fairy-stories' and more familiarly expressed in his letters are the strongest argument for my initial either/or claim – that *there is no magic in Tolkien at all*. What even he calls 'magic' or 'magia' is not what cultural history and anthropology, and by extension much fantasy literature mean by it.

Why then should we even bother (I ask after more than a dozen pages)? I think primarily because this needed to be said. And also, because it might be clear, but it is not at all evident from reading *The Hobbit* and *The Lord of the Rings*, but only after reviewing the thousands of pages of the textual history that became *The Silmarillion*. And finally, we should bother because despite the evidence, the question of magic in Tolkien just does not go away; and that is because of the other sort of magic that I referred to: the 'critical magic' in the fantastic. Shippey says Tolkien's problem was that he was not 'in' with the moderns (Shippey, *Author of the Century* 315-16); but he was not 'in' with the overwhelmingly dominant mode of literature, realism, and its critical backing either. So while critics approached him and the fantastic from such a standpoint, it always became the question of how these relate to 'consensus reality'. Todorov's either/or distinction is emblematic: if there is something in the story that is 'impossible' in reality, and is not explained somehow, it is the *marvellous* – magic (Todorov

41-42). The Aristotelian dictum that art is imitation, and the purpose of literature is to show the world, 'human nature', *as they are*, had led to 'mimetic' considerations overwhelming all others, to the point that an unreflected point of reference (like Todorov's) does not even register. Through its history leading back through modernism, rationalism, and ultimately Christianity (all having their reasons to privilege the 'real' and "denigrat[e] the non-real", Hume 3, see also 5-7 and 33-39), realism had become ideological: it tells you how things are, and does not ask your opinion. It is this ideologically entrenched critical orthodoxy that Tolkien (and the fantastic) upset. In 'On Fairy-stories', he says that "creative Fantasy is founded upon the hard recognition that things are so in the world as it appears under the sun" – a basically mimetic system of reference; but then he continues: "on the recognition of fact, but not a slavery to it" (*TOFS* 65). While critical and readerly practice assumes mimesis, and declares all non-mimetic elements 'magical', Tolkien insists on a different framework: on the *independence of fictional worlds*. His Secondary Worlds are not 'mimetic with some fantastic elements', but *radically different*, radically *fictitious* worlds that do not claim to be representations of the actual one.

But nothing ever can be that anyway: whatever you put in language will not *iconically* represent 'the world', because the world is 'out there', a non-linguistic reality – a*ny way of putting it* is just more or less conventional discourse about the world and the events in it. *All* literature is set in a fictitious world (insofar as it is a linguistic construct), but realistic literature purposely strives for it to be (or to be perceived as) *isomorphous* with the real one. This verisimilitude, however, is always an illusion: just one set of conventions that had been judged 'appropriate' to represent the world, in which readers (now trained mostly in the realistic tradition) can easily recognise what concepts of personality or motivation or interaction they hold in the real world (see Hume 37-39). *Magic* is something that is excluded, something that by definition *cannot* be part of verisimilitude, since, as we well know, it does not exist. But Tolkien's (and other fantastic) Secondary Worlds do not claim verisimilitude, in fact quite the opposite: "the fantasy world and the axioms that underlie it are *radically* unlike our own" (Attebery 110; italics mine). The author, says Tolkien, "makes a Secondary World which your mind can enter. Inside it, what he relates is 'true': it accords with the laws of that world" (*TOFS* 52). Here he foreshadows the theory of possible worlds, or its use in literary studies, in expecting not 'correspondence' (to the real world: mimesis), but 'consistency' (within the fiction). And 'critical magic' simply makes no sense here, since the frame of reference is the Secondary World and its own logic, not the Primary World and an ideologically prescribed mimetic logic. Not unless it can be described by another definition, like the cultural historical one I have been using, if that can be applied within the fiction. It then looks like there is no 'magic' in Tolkien at all: the either/or magic of cultural history he excised himself as the theological hierarchy of Middle-earth came to be more established; and the other has simply no business *being called* magic, when that simply signifies 'impossible in the real world, thus subverting realist convention'.

In actual practice, of course, one can probably never subvert *all* aspects of representing a world in language, and for other aspects one is not interested in one will fall back more or less on the conventions of realism. This is why fantastic works, Tolkien included, in some respects fit the requirements of the realistic ideology perfectly well. Descriptions, geography, some of the handling of time – most authors have no interest in going all the way to *Finnegans Wake* (an emblematically modernist text) and abandon language itself. Brian Rosebury, for example, argued persuasively that *The Lord of the Rings* in fact passes quite easily for a novel, if not a prominently realistic one. Significantly, about magic he says that it is "largely avoided [...] in favour of a putatively consistent system of powers and 'lore'" (Rosebury 115). Even the representation of the world and the story he finds tolerable by novelistic standards; one is reminded of Tom Shippey who said that *The Lord of the Rings*, like Ulysses, is "engaged in deep negotiation with the ancient genres of epic and romance" (Shippey, *Author of the Century* 311). And other worldviews, one could add: Tolkien's choice of a pansemiotic world certainly is quite unfitted for realism, because it presupposes meaning everywhere, while realism infuses with meaning (by the characters, their actions, their thoughts) a world that is otherwise meaningless. This all-pervasive meaning, if we will, is then also 'critically magical', since there is nothing like it in the Primary World. As John Garth put it in the discussion after this paper was originally delivered at the DTG Conference in Augsburg in October 2017, it is "either no magic or all magic." Seeing this un- or even anti-realist 'magic' in Tolkien is exactly like reading *Beowulf* in the way he so disapproved of – not at all on its own terms, not at all in the way it *works*.

Criticism has no problem with postmodernist experimentation, magical realism, or metafiction, often classed as 'fantastic', all of which resist the realist ideology and subvert realistic criteria of representation. Tolkien does that too, but in another way: he creates a huge, historical fiction which examines the ways language, knowledge, narrative and its various different forms are layered in a system across cultures, and together constitute the world and its past. Being a philologist, he does that in *texts*, so for Tolkien 'world-building' is really 'text-building': this is why he insists in 'On Fairy-stories' that literature is their prime medium, and that the art, the 'elvish craft' needed for it is not to be called 'magic'. It is not, because the term invokes cultural historical phenomena that are not there (after a while), and because it is defined by reference to an ideology of representation that fairy-stories by nature circumvent and subvert. Tolkien is certainly not a postmodernist, nor is his work 'postmodern' in this subversion. But that does not mean that the entire corpus cannot be seen from this perspective. For Tolkien, very much as for postmodernists, *the world is in a text*, and so his work "is always metafictional" (Attebery 41), questioning discourses of culture, negotiating between them, in the end showing how even the ultimate knowledge is only a matter of discourse, of privileged text. In this sense, he even queries his own theological hierarchy, representing that as merely one set of traditions, assigned the most authority. And that is even further from magic than a pansemiotic fictional world. It's not magic, it's philology; or maybe we should say *glamour*, and point everyone to the etymology.

About the Author

GERGELY NAGY (PhD) is an independent scholar who taught at the University of Szeged, Hungary, for 15 years. He wrote his dissertation on the 1977 *Silmarillion* and its basis in textuality, but even prior to that, argued in several articles and papers that textuality and the network of (fictional) texts is central to Tolkien's representation (and thus creation) of culture. He also published papers on Malory and Chaucer, and at the University of Szeged, taught courses on medieval English literature, 20th century fantastic literature and film (including Tolkien, Harry Potter, and science fiction), and 20th century popular music. He has been the member of the *Tolkien Studies* editorial board from the periodical's inception, and in the early 2000s, he was instrumental in creating the Hungarian Tolkien Society.

Abbreviations

LT I   Tolkien, J.R.R. *The Book of Lost Tales, Vol. 1*. New York: Ballantines, 1992.

LT II   Tolkien, J.R.R. *The Book of Lost Tales, Vol. 2*. New York: Ballantines, 1992.

FR   Tolkien, J.R.R. *The Fellowship of the Ring*. London: HarperCollins, 1991.

Hobbit Tolkien, J.R.R. *The Hobbit*. Boston and New York: HoughtonMifflin, 2007.

LB   Tolkien, J.R.R. *The Lays of Beleriand*. New York: Ballantines, 1994.

Letters Tolkien, J.R.R. *The Letters of J.R.R. Tolkien*. Ed. Humphrey Carpenter, with the assistance of Christopher Tolkien. London: George Allen & Unwin; Boston: HoughtonMifflin, 1981.

LR   Tolkien, J.R.R. *The Lost Road and Other Writings*. New York: Ballantines, 1996.

RK   Tolkien, J.R.R. *The Return of the King*. London: HarperCollins, 1991.

SME   Tolkien, J.R.R. *The Shaping of Middle-earth*. New York: Ballantines, 1995.

S   Tolkien, J.R.R. *The Silmarillion*. Boston and New York: HoughtonMifflin, 1999.

TOFS *Tolkien On Fairy-Stories*. Ed. Verlyn Flieger and Douglas A. Anderson. London: HarperCollins, 2008.

TT   Tolkien, J.R.R. *The Two Towers*. London: HarperCollins, 1991.

Bibliography

Attebery, Brian. *Strategies of Fantasy*. Bloomington and Indianapolis: Indiana University Press, 1992.

Bachmann, Dieter. 'Words for Magic: goetia, gûl, and lúth.' *Myth and Magic. Art according to the Inklings*. Ed. Eduardo Segura and Thomas Honegger. Zurich and Berne: Walking Tree Publishers, 2007. 47-55.

Clark Hall, John R. *A Concise Anglo-Saxon Dictionary*. 4th ed. Cambridge: Cambridge University Press, 1960.

Clarke, Arthur C. *Profiles of the Future: An Inquiry into the Limits of the Possible*. New York: Harper and Row, 1973.

FIMI, Dimitra. *Tolkien, Race and Cultural History. From Fairies to Hobbits*. London: Palgrave Macmillan, 2010.

HERBERT, Frank. *Dune*. New York: Berkley, 1977.

HUME, Kathryn. *Fantasy and Mimesis. Responses to Reality in Western Literature*. New York and London: Methuen, 1984.

KIECKHEFER, Richard. *Magic in the Middle Ages*. Cambridge: Cambridge University Press, 1989.

LOTMAN, Yuri. 'Problems in the Typology of Culture.' *Soviet Semiotics: An Anthology*. Ed. Daniel P. Lucid. Baltimore MD: Johns Hopkins University Press, 1977. 213-21.

RATELIFF, John D. *The History of The Hobbit. Vol. 1. Mr. Baggins*. Boston and New York: HoughtonMifflin, 2007.

ROSEBURY, Brian. *Tolkien. A Cultural Phenomenon*. London: Palgrave Macmillan, 2003.

SHIPPEY, Tom. 'Another Road to Middle-earth: Jackson's Movie Trilogy.' *Roots and Branches. Selected Papers on Tolkien*. Zurich and Berne: Walking Tree Publishers, 2007. 365-86.

'New Learning and New Ignorance: Magia, Goeteia, and the Inklings.' *Myth and Magic. Art according to the Inklings*. Ed. Eduardo Segura and Thomas Honegger. Zurich and Berne: Walking Tree Publishers, 2007. 21-46.

J.R.R. Tolkien, Author of the Century. Boston and New York: Houghton Mifflin, 2001.

TODOROV, Tzvetan. *The Fantastic. A Structural Approach to a Literary Genre*. Transl. Richard Howard. Ithaca: Cornell University Press, 1975.

TOLKIEN, J.R.R. *The Book of Lost Tales, Vol. 1*. New York: Ballantines, 1992.

The Book of Lost Tales, Vol. 2. New York: Ballantines, 1992.

The Fellowship of the Ring. London: HarperCollins, 1991.

The Hobbit. Boston and New York: HoughtonMifflin, 2007.

The Lays of Beleriand. New York: Ballantines, 1994.

The Letters of J.R.R. Tolkien. Ed. Humphrey Carpenter, with the assistance of Christopher Tolkien. London: George Allen & Unwin; Boston: HoughtonMifflin, 1981.

The Lost Road and Other Writings. New York: Ballantines, 1996.

The Return of the King. London: HarperCollins, 1991.

The Shaping of Middle-earth. New York: Ballantines, 1995.

The Silmarillion. Boston and New York: HoughtonMifflin, 1999.

Tolkien On Fairy-Stories. Ed. Verlyn Flieger and Douglas A. Anderson. London: HarperCollins, 2008.

The Two Towers. London: HarperCollins, 1991.

WEST, Richard C. 'Setting the Rocket Off in Story: The *Kalevala* as the Germ of Tolkien's Legendarium.' *Tolkien and the Invention of Myth. A Reader*. Ed. Jane Chance. Lexington CT: University Press of Kentucky, 2004. 285-94.

Renée Vink

Tolkien the Tinkerer: World-building versus Storytelling

Abstract

That J.R.R. Tolkien was a storyteller is obvious, given his authorship of books like *The Lord of the Rings* and *The Hobbit*. He has also, and rightly so, been hailed as a great world-builder. His world of Arda is full of details existing in their own right, regardless of their use in his various narratives. But simultaneously, it is not just any fantasy setting: it is our own world, only with a different past and history and seen from a specific angle. What happens when primary world realities enter the fantasy world of Arda through a back door? Does Tolkien's desire for realism never get in the way of his stories, his mythology?

The tension developing over time between Tolkien's world-building with everything this entailed on the one hand, and his storytelling with its (often religious) symbolism on the other, needs to be discussed more thoroughly, as does the balance between these two. In the later volumes of *History of Middle-earth* Tolkien is shown tinkering with his sub-created world, and occasionally backpedalling. He appears to have had second thoughts about several of his earlier concepts, such as, for instance, the cosmology of Arda and the concept of Death as the Gift of Men. Was Tolkien the storyteller and mythmaker in the process of disappearing behind Tolkien the world-builder during his later years?

At the end of the second chapter of *The Hobbit* the company of Thorin Oakenshield enters the cave of the recently petrified trolls. Inside they find all kinds of plunder, including a few swords. As the book states, "[t]wo caught their eyes particularly, because of their beautiful scabbards and jewelled hilts. Gandalf and Thorin each took one of these." (*H*, Ch. 2: 'Roast Mutton') Arriving at Rivendell, the company hears from Elrond that the swords were

> made in Gondolin for the Goblin-wars. [...] This, Thorin, the runes name Orcrist, the Goblin-cleaver in the ancient tongue of Gondolin; it was a famous blade. This, Gandalf, was Glamdring, Foe-hammer that the king of Gondolin once wore. (*H*, Ch. 3, 'A Short Rest').

People reading *The Hobbit* as their first book by Tolkien, probably won't give this passage any further thought. These names look like the author made them up on the spot to stress the importance of the swords and to point ahead to future fights and battles. That Glamdring is mentioned in *The Lord of the Rings* doesn't change this; if you are familiar with this work before reading *The Hobbit*, you'll simply think "so that's how Gandalf came by his sword". How the uncouth Trolls came by such an ancient, sophisticated royal blade must remain a matter of conjecture, as none of Tolkien's writings contain an explanation.

People who go on to read *The Silmarillion* will come across the name Gondolin there, but they won't encounter either Glamdring or Orcrist. Much of the *Silmarillion* material was already in existence before Tolkien conceived of *The Hobbit*, but these two swords weren't part of it. The Elven city of Gondolin played a role in his writings from the earliest stages on, as did its King. In *The Hobbit* this King's name is never mentioned, but it was and always remained Turgon. Both City and King appear frequently in the first volume of *The History of Middle-earth, The Book of Lost Tales I*. Elrond's information regarding the two swords in the third *Hobbit* chapter dates back verbatim to a late addition to the first, unfinished version of the book, the so called 'Bladorthin Typescript' (Rateliff 122), but no connection is made between Turgon and the anonymous owner of Glamdring, nor is Elrond identified as Turgon's great-grandson (123). The first time the names Glamdring and Orcrist are mentioned outside *The Hobbit* is in the drafts for *The Lord of the Rings* published in Volumes V-IX of *The History of Middle-earth*.

In other words, these swords and their names were indeed made up especially for *The Hobbit*. Yet websites like *The Tolkien Gateway* and *One Wiki to Rule them All*[1] do not doubt that Turgon wielded Glamdring in the disastrous fifth Battle of Beleriand, the Nirnaeth Arnoediad. Both assume that the description of Turgon's sword in 'Of Tuor and his Coming to Gondolin' (*UT* 56, note 31) applies to Glamdring. It wasn't necessary for Tolkien to make the identification: his secondary believers did it for him.

Likewise, it was in *The Silmarillion* of 1977 that it became clear Elrond Half-Elven was referring to his own great-grandfather when he mentioned the King of Gondolin in the passage in *The Hobbit*: the master of Rivendell turned out to be a son of Eärendil, the son of Idril daughter of Turgon. Now Elrond was

---

1 http://tolkiengateway.net/wiki/Glamdring; http://lotr.wikia.com/wiki/Glamdring

in all probability created specifically for *The Hobbit* in the early 1930s. His entry at 'The Tolkien Gateway' states this as a fact;[2] Christopher Tolkien's introduction to the 'Earliest Silmarillion' (*SME* 1, 11) does not, but contains no statements to the contrary either. Also, one would expect Elrond to have mentioned his family ties with the original owner of Glamdring if these had been established when *The Hobbit* was written, but he doesn't: there were no such ties yet. Tolkien merely told the story; the readers connected the dots.

Characters like Gandalf, Gil-galad and Galadriel provide yet more striking examples of added backstory. Gandalf first appeared in *The Hobbit* and returned with a vengeance in *The Lord of the Rings*. Everything else we know about him was written after the publication of the latter. An 'essay on the Istari' containing the account of Gandalf's mission to Middle-earth was written in the summer of 1954 as part of a projected index to *The Lord of the Rings* after this had been accepted for publication (*UT* 12, 388ff). Yet more background information is found in "very rapid jottings" and "a sketch of a narrative" (*UT* 392-93) not belonging to the essay, but possibly written after the projected index was cancelled because of the costs. Here we discover that Gandalf was a late addition to the group of wizards that the Valar sent to Middle-earth. His origins as a Maia by name of Olórin were added to the version of the 'Valaquenta' written in 1958 (*MR* 199f).

Gil-galad had hitherto only figured in one draft of the 'Fall of Númenor' but not in any of the First Age stories. At that stage, he was still a descendant of Fëanor (*LR* 29).[3] Later he briefly acquired Finrod Felagund for a father, ending up as the son of either Fingon son of Fingolfin, or Orodreth in his quality as Finrod's nephew, not his brother (see Vink).

In Gil-galad's case, an element appears that applies to Galadriel as well: conflicting information. The Lady of the Golden Wood is also wholly absent from the older material. Her presence in *The Silmarillion* (1977) is based on Tolkien's writings of the later 1950s and the 1960s. Once the *Ring* epic was published, Tolkien felt the need to incorporate this obviously very important Elvish lady in the history of the First Age. The textual material shows that it was less

---

2 http://tolkiengateway.net/wiki/Elrond
3 For the textual history of Gil-galad, see Vink.

clear to him in what way she was to be inserted: *Unfinished Tales* contains two different versions of Galadriel's departure from Valinor before the beginning of the First Age. In one, she fights against Feänor and his followers in the Kinslaying at Alqualondë together with her brother, Finrod (*UT* 230, based on a fragment in *MR* 128). The other version is markedly different and separates her altogether from the rebellion of the Noldor: she leaves Valinor together with her lover Celeborn (here a Teler, not a Sinda, with the unfortunate name of Teleporno), against the wishes of the Valar. This explains why she is exiled like all the other Noldor who left the Undying Lands (*UT* 232). But however contradictory this information may be, all of it dates from after the publication of *The Lord of the Rings*.

So, once his major opus became available to the public at large, Tolkien decided to reinforce the structure and the history of his secondary world by anchoring elements from the published books in the pre-existing, as yet unpublished texts about the Elder Days. Before, he hadn't felt the need to do so. A look at the publishing history of *The Lord of the Rings* tells us that he was so eager to see his *Silmarillion* in print along with the *Ring* epic, that he was prepared to turn his back on Allen & Unwin when they proved disinclined to do so. On discovering that other publishers did not want *The Silmarillion* along with *The Lord of the Rings* either, Tolkien fell back on Allen & Unwin; getting *The Lord of the Rings* published was more important to him in the end. But the *Silmarillion* version he offered the various publishers was one without Gandalf, Gil-galad and Galadriel. Back then, this does not seem to have bothered Tolkien overmuch. So why did he wish to amend these things after the publication of *The Lord of the Rings*?

One thing that changed between the pre- and post-*The Lord of the Rings* periods is that the reaction of the public came into play. Countless readers saw that Tolkien had not merely written a fantastic story, but had built an entire secondary world. In one fell swoop he had convinced them of its reality. Furniss, for instance, writes: "J.R.R. Tolkien's Secondary World is so convincing [...], that it might be reasonable to view him as not just a novelist, but a historian" (Furniss 9). He posits that *The Lord of the Rings* "(if not *The Hobbit* or *The Silmarillion*) could [...] defensibly be classified as historical fiction and not fantasy" (12). Many readers embraced the reality of Tolkien's world to such a degree, that they desired to immerse themselves further in it. As he wrote in 1956 to a reader:

> ... many like you demand *maps*, others wish for *geological* indications [...]; many want Elvish grammars, phonologies, and specimens [...]. Musicians want tunes, and musical notation; archaeologists want ceramics and metallurgy. Botanists want a more accurate description of the *mallorn* [...], and historians want more details about the social and political structure of Gondor; general enquirers want information about the Wainriders, the Harad, Dwarvish origins, the Dead Men, the Beornings, and the two missing wizards (out of five). (*Letters* 248)

In his 1939 essay 'On Fairy-stories' Tolkien had written about creating a "Secondary World" commanding "Secondary Belief", adding that this demanded "a special skill, a kind of elvish craft" (*TOFS* § 69). Clearly, he possessed this elvish craft: *The Lord of the Rings* did command widespread secondary belief and apparently possessed the "inner consistency of reality" he considered so difficult to achieve (*TOFS* § 68).

Yet his readers were not going to let him bask in the sun of this achievement – they were going to make him sweat, as the letter makes clear. He managed to supply some of the information his readers were asking for, like the origins of the Dwarves (*S* 43f), and some background for the two missing wizards (*UT* 393f). He wrote a great deal more on Elvish languages than he had already done (published on an ongoing basis in the linguistic journal *Parma Eldalamberon*).[4] But the sheer number of unfinished *Silmarillion* material seems to have been of more immediate concern to him than detailed descriptions of the *mallorn* tree, the social structure of Gondor, or the Beornings.

In 1951, a revised version of *The Hobbit* had been published. The changes Tolkien had made to the text brought it into accordance with *The Lord of the Rings*: Gollum had become a lot nastier than he was at first and his Ring, the Precious, stopped being the prize in a riddle contest: the Gollum of *The Lord of the Rings* wouldn't have dreamed of giving it away (for all the changes made to the book, see Rateliff). As *The Lord of the Rings* was the sequel to *The Hobbit*, achieving greater narrative consistency and removing obvious discrepancies was the logical thing to do.[5] However, after the *Ring* epic narrative consistency

---

4 http://www.eldalamberon.com/
5 Wolf discusses Tolkien's changes to *The Hobbit* as an example of world-building on page 130f in his study *Building Imaginary Worlds. The Theory and History of Subcreation*.

was only one of the things that mattered to Tolkien. Galadriel didn't actively partake in the wars of the Elves and Edain against Morgoth, but apparently now the Elder Days were no longer conceivable without her, as they had been at the time when Tolkien tried to get the *Silmarillion* published together with *The Lord of the Rings*. Could there be a link between the Glorfindel from 'The Fall of Gondolin' (*The Book of Lost Tales II*) and the one who appeared in *The Lord of the Rings*? Who and what exactly were the wizards, and who had sent them to Middle-earth? Etcetera. When Tolkien took it upon himself to answer such questions, the great rewrite of the Silmarillion began.

The conclusion seems warranted that the way many readers reacted to *The Lord of the Rings* played a crucial role in the endeavour of aligning the published works and the unpublished texts. It looks as though this type of reaction, perhaps in combination with the rejection of *The Lord of the Rings* as serious literature by a number of mainstream critics,[6] clinched Tolkien's status as a world-builder. Once the readers began to look over his shoulder, publishing the *Silmarillion* in the form it had at the time ceased to be an option for him, though the unexpected success of *The Lord of the Rings* made it financially viable. First, the legends had to be "made consistent" and "integrated with" the published works (*Letters* 333), though the way some fans reacted to *The Lord of the Rings* told him this would be a daunting task:

> [S]everal correspondents, have treated it [...] as if it was a report of "real" times and places, which my ignorance or carelessness had misrepresented in places or failed to describe properly in others. Its economics, science, artefacts [sic], religion and philosophy are defective or at least sketchy. (*Letters* 188)

He did have his doubts about the undertaking, pointing out that *The Lord of the Rings* is "in the ultimate analysis [...] a piece of literature, intended to have literary effect, and not real history" (*Letters* 188). The attraction of *The Lord of the Rings* was partly "due to the glimpses of a large history in the background: an attraction like that of viewing far off an unvisited island, or seeing the towers of a distant city gleaming in a sunlit mist [...] To go there is to destroy the magic" (*Letters* 333). The relative popularity of his *Silmarillion* among the fans

---

6 Of whom Edmund Wilson with his article 'Oo, Those Awful Orcs!' (*The Nation*, April 14, 1956) merely was among the first and most dismissive. Drout discusses several other early Tolkien bashers (109f).

of his secondary world, as opposed to Tolkien readers who predominantly love the *Ring* epic as a ripping good yarn, seems to prove him wrong. Not that his doubts ever stopped him from "going there" anyway.

Tolkien kept working on the material for about a dozen years after the publication of *The Lord of the Rings*, but as more time went by, the less likely it became that he would be able to finish the task. The question is, why was he unable to do so? For an attempt to answer this, it may prove useful to address the status of Tolkien's legendarium, the sum total of his writings about his secondary world of Arda.

As is well known, Tolkien started out wanting to write a mythology for England, to use a phrase he didn't coin himself, but which has become standard in Tolkien studies (for what he actually wrote, see *Letters* 144). This statement of intent firmly links his Middle-earth writings to our primary world. Originally, the 'Quenta Silmarillion' was to have been a frame narrative, the frame being a story about an Anglo-Saxon sailor, Ælfwine or Eriol, who found his way to Tol Eressëa and later returned to England with knowledge of the Elvish myths and legends he had heard during his sojourn there (*The Book of Lost Tales I & II*). This is a rough summary; things are, in fact, more complicated than that, and with 'The Notion Club Papers' (*LR*) Tolkien tried to create a rather different frame. But for the present paper this summary will do. Once Tolkien had more or less given up on his idea of a frame narrative (he never seems to have abandoned it entirely), the Elvish tales of the Elder Days were claimed to have been translated and transmitted by the humble hobbit, Bilbo Baggins. In his 'Foreword' to *The Lord of the Rings*, Tolkien himself posed as the translator of the 'Red Book of Westmarch', a large tome containing Bilbo's translations from the Elvish, his account of the Quest of Erebor, aka *The Hobbit*, and Frodo's and Sam's account of the War of the Ring, aka *The Lord of the Rings*.

As he pointed out, the world in which his stories are set is not imaginary; Arda is not a different planet, but our own. It is only the history he described or "translated" that was made-up; he constructed an imaginary time but not an imaginary place (*Letters* 244, 283). However, this became increasingly problematic. Tolkien started fretting about "how to reconcile the initial themes of his mythology, the history of the Elves and the Silmarils with an emerging urge to write not 'myth' anymore, but 'history', albeit feigned history or pseudo-history," as Fimi writes (125).

> The two problems that stand out are 1) the physical state of his sub-created world, something that seems to have struck him with full force when he picked up his writings about the Elder Days after the publication of *The Lord of the Rings*; and 2) its metaphysics. Ultimately, these problems turned out to be insurmountable for him and he died before the *Silmarillion* could be published in any form.

One important reason why Tolkien got stuck is that the cosmology of his secondary world is incompatible with that of our primary universe.[7] In the section 'Myths transformed' in *Morgoth's Ring* (367-431), Christopher Tolkien wrote about the inextricable tangle his father got himself into when he decided that "the art of the Sub-creator" should not extend to a cosmos that "runs counter to the known physical truths of his own days" (*MR* 371). The Sun and the Moon could never have been the last fruit and flower of two luminous supernatural trees and the Earth could never have been flat. The Valar, naturally familiar with the actual layout of the universe – our universe, as God had created it – must have informed the Elves of Aman about it, Tolkien decided. The matter of the *Silmarillion* was initially supposed to have been written by Elves, but he felt the need to change this: "It is now clear to me that […] the Mythology must actually be a 'Mannish' affair" (*MR* 370).

However, as Christopher writes, it was "remarkable that he never… seems to have felt that what he said in this present note provided a resolution of the problem that he believed to exist" (*MR* 371). Apparently, Tolkien found it very difficult to correct the "astronomically absurd" (ibid.) cosmology without rending the entire fabric of his myth – including a narrative core like the tale of Eärendil and the Silmaril that became the Evening Star. This contributed to his inability to finish the *Silmarillion*. He embarked on several rewrites, yet finished none of them. In his son's words these "are to be read with a sense of intellectual and imaginative stress in the face of such a dismantling and reconstruction, believed to be an inescapable necessity, but never to be achieved" (*MR* 369).

---

7 Discussed at more length by Fimi, 125-29.

The section of *Morgoth's Ring* describing his cosmological struggles also shows that he kept wrestling with the origins of the orcs and the matter of their free or enslaved wills, but without reaching a solution that was acceptable to himself, workable, and in accordance with *The Lord of the Rings*.[8] Further, a letter to Peter Hasting of September 1954 shows that Tolkien also realised the biology of Arda was at variance with primary world biology:

> Elves and Men are evidently in biological terms one race, or they could not breed and produce fertile offspring [...] But since some have held that the rate of longevity is a biological characteristic, within limits of variation, you could not have Elves in a sense "immortal" – not eternal, but not dying by "old age" – and Men mortal, more or less as they now seem to be in the Primary World – and yet sufficiently akin. (*Letters* 189)

As Fimi points out (152f), Tolkien contradicted himself here, as he gave Elves and Men different racial characteristics on various occasions and in one of his letters (*Letters* 204) assigned them different biological natures because of their different life spans. He solved this by declaring that his imaginary world had its own "biological dictum": biology did not work the same way in Middle-earth as it does in our primary world (Fimi 153, q. *Letters* 189).

Of course, sticking to known biology would have created a problem anyway, one that was almost as insurmountable as the original cosmology of Arda. If there are no Half-Elves, let alone Half-Elves able to procreate, the ending of the *Silmarillion* becomes impossible and even *The Lord of the Rings* will be affected. No Elrond, hence no Arwen of Half-Elven descent to marry Aragorn, who himself had a Half-Elven for an ancestor.

At the time, Tolkien solved the problem by stating: "This is a biological dictum in my imaginary world" (*Letters* 189). As this is the only feasible solution, it seems wise. But is it compatible with the notion that Middle-earth is basically our own world? This leads to all sorts of tricky questions regarding the scientific viability of Arda, whether this name denotes the entire Solar System or only Earth. Tolkien was aware of the problem; to repeat a quote given earlier:

---

8 This matter is discussed at length in Tyellas' paper and more briefly in Fimi (154f).

> [S]everal correspondents have treated [my work] as if it was a report of "real" times and places, which my ignorance or carelessness had misrepresented in places or failed to describe properly in others. Its economics, science, artefacts, religion and philosophy are defective or at least sketchy. (*Letters* 188)

Tolkien himself came to realise that no woods or flowers could have grown "on earth if there had been no light since the overthrow of the Lamps" (*MR* 375). Others have looked at his maps and criticised the flawed geology of Middle-earth (Yeskov, Acks), or questioned other details of his legendarium from a scientific point of view.[9] Why bother? one might ask. In a world rife with fire-breathing dragons, light-consuming spiders, and magic rings, a faulty mountain range or dubious demographics should not be too much of a surprise. The correct rejoinder to this kind of questions would be that the sub-creator knows best how things work. But when the sub-creator himself starts wondering, there will be no end.

Tolkien knew, of course, that he couldn't possibly render his sub-creation compatible with the state of the art in every field of science. New discoveries and developments could invalidate his constructions any time; it would have had a crippling effect on his creativity and imagination if he had dwelled on such things while writing his mythology in the 1920s and 1930s, or *The Lord of the Rings* in the late 1930s and the 1940s.

Problems like those sketched here appear to be direct consequences of the increasing primacy of worldbuilding over mythmaking and storytelling in Tolkien's post *The Lord of the Rings* writings. As Fimi puts it: "*The Hobbit* gave birth to *The Lord of the Rings* and inaugurated a new way of writing. Tolkien was not writing a mythology anymore, he was writing a novel" (119). He became overly concerned with getting his facts right and making things plausible. Instead of gradually giving way to history as had been his original intention, myth itself began to take on the guise of history, to be tackled with the tools of historiography and science. Symbolism made way for factuality. What started out as a myth depicting the creation of the Sun and the Moon threatened to fall victim to scientific correctness. When Eru Ilúvatar changed

---

9 See f.i. the contribution of SilentLion to this forum discussion about Elvish demography at The One Ring: http://newboards.theonering.net/search/Tolkien_Topics_C3/Reading_Room_F9/More_demography_P53005/.

the world in the cataclysm destroying Númenor, making a hitherto flat Earth round (*S* 279, 281), this neatly symbolised the discovery of the Earth's global shape, first by Greek astronomers and later by a more and more general public. If the Earth was round from the beginning, the symbolism is lost, and the story becomes the poorer for it. Invention threatens to take over imagination. As Christopher put it, his father "was devising [...] a fearful weapon against his own creation" (*MR* 371).

Philosophical and theological concerns still further complicated Tolkien's task of readying the *Silmarillion* for publication. Death as the Gift of Men came under fire in the text 'Athrabeth Finrod ah Andreth' (*MR* 301-66), which is part story, part treatise. Originally, the mortals of Arda could die of their own free will. They were given the grace to lay down their lives once they felt their time had come. Many did so, for instance Bëor (*S* 149), the first Númenorean Kings (*S* 266), and much later King Elessar (*The Lord of the Rings*, App. A, V). However, those who came under the shadow of Morgoth began to consider Death as a bad thing that had to be avoided. This change of attitude culminates in the story of the Downfall of Númenor, whose last ruler, Ar-Phârazon, leads an armada to the Undying Lands in a vain attempt to wrest immortality from the Valar (*S* 277ff).

The 'Athrabeth' puts an end to the notion of Death as a gift, replacing it by the more familiar concept of Death as a punishment found in the Book of Genesis. Instead of the Genesis story, Tolkien has his mortal character, Andreth, recount a Mannish myth, 'The Tale of Adanel'. This tells of Morgoth-worship among mortals, punished by Eru – here called "The Voice" – with the forced separation of soul and body (*MR* 347). In a letter of 1954 Tolkien still called Death a gift. Though, as he admitted, it might be bad theology, at the same time it was "an imagination capable of elucidating truth, and a legitimate basis of legends" (*Letters* 189). Around 1959, when he wrote the 'Athrabeth', he had obviously changed his mind and started backpedalling. That this would undermine an important element of the story of Númenor can hardly have escaped him, but he did it anyway.

His theological "tinkering"" is even more obvious in the suggestion, made by Finrod in the same text, that Eru, the One, will be incarnated in Arda someday.

In his own comments, Tolkien voices the concern that this could turn the story "into a parody of Christianity" (*MR* 356). One might guess that at some moment he considered introducing the Holy Trinity to his sub-created world.[10] Arda already contained the First and Third Persons of the Trinity – Eru Ilúvatar as God the Father and the Flame Imperishable as the Holy Spirit (Kilby 59), but as yet there was no equivalent of the Second Person, Jesus Christ. Whatever is the case, Tolkien apparently came to think it was not merely known physical truths his cosmos should adhere to, but Christian theology as well.

However, just like his views regarding cosmology, this creates problems. If Arda is basically our own world, the creation account in the Ainulindalë is at variance with Christian theology. According to the Bible, God saw that his creation was good (Gen. 1, *passim*). In our primary world, Tolkien says, "evil was brought in from outside, by Satan". This is not the case in his myth, he adds: there "the rebellion of created free-will precedes creation of the World (Eä); and Eä has in it, subcreatively introduced, evil […] of its own nature already when the *Let It Be* was spoken" (*Letters* 286). This is a possibility any sub-creator is free to explore, a piece of alternative metaphysics, the way the stories set in Arda are pieces of alternative (pre)-history. But the closer the metaphysics of a sub-created world move towards primary world creeds – in Tolkien's case with physical death as God's punishment for Men, plus a hint at a future incarnation of God on Earth – the greater is the chance that these creeds will become criteria to measure the sub-created world's compatibility with religious orthodoxy. Now, the symbolism of myth threatens to become the straightforwardness of doctrine. And the desire not to go against doctrine sets limits to pure storytelling. Looking over your own shoulder like a kind of inquisitor will set more bounds to your imagination and your sub-creating than old age will.

Writing to Peter Hastings, who had questioned Tolkien's theology after reading *The Lord of the Rings*, suggesting that a sub-creator ought to use the channels which he knew the creator to have used already, Tolkien showed himself aware of the basic issue:

---

10 Early signs of this are present in the Qenya Lexicon (published partly in *LT I* and in full in *Parma Eldalamberon* #12, 1998), which contains words for each person of the Holy Trinity. However, this Lexicon was written during the period when there was still a direct connection between Tolkien's stories and our own world in the form of the pseudo-historical character Eriol/Ælfwine.

> Liberation from the channels the creator is known to have used already is the fundamental function of "sub-creation", a tribute to the infinity of His potential variety [...] I am not a metaphysician: but I should have thought it is a curious metaphysic [...] that declared the channels known (in such a finite corner as we have any inkling of) to have been used, are the only possible ones, or efficacious, or possibly acceptable to and by Him! (*Letters* 188f)

Tolkien addressed one example of this liberation in his letter concerns Elvish reincarnation, the idea that Elves can be reborn. As it says in the essay 'Laws and Customs among the Eldar': "A houseless *fëa* [spirit] that chose or was permitted to return to life re-entered the incarnate world through child-birth" (*MR* 221). In the letter to Hastings Tolkien comments:

> "Reincarnation" may be bad theology [...] as applied to Humanity. [...] But I do not see how even in the Primary World any theologian or philosopher, unless very much better informed about the relation of spirit and body than I believe anyone to be, could deny the possibility of re-incarnation as a mode of existence, prescribed for certain kinds of rational incarnate creatures. (*Letters* 189)

More than fifteen years later, in 1970, discussing the return of Glorfindel from the Undying Lands to Middle-earth, Tolkien changed the concept of reincarnation and rebirth in what he called rehousing or re-embodiment, accompanied by a return to "the primitive innocence and grace of the Eldar" (*PME* 379-81). His reasoning was that the Glorfindel of the Third Age had to be identical with the Glorfindel of First Age Gondolin who fell to a heroic death, because the "repetition of so striking a name, though possible, would not be credible" (*PME* 380). That Glorfindel remained essentially the same person, precluded reincarnation. But to what degree is this change of tack due to the criticisms voiced years before by Peter Hastings? Did they make Tolkien reconsider, despite what he wrote in his answer? We don't know, but it does seem possible. If this is indeed the case, we witness Tolkien curbing his own freedom as a sub-creator once again. (Though I daresay here it was for the better, as re-embodiment is a more workable idea for Elves than reincarnation anyway.)

A concomitant danger of the developments sketched above would be that the line between primary and secondary reality begins to blur. The sub-created world becomes more and more aligned with the author's personal knowledge of, and assumptions about, the primary world. It appears that internal consistency is no longer the chief requirement for sub-created reality in the way Tolkien assumes it to be in 'On Fairy-stories' (*TOFS* § 68, 69). If primary world physics rule, how can the sun be green in a secondary world, as he thought possible in 1939? And even if "Elvish" craft could make green sun believable, or a flat Earth, or breathing one's last as a voluntary act, is it allowed to do so? The sub-creator's freedom is in danger of becoming restricted by natural laws and by his own creeds and convictions. The question arises whether the older Tolkien still believed in the sub-creative freedom his younger self had claimed, and even whether he did not come to consider the entire idea of sub-creativity misguided both from the viewpoint of a religious believer and of a stickler for hard scientific facts. During the post-*The Lord of the Rings* period he appears to have retired from the position held in his poem 'Mythopoeia' of 1931, where he claimed:

> Though all the crannies of the world we filled
> with Elves and Goblins, though we dared to build
> Gods and their houses out of dark and light,
> and sowed the seed of dragons, 'twas our right
> (used or misused). The right has not decayed.
> We make still by the law in which we're made. (*TOFS* § 77)

In 1954 he had answered his own question "Are there any 'bounds to a writer's job' except those imposed by his own finiteness?" by saying: 'No bounds, but the laws of contradiction, I should think' (*Letters* 194). Around the beginning of the next decade, when the gods of the Mythopoeia poem had become angelic Powers, he seems to have been less sure.[11] The writer became the spiritual watchdog of his own work, just like he became its material watchdog regarding scientific fact, making the task he'd set himself "of course an impossible one", as Vanderbeke & Turner write (11).

---

11 It was, after all, not Christians who had originally filled the world with Elves and Goblins. These, and the gods, and the dragons, were products of a human imagination unfettered and uncensored by Christian doctrine; pious Christians could and did borrow them from the pagans, but would they have invented them? In 'Mythopoeia', they were borrowed by a myth-loving Christian wanting to convince a myth-loving non-Christian that he wouldn't have to sacrifice myths and their populations if he converted. In other words, they were written with an agenda. Of course, it remains possible that Tolkien stood by his 1931 convictions even in the late 1950s and beyond. Nowhere does he retract his younger self's statements. But his second thoughts about a few theological issues do suggest a changed outlook.

How problematic is this really? In the afterword of the pocket edition of his novel *The Book of Lost Things*, John Conolly writes about his reluctance to reread his own book, not because he was ashamed of it,

> but because I was worried that I'd feel the urge to alter it, to tinker. Writers should never be allowed to return to their earlier books. Time passes, and writers change. They hope that they're getting better at what they do, but this may not be true. It may simply be something they tell themselves because it's reassuring, and the truth of their decline is too hard to face. (Conolly 321)

Can we apply this to J.R.R. Tolkien, the tinkerer of tinkerers?

In his defence, it needs to be pointed out that he only tinkered once with a published text: the 1951 edition of *The Hobbit*. For the rest he was merely rewriting unpublished drafts. As far as he knew, the *Silmarillion* remained in a state of flux, he could do with it as he saw fit, and he could not foresee that the earlier versions of his legendarium would be published along with the later ones. How much of a problem is it that we, his readers, encounter more than one version of events, character biographies, names, family trees, etc., in his writings? Some argue that it makes his one-man mythology look more realistic. Nagy, for example, suggests that "Tolkien's texts and the background mythological system they succeed in creating are essentially similar to real world mythological corpora" (Nagy 252). In neither case an original version exists on which all the variants are based.

Against this, Vanderbeke & Turner point out that knowledge can have two kinds of origins in Tolkien's secondary world: "[…] an invented past via a non-existent source, be it myth, tale of legend within Middle-earth, but on another level also […] an existing source in our own past" that Tolkien the scholar threw into the cauldron of his storytelling (Vanderbeke & Turner 7). It makes his mythology a hybrid to which Nagy's argument can't be applied unreservedly. Another argument against the suggestion that Tolkien wanted to achieve the diversity found in real world mythology is the relative uniformity of his tone:

> [A] general tone prevails in all the narrations, the melancholy or even gloomy feeling of loss and decay informs the narrative style no matter whether it is Elves or Men who transmit the tales. It can hardly be assumed that someone

as steeped in philology as he did not notice the predominantly monochromatic aspect in his works. Therefore it must be at least to some extent the result of a conscious choice. (Vanderbeke & Turner 15)[12]

A third factor undermining the likeness with primary world mythologies, also pointed out by Vanderbeke & Turner, is the fact that versions of the same tale allegedly told by narrators of different races, can be remarkably similar in outlook (13-16).

While this probably will remain a matter of debate, we must also realise that Tolkien's legendarium as it was published after his death does not look the way it does today by his own intent. It does so, because enough readers demanded "more Middle-earth" to make publishing his numerous manuscripts commercially viable. That his son Christopher, who used to work with him and probably knew Tolkien the mythmaker better than anyone, not only went along with this but dedicated the rest of his days to making its publication possible,[13] suggests that his father would not have been adamantly opposed to this We can't be entirely sure, though, that he wouldn't have thrown out at least some of the manuscripts if he had foreseen it happening. Would someone who believes that 'the laws of contradiction' set bounds to an author's work (*Letters* 194, as quoted above) have wanted to publish more than one version, let alone several *conflicting* versions, of the same tales?

Given his attempts to create a *Silmarillion* in accordance with *The Lord of the Rings*, Tolkien's own intention was to leave a consistent and, harmonious oeuvre to the world. But "[h]e could not satisfactorily 'integrate' two different visions of his invented world: the mythical [...] with the historical" (Fimi 194). His great epic and its predecessor, the only Middle-earth tales published during his lifetime, are internally and mutually consistent; the

---

12 In order to make their point, they exaggerate the "monochromatic aspect" (15) of his work. The tone of say, 'The Tale of Tinúviel' and other 'Lost Tales' in *The Book of Lost Tales II*, or *The Hobbit*, is markedly different from say, 'The Ainulindalë' or 'The Narn I Hîn Húrin'. The Lost Tales were obviously superseded by later versions of these stories, but this does not apply to *The Hobbit*. Christofari implicitly disagrees with Vanderbeke & Turner: "The legends remain [...] a hybrid compilation: too diverse to pass as the work of one author alone" (Christofari 185).

13 For Christopher Tolkien's personal reasons to publish *The Silmarillion* and *The History of Middle-earth*, see the 'Forewords' to these publications in *S* (7-9) and *LT I* (1-12). The latter contains, among other things, a defence against the allegation that he completed *The Silmarillion* with his own inventions.

one passage of which two conflicting versions existed at some point, Bilbo's account of how he came by the Ring, was harmonised (or retconned, as it would be called nowadays). In fact, the diversity and fragmentation which makes Tolkien's Legendarium resemble real world mythologies is a by-product of the decision to give the myriads of fans access to the Professor's hitherto unpublished work.

The final and major problem created by Tolkien's tinkering is, that his second thoughts about the texts written earlier in his life contributed to his inability to present a finished *Silmarillion*, this work so close to his heart, to an eagerly waiting audience. He was increasingly painting himself into a corner. Maybe this was indeed a matter of decline, to use Conolly's term. It has been suggested that Tolkien's craft was waning and that this is what his swan song, *Smith of Wootton Major*, is predominantly about. Tolkien called it "an old man's book" (*Letters* 389), and in 'Suggestions for the ending of the story' published in the extended edition of 2005 he writes: "a time comes for writers and artists, when invention and 'vison' cease and they can only reflect on what they have seen and learned" (*SWM* 81). Tom Shippey noted that "[d]efeat hangs heavy in Smith of Wootton Major" (243). This may very well have been an important factor. Perhaps Tolkien began to concentrate on theological tenets and scientific facts because the wellspring of his imagination was drying up.

This does not mean he became a bad storyteller: *Smith of Wootton Major* is among the best things he wrote, and some of the later additions to the *Silmarillion* are obviously inspired. For pages and pages the 'Athrabeth', the theological and philological discourse of Finrod and Andreth, is mainly of interest to hardcore Tolkien fans and scholars – until it culminates in a beautiful, tragic love story. A story that breathes life into the preceding debate and has inspired dozens of fanfics in several languages at Fanfiction.net, and over a hundred drawings at DeviantArt.[14] Even a Tolkien in decline was still a genius, but the decline should not be ignored.

---

14 https://www.fanfiction.net/search/?keywords=Andreth&ready=1&type=story
https://www.deviantart.com/whats-hot/?section=&global=1&q=andreth&offset=0

On the other hand, it is hard to imagine a Tolkien who never even considered rewriting the *Silmarillion* material of his younger years. Those were the days when the storyteller and the world-builder balanced each other out, the days that saw the birth of some of his greatest stories and the rise of Arda. That the worldbuilder later went a bit further than just rooting the Third Age tales and some of their characters more firmly in the storyteller's work seems less of a problem than if he had never tinkered at all.

About the Author

RENÉE VINK studied Scandinavian languages and German in Leiden and Gothenburg. She has translated several texts by Tolkien into Dutch, among them his *Beowulf*, the poetry in *The Legend of Sigurd and Gudrún*, and *Beren and Lúthien*. Also, she is a co-founder of Unquendor, the Dutch Tolkien Society, and has authored a number of papers on Tolkien for journals like *Tolkien Studies*, *Hither Shore*, and *Lembas Extra*. In 2012 her monograph *Wagner & Tolkien: Mythmakers* appeared. In the past Renée was active as an author of medieval mystery stories (in Dutch).

Abbreviations

H	TOLKIEN, J.R.R. *The Hobbit*. First published London: George Allen & Unwin, 1937. Revised edition 1951.
Letters	*The Letters of J.R.R. Tolkien*. Ed. Humphrey Carpenter with the assistance of Christopher Tolkien. London: George Allen & Unwin, 1981.
LR	TOLKIEN, J.R.R. *The Lost Road*. The History of Middle-earth, Vol. V. London: Unwin Hyman, 1987.
LT I	TOLKIEN, J.R.R. *The Book of Lost Tales I*. The History of Middle-earth, Vol. I. London: George Allen & Unwin, 1983.
MR	TOLKIEN, J.R.R. *Morgoth's Ring*. The History of Middle-earth, Vol. X. London: HarperCollins, 1994.
PME	TOLKIEN, J.R.R. *The Peoples of Middle-earth*. The History of Middle-earth, Vol. X. London: HarperCollins, 1996.
S	TOLKIEN, J.R.R. *The Silmarillion*. London: George Allen & Unwin, 1977.
SME	TOLKIEN, J.R.R. *The Shaping of Middle-earth*. The History of Middle-earth, Vol. IV. London: Allen & Unwin, 1986.

SWM   TOLKIEN, J.R.R. *Smith of Wootton Major*. Extended edition. Ed. Verlyn Flieger. London: HarperCollins, 2005.

TOFS   *Tolkien On Fairy-stories*. Expanded edition, with commentary and notes. Ed. Verlyn Flieger & Douglas A. Anderson. London: HarperCollins, 2008.

UT   TOLKIEN, J.R.R. *Unfinished Tales of Númenor and Middle-earth*. London: George Allen & Unwin, 1980.

Bibliography

ACKS, Alex. 'Tolkien's Map and The Messed Up Mountains of Middle-earth'. Tor.com, August 1, 2017. https://www.tor.com/2017/08/01/tolkiens-map-and-the-messed-up-mountains-of-middle-earth/ (accessed 15-10-2017)

'Tolkien's Map and the Perplexing River Systems of Middle-earth'. Tor.com, October 10, 2017. https://www.tor.com/2017/10/10/tolkiens-map-and-the-perplexing-river-systems-of-middle-earth/ (accessed 15-10-2017)

CHRISTOFARI, Cécile. 'The Chronicle Without an Author: History, Myth and Narration in Tolkien's Legendarium'. *Sub-creating Middle-earth. Constructions of Authorship in the Works of J.R.R. Tolkien*. Ed. Judith Klinger. Zurich & Jena: Walking Tree Publishers, 2012. 173-190.

CONOLLY, John. *The Book of Lost Things*. Illustrated paperback edition. London: Hodder & Stoughton, 2017.

DROUT, Michael D. C. *J.R.R. Tolkien Encyclopedia. Scholarship and Critical Assessment*. New York and London: Routledge, 2007.

FIMI, Dimitra. *Tolkien, Race and Cultural History. From Fairies to Hobbits*. Basingstoke and New York: Palgrave MacMillan, 2008.

FURNISS, Timothy R. *High Towers and Strong Places. A Political History of Middle-earth*. Toronto: Oloris Publishing, 2016. e-book version.

KILBY, Clyde S. *Tolkien & The Silmarillion*. Wheaton, Illinois: Harold Shaw, 1976

LAKOWSKI, Romuald I. 'The Fall and Repentance of Galadriel'. *Perilous and Fair. Women in the Works and Life of J.R.R. Tolkien*. Ed. Janet Brennan Croft and Leslie A. Donovan. Altadena: Mythopoeic Press, 2015. 153-167.

NAGY, Gergely. 'The Great Chain of Reading: (Inter)textual relations and the technique of mythopoesis in the Túrin story'. *Tolkien the Medievalist*. Ed. Jane Chance. London and New York: Routledge, 2003. 239-258.

Parma Eldalamberon. *Journal of the Elvish Linguistic Fellowship*. Ed. Christopher Gilson, 1988-

Rateliff, John D. *The History of The Hobbit*. (One Volume edition). London: HarperCollins, 2011.

Shippey, Tom. *The Road to Middle-earth*. 2nd ed. London: Grafton, 1992.

Tolkien, J.R.R. *The Hobbit*. First published London: George Allen & Unwin, 1937. Revised edition 1951.

The Lord of the Rings. London: George Allen & Unwin, 1954-55.

'Tree and Leaf'. In *Tolkien, Tree and Leaf, Smith of Wootton Major, The Homecoming of Beorthnoth*. London: Unwin Paperbacks, 1975. 7-102

The Silmarillion. London: George Allen & Unwin, 1977.

Unfinished Tales of Númenor and Middle-earth. London: George Allen & Unwin, 1980.

The Letters of J.R.R. Tolkien. Ed. Humphrey Carpenter with the assistance of Christopher Tolkien. London: George Allen & Unwin, 1981.

The Book of Lost Tales I. The History of Middle-earth, Vol. I. London: George Allen & Unwin, 1983.

The Book of Lost Tales II. The History of Middle-earth, Vol. II. London: George Allen & Unwin, 1984.

The Shaping of Middle-earth. The History of Middle-earth, Vol. IV. London: Allen & Unwin, 1986.

The Lost Road. The History of Middle-earth, Vol. V. London: Unwin Hyman, 1987.

The Return of the Shadow. The History of Middle-earth, Vol. VI. London: Unwin Hyman, 1988.

The Treason of Isengard. The History of Middle-earth, Vol. VII. London: Unwin Hyman, 1989.

The War of the Ring. The History of Middle-earth, Vol. VIII. London: Unwin Hyman, 1990

Sauron Defeated. The History of Middle-earth, Vol. IX. London: HarperCollins, 1992

Morgoth's Ring. The History of Middle-earth, Vol. X. London: HarperCollins, 1994.

The Peoples of Middle-earth. The History of Middle-earth, Vol. X. London: HarperCollins, 1996.

The History of Middle-earth Index. London: HarperCollins, 2002.

Smith of Wootton Major. Extended edition, ed. Verlyn Flieger. London: HarperCollins, 2005.

Tolkien On Fairy-stories. Expanded edition, with commentary and notes. Ed. Verlyn Flieger & Douglas A. Anderson. London: HarperCollins, 2008.

TYELLAS. 'The Unnatural History of Tolkien's Orcs' *Lembas Extra* 2010. Ed. Cecile van Zon. Tolkien Genootschap Unquendor, 75-85.

VANDERBEKE, Dirk & Allan TURNER, 'The One or the Many? Authorship, Voice and Corpus.' *Sub-creating Middle-earth. Constructions of Authorship in the World of J.R.R. Tolkien*. Ed. Judith Klinger. Zurich & Jena: Walking Tree Publishers, 2012. 1-19.

VINK, Renée, 'The Parentage of Gil-galad – a textual history.' *Lembas Extra* 2010. Ed. Cecile van Zon. Leiden: Tolkien Genootschap Unquendor, 35-44.

YESKOV, Kirill, 'Why I reimagined "LOTR" from Mordor's perspective.' SALON, 24-02-2011. http://www.salon.com/2011/02/23/last_ringbearer_explanation/ (accessed 01-09-2017).

Jonathan Nauman   199

Composition as Exploration: Fictional Development in J.R.R. Tolkien's *The Lord of the Rings*

Abstract

Tolkien's remarks about the composition of *The Lord of the Rings* often seem to imply that he experienced the writing of his heroic romance as exploration, encountering important figures and aspects of Middle-earth rather than intentionally inventing them. This paper compares these authorial contentions with evidence available in Christopher Tolkien's manuscript histories, focusing especially on the emergences of Treebeard and of Aragorn King Elessar, characters whose natures changed considerably as the narrative developed. The details of Tolkien's production and revision indicate a dynamic and revelatory approach to worldbuilding, the author accepting cues from his developing characters and their narratives in a manner analogous and relevant to his practices in linguistic invention.

When J.R.R. Tolkien received letters asking how he had managed to produce *The Lord of the Rings*, he would sometimes provide in reply memorable details from his two decades of composition: how some aspects of the narrative were long foreseen, how some figures and incidents had emerged unexpectedly, how the story had at certain points and times come to a halt.[1] He would also often express strong disapproval toward any attempts to read his work as topical commentary or veiled autobiography, observing that the plot of *The Lord of the Rings* had developed primarily to meet the practical challenges of creating a publishable sequel to *The Hobbit*, and that the consistency and imaginative atmosphere of the tale depended on longstanding linguistic and mythological constructs that he hoped to present more completely in work yet to be published. In many cases Tolkien would deliver along with these analyses and caveats brief narrative accounts of his own compositional experience, couched in terms one would normally associate with exploration and discovery rather than with authoring a story; indeed, Tolkien was inclined to highlight

---

1 These testimonies to the nature of his own artistic efforts were perhaps expressed most completely and succinctly in the 1965 Foreword to *The Lord of the Rings*, first printed in America for the new (authorized) Ballantine edition (*FR* 8-12).

this choice of terminology by explicitly contesting the idea that the mode of his writing was unusually inventive. "I have long ceased to *invent*," he wrote in one draft reply, a few months after the final volume of *The Lord of the Rings* emerged. "I wait till I seem to know what really happened. Or till it writes itself" (*Letters* 231).

One of Tolkien's more extensive experiential accounts of composition can be seen in a letter to W. H. Auden, answering a request for "a few 'human touches' in the form of information about how the book came to be written."[2] Following his usual pattern, Tolkien places his fictional work in the context of his linguistic inventions, denies "that the main idea of the story was a war-product," and proceeds to recount how he as writer experienced the transition from *The Hobbit* to *The Lord of the Rings*, adding some information about vagaries encountered during the composition of the heroic romance itself.

> I had no conscious notion of what the Necromancer stood for (except for ever-recurrent evil) in *The Hobbit*, nor of his connexion with the Ring. But if you wanted to go on from the end of *The Hobbit*, I think the Ring would be your inevitable choice as the link. If then you wanted a large tale, the Ring would at once acquire a capital letter; and the Dark Lord would immediately appear. As he did, unasked, on the hearth at Bag End as soon as I came to that point. So the essential Quest started at once. But I met a lot of things on the way that astonished me. Tom Bombadil I knew already; but I had never been to Bree. Strider sitting in the corner at the inn was a shock, and I had no more idea who he was than had Frodo. The Mines of Moria had been a mere name; and of Lothlórien no word had reached my mortal ears till I came there. Far away I knew there were the Horse-lords on the confines of an ancient Kingdom of Men, but Fangorn Forest was an unforeseen adventure. I had never heard of the House of Eorl nor of the Stewards of Gondor. Most disquieting of all, Saruman had never been revealed to me, and I was as mystified as Frodo at Gandalf's failure to appear on September 22. I knew nothing of the *Palantíri*, though the moment the Orthanc-stone was cast from the window, I recognized it, and knew the meaning of the "rhyme of lore" that had been running in my mind: *seven stars and seven stones and one white tree*. (*Letters* 216-17)

While Tolkien would not have been aiming for exactitude in this casual retrospective provided for human-interest publicity, comparison with Christopher Tolkien's findings in the manuscript histories of *The Lord of the Rings* seems

---

[2] From Humphrey Carpenter's headnote to Tolkien's 7 June 1955 letter to Auden (#163), summarizing Auden's request (*Letters* 211).

generally to confirm his recollections.³ And for the reflections and analyses that I intend to pursue here, it is especially interesting to note how Tolkien's conditional observations about the practicality of choosing the Ring as a link between *The Hobbit* and *The Lord of the Rings* modulate into narrative accounts of composition in which the Dark Lord appears "unasked," Strider's presence is "a shock," Fangorn Forest "unforeseen," Saruman unknown, and the *palantír* a sudden revelation. Tolkien clearly means to portray *The Lord of the Rings* as a text more emergent than foreseen, characters and events revealed in composition rather than being consciously designed or implemented.⁴ These descriptions, suggesting that the work had while underway a will of its own, are (again) largely corroborated in the manuscript histories, in which one can observe Tolkien following hints surfacing incidentally during composition and responding to cues for changes in character or plot emerging from the story, the tale itself evidently enabling its author to realize "what really happened." It might be said that, for Tolkien, world-building entailed an inclination to "sit and hearken" to his own narrative, a willingness to delegate to his own created characters abilities analogous to those given by Ilúvatar to the Ainur: "ye shall show forth your powers in adorning this theme, each with his own thoughts and devices, if he will" (*S* 15).⁵ Tolkien certainly considered all of his story to be his own creation – "it is written in my life-blood," he once observed, "such as that is, thick or thin" (*Letters* 122), and "I have exposed my heart to be shot at" (*Letters* 172). But as these metaphors would indicate, his attitude toward his fictional writings was not only or even primarily that of craftsman to artifact but quasi-parental; and his recounted and evident experiences in composition seem certainly to have contributed to his feeling that an author "has not much

---

3 Tolkien could be said to telescope his actual process in some of the examples, as will be noted below particularly in the cases of Fangorn and Strider. With regard to the *palantír*, for instance, Tolkien did change the nature of Wormtongue's missile in mid-composition, but the change occurred during a redraft, not during the first sketch of the scene (*WR* 65).
4 It might be noted that Tolkien did profess *The Lord of the Rings* to be "a fundamentally religious and Catholic work; unconsciously so at first, but consciously in the revision" (*Letters* 172). But for Tolkien this meant that there was no essential moral or philosophical contradiction between the clear human import of his fiction and the teachings of his Roman Catholic faith. During the writing of *The Lord of the Rings* he held that subcreated worlds could legitimately feature anthropologies and theologies differing from those of the primary world, and that such imaginary variants, proffered candidly as fictions, were "capable of elucidating truth" in their real-life contexts (*Letters* 189, footnote).
5 For Tolkien, characters truly subcreated would always possess "an incalculable element," differentiating them from allegorical types (*Letters* 233).

more share in his writings than in his children of the body" (*Letters* 122).[6] This perception of his unfolding narratives and emerging secondary world as a project more facilitated than controlled would also color his musings about the cultural phenomenon of the work's popular success, as surprising to Tolkien himself as it was to his publishers and to twentieth-century literary elites. When a visiting aficionado of *The Lord of the Rings* once challenged Tolkien about any pretensions he might have to being the exclusive originator and orchestrator of his heroic romance, Tolkien did not insist on his own agency, but instead took note that the visitor's admonitions resonated with the words of one of his legendarium's leading characters: here Tolkien considered himself to be listening externally to a voice that he had predictably treated during composition as authoritative and insightful.

> A few years ago I was visited in Oxford by a man whose name I have forgotten (though I believe he was well-known). He had been much struck by the curious way in which many old pictures seemed to him to have been designed to illustrate *The Lord of the Rings* long before its time. He brought one or two reproductions. I think he wanted at first simply to discover whether my imagination had fed on pictures, as it clearly had been by certain kinds of literature and languages. When it became obvious that, unless I was a liar, I had never seen the pictures before and was not well acquainted with pictorial Art, he fell silent. I became aware that he was looking fixedly at me. Suddenly he said: "Of course you don't suppose, do you, that you wrote all that book yourself?" Pure Gandalf![7] I was too well acquainted with G. to expose myself rashly, or to ask what he meant. I think I said: "No, I don't suppose so any longer." I have never since been able to suppose so. An alarming conclusion for an old philologist to draw concerning his private amusement. (*Letters* 413)

For Tolkien, subcreated characters not only provided aid in their own story's construction, but also could critique the writer himself.

It seems likely that any sort of literary composition pursued with the intensity necessary to induce what Tolkien called Secondary Belief would in some mode often feature the authorial experiences to which Tolkien testified: sudden emergence of images, changes in character, unexpected redirections in plot and action.

---

6 See also Tolkien's 1971 letter to Carole Batten-Phelps (cited below): "of course *The L. R.* does not belong to me. It has been brought forth and must now go its appointed way in the world, though naturally I take a deep interest in its fortunes, as a parent would of a child" (*Letters* 413).
7 Tolkien seems here to be remembering the last paragraphs of *The Hobbit*, in which Gandalf says to Bilbo Baggins, "You don't really suppose, do you, that all your adventures and escapes were managed by mere luck, just for your sole benefit?" (*Hobbit* 286).

Tolkien's persistent forays into intrinsically driven composition were remarkable not so much in their occurrence as in their genre, an observation anticipated in Tolkien's literary manifesto 'On Fairy-stories'. "The inner consistency of reality" necessary for Secondary Belief, Tolkien said,

> is more difficult to produce, the more unlike are the images and the rearrangements of primary material to the actual arrangements of the Primary World. It is easier to produce this kind of "reality" with more "sober" material. Fantasy thus, too often, remains undeveloped; it is and has been used frivolously, or only half-seriously, or merely for decoration: it remains merely "fanciful". (*TOFS* 60-61)

Tolkien acknowledged that it would not be easy for fantasy to achieve the seamless topographical, social, and psychological verisimilitudes generally praised as "realism" in the modern novel, but he suggested, probably on basis of ongoing experience, that labor, thought, and "special skill" could in fact accomplish this "most nearly pure form of narrative art" (*TOFS* 60), "storytelling in its primary and most potent mode" (*TOFS* 61). Clearly Tolkien owed some of the confidence with which he embraced the demanding labors required to produce consistent fantasy narratives to his earlier achievements in language creation, efforts that had included carefully warranted extensions of aesthetically generated linguistic motifs. In this creative activity he had been quite conscious of how ongoing individual, philological, and grammatical speculation and elaboration could intensify and enable linguistic effects he wished to produce (*ASV* 24-26). Mythological accounts and legends, which he considered cognates and living outgrowths of linguistic generation (*ASV* 23-24), could be pursued with a similar ramifying acumen on the narrative level.[8]

Looking more closely at some examples of Tolkien's practices in composing will I think both reinforce and clarify his claims about composition as exploration. Certainly *The Lord of the Rings* was not produced by following a 'Grand Design' foreseen by its author; and at its beginning it had little "in the way of a plan, or even of a conception" (Shippey 335, 108). The groundbreaking heroic romance seems rather to have emerged largely through Tolkien's ability to listen to his

---

8 Tolkien noted that previous modern invented languages had been abortive through failure to produce a body of legends. "Volapük, Esperanto, Ido, Novial, &c &c are dead, far deader than ancient unused languages, because their authors never invented any Esperanto legends" (*Letters* 231). Dimitra Fimi and Andrew Higgins provide accounts of each of these International Auxiliary Languages and of Tolkien's developing responses to them in *ASV* xlii-lii.

work in progress, following and (with earlier linguistic and mythological efforts in mind) synthesizing leads that the developing story helped to provide.[9] One can observe these dynamics at work in the development of two memorable characters in *The Lord of the Rings*: the important secondary figure of Treebeard the Ent, and the remarkable central figure of Strider the Ranger, Aragorn King Elessar. Tolkien mentions both of these figures repeatedly in recounting his experiences as a writer, and they exemplify how his legendarium grew around and through his characters not only by spontaneous emergence of materials under the force of narrative momentum but also through analytical and contextual troubleshooting, a process that was in fact just as 'work-driven' as the first.

It is quite fitting to start with the case of Treebeard, since the emergence of the Ents occasioned some of Tolkien's most extensive reflections on his own creative process. In the same letter to Auden that termed the Fangorn Forest narratives in *The Lord of the Rings* "an unforeseen adventure," Tolkien presented – as an amusing "*post scriptum*" – a testimonial note detailing his authorial relationship to the Ents.

> I did not consciously invent [the Ents] at all. The chapter called "Treebeard," from Treebeard's first remark on p. 66,[10] was written off more or less as it stands, with an effect on myself (except for labour pains) almost like reading someone else's work. And I like Ents now because they do not seem to have anything to do with me. I daresay something had been going on in the "unconscious" for some time, and that accounts for my feeling throughout, especially when stuck, that I was not inventing but reporting (imperfectly) and had at times to wait till "what really happened" came through. But looking back analytically I should say that Ents are composed of philology, literature, and life. They owe their name to the *eald enta geweorc*[11] of Anglo-Saxon, and their connexion with stone. Their part in the story is due, I think, to my bit-

---

9 The way I describe Tolkien's process here derives in part from the compositional directives and theories of American fantasist Madeleine L'Engle, who was inclined to characterize works of art as external entities with whom artists cooperate; see *Walking On Water* 22-23. Tolkien's own beliefs about composition, though in some ways similar to L'Engle's, actually entailed an even less transcendental and leading role for the author. As Tom Shippey has observed, "he thought that ideas were sent to him in dreams, and through the hidden resonances of names and languages," and that these dreams and ideas "did not come from his own mind but might [...] be the record or memory of something that once might have had an objective existence" (Shippey 339). Both Tolkien's and L'Engle's approaches to composition included preternatural and communicative assumptions that would connect successful fantasy less with personal invention than with good listening.
10 That is, Treebeard's greeting to the hobbits Merry and Pippin, "Almost felt you liked the Forest! That's good! That's uncommonly kind of you" (*TT* 82-83).
11 [Editorial note (*Letters* 445)] From the Anglo-Saxon poem *The Wanderer*, 87: "*eald enta geweorc idlu stonden*," "the old creations of giants [i.e. ancient buildings, erected by a former race] stood desolate."

ter disappointment and disgust from schooldays with the shabby use made in Shakespeare of the coming of "Great Birnam wood to high Dunsinane hill": I longed to devise a setting in which the trees might really march to war. And into this has crept a mere piece of experience, the difference of the "male" and "female" attitude to wild things, the difference between unpossessive love and gardening. (*Letters* 211-12)[12]

One notices here that, while Tolkien claims that the Ents emerged spontaneously during composition, he does not claim this about Treebeard in particular. A character by the name of "Giant Treebeard" had been invented years before the Fangorn episodes were written, appearing in preliminary drafts of *The Fellowship of the Ring* as a tree giant who, either on his own initiative (*RS* 363) or as Saruman's jailor (*TI* 71), had held Gandalf prisoner and prevented the wizard from coming to the Shire before the Black Riders arrived in pursuit of the Ring. Treebeard was foreseen to be a huge and malicious giant "in league with the Enemy" (*RS* 384); but quite early in Tolkien's plans for his narrative[13] another possibility had been contemplated.

> If Treebeard comes in at all – let him be kindly and rather good? About 50 feet high with barky skin. Hair and beard rather like *twigs*. Clothed in dark green like a mail of short shining leaves. He has a castle in the Black Mountains and many thanes and followers (*RS* 410).

---

12 The circumstances of this letter must again be noted, since they modify and help to explain its ambivalence – in this passage, a strong claim of authorial non-involvement with Ents, both during writing and after, paired with hypotheses of "unconscious" motivations and analyses that plausibly link authorial interests in "philology, literature, and life" to the invention of Ents – their name from the Anglo-Saxon, their attack on Isengard fulfilling a wish to better a scene in *Macbeth*, the debates between Ent and Entwife reflecting Tolkien's own observations of "unpossessive love and gardening" as two modes of relating to the natural world. Tolkien was basically opposed to biographical readings of his work, a sentiment he openly shared when Auden asked to write a book about him (*Letters* 367), and he also considered critical analyses of *The Lord of the Rings* otiose at best (*Letters* 414); but here, while carefully stating that he found "'interpretations' quite amusing; even those that I might make myself" (*Letters* 211), he willingly provided human interest material as requested for Auden's "talk about *The Lord of the Rings* on the BBC Third Programme" (*Letters* 211), and even for the moment consented to use along with Auden the word "Trilogy" for *The Lord of the Rings*, a term he was inclined to dismiss as "a fudge thought necessary for publication" (*Letters* 221). Auden had been one of Tolkien's students, and in the 1940s he had returned to Anglican Christian practice in part through the influence of Charles Williams (Lindop 276). Tolkien considered him "a critic of distinction" (*Letters* 239) and also a friend (*Letters* 412); but while appreciating Auden's support and praise, he did not think that Auden had found "the right way of considering either Quests in general or my story in particular" (*Letters* 239).

13 That is, during the unsettled but important, even pivotal flurry of proposals and revisions with which Tolkien's efforts with *The Lord of the Rings* resumed in summer and fall of 1939 (*RS* 369-87, *TI* 5-17).

Here Treebeard is still conceived primarily as a giant,[14] and his trees are "of *vast* height [...]. Say 500-1000 feet" (*RS* 410), but the focus has begun to shift toward his eponymous role as leader of the tree-folk, and as Christopher Tolkien notices (*RS* 411), there is a first anticipation of the future military role of the Ents in opposing the armies of Saruman and Sauron in the War of the Ring. Development of the episode advances even farther in story outlines written about a year later,[15] where it is proposed that

> Merry and Pippin come up Entwash into Fangorn and have adventure with Treebeard. Treebeard turns out a decent giant. They tell him their tale. He is very perturbed by news of Saruman, and more so by the fall of Gandalf. (*TI* 210)

In yet another set of notes, also evidently composed well before the 'Treebeard' chapter, Tolkien speaks of the Ents quite distinctively, querying, "Did first lord of the Elves make Tree-folk in order to or through trying to understand trees?" (*TI* 411); and in these preliminaries his phrasing clearly anticipates the text of his forthcoming chapter:

> Treebeard is anxious for news. He never hears much. But he smells things in the air. Prefers breath from South and West of the Sea. Too much East wind these days. He is bothered about Saruman: a machine-minded man. Fondest of Gandalf. Very upset at news of his fall. Only one of the wizards who understood trees. (*TI* 411)

One wonders, then, in retrospect, how Tolkien came to feel that the Ents had emerged spontaneously during composition, and even more how he found himself recalling, less than two years after publication of *The Two Towers*, that

> though I knew for years that Frodo would run into a tree-adventure somewhere far down the Great River, I have no recollection of inventing Ents. I came at last to the point, and wrote the "Treebeard" chapter without any recollection of any previous thought: just as it now is. And then I saw that, of course, it had not happened to Frodo at all. (*Letters* 231)

I would suggest that, in addition to speculative plots having quickly receded from conscious memory, Tolkien did in fact experience a decisive and unconscious turn while composing this chapter, as he spontaneously defaulted to describing

---

14 Tolkien had written to his publishers that a giant would be featured in his *Hobbit* sequel (*Letters* 42, footnote).

15 On Richard Creswell Rowland's examination script, dated August 1940 (*TI* 67, 79). Preliminary outlines of this kind were for Tolkien a perennial writing strategy; see, for instance, his notes for the later chapters of *The Hobbit* as foreseen during composition of the Eagles episode (Rateliff 229-30).

the Ents exclusively as Tree-folk, completely subordinating the fairy-tale giant motif which had been a major component of the "tree-adventure" when it had been anticipated as happening to Frodo. It seems likely that, until the actual writing, Tolkien had not consciously rejected the figure of "Giant Treebeard," even though the concept of the Tree-folk had in fact already begun to grow in his imagination.[16]

While Tolkien's experience with the development of the Ents and Treebeard provides a relatively straightforward example of emergent worldbuilding, plot and character undergoing an almost unintended change such that one model for the narrative fell away to make way for another without the author consciously willing it, the case of Strider the Ranger shows a much more gradual and complex process at work, and also a much more dramatic change. So central is the character and so great the breadth of the mutation from Strider's first-draft appearance as Trotter the rustic hobbit (*RS* 137-38) to Aragorn King Elessar receiving the crown in "The Steward and the King" (*RK* 302-04) that one is tempted to find in the sequence something of a pageant for the transformation of the world of *The Hobbit* into that of *The Lord of the Rings*.[17] Tolkien's statement to Auden that "Strider sitting in the corner at the inn was a shock, and I had no more idea who he was than had Frodo" (*Letters* 216)[18] remained remarkably true for a significant portion of the composition of *The Fellowship of the Ring*, with Tolkien repeatedly asking himself in his manuscript notes, "Who is Trotter?"[19] One approach Tolkien used to answer this question was to follow leads provided in the preliminary scene, where Bingo Bolger-Baggins (an early-draft name for the character that became

---

16 See also Verlyn Flieger, 'The Green Man, the Green Knight, and Treebeard', which relates the change from giant to tree-shepherd to Tolkien's philological interest in different meanings of the word 'ent', and sees in Treebeard's emergent character a modern re-presentation of the archetypal 'Green Man' as a guardian of nature. Christopher Tolkien notes that his father's claim that the 'Treebeard' chapter underwent no revision was not totally accurate, although "the first draft is for the most part extraordinarily close to the final form" (*TI* 414). An explicit consideration of Tom Bombadil by Treebeard seems to have given way to the discourses and poems on the Entwives (*TI* 416, 419-20), and the Ents's march on Isengard seems to have been a sudden decision that interrupted the draft (*TI* 418).
17 Elizabeth M. Stephen considers the development of the character of Aragorn along these lines and more extensively in *Hobbit to Hero* (2012).
18 Tolkien's description of this character's surprising intrusion is remarkably similar to Madeleine L'Engle's recount of the sudden appearance of Joshua Archer in *The Arm of the Starfish* (1965); see *A Circle of Quiet* 94 and *Walking on Water* 182-83.
19 See, for example, *RS* 210, 214, 223, 374; *TI* 6.

Frodo) consulted with Butterbur the innkeeper about a strange figure sitting at a distant table.

> Suddenly Bingo noticed that a queer-looking, brown-faced hobbit, sitting in the shadows behind the others, was also listening intently. He had an enormous mug (more like a jug) in front of him, and was smoking a broken-stemmed pipe right under his rather long nose. He was dressed in dark rough brown cloth, and had a hood on, in spite of the warmth, – and, very remarkably, he had wooden shoes! Bingo could see them sticking out under the table in front of him.
>
> "Who is that over there?" said Bingo, when he got a chance to whisper to Mr. Butterbur. "I don't think you introduced him."
>
> "Him?" said Barnabas,[20] cocking an eye without turning his head. "O! that is one of the wild folk – rangers we call 'em. He has been coming in now and again (in autumn and winter mostly) the last few years: but he seldom talks. Not but what he can tell some rare tales when he has a mind, you take my word. What his right name is I never heard, but he's known round here as Trotter. You can hear him coming along the road in those shoes: clitter-clap – when he walks on a path, which isn't often. Why does he wear 'em? Well, that I can't say. But there ain't no accounting for East and West, as we say here, meaning the Rangers and the Shire-folk, begging your pardon." Mr. Butterbur was called away at that moment, or he might have whispered on in that fashion indefinitely (*RS* 137-38).

Comparing this passage with the first notice of Strider in *The Fellowship of the Ring* shows quite clearly how Tolkien's revisions often transformed "the significance of events and the identity of persons while preserving those scenes and the words that were spoken from the earliest drafts" (*RS* 5).

> Suddenly Frodo noticed that a strange-looking weather-beaten man, sitting in the shadows near the wall, was also listening intently to the hobbit talk. He had a tall tankard in front of him, and was smoking a long-stemmed pipe curiously carved. His legs were stretched out before him, showing high boots of supple leather that fitted him well, but had seen much wear and were now caked with mud. A travel-stained cloak of heavy dark-green cloth was drawn close about him, and in spite of the heat of the room he wore a hood that overshadowed his face; but the gleam of his eyes could be seen as he watched the hobbits.
>
> "Who is that?" Frodo asked, when he got a chance to whisper to Mr. Butterbur. "I don't think you introduced him."

---

20 Butterbur, who in this draft was presented as a hobbit (*RS* 134), had first name Barnabas in most early drafts of *The Lord of the Rings*. His name was changed to Barliman after Aragorn's sobriquet "Trotter" was changed to "Strider" (*SD* 78).

"Him?" said the landlord in an answering whisper, cocking an eye without turning his head. "I don't rightly know. He is one of the wandering folk – Rangers we call them. He seldom talks: not but what he can tell a rare tale when he has the mind. He disappears for a month, or a year, and then he pops up again. He was in and out pretty often last spring; but I haven't seen him about lately. What his right name is I've never heard: but he's known round here as Strider. Goes about at a great pace on his long shanks; though he don't tell nobody what cause he has to hurry. But there's no accounting for East and West, as we say in Bree, meaning the Rangers and the Shire-folk, begging your pardon. Funny you should ask about him." But at that moment Mr. Butterbur was called away by a demand for more ale and his last remark remained unexplained. (*FR* 214)

The situation and even much of the phrasing for this momentous début remained intact from earliest extant sketch to published copy; but the adjustments in tone and intensification of artistry are remarkable. Most obviously, the comedic tenor is gone, displaced backward in the published story onto Pippin's uncircumspect but entertaining "account of the collapse of the Town Hole in Michel Delving" (*FR* 214); and Butterbur's sudden departure, at first a piece of caricature, has become foreboding. The stranger is a man, not a hobbit, shod in mud-caked leather boots rather than wooden shoes, and his cloak has changed from brown to dark green, the color of Bilbo's traveling cloak in *The Hobbit* (*Hobbit* 42, *FR* 57). His intermittent absences now recall Gandalf's visits to Bag End (*FR* 75), and his classification as a Ranger is now immediately capitalized.

The history and nature of this pivotal character would become, in the author's opinion, "part of the essential story" of *The Lord of the Rings* (*Letters* 237), a renewal of "the chief of the stories of the *Silmarillion*" (*Letters* 149), the mythos of Beren and Lúthien. But it took much listening to draft character interactions, much troubleshooting, and many false starts before these correspondences surfaced; and for most of the journey the character's colloquial name remained Trotter. Bingo's initial response to the vagabond hobbit's request to join his party would indicate the new character's status for much of the first phases of composition: Trotter "had a dark look – and yet there was something in it, and in his speech which often strayed from the rustic manner of the rangers and Bree-folk, that seemed friendly, and even familiar" (*RS* 154). After Trotter's successful leading of the hobbit party to Rivendell in the first draft, Bingo would become even more curious along similar lines. "It's an odd thing, you know," he would say there to Gandalf, "but I keep on feeling that I have seen him somewhere before – that,

that I ought to be able to put a name to him, a name different to Trotter" (*RS* 211). Here was a lead that Tolkien would consider and pursue in a number of different directions: perhaps Trotter was actually Bilbo Baggins himself (*RS* 223) – although this would be awkward in view of the earlier book's statement that Bilbo "remained very happy to the end of his days" (*Hobbit* 285); or perhaps he was "Folco Took (Bilbo's first cousin)" (*RS* 223), one of the young hobbits who had been inspired by Gandalf to go "off into the Blue for mad adventures" (*Hobbit* 19). But just as the concept of the Tree-folk had emerged as a background consideration during plans for a foreseen episode with "Giant Treebeard," another possibility for Trotter arose in the context of his being first sighted in Bree, a town over whose nature Tolkien had vacillated, envisioning it first as populated by a mixture of Big and Little Folk (*RS* 132), and then as an outpost inhabited entirely by hobbits (*RS* 133ff). In a series of notes entitled "Queries and Alterations," before returning to the beginning of the narrative for his "second phase" of composition, Tolkien entertained a third alternative, "Bree-folk are *not* to be hobbits" – and, immediately following, took this idea a step forward, "Rangers are best *not* as hobbits, perhaps" (*RS* 223). For the moment, this inferential possibility was left aside in favor of considering possible Hobbit backgrounds for Trotter, but the idea of Rangers as Men would begin to grow in Tolkien's imagination alongside the debates over Trotter's identity. A quick second phase of composition yielded to a third,[21] and Tolkien returned to his initial conception of Bree as a colony for both Men and Hobbits. This time "he found it difficult to achieve" a satisfactory description of Bree (*RS* 331), perhaps in part because of increased uncertainties about the Rangers and about Trotter.[22] Amidst repeated efforts to draft the first paragraphs of "At the Sign of the Prancing Pony" – Christopher Tolkien describes "version after version soon trailing off, to be replaced by the next" (*RS* 331) – Tolkien included in many cases a passage describing the Rangers as "mysterious wanderers that the Men of Bree regarded with deep respect (and a little fear),

---

21 The rewriting classified by Christopher Tolkien as the "second phase" proceeded only as far as the House of Tom Bombadil. Tolkien then returned to the beginning for a "third phase" of composition, which seems to have been started in late autumn of 1938 (*RS* 309). In this new draft, the name of the leading hobbit was Frodo rather than Bingo.

22 The discomfort could also be described as a divergence in overall imaginative direction for the story at large. While Tolkien was consciously pursuing a heritage for Trotter in *The Hobbit*, his feelings for the Rangers were beginning to lean toward earlier tales and the higher mythologies of *The Silmarillion*. In terms of Mark Wolf's theories of world-building, the author was poised between possible back-stories available within his developing legendarium (202-05).

since they were said to be the last remnant of the kingly people from beyond the Seas" (*RS* 331). However, this description was not finally chosen for the ongoing draft, which included instead a passage reinforcing the earlier idea of "Ranger" as a general term for a vagabond.

> In the wild lands east of Bree there roamed a few unsettled folk (men and hobbits). These the people of the Bree-land called Rangers. Some of them were well-known in Bree, which they visited fairly frequently, and were welcome as bringers of news and tellers of strange tales. (*RS* 332)

This choice was also pursued in Butterbur's revised description of Trotter, though the innkeeper's observations were much more ambivalent and tentative than in the first draft.

> He is one of the wandering folk – Rangers, we call them. Not that he really is a Ranger, if you understand me, though he behaves like one. He seems to be a hobbit of some kind. (*RS* 332)

In the "third phase" Tolkien would continue to depict Trotter along the lines given in the current version of Gandalf's reference letter,[23] and he would develop an identification of Trotter as Peregrine Boffin, a young hobbit who had acquired adventure "wanderlust" under the influence of Gandalf's and Bilbo's stories (*RS* 379, 384-86). In Rivendell Frodo would finally recall having met Peregrine long ago in Buckland (*RS* 392-93), and it would be discovered that the Ranger hobbit had suffered torture and disfigurement of his feet when "caught and imprisoned by the Dark Lord" during pursuit of Gollum on the marches of Mordor (*RS* 401),[24] thus explaining his need to wear wooden shoes.

Yet even as he pursued these efforts committed to developing Trotter's identity as a hobbit, Tolkien would experience a remarkable counter-movement. Christopher Tolkien explains: "At this point, while in the middle of writing the second text [of an account of Frodo asking about Trotter's shoes,] my father wrote across it: '?? Trotter had better not be a hobbit – but a Ranger, remainder of Western Men, as originally planned'" (*RS* 393). Evidently by this point the rejected alternative explanation for the Rangers had become strong enough in Tolkien's artistic

---

23 "*I am giving this to a ranger known as Trotter: dark rather lean hobbit, wears wooden shoes. He is an old friend of mine, and knows a great deal. You can trust him.*" (*RS* 352).
24 Tolkien also seems to have briefly envisioned Trotter's capture to have occurred in Moria (*RS* 437-38, *TI* 10), and some resonance of this supposition was carried forward into the final draft (*FR* 387).

consciousness to be offered briefly without qualification as the straightforward meaning of "Ranger"; furthermore, the usage had become convincing enough to be perceived by the author, for the moment, and apparently inaccurately, as the term's earliest intended meaning. This intrusion was a sudden aesthetic intuition, not a deliberate rational decision, for in the event Tolkien "did not follow up his directive" (*RS* 393).[25] Trotter would in the ongoing draft remain a hobbit, Peregrine Boffin, both during the sojourn in Rivendell and also through the first telling of the journey to Moria, where Tolkien's composition would come to its next major stopping-place "by Balin's tomb" (*FR* 9, *RS* 461). Nevertheless, this sudden impulse to make the Trotter character a "kingly" Ranger, intervening even as Tolkien was successfully troubleshooting Trotter's hobbit identity, shows perhaps even more than the later emergence of the Ents and transformation of Treebeard the openness of Tolkien's sensibility to the promptings of his own legendarium. As the story continued, it became clear that this burgeoning intuition about Trotter and the Rangers was to be accepted. In an outline of prospective action written as he was composing the Caradhras episode, Tolkien would itemize the loss of Gandalf, Gandalf's eventual return, and an expectation that Trotter would lead the party after Gandalf's fall (*RS* 462). But as Christopher Tolkien has noticed (*RS* 431), the hobbits's vulnerability in the snows on the mountain pass would potentially show that Trotter's unfolding role was becoming incommensurate with his hobbit identity.[26] After a short period of vacillation in which Tolkien briefly entertained an idea that Trotter was an elf in disguise (*TI* 6), composed an account of Trotter as a Man "of Elrond's household" named Aragorn (*TI* 6-7), and also made a final attempt to reimagine Trotter as Peregrine Boffin (*TI* 7-8), a list of "*Final Decisions*" was written on 8 October 1939 that included a mandate that seems indeed to have held true in Tolkien's subsequent composition: "Trotter is not a hobbit but a real *ranger* who had gone to live in Rivendell after much wandering" (*TI* 8). Much retrospective revision would be needed to implement the decision, and there would be considerable troubleshooting over Trotter's real name, as Tolkien had still not settled on a linguistic heritage for the Rangers (*TI*

---

25 One can also see the intrusion's status as a sudden artistic prompting in Tolkien's continued use of the word "ranger" in the old "vagabond" sense even when accepting Trotter's change from Hobbit to Man; see for instance *TI* 7, "Aragorn pretends he is a ranger and hangs about Bree."
26 As Tolkien would later explain, the hobbits's stature valuably exhibited "in creatures of very small physical power, the amazing and unexpected heroism of ordinary men 'at a pinch'"; but their height "ranging between two and four feet" best indicated "plain unimaginative parochial man" and would not easily epitomize nobility and good leadership in the legendarium (*Letters* 158, *FR* 21).

291, *RK* 507). Under the magical eaves of the Golden Wood and through drafts of Galadriel's gift-giving, Aragorn's name would mutate to Elfstone, to Ingold, back to Elfstone (*TI* 236, 277-78), and then back to Aragorn again in a redraft of Boromir's farewell at the point of death (*TI* 381). As Tolkien's composition moved into what would become Book III of *The Lord of the Rings*, the narrative would refer to Aragorn by his true name more and more consistently (*TI* 384), but his colloquial name, especially at ease among hobbits, would remain Trotter through Isengard (*WR* 38, 49), Dunharrow (*WR* 246), Minas Tirith (*WR* 390, 417), and even in conversations at the Prancing Pony in Bree during the hobbits's return to the Shire (*SD* 76). The change of Aragorn's sobriquet from Trotter to Strider, first implemented in corrections to a third-draft manuscript during the writing of Book VI (*SD* 77-78), coincided with another name change, "Cosimo Sackville-Baggins" to "Lotho Sackville-Baggins." These final adjustments in nomenclature, which seem to reflect Tolkien's preference for applicability over "allegory or topical reference" (*FR* 10),[27] would complete the narrative's migration away from the frivolous overtones of the Ranger's first appearance. Under the pressures of his own narrative, Tolkien had produced Aragorn son of Arathorn, a kingly Númenorean of genial strength whose character could bear legitimate tasks of leadership, the keeping of order and preservation of good custom in absence of the elvish visions of the legendarium's past (*RK* 307-08).

The manuscript histories seem clearly to show that for Tolkien, worldbuilding emerged dynamically through composition. What then is to be said of Tolkien's externally-oriented exploratory descriptions of the process? Explanations he occasionally offered that would ground his art in personal psychology seem convincing only in a limited way; indeed, Tolkien openly presented these gestures as amusing deflections of inquiry. Probably more salient are his repeated insistences basing all of his fiction in creative linguistics, a preoccupation that he did not in the end perceive as a private hobby only. Composition was for Tolkien a revelatory phenomenon emanating from his response to the history of language at large,

---

27 The change from Cosimo to Lotho avoided the Machiavellian resonances associated with Cosimo de Medici, and the change from Trotter to Strider, in addition to bringing the sobriquet in line with the character's use of boots rather than wooden shoes, avoided any reminiscence of the anti-Catholic slur word bogtrotter. Another important alteration, conceived earlier (*TI* 10) but not implemented until corrections were made to the final typescript (*SD* 78), was Butterbur's change of first name from Barnabas to Barliman, which avoided reference to a Christian saint in a story meant to render "what happened in B.C. year X" (*Letters* 246).

effectively a vatic occupation: "he felt his use of the word as well as his study of it had carried him beyond imagination into a real vision of what he wrote, that the word itself was the light by which he saw."[28] It seemed possible to him that his fictional visions were accurate visions, linguistically mediated exfoliations of earlier human experience, delivering a closer approximation to the primal creative unities of language than would normally be possible to modernity.[29] Far-fetched as these contentions can seem amidst the regnant post-Saussurean linguistics of the contemporary academy (*ASV* xiv), it is clear that Tolkien experienced them as remarkably productive.

About the Author

JONATHAN NAUMAN has authored *The Franklin Trees*, a children's book. As Secretary of the Vaughan Association (USA), he often speaks on seventeenth-century poetry in England, Wales, and America.

Abbreviations

ASV TOLKIEN, John Ronald Reuel. *A Secret Vice*. Ed. Dimitra Fimi and Andrew Higgins. London: HarperCollins, 2016.

FR TOLKIEN, John Ronald Reuel. *The Fellowship of the Ring*. New York: Ballantine Books, 1965.

Hobbit TOLKIEN, John Ronald Reuel. *The Hobbit*. New York: Ballantine Books, 1966.

Letters TOLKIEN, John Ronald Reuel. *The Letters of J.R.R. Tolkien*. Ed. Humphrey Carpenter. Boston: Houghton Mifflin, 1981.

RK TOLKIEN, John Ronald Reuel. *The Return of the King*. New York: Ballantine Books, 1965.

RS TOLKIEN, John Ronald Reuel. *The Return of the Shadow*. Ed. Christopher Tolkien. Boston: Houghton Mifflin, 1988.

---

28 Flieger, *Splintered Light* 9.
29 See Barfield 85-86: "the poesy felt by us to reside in ancient language consists just in this, that, out of our later, analytic, 'subjective' consciousness, a consciousness which has been brought about along with, and partly because of, this splitting up of meaning, we are led back to experience the original unity."

S	TOLKIEN, John Ronald Reuel. *The Silmarillion*. Ed. Christopher Tolkien. Boston: Houghton Mifflin, 1977.
SD	TOLKIEN, John Ronald Reuel. *Sauron Defeated*. Ed. Christopher Tolkien. Boston: Houghton Mifflin, 1992.
TI	TOLKIEN, John Ronald Reuel. *The Treason of Isengard*. Ed. Christopher Tolkien. Boston: Houghton Mifflin, 1989.
TOFS	TOLKIEN, John Ronald Reuel. *Tolkien On Fairy-stories. Expanded Edition with Commentary and Notes*. Ed. Verlyn Flieger and Douglas A. Anderson. London: HarperCollins, 2008.
TT	TOLKIEN, John Ronald Reuel. *The Two Towers*. New York: Ballantine Books, 1965.
WR	TOLKIEN, John Ronald Reuel. *The War of the Ring*. Ed. Christopher Tolkien. Boston: Houghton Mifflin, 1990.

Bibliography

BARFIELD, Owen. *Poetic Diction: A Study in Meaning*. Third edition. Middletown CT: Wesleyan University Press, 1973.

FLIEGER, Verlyn. *Splintered Light: Logos and Language in Tolkien's World*. Second edition. Kent OH: Kent State University Press, 2002.

'The Green Man, The Green Knight, and Treebeard: Scholarship and Invention in Tolkien's Fiction.' *Scholarship and Fantasy: Proceedings of The Tolkien Phenomenon, May 1992, Turku, Finland*. Ed. K.J. Battarbee. *Anglicana Turkuensia*, No. 12. Turku, Finland: University of Turku, 1993. 85-98.

LINDOP, Grevel. *The Third Inkling*. London: Oxford University Press, 2016.

L'ENGLE, Madeleine. *A Circle of Quiet: The Crosswicks Journal, Book I*. New York: Seabury Press, 1972.

Walking on Water: Reflections on Faith and Art. Wheaton IL: Harold Shaw, 1980.

RATELIFF, John D. *The History of The Hobbit. Part One: Mr. Baggins*. Boston: Houghton Mifflin, 2007.

SHIPPEY, Tom. *The Road to Middle-earth*. Revised Edition. London: HarperCollins, 2002.

STEPHEN, Elizabeth M. *Hobbit to Hero: The Making of Tolkien's King*. Moreton in Marsh, Gloucestershire: ADC Publications, 2012.

Tolkien, John Ronald Reuel. *The Fellowship of the Ring.* New York: Ballantine Books, 1965.

The Hobbit. New York: Ballantine Books, 1966.

The Letters of J.R.R. Tolkien. Ed. Humphrey Carpenter. Boston: Houghton Mifflin, 1981.

The Return of the King. New York: Ballantine Books, 1965.

The Return of the Shadow. Ed. Christopher Tolkien. Boston: Houghton Mifflin, 1988.

Sauron Defeated. Edited by Christopher Tolkien. Boston: Houghton Mifflin, 1992.

A Secret Vice. Ed. Dimitra Fimi and Andrew Higgins. London: HarperCollins, 2016.

The Silmarillion. Ed. Christopher Tolkien. Boston: Houghton Mifflin, 1977.

Tolkien On Fairy-stories. Expanded Edition with Commentary and Notes. Ed. Verlyn Flieger and Douglas A. Anderson. London: HarperCollins, 2008.

The Treason of Isengard. Ed. Christopher Tolkien. Boston: Houghton Mifflin, 1989.

The Two Towers. New York: Ballantine Books, 1965.

The War of the Ring. Ed. Christopher Tolkien. Boston: Houghton Mifflin, 1990.

Wolf, Mark J.P. *Building Imaginary Worlds: The Theory and History of Subcreation.* New York and London: Routledge, 2012.

Anahit Behrooz

Temporal Topographies: Mapping the Geological and Anthropological Effects of Time in J.R.R. Tolkien's Legendarium

Abstract

The many maps that J.R.R. Tolkien designed for his Middle-earth texts have been frequently considered in the context of worldbuilding and as tools for articulating the landscape, but their status as objects embedded with historical narratives has been largely overlooked. This paper positions Tolkien's maps as storytellers: as vehicles for depicting and negotiating Middle-earth's past ages. The ability of maps to record historical change becomes particularly important considering the unique relationship between the landscape and time in Tolkien's subcreation. Drawing on a catastrophic geological framework, each Age of Middle-earth is characterised by a cataclysmic change which entirely reconfigures the physical landscape. By considering the ways in which maps represent the passage of time and its effects on the physical landscape, and are thereby rendered historical documents, I aim to demonstrate how Tolkien exposes cartography's paradoxical attempt to fix a momentary interpretation of a world that is subject to the ravages of time, and how this works to articulate broader questions surrounding time, change, and loss.

Introducion

That the history of Middle-earth is predicated on enormous and consequential physical change is immediately obvious from Tolkien's framing of it as a "mythology for England". Tolkien's desire to create a "vast backcloth" of legends and tales for his country, and his insistence that Middle-earth should not be read as an "imaginary world" or another planet, but rather his own set in another, long ago time, immediately directs the reader's attention not only to the formation and existence of his subcreation, but also its inevitable destruction (*Letters* 144, 239). As John D. Rateliff succinctly put it,

> since Middle-earth is destined to become the world we see around us today, every wonder [...] [Tolkien] describes is doomed to pass away [...]. In a way, the whole epic of Middle-earth, from the Ainulindalë to the Restored Kingdoms of

Arnor and Gondor, is the world's longest line of dominos, set up with infinite care only to be knocked down. (Rateliff 67)

This geographical evolution is not only implicit in Tolkien's set-up of his world; it is illustrated at various points throughout the history of Middle-earth, a history which is marked by large-scale, often cataclysmic physical shifts. In this chapter, I will examine how Tolkien's Middle-earth maps both represent and speak to the physical changing of the world, and in particular the depiction of violent, geological change which characterises each Age of Middle-earth. By situating Tolkien's Middle-earth geology in a historical understanding of geological movements, I will demonstrate how his subcreation is based on a catastrophic model. I will then examine how certain Middle-earth maps respond to this geological framework and, more broadly, how the very existence of maps within such an extremely mutable world reveals the characters' own uncomfortable relationship with the passing of time and the changing of the world.

How does Middle-earth's landscape shift and change over the passing years? In the most extensive study of Middle-earth's invented geology, Gerard Hynes posits that Tolkien showed an awareness of new developments in the geological sciences in his depiction of the changing world, in particular drawing attention to how certain passages in the legendarium are reminiscent of the new theory of continental drift. Hynes argues that episodes such as Ossë dragging an island across the sea in *The Book of Lost Tales* and the thrusting away of Middle-earth from Valinor by the Valar in the 'Ambarkanta' gesture to the developing science of plate tectonics, demonstrating how the surface of the world can be mobile (Hynes 24). Hynes argues that Tolkien's embracing of such a contemporary scientific theory is emblematic of a wider geological framework in his legendarium: that of uniformitarianism.

A concept developed out of the Enlightenment, uniformitarianism argued that the world had been formed by gradual geological processes happening over deep time. This was in contrast to the other predominant belief, known as catastrophism, which theorised that the world was shaped by sudden, cataclysmic events. Catastrophism was largely informed by a desire to reconcile Christian narratives of the Flood and the Apocalypse with geology, and thus theorised a geological framework which incorporated, and was indeed based on, such violent catastrophes. It should be noted that catastrophists' theories were not necessarily overtly religious or supernatural; in his *Sacred Theory of the Earth* (1684-90), Thomas Burnet sought a theory that would explain the Flood without resorting to a *deus ex machina* explanation, arguing "They say in short, that God Almighty created waters on purpose to make the deluge, and then annihilated them again when the deluge was to cease; And this, in a few words, is the whole account of the business. This is to cut the knot when we cannot loose it"[1] (Gould 29). Thus, Burnet suggested instead that the earth's crust floated on a layer of water, which broke loose through the earth's surface at the time of the Flood. Nevertheless, despite such attempts at building scientific theses, religious beliefs remained fundamental to catastrophism. Thus, geological time frames of this period were based around biblical evidence: in the seventeenth century, Archbishop James Ussher tried to date the Creation, and thus the age of the earth, by using biblical genealogies, eventually calculating that the date of Creation was 4004 BC; John Lightfoot, vice-chancellor of Cambridge University, refined this to the morning of Sunday, October 23 4004 BC (Bowler 4).

Catastrophism, and the belief in what is now called Young Earth theory, persisted well into the nineteenth century. However, in the eighteenth century, uniformitarian beliefs were beginning to gain traction. The theory was developed and popularised by eighteenth-century geologist James Hutton and nineteenth-century geologist Charles Lyell, who noted that the earth was in a constant cycle of uplift and creation, and erosion and destruction, and that geological change was thus gradual rather than sudden (Gould 6). Hutton observed two key things: he recognised that granite, as an igneous rock, represented a counter to erosion, as new rock was constantly being created. He also theorised that the breaks in time represented by unconformities[2] found in the earth's crust were a result of a combination of erosion and new rock formation (Gould 6). Thus, Hutton theorised that as the earth was

---

1 There is an interesting parallel here between Burnet's conviction that God alone is not enough to explain cataclysms, and that a logical, scientific explanation is required, albeit underpinned by theological beliefs, and Tolkien's theories of subcreation. In 'On Fairy Stories', Tolkien asserts that it is not enough merely to create a world with a green sun; an "inner consistency of reality" is required to make the sun's greenness "credible" (*TL* 45).
2 An unconformity is defined as the meeting point of two layers of unconformable, that is to say periodically or materially different, strata (Allaby 523).

caught in these constant cycles of uplift and erosion, it could theoretically be millions of years old, thereby formulating the concept of deep time. Charles Lyell supported Hutton's theories in his three volume *Principles of Geology*, published 1830-33, by also linking the concept of a uniformitarian geology with the idea of deep time. Lyell compared the study of history to the study of geology; arguing that much as numerous events, both inconsequential and monumental, shaped the course of the former gradually over many years, the same principle of slow gradual change over time needed to be applied to the latter. This new conception of time naturally conflicted with the previous, biblically-motivated calculation. Although, as Peter J. Bowler notes, it would be a mistake to view uniformitarianism as entirely divorced from religion, particularly in the nineteenth century, the movement did represent a shift away from these theological models. With the arrival of the twentieth century came further uniformitarian discoveries which underlined the deep time theories of Hutton and Lyell and which removed religion from the equation entirely: in the early decades of the century it was discovered that certain elements were able to maintain the earth's central heat thanks to their radioactivity, and thus provide stable conditions for billions of years, thereby once more extending the timeline of the earth (Bowler 130). Around the same time, continental drift began to be theorised, which again supported the idea of topographical change occurring over long periods of time, and which moved even further from the previous religious model.[3]

Hynes argues that although much of Tolkien's work aligns with catastrophic ideas of world formation, his depiction of continental drift, itself a uniformi-

---

[3] Tolkien's own position on the age of the earth, particularly as a Catholic, is not as well established. In 1909, Pope Pius X ratified a decree which declared that the legitimacy of the first chapters of *Genesis* could not be questioned, particularly in regards to the creation of the world and the creation of man. Although the issue of a time frame is never specifically addressed, the decree nevertheless clearly advocated a literal reading. Anne M. Clifford suggests that this strict stance was an aggressive response to Darwin's theories of evolution which were undermining people's beliefs in the Creation story. However, throughout the eighteenth, nineteenth and twentieth centuries, an approach known as concordism was also practiced by many Christians of all denominations. Concordism attempted to reconcile Biblical and scientific theories; for example, the eighteenth-century scientist Buffon theorised that the six days of creation were in fact six "epochs", which would account for the long time frame required by new geological discoveries (Clifford 221-23). It is not known whether Tolkien subscribed to the Church's position or to the more liberal concordist approach. However, there is an interesting parallel between the concordist idea of the days of Creation lasting for epochs, and Tolkien's Valian Years, which were the measurement for time before the creation of the sun and the Awakening of Men, and which are much longer than a normal year span. It is therefore possible that Tolkien incorporated such religious frameworks within his own mythology.

tarian concept, and his comment in the 'Ambarkanta' on the earth changing "in the wearing and passing of many ages" (*SME* 240) is indicative of a uniformitarian perspective on geological change. As persuasive as Hynes' argument is, however, there is no doubt that Middle-earth's geological framework is a largely catastrophic one. Hynes himself acknowledges that episodes such as Ossë dragging an island or the Valar thrusting Middle-earth to sea, while hinting conceptually at uniformitarian theories such as plate tectonics, are nevertheless clearly catastrophic moments, isolated events in the history of the world instigated by powerful, uncontainable forces, rather than by constant and gradual natural forces. Tolkien's legendarium is filled with such moments. As discussed above, Tolkien describes how the Valar "thrust away Middle-earth at the centre and crowded it eastwards, so that it was bended [...] and the thrusting aside of the land caused also mountains to appear in four ranges" (*SME* 239), drawing a clear causal link between the foundation of new geological features (the mountains), and the action of the Valar. The word "appear" suggests an immediate effect, rather than a slow formation, again underlining the catastrophic nature of the act.

The end of the 'Ambarkanta' also touches on two of the fundamental catastrophic events which define the history of Middle-earth and its formation: the destruction of Beleriand at the end of the First Age and the drowning of Númenor at the end of the Second Age. In both instances, the world is described as being "broken" and "destroyed", highlighting how these events were unnatural, damaging, and negative, rather than part of a natural geological cycle. The 'Quenta' describes the destruction of Beleriand in greater detail:

> Thangorodrim was riven and cast down [...] so great was the fury of those adversaries that all the Northern and Western parts of the world were rent and gaping, and the sea roared in in many places; the rivers perished or found new paths, the valleys were upheaved and the hills trod down; and Sirion was no more [...] long was it ere [Men] came back over the mountains to where Beleriand once had been. (*SME* 157)

The sudden and entire destruction of this part of the world is emphasised through a language of reversal: low valleys are "upheaved", high hills are "trod down", and water both disappears from old river beds and appears in new places. The world has thus literally been turned upside down. The finality of "where Beleriand once had been" emphasises the cataclysmic nature of the event, and is echoed later in the 'Annals of Beleriand', which end with "and Beleriand was no more" (*SME* 310). Again, this works to portray this as a radical, seismic shift in the topography of Middle-earth.

The drowning of Númenor is both conceptually and descriptively as drastic an event. Both in terms of Middle-earth's worldbuilding and its mythology, the drowning of Númenor is a key moment, as it is here that the flat earth concept which Tolkien originally conceived is altered and the world changed into a globe. The description in 'The Fall of Númenor' is violent: Valinor is described as being "sundered" from the earth, causing a "rift" to appear in the sea (*LR* 15). Much like the description of the fate of Beleriand, the language here is one of absence, with parts of the old world being physically lost or removed. The description of the globing of the world is also very striking. Tolkien describes how "Ilúvatar gave power to the Gods, and they bent back the edges of the Middle-earth, and they made it into a globe" (*LR* 16). The use of the active voice emphasises how these changes are being enacted upon the earth by external forces, rather than from natural forces within, and thus emphasises the unusual, cataclysmic nature of the event.

What is also notable about each of these episodes is their unnatural, indeed their supernatural, character. While uniformitarian theory ultimately removed God from geology, catastrophism was very frequently linked with divine intervention, and Tolkien models Middle-earth's geology on this characteristic very closely. Each cataclysmic shift in Middle-earth's history is the result of the gods' actions, whether indirectly, such as the Great Battle where Beleriand is destroyed through a large-scale conflict between the deities, or directly, such as in the 'Ambarkanta' or 'The Fall of Númenor', where the Valar are instrumental in repositioning and restructuring the world. This works to reinforce the catastrophic nature of these events, by aligning them with other catastrophic events in the cultural consciousness caused by divine intervention, such as the Flood.

Moreover, it is not only the actual geological process which is important, but also the conceptualisation of time which it indicates. Stephen Jay Gould has suggested that the fundamental difference between catastrophists and uniformitarians is not scientific, but rather philosophical. Each group has an entirely different understanding of how time functions, and their geological theories are fundamentally informed by this difference. Gould argues that catastrophists have a linear view of time, which he terms Time's Arrow, where "history is an irreversible sequence of unrepeatable events […] moving in a direction" (11). Uniformitarians, on the other hand, have a cyclical view of time, termed Time's Cycle, where "time has no direction" and individual events are part of repeating cycles, and thus have no causality (11). Although Gould's book *Time's Arrow, Time's Cycle* was published in 1987, and thus could not have influenced Tolkien's understanding of geology, his framework is a key sensitising concept for understanding the relationship between geology and time in Tolkien's work. Tolkien's subcreation, and in particular its background mythology, has a very fatalistic character. Every cataclysmic event in the history of Middle-earth is a product of a single event in the world's prehistory: that is, Melkor's musical deviation from the rest of the Ainur during the 'Ainulindalë' and his introduction of discord and evil into the world. This act is a catalyst for each of the physically disruptive moments in Middle-earth's history: the distancing of Valinor from the rest of the world, the Great Battle which ends with Melkor's imprisonment, and the drowning of Númenor, which is a result of an uprising by the Númenóreans encouraged by Sauron, Melkor's second in command. This fatalistic character is underscored by Mandos' prophecy which is woven into many of Tolkien's drafts, in particular the 'Quenta' in *The Shaping of Middle-earth*. This prophecy states that Morgoth will eventually escape from his prison behind the Door of Night, destroy the Sun and the Moon and lay waste to much of Middle-earth before finally being defeated (*SME* 165). This framework echoes numerous catastrophist mythologies such as the Christian Apocalypse or the Norse Ragnarök. It constructs time as a teleological, linear framework which brings it in line with catastrophists' theories on time as an "arrow", and contrasts it with the uniformitarians, who believed that the ongoing formation of the world revealed a construction of time with "no vestige of a beginning – no prospect of an end" (Gould 63).

Having established the relationship between deep time and the physical landscape of Middle-earth, how do Middle-earth's maps work to articulate this relationship? As the scale of physical change being discussed in this paper is relatively large, the maps I will be focusing on are small-scale; namely the map of Middle-earth, the Silmarillion map, the Ambarkanta maps, and the Númenor map.

Firstly, each of these maps works to visualise the physical changes being described in the text. This visualisation works particularly on the level of the extradiegetic reader who can immediately cross-reference the maps with the texts detailing the shaping of Middle-earth and trace the changes. The ability of the map to chart the process of time is not immediately as obvious on a diegetic level, as very often an immediate comparison between maps is needed to make the change explicit. However, in a few instances, a reading is possible which suggests that the diegetic Middle-earth mapmaker and map reader is aware of the enormous shifts in their world, and is attempting to record them. The third diagram of the Ambarkanta maps bears the inscription, "The World after the Cataclysm and the ruin of the Númenóreans". Similarly, the revised Middle-earth map found in *Unfinished Tales* is labelled "The West of Middle-earth at the End of the Third Age". Both of these cartographic paratexts embed not only time into the map, but also a sense of history and of passing: the Ambarkanta map points to the idea of a before and after, and a need for remapping, while the Middle-earth map, while less explicitly cataclysmic, situates the map very firmly at the closing of an era. As Stefan Ekman comments, "Apart from instilling a sense of finality, it accentuates the fact that Middle-earth has a past (three ages of it, at the very least) as well as a future, a Fourth Age from which it is possible to establish the end of the previous age" (61). The label in conjunction with the map makes explicit the link between this history and the topography of the landscape; the representation of the world is correct but may not be (and probably will not be) in relation to other ages of Middle-earth.

Another more explicit visualisation of the enormous shifts in landscape also appears in the Middle-earth map, in particular when read alongside the Silmarillion map, which illustrates Middle-earth during the First Age. The Silmarillion map depicts a range of mountains named the Ered Luin, which wind down the entire eastern border of the map in a straight line from north to south. These mountains are the only topographical element from the Silmarillion map to also be depicted on the Middle-earth map. On the Middle-earth map, however, they are depicted in the extreme west, and their long, unhalting line through the landscape is now disrupted: they curve along the coast in the north western corner of Middle-earth, and are then interrupted by the Gulf of Lhûn, before resuming again as a short range named the Blue Mountains. To the west of the mountains, just off the coast, is a small island named Himling, a name linguistically very similar to the similarly positioned mountain of Himring on the Silmarillion map. Christopher Tolkien confirms in *Unfinished Tales* that "Himling was the earlier form of Himring [...] it is clear that Himring's top rose above the waters that covered drowned Beleriand" (*UT* 13-14). In a worldbuilding framework where the landscape is constantly under physical upheaval and nomenclatures constantly change, it is striking that traces of the Ered Luin mountains and Himring remain, that their names remain the same or recognisably similar, and that they are depicted on both maps. By visualising the presence of certain places, Tolkien suggests the absence of others, implicating what has been destroyed by showing what remains, and thereby demonstrating the map's attempt to record the past and to illustrate the extreme physical change which the Middle-earth landscape has undergone.

Despite these attempts, these maps are still at odds with a world that is constantly and radically in flux. In his seminal work *The Power of Maps*, Denis Wood discusses the ability of the map to encode temporalities. Wood argues that a commonly perceived paradox of mapping, that "every map is out of date before it's printed", is in fact not true, and that "anything that changes fast enough to render the map genuinely obsolete before it can reach its audience doesn't belong in the map in the first place" (125). However, in a catastrophic framework where the topography of the world can entirely change within a very short span of time, maps can indeed become not only out of date but entirely obsolete. This is illustrated in *Unfinished Tales* in 'A Description of the Island of Númenor'. The physical description of the island is preceded by a short introduction which explains that the information within is "derived from descriptions and simple maps that were long preserved in the archives of the Kings of Gondor" (*UT* 165). With Númenor entirely gone, these maps can no longer serve their original, intended function as navigational tools and have thus become obsolete as maps. Instead, they have turned into narrative artefacts – objects which can offer a window into the past, and which can speak to the catastrophic nature of the world's geology, but which are otherwise redundant. Their placement within the archives of Gondor underscores their inadequacy as cartographic objects. Unlike other examples of maps in Tolkien's legendarium, such as Thror's Map in *The Hobbit* which is carried around by the characters and is constantly in use, the maps of Númenor have become static and fossilised as records of history rather than geography, rendered useless by the catastrophic nature of Middle-earth's geology.

The analogy of maps as fossils is a relevant one, particularly considering the period in which Tolkien was writing. By the end of the eighteenth century, fossils had become curios and objects of both scientific and commercial interest. Areas of England where they were abundant, such as Dorset and in particular Lyme Regis, became tourist attractions, and residents of these areas frequently collected fossils from the beaches to sell to tourists (Cadbury 6). Not everyone appreciated the scientific and historical implications of fossils, however; at a time when theories of uniformitarianism and deep time were still on the cusp of being discovered, the presence of stone-like animal remains where no other such animals lived caused great curiosity and confusion. Many turned to a supernatural explanation: fossils were people turned into snakes for their crimes, petrified thunderbolts from God, or the material spirits of animals (7-8). However, some naturalists and scientists began to recognise them for what they were: remnants of a geological past. In particular, French naturalist and zoologist Georges Cuvier worked on classifying fossils, extrapolating from fossilised remnants what the original animal might have looked like. Although Cuvier himself was a catastrophist, his research on fossils nevertheless informed the simultaneous discovery of deep time. Cuvier theorised the idea of extinction, arguing that fossils were an undeniable proof of animals which simply no longer existed in the nineteenth century. Although fossilised remains of animals such as a woolly mammoth in Siberia and a mastodon in America had been recovered at the end of the eighteenth century, one of the prevailing theories at the time was that these belonged to new, undiscovered species, rather than to ones which no longer existed (Bowler 109). By examining and comparing numerous fossils with the bones of animals living in the nineteenth century, Cuvier demonstrated the realities of extinctions, and how fossils acted as a record for what was no longer there.

Throughout the nineteenth century, fossils gained more and more popularity among the public. The entire skeletal remains of an ichthyosaurus in Lyme Regis uncovered by 12-year old Mary Anning in 1812 was one of the most important fossil discoveries of the period; the specimen was sold to keen fossil collector Henry Hoste Henley, who eventually sold it to the British Museum for their new Natural History department (Torrens 259). The Natural History Museum in London opened in 1881; the Natural History Museum in Oxford had opened some decades previously in 1850, and by Tolkien's time, fossils and palaeontology had become a part of the public consciousness and popular culture.[4] Tolkien himself had at the very least a passing, childhood interest in fossils. He holidayed four times in Lyme Regis, twice as a child and twice as an adult; on his second childhood trip, Hammond and Scull note that he searched for fossils in the cliffs and found a prehistoric jawbone (Scull and Hammond 12). Although it is not certain that the parallels between maps and fossils was a deliberate choice, or that the substitution of the former for the latter was consciously done, the striking parallels between fossils and maps demonstrates that Tolkien turned to other devices to provide the same sort of historical residue which fossils were providing elsewhere in contemporary science and popular culture. Much like fossils, Tolkien's maps too are a material remnant of past geological eras, conserved for their historical value and acting as windows into the past. Moreover, the maps too speak to the age of the world, by reifying the time span between what they depict and their present condition, and providing tangible proof of this passage of time. Much as fossils are the relics of what was once alive and moving, maps too are frozen examples of a much more complex world. The static nature of maps such as the Númenor maps in the Gondorian archives, both in terms of making static the landscape they depict, and their own static position within the archive, lends them many of the connotations of fossils – inert, dead, extinct – and emphasises both the extreme gap between

---

4 In E. Nesbit's *Five Children and It* (1902), the Psammead, a sand fairy dating back to prehistoric times, explains that fossils are the remains of wishes granted by sand fairies, as wishes would always turn to stone at the end of the day; at the end of Arthur Conan Doyle's *The Lost World* (1912), the scientist Sumerlee retires from teaching to classify chalk fossils; in Noel Streatfield's *Ballet Shoes* (1936), three adopted sisters are called Pauline, Petrova, and Posy Fossil, so named after their adoptive uncle who is a palaeontologist; in Howard Hawks' *Bringing Up Baby* (1938), the main character is a palaeontologist, shown to be working on a brontosaurus skeleton. For more on palaeontology in the nineteenth- and twentieth-century popular imagination, see Laurence Talairach-Vielmas' 'Shaping the Beast'.

what they represent (the landscape of the past) and what they are now, and their inability to bridge this gap.

Both the maps' efforts and failures to represent a world on the cusp of extreme geological change therefore expose cartography's paradoxical attempt to fix a momentary interpretation of the world which is subject to the ravages of time. This paradox speaks to a wider tension within Tolkien's legendarium between Middle-earth's beings, their relationship with their world, and their experience of time. Tolkien famously summarised the essential theme of his writings in a letter to Joanna de Bortadano:

> the real theme for me is about something much more permanent and difficult: Death and Immortality: the mystery of the love of the world in the hearts of a race 'doomed' to leave and seemingly lose it; the anguish in the hearts of a race 'doomed' not to leave it, until its whole evil-aroused story is complete. (*Letters* 246)

For both races (Men and Elves respectively), their experience of time informs their relationship with the world and how they engage with it.

As has been established, Tolkien's cosmology is constructed around episodes of change, destruction, and ending. Yet Men, who struggle with the idea of mortality, actively resist this idea. The most famous example of their resistance to death and the passing of time is the fall of Númenor itself, an event precipitated by Men's desire for immortality. The Númenóreans were already blessed with greater life spans than most Men: in the first draft of 'The Fall of Númenor', Tolkien attributes this to the island's proximity to Valinor, and that the people had been "bathed in the radiance" of the land (*LR* 11); in later drafts, Tolkien explicates that these long life spans – and indeed the island of Númenor itself – were a reward for the Númenóreans' aid in the Great Battle against Morgoth. However, despite their longer life spans, the Númenóreans grow discontented, "they murmured against this decree [...] and their masters of lore sought unceasingly for the secrets that should prolong their lives, and they sent their spies to seek these in Valinor" (*LR* 15). Men's desire for longer life is shown to override all their other characteristics: towards the beginning of the tale, Númenóreans are portrayed as noble, wise, and close to the Eldar, yet within a short time span, they turn to subterfuge, treachery, and eventually violence, motivated by their desire for immortality, and their inability to let go and acknowledge their own brief presence in a changing world. It is ironic that this attempt at gaining immortality and possessing the world is what causes its radical physical change, and the concomitant loss of Men's relationship with the Eldar, as well as their prolonged lives. The Númenóreans' attempt to upset the natural order is shown to have cataclysmic results, thereby reinforcing Men's temporal limitations and their inability to escape a mortal life.

Men's uneasy relationship with time and their mortality can be translated through their cartography. Their need to map can be read as a representation of their refusal to acknowledge that the world will change, and change without them. The maps can be understood as another expression of their frustration with mortality: by concretising the world around them as it is, and preserving it in a material form, Men attempt to freeze time and the changing of the world, even if only on paper. Their attitude to older maps further indicates this: Tolkien describes how the Númenórean maps in the archive, despite providing some of the only records available for a now extinct land and civilisation, are crumbling into ruin because of "neglect", as "all but a few regarded study of what was left of its history as vain, breeding only useless regret" (*UT* 165). Thus, maps which no longer provide the comfort of a world which is still recognisable and obtainable, such as the old Númenor maps, are ignored. These maps act as a reminder of the changing world, the mortality of Men, and their insignificance within the wider cosmological sphere.

The Elves, meanwhile, have a different relationship with time due to their immortality. However, as Tolkien himself points out in a letter to Naomi Mitchison, their immortality does not embrace the passing of time, but rather freezes it: "[Elves] were 'embalmers'. They wanted to have their cake and eat it: to live in the mortal historical Middle-earth because they had become fond of it […] and so tried to stop its change and history, stop its growth, keep it as a pleasaunce, even largely a desert, where they could be 'artists'" (*Letters* 197). Thus, as Verlyn Flieger argues, "a timeless world is a frozen world […] beauty preserved is beauty embalmed" (6). One of the most striking examples of this attitude and its effects on the natural world is Lothlórien. Lothlórien is caught in a liminal space between the mortal world of Men and the immortal world of the Elves: it is a physical space which can be entered and which borders onto other, mortal spaces, yet it is also a space which unsettles the passage of time that the rest of Middle-earth experiences. The experience of crossing into Lothlórien reads similarly to crossings in portal fantasies: there is the sense of a threshold being traversed, and a new world discovered. Frodo senses this shift "as soon as he set foot upon the far book of Silverlode [...] it seemed to him that he had stepped over a bridge of time into a corner of the Elder Days [...] in Lórien the ancient things still lived on in the waking world" (*FR* 454-55). The disruption of the linearity of time is quite evident in this passage; Lothlórien does not recall the past, or even actively recreate it, but rather exists *within* it, so that the passage of time has effectively been halted.[5] Yet as Flieger argues, this creates a world which is "frozen" and "embalmed", that is to say a world which is, ironically, dead and unable to sustain life. This is underscored by Treebeard in *The Two Towers*, when he explains to the hobbits that the forest is "fading, not growing" (*TT* 608). The refusal of the Elves to acknowledge the need for change and their attempt to subvert natural order promotes an artificial stagnation which nevertheless will eventually succumb to the passage of time, thus failing to ease their complicated relationship with their own immortality.

The mapping of the world on the part of the Elves can be read as an extension of this need, similar to Men's, to resist the changing of the world by fixing it materially in a moment in time. The artificial fixity of mapping mimics the artificial fixity of Lothlórien, and reflects the map's ultimate inability to sustain itself within an evolving world. Flieger even points to the mapping of Lothlórien in her discussion of its timelessness, arguing "without doubt it is meant to be a real place. It is on the map" (81). However, the map fails to convey the discordance in time between Lothlórien and the rest of Middle-earth; rather, it portrays Lothlórien as a timeless place, and the rest of the world along with it. This works to depict the Elves' desire to preserve the entire world as it is; cartography thus becomes another tool in the Elves' arsenal, a tangible manifestation of the enchantment cast over Lothlórien. Reading the maps as an expression of this urge to stop time and thereby preserve the world reinforces understandings of the Elves' problematic relationship with their immortality and their fraught position within a mortal world.

---

5 Ekman (101-09) identifies Lothlórien as a typical example of a 'polder'.

Despite both races' resistance to time, their tragedy is that they must nevertheless eventually leave Middle-earth, whether individually through death, as with the race of Men, or as a species through fading, as is the case with the Elves. As with the Númenor maps and their depiction of a now destroyed land acting as a window into the past, the maps of Middle-earth act as vehicles for historical and specifically anthropological contemplation. They are a narrative record of history, except they do not only preserve and illuminate the geology of the past, and how the world physically looked, but also the traces of species who peopled these lands and presumably made and read these maps.

The analogy between maps and fossils is again pertinent here, especially in regards to the Elves, whose experience of leaving Middle-earth is effectively an extinction. As Rateliff argues, the framing of Middle-earth as a prehistory of our own world implies the death and extinction of all the species which no longer exist in it, and in the case of the Elves, this extinction is made explicit throughout the texts. It is first alluded to in the 'Quenta Silmarillion' draft in *The Shaping of Middle-earth*, where Tolkien describes how Lúthien faded "even as the Elves of later days faded, when Men waxed strong and usurped the goodness of the earth" (*SME* 134). A footnote referring to Men in the 'Quenta Silmarillion' draft in *The Lost Road* reads: "The Eldar [...] named them the Usurpers, the Strangers" (*LR* 245), furthering the idea that Men replaced Elves within the evolutionary hierarchy of Middle-earth, causing them to fade. *The Lord of the Rings* meanwhile focuses its narrative on the fading of the Elves: Gandalf speaks to Aragorn about how "the time comes of the Dominion of Men, and the Elder Kindred shall fade or depart" (*RK* 1272); the Appendices discuss how the Third Age was synonymous with the "fading years of the Eldar" (*RK* 1423); and the Prologue makes clear that by the beginning of the Fourth Age, the last of the High Elves – Elrond, Celeborn, and Galadriel – had departed Middle-earth, leaving it to the race of Men.

The concept of racial extinction was a popular one before and around Tolkien's time: by the eighteenth century it had become clear that certain races, in particular colonised indigenous peoples, were dying out, and Darwin's theory of evolution in the nineteenth century provided a framework to explain and largely excuse this endangerment (Qureshi 267). His 1871 *Descent of Man* commented that when "civilised nations come into contact with barbarians, the struggle is short" (Darwin 238). The parallels of this evolutionary model with the situation of the Elves in Middle-earth are clear. The Elves are cast as victims of a shift in their world's racial hierarchy, and their fading becomes an extinction. They become an irretrievable species, whose existence and cultural presence can only be traced through, as Rateliff argues, "a word or two, a few vague legends and confused traditions, a smattering of lines of nonsense nursey rhyme, and perhaps a single, battered book" (68). Maps can and should be added to this list: not only do they act as a physical, fossilised remnant of a cultural product from the time of these extinct species, but they also visualise the world that they lived in, and their place in it.

The extent to which maps can speak to the Elves' position in the world over time and their eventual fading away is greatly increased by the spatial aspect to their extinction. Due to their immortality, even when the Elves become extinct, they do not pass entirely out of existence, but are rather displaced from the mortal lands of Middle-earth, and move instead to the immortal, ethereal realm of the Undying Lands. The Undying Lands have a strange geographical character. They are portrayed as a distinctly physical space; this is demonstrated by descriptions throughout *The History of Middle-earth*, but particularly in the 'Ambarkanta', where the mountains, shores, and sloping lands of Valinor are described. It is also emphasised in 'The Fall of Númenor', when "Valinor was sundered from the earth" (*LR* 15), suggesting how the separation of the mortal and immortal lands was a physical process involving tangible objects. After the globing of the earth and the removal of the Undying Lands, the only path of access between them is effectively a road, which can only be crossed by the Gods and Elves, thereby separating Men from immortality both spatially and metaphysically. This road exists in a liminal space between the metaphorical and the physical. Its description in 'The Fall of Númenor' is very hesitant: the old line of the world is described as a "memory" which endures, and the path that remains is "likened" to a plain of air, a straight vision, and a bridge (*LR* 17), without ever establishing in concrete terms what it really is. Yet, much like the Undying Lands it accesses, the path also has a certain physicality: boats sail through it from the Grey Havens, and it is said that Elves and Gods can walk on it.

The slow extinction of the Elves, their fading trajectory through the long Ages of Middle-earth, and the destination of their immortality therefore have a physical and geographical manifestation in the road and the Undying Lands. The mapping of these spaces is striking. Valinor and the Undying Lands are represented in only a few of Tolkien's maps. The first is the I Vene Kemen map, found in *The Book of Lost Tales*. This is a particularly anomalous map within Tolkien's cartographic corpus: it is in the shape of a large ship, and Valinor is labelled near one of the helms. Maps IV and V of the Ambarkanta maps feature Valinor as a land mass towards the extreme west of the maps, with recognisably topographical features such as the mountains bordering it from the rest of the world. Diagram III of the Ambarkanta maps meanwhile features a line at a tangent to the circular world, cutting through the layers of water and air arranged in concentric circles around. This line is labelled "The Straight Path", and as this map is titled "after the Cataclysm", it is almost certainly the path to the Undying Lands. These lands and the path, despite their ethereal nature, therefore can be mapped. The path of the Elves' extinction, and their physical trajectory through the various Ages of Middle-earth can therefore be conveyed using cartography, allowing maps to speak to the time of the Elves, indicating the conclusion of their immortality and their passing through time, while also more broadly speaking to the geological and anthropological changes that happen in Middle-earth through deep time.

As this discussion shows, Tolkien's maps act as far more than mere paratext, or as a means for both external readers and characters to locate themselves geographically within the subcreated world. Both the maps and instances of map making and map reading within the texts intersect with many of the legendarium's most important themes and questions. In this case, the maps work to illustrate both the earth's evolution over time, and the characters' relationship with their surroundings as they change. The maps speak to the extreme changes in the earth's geology, while simultaneously acting themselves like geological fossils, providing clues to the parts of the world and its inhabitants which are no more. Tolkien's characterisation of his subcreation's geology as catastrophic pushes the idea of a changing world to the extreme, and thereby intensifies the tension already inherent in mapping between the fixity of the material map and the fluidity of the evolving world.

About the Author

ANAHIT BEHROOZ has an M.A. from the University of Oxford in French and German, and an M.Litt. from the University of St Andrews in Comparative Literature, where she wrote her dissertation on manifestations of fear in the short stories of E.T.A. Hoffmann and Edgar Allan Poe. Throughout her studies, Anahit has always been drawn to narratives of the fantastic, the supernatural, and the uncanny, which finally culminated in the decision to pursue a PhD on J.R.R. Tolkien's works. Her research examines cartographic practices in Tolkien's Middle-earth, exploring how these maps allow Tolkien to explore and expand on both geographical and cultural aspects of worldbuilding.

Abbreviations

FR	TOLKIEN, J.R.R. *The Fellowship of the Ring*. Vol 1 of 3. London: HarperCollins, 2008.
Letters	*The Letters of J.R.R. Tolkien*. Edited by Humphrey Carpenter. London: HarperCollins, 2006.
LR	*The Lost Road and Other Writings*. London: HarperCollins, 1987.
RK	*The Return of the King*. Vol 3 of 3. London: HarperCollins, 2008.
SME	*The Shaping of Middle-Earth*. London: HarperCollins, 1986.
TL	*Tree and Leaf*. London: George Allen & Unwin, 1964.
TT	*The Two Towers*. Vol 2 of 3. London: HarperCollins, 2008.
UT	*Unfinished Tales*. London: Grafton, 1991.

Bibliography

ALLABY, Michael. *A Dictionary of Geology and Earth Sciences*. Oxford: Oxford University Press, 2013.

BOWLER, Peter J. *Evolution: The History of an Idea*. Berkeley CA: University of California Press, 2003.

CADBURY, Deborah. *The Dinosaur Hunters: A True Story of Scientific Rivalry and the Discovery of the Prehistoric World*. London: HarperCollins, 2012.

CLIFFORD, Anne M. 'Creation.' *Systematic Theology: Roman Catholic Perspectives*. Ed. Francis Schüssler Fiorenza and John P. Galvin. Minneapolis MN: Fortress Press, 1991. 193-248.

DARWIN, Charles. *The Descent of Man and Selection in Relation to Sex.* Cambridge: Cambridge University Press, 2009.

EKMAN, Stefan. *Here Be Dragons: Exploring Fantasy Maps and Settings.* Middletown CT: Wesleyan University Press, 2013.

FIMI, Dimitra. *Tolkien, Race and Cultural History: From Fairies to Hobbits.* London and New York: Palgrave Macmillan, 2010.

FLIEGER, Verlyn. *A Question of Time: J.R.R. Tolkien's Road to Faërie.* Kent OH: Kent State University Press, 2001.

GOULD, Stephen Jay. *Time's Arrow, Time's Cycle: Myth and Metaphor in the Discovery of Geological Time.* Cambridge MA: Harvard University Press, 1987.

HYNES, Gerard. '"Beneath the Earth's Dark Keel": Tolkien and Geology.' *Tolkien Studies* 9 (2012): 21-36.

QURESHI, Sadiah. 'Dying Americans: Race, Extinction, and Conservation in the New World.' *From Plunder to Preservation: Britain and the Heritage of Empire, C.1800-1940.* Ed. Astrid Swenson and Peter Mandler. Oxford: Oxford University Press, 2013. 267-86.

RATELIFF, John D. '"And All the Days of Her Life Are Forgotten": *The Lord of the Rings* as Mythic Prehistory.' *The Lord of the Rings 1954-2004: Scholarship in Honor of Richard E. Blackwelder.* Ed. Wayne G. Hammond and Christina Scull, Milwaukee: Marquette University Press, 2006. 67-100.

SCULL, Christina, and Wayne G. HAMMOND. *The J.R.R. Tolkien Companion & Guide: Chronology.* London: HarperCollins, 2006.

TALAIRACH-VIELMAS, Laurence. 'Shaping the Beast.' *European Journal of English Studies* 17.3 (2013): 269-82.

TOLKIEN, J.R.R. *The Fellowship of the Ring.* Vol 1 of 3. London: HarperCollins, 2008.

The Letters of J.R.R. Tolkien. Edited by Humphrey Carpenter. London: HarperCollins, 2006.

The Lost Road and Other Writings. London: HarperCollins, 1987.

The Return of the King. Vol 3 of 3. London: HarperCollins, 2008.

The Shaping of Middle-Earth. London: HarperCollins, 1986.

The Two Towers. Vol 2 of 3. London: HarperCollins, 2008.

Tree and Leaf. London: George Allen & Unwin, 1964.

Unfinished Tales. London: Grafton, 1991.

TORRENS, Hugh. 'Presidential Address: Mary Anning (1799-1847) of Lyme; "The Greatest Fossilist the World Ever Knew".' *The British Journal for the History of Science* 28.3 (1995): 257-84.

WOOD, Denis. *The Power of Maps*. London: Routledge, 1992.

Robin Markus Auer

Sundering Seas and Watchers in the Water: Water as a Subversive Element in Middle-earth

Abstract

With Tolkien's extensive production of maps and the intricate detail of geology, flora, and fauna he provides, the basic elements of nature express not only the very physicality of the sub-created 'Middle-Earth' which makes it come to life in such depth of detail, but also an underlying network of motifs and ideas that often pervade story and action through what might be described as 'structural landscapes'. What is lacking, however, is a detailed and structured study of the natural elements, taking into account their immediate and constitutive physicality, their impact on, and role within the stories of Middle-earth, and the conceptual framework within which these elements manifest themselves in more abstract ways. This essay is a first step to fill this gap by providing an analysis of the role water plays in the creation of Middle-earth and its history. By taking a closer look at specific occurrences of water within the narratives as well as more subtle underlying motifs in *The Lord of the Rings* and Tolkien's other works, I will reveal how water works as the most subversive element of Tolkien's sub-creation through its often corrupted and corrupting qualities, and is essential to the unfolding of the story by adding ambiguity to an underlying meta-narrative of the elements.

> "Earth, air, water and fire are still the four elements of imaginative experience, and always will be." (Northrop Frye)

1 Sundering Seas and Watchers in the Water

One of the characteristic features of Tolkien's oeuvre, the maps and geographical and historical detail of Middle-earth have had a deep and lasting effect on the genre. What has often been overlooked, though, is the way this kind of very physical conceptualisation has not in fact been used to elaborate on the context and background of the narratives, but quite to the contrary forms the backbone of the underlying greater narrative that enables all the other narratives. Despite being fictitious, Middle-earth is incredibly physical and the elements of nature (mainly fire, water, earth, and air) work to highlight this physicality, and even form their own underlying narrative of elements, in which each element has its role and characteristics and is related to certain motifs and ideas that dominate the stories and are constantly reiterated and manipulated through the landscapes. But while these landscapes and their prominence in Tolkien's descriptions have often been noted negatively, they fulfil a crucial role as *structural landscapes* by interacting with and acting upon the people of Middle-earth and changing the course of events over and over again.

Apart from some attempts at looking at very specific characteristics of some of these elements,[1] and attempts to justify readings that ascribe agency to objects and elements in terms of an object-oriented ontology,[2] there have been no systematic attempts at analysing and presenting this underlying narrative and its influence on the story. In their immediacy, the elements are constitutive of the very fabric and fate of Middle-earth.[3] In an attempt to provide a reading that takes into account the role of water played in the major narratives, this essay is designed to take a first step towards this systematic framework of interpretation.[4] By taking a closer look at specific occurrences of water-related landscapes as well as more subtle underlying motifs in *The Lord of the Rings* and Tolkien's other works, the aim is to reveal how water works as the most subversive element of Tolkien's sub-creation through its often corrupted and corrupting qualities, and is essential to the unfolding of the story by adding ambiguity and subverting expectations repeatedly. Despite a clear tendency towards religious imagery, water is in fact treated in a more complex way that is ultimately closely interwoven with Tolkien's conception of mortality and the protagonists' choices as they venture "across the water".

2 From Geography to Structural Landscapes

In recent years, literary landscapes have become the focus of much research and scholarly endeavour. Yet in Tolkien, landscapes and their core components – the

---

1 For a reading of water as a vehicle for healing, see Silva Rivero (2015).
2 For this quite novel approach to Tolkien's ecology, see Roman (2015).
3 For a detailed analysis of the ways in which maps are used by Tolkien and others, see Ekman (2013).
4 According to Bachelard, "a material element must provide its own substance, its particular rules and poetics." (3) Bachelard in fact proposes a general poetics of water in his *Water and Imagination* (1942).

elements – acquire a metaphorical role so complex and essential that they become what I am going to call 'structural landscapes'.

Tolkien's extensive descriptions of landscapes and architecture are one of his most peculiar stylistic devices.[5] And indeed, his descriptive repertoire and detail are a frequent source of dismay for a considerable number of his readers. Stylistically, they often seem almost ekphrastic, that is, like poetic descriptions of actual pictorial representations, e.g. paintings of landscapes. If we take a look at the extensive collections of drawings, sketches and especially the maps reproduced for the books that Tolkien has produced, it seems almost plausible that his creative process might have involved a mediating stage of pictorial representation between imagination and literary (linguistic) description.[6] On the one hand, this is part of the overall process of making the created world more realistic and more immediately available to the readers' experience. On the other hand, it suggests that the created world is primary to the secondary process of literary verbalisation and in some way can be said to 'exist' before, and thus independently of the text. Tolkien himself described the experience of writing *The Lord of the Rings* as if "something had been going on in the 'unconscious' for some time, and that accounts for my feeling throughout, especially when stuck, that I was not inventing but reporting (imperfectly) and had at times to wait till 'what really happened' came through." (*Letters* no. 163)[7]

Thus, events in Tolkien's writing generally have to line up with the physical necessities and possibilities, down to such details as the moon phases observed by the protagonists in relation to the passing of the time in the story as a whole.[8] This is to some extent what is covered by referring to the geographical landscape of the secondary world, shaping the fates of the races and peoples that have to adapt to the specific requirements of their particular surroundings. Frequently, however, Tolkien passes even beyond this geographical aspect, introducing a framework

---

5 See, for example, Turner (2014).
6 Jeffrey MacLeod and Anna Smol 'see a recursive interplay between visual and verbal drafting, frequently used as a means of imagining the fictional territory into which Tolkien is moving his characters' (116). While MacLeod and Smol talk about actual physical drawings and sketches, Paul Tankard refers to Tolkien's more abstract original vision, and argues that much of Tolkien's interest in illustrations and drawings relating to his works was inspired by his curiosity about whether or not they resembled that "imagined and re-imagined […] vision of Middle-earth" (150).
7 Throughout this paper, letters will be cited by number of the letter rather than the page.
8 In one letter, Tolkien comments on spending an afternoon fixing problems with the moon phases (*Letters* no. 69).

of nature that is usually found in religious texts, where the elements of nature are manipulated by one or various deities, or natural events are interpreted as acts of such deities. Besides the more obvious claim that especially *The Silmarillion* is in a way the 'Bible of Middle-earth',[9] the similarities are revealing in that they show a sense of meaning pervading the physical makeup of the world. The landscapes and their basic elements serve both as environment and context, and as a means in and by itself, thus creating what Christopher Roman has called an "object-oriented ontology" (95). These landscapes provide basic structures that affect the stories Tolkien narrates to an extent that has prompted Tom Shippey, in his *The Road to Middle-earth*, to speak of "a cartographic plot" (73). In a way, the elements almost become agents of their own,[10] and their unfolding stories underscore, accentuate and counterpoint the histories of Hobbits, Elves, and Men. These aspects – primacy of the physicality of the created world before its narrative, metaphysical vitalism, and agency – are what characterise structural landscapes, as opposed to literary ones (the latter being a term used generally to describe the cultural and literary context of a specific time or place, as in Daiches and Flower's *Literary Landscapes of the British Isles*) or metaphorical landscapes (a term more aptly used to describe the way in which the setting is used as a metaphor for a certain general mood or characters' emotions, as often seen in Gothic novels, for example).

There is one further point that I want to stress here, one even more crucial to this essay than the notion of structural landscapes, and one that is especially interesting in a more specific Tolkienian context. Landscapes (and by extension the elements) create a space that can be characterised in a very specific cognitive way. "In spite of differences in [...] meanings, the different usages [of landscapes as poetic imagery] are still united by landscape as a cognitive category, being on the one hand related to the information received via sensory perception, and on the other hand, to certain conventions" (Sarapik 184). It is this conventional part that seems interesting in that it suggests (transferred from this pictorial background to the literary realm) that certain landscapes or elements may represent or create

---

9   This is not only true concerning the 'metaphysical content' in (especially) the first part, but also for its style (see Agøy 2011).
10 This happens often quite explicitly, as in *The Silmarillion*, or with the eagles and Ents in *The Lord of the Rings*. For most of *The Lord of the Rings* and *The Hobbit*, however, this agency is more subtle and implicit.

cognitive spaces, and that this in turn makes it possible and indeed rewarding to analyse and interpret them in terms of these cognitive spaces. Landscapes dominated by a specific element are therefore not just geographical, nor are they purely metaphorical in representing either the intervention of a higher force, or the mood and psychology of the protagonists, but in fact a structural as well as cognitive space.

Well-known examples of physical spaces that at the same time create this kind of cognitive space are the *locus amoenus* and its counterpart, the *locus terribilis*, both frequent literary *topoi* throughout antiquity and to this day.[11] These both create a separate or in-between space that is characterised in terms of its psychological impact rather than its physical properties. While a metaphorical landscape would express feelings, the cognitive space precedes and facilitates a decision or emotion.[12]

Landscapes, especially those of the Shire, Lórien, and Mordor have already been analysed in the context of environmental agendas, representations of home, etc.,[13] but it seems that a systematic account of the role of the elements is yet lacking. Over the course of this essay we will therefore take a closer look at how water, as one of the dominant natural elements, shapes the fate of Middle-earth; first as a structural landscape comprising the geographical feature, the metaphysical meaning as the realm of the water-deity Ulmo, and its explicit as well as implicit agency, and ultimately as a cognitive space that, more than any other, subverts expectations, hopes and fates, and constantly creates choices with which the protagonists are faced. Water is thus the most untypical of the elements in that it often evades the clear ontology that the other elements seem to invite, playing on the usual connotations of fluidity and physical anomalies. There are several types of general landscapes connected to water, namely seas, lakes, rivers, marshes, and mists. They each are connected to a specific kind of physicality and way of interacting with the people in the story, creating unique cognitive spaces.

---

11 In fact, there are even some examples of especially the *locus amoenus* in Tolkien's works; the first encounters of many major couples throughout the history of Middle-earth take place in such a *locus amoenus*: Thingol and Melian, Beren and Lúthien, Aragorn and Arwen. Túrin and Nienor journey from a *locus amoenus*, where they meet again without recognising each other and fall in love, to a *locus terribilis*, where they both ultimately die.
12 In other words, a metaphorical landscape is a symptom of a character's mental state or perception. A cognitive space creates or effects a certain mental state or emotion.
13 For an environmental reading of Tolkien, see especially the studies by Patrick Curry.

3 The Creation of Arda – Ulmo's Contested Realm

As one of the principal elements of nature, water is fundamental to the geography as well as history of Tolkien's sub-created world. In the Ainulindalë, we learn that in the vision of the world to come the Ainur "observed the winds and the air, and the matters of which Arda was made, of iron and stone and silver and gold and many substances: but of all these water they most greatly praised" (*S* 8). Water seems to play a special role and is held in high esteem by the quasi-angelic Ainur. There certainly seems to be a religious influence, if not quite an agenda here. Water is essential to life, a fact that has granted it a prominent role in many faiths and religions,[14] but with Tolkien there is obviously a markedly Christian influence, reminiscent of baptisms, holy water, and ritual washings.[15] This is further explicated in the statement that "it is said by the Eldar that in water there lives yet the echo of the Music of the Ainur more than in any substance else that is in this Earth"[16] (*S* 8) which again highlights the quasi-religious aspect,[17] namely the realisation of the creation in the substances of the world, where the created, and thus the creator, can be observed and experienced. There is, however, another aspect here, one that affects the stories more directly: the "echo of the Music of the Ainur" is a reference back not only to the act of creation, but also to the original plan, as played out in drama,[18] and thus water always recalls the course of events as designed by Eru Ilúvatar. This means that water will often serve – directly or through making people recall something of the original design – to steer events to the desired outcome, no matter how hopeless the situation may seem. And it is probably due to this echo that "many of the Children of Ilúvatar hearken still unsated to the voices of the Sea, and yet know not for what they listen." (*S* 8) The echo, which can only be properly understood by those who were there in the beginning, must be like a promise of hope and salvation, felt, even if not understood. It foreshadows the prominent role that water will play in the stories to come and in the lore of the peoples of Middle-earth. So even

---

14 For a general overview and introduction, see Shaw and Francis 2008.
15 Other references to holy water are Nienna's tears and Yavanna's song bringing forth the two trees (*S* 31) and Nienna's tears washing away the defilements of Ungolianth (*S* 83).
16 Water as restoring the course of events as it was supposed to be (according to Eru's plan).
17 It is of course well known that Tolkien endeavoured to drop all explicitly religious aspects within his works: "Myth and fairy-story must, as all art, reflect and contain in solution elements of moral and religious truth (or error), but not explicit, not in the known form of the primary 'real' world" (*Letters* no. 131).
18 "which they perceived first as a drama [...] and later as a 'reality'" (*Letters* no. 131).

in the very beginning, before the world is created, water already is crucial to the designed world and its future and fate.[19]

But even as early as that, before the world is actually made reality by Ilúvatar, water also acquires the ambiguous and indeed fluent role that it will play throughout the history of Arda in general, and Middle-earth in particular. For, quite clearly, this special position does not go uncontested. Ilúvatar, speaking to Ulmo, reveals "how here in this little realm in the Deeps of Time Melkor hath made war upon thy province" (*S* 8) even though, as we later learn, Melkor's attempts at subduing water to his will ultimately fail. He consequently always loathes and fears water, a sentiment often mentioned and apparently passed on to his thralls: "for at no time ever did Morgoth essay to build ships or to make war by sea. Water all his servants shunned, and to the sea none would willingly go nigh, save in dire need" (*S* 137). His hate extends to all those protected by and friendly towards Ulmo.[20]

More is revealed about Ulmo, the Lord of Waters, in the 'Valaquenta', and it is interesting to see in how far this already amounts to a description of the role of water (in the sense that his character traits are representative of those of the element of his domain)[21] that can be compared to the findings later on: "He dwells nowhere long, but moves as he will in all the deep waters about the Earth or under the Earth [...] he kept all Arda in thought [...] Ulmo loves both Elves and Men, and never abandoned them, not even when they lay under the wrath of the Valar" (*S* 17). This passage is interesting with regard to later events within *The Silmarillion*, *The Hobbit*, and *The Lord of the Rings* as this foreshadows the special link between water and the peoples of Middle-earth, even when there

---

19 With the *Silmarillion*'s posthumous editing and publishing, and major changes from the early drafts to the published text, it is difficult to judge the extent to which this conception of water is a constitutive or emergent feature of Tolkien's world, even though Tom Shippey, in *The Road to Middle-Earth*, notes that "[a] 'very high proportion' even of the detailed wording of this 1937 text remains in the published version. Much of *The Silmarillion*, then, could be seen as chronologically pre-*Hobbit*" (169). Besides, the motifs and conceptions identified are a matter of basic and underlying constitutive structures and concepts, not of placement in terms of an overall fixed outline, and thus valid independently of the exact history of writing and editing. Those interested in a more detailed account of the versions and drafts of the *Silmarillion* text should consult Douglas Kane's 2009 work *Arda Reconstructed. The Creation of the Published Silmarillion*.
20 "and Morgoth feared and hated the house of Fingolfin, because they had the friendship of Ulmo his foe" (*S* 233).
21 It seems important, however, to remember that this transfer of characteristics and projection onto the element of water is by no means a necessary or valid conclusion, but rather a proposition.

is no longer a clear connection between them and the other Valar (and thus elements). Further it is said that "at times he will come unseen to the shores of Middle-earth, or pass far inland up firths of the sea, and there make music upon his great horns" (S 17) which leaves us with another interesting, more symbolic, reference in the battle of the Pelennor Fields. The Rohirrim blow their horns when they finally arrive to aid Gondor in the battle, but the decisive stroke comes when Aragorn and his company arrive from the Sea, unexpectedly and unhoped for. Though not explicitly mentioned, it seems viable to at least consider this in terms of mirroring the two horns that Melkor ever feared, the Valaróma of Orome on his steed Nahar, and the Ulumúri of Ulmo;[22] similarly now Sauron's armies are trapped between the fierce riders with their big horns and the last remnants of the high Númenóreans coming from the sea aboard ships.[23] So indeed, "to all who were lost in that darkness [...] the ear of Ulmo was ever open; nor has he ever forsaken Middle-earth, and whatsoever may since have befallen of ruin or of change he has not ceased to take thought for it, and will not until the end of days" (S 34).

There are many Maiar following Ulmo and the rather short passage on the Maiar focuses to a great extent on the two major ones, Osse and Uinen, again highlighting the central importance of water. "[O]f all the Maiar Osse and Uinen are best known to the Children of Ilúvatar" (S 21). Especially Uinen's close relationship to mariners among Elves and Men is highlighted: "to her mariners cry, for she can lay calm upon the waves, restraining the wildness of Osse.[24] The Númenóreans lived long in her protection, and held her in reverence equal to the Valar" (S 22). They both seem to have quite essential, if restricted domains, and also very different tempers, relating to the fact that water can be quite deadly in a raging storm, but calm and soft at other times. Even Melkor valued their power, especially that of Osse, obviously for his destructive potential. "Melkor hated the Sea, for he could

---

[22] While it is true that it is nowhere explicitly stated that Melkor fears the Ulumúri in the same way he does the Valaróma, it seems safe to assume that their sound would not bode well for him as Ulmo is often his main rival in the events in Middle-earth.

[23] Even though there are no actual horns announcing their arrival, the scene does invite this interpretation: "and the mirth of the Rohirrim was a torrent of laughter and a flashing of swords, and the joy and wonder of the City was a music of trumpets and a ringing of bells" (RK 1109). Thus the joy of the Rohirrim upon receiving help from the ships is instantly framed in relation to water, suggesting a connection between the laughter announcing the turning of the tide of battle and the music of water, which – read against the backdrop of *The Silmarillion* – seems almost rather obvious.

[24] In an earlier conception revealed in *The Book of Lost Tales*, Osse was indeed a Vala himself.

not subdue it. It is said that in the making of Arda he endeavoured to draw Osse to his allegiance, promising to him all the realm and power of Ulmo, if he would serve him" (*S* 22). Osse is arguably the more dangerous and less trustworthy of the two, and yet he is never described as wilfully evil, as "those who dwell by the sea or go up in ships may love him, but they do not trust him" (*S* 22). Interestingly, Ulmo is the only Vala who does not dwell in Valinor and is thus more readily situated within Arda as a whole.

4 Cast it into the Sea – Water in *The Hobbit* and *The Lord of the Rings*

Now that we have a clearer idea of the role water plays in the events leading up to the two major narratives of *The Hobbit* and *The Lord of the Rings*, it is time to examine in how far the role of water undergoes changes and becomes more subtle in the more realistic, historiographical setting of especially *The Lord of the Rings*.[25] With the withdrawal of the higher powers of the West from the physical world, the natural elements finally emerge as agents of their own, no longer as manifestations of divine power. Therefore, the more individual aspects of the structural landscapes and cognitive spaces move into the foreground as the mythical aspects become secondary and symbolical at best. It is also here that the ambiguous character and subverting of expectations and hopes becomes apparent in its clearest form by directing action and story in unexpected ways.

As Bilbo rightly points out, adventures are something sought only by those who live "across the Water", and of course, his adventure begins the very moment he makes up his mind and crosses the Water to meet with Thorin and his company. The use of the name of the river coinciding with the name of the element is almost programmatic. It attaches to water a notion of queerness and otherness, a separation between the realms of the everyday and normal on the

---

25 Dimitra Fimi also notes that with *The Hobbit*, there is a "shift of Tolkien's creative writing from a 'mythical' to a 'historical' mode" (120). It is therefore not surprising that prominent mythical aspects (like the deities and their strong connection to certain elements) would have to attain a new character or mode as well. Fimi (124) also notes the importance of the sea as a geographical feature in the reshaping of the world and the transition from a flat to a round conception, which will be discussed in a slightly different context later in this chapter.

one side, and the strange and exceptional on the other side.²⁶ Hobbits dislike water as it seems to them unreliable and dangerous, connected with "boating" and other mad adventures. And though this separation between possibility and reality is characteristic of the role water plays in Tolkien's works, it is not always as straightforward as in this instance. While there are numerous instances in which water landscapes affect the plot in both stories, I will limit the discussion to a few exceptional cases and more general types.

One of the initial incidents brought about by the intervention of water is the fight with the trolls after a river has swallowed much of Thorin and his company's supplies. Over and over again, the obstacles and inconveniences posed by water divert their journey in unexpected, yet often (ultimately) beneficial ways.²⁷ A bit later on, Rivendell marks the transition into the wilderness proper. Here, as well as later in *The Lord of the Rings*, the valley with its numerous waterfalls serves as a place where advice is given and contemplation is made possible: over and again, travellers in Rivendell are faced with the choice to turn away from their path, or to continue.²⁸ Up in the Misty Mountains, another storm prevents the dwarves from lighting a fire and urges them to seek out a dry cave, resulting in their capture by the goblins, the death of the Great Goblin, and ultimately the finding of the Ring by Bilbo, apart from changing the route of the company. Down in Gollum's cave, on the edge of the water, Bilbo's fate is changed dramatically, and it is worth noting that both known instances of the

---

26 In her book on *Perilous Realms*, Marjorie Burns talks about "a variety of boundary markers and gateways" (45). She acknowledges the important role water often plays ("water is crossed, and the familiar gives way to the strange", 50) and rightly recognises the many parallels in tales of the Celtic 'Otherworld' or Norse mythology. And yet, while her assessment seems appropriate as far as most of *The Hobbit* is concerned (especially her focus on how Bilbo has to cross "not just any water but *The Water*", 55), there is a crucial difference between some of the water landscapes and the simpler "bridges, gates, and doors" (ibid.): the water landscapes also function as places in themselves. While with gates and doors, one usually has to be *on one side or the other*, many of the water landscapes also allow for being *in*, creating an additional space that is neither one, nor the other, or what Stefan Ekman calls "a borderland" which "serves as a 'marker, resting place or toll-gate between two differing kinds of reality'" (68-69). I will, however, not adopt this term, as it seems to be a special case of the more general structural or cognitive space.
27 Not only does it lead to the discovery of several items crucial to later events, but it also offers Bilbo a chance to prove his questionable usefulness by the choices he makes.
28 This is not only true for travellers, but also for those dwelling there. Rivendell with its waterfalls is a place of in-between-ness that is a home not only to Elrond the Half-Elven, a descendant of Eärendil, but also for a while to Aragorn, another descendant of Eärendil who grows up in anonymity and exile until he later emerges as the heir to the throne of Gondor and Arnor, and Arwen, the first Elf since Lúthien to forsake her innate immortality for love.

Ring abandoning and betraying its master (Isildur and Gollum, respectively) are connected to water.

In Mirkwood, the forest river poses a serious obstacle, especially after it causes Bombur to fall into a slumber full of dreams foreshadowing their later capture by the Elves. Here, the psychological and cognitive impact of water is made explicit, giving the cognitive space overt primacy over the structural landscape. In captivity and without much hope of escaping from the halls of Thranduil, it is through the river gate and in barrels that they escape, even though their fate is only revealed once they have left the water again. While this escape finally establishes Bilbo as the secret leader of the company, it is the title of barrelrider that, among the many poetic titles Bilbo assumes in his conversation with Smaug, provides the crucial clue to Smaug. This prompts his attack on Lake Town and his undoing at the hands of Bard. The clue pointing towards the river here betrays first Bilbo, who causes great harm for the people of Esgaroth, but ultimately also Smaug, who dies in the lake.

As the narrative style shifts from fairytale towards the more elevated style of *The Lord of the Rings*, the role of water as an agent as well as a cognitive space is expressed even more subtly. As soon as it becomes clear that Frodo and his companions are being chased by the Black Riders, they use the river Brandywine to escape: Bucklebury ferry provides a vital shortcut, the next bridge being ten miles up the river. Inside the Old Forest, the Withywindle provides a landmark by which the hobbits try to navigate (by avoiding it). Sitting on a high hill and at a loss for a clear direction, the hobbits find themselves "on an island in a sea of trees, and the horizon was veiled" (*FR* 149). This clear reference back to Bilbo climbing up the trees in Mirkwood frames their sense of loss of direction in terms of the sea as a landscape, stressing the problem of navigating it due to a lack of landmarks. All in all, however, *The Lord of the Rings* is usually focused more on the rivers than unmoving bodies of water (such as lakes or seas), so that they end up following the Withywindle after all, even though they are aware that it is "the centre from which all the queerness comes"[29] (*FR* 149) and that, further expanding the reference to

---

29 This recalls earlier notions of queerness and transgression. The hobbits hold the water responsible for bringing the trees to life.

Bilbo's experiences in Mirkwood, it makes them drowsy and has a marked effect on their psyche, bringing them to Old Man Willow, who pushes Frodo into the water and traps Merry and Pippin. They are saved and invited by Tom Bombadil to join him and Goldberry (the daughter of the river) at their home. After the mist on the South Downs has delayed them once again,[30] Frodo is saved from the Black Riders as they try to cross the ford of the river Bruinen and are swept away by the floods, once again justifying Sauron's thralls' fear of water. So for the second time now, Frodo has been saved from the Nazgûl by a river.[31] In Rivendell, contrary to their expectations, the hobbits are faced with another choice, that of returning to the Shire or going on the quest to destroy the Ring. In the council of Elrond, the possibility of throwing the Ring into the sea or sending it across the ocean is entertained briefly, but quickly dismissed, as "they who dwell beyond the Sea would not receive it" (*FR* 347) and "there are many things in the deep waters; and seas and lands may change" (*FR* 347). This limits the action to Middle-earth, shifting the landscapes of interest from oceans and lakes to the more agile rivers and mists, moving and making accessible new routes of travel, while also foreshadowing the events at the gates of Moria.

There, Frodo is attacked by the Watcher in the Water, forcing the fellowship to retreat into the mines with no other option. As a consequence, Gandalf falls at the bridge of Khazad-dûm. Soon afterwards, Frodo and Sam catch glimpses of the future and the past, of possibilities and dangers in Galadriel's mirror, in what is a scene of outstanding importance. The workings of the mirror are never explained. What is clear, however, is that the mirror works in mysterious ways, subverting prior expectations of what one will see when looking into it,

---

30 Mist is not exactly a type of landscape, but invades other landscapes and changes their cognitive aspects. On several occasions, mists hide travelers from sight, and while on most occasions this is favourable to the travelers (as in hiding the Rohirrim under Eorl the Young riding to aid Gondor, and making them go faster than expected while at the same time leaving them refreshed), this time it leads to the hobbits being captured and put under a spell, recalling the way Glaurung used the mist to put Turin's sister Nienor under his spell. Frodo's getting lost in the mists and finding himself in a dangerous and otherworldly setting is reminiscent of an incident in the Welsh *Mabinogion*, as Marjorie Burns clearly recognizes (even though she does not explicitly point out the parallel, 53).
31 This is brought about by Gandalf and Elrond, who both are connected to water by their status as queer beings. Frodo, wounded by the Morgul-blade and slowly passing over to the spirit-world that the Nazgûl inhabit, ends up on the opposite side of the river, indicating his rescue. For a more detailed discussion of water as separating the worlds of the living, the dead, and the immortals, see section 6 on 'Mortality and the Sundering Sea'.

as well as generally revealing possibilities rather than realities. It is the cognitive space opened up by water made into reality. Galadriel is of course also the keeper of the ring of water, Nenya. She plays a crucial role by sheltering the Fellowship and affecting their individual decisions. She also hands Frodo the light of Eärendil in a phial. This gift links him to water and to Eärendil and marks him as a traveller between the worlds, hinting at his fate of ultimately sailing West against all odds.

Travelling down the Anduin to delay the decision over the route again explicitly highlights the in-between-ness of water landscapes. The breaking of the Fellowship and the death of Boromir separate the remaining fellowship by placing them on opposite sides of the river. Contrary to his initial plans, Frodo is accompanied by Sam, who leaps into the water in order to follow him despite not being able to swim. Deep in Fangorn, Merry and Pippin drink from the water that makes them grow. Frodo and Sam meanwhile reach the Dead Marshes[32] together with Gollum, are captured by Faramir, and taken back to his camp behind a waterfall, their fate once again unclear and hidden behind water. Unexpectedly, however, they find a friend in Faramir, who is more alike to the Númenóreans than most Men of the age. At Helms Deep, the small brook leaving the keep is used to breach it, almost resulting in defeat. This brook here exemplifies the ambiguous nature of water: while it is vital to the defenders as a source of water in a siege, it presents the attackers with a welcome weakness in the otherwise solid wall. At the same time, ironically, Isengard is overthrown by the Ents who free the river Isen so that Isengard is flooded. On their way to Minas Tirith, Aragorn and his company take the Paths of the Dead but ultimately emerge from the corsair ships meant to support Sauron's attack on Minas Tirith and turn the tide of the battle of the Pelennor Fields. Finally, Frodo and the other ringbearers leave Middle-earth on a ship sailing from the Grey Havens, only for Sam, Legolas and Gimli to follow later on.

---

32 The Dead Marshes reveal another landscape that makes several appearances, but here in corrupted form. Due to its peculiar placing of the fallen in-between life and death, the Dead Marshes have a marked effect on Frodo, who seems especially sensitive to psychological influences. In turn, the marshes keep away the Nazgûl, as before in the Shire.

5 Navigating the Sundering Seas – Water-Journeys from Fëanor to Frodo

Let us now take a closer look at how waterways interact with those travelling across them, as these journeys allow us to examine water in terms of both a structural landscape, as well as a cognitive space. Furthermore, there is an overall narrative of the struggle between choice and fate that is central to Tolkien's cosmology and largely negotiated in the treatment of sea-journeys. Not only does this result in a very specific localisation of both choice as well as fate in the physical world, but by providing a framework for journeys of will and journeys of fate, a whole new reading of the quest-and-return narratives of the two major works, *The Hobbit* and *The Lord of the Rings*, becomes possible. But let us first take a look at how this narrative emerges in *The Silmarillion*.

Following the summons of the Valar, the Elves are repeatedly faced with a choice between journeying on and staying behind, especially when faced with bodies of water (rivers, lakes, seas), which offer them cognitive spaces of hesitation and contemplation. Beginning at the very place of their awakening, lake Cuiviénen, there is frequent sundering among the Elves. The different tribes of the Elves, with their linguistic and historical differences, thus emerge from the choices of going or not going "across the water". But while the rivers and lakes merely provide temporary delay, the sea is a major obstacle that initially requires divine intervention. The Valar, beings that by their very nature exist 'in-between', do not require any vessels to cross a physical boundary like the ocean. The Elves, however, have to be ferried across on an island, and it is only through a final act of hesitation which leaves some of the Elves on the island of Tol Eressëa[33] that they are taught the craft of shipmaking from Ossë.[34] It is one of the first (and few) instances of the initial design being changed to reflect the choices made by the inhabitants of Arda.

---

[33] Dwelling on an island is in fact explicitly introduced in terms of permanent in-between-ness as the Elves wish to forsake neither Aman nor Middle-earth. This motif of the permanent in-between-ness of islands is evoked repeatedly throughout Tolkien's stories both implicitly and explicitly, as for example in Númenor, Mirkwood, Old Forest, Lórien, and Osgiliath.
[34] Ulmo sends "Osse, their friend, and he though grieving taught them the craft of ship-building" (*S* 61) so that they and their ships can be drawn from Eressëa to the shores of Valinor across the windless sea by swans.

When later Fëanor rallies the Noldor, he recalls Cuiviénen in his speech leading many of the Noldor to follow him across the sea to Middle-earth: "In Cuiviénen sweet ran the waters under unclouded stars" (*S* 88). Faced with a choice between building ships and daring the northern passage, he turns to the Teleri, whose refusal to help Fëanor ends in the tragic first kinslaying at Alqualonde. As a result, the Doom of the Noldor is revealed and many Noldor die as some of the ships are destroyed by Uninen's tears for the dead mariners.[35] Their doom is settled by the burning of the ships (a proverbial "burning of bridges" in many ways) and Fëanor's betrayal of Fingolfin. Fingolfin and his host "finding no other way [...] endured at last the terror of the Helcaraxë and the cruel hills of ice" (*S* 97-98). The ban is enforced by changing the geographical landscape in a way that makes the sea an impassable structural landscape rather than keeping them out by active force: "And in that time also [...] the Enchanted Isles were set, and all the seas about them were filled with shadows and bewilderment" (*S* 113). This is also expressed in terms of a change in the cognitive space: "waves sighed for ever upon dark rocks shrouded in mist [...] great weariness came upon mariners and a loathing of the sea; but all that ever set foot upon the islands were there entrapped, and slept until the Change of the World" (*S* 114).[36] While this physical barrier may at first seem more permanent than an actual keeping guard of Ulmo or Osse, it already contains a spark of hope in that its physicality suggests that it might be overcome, given the appropriate combination of skill and will.

Eärendil, whose story begins in Gondolin before its fall, embarks on the journey by his own will.[37] As Fëanor's sons try to reclaim the Silmaril held by Elwing, she casts herself into the sea and is saved by Ulmo and sent out to Eärendil on his ship, when he is already heading west. This may be seen not only as an act

---

35 It may seem surprising that they are avenged by Uinen instead of Osse, but the echo of Nienna's tears washing away the defilements of Ungolianth makes clear the gravity of Fëanor's deeds.
36 There are repeated attempts by the Noldor in Middle-earth to send emissaries: "they built ships, and set sail into the uttermost West [...] seeking for Valinor, to ask for pardon and aid of the Valar [...] the seas were wild and wide, and shadow and enchantment lay upon them; and Valinor was hidden" (*S* 186). In the context of the passage above I think it seems legitimate to read this in terms of the landscape acting by enchanting (that is, by having a psychological impact onto) the mariners.
37 With Eärendil, there is from the beginning a very explicit focus on his relation to water, as well as his special status as a Half-Elven. It might also be interesting to consider this in-between-ness in terms of race in relation to the elementary in-between-ness of water (both in terms of geography, as well as the fact that it expands not only when heated, but also when cooled, a characteristic called negative thermal expansivity).

of intervention by Ulmo, but indeed a granting of passage for the westward journey. Hence their journey is successful: "Eärendil, first of living Men, landed on the immortal shores" (*S* 297). This reading is further supported by Ulmo's plea in the ring of doom: "Ulmo said: 'For this he was born into the world. And say unto me: whether is he Eärendil Tuor's son of the line of Hador, or the son of Idril, Turgon's daughter, of the Elven-house of Finwë?'" (*S* 299).[38] Eärendil and his ship are consequently elevated to the heavens as a sign of the forgiveness of the Valar and the end of the ban, symbolically pointing towards Valinor: "Now when first Vingilot was set to sail in the seas of heaven, it rose unlooked for, glittering and bright; and the people of Middle-earth beheld it from afar and wondered, and they took it for a sign, and called it Gil-Estel, the Star of High Hope" (*S* 301).[39]

The final great sea-journey in *The Silmarillion* is the one undertaken by the Númenóreans. It is the final step in the historical progression from the domination of Elves to Men (coinciding with a shift in narrative perspective), and similarly the ultimate step in changing the physical landscape of the sea (and indeed the whole of Arda). Fittingly, it also presents both directions of sailing in contrast: the two parties – that of Ar-Pharazôn, and that of Elendil and the faithful – mirror the previous journeys in terms of their direction. Another parallel is that there is in fact a ban against the Númenóreans not to sail west towards Valinor. The westward journey can thus be seen as an act of rebellion while the eastward journey is an act of conformity or even loyalty, especially as it goes against the direct orders of the king. This time, there is no physical barrier (following the lifting of the ban against the Noldor). Instead, the ban is now purely spiritual in nature: "Thus the fleets of the Númenóreans moved against the menace of the West; [...] and the sea was still, while the world waited for what should betide" (*S* 333). Successfully sailing west, "they broke the Ban of the Valar, and sailed into forbidden seas, going up with war against the Deathless, to wrest from them everlasting life within the Circles of the World" (*S* 333). By breaking the ban, they evoke the wrath of Eru himself, and

---

[38] There has been no room to examine in more detail the relationship between Ulmo and the house of Hador, which is elaborated in great detail in *The Silmarillion* and the *Unfinished Tales*, as well as several other publications.

[39] Eärendil's never-ending journey is also related in poetic form in *The Lord of the Rings*, as Bilbo recites the 'Song of Eärendil the Mariner' in Rivendell, reminding the fellowship and reader alike of the goodwill of Ulmo and the other Valar.

their doom unfolds in their undoing and the sinking of the isle of Númenor. The Faithful are spared from the downfall of their people quite explicitly: "And the deeps rose beneath them in towering anger, and waves like unto mountains moving with great caps of writhen snow bore them up amid the wreckage of the clouds, and after many days cast them away upon the shores of Middle-earth" (*S* 335-36). In this final reshaping of the world, even the otherwise consistent narrative of fate and will is inverted, suggesting that the Númenóreans forfeited their right to sail east at their will by going against the will of the Valar in claiming for themselves the westward passage.

As the clear east-west dichotomy of water-journeys in *The Silmarillion* is dissolved by removing the true West from the physical world, the people of Middle-earth become free in terms of the direction of travel. There is now a categorical difference between sailing west (which now ultimately leads back to the eastern shores) and sailing into the West (now entirely a matter of divine grace). Therefore, the journeys undertaken on water by Bilbo in *The Hobbit*, and by the Fellowship, Frodo and Sam, and Aragorn and his company in *The Lord of the Rings* do not qualify for an analysis in the same terms. Nonetheless, however, they serve to prove a further point. The characters, while using the waterways in order to get closer to their designations, are usually safe from outside interruption while actually travelling on the water. Water as a landscape is remarkably free from evil influence,[40] so that against all odds, Bilbo's barrel-riding, Frodo and Sam's crossing of the Anduin to the arguably more dangerous shore, and Aragorn's approach to the battle at Minas Tirith, go remarkably well. Rivers and lakes, by effectively providing routes only to those free from evil, serve as a way of integrating water landscapes into the wider network of landscapes in Middle-earth. In a quest that is first and foremost grounded in secrecy and stealth rather than military might, exclusive access to these landscapes becomes a decisive advantage.

There clearly emerges a general trend as to the direction of the voyages. Westward passage (in terms of the true West), in order to be successful, has to

---

40 Even the Watcher in the Water, as argued earlier, while surely treacherous, is not exactly a force for evil. Instead, water-dwellers often seem to showcase the same ambiguity and in-between-ness as the element they inhabit (this is especially true for Gollum/Smeagol, who could be said to inhabit both water and earth).

be granted and cannot be achieved against the will of the Valar, as proven by the fate of the messengers during the ban and the fate of Ar-Pharazôn's fleet and Númenor. By contrast, eastward journeys are generally an expression of free will, and successful independently of the will of the Valar (with the exception of Elendil's journey). This spatial aspect of the structural landscape of the sea is slowly being transferred into a more spiritual sphere, with every act of rebellion causing repercussions and changing the geographical landscape (and indeed also marking the progression from a flat to a spherical conception of the world), which ironically constitutes the ultimate physical barrier (in the sense of being an insurmountable barrier to physical beings). Thus when Frodo and the other ring-bearers leave Middle-earth at the end of *The Lord of the Rings*, the granting of passage is especially meaningful, as this passage is by birthright only granted to the Firstborn, acknowledging Frodo's (and later Sam's) outstanding role in the saving of Middle-earth. This is the making-explicit of Tolkien's often cited "ennoblement of the ignoble" (*Letters* no. 165), one of his major concerns and motifs, here realised in its most definite and tangible form.

6 Mortality and the Sundering Sea

While at first sailing into the West is a physical journey, the changing of the shape of the world and physical removal of Aman changes the meaning of sailing into the west completely, as Tolkien explains in a 1971 letter: "if any keen-eyed observer from that shore had watched one of these ships he might have seen that it never became hull-down but dwindled only by distance until it vanished in the twilight: it followed the straight road to the true West and not the bent road of the earth's surface. As it vanished it left the physical world" (*Letters* no. 325). In the same letter, Tolkien lays out the distinction between immortals and mortals:

> As for Frodo or other mortals, they could only dwell in Aman for a limited time – whether brief or long. The *Valar* had neither the power nor the right to confer 'immortality' upon them. Their sojourn was a 'purgatory', but one of peace and healing and they would eventually pass away (*die* at their own desire and of free will) to destinations of which the Elves knew nothing. (*Letters* no. 325)

All this seems to point towards a semi- or quasi-physical setup, even though Tolkien concedes that this should not be taken "geologically or astronomically 'true'" (*Letters* no. 325).

Tolkien's conceptualisation of the removal of Aman from the physical world seems to have undergone slight changes over time. In an earlier letter from around 1951, Tolkien reveals that "the world is round, and finite, and a circle inescapable – save by death. Only the 'immortals', the lingering Elves, may still if they will, wearying of the circle of the world, take ship and find the 'straight way', and come to the ancient or True West, and be at peace" (*Letters* no. 131). This clearly appears to be a more physical solution to the issue, but at the same time more problematic in that there are obvious inconsistencies in terms of geography and narrative. In editing *The Silmarillion* for publication, Christopher Tolkien seems to have preferred the semi-physical solution, which is also more consistent with the water-related symbolism involved.

There is of course a rich tradition of bodies of water separating the lands of the living from those of the dead, as in the river Styx that has to be crossed to get into Hades, but once more the Celtic and Norse influences seem more central to Tolkien's conception. For beyond the sea lie the "immortal shores" that Eärendil reaches, a land filled with Valar, Maiar and Elves that is once more reminiscent especially of the Celtic Otherworld. Even the realms of the Elves within Middle-earth are set apart by rivers and streams that indicate passage and crossing over into an otherworldly sphere (where often even time passes differently).[41] These are in-between places, little islands of the Otherworld within the world of the mortals. As Burns notes, "such crossings of mortal and fairy worlds, occur most often at twilight, in the mist, or at the margin of rivers" (62) and "[a]long with fords, ferries, and water crossings in general, literary or mythological bridges serve [...] to represent spiritual transition, the traversing of space or time, of barrier or gap, that lies between two worlds" (54). In this Celtic context, the placement of the pantheon of

---

41 Burns lists here the ford of Bruinen which has to be crossed to enter Rivendell, the stream in front of the gates of the halls of the Elven king in Mirkwood, and the numerous little streams that shield Lórien in the west, while it borders the river Anduin in the east. For a more detailed discussion, see Burns (68).

minor gods and other immortals beyond the sea is not surprising at all. While water structures Tolkien's narratives in quite distinctive ways, the crossing of water not only marks the passage into stranger, more otherworldly tales, but also crucially separates mortals from immortals. There are even some places that represent a more permanent in-between-ness (like the Dead Marshes). In the end, however, characters tend to end up on either side of this seemingly binary opposition of mortality and immortality. For the mortal characters, the Otherworld can always only be an ephemeral abode, while the immortals similarly have to leave Middle-earth. The most noteworthy, and one of only a few exceptions, concerns Eärendil and his descendants: Inherently bound to a life on the sea, Eärendil spends most of his time in-between the worlds. Similarly, his descendants on the side of Elros inhabit the island of Númenor between Middle-earth and Aman. Their status as a kind of hybrid between mortal and immortal is symbolically expressed in their longevity and the mode of their passing. Repeatedly, we are reminded that they tired of life in a way more alike to some Elves than that of other Men. Ironically, it is only in their striving for immortality proper that they are again reduced to human proportions. They are either stranded for ever on the mortal shores, or dead on the immortal shores. To them, the sea as a habitat and landscape collapses into a boundary and finally settles their fate on this side.

Yet beyond the Otherworld of Aman lies the Outer Sea, another boundary, the only border those waiting in the Halls of Mandos have not yet crossed. In its final form, then, "across the water" transforms into a synonym for the final unknown. So while the Elves, the immortal Firstborn Children, return to the Halls of Mandos, Men pass even further. Ilúvatar's gift means that they are set apart in the Halls of Mandos, to finally journey on into the unknown. "Mandos under Ilúvatar alone save Manwë knows whither they go after the time of recollection in those silent halls beside the Outer Sea" (*S* 117). This is in a way the final uncertainty, the final doubt. For whatever comes after, it will have to be sought even beyond the Outer Sea.

7 Conclusion

As we have seen, water as an element of Tolkien's secondary world has its very own crucial role that is characterised above all by its fluidity in constantly changing the course of events in unexpected ways and interacting with individuals and groups. It does so by enacting its physicality within Tolkien's major narrative works as a structural landscape and by playing with the expectations, hopes, and by repeatedly offering choices to the people journeying across Middle-earth and beyond. While it would have been interesting to also look at Tolkien's poetic renderings of stories like that of Eärendil or Tom Bombadil, this would have exceeded the limitations of this essay.

By examining its initial role within the created world and then tracking its role and development throughout the history of Middle-earth and within the major narratives, it has been possible to identify a meta-narrative of water as an element that is – more than that of any other element – representative of the shift in the overall conceptualisation of Arda. From enacting Ulmo's will and power to a more secular structural landscape rejecting a clear moral grounding, its transition lends coherence to the stylistic development that makes the various narratives so distinctly recognisable, while at the same time elaborating on the created world in a tone consistent with its ontology.

A further layer of meaning has been identified in the relation between the direction of sea-journeys and the tension between fate and free will, which is also closely related to the issue of mortality, and which is negotiated within the context of a westward calling. As for the unknown fate of Men, the uncertainty attached to their mortality and the refusal to offer conceptual closure is yet again explained in terms of lying beyond the (Outer) Sea. In the end, and judging by what we have learned about water, there is undoubtedly reason for hope, even without certainty. If we want a definite answer as to the nature of the final adventure, as humans and readers of Middle-earth, we may have to go across the Water to find out.

About the Author

ROBIN MARKUS AUER is reading Philosophy at Heidelberg University for an MA. He holds a BA from Heidelberg in English and Philosophy and an MSt in English (650-1550) from Merton College, Oxford. His academic interests include cognitive poetics, narratology, evolutionary approaches to literary theory, Anglo-Saxon literature, and Tolkien. Graduating from Heidelberg in 2015 with a thesis on '"The Tales That Really Mattered" – Frame Narrative and Identity in J.R.R. Tolkien's *The Lord of the Rings*', he has also contributed a paper on Tolkien titled 'Tolkien's Middle-Earth: A Myth in a Test Tube' to a student conference on the topic of myth in Gießen in the same year. At Oxford, he completed his thesis on 'Distribution, Form and Function of hapax legomenon-compounds in the riddles relating to the Anglo-Saxon scriptorium' under the supervision of Rawlinson & Bosworth Professor of Anglo Saxon, Andy Orchard. He is currently working on theories of literary criticism and cognitive science in preparation for a PhD project on cognitive and neuroscientific approaches to literature.

Abbreviations

FR   TOLKIEN, J.R.R. *The Fellowship of the Ring.* London: HarperCollins, 2007.

Letters   *The Letters of J.R.R. Tolkien.* Ed. Humphrey Carpenter, with the assistance of Christopher Tolkien. London: HarperCollins, 2006.

RK   TOLKIEN, J.R.R. *The Return of the King.* London: HarperCollins, 2007.

S   TOLKIEN, J.R.R. *The Silmarillion.* Ed. Christopher Tolkien. London: HarperCollins, 1999.

Bibliography

AGØY, Nilv Ivar. 'A Question of Style. On Translating *The Silmarillion* into Norwegian.' *Tolkien in Translation.* Ed. Thomas Honegger. Second edition. Zurich and Berne: Walking Tree Publisher, 2011. 31-43.

BACHELARD, Gaston. *Water and Dreams. An Essay on the Imagination of Matter.* Translated from the French original L'eau et ses rêves (1942) by Edith R. Farrell. Dallas: The Dallas Institute of Humanities and Culture, 1983.

BURNS, Marjorie. *Perilous Realms. Celtic and Norse in Tolkien's Middle-earth.* Toronto: University of Toronto Press, 2005.

CURRY, Patrick. *Defending Middle-earth: Tolkien: Myth and Modernity.* London: HarperCollins, 1998.

Deep Roots in a Time of Frost. Essays on Tolkien. Zurich and Jena: Walking Tree Publishers, 2014.

DAICHES, David and John FLOWER. *Literary Landscapes of the British Isles: A Narrative Atlas.* New York: Paddington, 1979.

EKMAN, Stefan. *Here Be Dragons: Exploring Fantasy Maps and Settings.* Middletown: Wesleyan University Press, 2013.

FIMI, Dimitra. *Tolkien, Race and Cultural History.* Basingstoke: Palgrave Macmillan, 2009.

MACLEOD, Jeffrey J. and Anna SMOL. 'Visualizing the Word: Tolkien as Artist and Writer.' *Tolkien Studies* 14 (2017): 115-31.

ROMAN, Christopher. 'Thinking with the Elements: J.R.R. Tolkien's Ecology and Object-Oriented Ontology.' *Representations of Nature in Middle-earth.* Ed. Martin Simonson. Zurich and Jena: Walking Tree Publishers, 2015. 95-118.

SARAPIK, Virve. 'Landscape: The Problem of Representation.' *Proceedings of the Estonian Academy of Arts* 10 (2000): 183-99.

SHAW, Sylvie and Andrew FRANCIS (eds.). *Deep Blue: Critical Reflections on Nature, Religion and Water.* Oakville CT: Equinox, 2008.

SHIPPEY, Tom. *Roots and Branches. Selected Papers on Tolkien.* Zurich and Berne: Walking Tree Publishers, 2007.

The Road to Middle-earth. London: Allen & Unwin, 1982.

SILVA RIVERO, Gabriela. '"Behind a grey rain-curtain": Water, Melancholy and Healing in *The Lord of the Rings.*' *Representations of Nature in Middle-earth.* Ed. Martin Simonson. Zurich and Jena: Walking Tree Publishers, 2015. 49-71.

TANKARD, Paul. '"Akin to my own Inspiration": Mary Fairburn and the Art of Middle-earth.' *Tolkien Studies* 14 (2017): 133-54.

TOLKIEN, John R.R. *The Fellowship of the Ring.* London: HarperCollins, 2007.

The Hobbit. London: HarperCollins, 2006.

The Letters of J.R.R. Tolkien. Ed. Humphrey Carpenter, with the assistance of Christopher Tolkien. London: HarperCollins, 2006.

The Return of the King. London: HarperCollins, 2007.

The Two Towers. London: HarperCollins, 2007.

The Silmarillion. Ed. Christopher Tolkien. London: HarperCollins, 1999.

Unfinished Tales. Ed. Christopher Tolkien. London: HarperCollins, 2014.

TURNER, Allan. 'Tolkien's Living Landscapes.' *Hither Shore* 11 (2014): 8-17.

Michaela Hausmann

Lyrics on Lost Lands:
Constructing Lost Places through Poetry in J.R.R. Tolkien's *The Lord of the Rings*

Abstract

This paper analyses selected poems from *The Lord of the Rings* in which 'lost places' like Valinor or Beleriand are depicted in order to show how these places are constructed by means of poetic techniques of world-building. On the one hand, those lyrics on lost lands therefore contribute to the overall subcreation of Arda as a complex Secondary World, but, on the other hand, they also have an impact on the immediate diegetic context and the characters in *The Lord of the Rings* because the representation of such lost places is always filtered through the personal and cultural perspective of the singer and mediated to an unknowing audience. The following paper will therefore look at the world-building potential as well as the performance contexts of these lyrics on lost lands in *The Lord of the Rings*.

1 Introducion

In his essay 'On Stories', C. S. Lewis claimed that he "want[s] not that momentary suspense" a story can create but "that whole world to which it belonged" (5). With this statement, he acknowledged the importance of setting as a spatio-temporal dimension which has come to be considered one of the major constituents of a story next to events and characters (Chatman, 19). This is particularly true for fantasy literature, where "the special role of setting and geography [...] has been amplified and developed in the work of nearly all the major writers [...]" (Mathews 39), because "the ability of fantasy to generate wonder [...] is closely tied to both setting and story line" (Attebery 128). As a result, the subcreation of fantastic Secondary Worlds has become a major feature of many works of fantasy literature and Tolkien's fictional world of Arda is often perceived as an unparalleled example.

His *Silmarillion* contains an account of the genesis of this world in form of a fictional creation myth. According to this, the Secondary World of Arda is literally *sung* into existence by the divine Eru and the angelic Ainur (S 3-12) which accentuates the direct correlation between song or poetry and subcreation in Tolkien's works. It is therefore justifiable to assume that the embedded poems in the other works of his *legendarium*, *The Hobbit* and *The Lord of the Rings*, also contribute to literary world-building in the overall narrative. With regard to the success of his fictional world and his literary works in general, Tolkien himself argued that "part of the attraction of L. R" lies in its evocation of "glimpses of a large history in the background [...] viewing far off an unvisited island, or seeing the towers of a distant city gleaming in a sunlit mist" (*Letters* 333).

My argument in this essay is that poems that are concerned with lost lands poetically construct such "unattainable vistas" (*Letters* 333.) and therefore exemplify techniques of literary world-building. In turn, the shaping of individual places also contributes to a complex and detailed mental construction of the entire Secondary World to which they belong, so that 'lyrics on lost lands' assume a general world-building function. As such, they arguably belong to those storytelling elements "that do not advance the story but which provide background richness and verisimilitude to the imaginary world" (Wolf 2).

Yet such poems simultaneously convey a very personal perspective of the diegetic performers towards the world they inhabit. Insofar, the embedded poems seem to cater to two aesthetic effects Tolkien described to his son Christopher as follows:

> There are two quit [sic] diff. emotions: one that moves me supremely and I find small difficulty in evoking: the heart-racking sense of the vanished past [...]; and the other the more 'ordinary' emotion, triumph, pathos, tragedy of the characters. [...] A story must be told or there'll be no story, yet it is the untold stories that are most moving. (*Letters* 110-11).

The second emotion corroborates Tolkien's insistence that his verses "are all dramatic" being "fitted in style and contents to the characters in the story that sing them, and to the situations in it" (*Letters* 396). This means that, even though they build images of lands lost in the distant past, these poems have an impact on the concurrent action and also communicate a character's emotions to which a reader can relate.

The following analysis of three 'lyrics on lost lands' will therefore examine the world-building potential of selected embedded poems in *LotR* in terms of constructing and mediating images of particular places in Arda from a certain perspective in a specific narrative situation. At first, a theoretical framework will be provided drawing on central aspects of Wolf's landmark publication *Building Imaginary Worlds* and applying them to the analysis of poetry. Afterwards, a definition of 'lost lands' in the context of this paper will be given in order to explain the selection of poems before an in-depth analysis of Galadriel's two Lothlórien songs and Treebeard's 'In the Willow-Meads of Tasarinan' will be conducted. Finally, a concluding statement shall serve to summarise and reflect on the world-building potential of these embedded lyrics on lost lands in *LotR*.

2 Literary World-building in Poetry: Theoretical Framework

Two essential terms with regard to world-building in fantasy literature, namely 'subcreation' and 'Secondary World', derive from Tolkien's influential essay 'On Fairy Stories' (OFS) where subcreation is described as the invention of "a new form" through the artistic combination of existing material and the artist's imagination. As a result, a fantastic otherworld, or "Secondary World" as Tolkien calls it, may take shape "which your mind can enter" (OFS 132). According to Tolkien's Christian perspective, the supreme and only truly creative act was the divine creation of our world. A human artist's creative power can therefore only ever be subordinate, only ever echo this primary act of creation, and it is therefore called subcreative art. Likewise, the material used by the subcreative artist to build an imaginary world necessarily derives from our real world, and can only be imaginatively transformed. In order to stress this causal relation, Tolkien uses the term "Primary World" for our perceived reality, and "Secondary World" for the imaginative otherworld (OFS 132). The capacity for subcreative art is given to all human beings through the power of language and the imagination by which we can "make the rare and terrible blue moon to shine; or we may cause woods to spring with silver leaves and rams wear fleeces of gold, and put hot fire into the belly of the cold worm" (OFS 122).

Based on Tolkien's theoretical delineations, Mark Wolf's *Building Imaginary Worlds* continued to examine the nature and construction of Secondary Worlds and the process of subcreation. He expands the definition of Secondary Worlds significantly, claiming that a Secondary World must be "a fictional place", either an entire world or something on a smaller scale such as a forest or village; and that it must be set apart from the Primary World but related to it. Wolf further argues for three central principles each Secondary World should observe: "it will need to have a high degree of invention, completeness, and consistency" (OFS 33). The latter renders a Secondary World believable, which is the essential quality any Secondary World should possess according to Tolkien: "the moment disbelief arises, the spell is broken; the magic, or rather art, has failed. You are then out in the Primary World again, looking at the little abortive Secondary World from outside" (OFS 132). Therefore, the Secondary World should be without internal contradictions in terms of physical laws and invented features. Completeness denotes the detail with which a Secondary World is imbued and suggests a bigger picture than can be presented within the narrative constraints of a story, such as "infrastructures, ecological systems, and societies and cultures [...]" and the "sense that a world has a past history [...]" (Wolf 42). Invention is the principle that endows a Secondary World with a unique design and demarcates it from the Primary World. Wolf differentiates four categories in which secondary-world invention can occur: (1) "the nominal realm, [...] in which new names are given for existing things", (2) "the *cultural* realm, which consists of all things made by humans (or other creatures)," (3) "the natural realm, which includes not only new landmasses (or other places like underground regions), but new kinds of plants and animals, and new species and races of creatures", and (4) "the ontological realm itself, which determines the parameters of a world's existence, that is, the materiality and laws of physics, space, time, and so forth that constitute the world" (Wolf 35-36).

Wolf adds another important requirement for each Secondary World, claiming that it must not be "simply geographical but *experiential*; that is, everything that is experienced by the characters involved, the elements unfolding someone's life (culture, nature, philosophical worldviews, places, customs, events, and so forth)," (Wolf 25). Without an experiential anchoring, world-building is much less effective and runs the risk of becoming an endless enumeration of invented features without meaning. As vehicles of subjective perspective, embedded poems could contribute significantly to this experiential quality enabling a reader to relate to the Secondary World.

As autonomous texts, poems may seem ill-equipped for the successful creation of an elaborate setting, let alone a full-scale Secondary World, because there is necessarily a reduced number of spatio-temporal cues in poetry in comparison to dramatic and narrative texts (Petzold 125-27). Indeed, poetry's "tendency to relative brevity" and the reduction of the subject matter, which impairs detailed world-making (Werner Wolf 265-67), seems irreconcilable with the abovementioned criterion of completeness. Moreover, a limited number of lines also reduces the principle of secondary-world invention to a sketchy idea of an otherworld. Here, the stylistic device of *embedded* poems proves an effective artistic solution to the problem. Due to the overarching prose narrative, the poems are no longer self-contained pieces of art, so that potential gaps and sketchy pieces of information in the poems can often be contextualised and disambiguated. By being integrated into the prose narrative, the poems lose the problematic feature of self-referentiality and can enrich the prose narrative by, for example, imparting additional information on the "different cultures, traditions and time-periods" in the narrative (Drout 4).

All these aspects contribute to the *completeness* of a Secondary World, but the poems in Tolkien's *LotR* can furthermore contribute to secondary-world *invention* by furnishing the constructed places with idiosyncratic features. For the purpose of the analysis, the exemplary poems will be scanned for references corresponding to Wolf's realms of secondary-world invention:

Realms of Invention (Wolf)	⇒	References in the poems to:
nominal realm	⇒	Arda's specific names and languages etc.
cultural realm	⇒	Arda's peoples, their customs, history etc.
natural realm	⇒	Arda's vegetation, geography and life forms
ontological level	⇒	Arda's physical laws and development

The last category will comprise references to the fundamental changes in Arda's design on the surface level because in Tolkien's *legendarium* such shifts of continents, etc., always have metaphysical implications. These changes affect the ontological dimension because of the significant physical and psychological consequences for the Secondary World of Arda and its inhabitants.

As mentioned above, all secondary-world invention works primarily by combining new things with primary-world material, so that the individual references found in the poem have to be considered in relation to the primary-world features from which they borrow or deviate. In order to examine whether the principles of secondary-world consistency as well as intertextual consistency are observed, the statements and descriptions in the poems of *LotR* will be compared with representations of the respective places in the prose narrative as well as with maps and narrative descriptions from *The Silmarillion* which belong to the diegetic pre-history of *LotR*.

Whenever space in literary text is analysed, however, it should be kept in mind that the representation of space is usually a double-edged sword because the mediation of a material, geographical place is always influenced by a speaker's or focaliser's personal, social and cultural concepts. Although this enables experiential anchoring, it also distorts the representation of the constructed place. This in turn sheds light on the performer's personality as well as on the relationship between performer and listener, as Joanna Kokot argues:

> The poems [...] communicate the performer's unique interpretation of reality. They not only express the performer's wishes and thoughts, his understanding of the world, or his reactions to his actual situation, but they enable the listeners to experience a contact with the performer, which is different from that acquired in common talk or through direct observation. (194)

Thus, the performance contexts need to be taken into account as well as the speakers' and audiences' perspectives.

3 Defining Lyrics on Lost Lands in the Context of Tolkien's Works

Among the various poems in *LotR* that point to a distant past, there are some that are concerned with a very particular aspect of world-building, namely with the representation of lost lands. Those 'lyrics on lost lands' refer to places which appear lost from the diegetic context of *LotR* both chronologically and spatially. They hace vanished from the surface of Arda by the Third Age in which the story of the *LotR* is set and cannot be accessed by the characters anymore. In *LotR* such lost places include the lands of Beleriand which had once been a significant part of Middle-earth until they were drowned in the cataclysmic War of Wrath at the end of the First Age (*S* 303). In the course of the Second Age, the large island Númenor suffered a similar fate. Together with most of its inhabitants, it was submerged under the wave as a punishment for their blasphemic pride and desire for immortality (*S* 334). The Undying Lands, consisting of the continent Aman and the Elvish island Tol Eressëa, present a borderline case. After the exile of the Noldor during the First Age, the Undying Lands were "shut against the Noldor" and anyone coming from Middle-earth in an event called the "Hiding of Valinor" (*S* 113-14). Since the sailors of Númenor nevertheless threatened to attack the Undying Lands, those lands were irrevocably removed from the circles of the world after the Second Age and thus became inaccessible to anyone except the Eldar (*S* 334-38).

Such lyrics on lost lands are interesting cases of world-building for various reasons. For one, the implied former existence of such lost lands endows Arda with a past history and geological development, thereby contributing to its completeness. Most characters in *LotR*, except for the Istari and some of the High-Elves like Galadriel and Elrond, lack prior knowledge or even personal memory of these places. For them and for us as readers, the poems often provide the sole or primary source of information about these places. As they can no longer function as actual settings in *LotR*, they do not feature in the prose passages. The representation of lost places is confined to the poems. Lyrics on lost lands therefore allow for a more condensed analysis of the relevant world-building principles than poems whose places correspond to actual settings in *LotR*.

However, the poems nevertheless have implications for the immediate plot and the characters in *LotR*, so that, contrary to what Raffel said (232), skipping those poems would result in a substantial loss to the overall tale. Hence, the performance contexts and the artists' and audiences' perspectives of these embedded poems and their construction of literary space need to be considered. With regard to lyrics on lost lands, there is a noticeable knowledge discrepancy between the performers and their respective audiences. Usually, the characters who recite or sing the poems, actually remember these places they sing about from personal memory and experience. Such characters function as temporal links in whom the memory of the past is preserved and mediated to an unknowing audience. But neither the diegetic listeners nor the readers who are not familiar with the entire *legendarium* can verify the images conveyed by these poems. Their knowledge entirely depends on the information transmitted in the poems which, however, always function as vehicles of the composers' subjective perspectives. The singers, of course, are aware that they are not creating a new world but that the poetic construction of lost lands in poetry is always the product of their own artistic re-creation and manipulation. For the audiences, on the other hand, the images of these lost lands as constructed through the poems could be seen as instances of subcreated subcreation, i. e. subcreations by characters within Tolkien's own fictional subcreation.

Wolf only discusses those types of subcreated subcreations that can be entered physically and hold real dangers for the visitors (233-34). This would exclude Tolkien's singers of lyrics on lost lands because they do not actually make a world but rather create poetic portals across time to a world that had already been there before (Wolf 236). On the other hand, one could argue that the lost lands have the necessary features of remoteness and inaccessibility. Moreover, at the moment of the performance, a concise image of a place is imaginatively created for the listeners and they can enter these worlds mentally. Insofar, the lost lands should not be considered material subcreated subcreations but imaginative subcreated subcreations, just as any literary text is an imaginative subcreation. In Tolkien's fictional cosmos, the poetic speech act becomes a subcreative act, and songs and poems become subcreative tools that constantly echo the music of Eru and the Ainur, albeit with diminished creative power.

For these reasons, the lyrics on lost lands in *LotR* promise insights into the processes involved in literary world-building and the artists' and audiences' individual perspectives through which the presentation of space is constantly filtered. The three poems chosen for the analysis belong to the category of lyrics on lost lands and offer the greatest variety of references to secondary-world invention, thereby promising the greatest potential of exemplifying processes of literary world-building. 'I Sang of Leaves' and 'Namárië' are both sung by Galadriel and complement each other in the poetic construction of Aman, so they should be considered in tandem, while Treebeard's 'In the Willow-meads of Tasarinan' is concerned with the lands of Beleriand.

4 Analysis

4.1 Galadriel's 'I sang of leaves' and 'Namárië'

Galadriel's songs, 'I sang of leaves' and 'Namárië', both occur in the chapter 'Farewell to Lórien' and are both concerned with Lothlórien as an immediate setting of the narrative, and with the Undying Lands. In *The Silmarillion*, the Elves' connection to this place is delineated. After their awakening in Middle-earth, the Elves were invited by the Valar to live with them in Valinor. Those Elves who accepted the invitation subsequently came to be known as High Elves or Calaquendi because they lived in the Blessed Realm. One Elvish race, the Noldor, rebelled against the Valar, and, being exiled from the Undying Lands, came to live in Middle-earth until they were pardoned and allowed to return after the First Age (*S* 94; 305). Hence, the Undying Lands are considered the ancient home of the Elves for which those yearn who still linger in Middle-earth, uncertain whether they will be able to return at some point.

One of those Noldorin exiles is Galadriel who was born in the Undying Lands and chose to stay in Middle-earth after the First Age (*S* 306). She is consequently one of the oldest living characters in Middle-earth by the time of the Third Age and remembers Aman from personal experience, so that the poetic construction of the Undying Lands is strongly filtered through her experiential memory. Her audience for both songs, on the other hand, has little or no knowledge about the Undying Lands, let alone personal memories. Among the diegetic audience, only the Elves of Lothlórien, Legolas, and Aragorn would understand the songs' references to the Undying Lands as they have at least some rudimentary knowledge of Elvish history and lore. Gimli, Boromir, and the Hobbits, who are the main focalisers in *LotR*, however, would only know about the West as a fabled place to which the Elves sail after their departure from Middle-earth (*LotR* 104).

The two songs frame the farewell feast of the Fellowship and their hosts, Celeborn and Galadriel. While the Fellowship practise for their imminent journey in the Elvish boats on the river, Galadriel and Celeborn approach with their ship in the likeness of a swan. Galadriel sings 'I sang of Leaves' in the common tongue understood by everybody, so that it can be assumed to be directed to the Fellowship.

> *I sang of leaves, of leaves of gold, and leaves of gold there grew*
> *Of wind I sang, a wind there came and in the branches blew.*
> *Beyond the Sun, beyond the Moon, the foam was on the Sea,*
> *And by the strand of Ilmarin there grew a golden Tree.*
> *Beneath the stars of Ever-eve in Eldamar it shone,* 5
> *In Eldamar beside the walls of Elven Tirion.*
> *There long the golden leaves have grown upon the branching years,*
> *While here beyond the Sundering Seas now fall the Elven-tears.*
> *O Lórien! The Winter comes, the bare and leafless Day;*
> *The leaves are falling in the stream, the River flows away.* 10
> *O Lórien! Too long I have dwelt upon this Hither Shore*
> *And in a fading crown have twined the golden elanor.*
> *But if of ships I now should sing, what ship would come to me,*
> *What ship would bear me ever back across so wide a Sea?*
> (*LotR* 485-86, my line numbers)

In light of the aforementioned interrelationship between music and subcreation in Tolkien's *legendarium*, the first two lines are significant because the first person speaker, who can be identified as Galadriel, self-reflects on her role as a subcreated subcreator whose song produced actual changes in the singer's reality. The golden leaves are a reference to the mallorn trees which had been introduced as a unique feature of Lothlórien's vegetation upon the Fellowship's arrival (*LotR* 435, 444). Since there is no equivalent to any tree in our Primary World, the mallorn trees are an invention in the natural realm of the Secondary World of Arda. Although it was not Galadriel who invented the mallorn trees, she made the seeds blossom in Lothlórien with the power of her Elven ring Nenya.

After this introductory couplet, the song's focus shifts from Lothlórien to the Undying Lands in lines 3-7. Since the preposition "beyond" usually indicates spatial distance, its conjunction with Sun and Moon initially suggests that the places subsequently described – "the strand of Ilmarin", the "golden Tree", "Eldamar" and "Elven Tirion" – must be located somewhere outside of Arda in outer space. As a result, this place attains an almost fairy-tale quality to the unknowing listener which is corroborated by the strange proper names that cannot be found anywhere on the maps in *LotR*. Readers familiar with *The Silmarillion* and Galadriel herself, however, know that "beyond" marks temporal distance here, placing the image of the Undying Lands constructed in lines 3-7 into the far past. The proper names are geographical references to places in the Undying Lands: Ilmarin is the dwelling place of the Valar Manwë and Varda, two of the most powerful subcreative powers that had shaped Arda, Eldamar is the land of the Elves on the continent of Aman, and the reference to the walls of Elven Tirion identify the latter as a chief Elvish city in the Undying Lands.

All the other aspects in these lines are references to the ontological realm because they define objects of light and time-reckoning in their cosmic genealogy. Since the Undying Lands are described in their state beyond or before the Sun and Moon, these two celestial bodies did not belong to the Secondary World of Arda from the beginning. Consequently, there had been no concept for "day" and everything was "Ever-eve" and stars were the only heavenly source of light (l. 5). Apart from these, the song refers to "a golden Tree" which radiates light as it "shone" beneath the stars. According to Arda's history in *The Silmarillion*, the Trees of Light were the original sources of light from which the brightest stars were made when the Elves awoke in Middle-earth. The golden Tree, Laurelin, and its silver counterpart, Telperion, grew in Valinor and afforded Arda with a concept of time reckoning due to their waxing and waning hours (S 31-32). Line 7 indicates this connection between the Two Trees and chronology through the metaphor of "branching years". After the Trees' destruction through Melkor, Varda took a last piece from each of the dying trees, and made the sun from Laurelin and the moon from Telperion; and both sources of light continue the chronological function. Since the trunks of the mallorn trees in Lothlórien are compared to "silver pillars" with golden leaves (*LotR* 435), they are clearly modeled on the silver and golden light of the Two Trees (S 31), so that the poem not only makes references to Arda's invented vegetation but also provides these invented trees with their own evolution in the subcreated world.

The lines on Aman build up a tentative image of a place within Arda with concrete geographical references that work like a scaffold for the audience's imagination. In addition, the cosmic development of the entire Secondary World is hinted at. In the context of *LotR*, this is nowhere made more explicit than in Galadriel's song which thereby becomes a small window across time and space for the audiences, deepening the characters' own understanding of the world they live in, and providing the reader with a brief extract of cosmic history of the subcreated world they have imaginatively entered.

Structurally, Galadriel's song is written in seven couplets of connected thoughts that form the following pattern: The first couplet encapsulates Galadriel's reflection on her own past subcreative acts, the second and third couplet provide a description of the Undying Lands in a past state, the fifth and sixth couplet present an image of Lothlórien's and Galadriel's present and future state, and the final couplet is a rhetorical question about Galadriel's uncertain personal future. The temporal and spatial shifts are enunciated in the fourth couplet (lines seven and eight). While line seven completes the description of the Undying Lands, line eight moves the focus to the speaker's immediate situational context, i.e. Lothlórien and the Fellowship's departure, by using the past tense in line seven but the present tense and temporal adverb "now" in line eight. The spatial deictic markers ("there" and "here") furthermore underline the gulf between the past image of the Undying Lands and the present state of Lothlórien. It is certainly no coincidence that this divide is conceived in the image of the "Sundering Seas" because, on the one hand, the seas are, in fact, between Middle-earth and the Undying Lands in Tolkien's Arda, but the sea is also metaphorically charged with notions of spatial distance and time in perpetual motion.

The reference to the Elven-tears in Middle-earth convey the sadness, the pains of exile and nostalgia of the Elves for the Undying Lands, sentiments which Tolkien had defined as central characteristics of Elves (*Letters* 236). All these emotions govern the presentation of Lothlórien as an imperfect place that is no longer immune to change because the destruction of the One Ring would also destroy the preserving power of Galdriel's ring Nenya. Just as Galadriel informs Frodo that "the tides of Time will sweep it [Lothlórien] away" (*LotR* 475) should he be successful, lines nine and ten express metaphorically how Lothlórien's glory – the golden leaves of the mallorn trees – will be washed away by the river, the symbol of time. Likewise, winter as the season of barrenness will come to Lothlórien whereas its spring and summer "are gone by, and they will never be seen on earth again save in memory" (*LotR* 489). The two apostrophes at the beginning of lines 9 and 11 emphasise the song's function as a lament for Lórien and corroborate "the *ubi sunt* motif" that is frequently found in "Old English elegiac poetry" (Donovan 239). While the first apostrophe introduces a description of Lórien's fate in general, the second moves to Galadriel's personal fate which is closely tied to Lórien's.

Lines 11-14 are consequently characterised by a heightened degree of subjectivity due to the use of the first person pronoun in each of them. It becomes apparent that Galadriel perceives that her own time in Middle-earth ("this Hither Shore") is coming to an end. Likewise, her efforts to defend Lothlórien's beauty against the effects of time – here expressed by the metaphor of Galadriel twining the golden flower elanor in a fading crown – must eventually be in vain (l. 12). Galadriel's status as an exile in Middle-earth is only hinted at while *The Silmarillion* presents it in more detail. Her own tragedy is that she had shaped Lothlórien as a place of timeless perfection, and that she now has to sacrifice it in order to defeat Sauron and to be re-admitted into the Blessed Realm (*LotR* 476). Since Lothlórien and its mallorn trees are an after-image of the Undying Lands and the Two Trees, Galadriel's sadness about losing Lothlórien reminds her of the loss of her ancient home in the Undying Lands. The final couplet, however, expresses her fear that, in spite of her sacrifice, there may be no ship to carry her across the sea to the Undying Lands. This concluding rhetorical question remains unanswered until the end of the entire narrative.

The mentioning of boats at the end of Galadriel's first song brings the audience back to the immediate narrative context of *LotR* and the Fellowship's imminent journey on the river Anduin. With its consistent iambic heptametre, the poem imitates the regularity of the flowing river, so that the formal aspects as well as the song's subject matter contribute to the overall impression of the inexorability of time in flux which dominates the entire chapter on Lothlórien. As the Fellowship leave Lothlórien in their boats, they look back at Galadriel and it seems to them that "Lórien was slipping backward, like a bright ship masted with enchanted trees, sailing on to forgotten shores, while they sat helpless upon the margin of the grey and leafless world" (*LotR* 491). Flieger interprets this impression as a convergence of temporal dimensions: once their boats reach the Anduin, the Fellowship are back in the flux of progressive time which relentlessly leads them to the future, whereas Lothlórien, a place of Elvish or "suspended time" drifts into the past and fading memory (Flieger 97-98). It emulates Frodo's earlier view of Galadriel as "present yet remote, a living vision of that which has already been left far behind the flowing streams of Time" (*LotR* 486). The Elves' eventual departure from Middle-earth and their return to a past and lost land, which only they can reach, is anticipated here, whereas those remaining in Middle-earth have no means to sail against the tides of time but are driven by them. Such curious overlaps of time are also exemplified by the embedded poems themselves which Zimmermann argues to be "places where the linearity which prevails in the novel is suspended and where past, present and sometimes future merge" (81).

Galadriel's second song, which is mediated through Frodo as a focaliser, continues the construction of the Undying Lands in a past state. The song is rendered in Quenya (*LotR* 492), the fictional language of the High Elves, so that this poem is in itself a direct reference to the invented languages of Arda and what Wolf defines as the nominal realm. Moreover, the text does not show any of the structural regularities of Galadriel's previous song in Westron, such as end rhymes or regular metre, so that an older tradition of Elvish poetry with its own specific conventions is implied. Frodo's perspective creates a problem of transmission and interpretation for the reader because, just as Frodo "did not understand the words" (*LotR* 491) neither do readers unless they have learned Quenya prior to their reading experience. However, the words "remained graven in his [Frodo's] memory, and long afterwards he interpreted them as well as he could" (*LotR* 492). Hence, we are faced with the danger of words and meaning becoming lost in Frodo's fictional translation and have to rely on his interpretation. To increase the problem of understanding, the language is said to be "that of Elven-song" and to speak "of things little known on Middle-earth" (*LotR* 492). These statements reveal the Elvish perspective in the poem and indicate the audience's ignorance regarding the subject matter of the song:

> Ah! like gold fall the leaves in the wind, long years numberless as the wings of trees! The long years have passed like swift draughts of the sweet mead in lofty halls beyond the West, beneath the blue vaults of Varda wherein the stars tremble in the song of her voice, holy and queenly. Who now shall refill the

cup for me? For now the Kindler, Varda, the Queen of the Stars, from Mount Everwhite has uplifted her hands like clouds, and all paths are drowned deep in shadow; and out of a grey country darkness lies on the foaming waves between us, and mist covers the jewels of Calacirya for ever. Now lost, lost to those from the East is Valimar! Farewell! Maybe thou shalt find Valimar. Maybe even thou shalt find it. Farewell! (*LotR* 492-93)

The second song also uses the mallorn leaves that fall "like gold" as a symbol of time and transience, conflating the autumnal metaphor of falling leaves with the fading of Lothlórien and the loss of the Two Trees. Thereby, the subcreated genealogy of these invented trees is once more alluded to while our primary-world concept of autumn is necessary to ensure understanding on the reader's part. Another simile compares the passing of years with the "swift draughts of sweet mead" with which Galadriel shifts the song's focus from Lothlórien to the Undying Lands. By making mead the traditional beverage of "the lofty halls beyond the West", a whole repertoire of cultural references is opened up for the primary-world reader who is familiar with Norse mythology. In the context of the former, mead is depicted as the ritual drink enjoyed in Valhalla (Mortensen 34) and the "mead of poetry" also bestows the gift of poetry to anyone who drinks it (Lindow 224-27). Both references resonate with associations of immortality and afterlife which can be applied such to the construction of the Undying Lands in Galadriel's song.

While the concept of mead is directly transmitted to the Secondary World of Arda, the frequent mentioning of Varda in the song constitutes a case of secondary-world invention with regard to the cultural realm. The various epithets like "Queen of the Stars", "Kindler" as well as the description of her voice as "holy and queenly" signify a religious reverence with which Varda is regarded in the song. Although the unknowing audience would thus be able to deduce her quasi-divine status in Elvish culture, not much about her role in Arda is disclosed in these lines. Even a short sentence that reads like an editorial comment after Frodo's translation of Galadriel's song is vague. It only explains that "Varda is the name of that Lady whom the Elves in these lands of exile name Elbereth" (*LotR* 493), and thus creates an intertextual link to the Elvish song the Hobbits hear in the Shire (104) and reveals that Middle-earth is a place of exile to the Elves. *The Silmarillion*, however, introduces Varda as one of the angelic Valar. She made the stars, and the sun and the moon, for which she is loved by Elves in particular. With this knowledge, the "blue vaults" in the poem can be interpreted as the sky over the Undying Lands and the stars react to the sound of her voice because they are her creations. Therefore, the poem makes a cultural reference to the Elves' religious reverence for Varda and an ontological reference to her as one of the Arda's main mythical subcreators.

In addition to the cultural realm of secondary-world invention, there are also many references to the natural level in form of geographic places in the Undying Lands such as Mount Everwhite, Calacirya, and Valimar. Although none of these places is defined more closely in the poem, their proper names reveal attributes that help construct an image of the Undying Lands. Mount Everwhite's name suggests a considerable height denoting an almost fairy tale superlative. This is corroborated by the mountain's function as the highest peak in Arda and the dwelling place of Manwë and Varda in *The Silmarillion*. Calacirya, is said to have jewels in the poem. *The Silmarillion* gives its translation as "Pass of Light" and relates its significance as the main gap in the mountain range of the Pélori in the Undying Lands through which the light of the Two Trees could reach the Elvish dwelling places at the coast (*S* 59). Valimar can be understood in analogy to Eldamar as 'home of the Valar' and denotes the chief city in the Undying Lands, where many of the Valar and Maiar lived. In Galadriel's song, the yearning for Valimar is expressed through repetition.

All these geographic places furnishing the image of the Undying Lands in the poem are inextricably linked to loss: The jewels of Calacirya are lost in mist, on Mount Everwhite Varda's hands resemble obscuring clouds, and Valimar is lost to those in the East because all paths are "drowned in shadow". These metaphors of veiling and loss are references to the ontological realm of invention because they hint at the drastic changes in Arda's geographic design. The lines about Varda who "has uplifted her hands like clouds, and all paths are drowned deep in shadow; and out of a grey country darkness lies on the foaming waves between us" allude to the Hiding of Valinor when "the seas [...] were filled with shadows and bewilderment" (*S* 113). By attributing the making of the Shadowy Seas to Varda, the poem adds essential information nowhere else to be found in Tolkien's *legendarium*. Galadriel's subsequent affirmation that "now lost, lost to those from the East is Valimar!", though, refers to Aman's final removal from the circles of Arda after the Second Age. Again, the contrastive pairs (then and now; West and East) are used to illustrate the great divide between the Undying Lands and Middle-earth where Galadriel and the Fellowship are located.

As in the previous song, Galadriel's subjective perspective is communicated by a rhetorical question: "*Who now shall refill the cup for me?*" stressing her former life in the Undying Lands, its subsequent loss, and her fear of not being allowed to return to the Elvish community there, here expressed by the social rite of cup-bearing. In both of her songs, Galadriel constructs an image of Aman full of concrete references to all spheres of secondary-world invention, from the nominal to the cultural, geographical, natural and even ontological realm, so that her audience can imaginatively enter this lost land. But for the diegetic audience as well as for us as readers, the image of this 'lost place' is tainted by Galadriel's nostalgia and her subjective desire to return to Valinor. Both poems communicate Galadriel's personal feelings, something she only does to that extent in her poems. These poems are therefore crucial instruments of her characterisation in the narrative. But the songs also fulfil another function because, on a more abstract level, the Elves' and Galadriel's loss of Aman mirrors the Fellowship's loss of Lothlórien. In both cases, a paradisal place becomes lost to characters that have enjoyed it for a while but must leave it with little hope to return. Galadriel's Elven-tears in her first song are reflected in the Fellowship's tears after their departure (*LotR* 493). The poems thus serve to establish a bond of empathy and mutual experience. Yet Galadriel's second song ends by expressing the possibility that "maybe even thou shalt find Valimar". In spite of overwhelming sadness, the poems thus sustain a faint but prevailing sense of hope.

4.2 Treebeard's 'In the Willow-Meads of Tasarinan'

'In the Willow-meads of Tasarinan' is sung by Treebeard in book 3 of *LotR* when he carries Merry and Pippin to his home in the heart of Fangorn. It concludes their conversation about the danger of the forest and the nature of Ents; and Treebeard explains that Ents have much in common with Elves. Both races are dwindling and, like Elves, who "hid themselves, and made songs about days that would never come again", Treebeard also uses a song to lament the past when "there was all one wood" covering the entire face of Middle-earth (*LotR* 610). The song focuses on the forests of Beleriand with their different tree types and poetically traces the speaker's journey through the seasons of the year – a journey which Treebeard seems to have made in his youth. Since Ents are invented creatures that embody nature in general and trees in particular, the Entish perspective in Treebeard's song is quickly exposed by the subject matter: The abstract concept of time and history is conceived in the natural image of seasonal progress from spring to winter instead of historical events, and Treebeard's profession as a tree-shepherd also accounts for the poem's preoccupation with different tree-species and their natural conditions. Thus, Treebeard's song only mediates those parts of lost Beleriand to which he has a personal connection.

Merry and Pippin, on the other hand, have no personal memory of Beleriand and know very little, if anything, about it – just as many readers. Hence, the Hobbits' and our mental construction of these lands relies exclusively on the information gleaned from Treebeard's song. But the trees mentioned in the lyrics – willows, elms, beeches and pines – correspond to trees known by the Hobbits and in our Primary World, too. By applying this knowledge to the space evoked in the poem, the audiences can get an idea of the type of landscape represented by these lost forests of Beleriand. The map in the posthumously published *Silmarillion* is very consistent with the idiosyncratic conditions required by each of the forests in the poem, and therefore exemplifies the intertextual consistency across Tolkien's *legendarium*.

Structurally, each forest is rendered in the space of three lines, the first introducing the proper name and the season associated with it, the second elaborating on the specific set of sensory impressions which invests the respective forest with a particular mood and sensation. This emotional quality is always announced by the interjection "Ah". The third line of each descriptive triplet contains a qualitative evaluation that is matched with cognitive and emotional processes and their expression:

> And I said that was good.
> And I thought that was best.
> It was more than my desire.
> My voice went up and sang in the sky. (ll. 3, 6, 9, 12)

Through this parallelism, a progressive enhancement of Treebeard's emotional elevation is effected from speech act, to cognitive process, to emotional process, culminating eventually in a song which is thereby rendered the ultimate mode of individual expression and praise. Since the song is lifted to the sky, the spiritual boundary between Arda and its divine creator is overcome and Treebeard's song amounts to a form of giving praise to Eru. Although as a literally earth-bound character Treebeard is tied to the physical limitations of Arda, he can experience "a joy that crosses the borders of the self and thus enables the subject to transcend its own existence" (Eilmann 111).

Treebeard's first mentions the "willow-meads of Tasarinan" where he "walked in the Spring" (l. 1). Willows and meads, i.e. meadows, suggest proximity to water, and the map of Beleriand in *The Silmarillion* confirms this by locating Tasarinan at the confluence of the rivers Narog and Sirion. Being the forest associated with spring, the season of budding life and blossoms, Tasarinan especially caters to the senses of sight and smell (l. 2).

Lines four to six are subsequently concerned with "the elm-woods of Ossiriand" (l. 4). As elms are a deciduous species that prefers partly flooded areas, their connection to the season of summer as well as the forest's location "by the Seven Rivers of Ossir" contribute to a consistent and convincing environment. Moreover, the water of the many rivers is also a plausible source for the "light and music" governing the sensory impressions of this constructed space (l. 5). The sense of music is also preserved in the land's later name Lindon – land of music – adding even more consistency to Arda's geographic and linguistic design.

Treebeard continues his poetic recollection with the season of autumn that is linked to Neldoreth, a forest full of beeches (l. 7). Beeches are known in our Primary World for their particularly wonderful golden and red leaves in autumn – a concept that is adopted in Tolkien's subcreated world, too. Hence, these colours are also vivid in Treebeard's memory of Neldoreth in Beleriand. As a second sensory input, "the sighing leaves" (l. 8) could allude to the melancholy typically associated with autumn in general or the sad fates of Doriath, and Beren and Lúthien which are all tied to the forest of Neldoreth.

Treebeard's seasonal journey through the forests of Beleriand ends among "the pine-trees upon the highland of Dorthonion" Treebeard "climbed in the Winter" (l. 10). Knowing from the Primary World that pines are common in colder and low-nutrient regions, even Merry and Pippin would be able to construct an image of Dorthonion as a northern and mountainous landscape. This image is further substantiated by the geographical reference to a mountain named Orod-na-Thôn. In addition, a concise but effective impression of a wintry environment is evoked through the "wind" and the visual contrast of "whiteness" and "black branches" (l. 12).

In the final lines of the song, the glorious image of these lost forests of Beleriand is strongly contrasted with the bleaker present in the remaining parts of Middle-earth. The adverb "now" in line thirteen introduces this shift to the present tense with the statement that "now all those lands" Treebeard had previously described "lie under the wave" (l. 13). After the War of Wrath at the end of the First Age, the Valar from Aman fought against Melkor, and the fight between these titanic forces destroyed the lands of Beleriand, so that the sea eventually swallowed it. Hence, the line is a reference to the ontological realm. Having lost the forests of Beleriand, Treebeard is now confined to the forest of Fangorn in Eriador, whose alternative names, "Tauremorna", "Aldalómë", and "Tauremornalómë" (ll. 14, 18), translate into images of a dark forest and twilight because of their Elvish morphological components for tree (*alda*), forest (*taur*), dark (*mor*) and dusk (*lómë*) (*S* Appendix 430, 442, 438). Thereby, Fangorn in the Third Age constitutes a drastic counterpart to the lost forests of Beleriand. All the forests in Treebeard's song have names of Elvish origin, either Quenya or Sindarin, and are therefore references to the nominal realm with Arda's invented languages and etymology. By using them, Treebeard seems to corroborate his previous remark that the Ents had learnt their language from the Elves (*LotR* 610), adding consistency to Tolkien's Secondary World.

Being a tree-shepherd, Treebeard considers trees and forests as his "friends" and to be under his personal charge (*LotR* 617). Experiencing the loss of Beleriand's forests in person, must consequently have been very traumatic for him. Therefore, his poem is suffused with an air of melancholy and nostalgia like Galadriel's songs. In addition, the lost forests of Beleriand signify the general diminishing of forests and Ents. This sense of transience permeates the last lines of the song and culminates in the autumnal metaphor of bygone years that "lie thicker than leaves" heralding the inevitable end of the world and carrying no promise of renewal. From Treebeard's personal perspective, this metaphor also illustrates the doom of his race which is subject to fading as there seem to be no Entwives and Entings left in Middle-earth (*LotR* 618, 634).

5 Conclusion

The preceding analyses showed that 'lost lands lyrics' in *LotR* construct images of places in Arda that have vanished from the surface of the world by using central principles of literary world-building. In that respect, the principle of secondary-world invention plays a significant role because the poems contain references to various realms of invention and combine primary-world concepts with imaginative modifications or additions. Therefore, they exemplify world-building processes in a nutshell. Those reconstructed places in turn, however, contribute to the overall secondary-world design of Arda by filling in blank spots on the map and in the historical record. They are thus conducive to the completeness of Arda as a complex Secondary World with an idiosyncratic chronological and spatial development whose consistency is maintained across the various textual manifestations in Tolkien's *legendarium*. Since the diegetic audience of the poems within the story, as well as the reader, lack previous knowledge about these places, the 'lyrics on lost lands' constitute instances of subcreative art from the audience's perspective, and echo the diegetic creation of Arda by Eru and the Ainur.

But the construction of lost lands through poetry is always refracted by the singers' perspective whose personal memories pervade the songs. Although this personal link manipulates the audience's construction of lost places, it is essential to endow these places with an experiential quality in order for the audience to fill these places with meaning through empathy, and in order to make the poems relevant for the narrative context of *LotR* in terms of characters and situations.

All three analysed songs express the singers' yearning for a glorious yet irretrievable past, and evoke the emotion of nostalgia, the "heart-racking sense of the vanished past" (*Letters* 110). This sentiment is conveyed in each song by the overarching metaphor of autumn. But the loss of those places in the poems always correlates with the imminent loss of a land or space on the diegetic level of *LotR*. The loss of the Undying Lands is emulated by the approaching loss of Lothlórien, and the loss of the forests of Beleriand in Treebeard's song foreshadows the gradual vanishing of the old forests and the Ents. Due to these relations to the immediate setting and the characters in *LotR*, the latter are likewise affected by the sense of melancholy communicated by the poems. To Frodo, Galadriel's song seemed "fair […], but it did not comfort him" (*LotR* 491); and Merry and Pippin are confronted with an omnipresent silence in the wood after Treebeard's song (*LotR* 611).

But this is not the final word. Later in the narrative, the hope at the end of "Namárië" is fulfilled because there is a ship that carries Galadriel back to Valinor across the Sundering Seas and even Frodo finds Valimar (*LotR* 1347-48). Similarly, the farewell conversation between Treebeard and Galadriel suggests that even the drowned landmasses of Beleriand might one day be "lifted up again" so that "[t]hen in the willow-meads of Tasarinan we [Galadriel and Treebeard] may meet in the Spring" (*LotR* 1285). Insofar, the poems also sustain the hope that these lost lands may one day be restored.

In conclusion, lyrics on lost lands do have an immediate function for the diegesis of *LotR* in terms of narrative events and characterisation. They therefore express the "tragedy of the characters" (*Letters* 110). But, more importantly, the poems provide the aesthetic experience of "viewing far off an unvisited island or seeing the towers of a distant city gleaming in a sunlit mist" (*Letters* 333). Thereby, these poems contribute to the construction of Arda as a complete, consistent and inventive secondary worlfd, a major factor in the overall aesthetic effect in Tolkien's works. Although Tolkien further maintains that these lost places should remain inaccessible, because "to go there is to destroy the magic" (*Letters* 333), the lyrics on lost lands and their narrative context insist on a hope for an ultimate eucatastrophe which is "the true form of fairy-tale, and its highest function" (OFS 153).

About the Author

MICHAELA HAUSMANN is a research assistant and lecturer in English Literary Studies at the University of Vechta (Germany). She currently writes her PhD thesis on embedded poems in fantasy narratives of the nineteenth and twentieth century, and she has presented and taught on Tolkien's works for the past two years. Her other research interests include fantasy literature in general, Romantic, Victorian, and early twentieth-century literature, literary constructions of space, and film studies.

Bibliography

ATTEBERY, Brian. *Strategies of Fantasy*. Bloomington & Indianapolis: Indiana University Press, 1992.

CHATMAN, Seymour. *Story and Discourse: Narrative Structure in Fiction and Film*. Ithaca: Cornell University Press, 1978.

DONOVAN, Leslie A. 'The Valkyrie Reflex in J.R.R. Tolkien's *The Lord of the Rings*: Galadriel, Shelob, Éowyn, and Arwen.' *Perilous and Fair: Women and the Works of J.R.R. Tolkien*. Ed. Janet Brennan Croft and Leslie A. Donovan. Altadena: Mythopoeic Press, 2015. 221-257.

DROUT, Michael. 'Introduction: Reading Tolkien's Poetry.' *Tolkien's Poetry*. Ed. Julian Eilmann and Allan Turner. Zurich and Jena: Walking Tree Publishers, 2013. 1-8.

EILMANN, Julian. 'I Am the Song: Music, Poetry, and the Transcendent in J.R.R. Tolkien's Middle-earth.' *Light beyond All Shadow: Religious Experience in Tolkien's Work*. Ed. Paul E. Kerry and Sandra Miesel. Madison: Fairleigh Dickinson University Press, 2013. 99-117.

J.R.R. Tolkien: Romanticist and Poet. Zurich and Jena: Walking Tree Publishers, 2017.

FLIEGER, Verlyn. *A Question of Time: J.R.R. Tolkien's Road to Faërie*. Kent: The Kent State University Press, 1997.

GARTH, John. 'How Tolkien Discovered Fairy-tale through Beowulf and War.' 18 February, 2015. <http://www.scififantasynetwork.com/how-tolkien-discovered-fairy-tale-through-beowulf-and-war/>.

KOKOT, Joanna. 'Cultural Functions Motivating Art: Poems and Their Contexts in *The Lord of the Rings*.' *Inklings-Jahrbuch* 10 (1992): 191-204.

LEWIS, C.S. 'On Stories.' *On Stories and Other Essays*. Ed. Walter Hooper. San Diego: Harcourt, 2002. 3-20.

LINDOW, John. *Norse Mythology: A Guide to the Gods, Heroes, Rituals, and Beliefs.* Oxford: Oxford University Press, 2001.

MATHEWS, Richard. *Fantasy: The Liberation of Imagination.* New York and London: Routledge, 2002.

MORTENSEN, Karl. *Handbook of Norse Mythology.* Transl. A. Clinton Crowell. Chesterville: Kellscraft, 2011.

PETZOLD, Jochen. *Sprechsituationen lyrischer Dichtung: Ein Beitrag zur Gattungstypologie.* Würzburg: Königshausen & Neumann, 2012.

PHELPSTEAD, Carl. '"With chunks of poetry in between": *The Lord of the Rings* and Saga Poetics.' *Tolkien Studies* 5 (2008): 23-38.

RAFFEL, Burton. '*The Lord of the Rings* as Literature.' *Tolkien and the Critics: Essays on J.R.R. Tolkien's The Lord of the Rings.* Ed. Neil D. Isaacs and Rose A. Zimbardo. Notre Dame & London: University of Notre Dame Press, 1976. 218-246.

TOLKIEN, J.R.R. *The Letters of J.R.R. Tolkien.* Ed. Humphrey Carpenter with the assistance of Christopher Tolkien. Boston: Houghton Mifflin, 1981.

The Lord of the Rings. London: Harper Collins, 2007.

'On Fairy-Stories.' *The Monsters and the Critics and Other Essays.* Ed. Christopher Tolkien. London: George Allen and Unwin, 1983. 109-61.

The Silmarillion. London: Harper Collins, 1999.

WOLF, Mark J.P. *Building Imaginary Worlds: The Theory and History of Subcreation.* New York and London: Routledge, 2012.

WOLF, Werner. 'Aesthetic Illusion in Lyric Poetry?' *Poetica* 30 (1998): 251-89.

ZIMMERMANN, Petra. '"The glimmer of limitless extensions in time and space": The Function of Poems in Tolkien's *The Lord of the Rings*.' *Tolkien's Poetry.* Ed. Julian Eilmann and Allan Turner. Zurich and Jena: Walking Tree Publishers, 2013. 59-88.

Hamish Williams

Mountain People in Middle-earth: Ecology and the Primitive

Abstract

This paper identifies and interprets the relationship between mountains and the various ethnicities who originate from this space in Tolkien's Middle-earth. My analysis is divided into four sections: the first gives a background of exemplary *ethno-topographic* theories in antiquity; the second revises relevant Tolkien scholarship on worldbuilding (particularly, the relationship between the natural world and its inhabitants); the third illustrates how mountains in Middle-earth provide a coherent pool of common racial characteristics for those inhabitants who originate from these spaces; and the fourth searches for functions behind this close structural relationship.

1 Ethno-Topographic Thought in Antiquity

It is worth reflecting on the precedent in Western thought of what I term *ethno-topography* – the notion that a specific type of land or demarcated place characterizes an ethnicity which originates from this space.[1] While ethno-topographic ideas can be found in pre-modern texts across several world regions, including the Middle East, China, and South America (Talbert and Raaflaub 4-5), this survey confines itself to three Ancient Greek foundation texts[2] on the subject (Herodotus, Plato, and Strabo). In tandem with my study of ethno-topography in Tolkien, this review illustrates the scope of racial characteristics dictated by designated locations (including physical features, disposition, military abilities, social customs, economic/production activities, etc.) and suggests underlying functional motives for these classifications.

---

1 It should be noted that ancient writers often examine the effect of climate/weather (not just *topos* or 'place') on people.
2 "Division of the globe by continents, climates and cultures became a topic that engaged a long succession of Greek writers, who in turn later influenced Jewish, Roman and medieval thinking in East and West" (Talbert and Raaflaub 3-4; cf. Romm 215-16).

Herodotus, writing in the mid-5th century BCE, provides detailed descriptions of various territories around the Hellenic world and of their local inhabitants. In the discussion of Egypt in Book 2, the character of the land is related to that of the people:

> I am going to talk at some length about Egypt, because it has very many remarkable features and has produced more monuments which beggar description than anywhere else in the world. [...] In keeping with the idiosyncratic climate which prevails there and the fact that their river behaves differently from any other river, almost all Egyptian customs and practices are the opposite of those of everywhere else. (Herodotus *Histories* 2.35; Waterfield [trans.] 108)

This "idiosyncratic" (2.35; 108) physical behaviour of the Nile includes its propensity to flood in summer, while, on the other hand, staying low in winter, and its lack of natural winds (2.19). The uniqueness of the Egyptian climate relates to the intense heat and dryness (2.26). The social customs and normal protocols inverted from Greek behaviour include, among others: gender roles (women trade, men weave), personal hygiene 'activities' (undertaken at home, not in public), the physical appearance of priests (being bald-headed, not hirsute), the place of domestic animals (not separated from people), and the manner of writing style (from right to left) (2.35-36). Thus, just as the Egyptian river and climate are strangely different from those of all other lands, so the customs of the Egyptians are strangely inverted from normal, Greek social expectations (Romm 219). Topography and climate become a means of exoticizing or othering the inhabitants.[3]

In the fourth book of Plato's *Laws*, written in the mid-4th century BCE, an unnamed Athenian Stranger discusses two types of topography – coastal land and hilly inland – as potential sites for a city (*polis*). Each location characterizes its native populace with respect to disposition, economic activities, and military endeavours. According to the Athenian Stranger, a *polis* built in a hilly interior is conducive to "the acquisition of virtue" (704D; Bury [trans.] 257) among its citizens, while a littoral settlement is most likely to have "luxurious and depraved habits" (704D-E; 257) and to lead its population to "knavish and tricky ways" (705A; 257). In terms of economic activities, coastal settlements are depicted as being concerned with mercantile trade and thus the acquisition

---

3 For similar ethno-topographic 'othering' across world regions, cf. Talbert and Raaflaub 4-5.

of goods from foreign lands (leading to a decadent disposition); on the other hand, inland regions are characterized as being more concerned with the actual production of commodities from natural resources (704C-705B). In terms of military activities, the Athenian Stranger argues that marines (coastal soldiery) are naturally accustomed to a manner of skirmishing which valorizes retreat to ships and flight over the seas rather than standing ground, fighting, and dying, in the manner of landlocked soldiers (706C-707D). The contrast is between the nobility and honour of the landlocked soldiers[4] and the cravenness of the coastal marines.[5]

As to why the Athenian Stranger (and Plato) has created such an ethno-topography, it is perhaps not coincidental that an origin myth of the city of Athens (a coastal settlement) is referenced in this part of the dialogue (that of King Minos and the periodic ransom of Athenian youth to the Minotaur [706A-C]). Despite the heavy cost of Minos' ransom, the Stranger insists that Athens was in a better moral state in those foundational times, before it started capitalizing on the potential (especially, military) of its coastal position (706B-C). The generic narrative of moral lapse or decline in a coastal settlement, in tandem with 'international' economic growth and greater focus on maritime endeavours, is suggestive of the historic decline of Athens herself in Plato's lifetime.[6]

The Greek geographer Strabo, at the start of the 1st century CE, classifies land (and the corresponding climate) into two opposing categories: the mountainous with cold climate[7] and the more habitable plains and coastal regions with milder climate (*Geographica* 2.5.26). The mountainous, wintry parts breed a race of men who are naturally disposed towards either savagery or theft, who are ignorant of commercial activities, and who are inclined towards martial bravery and warfare; the low-lying, coastal, mild-weather parts nurture men who have a profound understanding of the civilized arts and institutions of government, who are accomplished in economic activities and trade, and who are inclined towards peace (2.5.26). Thus, according to Strabo, the European continent, divided as it is between the mountainous/cold parts and the low-lying/

---

4 In the concept of the hero in early-Greek society, fame (*kleos*) was associated with death in battle.
5 For the relationship between climate and military strength in Herodotus, cf. Romm 220.
6 For other ideas on geography/climate and people in Plato, cf. Romm 224-25.
7 On the importance of climate (temperature, winds) to ethnic character in early-Greek thought, cf. Romm 220-23.

coastal/warm parts, achieves an ideal balance in the character of its ethnicities (2.5.26). Strabo's ethno-topography of mountainous, harsh-weather inhabitants and coastal/plain, mild-weather dwellers is based upon an opposition between the savage and the civilized, which must be contextualized within a period of rapid Roman imperial,[8] 'civilizing' expansion across the European continent – in particular, through the harsher climate and alpine topography of northern regions beyond the coastal ring of the Mediterranean (Dueck 242-44).

2 Building Nature and Culture in Middle-earth

Michael Brisbois, whose study of Middle-earth is themed according to the traditional division of nature and culture (197), introduces a third category, "imaginary nature" (198), to be divorced from 'real nature', as perceived by our senses, and 'human culture' (198). According to Brisbois (198-200), real nature in Middle-earth is visible in several respects: familiar, real-world natural phenomena (e.g. seasons) and objects function or exist normally and consistently in Middle-earth;[9] Tolkien furnishes his stories with an onomastic depth (e.g. place names) which is, seemingly, as rich as that of our own world; and we perceive real-world environmental problems in Middle-earth (e.g. deforestation). Furthermore, according to Campbell (433-35), Tolkien's "descriptive mode" (434) is also achieved by an ecological vision which depicts a certain interconnectedness in nature between the individual parts. Over the "primary belief" (Brisbois 198)[10] which these authorial gestures towards realism install in the reader's mind there is asserted the symbolic meaning of nature, 'imaginary nature', which "allows us to perceive the hidden meanings behind the natural images and events of the novel" (206-07).

Much of the appeal of Middle-earth (alongside mythic, medieval intertexts) resides in the sheer depth and aesthetic wonder of its natural world (Campbell 431); this realism, however, should not blind us to the cultural meaning which land and nature attain. There have been various symbolic interpretations into specific representations within or the organization of Tolkien's natural world:

---

8 On Strabo's ambiguous stance on Roman imperialism as a Greek, cf. Dueck 242-44.
9 Cf. Curry 60
10 Cf. Curry 60

Brisbois, for example, evaluates Middle-earth with respect to certain manufactured natural laws which are reflective of Tolkien's stout Catholicism (201-08),[11] whereas Lobdell explores the connotations of the cardinal divisions (north, west, east) of Tolkien's geography – thus the west is associated with general benevolence, salvation, notions of paradise, and a tension between death and (re)birth (49-68).

The symbolic interpretation of nature and geography in Tolkien shows how a given sphere garners our hermeneutic interest because of the cultural associations with which it is imbued. Equally, though, in Tolkien's world it is evident that, in many cases, culture is determined and shaped by a dominant environment or natural sphere. In other words, nature is as much a symbol for culture as culture is for nature. The relationship is often reciprocal:

> The complex relationship between Elves and forests and Dwarves and mountains makes defining nature even more complex. Sam knowingly comments about the Elves of Lothlórien: "they seem to belong here, more even than Hobbits do in the Shire. Whether they've made the land, or the land's made them, it's hard to say, if you take my meaning" (*FR*, II, vii). The subtle magic that infuses the Elves is intertwined with the land they live in, suggesting they do not make clear distinctions between culture and nature. (Brisbois 197-98)

On the subject of ethno-topographic analyses in Tolkien scholarship, while there has not as yet been a comprehensive analysis of how a feature of land *generically* characterizes races which originate or dwell in such a space (e.g. profiles of mountain/river/forest people), the close relationship between the character of *specific* races and the landscape they inhabit has been acknowledged: "Dwarves with mountains, Hobbits with pastoral countryside, Elves with the woods and trees, and even Orcs with desolate places where nature is under siege" (Campbell 436).[12]

In the case of hobbits, their agrarian landscape informs many of their racial characteristics, rendering them a people associated with the soil or the earth (Dickerson and Evans 90). Many hobbits live underground, within the soil, and their bare feet demonstrate their close physical connection with the earth

---

11 Campbell 435-36.
12 Curry 61-62.

(12-13, 90). On their names, *hobbit* means "hole-builder" (*RK* 511), while young girls are given floral-based names (Dickerson and Evans 13). Their economy is founded on small-scale, pre-modern, hands-on subsistence farming (90), tokens of which are visible throughout the novels (72). Heroic accomplishments and acts of valour are often realized by hobbit farmers (72-73, 75, 85-87). And lastly, there might even be an agrarian quality to the disposition of hobbits, that they perceive of their identity as ineluctably 'rooted' to the earth and that which grows on it (cf. 90).

It is also worth observing that the relationship between place and inhabitants in Middle-earth is not only apparent on an ethnic level but can also be demonstrated through specific individuals (e.g. Goldberry, Bombadil, Treebeard) who assimilate into their environment (Campbell 436-37). Certainly, the environmental message(s) of Tolkien's work has become an increasingly popular subject in recent times (Flieger 2012, 262-63),[13] and the ecological function of ethno-topography in Tolkien, in allowing inhabitants to assimilate into their environment, is discussed in the fourth section of this paper; equally, though, I examine how such ethno-topography is underscored by certain cultural beliefs.

3 A Catalogue of Orogenetic Characteristics

Tolkien described a number of *orogenetic*[14] people – those originating from, within, or near mountains – in Middle-earth: (1) dwarves, (2) trolls, (3) goblins/orcs, (4) Drúedain, (5) Harfoots, and (6) the men of Lossarnach.[15] In the first part of this section (3.1), I cite the mountain origin stories of the six ethnicities I am examining. In the second part (3.2), my analysis is divided according to 7 categories (3.2.1, 3.2.2, etc.), in each of which I provide textual evidence which demonstrates the existence of common or racial characteristics among the respective orogenetic people.

---

13 For further discussions on environmentalism in Middle-earth, cf. Campbell 437-40; Curry 64-66, 74-98; *contra* Flieger 2012, 262-74.
14 A coinage. Its normal use is geological, cf. "orogenesis" in *Oxford English Living Dictionaries* (henceforth, *OELD*). https://en.oxforddictionaries.com/
15 This classification excludes: (i) non-ethnic/non-humanoid entities (e.g. Valar, animals); (ii) ethnicities who are found but do not necessarily originate in mountains; and (iii) individuals/specific heroes. Individualization naturally occurs within ethnic groups in Tolkien's world, cf. Chism 2007a, 555-56; Evans 213-14; Schneidewind 2005a, 66; Vink 129-30.

3.1 Mountain Origin Stories

3.1.1 *Dwarves*. The dwarves are orogenetic both in a constitutive and topographic sense, having been fashioned from mountain stone and having been born under the mountains in a great hall of Aulë (*LR* 143; *S* 37, 39).[16] The dwarves first enter the elf-centered landscape of *The Silmarillion* by coming over and down from "the Blue Mountains of Ered Luin into Beleriand" (100).

3.1.2 *Trolls*. Trolls are similar to dwarves in that their orogenesis is constitutive and topographic. The narrator of *The Hobbit* provides the clearest exposition of the genesis and destruction of individual trolls: "For trolls, as you probably know, must be underground before dawn, or they go back to the stuff of the mountains they are made of, and never move again" (50). And thus trolls are most often encountered on, under, or close to mountains in Middle-earth (e.g. *FR* 425-26, *Hobbit* 40, *RK* 112, 513).

3.1.3 *Orcs*. The 'creation' of the first orcs[17] or goblins under the Iron Mountains in the North can be reconstructed from *The Silmarillion*: "Now Melkor began the delving and building of a vast fortress, deep under Earth, beneath dark mountains where the beams of Illuin were cold and dim. That stronghold was named Utumno" (29); "[Captured elves] were put in prison [in Utumno], and by slow arts of cruelty were corrupted and enslaved; and thus did Melkor breed the hideous race of the Orcs in envy and mockery of the elves" (47). Moreover, in a note on the language of orcs, Tolkien associates their origins, that is, where their older clans live, with the Misty Mountains and those of the North (*RK* 512-13).

3.1.4 *Drúedain*. In *Unfinished tales*, the Drúedain are said to have accompanied the people of Haleth during their migration into Beleriand (487-88; cf. *S* 166). These Drúedain in Beleriand eventually dwindled (*UT* 488). Importantly, though, in a short note, Tolkien confirms that this branch of Drúedain originally hailed from a parent tribe in the White Mountains (494), the ancestors of the tribe of Ghân-buri-Ghân and represented by the forgotten statues of Dunharrow in Rohan (494-95). The Drúedain claim to be the original inhabitants of the White Mountains (495).

---

16 For similarities with Norse dwarves (including chthonic genesis), cf. Vink 124-25, 131.
17 On the uncertain ontology of orcs, cf. Chism 2007a, 556; Fimi 154-57; Schneidewind 2005a, 49-50.

3.1.5 *Harfoots*. Tolkien divides hobbits into three original strains or varieties: Harfoots, Stoors, and Fallohides. Stoors dwelt on riverbanks and Fallohides near woodlands (*FR* 4-5), while Harfoots "preferred highlands and hillsides" and "long lived in the foothills of the mountains" (4).

3.1.6 *Men of Lossarnach*. Upon sighting the men of Lossarnach and their captain, young Bergil claims his kinship to them: "old Forlong the Fat, the Lord of Lossarnach. That is where my grandsire lives" (*RK* 36). Earlier Bergil's father, Beregond, remarks to Pippin how unusual it is for him to see a horse such as Shadowfax: "I love beasts, and we see them seldom in this stony city; for my people [i.e. those of Lossarnach] came from the mountainvales" (25). Later, Beregond points out to Pippin the path of the refugees: "That is the road to the vales of Tumladen and Lossarnach, and the mountain-villages, and then on to Lebennin" (27); dwellings in the mountains are accessed by travelling into Lossarnach. In a letter from 1955, Tolkien compared his realm of Lossarnach to the Italian town of Assisi, built on a high spur of Mount Subasion (Hammond and Scull 2006, 462).

3.2 Orogenetic Characteristics

The following analysis presents seven categories, wherein common or racial characteristics are attributed to several orogenetic ethnicities. The categories include: physical features, dwelling places, language abilities, disposition, production activities, heroism, and manner of death.[18]

3.2.1 Physical Features

Tolkien's mountain people are short and of broad stature. The elves of Beleriand call the dwarves the "Naugrim, the Stunted People" (*S* 100). Although some exceptional orcs are described as being large or as tall as men (*FR* 425, 426), the association between mountainous origins and a generic shortness of orcs is clear in the chapter 'The Uruk-hai' from *The Two Towers*, wherein the "many" (50) goblins who have pursued the Fellowship from Moria in the Misty Mountains are perceived by Pippin as being "smaller" (50) than the

---

18 By *race*, I am denoting 'ethnic groups', similar in 'physical characteristics' and 'sharing the same culture, history, language, etc.' (cf. 'race', 1, 1.2, *OELD*).

modified Uruk-hai and orcs of Sauron. Regarding orc body shape, Tolkien describes Grishnákh as "a short crook-legged creature, very broad and with long arms that hung almost to the ground" (50). The Drúedain are "stumpy (some four foot high) but very broad, with heavy buttocks and short thick legs" (*UT* 488), while Merry sees Ghân-buri-Ghân as "a strange squat shape, [...] short-legged and fat-armed, thick and stumpy" (*RK* 116), standing beside Éomer and Théoden. Harfoots are the smallest and shortest of the three hobbit subgroups (*FR* 4). And the men of Lossarnach "were shorter [...] than any men that Pippin had yet seen in Gondor" (*RK* 36). Their leader, Forlong the Fat is notable for his "wide shoulders and huge girth" (*RK* 36); no mention of height is made.

Many of these orogenetic ethnicities attain darker pigmentation, whether of the skin and/or the eyes. The orc-chieftain in Moria has a "swart" (*FR* 426) face, an archaic term for dark-complexioned,[19] while his eyes are compared to "coals" (*FR* 426). The eyes of the Drúedain are described as being so black that the pupils cannot be distinguished, except when they shine red in wrath (*UT* 488), and Tolkien's original Drúedain, in his initial draft of the 'Ride of the Rohirrim', were called the "dark men of Eilenach" (*WR* 343-44).[20] The Harfoots "were browner of skin" (*FR* 4) than the other two hobbit tribes. And the men of Lossarnach are "somewhat swarthier" (*RK* 36) than other Gondorians.[21]

3.2.2 Dwelling Places

Orogenetic people mainly live in underground homes (holes, caves, tunnels, or great subterranean chambers).[22] Thus dwarves live in "great halls and mansions" (*S* 100) delved into the mountains. Trolls are encountered as cave dwellers (e.g. *FR* 425-26). Goblins, apart from Uruk-hai and other larger orcs, live and are encountered in subterranean caverns and tunnels within mountains (e.g. *Hobbit* 71-72). The Drúedain originally slept in caves or even in the open air in the

---

19 Cf. 'swart', *OELD*.
20 'Dark', to be fair, could denote physical appearance, a malevolent disposition, or being from a dark (age) history.
21 Dwarves are dark-skinned in Norse mythology (Vink 124).
22 Several elvish clans also dwelt in underground dwellings, a defensive necessity against enemies (Dickerson and Evans 103).

White Mountains (*UT* 499-500). And the Harfoots are the strain of hobbit who longest maintained underground dwellings, even when they no longer lived on mountains and became agrarian people in Eriador (*FR* 4).

3.2.3 Language Abilities

Mountain people in Middle-earth are characterized as having limited or unsophisticated (infantile) communicative abilities. The language of the dwarves is unintelligible to the elves, for whom it is "cumbrous and unlovely" (*S* 101; cf. *LR* 194-95; *RK* 514).[23] Trolls "had no more language than beasts" (*RK* 513) and usually act without speech (e.g. *FR* 425-26; *RK* 112, 197; *S* 232). Some trolls, under Sauron's educating hand, "spoke a debased form of the Common Speech" (*RK* 513), while even the 'improved' Olog-hai "spoke little" (514).[24] Orcs have no real language of their own but have perverted other languages into their speech (512). Non-verbal, onomatopoeic articulations are also commonly attributed to them: "The yells and yammering, croaking, jibbering and jabbering; howls, growls, and curses; shrieking and skriking" (*Hobbit* 76; cf. 72). The Drúedain show a general disclination towards language, exemplified by their characteristic stone-still silence. Their communication is marked by non-verbal utterances (*RK* 120, *UT* 492), their "halting fashion, and uncouth words" (*RK* 116), their lack of written communication, and physical hand signs (*UT* 489). Lastly, the men of Lossarnach are depicted as nonverbal warriors – "grim-faced" (*RK* 36) and silent.

3.2.4 Disposition

The grim disposition of the men of Lossarnach is attributable to both dwarves and Drúedain (*UT* 494). Indeed, the ethno-topographic notion that mountain men are customarily grim is reinforced when, in the catalogue of soldiers entering Minas Tirith, Tolkien describes another group of soldiers "from Lamedon" as "a few grim hillmen without a captain" (*RK* 37).

---

[23] The elves bestow upon themselves the name *Quendi*, which denotes "those that speak with voices" (Evans 198); their identity is declared through their possession of language (198).
[24] In *The Hobbit* there are some contradictions in the coherence of Tolkien's mythology as early fairy-story elements (such as the silly cockney trolls [cf. *Letters* 191]) crept into that narrative (*Letters* 296-99; cf. *TOFS* 49-59).

3.2.5 Production Activities

Tolkien's orogenetic people can be regarded as supreme manufacturers – *manufacere* in the Latinate sense of "to make with the hand". The dwarves, who are dubbed "Gonnhirrim, Masters of Stone" (*S* 100), are depicted as expert crafters (39), having "marvellous skill with metals and with stone" (102).[25] Goblins too have similar manufacturing abilities, being able to dig into the earth, mine, and thus make many practical instruments (*Hobbit* 73-74). The Drúedain are referenced as gifted stone-craftsmen (*UT* 489).[26] The Harfoots have the greatest manufacturing potential of the hobbits. Tolkien chooses to describe the appendages of Harfoots from a qualitative perspective: "their hands and feet were neat and nimble" (*FR* 4); both adjectives imply a great degree of skill and precision.[27] The appendages of the Stoors, however, are given only quantitative attributes (*FR* 4), whereas the Fallohides are deficient in "handicraft" (4), compared to their elf-like linguistic and singing abilities. The tension between higher-level manufacturing ability (skillful hands) and lower-level linguistic skills can be detected in the ethnic profiles of dwarves (*LR* 195), goblins, and Drúedain. There is also, in some cases, a tension among orogenetic people between manufacturing things and growing things. Dwarven smithery is contrasted with their lack of understanding for growing and living things in their creation story (*S* 39). In one of the more allegorical texts in Tolkien's writings (*Hobbit* 73-74), there is a correlation between the goblins' expertise in handcraft and their 'industrial' destruction of the natural world (74).

3.2.6 Heroism

Orogenetic people achieve victory through physical prowess – sheer strength and hardiness. In the dwarven creation story, we learn that Aulë made the dwarves "strong to endure" (*S* 39), "stone-hard" (39), and able to "suffer toil and hunger and hurt of body more hardily than all other speaking peoples"

---

[25] On craftsmanship as a 'Jewish' quality, cf. Vink 124, 126-27; against dwarves as antisemitic caricatures, cf. Vink 129-42.
[26] They are also wood-craftsmen, which, along with their tracking abilities, botanical knowledge (*UT* 489), and poison darts (*RK* 115-16), is an important marker of their being forest people (cf. Hammond and Scull 2005, 555).
[27] "Done with or demonstrating skill or efficiency" (cf. 'neat', *OELD*). "Quick and light in movement or action; agile" (cf. 'nimble', *OELD*).

(39). Moreover, this focus on physicality is fashioned for heroic/martial contexts, aimed at countering the hostilities of Melkor (39; e.g. 229-30). Trolls are also imbued with rock-hard strength and physical toughness. In the appendices, the Olog-hai are described as "harder than stone" (*RK* 513). And this quality is demonstrated in the fight in the Chamber of Mazarbul, in the Moria sequence, when Boromir attempts to strike a cave troll: "[he] hewed at the arm with all his might; but his sword rang, glanced aside, and fell from his shaken hand. The blade was notched" (*FR* 425-26). The fact that Boromir, often represented as the most physically strong of the Fellowship (Librán-Moreno 16-17, 31-32), cannot in any wise harm the troll through force exemplifies the stone-like toughness of the troll's constitution. The men of Lossarnach resemble dwarves in: their "great battle-axes" (*RK* 36; cf. *S* 230), their heavy armour (*RK* 36; cf. *S* 104), and the headgear of their leader (*RK* 36, cf. *S* 229-30, *UT* 98). The resemblance to and connotations of dwarven gear and physique suggests that the men of Lossarnach primarily operate as men of physical hard(i)ness.

3.2.7 Manner of Death

Physical or symbolic/cultural petrification (being turned into stone) occurs after death for three orogenetic people. Three beliefs are suggested for the fate of dwarves after death (*S* 39); of these, one, propagated by elves, is that the 'spiritless' dwarves return to the stone from which they were made after they die – the original *Lost Road* version of the myth (*LR* 143, 195).[28] The nature of the trolls' genesis and their petrification upon death mirrors *The Lost Road* story of the dwarves.[29] The modified trolls of Sauron, unlike the so-called stone-trolls (cf. *Letters* 191), did not experience a literal petrification; Tolkien, however, still implies a symbolic petrification when they die: after the troll chief at the battle before the Black Gate is struck down by Pippin, he "came crushing down like a falling rock" (*RK* 197).

The Drúedain possess a stone-like quality to their natural constitution. The body of Ghân-buri-Ghân is "gnarled as an old stone" (*RK* 116), and, upon seeing

---

28 On the ambiguous eschatology of the dwarves, cf. Vink 131-32.
29 The aversion to sunlight in Norse mythology is a characteristic of dwarves (cf. *Alvíssmál* 16, 35).

him, Merry is reminded of the stone statues of the púkel-men in Dunharrow, "brought to life" (116). The rocky constitution of the Drúedain is best realized in *Unfinished Tales*, wherein their capacity to become seemingly petrified, as still and quiet as stone, for long periods of time is dramatized in a short anecdote. A forester strolls past two Drûgs, greets them, but then realizes that they are mere statues; several days later he returns to the same statues and takes a nap under one of them, at which point one statue-Drûg greets the man; this Drûg had carved one stone statue in memory of his dead father and was himself standing statue-still beside the memorial to his father (490-91).[30]

In Dunharrow, nothing of the Drúedain is known by the present occupiers of the land, the Rohirrim, and all that remains of this lost, nameless society are the stone statues; cultural death is here represented through petrification. In the forester-statue anecdote, the congruence between the inanimate stone statue, representing a dead Drûg, and the animate, stone-still Drûg, quite alive, simulates a petrifying transformation upon death, wherein the live Drûg harmonizes with the 'dead' Drûg, ritually becoming or performing a stone like his 'dead father'.

3.3 Summary of Characteristics

The extent of the similarities in this analysis suggests that mountains are notable ethno-topographic structures in Tolkien's Middle-earth. Mountains provide a set of characteristics from which a given people, who have their origins in these spaces, can be described.

	Physical Features	*Dwelling Places*	*Language Abilities*	*Disposition*	*Production Activities*	*Heroism*	*Manner of Death*
Typical Character	Short, Squat, Dark	Underground	Simple, Mute, Uncouth	Grim	Manufacturing	Physical Prowess	Petrification

It is important to note here that this structural analysis is not asserting that these orogenetic characteristics are comprehensive for each individual ethnicity in their entirety. Mountains provide a wide pool of possible characteristics, from

---

30 For the inversion of this story, where a stone temporarily becomes a Drûg, cf. *UT* 491-93.

which these ethnic groups, which originate from this space, can be described. The character of each individual race in Middle-earth is not only a product of their topographic origin but also, for example, of their creation myth in Tolkien's universe, of their relationship with other historical models of this race,[31] or of their topographic development in Tolkien's world.[32]

4 Mountains and Meaning in Middle-earth

In this section, I examine some functional values of these orogenetic characteristics: firstly, from an ecological perspective, wherein the people become part of the land; and secondly, from a cultural perspective, in creating an opposition between the 'primitive' and the 'civilized'.

4.1 Environmental Assimilation: The Ecological Function of Mountains

The traits of orogenetic people are, by and large, extensions of an existence imagined in close harmony with the mountains and of the physical substance of mountains. On the first point, the fact that mountain people live in caves and occupy themselves with stonemasonry appears to be a manifest product of their orogenesis – caves are the most ready natural shelter in mountains and stone the most abundant substance for industry. On the second point, many features of the orogenetic people seem imbued with a stone-like quality, which Tolkien alludes to on several occasions.

With regard to language and communication, in *The Hobbit* the goblins "laughed in their horrible stony voices" (72); and in the sequel the orc voices are described as follows: "There was a rush of hoarse laughter, like the falling of sliding stones into a pit" (*FR* 425). A typical natural sound of the mountains, the falling of rocks, is transferred to the vocal qualities of an orogenetic people, who laugh in their "stony voices" or like "sliding stones". The linguistic connotations of having a stony, mountainous voice are plainly negative: "horrible" and "hoarse". Stones are rough, jagged, unsmooth objects, and their move-

---

[31] On other literary-mythic influences: for dwarves, cf. Vink; for the Drúedain, cf. Flieger 2003.
[32] Harfoots become lowlanders; some Drúedain become woodland people.

ments convey these qualities through a "hoarse", unsmooth, and so unpleasant sound. Equally, the propensity for mountain people to be simply non-verbal or non-communicative is exemplified by the mute quasi-petrification of the Drúedain, as in the example of the forester, where the silence and stillness of the 'stony-fied' Drûg deceives the man (*UT* 490-91). To be turned into stone implies the loss of speech and movement.

That mountain people display heroism through physical strength and endurance is a simple extension of the natural quality of stones. This is self-evident in the dwarven creation story where the "stone-hard" (*S* 39) dwarves are designed to be both physically "strong" (39) and enduring – "[suffering] more hardily than all other speaking people" (39). Stones are, of course, physically hard objects and tend to last a very long time (hence, endurance or hardiness). Importantly, as earlier cited, this stone-hard(i)ness of dwarves occurs in the context of their imminent skirmishes with Melkor (39); it informs their means of heroic endeavours. This rocky constitution of orogenetic people, as evidenced in the cases of the dwarves, trolls, and Drúedain, even informs the birth and/or death of these people – whether, they literally petrify upon dying or whether their death is associated with rocks on a symbolic or cultural level.

In terms of disposition, presumably the senses which underlie such expressions in English as *stony-faced* and *stone-hearted*, both denoting a lack of emotion or feeling, are at the root of the grim or serious disposition of these mountain people.[33] Certainly, specifically with respect to the disposition of the dwarves, Tolkien does seem to interrelate their "stony-hard" quality (*S* 39) with their "stubborn[ness]" (39), by juxtaposing these two words in their creation story. The implication of stubborn people as (stone-)hardheaded is implied. With respect to their lack of concern for growing things, the tension between stone as inorganic matter and forests as organic matter is probably relevant.

Thus many of the racial characteristics of orogenetic people in Tolkien – including their dwellings, language abilities, production activities, forms of heroism, disposition, and birth/death – are natural extensions of their mountainous

---

[33] The Arkenstone is both "the Heart of the Mountain" (*Hobbit* 314) and "the heart of Thorin" (314). The dwarf's love for the stone overrides any compassion for the refugees from Lake-town (310) or Bilbo (319).

environment. They literally and symbolically embody the quality of their land and adopt a form of life which is most suited to this space. Mountains in Middle-earth, along with other features of the landscape such as forests and pasture, therefore have an ecological function[34] in assimilating the inhabitants of a domain with the physical composition of their environment. Land determines character in Tolkien.

4.2 Mountains and Racial Hierarchies: Markers of the Primitive

In *Tolkien, Race and Cultural History: From Fairies to Hobbits*, Dimitra Fimi separates Tolkien's ideas about race[35] articulated in his personal/scholarly life from the racial hierarchies represented in Middle-earth (157). With regard to the former, although the juvenile Tolkien is recorded as having once made what would certainly now be regarded as a racist speech at a school debate (134), this would have to be put in the context of his educational upbringing in Late Victorian England, where the physical anthropology of race (combined with theories of corresponding mental abilities and perceived natural hierarchies) was an accepted scientific study (132-35). Conversely, as he matured and as scientists began to question the accuracy of such studies (134-37), Tolkien expressed several more progressive judgements on race: on discrimination against black Africans in South Africa (e.g. *Letters* 73) and at the supposed Aryan/Nordic superiority (and Jewish racial inferiority) (*Letters* 37-38, 375; cf. Fimi 135-37; Vink 134-35). Tolkien, however, was still very much a product of his field of philological and historical study (Fimi 138-39)[36], and he seemed to have romanticized the more positive-oriented aspects of racial categorizing, encapsulated by his love of the "noble northern spirit" (*Letters* 56) and his concern with his own Anglo-Saxon ancestry (*Letters* 108; Fimi 139-40).[37]

---

34 Ecology is "the branch of biology that deals with the relations of organisms to one another and to their physical surroundings" (cf. 'ecology', *OELD*).
35 There is a frequent conflation in Tolkien's texts between terms such as *races, peoples*, and *kindreds*, cf. Fimi 132; Schneidewind 2005a, 42-43. On Tolkien's misunderstanding of the biological denotations of race, cf. Schneidewind 2005a, 41-44. And for an evolutionary-biology reading of peoples in Middle-earth, cf. Schneidewind 2005b.
36 On language and race, cf. Bachmann and Honegger 15-21.
37 Cf. Schneidewind 2005a 45-46.

This paper does not aim to reconcile the progressive attitudes of Tolkien with his more romantic, personal, and philologically-inspired notions regarding ethnicity, nor will I try to connect the literary work with the personal (cf. Fimi 157).[38] Rather, I am concerned with the ethnographic imagination within Middle-earth. On the basis of my structural analysis in the third section, orogenetic characteristics can be interpreted as *markers of the primitive* in Middle-earth. This can be validated: (i) by comparing the typical orogenetic characteristics with anthropological ideas of primitive race which were being popularized around the turn of the twentieth century; and (ii) by consulting Tolkien's text, which provides a system of racial oppositions and narrative exchanges between the primitive and civilized.

(i) Anthropological thought in Victorian times and in the early twentieth century was greatly concerned with the question of racial difference. Different races are, according to Madison Grant's influential book *The Passing of the Great Race* (1936), governed by fixed "somatological" (xix) and "psychical" (xix) characteristics. These definite physical and mental capacities ensure that some groups of men exist in a more 'primitive' or less developed manner, while others attain superiority over the former, ushering in a more 'civilized' state of affairs. According to Grant, human history is a series of cycles by which the more newly-evolved race (ultimately for him, of Nordic stock) gains mastery over the more primitive types (xxii). This early anthropological study was of course tendentiously designed to assert the cultural superiority of Europeans ('Caucasoid') over non-Europeans.

Part of this racial imagination in anthropological thought at the time entailed the cultural creation or *caricature of the original primitive*, which may variously be termed Eolithic, Palaeolithic, or Stone Age man, and of which the Neanderthals seems to have been regarded as a typical example. These early Stone Age men and Neanderthals were characterized as: having a central preoccupation with "the manufacture of tools" (Grant 104); living "in caves or rather in their entrances" (107); having non-white, darker, or browner skin pigmentation (107) or being "gorilla-like" (108); and being short and thickset

---

38 On Tolkien and racism, cf. Bachmann and Honegger 32-37; Chism 2007b; Fimi 157-58; Schneidewind 2005a, 46-50; Vink 129.

(107; Osborn 220, 237-38), especially as compared with the exceptionally tall, and more 'modern' Cro-Magnons (Grant 108-09) – thus equating shortness with the generic primitive man.[39]

Together with these characteristics can be partnered certain dispositional, linguistic, and religious features which anthropologists, such as John Lubbock in his *The Origin of Civilization and the Primitive Condition of Man: Mental and Social Condition of Savages* (1882), deemed to fall under the designation of the 'original primitive', and which were to be analogously identified among contemporary, savage peoples (1-3). In terms of disposition, Lubbock characterizes savages as acting out of physical, violent, murderous impulse, in an absence of moral and intellectual interior (388-410, 499; cf. Fimi 150). Under linguistic features Lubbock lists: the absence of language (411), the use of physical gestures/signs instead of verbalization (411), child-like communication (415), a general paucity of words (417), onomatopoeic words and animal mimicry (418-20), and an absence of abstract language (420, 431-33). In terms of religious activities, Lubbock broadly characterizes primitive cultures as materialist: in that these societies did not have a modern, Western sense of a spiritual, immaterial afterlife beyond the physical realm (202, 209); that they invested the physical world and objects therein (often including stones and mountains [301-12]) with 'spiritual' or magical significance (206, 283); and that their eschatological rituals were articulated through a material form (284-86).

Tolkien's mountain people strongly resemble the nineteenth and early-twentieth century imagination of the primitive Stone Age man: a short, squat frame; darker pigmentation; cave-dwelling; occupied with manufacturing (particularly, of stone); linguistically crude or child-like; inclined to physical violence over and above intellectual exploits; and having (indeed, sometimes embodying) a materialist perspective of life and death. But why did mountains, in particular, come to represent a space of the primitive in Tolkien's imagination? In European ethno-topography, the Alpine mountains seem to have represented a barbaric/uncivilized 'other', especially in their opposition to the civilized powers of the Greco-Roman world along the Mediterranean and later the British Empire

---

39 The shape and size of the skull was also an important marker in physical anthropology of the time, cf. Grant 19-24; Ripley 37-57.

in the west. Such an opposition was captured in the ancient world in Strabo's division of coastal people and mountain people, the latter of whom were stylized as *barbaroi* (2.5.26).

An ethno-topographic theory more contemporaneous with Tolkien was that of William Ripley, whose *The Races of Europe* (1899) divided Europe ethnically between the Teutonic (or Nordic), the Alpine, and the Mediterranean people. The analysis entailed the categorization of somatic types (including head shape, hair and eye colour, and height [121]) according to certain races, who were distributed in different parts of Europe; thus the Alpine race comes, of course, from "the Alpine highlands of mid-western Europe" (124); "it is, therefore, pre-eminently a mountain type, whether in France, Spain, Italy, Germany, or Albania; it becomes less pure as we go east [...] across the great plains" (128). These physical differences apparently engendered certain dispositional and cultural differences among the three races. The Alpines are, according to Ripley (549-50), characterized by a sedentary nature, an intellectual inferiority which contrasts poorly with the natural political vigour of the Teutons and the artistic Mediterraneans. The Alpines are a simple, peasant people. They are less developed, less civilized, and this shows in their propensity to stay in the mountainous countryside and away from the cities, which Ripley regards as the primary sites for societal competition between races, and where civilization is thus enhanced (and the superior Nordic race establishes its authority) (550-51).

A possible tripartite ethno-topography such as Ripley's in Tolkien's Middle-earth has been suggested by Dimitra Fimi (145), and certainly Tolkien seems to have been fond of catalogues of three in marking different races or groups of people (143-46). With respect to my own classification of orogenetic characteristics, there does not appear to be a direct link in specific racial characteristics: Tolkien's 'Alpine' people seem a physical mesh between Ripley's Alpines and Mediterraneans, they are grim, tough warriors rather than soft-minded peasants, and they are concerned with manufacturing things rather than farming the land. Nevertheless, both Ripley's and Tolkien's 'Alpine people' are marked out as 'uncivilized', although this savage aspect is articulated in a different opposition: for Ripley, through their anti-urban, pastoral, anti-intellectual character, and because, to put it bluntly, they are not ethnically Nordic/Teutonic; for Tolkien, this othering is articulated through a model of a primitive,[40] material-based, Stone Age man, and in opposition to a model, which, as I describe in (ii) below, seems manifestly elven.

(ii) That mountains in Middle-earth characterize indigenous ethnicities in primitive terms is further illustrated by a certain duality which is created when mountain people encounter, react to, or, otherwise, are described with respect to non-mountain people. A set of racial binaries is apparent: short versus tall;[41] darker versus lighter pigment;[42] cave-dwelling versus non-cave (tree/city) dwelling; low versus high linguistic levels;[43] manufacturing aptitude versus an understanding of nature; physical violence versus intelligence and communication; material existence versus higher spiritual voyage.[44] These racial oppositions can be found (in different proportions) in the contrasts between: dwarves and elves; Drúedain and other men (including Rohirrim and men of Haleth); Harfoots and Fallohides, and the men of Lossarnach and men of Dol Amroth. These comparisons are not meaningless but point to a hierarchical opposition between the 'primitive' and the 'civilized' in Tolkien's works.

'Civilized' is always a relative term since a given society can only be deemed superior/advanced with respect to another more backward, 'primitive' society. In Middle-earth this superiority can be manifested in different respects; there are different realizations of cultural superiority. One realization is hierarchical dominance. When two or more races are grouped together, the superior civilized race takes socio-political control and is dominant over the more primitive race.[45] Tolkien provides an example of this in the origin story of hobbits (*FR* 4-5). Harfoots attain primitive, orogenetic characteristics, in that they are of short stature and brown skin, have manufacturing ability, live in holes, and are friends with other orogenetic people (dwarves); Fallohides are naturally taller, have pale skin,[46] are linguistically-oriented and musical, and are friends with the super-civilized elves. The racial differences relate to

---

40 On Tolkien as against notions of the 'primitive' as being inferior to a 'civilized class', cf. *TOFS* 44, note 2; Mitchell 7-8.
41 Cf. Fimi 147.
42 Cf. Fimi 146-50.
43 Cf. Fimi 145-46.
44 On the (medieval-inspired) hierarchy according to 'spirit' and 'matter' in Tolkien, cf. Fimi 141.
45 Cf. Grant 46, 139-42, 228; Ripley 549-50, 554.
46 The roots of *fallohide* denote 'pale brown' (cf. 'fallow', *OELD*) and 'skin' (cf. 'hide', *OELD*).

specific positions in the hierarchies once the various groups of hobbits merge. The Harfoots "were the most normal and representative variety of Hobbit, and far the most numerous" (4). They are common and unremarkable, in stark contrast to the Fallohides, "[who] were often found as leaders or chieftains among clans of Harfoots or Stoors. Even in Bilbo's time the strong Fallohidish strain could still be noted among the greater families, such as the Tooks and the Masters of Buckland" (4-5). Primitive, orogenetic characteristics are associated with a lower level on the social hierarchy, with less potential to gain social distinctions and elevation.

It is indeed the Tookish/Fallohide strain in Bilbo Baggins which induces him to leave his hobbit hole (a physical feature reflecting his Baggins/Harfoot background), to leave behind his existence of simple comforts and pleasurable routines (Stevens and Stevens 21), and to undertake his great adventure of discovery in *The Hobbit* (Ruud 111). At the end of the children's story, Gandalf informs Bilbo: "Something is the matter with you! You are not the hobbit that you were" (*Hobbit* 347). He is regarded as something of an outsider by his fellow hobbits, "except by his nephews and nieces on the Took side" (348), whereas, on the other hand, the Sackville-Bagginses, who are after inheritance and estate, believe that an imposter and not the genuine "Baggins" (348) has returned. And, in both a nominative and connotative sense, they are quite correct. The Tookish/ Fallohide strain has distinguished Bilbo 'Baggins' beyond the bourgeoisie of the commoners, and his Baggins/Harfoot background.

A second way in which civilized races can be presented as superior over primitive groupings is through the juxtaposition of social structures of two different ethnicities. In the 'Homeric' catalogue of soldiers who enter Minas Tirith (*RK* 36-37), there is a contrast drawn between the primitive, orogenetic features of the men of Lossarnach, who are short, swarthy-skinned, silent and grim (not language people), and physically-oriented individuals (hence, axes, heavy armour), and the men of Dol Amroth, who are tall and who arrive at Minas Tirith singing (language people). The contrast between the primitive and the civilized is further mapped in terms of class distinctions. The men of Dol Amroth are "tall as lords" (37); they have a developed equestrian class ("a company of knights in full harness riding grey horses" [37]); and they have a clear token of heraldry ("gilded banners bearing his token of the Ship and the Silver Swan"

[37]). The men of Lossarnach, however, are lacking in these respects: their shortness naturally connotes a lack of nobility (hence, the evaluative phrase, "tall as nobles" [37]); they do not have beautiful tokens of heraldry but are covered in dust (a "dusty line of men" [36]); and apart from their leader, they do not have cavalry, and hence no equestrian class.

Their leader, who attains a quasi-noble status through horse ownership, is given the bathetic title of Forlong the Fat. In Middle English, one possible modern sense of "forlangen" is "to long for" (Mayhew and Skeat 90). It is a not unfitting name therefore, and a typical etymological quip by Tolkien, for an old man of "huge girth" (*RK* 36). Even poor Forlong's horse has to be "thick-limbed" (36) to carry the hefty fellow. The failure of this thick-limbed man and his inelegant horse to arrive at the proper image of the noble is the butt of the joke here. And so in their failure to match the class criteria of the civilized men of Dol Amroth, the more primitive men of Lossarnach are rendered humorous and so inferior. Nevertheless, in spite of this cultural deficiency, they fight to the last man in the Battle of Pelennor Fields (*RK* 139), fulfilling the role of steadfast, trustworthy barbarians, a variant of the noble savage.[47]

A third way to mark the superiority of the civilized over the primitive is to incorporate one or more racial characteristics of the civilized in the very process of defeating a primitive entity: narratives involving light defeating darkness, the spiritual defeating the material, or language defeating dumbness. Regarding the last of these, it is notable that the mountain-dwelling trolls, as physically-oriented, linguistically-crude beings (tokens of the primitive) are defeated primarily by acts of communication and elvish magic (tokens of the civilized) in Middle-earth.

It takes the most physically weak, vulnerable member of the Fellowship, Frodo, armed with a magical elven dagger from Gondolin (*Hobbit* 82), to draw black

---

47 The image of the noble savage (e.g. the Drúedain [Fimi 150-51]) represents people as developmentally inferior through the child-adult metaphor (cf. Lubbock 516-19), while at the same time pointing to their essential, natural goodness (Fimi 151). In this regard, it is important to distinguish between the power-based hierarchy of primitive-civilized in Tolkien, which is governed by racial characteristics, and an ethical hierarchy of good-evil. As Schneidewind 2005a (50-62) illustrates, there is a reoccurring complexity to the moral fabric of individuals within Tolkien's races which undermines any comprehensive association of race with morality.

blood from the cave troll (*FR* 426). In *The Hobbit*, it is not the crude, physical, bellicose attempts of the dwarves (46), their typical form of heroic endeavour, but rather Gandalf's verbal gymnastics of mimicry (48-49) and then cunning thinking to delay the three trolls until dawn (49-50) which lead to the destruction and petrification of Tom, Bert, and William. At the battle before the Black Gate, Pippin manages to draw the black blood of the troll chief who has struck down Beregond; and he achieves this not through physical strength, being a mere hobbit and not a heavily-armed Gondorian soldier like Beregond, but because like Frodo he possesses an ancient sword, "the written blade of Westernesse" (*RK* 197). It is the "written"[48] language engraved on the sword which connects it to its powerful past in Númenor and thus lends it power.

The trolls are primarily figures of great physical force, and this strength is most readily defeated by protagonists who display superior communicative skills (Gandalf's mimicry) or who possess potent objects which can communicate with the past (Frodo's sword with Gondolin, Pippin's blade with Númenor). Gandalf, Frodo, and Pippin triumph in each instance through forms of inter-cultural communication which transcend the dumb physicality of trolls: Gandalf defeats the trolls by becoming a troll himself, Frodo 'summons' the help of Beleriand, Pippin that of Westernesse.[49]

The study of the ethno-topography of mountains in Middle-earth reveals the reciprocal relationship between land and people in Tolkien. Ethnicities which originate from mountains tend to display features which are physically imbued with the substance of this terrain and to undertake a life which is closely adapted to their surroundings. Mountains thus have an ecological function. But as much as people are a product of the land, the land becomes a sphere of human culture. A study of orogenetic features in Tolkien presents a comprehensive profile of racial characteristics which are suggestive of a nineteenth and early twentieth century vision of the original primitive, Stone Age man, in partnership with stereotypes of contemporary 'savages'. These orogenetic

---

48 Cf. Hammond and Scull 2005, 598.
49 A fourth way of indicating the superiority of the civilized in Middle-earth is created through the notion of the 'pure blood' of an advanced race being diluted by an inferior race (Fimi 147-48). For the idea in the physical anthropology of race, cf. Grant 76-94; Lubbock 515-16; Ripley 569-71. *Contra*, on the advantage of 'cross-breeding' in Middle-earth, cf. Fimi 151-54.

features in Tolkien are often contrasted with opposing racial characteristics, creating hierarchical narratives where the 'primitive' is measured, in different respects, against the 'civilized'.[50]

About the Author

HAMISH WILLIAMS holds a PhD in Classics from the University of Cape Town (South Africa) and is currently a guest researcher at Leiden University (the Netherlands). His doctoral dissertation entailed a connotative study of the *Odyssey*, while his current postdoctoral project is centred on the reception of Classical mythology in Tolkien. His research is spread between the subfields of epic poetry, early Greek literature, comparative mythology, classical reception, popular fiction, and fantasy literature. Thematically, his work has examined topics such as hospitality, space, humour, and heroism.

Abbreviations

FR   see Tolkien 2001a
Hobbit see Tolkien 2006a
Letters see Tolkien 2006b
LR   see Tolkien 1987
RK   see Tolkien 2001c
S   see Tolkien 2002
TOFS   see Tolkien 2014a
TT   see Tolkien 2001b
UT   see Tolkien 2014b
WR   see Tolkien 2000

---

50 I would like to thank: Thomas Honegger and Dimitra Fimi for their comments in helping me to restructure and revise this paper; the Dutch Tolkien Society (Unquendor) for listening and responding to an initial draft of this work (and for a most hospitable evening at the Herberg in Zutphen); and Ksenia for her encouragement. All views and conclusions arrived at are the author's own.

Bibliography

BACHMANN, Dieter and Thomas HONEGGER. 'Ein Mythos für das 20. Jahrhundert: Blut, Rasse und Erbgedächtnis bei Tolkien.' *Hither Shore* 2 (2005): 13-40.

BRISBOIS, Michael J. 'Tolkien's Imaginary Nature: An Analysis of the Structure of Middle-earth.' *Tolkien Studies* 2 (2005): 197-216.

CAMPBELL, Liam. 'Nature.' *A Companion to J.R.R. Tolkien*. Ed. Stuart D. Lee. Chichester: Wiley Blackwell, 2014. 431-45.

CHISM, Christine. 'Race and Ethnicity in Tolkien's Works.' *J.R.R. Tolkien Encyclopedia: Scholarship and Critical Assessment*. Ed. Michael D.C. Drout. London: Routledge, 2007a. 555-56.

'Racism, Charges of.' *J.R.R. Tolkien Encyclopedia: Scholarship and Critical Assessment*. Ed. Michael D.C. Drout. London: Routledge, 2007b. 558.

CURRY, Patrick. *Defending Middle-earth. Tolkien: Myth and Modernity*. London: HarperCollins, 1997.

DICKERSON, Matthew and Jonathan EVANS. *Ents, Elves, and Eriador*. Lexington CT: The University Press of Kentucky, 2006.

DUECK, Daniela. 'The Geographical Narrative of Strabo of Amasia.' *Geography and Ethnography: Perceptions of the World in Pre-Modern Societies*. Ed. Richard J.A. Talbert and Kurt A. Raaflaub. Chichester: Blackwell, 2010. 236-51.

EVANS, Jonathan. 'The Anthropology of Arda: Creation, Theology, and the Race of Men.' *Tolkien the Medievalist*. Ed. Jane Chance. London: Routledge, 2003. 194-224.

FIMI, Dimitra. *Tolkien, Race and Cultural History: From Fairies to Hobbits*. Basingstoke: Palgrave Macmillan, 2009.

FLIEGER, Verlyn. 'Tolkien's Wild Men: From Medieval to Modern.' *Tolkien the Medievalist*. Ed. Jane Chance. London: Routledge, 2003. 95-105.

Green Suns and Faërie: Essays on J.R.R. Tolkien. Kent OH: The Kent State University Press, 2012.

GRANT, Madison. *The Passing of the Great Race: Or the Racial Basis of European History*. New York: Charles Scribner's Sons, 1936.

HERODOTUS. *The Histories*. Trans. Robert Waterfield. Oxford: Oxford University Press, 2008.

LIBRÁN-MORENO, Miryam. 'Parallel Lives: The Sons of Denethor and the Sons of Telamon.' *Tolkien Studies* 2 (2005): 15-52.

LOBDELL, Jared. 'In the Far Northwest of the Old World.' *Bloom's Modern Critical Interpretations: J.R.R. Tolkien's The Lord of the Rings*. Ed. Harold Bloom. New York: Infobase Publishing, 2008. 49-68.

HAMMOND, Wayne G. and Christina SCULL. *The Lord of the Rings: A Reader's Companion*. London: HarperCollins, 2005.

The J.R.R. Tolkien Companion and Guide: Chronology. London: HarperCollins, 2006.

LUBBOCK, John. *The Origin of Civilization and the Primitive Condition of Man: Mental and Social Condition of Savages*. London: Longmans, Green & Co., 1882.

MAYHEW, A.L and Walter W. SKEAT. *A Concise Dictionary of Middle English from A.D. 1150 to 1580*. Oxford: Clarendon Press, 1888.

MITCHELL, Philip I. '"Legend and History Have Met and Fused": The Interlocution of Anthropology, Historiography, and Incarnation in J.R.R. Tolkien's "On Fairy Stories".' *Tolkien Studies* 8 (2011): 1-21.

OSBORN, Henry F. *Men of the Old Stone Age: Their Environment, Life and Art*. New York: Charles Scribner's Sons, 1915.

PLATO. *Laws*. Trans. Robert G. Bury. Cambridge, Massachusetts: Harvard University Press, 1956.

RIPLEY, William Z. *The Races of Europe: A Sociological Study*. London: Kegan Paul, Trench, Trübner & Co., 1899.

ROMM, James. 'Continents, Climates, and Cultures: Greek Theories of Global Structure.' *Geography and Ethnography: Perceptions of the World in Pre-Modern Societies*. Ed. Richard J.A. Talbert and Kurt A. Raaflaub. Chichester: Blackwell, 2010. 215-35.

RUUD, Jay. *Critical Companion to J.R.R. Tolkien: A Literary Reference to His Life and Work*. New York: Facts On File, 2011.

SCHNEIDEWIND, Friedhelm. 'Biologie, Abstammung und Moral.' *Eine Grammatik der Ethik*. Thomas Honegger, Andrew J. Johnston, Friedhelm Schneidewind, and Frank Weinreich. Saarbrücken: Verlag der Villa Fledermaus, 2005a. 39-66.

'Biologie, Genetik und Evolution in Mittelerde.' *Hither Shore* 2 (2005b): 13-40.

STEVENS, David and Carol D. STEVENS. 'The Hobbit.' *Bloom's Modern Critical Views: J.R.R. Tolkien*. Ed. Harold Bloom. New York: Infobase Publishing, 2008. 17-26.

TALBERT, Richard J.A. and Kurt A. RAAFLAUB. 'Introduction.' *Geography and Ethnography: Perceptions of the World in Pre-Modern Societies*. Ed. Richard J.A. Talbert and Kurt A. Raaflaub. Chichester: Blackwell, 2010. 1-8.

Tolkien, John R.R. *The Lost Road and Other Writings*. Ed. Christopher Tolkien. London: HarperCollins, 1987.

The War of the Ring. Ed. Christopher Tolkien. [1990]. London: HarperCollins, 2000.

The Lord of the Rings: The Fellowship of the Ring. [1954]. London: HarperCollins, 2001a.

The Lord of the Rings: The Two Towers. [1954]. London: HarperCollins, 2001b.

The Lord of the Rings: The Return of the King. [1955]. London: HarperCollins, 2001c.

The Silmarillion. Ed. Christopher Tolkien. [1977]. New York: Ballantine Books, 2002.

The Hobbit. [1937]. London: HarperCollins, 2006a.

The Letters of J.R.R. Tolkien. Ed. Humphrey Carpenter. [1981]. London: HarperCollins, 2006b.

Tolkien On Fairy Stories. Ed. Verlyn Flieger and Douglas A. Anderson. [1947]. London: HarperCollins, 2014a.

Unfinished Tales. Ed. Christopher Tolkien. [1980]. London: HarperCollins, 2014b.

Vink, Renée. "'Jewish' Dwarves: Tolkien and Anti-Semitic Stereotyping.' *Tolkien Studies* 10 (2013): 123-45.

Timo Lothmann, Arndt Heilmann, Sven Hintzen

Then Smaug Spoke:
On Constructing the Fantastic via Dialogue in Tolkien's Story Cosmos

Abstract

In this study, we have a closer look at dialogue in a representative set of texts from the Middle-earth legendarium in order to inspect the functional potential of dialogue and its world-building capacity. We combine corpus-analytical tools from linguistics with a cognitive approach. The quantitative and qualitative analysis of prominent linguistic features of selected examples of dialogic interaction (e.g. the Smaug–Bilbo colloquy from *The Hobbit*) points to salient differences in the setup and the function of the dialogues. The detected patterns eventually lead to a function-based classification into four main dialogue types in the Tolkien corpus under investigation, namely the *bantering, personalising, story-propelling*, and *historicizing* types. These types are modelled to cover the range of styles and topic dimensions from a micro- to a macro-level of systematic foregrounding, thus representing their complementary impact on world-building density and coherence. In this respect, there is a high potential for follow-up studies using eye-tracking methodology. Ultimately, our presented model is meant to offer opportunities for the study of dialogue as a versatile and strategic device in fictional literature beyond Tolkien.

> the story has to be told, and the dialogue conducted in a language
> (Tolkien, *Letters* 144)

1 Introduction and scope

We intend to have a closer look at dialogue in a representative set of texts from the Middle-earth legendarium in order to inspect the functional potential of dialogue in general, and its world-building capacity in particular. The analysis of selected examples of dialogic interaction (e.g. the Smaug–Bilbo colloquy from *Hobbit*) points to salient differences in the setup and the function of the dialogues under concern. The detected patterns lend themselves to be fed into a model of dynamic dialogue types which we will offer as an intermediate summary of this research project.

In the course of the quantitative and qualitative inspection of dialogue patterns, we combine corpus-analytical tools from linguistics with a cognitive approach. For instance, we include an exemplary discussion of metaphors in dialogue and their eventual significance in the world-building process at hand. With this study, we want to contribute to a better and in-depth understanding of the fabric of Tolkien's worlds, and of the fantastic in secondary worlds in general, by text researchers as well as fantasy literature enthusiasts. In this context, we will provide link-ups to the theoretical concept of subcreation (Tolkien, *TOFS*; Wolf) and to the framework of verbal art (Hasan, *Verbal Art*).

2 Approaching dialogue

With respect to the wide functionality of dialogue, Mildorf and Thomas (2) state:

> [Dialogues] play a formative role by creating characters and presenting them in interaction, by puncturing as well as building narrative structures, by affording positions for interactions between characters or narrators and their audiences […].

Being aware of the diversified, dynamic and overlapping functions such as the sociocultural negotiation of power hierarchies, commonality, tradition, emotion, or viewpoints, we assume that authors or narrators present crucial, representative bits of intersubjective language behaviour so readers can use these instances to mentally build and modify fictional characters and the social fabric they act in. Consequentially, we see dialogue as a building block of the conceptualisation of the secondary world (Tolkien, *TOFS*; Wolf), hence as a fundamental element of fictional world-building. In this context, Ekman and Taylor rightfully remind us that the term world-building has been employed widely and for different purposes, thus blurring its explanatory potential. We want to refer to world-building as the joint, yet individual enterprise in the author's and the readers' minds to the end that an imaginary, non-primary story world becomes real on the basis of the 'laws' of that world combined with the author's and the readers' diversified experience. Seen in this way, the argument comes full circle: world-building is a concerted dialogic activity in itself.[1] It involves both a subcreating text author and engaged text readers.[2]

Ideally, the author offers world-building blocks that are stable enough to be identified as reliable and consistent secondary world elements by readers who may then become agents in the dynamic process by picking these blocks up, filling possible gaps (e.g. typical traits of a certain story character) during immersion[3] and potentially re-using them in new subcreational contexts.[4] Rebounds into the primary, 'real life' world are possible as well, where meanings may be constructed and negotiated on the basis of primary and secondary world experience combined.[5] The analysis of concrete language use, or *verbalisation* (Hasan, *Verbal Art* 96-97), is our key to come to terms with the elusive building processes. Character-to-character dialogue with all its performative pragmatics constitute, as hinted at above, environment-transforming events per se, which are mediated within a narrative framework. Along these lines, we want to look into dialogue as a meaningful formative tool.

3 Text basis and method

For the present study, we consider the texts *The Silmarillion* (*S*), *The Hobbit* (*Hobbit*), and *The Lord of the Rings* (*LotR*) a representative cross section of Tolkien's oeuvre related to Arda, and Middle-earth settings in particular. A fully machine-readable corpus was thus compiled to serve the purpose of investigation at hand. The corpus is constituted of 712,930 words in total and comprises OCRed versions of the full *S*, *Hobbit*, and *LotR* according to

---

[1] See Bakhtin's notion of *dialogism* as a structuring force that generates discourse via literary art. Applied to the Tolkien context, Saxton (170) states in this regard that "Middle-earth is, indeed, a remarkably dialogic space."
[2] *Subcreation* is used in the Tolkenian sense here of reinstantiating the divine act of creation by means of text (Tolkien, *Letters* 153; *TOFS* 52); see also Wolf.
[3] In the context of immersion, Lothmann and Scholz have offered a fruitful approach to the building of stable secondary worlds based on Blending Theory (according to Fauconnier and Turner). On gaps as potential story loci and the incompleteness of imaginary (secondary) worlds, see Doležel.
[4] Examples of such new subcreation are texts that fall under the heading of fanfiction. These are based on continuation or resistance of the authority of the original author. More often than not, the emotional investment, for instance in the continuation of building fictional characters, is considerable; see Barnes.
[5] Pervasive effects of fiction on readers' primary world lives are described as a consequence of immersion by e.g. Green and Dill. The far-reaching effects may offer new perspectives and even include personality changes; see Caracciolo (*Virtual Body*); Djikic and Oatley.

Tolkien without prefaces, appendices and commentaries.[6] Notably, spoken parts constitute 37.6% of the entire corpus (Fig. 1), varying between 11.6% in *S* and 46.8% in *LotR*.

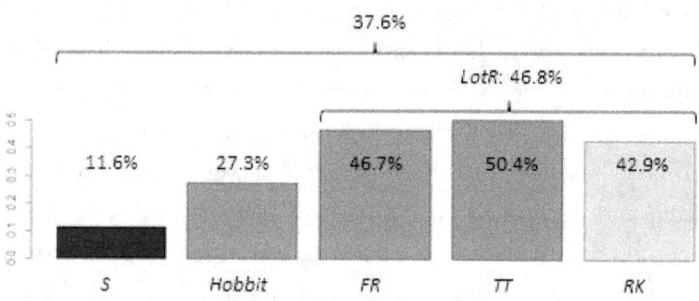

Fig. 1: Ratio of spoken parts in the corpus[7]

For our investigation, we operationalised 'dialogue' as every string of characters within quotation marks and assigned the remainder to a category 'narrative'. Using *Python* (version 3.6) and its package *re* (version 62) we identified such 'dialogue' and 'narrative' by means of regular expressions.[8] The extracted stretches of text were automatically tokenised and tagged for part-of-speech (PoS) with *TreeTagger* (version 3.2.1; see Schmid). This allowed us to count the number of words and calculate the ratio of dialogue in the corpus.

Further, in order to address dialogue from different directions, we were interested in the relation of dialogue and text complexity. In this respect, the number of syntactic clauses contained in a text can be an indication for its idea complexity.[9] We employed *UAM CorpusTool* (O'Donnell) to annotate automatically clausal structures within the speech parts and the (non-speech) narrative parts of the

---

[6] Though *S*, *Hobbit*, and *LotR* are stylistically diverse, we do not go so far here to treat the texts as registerially diverse. While *S*, for instance, is rather a compilation in terms of narrative organisation and leaves considerable gaps for the reader to fill in terms of world-building, we assume a wide-ranging cohesion of subcreation across all these texts that cover millennia of secondary world history; see the concept of 'inner consistency of reality' in Tolkien (*TOFS* 59).
[7] Fictional literature for the younger often features a higher proportion of external representation via direct speech (Joy); within our corpus, *LotR* would fall more into this logic than *Hobbit*.
[8] See Python Software Foundation. 'Regular expressions' are (abstract) character strings that can be used to generate search patterns for searching an input text.
[9] In our context, 'idea' refers to the relation of events and constellations expressed by grammatical means.

corpus (see Fig. 2 for an example of the annotation). We counted the occurrence of clauses in both conditions and normalised them per 1,000 words for the sake of comparison. We found a pronounced difference between speech (149.45 clauses per 1,000 words) and narration (126.03 clauses per 1,000 words), which gives rise to the interpretation of corpus speech, i.e. including dialogue, being more syntactically explicit than non-speech.

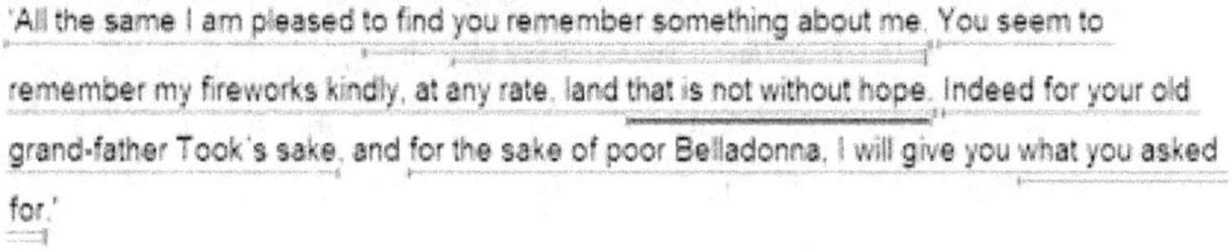

> 'All the same I am pleased to find you remember something about me. You seem to remember my fireworks kindly, at any rate. Iand that is not without hope. Indeed for your old grand-father Took's sake, and for the sake of poor Belladonna, I will give you what you asked for.'

Fig. 2: Complexity annotation example (see *Hobbit* 6)

This finding may stand against the intuition that speech in fictional texts features a comparably 'simpler' syntax in order to mirror conversational behaviour readers know from daily practices. Tolkien made the characters use edited speech, in a sense, thus providing another particular jigsaw piece for the world-building process. We will take up this point later on.

For the additional comparison of the conditions 'spoken' and 'narrative' on a word level we used linear mixed regression modeling.[10] The variables under investigation were *relative number of pronouns*, *lexical density*, and *type-token ratio*. In this respect, pronouns exemplify recurring references to characters. Further, pronouns usually occur in the phrasal or clausal context of attributes, events, and locations. Lexical density, a measure of the proportion of lexical words in a text, was chosen as it serves as an indicator of the centrality of attributes, characters, places, and events in the discourse under concern. Lastly, the type-token ratio represents the ratio between unique words to the total amount of words. It is a diversity measure which is indicative of newly introduced characters, places, or events. On this basis, we assume that the

---

10 The statistical analyses were performed in *R* (R Core Team) using generalised linear mixed models with the package *lme4* (Bates et al.). The mixed model allows to factor in idiosyncrasies of the different corpus texts with respect to the investigated feature.

variables under investigation capture basic aspects of world-building on an abstract level.

We added a random effect to capture different baselines of each measure per corpus part (*S, Hobbit, FR, TT, RK*), and we added fixed effect to control for the progression within the parts. This progression measure was based on chapters and was normalised so that, for instance, the last chapters and the middle chapters of each corpus part corresponded to one another.[11] One result was that pronoun use is significantly higher in the spoken parts of the corpus (of all words) than in the narrative (11.9% vs. 7.9% of all words; χ^2=372.12, p<0.001). Further, spoken parts are lexically denser than the narrative ones (63.3% vs. 61.1%; χ^2=98.5, p<0.001); see Fig. 3.

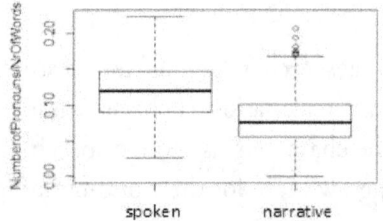 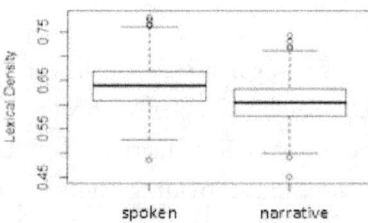

Fig. 3: Ratio of pronouns and lexical density in 'spoken' vs. 'narrative'[12]

Additionally, the type-token ratio revealed the spoken parts to be slightly yet significantly more diverse[13] than the narrative parts (66.6% to 64%; χ^2=46.44, p<0.001) in our corpus. The data illustrate how spoken and narrative parts differ notably in Tolkien's work under concern. In total, with further investigation required, the results point to a decisive role of speech (and thus dialogue) in world-building, thus complementing and specifying the function of the narrative parts in the process.

Clearly, the category 'spoken' as identified above includes all 'true' dialogue instances which are seen here as purposeful spoken conversation with at least

---

11 Normalisation was done by converting the chapter to z-scores, i.e. standard deviations above and below the mean.
12 Here only 'spoken' or 'narrative' text stretches of more than 100 words inform the analysis.
13 The higher the type-token ratio, the more lexically diverse the respective text is. Here, the type-token analysis considers text stretches of more than 100 and less than 200 words.

two participants and at least two conversational turns, i.e. the participants add an active spoken contribution to a particular conversational exchange context. Basing on this working definition, we extracted instances for exemplary analysis. We did so under the premise that "crucial structural and functional principles and patterns are at work in fictional dialogue as they are in natural conversation" (Toolan 193).[14] Further, as dialogue is reported to function as a "gear-shifting" technique (Page in Thomas, *Dialogue* 84) that is employed at "seminal moments" in Tolkien's work in particular (see Joy 76), it deserves to be in the focus in what follows in part 4.

Via the grammatical tagging for PoS,[15] the corpus data were analysable for word class distribution. The data could then be processed with the help of the corpus tool AntConc (Lawrence). We selected the four main lexical word classes, i.e. nouns, verbs, adjectives and adverbs, plus pronouns as we expect all of these to serve key roles in dialogue. We now want to move on to highlight these roles by inspecting dialogue examples from across the corpus of *S*, *Hobbit*, and *LotR*.

4 Dialogue: examples and patterns

Example: *S* 39-42 (dialogue only, 661 words)

The participants of the dialogue are the Valar Yavanna, Aulë, and Manwë discussing aspects of creation. In this passage from *S*, there is one particularly dominating word class (Tab. 1). Nearly 26% of all words in this dialogue are nouns, which is more than 5% higher than the highest percentage of nouns in the other dialogue examples (see Tab. 2-4).

---

[14] These principles and patterns include socio-pragmatic cooperative routines that are guided by (authors' and readers') individual relevance judgements based on experience with dialogic contexts. An extension from actual spoken to fictional written-as-spoken dialogue is thus considered productive here. On possible striking differences of (constructed) fictional dialogue and everyday conversation, however, see the exemplary overview in Nykänen and Koivisto and the corpus study by Oostdijk. See also footnote 20.

[15] The annotation tool *TreeTagger* (Schmid) was chosen for its low error rate (3%). After the automated annotation, the data were post-corrected manually to exclude errors. *TreeTagger* uses the Penn Treebank tagset to assign PoS tags to the individual words.

	nouns	verbs	adjectives	adverbs	pronouns
S 39-42	**25.94%**	15.58%	4.40%	6.72%	11.31%

Tab. 1: Part-of-speech ratio of *Silmarillion* dialogue

Contentwise, the passage is concerned with mythological topics and puts historical events into the perspective of the story world cosmos. In this context, the finding above is in line with the fact that concepts and (fictional) states of affairs including mythical or mythological actors, places and conceptualisations are ideas that usually find their expression in texts via nouns.[16] In terms of the function of the nominal word class as representing material or non-material entities in the world, we can state that the world-building potential of this word class finds emphasis in this dialogue example. Simply put, Tolkien relied particularly on nouns here in order to construct relevant features of his legendarium such as creation myth as a constitutive and cohesive cultural element.

Example: *LotR* 261-64 (dialogue only, 1,419 words)

Elrond's Council at Rivendell in *FR* is a milestone of the story development of *The Lord of the Rings* due to the influential resolutions resulting from a joint interaction of multiple parties. In this passage, the involved locutors, all members of different cultures with assumedly dissimilar discussion traditions yet overlapping interests, engage in "intertraditional dialogue" (Simonson 175) out of political necessity. The dialogue (or polylogue to be specific) features the exchange of cultural customs and stereotypes via the speech of their representatives.

The quantitative analysis of the passage shows the relative weightiness of one word class, here verbs, compared to the other investigated examples (Tab. 2; see Tab. 1, 3-4). The verbal class is usually exploited to express processes or actions. Coinciding with a relatively high amount of verb-specifying adverbs, the verb ratio in this example hints at a rather action-

---

16 Here, 'text' denotes all linguistic forms of a communicative act, i.e. spoken and written.

driven motivation of the dialogue function, thus having the potential of pushing the story forward. This function is skilfully embedded by Tolkien in the multicultural dialogue.

	nouns	verbs	adjectives	adverbs	pronouns
LotR 261-64	20.31%	**18.99%**	5.15%	8.39%	13.9%

Tab. 2: Part-of-speech ratio of *Lord of the Rings* dialogue

Example: *Hobbit* 222-27 (dialogue only, 933 words)

The Smaug–Bilbo interaction takes up considerable space in *Hobbit*. This hints at its decisive importance in the text (see also Jakobsson), also in view of the fact that *Hobbit* predominantly consists of non-spoken (narrative) parts (see Fig. 1). The significance of this dialogue relates to character development in particular. The dialogue qualifies as a case of subcreation within subcreation as the dragon becomes a narrative agent by constructing *himself* as a complex character. Drawing on Lakoff and Johnson's Conceptual Metaphor Theory, a recent study (Lothmann) has shown that this self-construction is effected by metaphorical conceptualisations in particular that underlie Smaug's verbose language use in the dialogue passage. Foregrounded examples such as DRAGON IS HUMAN WARRIOR (*Hobbit* 226) and DRAGON IS KING (later in *Hobbit* 233) do not only underscore the awareness of his individuality, but render Smaug's elusive Faërie nature (Tolkien, *TOFS* 55) and motivations for action more conceptualisable within the logic of the secondary world for both his collocutor Bilbo and the reader. The Smaug–Bilbo dialogue is thus functional in character-constituting terms. It further serves as a natural frame of a challenge between interlocutors on intellectual par in lieu of a physical fight.[17] This function is supported by the PoS data (Tab. 3).

---

17 While Bilbo's riddling talk skills are already established at this point of the story (see *Hobbit* 73-79), Smaug's wit and inquisitiveness are given considerable space. Smaug utters no less than 643 words in this dialogue context.

	nouns	verbs	adjectives	adverbs	pronouns
Hobbit 222-27	19.39%	18.58%	6.73%	9.07%	16.7%

Tab. 3: Part-of-speech ratio of *Hobbit* dialogue (1)

Among the selected examples, this dialogue features the highest ratio of three word classes, namely adjectives, adverbs, and pronouns. The findings match the focus on character, as especially adjectives (and their potential adverb specifiers) are used to attribute features to entities including story characters. The high pronoun ratio, i.e. here the usage of first person pronouns by Smaug in particular, supports his self-construction within the conceptual confines of the story world, hence guiding the reader to build the story world accordingly.[18]

Example: *Hobbit* **4-12 (dialogue only, 1,006 words)**

This dialog example consists of the first Gandalf–Bilbo exchange and the first conversational turns of Bilbo and members of the dwarves visiting his house. Interestingly, the PoS analysis of these introductory dialogues from Hobbit revealed no domination of a particular word class (Tab. 4) in view of the other examples under concern (see Tab. 1-3).

	nouns	verbs	adjectives	adverbs	pronouns
Hobbit 4-12	20.7%	17.71%	6.12%	6.83%	16.07%

Tab. 4: Part-of-speech ratio of *Hobbit* dialogue (2)

All percentages were neither the highest nor the lowest across all categories, seemingly making it the most 'ordinary' example dialogue. However, nouns, adjectives and pronouns in this dialogue have the second-highest ratios among the examples. We may claim that the relatively high percentage of adjectives

---

[18] 43 of the 157 personal pronouns (and 9 of the 29 possessive pronouns) in this dialogue refer to the first person singular, i.e. the speaker Smaug.

and pronouns hint at a function of additionally supporting the description of entities including story characters.

In the following part, we will attempt to resume the threads offered by the data and their analysis. The incipient interpretations provided here will feed a systematic framework.

5 Towards a model of dialogue and dialogue functions

Realities, primary or secondary, exist because of conceptualisations and their rendering by means of words. As well, creation within the Middle-earth legendarium basically proceeds via language (see Keene; Tolkien, *TOFS*; Zimmer). In terms of pragmatics, world-building is a perlocutionary effect in the individual's mind as a reaction to such directed language use. Dialogue has a considerable role in this creation, given that there is the willingness to mentally perform it on the one hand, and that it follows an explicable, consistent logic on the other. On the basis of the depicted linguistic patterns (see part 4) and PoS analysis in particular, we want to set forth a classification of dialogue according to four types that all inform the construction of meaning within the fictional world settings (Fig. 4). We are suggesting that the identified types can be applied broadly to analyses of fantastic story worlds, and of fictional literature in general.

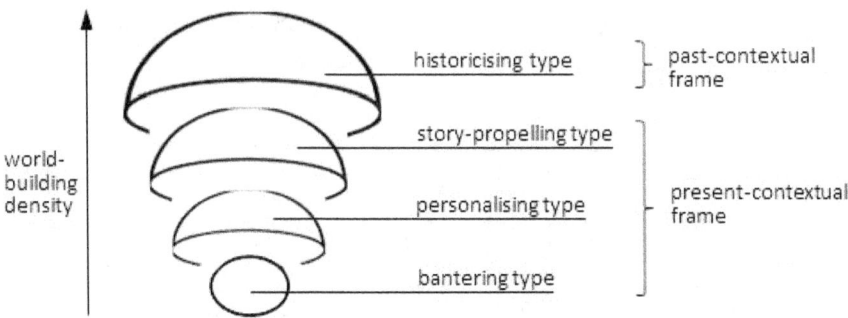

Fig. 4: Model of dialogue classification according to examples from *S*, *Hobbit*, and *LotR*

The types are modelled along their main functional purpose within the story fabric, which corresponds to their verbal impact on world-building, or world-building density.[19] Clearly, the types may dynamically overlap and occur in degrees within dialogue situations and contexts. The confines of the respective types, however, root in our quantitative data.

a) The *bantering* type

More than dialogues of other types, *bantering* dialogues are used to bring an 'everyday touch' to the conversational behaviour of the story world characters. We as readers may take up *bantering* dialogues as a tool to construct the sociopragmatic conventions of the speakers including phatic expressions such as politeness formulae to foster social bonds, humour, casualness, playfulness, and swearing. As in primary world contexts, dialogue appears to be a natural locus of such functions in secondary worlds.[20]

The initial Gandalf–Bilbo exchange in *Hobbit* is an example of this type. It is particularly this example which, however undirected and marginal it may seem for the larger framework and the development of the story plot, lends itself well as an entry gate to the secondary world which the interlocutors are part of, and of which first readers still know little at this point. Readers may initiate and supplement their construction of fictional characters on the basis of the characters' behaviour in bantering dialogues.[21] In terms of PoS, this is supported by their featuring high percentages of pronouns and character-descriptive adjectives. In this respect, the *bantering* type overlaps with the following one, i.e. the personalising type.

---

19 We are aware that world-building can be sparked, supplemented, or rely as well on paratexts such as maps, illustrations, etc. Here, with our corpus being based on language only, we focus exclusively on verbally transported world-building, and world-building density, respectively.
20 Note that the *bantering* dialogues in the Tolkenian context are, as are other dialogue types mentioned in this part, characterised by an edited quasi-mimesis that is likely to be influenced by novel writing conventions (see Mepham 412) as well as by non-fiction dialogue practices of the time. Specifically put, the dialogues do not involve an imitation of everyday primary world speech as readers would employ it in their speech behaviour. Thus, the corpus dialogues miss out on demotic vernacular, hesitation phenomena, tags, or features of spoken grammar in general that readers are used to. See also Oatley (*Taxonomy*).
21 In this context and with particular respect to the Gandalf–Bilbo exchange in *Hobbit*, see Wegener and Lothmann. Dialogue per se is helpful in the event of coming to terms with the secondary world as dialogue is a tool that connects the readers' daily habits and communicative experiences with the story characters' life spheres.

Bantering dialogues can be found throughout the corpus. An additional example are the recurring references to the Orc-slaying contest between Gimli and Legolas (*LotR* (*TT*) 524; 530) who are counting and comparing the number of defeated enemies. These dialogue passages add a particularly humorous, tension-relieving dimension to the seriousness of the depicted war events.

b) The *personalising* type

Via this dialogue type, the fictional self can be transactionally constructed (see Magnusson in Thomas, *Fictional* 60). Here, the self vis-à-vis the other is stressed in the light of characters being pivotal anchors within secondary world settings.[22] The reader may thus obtain insight into the characters' nature and motivations. The quantitative PoS analysis showed a connection between such a *personalising*, i.e. character-building, function and dialogues with the highest percentage of adjectives, adverbs, and pronouns.

The Smaug–Bilbo exchange in *Hobbit* is an example of the *personalising* dialogue type. There, Smaug conceptualises himself as a deep and dynamic individual character, even as a cultural representative and moral authority. World-building (including an understanding of the Faërie logic of the secondary world) thus gains density on a micro-level.[23] Still, this is to be separated from dialogue types in which processes or historical contextualisations are in functional focus; see c) and d) below.

Further examples of *personalising* dialogues are the beginning of the Gollum–Bilbo interchange in *Hobbit* (72-73) and Gandalf's self-characterisation when re-encountering the party after the battle with the Balrog (*LotR* (*TT*) 484).

---

22 See similarly Caracciolo (*Narrative Space* 425).
23 The *personalising* function includes the display of ideolectal, ethnolectal or multilingual competence; see the use of lexical and grammatical archaisms by Theoden in *LotR* (*TT*) (507) or the pronunciation particularities of the Rohirrim in general (*LotR* (*TT*) 496-97) which are intended to be added to character (or group) conceptualisation by the reader. On the link-ups of language and landscape, see Smith (74). On different stylistic features of the speech of *LotR* protagonists, see Shippey.

c) The *story-propelling* type

Story-propelling dialogues are used in order to push the story forward and to highlight decisions and actions made in the present context. As actions may be described, planned and executed by more than one individual and may refer to a historical chain of events, this dialogue category is in between the micro- and macro-levels of building the secondary world. The PoS analysis supports the separate *story-propelling* type, which features a significantly high ratio of verbs and thus a clear focus on processes.

The Council of Elrond dialogue may serve as an example of this type. In this example, intercultural negotiation leads to collaboration.[24] Importantly, the main course of story actions is set via dialogue, which itself adds coherence to both story and the story world (see Simonson 178). Sharing opinions and stories is intrinsic to *story-propelling* dialogues as a process itself that leads to further meaning-making processes (i.e. action) within the secondary world context. This includes intra- and intercultural aspects as well as the techniques of poetry and song.

Another *story-propelling* dialogue that also has decisive function for the course of the story is the dialogue between Boromir and Frodo (*LotR* (*FR*) 388-90). It is connected to the breaking of the Fellowship and thus the split of the narrative into two main strands.

d) The *historicising* type

Our model includes a historicising category that comprises the dialogues with a macro-level and high-density world-building function. In the Tolkien context, matters of history including myth and cosmology are discussed here to be taken up as a basic temporal and moral framework that the concerned (fantastic) story characters are subject to. An example of this is the Yavanna–Aulë–Manwë dialogue in *S*. Further, the Galadriel–Melian–Thingol dialogue (*S* 145-47) and Treebeard's story of the Entwives (*LotR* (*TT*) 464-65) qualify as examples of this

---

24 The Council of Elrond may represent one of the so-called recognition events which are, according to Clute and Grant, pivotal to the structure of fantasy in general. As such recognition centres around past and future actions, we can indeed expect verbs to dominate in such contexts. We are indebted to an anonymous reviser for bringing up this connection.

type.²⁵ *Historicising* dialogues are particularly instrumental when story characters encounter individuals who, by conversing, fill them in on previously unknown historical contexts. The effect is a broadening of their (and eventually the reader's) limited story-relevant background knowledge and cultural perspective.

Nouns prevail as the by far most significant PoS in dialogues of this type, which suits the function of conveying concepts, actors, places, and states of affairs from story times past, including Faërie ones. Nonetheless, they help provide a past-contextual frame for the story present and are decisive in terms of story world coherence, or *Überbau*. In the context of Tolkien in particular, *historicising* dialogues add depth to the subcreational construct in terms of a diachronic story dimension, as well as its deeper moral significance throughout.²⁶ This dialogue type and function is in line with Hasan's theme within her linguistics-based framework of verbal art (see Hasan, *Verbal Art; Private Pleasure*). In this vein, the *historicising* type is used to act, as a high-order meaning-organisational instrument and via a systematic patterning of linguistic choices, towards an informed engaging with a story-encompassing *theme* by the reader.²⁷ The framework implies that a systematic patterning within a text, or foregrounding (see Hasan, *Verbal Art* 96, 101), fosters the perception of that very text as a coherent unit. Dialogue of the types described in this part, i.e. types b), c), and d) in particular, feature such patterning on the basis of PoS. It is stated in general here that dialogues contribute to a consistent foregrounding that promotes, if not eases, effective secondary world-building. Overlapping of types is assumed to be frequent and boundaries are fuzzy, for instance at the Council of Elrond when Elrond 'historicises' by creating context in space and time across a longer text passage (*LotR* (*FR*) 237-39) to ratify the intercultural connections of the dialogue participants. Clearly, he does so for the reader as well.

---

25 An interesting additional example is the debate of Finrod and Andreth, which was not part of our corpus design as this dialogue (Tolkien, *MR* 307-25) is an editorially later addition to the *Silmarillion* story repository. The epochal scope of this dialogue, however, is unparalleled in Tolkien's Middle-earth legendarium. The *historicising* type as proposed here features conceptional overlaps with the *mythos* and *ethos* categories by Honegger.
26 In Tolkien's *historicising* dialogues, the temporal dimension is stressed by the occasional use of antiquated verb and pronoun forms, which further adds a certain exaltedness to the conversational context; see e.g. "If thou hadst thy will" (*S* 40).
27 According to Hasan (see *Verbal Art* 100), the *theme* or deeper meaning relates to an issue that is of relevance for the author's and the readers' (shared) cultural community as a whole, including norms of social (co-) existence, and ontological worldviews in general. Tolkenian *themes* deal, among other things, with hope and loss, mortality, ethical imperatives, enchantment, or the evil within. On linguistic choice, see Halliday; Hasan (Choice).

6 Conclusion and outlook

A statistical analysis of prominent linguistic features, i.e. part-of-speech in particular, has led to a function-based classification into four main dialogue types in the Tolkien corpus under investigation. These *bantering, personalising, story-propelling*, and *historicising* types have been modelled to cover the range of styles (from colloquial to solemn) and topic dimensions (phatic communication, character, plot development, or mythohistorical contextualisation) from a micro- to a macro-level of systematic foregrounding, thus representing their complementary impact on world-building density and coherence. In this regard, dialogue shows to be more than a technique, i.e. more than a mere alternative container of story material. Dialogue as identified here is used as a frequent, versatile and strategic device that has a decisive share next to non-dialogue in the building of a secondary world setting. Our presented model is meant to offer opportunities for the study of fictional literature beyond Tolkien's Middle-earth story cosmos.

Spoken words in dialogue add relevant meaning-making potential to the reader's individual world-building approaches. Dialogue, and this means not only instances in pivotal story scenes, may be seen in this respect as a catalyst that adds 'architecture' in terms of depth, detail, and consistency on the basis of conceptual and according linguistic choices by the author. With respect to Tolkien's fictional fantasy where "all magic is linguistic in inspiration" (Zimmer 65), dialogue is a major skeleton key to unlock the workings of Faërie, for instance to learn about Smaug's complex personality directly from his own utterances, and to bring that character construction into line with the secondary world reality that surrounds him. Tolkien's agents within the secondary world across several texts (here: *S*, *Hobbit*, *LotR*), act within "a world for the languages" (Tolkien, *Letter* 165), thus also within a world for dialogue. Dialogue represents an offer to the reader to engage in the world-building process.

For a better understanding of the nature of dialogue and its functional breadth in fictional texts, it is as advisable as it is promising to continue this project. We intend to validate and strengthen the corpus findings with experimental methods. For instance, we expect different sets of reading behaviour for the four dialogue types presented here. By using eye-tracking as a next step, we want to contribute to making world-building, and the elusive conceptualisations involved therein, visible and thus render it a more quantifiable object of research. Further, via eye-tracking means, we can move away from an idealised, modelled reader to the actual readers in the flesh, as it were. A prior, related pilot study by Wegener and Lothmann has shown that the dialogue parts in the initial text passages of *The Hobbit* feature not only significantly less eye-fixation duration during reading than the surrounding narrative passages, but also quantitatively less elements from Faërie (Tolkien, *TOFS*) than the non-dialogue. These data suggest that Tolkien as the author uses descriptive narrative to guide the reader in and into the secondary world of the story with its fantastic strangeness, while the dialogic passages are closer to the reader's primary world experience. With more insights from such interdisciplinary approaches and by enhancing the corpus beyond Tolkien and beyond fictional fantasy genre restrictions, it will be interesting to see the particular impact of dialogue also on readers' immersion.[28]

After all, world-building is part of our "craft[ing] shared stories" (Saxton 165). We can safely assume that this co-architecturing[29] of the fantastic by author and readers relies to a significant extent on systematic cognitive and linguistic patterning. In the event of crafting, we have the opportunity to appreciate the art-ness of texts (see Hasan, *Verbal Art*) and, even more so, secondary worlds as cultural artifacts.

About the Authors

TIMO LOTHMANN is a post-doc researcher and lecturer of English linguistics at RWTH Aachen University. He has also taught at the universities of Münster and Paderborn. His research interests include cognitive approaches to language, reading and translation processing, pidgin and creole languages, early English poetry, and J.R.R. Tolkien's oeuvre. He lays particular stress on interdisciplinary perspectives. Recent publications comprise a metaphor approach to the Beowulf dragon and an analysis of Tolkien's concept of Faërie as a framework for the blending of story rooms. He currently focuses

---

28 In terms of links to further study, Hyde provides us with corpus data on verbs that introduce a spoken sequence in *Hobbit* and *LotR*, indicating *how* the utterance is performed. He shows that intracultural consistency as well as individuality and development of characters are systematically fostered by these introductory verbs. This is interesting all the more as readers simulate a character's voice in their minds when reading dialogue; see Yao and Scheepers.
29 This process reminds of Oatley's 'novelising' conversational utterances; see *Meetings* (442-43).

on fields of application of conceptual metaphor and blending theory. Among these fields, it is the imaginary worlds in the literature of the fantastic which he has been intrigued by in particular.

Contact: timo.lothmann@ifaar.rwth-aachen.de

ARNDT HEILMANN is a PhD student of English linguistics at RWTH Aachen University. His research foci are translation process studies, psycholinguistics and corpus studies. He is mainly interested in quantitative assessment and statistical analysis of linguistic phenomena and their effect on physiological measures, such as eye-tracking and keystroke-logging data, but also on functional linguistic theories. In his PhD project he investigates the influence of expertise on translation processes and products.

arndt.heilmann@ifaar.rwth-aachen.de

SVEN HINTZEN is an MA candidate of English Studies at RWTH Aachen University. He currently works as a student assistant at the department of English Linguistics. His research interests are in translation studies as well as in cognitive and systemic-functional approaches to metaphor.

sven.hintzen@rwth-aachen.de

Abbreviations

Hobbit	TOLKIEN, J.R.R. *The Hobbit or There and Back Again*. Rev. ed. New York: Ballantine Books, 1982.
Letters	TOLKIEN, J.R.R. *The Letters of J.R.R. Tolkien*. Ed. Humphrey Carpenter. London: Allen and Unwin, 1981.
LotR	TOLKIEN, J.R.R. *The Lord of the Rings*. London: HarperCollins, 1995.
MR	TOLKIEN, J.R.R. *Morgoth's Ring*. Ed. Christopher Tolkien. London: HarperCollins, 2015.
S	*The Silmarillion*. Ed. Christopher Tolkien. London: HarperCollins, 2008.
TOFS	*Tolkien On Fairy-stories*. Ed. Verlyn Flieger and Douglas A. Anderson. London: HarperCollins, 2014.

Bibliography

BAKHTIN, Mikhail. *The Dialogic Imagination: Four Essays*. Austin: University of Texas Press, 1982.

BARNES, Jennifer L. 'Fanfiction as Imaginary Play: What Fan-written Stories Can Tell Us about the Cognitive Science of Fiction.' *Poetics* 48 (2015): 69-82.

BATES, Douglas et al. 'Fitting Linear Mixed-effects Models Using {lme4}.' *Journal of Statistical Software* 67 (2015): 1-48.

CARACCIOLO, Marco. 'The Reader's Virtual Body: Narrative Space and Its Reconstruction.' *Storyworlds* 3 (2011): 117-38.

'Narrative Space and Readers' Responses to Stories: A Phenomenological Account.' *Style* 47 (2013): 425-44.

CLUTE, John and John GRANT. 'Fantasy.' *Encyclopedia of Fantasy*. Digital version. Ed. John Clute et al. 1999. 11 Jan. 2018 <http://sf-encyclopedia.uk/fe.php?nm=fantasy>.

DOLEŽEL, Lubomir. *Heterocosmica: Fiction and Possible Worlds*. Baltimore: Johns Hopkins University Press, 1998.

DJIKIC, Maja and Keith OATLEY. 'The Art in Fiction: From Indirect Communication to Changes of the Self.' *Psychology of Aesthetics, Creativity, and the Arts* 8 (2014): 498-505.

EKMAN, Stefan and Audrey I. TAYLOR. 'Notes towards a Critical Approach to Worlds and World-building.' *Fafnir: Nordic Journal of Science Fiction and Fantasy Research* 3.3 (2016): 7-18.

FAUCONNIER, Gilles and Mark TURNER. *The Way We Think: Conceptual Blending and the Mind's Hidden Complexities*. New York: Basic Books, 2003.

GREEN, Melanie C. and Karen E. DILL. 'Engaging with Stories and Characters: Learning, Persuasion, and Transportation into Narrative Worlds.' *The Oxford Handbook of Media Psychology*. Ed. Karen E. Dill. Oxford: Oxford University Press, 2013. 449-61.

HALLIDAY, M.A.K. *An Introduction to Functional Grammar*. London: Arnold, 1989.

HASAN, Ruqaiya. *Linguistics, Language, and Verbal Art*. 2nd ed. Oxford: Oxford University Press, 1989.

'Private Pleasure, Public Discourse: Reflections on Engaging with Literature.' *Language and Verbal Art Revisited: Linguistic Approaches to the Study of Literature*. Ed. Donna R. Miller et al. London: Equinox, 2007. 13-40.

'Choice, System, Realization: Describing Language as Meaning Potential.' *Systemic Functional Linguistics: Exploring Choice*. Ed. Lise Fontaine et al. Cambridge: Cambridge University Press, 2013. 269-99.

HONEGGER, Thomas. 'The Four Pillars of Worldbuilding: Mythos – Topos – Ethos – Praesentatio.' Paper given at *Tolkien Seminar 2017: Fantasy, Science Fiction und literarische Weltschöpfungen*. Augsburg, October 2017.

HYDE, Paul N. "Gandalf, Please Should not 'Sputter'.' *Mythlore* 13.3 (1987): 20-28.

JAKOBSSON, Ármann. 'Talk to the Dragon: Tolkien as Translator.' *Tolkien Studies* 6 (2009): 27-39.

JOY, Louise. 'Tolkien's Language.' *J.R.R. Tolkien: 'The Hobbit' and 'The Lord of the Rings'*. Ed. Peter Hunt. Basingstoke: Palgrave Macmillan, 2006. 74-87.

KEENE, Louise E. 'Restoration of Language in Middle-earth.' *Mythlore* 20.4 (1995): 6-13.

LAKOFF, George and Mark JOHNSON. *Metaphors We Live by*. Repr. Chicago et al.: University of Chicago Press, 2003.

LAWRENCE, Anthony. *AntConc*. Version 3.4.4. Software. 2017. 23 Oct. 2017 <http://www.laurenceanthony.net/software/antconc>.

LOTHMANN, Timo. 'The Ravaging and Hoard-guarding Antagonist: A Cognitive Approach to 'Dragon' Conceptualisations in *Beowulf* and Selected Writings of Tolkien.' *Fastitocalon* 6 (2016): 169-84.

LOTHMANN, Timo and Janek SCHOLZ. 'Derived from and Flowing into Reality: Faërie as a Conceptual Framework for the Blending of Story Rooms.' *Hither Shore* 12 (2016): 8-20.

MEPHAM, John. 'Novelistic Dialogue: Some Recent Developments.' *New Developments in English and American Studies: Continuity and Change. Proceedings of the Seventh International Conference on English and American Literature and Language*, Kraków, March 27-29, 1996. Ed. Zygmunt Mazur et al. Kraków: Universitas, 1997. 411-31.

MILDORF, Jarmila and Bronwen THOMAS. 'Introduction: Dialogue across Media.' *Dialogue across Media*. Ed. Jarmila Mildorf et al. Amsterdam et al.: Benjamins, 2017. 1-15.

NYKÄNEN, Elise and Aino KOIVISTO. 'Introduction: Approaches to Fictional Dialogue.' *International Journal of Literary Linguistics* 5.2 (2016): 1-14.

OATLEY, Keith. 'A Taxonomy of the Emotions of Literary Response and a Theory of Identification in Fictional Narrative.' *Poetics* 23 (1994): 53-74.

'Meetings of Minds: Dialogue, Sympathy, and Identification in Reading Fiction.' *Poetics* 26 (1999): 439-54.

O'Donnell, Mick. *UAM Corpus Tool*. Software. 2017. 23 Oct. 2017 <https://www.uam.es/departamentos/filoyletras/filoinglesa/Personal/michael.odonnell>.

Oostdijk, Nelleke. 'The Language of Dialogue in Fiction.' *Literary and Linguistic Computing* 5 (1990): 235-41.

Python Software Foundation. *Python*. Software. 2017. 23 Oct. 2017 <https://www.python.org>.

R Core Team. 'R: A Language and Environment for Statistical Computing. R Foundation for Statistical Computing.' 2017. 23 Oct. 2017 <http://www.R-project.org/>.

Saxton, Benjamin. 'Tolkien and Bakhtin on Authorship, Literary Freedom, and Alterity.' *Tolkien Studies* 10 (2013): 165-81.

Schmid, Helmut. 'Improvements in Part-of-Speech Tagging with an Application to German.' *Proceedings of the ACL SIGDAT-Workshop*. Dublin, 1995.

Shippey, Tom. *J.R.R. Tolkien: Author of the Century*. London: HarperCollins, 2001.

Simonson, Martin. *The Lord of the Rings and the Western Narrative Tradition*. Zurich and Jena: Walking Tree Publishers, 2008.

Smith, Ross. *Inside Language: Linguistic and Aesthetic Theory in Tolkien*. Zurich et al.: Walking Tree Publishers, 2007.

Thomas, Bronwen. 'Dialogue.' *The Cambridge Companion to Narrative*. Ed. David Herman. Cambridge: Cambridge Univ. Pr., 2007. 80-93.

Fictional Dialogue: Speech and Conversation in the Modern and Postmodern Novel. Lincoln et al.: University of Nebraska Press, 2012.

Tolkien, J.R.R. *The Letters of J.R.R. Tolkien*. Ed. Humphrey Carpenter. London: Allen and Unwin, 1981.

The Lord of the Rings. London: HarperCollins, 1995.

The Hobbit or There and Back Again. Rev. ed. New York: Ballantine Books, 1982.

The Silmarillion. Ed. Christopher Tolkien. London: HarperCollins, 2008.

Tolkien On Fairy-stories. Ed. Verlyn Flieger and Douglas A. Anderson. London: HarperCollins, 2014.

'Athrabeth Finrod ah Andreth.' *Morgoth's Ring*. Ed. Christopher Tolkien. London: HarperCollins, 2015. 301-66.

Toolan, Michael. 'Analysing Fictional Dialogue.' *Language and Communication* 5 (1985): 193-206.

WEGENER, Rebekah and Timo LOTHMANN. 'That's not Normal Rabbit Behaviour: On the Track of the Grammar of Fictional Worlds.' *On Verbal Art: Essays in Honour of Ruqaiya Hasan*. Ed. Rebekah Wegener et al. London: Equinox, 2018. Chapter 11.

WOLF, Mark J.P. *Building Imaginary Worlds: The Theory and History of Subcreation*. New York et al.: Routledge, 2012.

YAO, Bo and Christoph SCHEEPERS. 'Contextual Modulation of Reading Rate for Direct versus Indirect Speech Quotations.' *Cognition* 121 (2011): 447-53.

ZIMMER, Mary. 'Creating and Recreating Worlds with Words: The Religion and the Magic of Language in *The Lord of the Rings*.' *Seven: An Anglo-American Literary Review* 12 (1995): 65-78.

Maureen F. Mann

Artefacts and Immersion in the Worldbuilding of Tolkien and the Brontës

Abstract

This paper provides a preliminary study of worldbuilding theory in the imaginary world of the four Brontë siblings – Charlotte, Branwell, Emily, and Anne – and compares it with that of J.R.R. Tolkien. Despite the differences of age and historical period, the delight of these writers for worldbuilding begins in their adolescence and involves play with script and language. Glass Town and Angria share many similarities with Middle-earth as these worldbuilders authenticate their worlds and establish artefacts for it. However, the two worlds have very different ethos, with Tolkien's being theorised by Mark J.P. Wolf as the definitive example of a fully realised world with consistent and plausible verisimilitude. In contrast, the Brontës create an imaginary space for literary exploration and apprenticeship which challenges early nineteenth century realism. The paper concludes with a study of how deeply immersive their imaginary worlds became for Tolkien and all the Brontës.

An unexpected comparison

This paper provides a preliminary comparison between authors separated by historical period and by age who yet shared the same delight in worldbuilding.[1] Tolkien's worldbuilding has been theorised as a defining example of a complete and consistent, plausible and credible imaginative world, with an emphasis on verisimilitude (*BIW* 6, 23-25, 130-34). Tolkien himself wrote to Milton Waldman that he aimed for "an illusion of historicity" (*Letters* 143, no. 131). The Brontës' worldbuilding, on the other hand, aims for what might be called an illusion of literary culture; it is a different kind of fictional writing, with a different ethos. An imagined writing space for mimicking and mocking the literary conventions of the time, shared privately only amongst each other,

---

1 A similar delight is the conversations I have shared about worldbuilding with Thomas Honegger, Dimitra Fimi, Shelley King, and Tony Wood, all of whose ideas have ably facilitated this paper, as well as information from Alan Reynolds and Gordana Maria Santo.

the Brontë worldbuilding plays with literary forms and quite often questions aspects of early nineteenth century realism.² Yet Glass Town and Middle-earth have several similarities. Both demonstrate the profound linguistic curiosity and creativity of their creators. Their worldbuilding includes authenticating the world and creating artefacts of the world. In providing a place for profoundly creative imaginations to find expression, worldbuilding imbues these writers with a deeply immersive activity.³

The Mustard Seed⁴

In the beginning was adolescent play. The Brontë children were 6 to 10 years of age when their oral play began in 1826. They started writing down the plays (or at least Charlotte and Branwell did) three years later. Tolkien began creating Nevbosh with his cousin Marjorie Incledon at the age of 15, although they had been indulging in Animalic before that (1907) (*ASV* xiv). Tolkien readers will be well aware of how language invention led to the creation of Middle-earth, but they may not be aware of the genesis of the Brontë worldbuilding. Their imaginary world was inspired by a gift of 12 toy soldiers from their father, the Reverend Patrick Brontë. For three years, play with these toys involved real childhood playmaking of games and toy soldier battles; the siblings' 'let's pretend', however, developed into what Carol Bock describes as "collaborative performances" (Bock 1). This collaboration was complex. The four siblings played multiple roles as authors,

---

2 Four Brontë siblings shared in the worldbuilding. Charlotte is of course well known for the novels *Jane Eyre*, *Shirley*, *Villette*, and *The Professor*, and Emily for *Wuthering Heights*. Anne was to see two novels published before she died, *Agnes Grey* and *The Tenant of Wildfell Hall*. Branwell published over sixteen poems in reputable local newspapers during his lifetime while his lauded translations of Horace's *Odes* were not published until after his death; he is largely remembered for his tragic position in the family, although current critical thought suggests he could have become a respected regional poet had he survived. Neufeldt, 'Introduction', *WPBB* xv.

3 There is no standard or accepted way to discuss authors from family groups in papers which discuss them concurrently. The difficulty exists for JRR Tolkien and Christopher Tolkien while it is fourfold with the Brontës, with the added problem that female authors have often been dismissed with patronising use of first names. This paper discusses the collaborative worldbuilding of four young members of the same family and for that reason I will forsake overly-repeated use of the patronymic and refer to the siblings, with no denigration, by their given names. I will do so also with Christopher Tolkien and Hartley Coleridge when necessary.

4 Charlotte in 1835 prominently used two biblical metaphors to describe the siblings' worldbuilding, the mustard seed and the almond rod, in an untitled manuscript now called 'We wove a web in childhood', from the first line. *SW* 151-57.

editors, characters, participants, and audience in the Glass Town saga; they were both producers and consumers of their worldbuilding, self-reflectively commenting on it and each other and creating the caricatures of Benjamin Patrick Wiggins and Charlotte, Jane (i.e. Emily Jane), and Anne Wiggins and setting themselves up as the presiding genii loci with supernatural powers, Genii Talli, Branni, Emmi, and Anni.

When the siblings began writing down these performances, they used the literary form of dramatic plays; play led into plays. The Young Men's Play, Our Fellows Play, and the Islanders' Play then fed into the worldbuilding. The Glass Town Confederacy involved a fictional colonial invasion into the historical area of Guinea on the African Gold Coast, the land of the Ashantees; it developed into four kingdoms, one for each sibling, Sneaky's Land, Wellington's Land, Parry's Land, Ross's Land (named after the toy soldiers – Bonaparte became Sneaky after Napoleon's death), with each kingdom having its own capital or Glass Town and each kingdom depicted as a bustling society of business and industry, military development and high society intrigue. A falling apart of the collaborative authorship after five years (when Charlotte left Haworth to attend boarding school) saw Emily and Anne withdraw from Glass Town to create the new kingdoms of Gondal and Gaaldine in the North and South Pacific while Charlotte and Branwell invented the new kingdom of Angria that bordered the Confederacy to the east; Gondal appears to have comprised four kingdoms ruled by rival and warring families where mutiny and imprisonment are main themes, with a focus on female figures of power and authority; little is heard of Gaaldine, which was subject to the northern island; the Angrian saga was conceived as a power struggle between the passions and ambitions of two brutal and ruthless men, Northangerland and Zamorna, within the concept of a rise and fall of empire and against a backdrop of aristocratic malevolence and decadence.[5]

---

5 'A Leaf from an Unopened Volume', a prophetic story dictated to Charles Wellesley by a strange "Unfortunate Author", foretells the despotic and unscrupulous nature of the Angrian empire, the dissolute and malicious behaviours of Zamorna's family, and the future regicide of his heir twenty-five years in the future, suggesting how far in advance both Charlotte and Branwell imagined Angria's history (*EEW* II, 1, 323-78). Branwell's 'The Life of Alexander Percy', narrated by Captain John Bud, records some of the darkest events and vices from Northangerland's life (*WPBB* II, 92-190).

Authenticating the Worldbuilding

The 12 toy soldier were to become The Twelves, adventurers and colonial founders of the Glass Town Federation. (Charlotte's Ninepins represented the Ashantee tribesmen (*WPBB* I, 153) but few Ashantee characters were ever named despite the wars with the original inhabitants.) Charlotte and Branwell both describe the choosing of the soldiers intriguingly as fictional events within the history of the Glass Town Confederacy itself, told from the point of view of a toy soldier. The first and foremost artefacts of the Glass Town saga are of course these toy soldiers. Branwell shared his gift of toy soldiers, with each child eagerly claiming a soldier; Charlotte named hers Wellington while Branwell named his Bonaparte and thereby they named their rivalry or what might also be called cooperative competition; Charlotte stated that Emily's was named Gravey by a royal 'we' (because he was a "grave looking fellow") and Anne's was given the name Waiting Boy (because he was "a queer looking thing" like she was) (*EEW* 1, 5); therein begins the tale of the dominance of the elder siblings. The naming of the toys is an exuberant event in all the recorded versions of the choosing; the significance of the event reflects Tolkien's own assertion about names in his worldbuilding: "To me a name comes first and the story follows" (*Letters* 219, no. 165).[6] Eventually Emily and Anne claimed their right to name their soldiers and they chose Ross and Parry, after the renowned Arctic explorers Sir William Edward Parry and Sir James Clarke Ross. Eventually all the Twelves were named and given roles in the worldbuilding.

Their identity as toy soldiers is not, however, simply forgotten as the worldbuilding develops; their nature as small toys forms significant parts of stories. In an early story, Branwell recounts how the toys felt about the choosing and their possible separation (*WPBB* I, 150). In later events, once the siblings leave behind the initial small magazine format, they write stories which highlight the nature of the toys in relation to their authors. In Charlotte's 'The Three Old Washerwomen of Strathfieldsay' the Genii (in their guise as the Little King and Queens) become washerwomen and a mischievous "brownie" who interact with the Wellington toy and his family; their intrusion frightens one of the sons,

---

6 Tolkien revisits the linguistic connection between name and phenomenon in his discussion of Thórr and thunder in 'On Fairy-stories'; as Flieger explains, "without the name, we cannot identify the phenomenon or our experience of it" (*TOFS* 104).

Charles Wellesley, and they try to calm him by identifying their washerwomen characters as "enchantments" (*EEW* I, 203). And Charlotte's 'Strange Events' recounts Charles' macabre hallucination of being just a character in someone else's mind, without a real life of his own: "It seemed as if I was a non-existent shadow, ... I was the mere idea of some other creature's brain" (*EEW* I, 257); he contemplates that he, his father and family, indeed all of Glass Town itself are someone else's mere copy of another different land, with "visionary fairies, elves, brownies, the East Wind" (*EEW* I, 258); he sees himself picked up by a giant so large her hand could grasp the Tower of All Nations (a significant architectural feature of Glass Town which combines traits of the Tower of Babel and the Tower of London);[7] this large, strange figure is unnamed but obviously is the Geni Talli looking down on her toy soldier. Here, Charlotte writes a metafictional story about how these toy characters might feel about their creators. These artefacts provided not just inspiration for play but became topics in the narrative in their toy status as well as personages and feigned authors in the imaginary world.

Tolkien's adult compositions of course never incorporated any of his own toys in his secondary world, but it is interesting how many of his stories outside Arda involved his children's toys. *Roverandom*, written at around the same time as *The Hobbit*, is a Toy in the Moon fairy tale written to console his son Michael for the loss of his stuffed dog. *Mr. Bliss*, written and illustrated circa 1928-31, was reportedly inspired by Christopher's favourite toy at the time and the three brothers' stuffed bears.[8] Tolkien 'forged' letters complete with North Pole stamps from Father Christmas for his children – not part of Arda, but

---

7 The pervasive references to this Tower, along with the depictions of the Genii with Pentecostal insignia, deserve more analysis than is possible in this paper. Charlotte was particularly intrigued by the confusion between Babel and Pentecost; the worldbuilding names Babylon many times over. In addition to traditional exegesis of the biblical story, Babel also figured highly in Masonic lore and conspiracy fictions. (Personal communication, Jay MacPherson, Graduate Seminar in Conspiracy Fiction, Department of English, University of Toronto, 1983. Mann 15-17, 47, 169-70, 251-56). Branwell was secretary of the Three Graces Masonic Lodge of Haworth (Barker 267, 287). As a second fall, Babel has repercussions for the ultimately ruinous nature of Angria; Glass Town has the sinister element of two secret societies (Barker, 224). The Tower of All Nations is one of the most complicated links to the Primary world.

8 Scull and Hammond report the letter written by Joan Tolkien to the *Sunday Times* (10 October 1982, 25) that *Mr. Bliss* was inspired by a new toy car for Christopher and stuffed bears that belonged to the three sons (*Reader's Guide* 590-91). Scull and Hammond also report that Tolkien was so respectful of his daughter Priscilla's attachment to her stuffed bears that he filled a car with luggage and her toys while other members of the family took the train or rode bicycles to a family holiday in Sidmouth (*Reader's Guide* 161). Toys were greatly respected by Tolkien.

involving toys and his depiction of the polar world, for twenty years. There is, however, one character in *The Lord of the Rings* whose name at least and physical description are derived from one of the Tolkien children's toys, the Dutch doll Tom Bombadil. It is not known how the doll acquired that name, but Tolkien used the name to establish a character in a poem published in the *Oxford Magazine* years before *The Lord of the Rings* was written; Tolkien then inserted the "particular, individual, and ridiculous name" in the Ring story in order to develop the narrative before the hobbits arrive at Rivendell for their meeting with Elrond (*Letters* 192, no. 153). Tolkien in this letter even insists that Goldberry's response to Frodo about who Tom is, and Tom's own comments about his name, are related to "the mystery of *names*" (italics in the original). In keeping with Tolkien's other comment about names, it would appear that the Bombadil story began with the name, the name of a toy. Toys were not central artefacts of Tolkien's worldbuilding as they were of the adolescent Brontës' but they certainly provided inspiration for his play in his narratives for children. Play, true imaginative sport and beguilement, is a significant factor in both the Tolkien and Brontë impetus to worldbuilding.

The second and more significant artefact in Glass Town is, again quite literally, a physical object – or rather many of them. When the two elder siblings[9] started writing down their plays in 1829, initially they used loose sheets of paper, but their writing quickly took the form of tiny, miniature books, no larger than 4.5 cm by 3.5 cm (postage stamp sized), a size that was intended to be books that the twelve inch high toy soldiers could hold and read; they were also to contain articles written by the toy characters as authors, poets, men about town, career military officers, businessmen and industrialists and book publishers in Glass Town. The tiny books authenticated the worldbuilding. The two elder siblings created these books from January 1829 to the end of 1830, with Charlotte taking over the editorship from Branwell once he was to become the publisher of the 'Monthly Intelligencer' newspaper, which gave him more scope for reporting on the political scene;

---

9 The surviving tiny manuscripts are the work of Charlotte and Branwell alone and only three of Branwell's are extant (Alexander, *Early Writings* 36-37). No prose manuscripts remain of the early contributions from Emily and Anne to Glass Town, nor even of their prose manuscripts for Gondal. Juliet Barker believes the Gondal saga was as extensive and detailed as the Angrian one (273). Emily and Anne continued to write collaboratively about Gondal until their deaths, well after *Wuthering Heights* and Anne's two novels had been published.

this newspaper was said to be one of the newspapers taken by Bravey's Inn, a centre for the intelligentsia in GlassTown (Barker 191) and so it became a reported artefact. The books are an imitation of the influential print culture of the time, as represented particularly by the very popular *Blackwood's Edinburgh Magazine*, which as a periodical review published extracts of poetry, fiction, biography, history, travel memoirs, comic character sketches, antiquarian studies, burlesques, parodies, lampoons, reports of celebrated trials, macabre tales of horror and the supernatural, synopses of parliamentary speeches, economic reports, new findings in medical arts and scientific shams, affairs both foreign and current, and imaginary conversations – an exceedingly diverse range of discourse, the tone of which varied from the serious to the frivolous. Charlotte's 'The History of the Year' (written in large script before the beginning of the worldbuilding) describes the magazine as "the most able periodical there is" (*EEW* 4). The initial title of the miniature magazine, *Branwell's Blackwoods Magazine* (*WPBB* I, 11), speaks to the influence, which can also be seen in the many forms of discourse which the siblings included in their magazine. Branwell was to describe the excitement he felt reading *Blackwoods* as a child when writing to the editor of the magazine in the hopes of becoming a contributor: "I cannot express, though you can understand, the heavenliness of associations connected with such articles as Professor Wilson's, read and re-read while a little child, with all their poetry of language and divine flights into that visionary region of imagination which one very young would believe reality, and which one entering into manhood would look back upon as a glorious dream" (Alexander, *Early Writings* 20). It is *Blackwoods* which sets the rules for this initial stage of the Brontë worldbuilding and defines that world as an imagined literary space where the siblings explored "the conventions of their culture" (Glen 4), a current culture rather than a past culture, unlike Tolkien's adult worldbuilding. Both elder siblings had made hand sewn books for earlier stories. However, their book making took on full scale appropriation of *Blackwoods* with the move into the Glass Town saga proper; the Scottish magazine functions as a hypotext for the initial development of the imaginary world, a world ironic and heteroglossic.[10] The little books provide a wealth of paratextual detail about the Secondary

---

10 All of the siblings were voracious readers and as the Glass Town world grew, so did the print and literary models for their imaginative space, but *Blackwoods* was their initial inspiration.

world – title pages with publishers, tables of content, sales advertisements, street addresses of companies, in addition to the individual contributions; even when the little magazine format was dropped, Charlotte continued to design the paratextual detail of title pages.

Locating the Worlds

The Brontë siblings were thinking of other features of their worldbuilding from very early on. Charlotte's first extant book, written for Anne sometime between 1826 and 1828, includes a small map of the countries 'Taley, Vittoria, Brany and Waiting'; 'Vittoria' shows Emily's interest even as a young girl in the Princess Victoria while 'Waiting' clearly names the country for Anne's toy soldier. This map likely represents the incipient thoughts about the Glass Town worldbuilding, for it is followed by two pages of geographical notes about 'Wellington' and 'Parry' including a census and a list of names of Primary world lands under the imaginary lands (*EEW* I, 3). Even before the tiny manuscripts appropriated *Blackwoods*, Charlotte at least at 10 was thinking about where hers and her siblings' play could happen, other than in their 'backyard', the moors of Yorkshire.

The hypotext, *Blackwoods*, was to provide that, as well as their Primary world via the popular geography book, J. Goldsmith's *Grammar of General Geography* (1823). The map of Glass Town appeared in Branwell's *The History of the Young Men*, December 1830 – May 1831, as a double paged map used as the frontispiece in the hand-sewn booklet. (Branwell writes of events a year after Charlotte does and his purported author Capt. John Bud in fact refers to her "Romantic Tales" as a source from 20 or 30 years prior to his writing.) Bud describes the site on the Gold Coast of Africa (*WPBB* I, 139) and then continues with a pseudo-historical conjecture about the colonial intrusion into Guinea,[11] leading up to an imaginary version of the battles between the Ashantees and the British invaders. Neufeldt, Branwell's editor, notes that Branwell could have known the reports of the First Anglo-Ashantee War (1823-31) which

---

11 For a post-colonial analysis of the worldbuilding, see Azim. Despite the colonial battles, Branwell does at one point mention the "haughty despotism" of the European, Middle-eastern, and American adventurers who made Verdopolis such a bloody and unstable place (*WPBB* II, 98).

were widely published in British newspapers. He also notes that Goldsmith's *Grammar* (1823) includes the map on which Branwell's is based, a map which shows the Kingdom of Ashantee; the Parsonage library included Goldsmith's *Grammar*, which was well annotated by all the siblings. (Anne added notations to it to include places in Gondal in Goldsmith's alphabetical list of places in the world; *SW* 494-95.) As well, the *Blackwoods* issue for June 1826 includes the article 'Geography of Central Africa. Denham and Clapperton's Journals' which included a very detailed map of the region. So the Glass Town Confederacy map did not function as a working map (although it might have to some degree), such as the initial maps Tolkien used (*SME* 219); sewn into one of the issues of *The History of the Young Men*, the Glass Town map became an authenticating artefact of the worldbuilding, similarly to how Thrór's map functions in *The Hobbit* (but not the Wilderland map). Branwell's map is part of the sibling's appropriation of *Blackwoods* (or of Goldsmith).

No map for Angria has ever been found but Alexander, Charlotte's editor, has editorially amended the Glass Town map to include Angria on the eastern most boundary. What does exist is Branwell's 1834 description of the provinces of Angria in a manuscript fragment of 12 pages, folded but never stitched; Neufeldt reports that one sheet is missing, likely containing the listing for Adrianopolis, the new capital, and possibly another province, Gordon. Branwell lists seven provinces by name with geographical size, provincial capital city, the leader or ruling politician, and a census, giving Angria an overall population of almost five million people (*WPBB* II, 199). This list introduces what is a letter from the Ambassador of Verdopolis (as Glass Town is renamed after the Confederacy becomes more sophisticated); this is Capt John Flower, now Viscount Richton, reporting on the "Advent" of the "rising nation" with the coronation of Zamorna as King of Angria.[12] Of later reports (titled by the editors 'Angria and the Angrians', by volume number) Neufeldt observes that "Branwell's geography is somewhat fanciful" or "confused", with named rivers not being depicted with historical accuracy (*WPBB* II, 652-53).

---

12 The reports provide a way for Branwell, through his narrator, to present a different perspective and foretell the tyranny and treachery of Zamorna and the unrest which will lead to the War of Encroachment and other civil wars.

Geography is not often a significant feature of the events, except for the initial story where the adventurers' ship is blown off course and for a story about moon travel. More commonly, the topography of the Confederation is a subject for observation and description and is not consistently exotic – more picturesque in the European traditions of landscape. One story at least, 'A Day at Parry's Palace' (*EWW* I, 229-33), suggests that Emily's and Anne's kingdoms of Ross and Perry resemble the settings of Yorkshire and Scotland (which the narrator derides as unromantic). Charlotte in particular describes landscapes, caves, forests, and mountains as fairy regions with supernatural features such as pillars of gemstones, ever blooming plants, strange sources of light, and sublime music while Branwell is much more given to describing architectural features when he isn't chronicling battles. Charles Wellesley, to entertain his brother Arthur (who becomes Zamorna), invents a story of travel to the moon which includes walking trees and a "moon eagle" who flies the main character back to earth. Charles includes a description of Earth seen from the moon. Glass Town and more particularly Angria do not in fact represent an actual kingdom or British colony in Africa, even though the worldbuilding map had overtraced a real world map. Angria itself was simply an imagined geographical extension east and its imperial expansion and civil wars become increasingly fictional, caused by the rivalry of the characters. The imaginary world did not stay directly and specifically tied to the Primary world geographically; Branwell's descriptions of these later internecine battles resemble those described in classical literature while Charlotte's later Angrian tales show her alertness to "the literary, linguistic and cultural life of her time [...] playing wittily with contemporary literary fashions" (Glen, *TA* x). The Brontës did not attempt to create an alternate historical world so much as an imagined fictional space to explore writing as creativity – and as apprenticeship.

This mapping was, quite naturally given the very different ages and maturities of the worldbuilders, different from Tolkien's charting of Middle-earth. Tolkien used highly detailed, precise working maps extensively for *The Lord of the Rings* but the relationship to the Primary world was not initially a fixed structure for him. His son Christopher has reproduced the first Silmarillion maps which are detailed about topography (elevations, mountains, forests, rivers, marshes, the dwarf-road) but which do not provide any hint of how the area relates to the Primary world. Even the hastily sketched Westward Extension, which names the Western Seas, and the similar Eastward Extension, do not establish a relationship with north west Europe (*SME* between 220-21, 228, 231), except to place the lands east of a sea. The later diagrams and maps of the Ambarkanta, as products of the very early cosmology, are wholly imaginary (*SME* 243-52). The early legends of *The Book of Lost Tales*, which were part of Tolkien's initial efforts to devise his legendarium and which placed it in England, included a very early rough draft of that cosmology in which the earth is cocooned or "globed" within unseen walls (*Lost Tales*, I, 81, 227). Some passages of Old English show an attempt to authenticate this placement, but Tolkien came to abandon that specific attempt. Yet as Fimi has demonstrated, after *The Lord of the Rings*, "Tolkien started making a 'claim to history': talking about Middle-earth not as an imaginary world, but as Northern Europe in a very remote past in history, lost in the mist of myth and legend" (Fimi 50). In 1956 Tolkien wrote to Auden:

> I am historically minded. Middle-earth is not an imaginary world. The name is the modern form [...] [for] the objectively real world, in use specifically opposed to imaginary worlds (such as Fairyland) or unseen worlds (as Heaven or Hell). The theatre of my tale is this earth, the one in which we now live, but the historical period is imaginary. (*Letters* 239, no. 183)

While Tolkien might have been using the military definition of 'theatre', for the Brontës, their theatre was that of play and drama (even given Branwell's penchant for battle scenes).

Fonts of fun and appropriation

As if to focus on this space of imaginative discourse, these miniature books were produced using a miniscule, italic-like script which often today requires a magnifying glass to read or even a microscope (Alexander, *Early Writings* 3). Even as Charlotte and Branwell moved away from the tiny books and into quarto-sized pages (starting in 1832 with the creation of the new kingdom of Angria), Charlotte continued to use this tiny script and Branwell abandoned it only when he abandoned Angria in 1839 (Neufeldt, 'Introduction', *WPBB* I, xxvii). It came to stand for the literary nature of the imagined world as something different from communication in the Primary world, not an escape from that world but as a sign of a different, creative space. In addition to this print form, Branwell also played with other scripts; in the July 1829 edition of *Branwell's Blackwoods Magazine* he created a strange mix of letters and numbers designed to look like an ancient writing system.[13] This is particularly interesting because it occurs in a passage of his review of the works of Ossian which Branwell's narrator Bud is said to publish; the controversy over the authenticity of Macpherson's poetry as well as the book itself became a feature of the imaginary world.[14] The volume of Macpherson's *Poems of Ossian* which the family owned (and which contains annotations from all the siblings, along with many marked passages; Alexander, *Early Writings* 19) contained Hugh Blair's defense of the authenticity of the poems (*WPBB* I, 28, fn. 16) so obviously the siblings were aware of the controversy over Macpherson's 'forgery' and thus were aware of the concept of creating or imitating documents from another time and culture.[15] The siblings' most common habit was a practice of lettering with both thick and thin strokes, using quill pens and ink, and designed to look as much as possible like print. However, as Alexander and Sellars have claimed, "The Brontës used a bewildering variety of handwritings and forms of signature over a number of years, and often within the same year (*AB* 4).[16]

---

13 Neufeldt has attempted an "imperfect rendition" of Branwell's imitation using letters, italics, numbers, pi, swa, and the obelus (*WPBB* I, 28).

14 *Branwell's Blackwoods Magazine* for June 1829 also includes this letter to the Editor from Bud, dated June 1, 1829: "SIR I write this to accqaint you of a circumstance which has happened to me & which is of great importance to the world at large. On May 22, 1829 the Chief Genius Taly came to me with a small yellow book in her hand she gave it to me saying it was the POEMS of that Ossian of whom so much has been said about whose works could never be got – upon an attentive perusal of the above said works I found they were most sublime and excellent I am engaged in publishing an edition of them in Quarto – 3 Vols – with notes commentary &c I am fully convinced that it is the work of OSSIAN who lived 1000 years ago – and of no other there is a most intense anxiety prevailing amongst literary men to know its contents in a short time they shall be gratified amongst literary men to know its contents." The letter is copied to "the Chief Genius Brany" (*WPBB* I, 14). Fimi (56-57) discusses Ossian's famous worldbuilding forgery in comparison with Tolkien.

15 Branwell's comment on Bud's edition of Ossian reads: "this is one of the most long winded Books that have ever been printed we must now conclude for we are dreadfully tired." (*WPBB* I, 29). The conversation in this edition of the tiny magazine contains references and quotations to Ossian, again demonstrating the siblings' desire to appropriate contemporary topics in the print culture.

16 Branwell would also occasionally throw in letters of the Greek alphabet, such as delta, theta, and eta, not necessarily in a meaningful way but to display his knowledge of the alphabet (*SW* xviii). He also attempted to reproduce Yorkshire dialect in characters' spoken language but this was not taken up by his sisters. Alexander's decision to normalise the siblings' spelling and punctuation for the *Selected Writings* removes the evidence of how the siblings used Tolkien's "visible marks" (*ASV* 10) to represent their language.

In *A Secret Vice* Tolkien had suggested that play with such marks for writing sound was a way of appreciating language as an art rather than a regular means of communication:

> The faculty for making visible marks is sufficiently latent in all. […] It is more highly developed in others, and may lead not only to heights of illumination and calligraphy for sheer pleasure, but it is doubtless allied in many ways to drawing. (*ASV* 10)

Tolkien's interest in the visible representation of language is shown in three places where he creates physical artefacts for his Secondary world, facsimiles of three burnt, torn, and blood-stained pages from the *Book of Mazarbul*, a copy of Thorin's contract with Bilbo, and a facsimile of Aragon's letter to Sam Gamgee.[17] Dimitra Fimi has discussed at length the role of these artefacts in Tolkien's worldbuilding, suggesting they demonstrate how deeply immersed Tolkien was in his mythology and how dedicated to creating "feigned palaeography" that would authenticate his world (Fimi 59). The interest in script as authentification is also shown in Emily's work. She decorated the first page of her Gondal notebook with the paratextual heading 'Gondal' in a stylised script and surrounded by decorative leaves and swirls while the poems themselves employ the tiny italic-like script (*SW* 393). Both Tolkien's own work and that of the Brontës supports his idea that this play with script and the visual representation of language sounds suggests a talent that leads to drawing.

According to Wolf, drawing, or artwork of any kind, is part of the framework of information for a Secondary world (*BIW* 154), the implication being that a "concrete image" helps delineate the world. This may hold true for Tolkien's world, but it does not quite characterise the role of art in the Brontës' worldbuilding. Tolkien's work is extensively known through his own illustrations for *The Hobbit* and the two editions by Hammond and Scull, *J.R.R. Tolkien: Artist and Illustrator* and *The Art of The Lord of the Rings by J.R.R. Tolkien*. The best known illustrations for *The Hobbit* were undertaken with considerable discussion between Tolkien and his publisher, but Tolkien also

---

17 Tolkien's idea that the visible representation of language itself carries meaning is suggested by the observation of Arne Zettersten (124), who notes that Tolkien "changed his handwriting in order to draw my attention to a particular passage" in a personal letter.

discussed the illustrations with at least his daughter Priscilla. (The "home manuscript" (Hammond & Scull, *Artist* 95) – Tolkien's term for the copy lent to friends before interest from the publisher – included maps and an unknown number of illustrations.) Hammond and Scull (Artist 95) say that "the text does not depend upon pictures, but it often benefits from them", due to the lack of detailed description of place in Bilbo's tale. Tolkien also took a keen interest in choosing illustrators for his published works, favouring Pauline Baynes for books such as *Farmer Giles of Ham*, *The Adventures of Tom Bombadil*, and *Smith of Wootton Major*, and cover art and slip cases for *The Hobbit* and *The Lord of the Rings* because of the whimsical nature of her style without being sentimental.[18] The role of visual culture in the Brontës' worldbuilding, however, is quite different from that in Tolkien's as it does not provide pictorial representation. Rather, it reflects the imaginative space of the worldbuilding.

The Brontë siblings were given art lessons in what was the expected level of training and skill for middle class children in early Victorian England, particularly the sisters. Branwell studied with William Robinson as preparation for a career as a portrait artist, which he pursued for a short time and possibly until the age of twenty Charlotte considered a career as a miniaturist (*AB* 11). The significant point of their training for worldbuilding is that at least Charlotte had a profoundly visual imagination which shows in the Glass Town and Angrian writing. Alexander suggests that at least some of the frenzied periods of worldbuilding coincide with increased drawing (*AB* 1). However, *The Art of the Brontës* lists only 30 out of the 368 plates from the four siblings as related to the worldbuilding. None of those plates bear any resemblance to Jane Eyre's unusual paintings which so piqued Rochester's interest.

Branwell's manuscripts are covered with small sketches of faces, figures, architecture, buildings, machinery, landscape, and colophons. Charlotte's work, however, shows her translating her visual imagination into writing. Her early work included two pencil sketches for the single page manuscript of the fairy tale 'The Keep of the Bridge' (1829) (*EEW* I, 37) but there are not many full illustrations of Glass Town landscapes or architecture from

---

18 See also the recent articles by Tankard, and by MacLeod and Smol, respectively.

any of the siblings. There are illustrations of characters – a peasant woman, some brief sketches of heads, and fuller drawings of main characters such as Zamorna and Northangerland. Several depictions of female characters are copies of famous engravings, a trait which shows the influence of Charlotte's art training. What are far more common are written descriptions and explicit scenes or vignettes. Perhaps this is because the hypotext, *Blackwood's*, did not print illustrations but descriptions of artwork and discussions of current art theory.

An article in *Blackwood's Young Men's Magazine* of December 1829 (Alexander's title) provides a review of the "glorious picture", 'The Chief Genii in Council', by the Glass Town artist Edward De Lisle. There are no extant drawings of this painting and no editorial references such a work. Yet Charlotte's description (the review is signed by her and not by any of her other narrators) is so immensely detailed that readers can easily picture the entire scene in their own imagination, especially with the cues Charlotte provides for how to read the painting. The light "irradiating" from the Genii's jeweled thrones "reminds you that you are gazing on the production of a mighty imagination. In the centre hangs a sun-like lamp and you can hardly bring yourself to believe that is not a reality [...]" (*EEW* I, 114). The same address to the reader appears in the review of 'The Spirit of Cawdor Ravine' by the Glass Town painter and master of the sublime George Dundee. "The stream running through the ravine is so natural that you fancy you hear the sound of its roaring." Again, this review is signed "Charlotte Brontë" (August 21, 1829. *EEW* I, 64). Charlotte's descriptions of landscape are numerous – as numerous and as observant as Tolkien's in *The Lord of the Rings* – and many of them demonstrate knowledge of art theory in the discussion of perspective and the picturesque as well as colour, light, and shadow (*AB* 16). Alexander and Sellars claim that Charles Wellesley's description of the reproductions in 'Tree's Portrait Gallery of the Aristocracy of Africa', in Charlotte's 'A Peep into a Picture Book' (*EEW* II, ii, 85-96) suggests her familiarity with the style of the Finden brothers' portraits (*AB* 17). However, Charlotte's later Angrian writing extends this use of the visual arts beyond description into a narrative structuring device. Heather Glen has shown how these last tales use "a sharply pictured scene" to suspend the action and reflect upon it in an interplay of story and visual moment (*TA* xxxv); they are an experiment with aesthetic form; such "suspension of narrative in 'scene'" shows Charlotte playing with a familiar characteristic of the fiction of the 1830's (*TA* xxxvi) and demonstrates once again that the worldbuilding is an imagined literary space for creative expression.[19]

Perhaps reflecting the importance of the visual arts to the siblings, artists are given exceptionally high status in the aristocratic society of the worldbuilding. De Lisle and Dundee in particular rise to important positions in the aristocracy, earning titles as well as important patronages. The Angrian tale 'A Leaf from an Unopened Volume' (January 17, 1834) involves the acclaimed painter William Etty in a series of escapades and events which form the main plot of the story. Etty, who is named after the historical Yorkshire painter William Etty, has followed Zamorna to the newly created kingdom of Angria and is knighted by Zamorna for his service to art in the kingdom. As it turns out, Etty is the disowned son of Northangerland (disowned sons are a recurrent theme); his lineage is finally acknowledged only at the end of the story, thus allowing the resolution of a happy marriage. The story includes a description of his studio with "all the paraphernalia" of an "eminent artist" (*EEW* II, i, 327) such as an artist's lay figure and a *camera lucida* as well as paintings, sketches, sculptures, busts, and various crayons, paints, and tools. The studio is part of a large marble mansion which Zamorna has erected near the royal park (one mansion for each of the nine classical muses – obviously not a feature of British of colonial expansion); of the description of the surrounding landscape, Alexander says, "Charlotte Brontë's natural scenes now show evidence of familiarity with eighteenth-century landscape garden design" (*EEW* II, i, 328, fn. 18). Etty's involvement with the story extends far beyond his easy familiarity with the aristocracy and his portrait of the consort of Zamorna's heir; it reaches into the machinations of Zamorna's political intrigues. The intricate and intimate way that his position as an artist is intertwined with his true fictional identity and the plot of the story demonstrates the significance of the cultural infrastructure of the worldbuilding. The story is doubly significant as well because

---

19 The narrator of 'Mina Laury' (Charles Wellesley, with fuller characterisation and now called Charles Townsend), begins with "I have a great partiality for morning pictures" and provides a frozen tableau before the characters enter (*TA* 7; see also *TA* 123, 218-19, 223, 305-06, 231, 255-56, 321-22).

it claims to foretell the fall of the Angrian empire through rebellion, with coins and statues detailing the profile and figure of the deceased Emperor being one of the authenticating details (*EEW* II, i, 360). One other significant use of an aristocrat using an incognito as an artist occurs in 'The Green Dwarf' where the Earl of St. Clair masks himself as a humble artist, Mr. Leslie. Charlotte's early story 'The Swiss Artist', of a young Swiss boy taken by a mentor to Paris to view the Louvre, reworks a line from Shakespeare to refer to artists as "geni-gods" (*EEW* I, 116). Artwork provides more than just pictorial information for the Glass Town and Angrian worldbuilding.

Scriblomania

Charlotte and Branwell used four different terms for their worldbuilding. Critical reception has focussed on the phrases "the world below" and "the infernal world", yet whether the siblings meant Angria itself with its unscrupulous and scandalous denizens or their entire worldbuilding activity has never been addressed. They referred more positively to their worldbuilding as "the mighty phantasm", almost a religious creed, and, humorously, "scriblomania" (*SW* 163, 165) (a contemporary term, which Coleridge himself used to refer to his urge to write, *OED*). One of Tolkien's colleagues, Arne Zettersten, who worked with Tolkien on the medieval manuscripts of the *Ancrene Wisse* and who has also written on the role of language in Tolkien's work, notes a linguistic tendency in Tolkien that can also be observed in the siblings. Zettersten says Tolkien "could dwell in both worlds at the same time or enjoy an interplay between them. These tracks between the two worlds ran very closely together and Tolkien could rush along them simultaneously" (Zettersten 25). To explain this ability to move rapidly between the Primary and Secondary worlds, Zettersten refers to the linguistic term "*code switching*" (113), the ability of speakers to move rapidly between two languages, two dialects, or two registers. This capacity for code-switching is what Zettersten thinks allowed Tolkien to enter his Secondary world so freely that it was real for him. This metaphor of code switching is also helpful in providing a positive way to understand the Brontës' involvement in their invented world. Their various forms of participation in the imaginary world made code switching highly likely for them.

Birthday notes, written quite informally by Emily and Anne every three or four years from 1834 to 1845, demonstrate this code switching particularly strongly. They are not manuscripts of Gondal but biographical remembrances that happen to include comments about the worldbuilding. They were intended to be used as personal time capsules and it is probably significant that they were signed by both sisters who were conversing with each other in the world in which each was fluent. The first note from 1834 includes many homey details of domestic activities interlaced with events in worldbuilding: "papa […] gave Branwell a Letter saying here Branwell read this and show it to your Aunt and Charlotte – The Gondals are discovering the interior of Gaaldine Sally Mosley is washing in the back kitchin" (*SW* 485). The 1837 paper moves back and forth between Parsonage life and Gondal without skipping a beat:

> Charlotte working in Aunt's room Branwell reading Eugene Aram to her Anne and I writing in the drawing room […] I Agustus – Almedas life 1st vol – 4th page from the last a fine rather coolish thin grey cloudy but sunny day Aunt working in the little Room papa – gone out. Tabby in the kitchin – the Emprerors and Empresses of Gondal and Gaalddine preparing to depart from Gaaldine to Gondal to prepare for the coronation which will be on the 12th of July Queen Vicctiora (sic) ascended the throne this month Northangerland in Monceys Isle – Zamorna at Eversham. (*SW* 487)

The notes from 1841 provide a little more structure by separating Primary and Secondary worlds into different paragraphs. However, Emily's 1845 note recounts hers and Anne's trip to York when they pretended they were various characters from the Gondal saga:

> during our excursion we were Ronald Macelgin, Henry Angora, Juliet Angusteena, Rosabelle [?Esmaldam], Ella and Julian Egramon[t] Catherine Navarre and Cordelia Fitzaphnold escaping from the palaces of Instruction to join the Royalists who are hard driven at present by the victorious Republicans – The Gondals still flo[u]rish bright as ever I am at present writing a work on the First Wars […] We [includes Anne] intend sticking firm by the rascals as long as they delight us which I am glad to say they do at present. (*SW* 490)

And Anne's 1845 paper considers the fate of Gondal in the same thought as the future of the siblings: "The Gondals in general are not in first rate playing condition – will they improve? I wonder how we shall all be and where and how situated on the thirtieth of July 1848" (*SW* 492-93).

This is extremely similar to Zettersten's observation that Tolkien could 'dwell in both worlds at the same time" (25). A further similarity is that Branwell published his poems in local newspapers under the pseudonym 'Northangerland', the arch rival of Zamorna, even though he had contacted the publisher using his real name (Barker 437, 1060-61). That may not be a pure example of code switching but it demonstrates the degree to which Branwell was comfortable with relating his Primary and Secondary worlds, something similar to Tolkien including the names of Beren and Lúthien on his own and Edith's gravestone.

Characterising Charlotte's immersion in the worldbuilding is more complex because she left more historical documents about the worldbuilding, most of which have been traditionally interpreted to denigrate her involvement with the sagas. The most anthologised of these pieces date from her time teaching at Roe Head, where her great unhappiness over the uncongenial teaching was also combined with the absence of her close, collaborative writing partner Branwell (who was furiously writing back home at Haworth about precipitate events in Angria and was about to kill off one of her favourite characters) and where for the first time in her life she had no opportunity to write. Yet these fragments do demonstrate her self-reflexive awareness of the relationship between the created world and the real world; they are not unmediated autobiography but literary performances. As Heather Glen argues, Charlotte's voice was not that of "escapist romance" but one "almost 'preternaturally'" alert to the powers of writing (Glen 3). The preliminary nature of this paper excludes a thorough analysis of all these accounts, except to point out that the prompts Charlotte mentions which inspire her despite her frustrations with teaching are iconic literary tropes of inspiration, especially from the Bible. They articulate how she moves from her condition in the real world to the creativity of her worldbuilding and writing (*SW* 158-60, *passim*). Even her often anthologised 'Farewell to Angria' appropriates the common literary trope of "farewell to youth" used by the writers she was familiar with, Byron, Coleridge, Keats, and Wordsworth (Glen 22). The most explicit statement of Charlotte's awareness of worldbuilding, however, lies in her letter to Hartley Coleridge, written four years later than the journal fragments.

Hartley had complimented Branwell's translations of Homer's Odes and invited him to visit Hab Cottage in May 1840. With this positive example in front of her, Charlotte sent Hartley (pseudonymously) part of an Angrian tale disguised by being reset in Yorkshire with Zamorna under a new name (Barker 395). Clearly, he had been negative about the work. Given he himself continued to create the imaginary world of Ejuxria throughout his adulthood, her comment to him about worldbuilding is intriguing.[20] Because this letter is not often anthologised, this relevant paragraph deserves full quotation.

> It is very edifying and profitable to create a world out of one's own brain and people it with inhabitants who are like so many Melchisedecs – "without father, without mother, without descent, having neither beginning of days, nor end of life". By conversing daily with such beings and accustoming your eyes to their glaring attire and fantastic features – you acquire a tone of mind admirably calculated to enable you to cut a respectable figure in practical life – If you have ever been accustomed to such society Sir you will be aware how distinctly and vividly their forms and features fix themselves on the retina of that "inward eye" which is said to be "the bliss of solitude". Some of them are so ugly – you can liken them to nothing but the grotesque things carved by a besotted pagan for his temple – and some of them so preternaturally beautiful that their aspect startles you as much as Pygmalion's Statue must have startled him – when life began to animate its chiselled features and kindle up its blind, marble eyes. (Ch. Brontë, *Letters* 26)

Charlotte here uses three literary allusions to defend the condition of worldbuilding, from the Bible, from the poet Wordsworth (the romantic spiritual vision of "I wandered lonely as a cloud" becomes almost literal), and from Greek mythology and all suggest a profound and intense, almost virtual experience. (The Melchisedecs allusion is particularly intriguing, for Glass Town and Angria have relatively little history, compared with the long ages of Middle-earth.) While the paragraph does not demonstrate the code switching of Emily's and Anne's birthday papers, it does describe a condition under which code switching can happen. As Charlotte wrote in the 'Farewell to Angria', the music of an imagined event in Angria "came thrillingly to my mind's – almost to my body's – ear" (*SW* 156).

---

20 Neither her first letter to him nor his response is extant and there is no historical evidence, just wild speculation, whether Branwell and Hartley might have discussed worldbuilding. There is no mention in Barker's extensive family biography of Branwell ever mentioning knowledge of Ejuxria to Charlotte.

Sic Transit etc.

Charlotte wryly borrowed this Latin tag in her recollection of how a student interrupted one of her reveries of Angria (*SW* 157); its use affirms the worldbuilding while ironically commenting on it. Sometimes the Primary and Secondary worlds do not run closely on Zettersten's two tracks. Nor does all worldbuilding aim for Tolkien's "illusion of historicity". The Brontës's subcreation had a different ethos; they created a world which allowed them to experience their participation in the literary culture of their time. Exploring Glass Town and Angria provides a fuller understanding of worldbuilding than has been theorised via Tolkien's Middle-earth and other contemporary worlds. Going elsewhere can be to an imagined literary space as well as to a different destination. However, despite this different ethos between Middle-earth and that of Glass Town and Angria, creators of both worlds appear ultimately to inhabit their created worlds imaginatively as co-extensive with their real world.

About the Author

MAUREEN F. MANN holds a PhD in English literature from the University of Toronto and taught at Wilfred Laurier University, York University, and the University of Toronto before retiring. Her specialty was Romantic theories of the imagination in the novels of Charlotte Brontë while she also taught Canadian and 18th Century British literature, as well as the history of the language, with other interests in medieval literature, science fiction, and fantasy. She is co-editor of *Laughter in Middle-earth: Humour in and around the Works of Tolkien*, to which she contributed an article on Nonsense in Tolkien and has recently contributed "Musicality in Tolkien's Prose" to the forthcoming *Music in Tolkien's Work and Beyond*. Her current research interest is early Victorian fairie in the Brontës.

Abbreviations

AB   ALEXANDER, Christine and Jane SELLARS. *The Art of the Brontës*.
ASV   TOLKIEN, J.R.R. *A Secret Vice: Tolkien on Invented Languages*.
EEW   BRONTË, Charlotte. *An Edition of the Early Writings of Charlotte Brontë*.
Letters   TOLKIEN, J.R.R. *The Letters of J.R.R. Tolkien*.

MUW	BRONTË, Charlotte and Patrick Branwell BRONTË. *The Miscellaneous and UnpublishedWritings of Charlotte and Patrick Branwell Brontë.*
SME	TOLKIEN, J.R.R. *The Shaping of Middle-Earth.*
SW	BRONTË, Charlotte et al. *Tales of Glass Town, Angria, and Gondal: Selected Writings.*
TA	BRONTË, Charlotte. *Tales of Angria.*
TOFS	TOLKIEN, J.R.R. *Tolkien on Fairy-stories.*
WPBB	BRONTË, Patrick Branwell. *The Works of Patrick Branwell Brontë.*

Bibliography

ALEXANDER, Christine and Jane SELLARS. *The Art of the Brontës.* Cambridge: Cambridge University Press, 1995.

ALEXANDER, Christine. *The Early Writings of Charlotte Brontë.* Oxford: Basil Blackwell, 1983.

AZIM, Firdous. *The Colonial Rise of the Novel.* London: Routledge, 1993.

BARKER, Juliet. *The Brontës.* London: Abacus, 2010.

BOCK, Carol. *Charlotte Brontë and the Storyteller's Audience.* Iowa City: University of Iowa Press, 1992.

BRONTË, Charlotte. *An Edition of the Early Writings of Charlotte Brontë.* Two volumes. Ed. Christine Alexander. Oxford: Basil Blackwell for the Shakespeare Head Press, 1987.

Selected Letters of Charlotte Brontë. Ed. Margaret Smith. Oxford: Oxford University Press, 2007.

Tales of Angria. Ed. Heather Glen. London: Penguin, 2006.

BRONTË, Charlotte and Patrick Branwell BRONTË. *The Miscellaneous and Unpublished Writings of Charlotte and Patrick Branwell Brontë.* Two volumes. Oxford: Shakespeare Head Press, 1938.

BRONTË, Charlotte et al. *The Brontës: Their Lives, Friendships, and Correspondence in Four Volumes.* Ed. T.J. Wise. Oxford: Shakespeare Head Press, 1933.

Tales of Glass Town, Angria, and Gondal: Selected Writings. Ed. Christine Alexander. Oxford: Oxford University Press, 2010.

Brontë, Patrick Branwell. *The Works of Patrick Branwell Brontë: An Edition*. Three volumes. Ed. Victor A. Neufelt. New York: Garland, 1977.

Fimi, Dimitra. 'The Past as an Imaginary World: The Case of Medievalism.' *Revisiting Imaginary Worlds: A Subcreation Studies Anthology*. Ed. Mark J.P. Wolf. New York: Routledge, 2017. 45-65.

Genette, Gérard. *Paratexts: Thresholds of Interpretation*. Trans. Jane E. Lewins. Cambridge: Cambridge University Press, 1997.

Glen, Heather. *Charlotte Brontë: The Imagination in History*. Oxford: Oxford University Press, 2002.

Hammond, Wayne G. and Christina Scull. *The Art of The Lord of the Rings by J.R.R. Tolkien*. Boston: Houghton Mifflin Harcourt, 2015.

J.R.R. Tolkien: Artist & Illustrator. Boston: Houghton Mifflin, 2000.

The Lord of the Rings: A Reader's Companion. London: HarperCollins, 2014.

The J.R.R. Tolkien Companion and Guide: Reader's Guide. Boston: Houghton Mifflin, 2006.

Mann, Maureen Forbes. *The Authority of Language in the Novels of Charlotte Brontë*. Diss. University of Toronto, 1988.

MacLeod, Jeffrey J. and Anna Smol. 'Visualizing the Word: Tolkien as Artist and Writer.' *Tolkien Studies* 14 (2017): 115-31.

Root-Bernstein, Michele. *Inventing Imaginary Worlds: from Childhood Play to Adult Creativity Across the Arts and Sciences*. New York: Rowman & Littlefield, 2014.

Tankard, Paul. '"Akin to my own Inspiration": Mary Fairburn and the Art of Middle-earth.' *Tolkien Studies* 14 (2017): 133-54.

Tolkien, J.R.R. *A Secret Vice: Tolkien on Invented Languages*. Ed. Dimitra Fimi & Andrew Higgins. London: HarperCollins, 2016.

Mr. Bliss. London: Allen & Unwin, 1982.

The Book of Lost Tales. Part One. Ed. Christopher Tolkien. London: HarperCollins, 2002.

The Lord of the Rings. London: HarperCollins, 1995.

The Letters of J.R.R. Tolkien. Ed. Humphrey Carpenter. London: HarperCollins, 2006.

The Shaping of Middle-earth. Ed. Christopher Tolkien. London: Allen Unwin, 1986.

Tolkien on Fairy-stories. Expanded edition, with commentary and notes. Ed. Verlyn Flieger & Douglas A. Anderson. London: HarperCollins, 2014.

WOLF, Mark J.P. *Building Imaginary Worlds: The Theory and History of Subcreation.* New York: Routledge, 2012.

ZETTERSTEN, Arne. *J.R.R. Tolkien's Double Worlds and Creative Process: Language and Life.* London: PalgraveMacmillan, 2011.

Bradford Lee Eden

Sub-creation by any Other Name: The Artist and God in the Early Twentieth Century

Abstract

This contribution will examine other writers and philosophers of the late-nineteenth and early twentieth-centuries who wrote or discussed various ideas and thoughts around man's role as a sub-creator and inventor. Many of these individuals were Tolkien's contemporaries or were influences on Tolkien: Francis Thompson (1859-1907), James Joyce (1882-1941), Jorge Luis Borges (1899-1986), Jacques Maritain (1882-1973), and David Jones (1895-1974). All wrote about their views regarding man in relation to God, especially as imitators, artists, writers, and sub-creators. This paper will provide more information on what each of these individuals felt and said, and what influence they may/may not have had on Tolkien and his theory of sub-creation.

Introducion

As I have explored the role and influence that 'Third Spring' authors and their writings (that is early twentieth-century British-Anglican converts to Roman Catholicism) had on the thoughts and writings of J.R.R. Tolkien, various threads and tangents of other late-nineteenth and early-twentieth century writers and their comments on man's role as artist in relation to God have peaked my curiosity.[1] Granted, I am not an expert on early modern literature nor do I claim to have acquired a broad-based scholarly knowledge of the individuals and their writings that I am about to discuss. I have, however, felt that Tolkien scholars need to expand outside of their comfort zones and begin to discuss the wider social, cultural, political, and literary influences outside of Tolkien's documented sources. As such, I am willing to step outside my own comfort zone with this chapter, and begin the process of exploration and brainstorming about how the Tolkien scholar community

---

1 So far, this exploration has been presented in four separate unpublished papers: Eden (2017a), Eden (2017b), Eden (2017c), and Eden (2017d).

can and should examine early modern writers and their ideas which probably influenced Tolkien's own thought processes but aren't as well documented as those already researched.

We already know that Tolkien was a voracious reader, as is recorded in the areas of astronomy by Kristine Larsen, time travel by Verlyn Flieger, and now language creation by Dimitra Fimi and Andrew Higgins, to name but a few (Larsen 2014; Flieger 2004; Tolkien 2016). Tolkien was especially interested in the writings of the 'Third Spring' authors such as Graham Greene, Christopher Dawson, G.K. Chesterton, and David Jones. Dawson's book *Progress and Religion* had an especially strong influence on Tolkien's essay 'On Fairy-Stories' (Tolkien 2008; Ryan 2009a). But there were also other major writers during Tolkien's lifetime who expounded their viewpoints on the role of man as artist, inventor, and sub-creator in relation to God. I want to provide just a glimpse of some of these authors and their ideas, again not as an expert but in order to provoke discussion and hopefully full-fledged research on their interconnections with and influence on Tolkien's thoughts surrounding this topic. Some of these influences are better documented than others; for some there may be no documentation whatsoever. In any event, knowledge of these similar ideas can only lead to more questions and hopefully more in-depth examination and research.[2]

Francis Thompson (1859-1907)

Let me start first of all with Francis Thompson. We all know that Thompson's life and poetry had a strong influence on Tolkien as a young undergraduate at Oxford, and that he even purchased his *Works* in 1913 and 1914. Andrew Higgins discusses many of the influences which Thompson's poetry had on Tolkien (Higgins 2015; especially 131-44). In my own delvings into Thompson's poetry to find connections to Tolkien's works, I have discovered a little-known reference in one of Thompson's biographies to an unpublished manuscript titled 'On an analogy between God, Man and the Poet', a fourteen-page handwritten document in which Thompson expounds his ideas on this topic. Now obviously

---

[2] Many others have already been documented or mentioned in other contexts: George MacDonald, John Ruskin, W.H. Auden, Martin C. D'Arcy, Mircea Eliade, Paul Tillich, G.K. Chesterton, and Samuel Taylor Coleridge to name but a few. For some introduction to the immensity of this topic, see Ryan, J.S. (2009b); Phelpstead (2014); and Wolf (2012).

Tolkien would not have known of this manuscript, but I have been able to obtain a copy of this manuscript, which I am in the process of transcribing and will be discussing at the Popular Culture Association/American Culture Association conference in March 2018 in Indianapolis, Indiana. Thus far, I have been able to glean that Thompson's thoughts on the relationship between God, man, and the artist are quite similar to Tolkien's concept of sub-creation. Again, Tolkien would not have known of this document, but it goes to show that many individuals in the late nineteenth/early twentieth century were thinking and writing on this topic, and that Tolkien was not the only one.

James Joyce (1882-1941)

Moving on then to James Joyce. Hiley (2015) has documented that Tolkien read Finnegan's Wake, and recorded some of his thoughts on the book in MS Tolkien 24, fol. 44-45 in the Bodleian Library at Oxford University.[3] Hiley makes some thoughtful comments on Tolkien's analysis and comments regarding Joyce's use of language, and that Tolkien's criticism of *Finnegans Wake* was not "because Joyce was too radical or pretentious (as Tolkien's colleague C.S. Lewis did, dismissing Joyce's writing as *'steam* of consciousness'), but because Joyce was not radical enough in his application of 'pure sound' in language" (Hiley 118). It would be interesting to know if Tolkien's reading and comments regarding *Finnegan's Wake* were close in time to his 1930's speech on invented languages in Tolkien (2016).

In any case, I am not an expert on Joyce, but I do have advanced degrees in musicology, and was astounded in my initial examination of Joyce's works with the extensive musical allusions he incorporated into his writings. As I read much of the scholarship surrounding Joyce's works, I was reminded of Fimi and Higgin's edition of *A Secret Vice* concerning the 'Essay on Phonetic Symbolism' that Tolkien wrote in the 1930s. Much of what is said in that essay reverberates with Joyce's extensive quotation and allusion to music and musical works in his writings. One especially interesting article called 'Sound and sense: James Joyce's aural esthetics' makes links between the medieval Celtic penchant for rhymes, grammar, and

---

3 Thanks to Massimiliano Izzo for pointing out this article to me.

sound, and Joyce's use of aural stylistic devices (Tymoczko 2005). I have written extensively on the importance of musical allusion in Tolkien's works, especially his early versions of his legendarium stories, so discovering Joyce's conscious use of musical allusion excited me in wondering whether Tolkien ever read Joyce, and when. So again, another challenge to the Tolkien scholar community for exploration. For those who have done research on Tolkien's language invention and use of language, the book *Joysprick: An Introduction to the Language of James Joyce* by Anthony Burgess is a great place to see how another early twentieth-century writer consciously used his heritage (that is, Irish) and his love of music in various ways and methods throughout his oeuvre (see also Weaver 1998). Joyce became progressively blind towards the end of his life, and it is known that he dictated and sang his notes for *Finnegan's Wake* to his closest friends. I point this out, because the next writer also had issues with eyesight.

Jorge Luis Borges (1899-1986)

Jorge Luis Borges was born in Argentina, and was taught at home until the age of eleven. He was bilingual in both Spanish and English, and his father's personal library contained over 1,000 volumes. He was quoted as saying "if I were asked to name the chief event in my life, I should say my father's library." Borges' best known stories were on fantastical themes, such as a library that contained every 410-page text, a man who forgets nothing he experiences, an artifact through which the user can see everything in the universe, and a year of still time given to a man standing before a firing squad. Major topics that fascinated Borges included dreams, labyrinths, libraries, mirrors, fictional writers, philosophy, and religion. Similar to Tolkien, he also employed the devices of literary forgery (i.e. second and third-level narrators) and even the review of an imaginary work, both forms of modern pseudo-epigrapha. Borges was completely blind by the age of 55 (1954); even so, he was Director of the Argentine National Library from 1955-73. He never learned braille, so he became unable to read. His mother became his personal secretary and reader. Scholars have suggested that his progressive blindness helped him to create innovative literary symbols through imagination. Borges spent the remainder of his life translating anything and everything into

Spanish; he initiated his study of Old English and Old Norse after going blind. When Borges died in 1986, he was buried in Geneva, Switzerland, where his headstone is adorned with carvings derived from Anglo-Saxon and Old Norse art and literature.

Borges' view of literary creation has been dubbed the "Borgesian conundrum" which is the ontological question of whether the writer writes the story, or it writes him. According to one writer "the basic contention was that fiction did not depend on the illusion of reality; what mattered ultimately was an author's ability to generate 'poetic faith' in his reader." Borges described his philosophy and experience of writing in a 1971 lecture at Columbia University:

> This is a kind of central mystery – how my poems get written. I may be walking down the street, or up and down the staircase of the National Library [...] and suddenly I know that something is about to happen. Then I sit back. I have to be attentive to what is about to happen. It may be a story, or it may be a poem, either in free verse or in some form. The important thing at this point is not to tamper. We must, lest we be ambitious, let the Holy Ghost, or the Muse, or the subconscious – if you prefer modern mythology – have its way with us. Then, in due time, if I have not bamboozled myself, I am given a line, or maybe some hazy notion – a glimpse perhaps – of a poem, a long way off. Often, can barely make it out; then that dim shape, that dim cloud, falls into shape, and I hear my inner voice saying something. From the rhythm of what I first hear, I know whether or not I am on the brink of committing a poem, be it in the sonnet form or free verse [...] All this boils down to a simple statement: poetry is given to the poet. I don't think a poet can sit down at will and write. If he does, nothing worthwhile can come of it. I do my best to resist this temptation. I often wonder how I've come to write several volumes of verse! But I let the poems insist, and sometimes they are very tenacious and stubborn, and they have their way with me. It is then that I think, "If I don't write this down, it will keep on pushing and worrying me; the best thing to do is to write it down." Once it's down, I take the advice of Horace, and I lay it aside for a week or ten days. And then, of course, I find that I have made many glaring mistakes, so I go over them. After three or four tries, I find that I can't do it any better and that any more variations may damage it. It is then that I publish it. (Mualem 2012, 170-71)

As an aside, if you don't already, Umberto Eco based the blind librarian in his *Name of the Rose* on Borges.

Jacques Maritain (1882-1973)

Jacques Maritain was a convert to Catholicism after having been raised a Protestant, and after a period of agnosticism discovered the writings of St. Thomas Aquinas. Maritain's extensive career and writings were inspirational to many humanists and Catholics in the mid-twentieth century, and his thoughts on metaphysics, epistemology, the philosophy of nature and natural theology, moral and political philosophy, and aesthetics and the philosophy of art influenced the direction of Catholic thought and apology up to and including the Vatican II Council in the 1960s. His ardent defense of human rights during World War II and beyond were well ahead of his time.

There are many connections between Tolkien's sub-creation theory and Maritain's invocation of secondary creation expounded in his book *Creative Intuition in Art and Poetry* (1953). Both (Milbank 2009) and (Caldecott 2003) discuss the many philosophical and aesthetic links between Tolkien and Maritain. Although there is scant evidence of whether Tolkien read Maritain, Jonathan McIntosh (McIntosh 2009) specifically queried Christopher Tolkien on his father's knowledge of Maritain's work, to which he received a positive reply in a personal email of 12/6/2008 from the Tolkien Estate.[4] McIntosh spends a considerable part of his dissertation exploring similarities between Tolkien and Maritain in their thoughts on the responsibility of art to communicate truth to the intellect, art's freedom from and yet imitation of nature, and the simultaneous practicality yet integrity and dignity of the work of art. I think that there are many opportunities for Tolkien scholars to delve into the possible interconnections of Tolkien's and Maritain's philosophies regarding God, man, and art.

David Jones (1895-1974)

Finally, I want to discuss David Jones. I have mentioned Jones' close links to Tolkien in my 'Third Spring' authors papers, where I have indicated that there was a "mutual admiration" club between these two. Jones has been called the greatest Roman Catholic poet in English of the 20th century, and the most important native British poet of the 20th century. He spent time with Eric Gill in

---

4   Thanks again to Massimiliano Izzo for directing me to this reference.

the early 1920s, was strongly influenced by Jacques Maritain and his book *Art and Scholasticism* (London: Sheed & Ward, 1946), as well as Thomas Aquinas and Buddhism. Jones argued that people are fundamentally artists, very similar to the sub-creation theory of Tolkien, and that myth is intimately tied to tradition (for instance, the dying god, and the sense of orthodox Christianity's transforming power over myth and fact which Chesterton, Lewis, and Tolkien felt was captured in the only 'true' myth). In his book *Anathemata* (1965), which Auden called "the finest long poem in English in the 20th century," Jones lists Tolkien among the fifty most important living or recently living authors to whom he is indebted. Barton Friedman discusses connections between Jones and Tolkien in his article 'Tolkien and David Jones: the Great War and the War of the Rings' which surprisingly was not consulted or cited by John Garth in his *Tolkien and the Great War* book (Friedman 1982). Friedman spends time discussing the use of war images in both Jones's and Tolkien's writings. Jones' book *Epoch and Artist* (1959) is a compilation of letters, reviews, prefaces and essays from 1937-58. It includes a 'Myth of Arthur' chapter in which references to both Charles Williams and Tolkien are included, as well as a chapter titled 'The Arthurian Legend' which is a review of Williams' *Arthurian Torso* as well as a tribute since it was published after Williams' death. The summation of Jones's philosophy is the close association of art to sacrament and religion. The 1955 essay 'Art and Sacrament' is the most complete examination by Jones of the relation between his aesthetics and his religious philosophy. God is the ultimate artist, and man is the unique functioning artist on earth (since lower animals nor angels can 'make'). Jones, interestingly enough, provides four categories of how man 'makes', and here I think there is a possible influence on Tolkien's story *Smith of Wootan Major* which has gone undocumented thus far. The four examples are: strategy, the celebration of the Eucharist, Hogarth's painting *The Shrimp Girl*, and finally the preparing of "Susan's birthday cake." As one listens to Jones explain how the preparation of Susan's birthday cake is an example of how man 'makes' as a reflection of God, think about Tolkien's description of the birthday cake in *Smith of Wootan Major*:

> You would be witness of something not dissimilar from what you witness in the kitchen where the cook is making a cake patterned with icing-sugar. If the cook should say: 'This is for Susan's birthday – don't you think it is a work of art?' You may or may not agree with the cook's notion of beauty but

you would not be able to deny the 'art'. For leaving aside the art of cooking and the supererogatory art of icing, in so far as the cake is 'made for Susan's birthday' it is 'made over' in some sense. By every possible test it belongs to Ars. It belonged to Ars, or rather it was pre-ordained to Ars, from the first movement of the cook's mind to make something that should be significant of Susan's birth [...] There is making, there is added making, there is explicit sign, there is a showing forth, a re-presenting, a recalling and there is gratuitousness and there is full intention to make this making thus. Moreover this particular making signifies a birth. It recalls a past event and looks back at some anniversaries and looks forward to future anniversaries, it is essentially celebrative and festal: it would be gay. [...] It was pure good fortune that we stumbled on this example in the kitchen, for indeed we might have searched further and fared far worse. For probably there are not many arts that would so simply and conclusively show forth to us the nature and function of Ars [...] (Jones 1959, 163-64)

While nothing exists to indicate that Tolkien read Jones, we know that he was a voracious reader of anything and everything, and Jones was a prominent writer in the Catholic convert tradition. It is difficult not to see a connection here between the idea presented in *Smith of Wootan Major* of a large cake as part of the entrance into Faerie, and Jones's example of Susan's birthday cake, which I am sure had a special place in the back of Tolkien's mind when he was struggling with the story of *Smith of Wootan Major*.

Conclusion

To sum up, I would like to heartily recommend (Wolf 2012), which spends a considerable amount of time on Tolkien, the concept and development and stages of subcreation, and other subcreationists. I would like to end with a number of quotations, first from James Joyce on his novel *Ulysses*:

> I've put in so many enigmas and puzzles that it will keep the professors busy for centuries arguing over what I meant, and that's the only way of insuring one's immortality. (Joyce quoted in Ellann 1982, 521)

From Philip K. Dick's 'How to build a universe that doesn't fall apart' (greatly redacted):

> It is an astonishing power: that of creating whole universes, universes of the mind. I ought to know. It is my job to create universes, as the basis of one novel after another. And I build them in such a way that they do not fall apart two days later. However, I will reveal a secret to you: I like to build universes which

> do fall apart [...] do not assume that order and stability are always good, in a society or in a universe [...] that is part of the script of life. Unless we can psychologically accommodate change, we ourselves begin to die, inwardly. (Wolf 2012, 197)

Finally, Wolf's final words in his book sum it up best:

> Subcreation is not just a desire, but a need and a right; it renews our vision and gives us new perspective and insight into ontological questions that might otherwise escape our notice within the default assumptions we make about reality. Subcreated worlds also direct our attention beyond themselves, moving us beyond the quotidian and the material, increasing our awareness of how we conceptualize, understand, and imagine the Primary World. And the more aware we are of it, the better we can appreciate the Divine design of Creation itself and our place in it. (Wolf 2012, 287)

About the Author

BRADFORD LEE EDEN is Dean of Library Services at Valparaiso University. He has a masters and Ph.D. degrees in musicology, as well as an MS in library science. His recent books include *Middle-earth Minstrel: Essays on Music in Tolkien* (McFarland, 2010); *The Associate University Librarian Handbook: A Resource Guide* (Scarecrow Press, 2012); *Leadership in Academic Libraries: Connecting Theory to Practice* (Scarecrow Press, 2014), *The Hobbit and Tolkien's Mythology: Essays on Revisions and Influences* (McFarland, 2014), and the ten-volume series *Creating the 21st-Century Academic Library* (Rowman & Littlefield, 2015-17). He served as president of the Library Publishing Coalition (LPC) in 2015-16. He is also editor of the *Journal of Tolkien Research*, an online peer-reviewed journal available at http://scholar.valpo.edu/journaloftolkienresearch

Bibliography

BURGESS, Anthony. *Joysprick: An Introduction to the Language of James Joyce.* New York: Harcourt Brace Jovanovich, 1973.

CALDECOTT, Stratford. *Secret Fire: The Spiritual Vision of J.R.R. Tolkien.* London: Darton Longman & Todd, 2003.

EDEN, Bradford Lee. 'The 'Third Spring' authors: a neglected thread of Tolkien scholarship.' Popular Culture Association/American Culture Association conference, San Diego, CA, April 11-15, 2017a. Unpublished paper presentation.

'The 'Third Spring' authors: new discoveries and connections.' 52nd International Congress on Medieval Studies, Kalamazoo, Michigan, May 11-14, 2017b. Unpublished paper presentation.

'Third Spring authors: 20th-century Catholic converts and their influence on Tolkien.' Roundtable paper, 2017 International Medieval Congress, Leeds, UK, July 3-6, 2017c. Unpublished paper presentation.

'Third Spring authors: British Catholic converts and American contacts.' Midwest Conference on British Studies, St. Louis, MO, September 28-30, 2017d. Unpublished paper presentation.

ELLMANN, Richard. *James Joyce*. 2nd ed. Oxford: Oxford University Press, 1982.

FLIEGER, Verlyn. 'Do the Atlantis story and abandon Eriol-Saga." *Tolkien Studies* 1 (2004): 43-68.

FRIEDMAN, Barton. 'Tolkien and David Jones: the Great War and the War of the Rings.' *CLIO* 11.2 (1982): 115-136.

HIGGINS, Andrew S. *The Genesis of J.R.R. Tolkien's Mythology*. Ph.D. dissertation, Cardiff Metropolitan University, 2015.

HILEY, Margaret. "Bizarre or dream like': J.R.R. Tolkien on Finnegans Wake.' *Joycean Legacies*. Ed. Martha C. Carpentier. New York: Palgrave Macmillan, 2015. 112-126.

JONES, David. *The Anathemata: Fragments of an Attempted Writing*. New York: Viking Press, 1965.

Epoch and Artist: Selected Writings by David Jones. Ed. Harman. Grisewood, New York: Chilmark Press, 1959.

LARSEN, Kristine. "It passes our skill in these days': Primary World influences on the evolution of Durin's Day.' *The Hobbit and Tolkien's Mythology: Essays on Revisions and Influences*. Ed. Bradford Lee Eden. Jefferson, NC: McFarland, 2014. 40-58.

MARITAIN, Jacques. *Art and Scholasticism, and the Frontiers of Poetry*. London: Sheed & Ward, 1930.

Creative Intuition and Poetry. New York: Pantheon Books, 1953.

MCINTOSH, Jonathan S. *The Flame Imperishable: Tolkien, St. Thomas, and the Metaphysics of Faërie*. Ph.D. dissertation, University of Dallas, 2009.

The Flame Imperishable: Tolkien, St. Thomas, and the Metaphysics of Faërie. Kettering, OH: Angelico Press, 2017.

MILBANK, Alison. *Chesterton and Tolkien as Theologians: The Fantasy of the Real*. London: T&T Clark, 2009.

MUALEM, Shlomy. *Borges and Plato: A Game with Shifting Mirrors*. Madrid: beroamericana, 2012.

PHELPSTEAD, Carl. 'Myth-making and sub-creation.' *A Companion to J.R.R. Tolkien*. Ed. Stuart Lee. Maldon, MA: Wiley Blackwell, 2014. 79-91.

RYAN, John S. 'Dynamic metahistory and the model of Christopher Dawson.' *Tolkien's View: Windows into his World*. Zurich and Jena: Walking Tree Publishers, 2009a. 141-151.

— 'Folktale, fairy tale, and the creation of a story.' *Tolkien's View: Windows into his World*. Zurich and Jena: Walking Tree Publishers, 2009b. 153-177.

TOLKIEN, J.R.R. *Tolkien on Fairy-stories*. Expanded edition with commentary and notes, edited by Verlyn Flieger & Douglas A. Anderson. London: HarperCollins, 2008.

— *A Secret Vice: Tolkien on Invented Languages*. Ed. Dimitra Fimi and Andrew Higgins. London: HarperCollins, 2016.

TYMOCZKO, Maria. 'Sound and sense: James Joyce's aural esthetics.' *Heroic Poets and Poetic Heroes in Celtic Tradition: A Festschrift for Patrick K. Ford*. Ed. Joseph Falaky Nagy, Leslie Jones, and Patrick K. Ford. Dublin: Four Courts Press, 2005. 359-376.

WEAVER, Jack W. *Joyce's Music and Noise: Theme and Variation in his Writings*. Gainesville: University Press of Florida, 1998.

WOLF, Mark J.P. *Building Imaginary Worlds: The Theory and History of Subcreation*. New York: Routledge, 2012.

Kristine Larsen

A Mythology for Poland: Andrzej Sapkowski's *Witcher* Fantasy Series as a Tolkienian Subcreation

Abstract

Andrzej Sapkowski's (1948 -) Witcher fantasy series featuring the adventures of the chemically-modified monster killer for hire (or "Witcher") Geralt, his sorceress lover Yennifer, and Ciri, the eugenically-engineered child of destiny, is an award-winning best seller in his native Poland and has a devoted audience across the globe. Featuring a bestiary of fantastical creatures from classical mythology, and, more importantly, mythological creatures from Polish and Slavic mythology, Sapkowski also interweaves Arthurian legend with Polish folktales, magic with genetic engineering, and environmentalism with court intrigue. The result is a detailed, self-contained Secondary World (to use Tolkien's terminology) crafted especially for the author's Polish audience. But it will be argued that Sapkowski's work nearly succeeds as a subcreated mythology for modern Poland (similar to Tolkien's original desire for his legendarium to serve as a mythology for England).

1 Introduction: A Mythology for England

In a 1951 letter to Milton Waldman, J.R.R. Tolkien explains "I was from early days grieved by the poverty of my own beloved country: it had no stories of its own (bound up with its tongue and soil), not of the quality that I sought, and found (as an ingredient) in legends of other lands. There was Greek, and Celtic, and Romance, Germanic, Scandinavian, and Finnish (which greatly affected me): but nothing English, save impoverished chap-book stuff" (*Letters* 144). In his mind, even the great epic Beowulf is not truly an English mythology, as it is not set on English soil. But as Hostetter and Smith argue, Beowulf does "demonstrate that the Anglo-Saxons had a mythology from which such an epic could be formed" (281). In response to this lacuna, Tolkien had once thought to "make a body of more or less connected legend, ranging from the large and cosmogonic, to the level of romantic fairy-story [...] which I could dedicate simply to: to England; to my country" (*Letters* 144). What would such a "mythology *for England*" (Carpenter, *Tolkien* 100) entail? Tolkien believes it should be

> somewhat cool and clear, be redolent of our 'air' (the clime and soil of the North West, meaning Britain and the hither parts of Europe [...] and, while possessing (if I could achieve it) the fair elusive beauty that some call Celtic (though it is rarely found in genuine Celtic things), it should be 'high', purged of the gross, and fit for the more adult mind of a land long now steeped in poetry. (*Letters* 144-45)

While Tolkien had to abandon what he later admitted was an arrogant task (*Letters* 230), as Tom Shippey has noted, there are "two very clear national self-images in 'the Shire' and 'the Mark,' both in their different ways identifiably English terms" (92). In addition, Honegger points out that both hobbits and the Shire (although pictured by Tolkien as occupying the distant past of our own Primary World) represent "the epitome of (modern) Englishness on several levels. First, they speak the clearly recognizable English dialect of the Oxford Warwickshire area. Secondly, their cultural and technological know-how is similar to that of an idealized rural Victorian England" (24).

Although not as well known to American audiences, Andrzej Sapkowski's *Witcher* (Polish *Wiedzmin*) fantasy series is comprised of four collections of short stories and a sequence of five novels originally published in his native Polish from 1992-2013. The works were best sellers in Poland and Sapkowski has a devoted audience across the globe. Although the Polish television series adaptation and resulting film (constructed by condensing the series) were largely panned by fans and critics, the video games based on the series are wildly popular and continue to introduce new fans to the literary source material. In fact, a series based on Sapkowski's franchise is currently under development by Netflix (Kettley). Sapkowski explains of his adventures of the genetically-modified monster killer (or "Witcher") Geralt, his sorceress lover Yennifer, and Ciri, the eugenically-engineered child of destiny, "when I began to write in Poland there was no one, I was the pioneer. That is not immodesty, it is the truth: I had to create Polish fantasy" (Nolen, 'Part I'). Sapkowski further believes that his Polish audience is "extremely discerning, [and] was not going to accept hybrids of the middle road between Fantasy and other genres, or a simple copy of Tolkien. S/he is searching for something new, special. And that eagerness for creating something new, special, that is what drove me to write"

(Nolen, 'Part I'). This essay will explore Sapkowski as an effective subcreator, to use Tolkien's terminology, and argue that his "Polish fantasy" was embraced by his culture due to its updating and revisioning of the already extant Polish mythology. In the process, Sapkowski has not only created a uniquely modern fantasy for a modern Poland, but nearly reached Tolkien's personal goal of creating a new mythology for his homeland.

2 The *Witcher* Series: Sapkowski's Subcreation.

Andrzej Sapkowski (1948 -) initially introduced his mythical world of mutants and monsters in a short story published in *Fantastyka*, a Polish science fiction and fantasy magazine. The eponymous first Witcher story, "Wiedzmin," was penned by the economics-trained travelling furs salesman and polyglot as a one-off written in 1986 for the magazine's contest (Purchese). After it won third place, additional short stories continued to appear in the magazine until they were published as book-length collections in 1992 (*Sword of Destiny* [*Miecz przeznaczenia*]; English translation 2015) and 1993 (*The Last Wish* [*Ostatnie Życzenie*]; English translation 2007). A series of five subsequent novels followed: *Blood of Elves* (*Krew Elfów* 1994; English translation 2008), *The Time of Contempt* (*Czas Pogardy* 1995; English translation 2013), *Baptism of Fire* (*Chrzest Ognia* 1996; English translation 2014), *The Tower of the Swallow* (*Wieża Jaskółki* 1997; English translation 2016), and *The Lady of the Lake* (*Pani Jeziora* 1999; English translation 2017).[1] *Season of Storms* (*Sezon Burz*), a set of short stories set in the same time period as *The Last Wish*, appeared in Polish in 2013 (English translation 2018). Drenda (180) argues that the delay in publishing *Witcher* novels was due to the fact that Polish fantasy only became seen as a viable genre in the 1990s after the fall of Communism in Poland due to "the introduction of a free market economy and freedom from censorship." In this way Sapkowski's work was revolutionary, and Drenda terms Geralt not only "one of the first heroes of the new generation" but a "beacon heralding a new age in the history of Polish literature – the age of fantasy (heroes)" (180).

---

[1] Another collection of short stories, *Something Ends, Something Begins* (*Coś Się Kończy, Coś Się Zaczyna*) appeared in Polish in 2000, but only two of the stories relate to Geralt; it currently only exists in English in fan translations.

In the mythology of the series, Witchers are taken from their families as children and mutated using a variety of herbs, chemicals, and magic. Those who survive the painful and lengthy process are trained in martial arts, magic, and monster physiology and taxonomy. In return they are rewarded with superhuman strength, agility, and senses, an extremely long lifespan, and resistance to disease. However, they are sterile and are said to be without emotion (although Geralt's deep feelings for those he cares for are central to the plot). Witchers are social outcasts, equally looked down upon by humans, elves, dwarfs, and other humanoid creatures who reluctantly rely on the mutants to do their dirty work for them. Geralt is cursed as a "Mutant, Monster, Freak. Damned by the gods, a creature contrary to nature," (Sapkowski, *Blood of Elves* 64), as well as called a "freak of nature. You hell spawn" (Sapkowski, *Baptism of Fire* 181). Geralt is deemed a monster whose job is to act as the judge, jury and executioner for other monsters, although his personal creed prevents him from killing creatures that demonstrate intelligence or do not pose a direct threat to humans. On the other hand, Geralt is most often faced with monstrosities in human form, whom he also dispatches when necessary. Despite his grisly reputation, Geralt is a hero, albeit an admittedly flawed one, and as the series unfolds, the reader comes to appreciate that Geralt is far less monstrous than many members of the various species (both humanoid and not) that he relies upon for his livelihood.

The series has received three Zajdel Awards for Excellence in Polish Science Fiction/Fantasy, for the short stories 'The Lesser Evil' (1990) and 'Sword of Destiny' (1992), and for the novel *Blood of Elves* (1994), which also received the (more international) 2009 David Gemmell Legend Prize. However, commercial success is not necessarily synonymous with masterful subcreation in the Tolkienian sense. For as Tolkien explains in his famous essay "On Fairy-stories," a true Secondary World is one "which your mind can enter. Inside it, what he [the author] relates is 'true': it accords with the laws of that world. You therefore believe it, while you are, as it were, inside" (*TOFS* 52). Therefore, as Mark Wolf expands, consistency, or "the degree to which world details are plausible, feasible, and without contradiction," is key (43). This necessitates "a careful integration of details and attention to the way everything is connected together" (Wolf 43). Sapkowski not only concurs, but boasts "My vision of Fantasy is almost real.

You have to believe that which occurs in the stories, because they are not a fairy tale. [...] I have turned to construct the fantasy story: it is almost real, you have to feel it, to believe all. It is not the typical fair[y] tale [...]" (Nolen, 'Part I').

But it is not merely consistency that defines a successful subcreation, but also the completeness of the Secondary World. Wolf (35-36) describes this as including not only the creation of new names for people, places, and things (which leads to the creation of language), but unique cultures and natural environments (in terms of geography/geology, astronomy and biology). The very laws of nature (including any magical properties) can differ from our Primary World as well. Aiding the reader in understanding the sometimes complex relationships between all these factors can be maps, timelines, and genealogies, sometimes included (as in the case of Tolkien) in appendices or front/back matter. A truly complete Secondary World also extends beyond the margins of what is explicitly shown within the tale, both in time and space. This necessitates a past history, a background that is often incomplete, mysterious, or steeped in legend and myth. Tolkien's late explanation for the "astronomically absurd" cosmology of the *Silmarillion* texts as being the legends told by the Númenóreans is an excellent example (*MR* 370).

To what extent does Sapkowski's fictional world satisfy these requirements? The world of Geralt certainly does contain references to not only a mythic past, but entire parallel universes that lie "off the map," as it were. The first full-length novel in the series, *Blood of Elves*, begins with a quotation from a famous (within the fictional world) prophecy, the Aen Ithhlinnespeath: "The world will die amidst frost and be reborn with the new Sun. It will be reborn of the Elder Blood of Hen Ichaer, of the seed that has been sown. A seed which will not sprout but will burst into flame" (1). The first part of the myth is a nod to the Norse legend of Ragnarok, while the second refers to Ciri, including her genetically engineered pedigree and her uncontrolled magical powers. The prophecy suggests that the chosen child will be able to open a doorway in space-time to a parallel world (universe) before their own world is completely frozen. The existence of multiple universes is central to the history of the unnamed world on which Geralt lives, not only because of the prophecy and Ciri's ability in the later novels to travel (albeit uncontrollably) from universe to universe, but because the initial entrance of mankind, magic, and monsters into Geralt's world from another universe is, according to Elvish lore, due to a shadowy catastrophic event in the mythical past termed the Conjunction of the Spheres.

As in the case of Aragorn, Thorin, Fëanor, and Eärendil in Middle-earth, bloodlines undoubtedly drive much of the plotlines in Sapkowski's series. Nowhere is this more important than in Ciri's bloodline (which is recounted in expositional detail in the novel *Baptism of Fire* [264-71]). Here sorceress Sheala de Tancarville offers that "Even elven legends and prophecies, which I in no way disregard, consider the Elder Blood to be utterly atrophied. Extinct," to which fellow sorceress and Queen of the Elves, Enid an Gleanna/Francesca Findabair, answers that the tale of the love affair between the elven sorceress Lara Dorren aep Shiadhal and the human sorcerer Creggennan of Lod is true but "so overgrown with fairy-tale ornamentation it is difficult to recognize. There is also enormous variance between the legend's human and elven versions; chauvinism and racial hatred can be heard in both of them, though" (264). This is confirmed in excerpts from two versions of the legendary death of Lara (one human and one elven) that open this chapter of the novel (235).

In order to fully flesh out a subcreated world, astronomy and geography/geology are also required. As in the case of Tolkien's Elves, Sapkowski's Ciri knows a number of her world's constellations, such as "the Seven Goats, the Jug, the Sickle, the Dragon, and the Winter Maiden" (Sapkowski, *The Time of Contempt* 266) and she utilizes the stars to navigate through unfamiliar territory. She also uses the night sky to determine whether or not she has teleported into another part of her own world, or to a different planet altogether.[2] In her travels Ciri encounters deserts, lakes, frozen wastelands, and other geographical extremes, and while Sapkowski has not issued an official map for his unnamed Continent, he did consult with the videogame makers on their maps (work largely based, in turn, on fan-drawn maps) (Whitbrook). This lack of official cartography sets Sapkowski's work apart from Tolkien's, as does the fact that the former author never created an entire language. So-called Old Speech, or Hen Llinge, is included in the series as phrases or individual words spoken by Elves and then translated into Common Speech. The language appears to draw heavily from

---

2 For more detailed analysis, see Larsen (2014).

Welsh and Gaelic, with additional influences from English, French, and Latin (Rogers 213-14). Given Tolkien's vocation as a philologist versus Sapkowski's training in economics, this disparity is not surprising.

But language is only one aspect of culture. Religion (both of the characters and the author) may also play an important role in the Secondary World. While some cultures have deities and religious practices within the world of the Witcher series, similar to the case of Tolkien, religious beliefs do not play a central role in the story, nor is there identifiable Christianity. This is interesting, given that Sapkowski, like Tolkien, is a devout Catholic (Sims). However, as in the case of Tolkien's works, literary critics find Catholic themes and strands within Sapkowski's series. For example, Tighe (191) argues that in Sapkowski's depiction of "the solitary man fighting his way through a world populated by tricky demons and blood sucking temptresses" we see echoes of "Catholic parables about the developing battle between good and evil or, equally, parables about the demons and denizens of capitalism, which have of late much troubled the realm."

Sapkowski's subcreation is also fleshed out by various quotations found at the start of many chapters. Some are fictional writings by characters who appear in the series itself (such as Dandelion's *Half a Century of Poetry* and Tissaia de Vries' *The Poisoned Source*) while others are attributed to characters who are not mentioned elsewhere. Among these are Nicodemus de Boot's *Meditations on Life, Happiness and Prosperity*, which grants readers insight into the morals and prejudices of Sapkowski's Secondary World, Flourens Dellanoy's *Fairy Tales and Stories*, which recounts fairy tale versions of Geralt's adventures, and the notoriously unreliable *Encyclopedia Maxima Mundi* of Effenberg and Talbot, allegedly written several centuries after the events in the novels. Through the latter two, Sapkowski pokes fun at sanitized versions of legends told to children (versions that often alter the darkness of the original tale), and self-assured historians who believe that they have an accurate picture of past events and personalities (not unlike the epilogue to Margaret Atwood's 1986 novel *The Handmaid's Tale*). Perhaps the most interesting of the self-referential works is an excerpt from the fictional newspaper *The Inverness Weekly* dated March 18, 1906. This describes a reported dreamlike sighting of a girl on horseback accompanied by a white unicorn (Ciri and Ihuarraquax) seen by known single malt scotch drinker "Mr. Malcolm Guthrie of Braemore" while fishing on Loch Glascarnoch. The editor of the paper opines that Guthrie's drinking explains "the seeing of white unicorns, white mice and monsters from lochs," an obvious reference to sightings of the Loch Ness Monster (Sapkowski, *The Lady of the Lake* 241).

There is also the occasional reference to Primary World writings, including the Bible and Johann Goethe's poem 'Erlkönig,' both references that would have been appreciated by his Polish readers. This leads us to consider the intended audience of Sapkowski's works. For although his highly coherent and complete subcreated universe has captured the attention and affection of millions of readers and gamers worldwide, his original intentions were far more local – he set out to define Polish fantasy. If this is true, then we should examine what specific aspects of the Witcher universe make it a uniquely Polish fantasy, and, even more importantly, a fantasy *for* Poland.

3 A Fantasy for Poland

Dorota Guttfeld (69-71) details the widespread introduction of Western science fiction into Poland in the late 1950s and early 1960s, including Polish translations of *The Hobbit* and *The Lord of the Rings*. Among the early readers of Tolkien in Poland was Andrzej Sapkowski, who describes also being influenced by the works of Ursula Le Guin, Roger Zelazny, Michael Moorcock, and Marion Zimmer Bradley (Cutali). Kowalik (6) explains Tolkien's popularity among Polish readers as due to both the contrast between the fantastical Middle-earth and "the drab reality of everyday life" in Communist Poland as well as Tolkien's distinctively Catholic themes. In particular, themes of redemption and self-sacrifice (especially Frodo's) are argued to resonate particularly well with Polish Roman Catholics. Kowalik also points out that "innocent suffering and self-offering has long been part of their cultural tradition, which renders them particularly sensitive to the Romantic underpinnings of Frodo's incurable wound and his simultaneous attraction to and struggle with Sauron" (6). If this is true, then Sapkowski turns this concept on its head in the end of his Witcher series, as Ciri, the child who is foretold to save the world through her magical bloodline, refuses to offer herself as a sacrifice and fulfill the prophecy that drives much of the major subplot of the series.

By the 1980s, the popularity of Tolkien and other Anglophone science fiction/fantasy (SFF) authors drove fans to create their own translations of classic works that had not yet been translated into Polish, largely through fan clubs called "klubówki" (Guttfeld 81).[3] After the fall of Communism in 1989, there was an explosion of works officially published in Polish, but the majority of them were translations from English. In this new era of publishing, "Polishness" became seen as a "hindrance" (Guttfeld 87). To circumvent these stereotypes, some Polish authors wrote under English pen names, or published works naming themselves merely the translators of works written by non-existent Anglophone writers (Guttfeld 88-89). But the other consequence of this prejudice was that there were very few Polish works of SFF translated into English. This is the culture that spawned (and was openly challenged by) Sapkowski's Secondary World, not only in its open integration of both Slavic and Western traditions and cultural references, but his open flaunting of the accepted rules for publishing success in Poland.

Aleksandra Mucha points out that in the case of Secondary Worlds, "some elements are taken from the author's culture or the ones known to him/her. These can be creatures from various mythologies, quotations from famous works, or allusions to items existing in the real world." (61). As previously explained, quotations from both Sapkowski's Primary and Secondary Worlds appear in the Witcher novels, including parodic works and humorous self-references. In his undergraduate thesis on humor in the amateur translations of the Witcher series, Maciej Saj (27) notes that much of Sapkowski's humor is grounded in Polish culture; therefore it cannot be readily translated into other languages divorced from the cultural context.[4] Sapkowski's dependence on Polish humor does fit with his intention to make a Polish fantasy.

Another important area in which Sapkowski embraces his Polish heritage is in naming characters. Among the "seven deadly sins of Polish science fiction"

---

[3] The tradition continues, although now often in reverse; during the delayed publication of Sapkowski's series into English, fan translations available on the Internet filled the need.
[4] A specific example noted by the author of this essay will be described later in this section.

noted by Marek Oramus is the trend in the 1970s and 1980s to give characters (especially major ones) "names of undetermined origin" rather than recognizably Polish names (Guttfeld 74). Guttfeld (75) suggests that this trend was due in part to efforts to evade censors by setting the stories outside of Poland, but also reflected the technological dominance of the English speaking world. Piotr Gociek argues that it was therefore a natural step to move from culturally neutral invented names that sound futuristic "such as Nep, Urg, or Fot," to stereotypically English "Smiths, Joneses and Martins" (Guttfeld 75). Guttfeld (76) points out that Sapkowski played a seminal role in reversing this trend, as the Witcher series features both minor characters with traditional Polish names (such as Biruta, Piotr, Karolina, and Jan), as well as major characters with names that would have been familiar to Polish readers, such as Leo Bonhart, Stefan Skellan, and Maria/Milva.

But Sapkowski's characters are not only Polish in name, but in spirit as well. As he explains in a 2008 interview, when he "began 13 years ago, all the world in Poland was absolutely sick of superhero stories and they wanted a story of a man which was not omnipotent" (Nolen, 'Part II'). Drenda argues that the mysterious loner Geralt is the "pioneer-hero of Polish fantasy" and therefore cannot be compared to other Polish fantasy heroes, but instead with heroes in other types of Polish literature and folklore. In particular, Drenda singles out a similar archetype made popular by the Polish Romantic poet Adam Mickiewicz (181). One important characteristic of the typical Polish heroic figure used by Mickiewicz is scarring, both physical and mental (Drenda 183). Not only is Geralt often scarred in his myriad battles, but Ciri receives a permanent, disfiguring facial scar while escaping from bounty hunter Leo Bonhart and his nefarious employer Stefan Skellan. The sorceress Trish Marigold is mentally scarred (and perhaps physically so) from nearly dying at the Battle of Sodden Hill, and it is suggested that Yennifer is a hunchback who uses magic to hide her deformity from the eyes of others. Drenda (184) also points out that the wounded hero is central to the late 19th century works of Henryk Sienkiewicz, termed the father of the Polish epic novel. While Geralt does not exhibit the patriotism to country that Sienkiewicz's heroes demonstrate, Drenda (185) argues that Geralt (who has no country or homeland to be patriotic to) is instead deeply committed to his code and to his duty – to protecting innocents from monsters of all varieties (even those who wear a human face).

But Polish literature is not the sole Polish influence on Sapkowski's work. In an influential 1993 essay Sapkowski ironically argues that Slavic mythology lacks the potential found in Celtic and Germanic mythology to be the basis for successful fantasy (paralleling Tolkien's earlier criticism of English mythology). Guttfeld (91) gives the crux of Sapkowski's argument as that "there is no genuine fantasy in Poland, save few exceptions that prove the rule. Poland has no fantasy, Sapkowski arguments, because, first of all, it has no fantasy archetypes. Slavic mythology is a set of half-forgotten, emotionally empty names, which neither authors nor readers ever feel projecting on their dreams." Perhaps for this reason, Sapkowski also draws upon many other mythological traditions, for example Roman fauns and satyrs, Celtic kelpies, Arabic ghuls, and Portuguese bruxa (Mucha 63). But while Sapkowski openly draws from classic myths, legends, and fairy-tales, it is always with an evolutionary eye that reimagines ancient stories in a fresh (and often satirical) way.

For example, the classic tale of Snow White and the Huntsman is adapted in his short story 'The Lesser Evil' (*The Last Wish*). In Sapkowski's revision, the princess Renfri escapes from an evil sorcerer who has conducted experiments upon her, and survives both being raped by the huntsman sent by her stepmother to kill her (complete with the obligatory command to bring back the girl's heart) and being poisoned by an apple. Renfri takes revenge on her tormenters, first with her gang of seven ill-natured dwarfs, and later a band of human cutthroats. The tale of Beauty and the Beast receives two separate make-overs by Sapkowski. In the short story 'A Grain of Truth' (*The Last Wish*) a young man, Nivellen, is cursed after raping a priestess, a curse that can only be lifted if he wins the love of one of the merchants' daughters who are paid to stay with him for a year at a time. Geralt is forced to kill Nivellen's most recent companion, Vereena, who is revealed to be a bruxa (vampire) who has been using the man-beast for her own devices. In an interesting twist to the trope, Nivellen is cured of his curse when he is splattered with Vereena's blood. In Geralt's words, there is a "grain of truth in every fairy tale," in this case that the cure is brought about by true love, but in this case on the side of the man-beast (Sapkowski, *The Last Wish* 88).

Another retelling of Beauty and the Beast is found in the short story 'A Question of Price' (*The Last Wish*). Unbeknownst to her mother, Queen Calanthe, young Princess Pavetta has been having an affair with Urcheon/Duny, a nobleman cursed to have a hideous beastlike face from sunrise to midnight. Urcheon claims that Pavetta had been promised to him years earlier under the Law of Surprise, when he had saved Calanthe's husband, King Roegner. Urcheon wooed Pavetta in secret because he had been told that a "child-surprise could free me from the curse," although the curse is actually lifted when Pavetta's mother freely offers her daughter to him (Sapkowski, *The Last Wish* 195). Geralt is the one to reveal the fulfillment of the Law of Surprise to all involved when, as his price for controlling Pavetta's sudden magical outburst, he demands the child-surprise that only Pavetta knew she was carrying, the aforementioned Ciri. In describing the Law of Surprise (specifically in the case of a "child marked out by destiny"), several "factual" examples are noted, including "Zivelana, who became the Queen of Metinna with the help of the gnome Rumplstelt, and in return promised him her firstborn" (Sapkowski, *The Last Wish* 179-80). There is also a reference to Cinderella in the same story, when Geralt explains to Queen Calanthe that Prince Hrobarik "tried to hire me to find a beauty who, sick of his vulgar advances, had fled the ball, losing a slipper" (Sapkowski, *The Last Wish* 163).

There are also a number of other classic legends and fairy-tales referenced and reworked by Sapkowski in the series. For example, the titular tale of the first collection of short stories, 'The Last Wish,' plays with the tale of Aladdin and the enchanted lamp. Arthurian legend is featured in the last novel of the series, *The Lady of the Lake*. The work begins begins with Galahad coming upon Ciri as she is bathing in a lake (presumably in our Primary World) and he believes her to be Nimue, the Arthurian Lady of the Lake, offering him a sword. She tells the knight her story, which unfolds as the novel, and ends with her riding with him toward Camelot. The other Lady of the Lake is the novel is actually named Nimue, a sorceress from the future of Ciri's world who is obsessed with the legend of Ciri and Geralt. When Ciri flees between worlds and centuries, she encounters Nimue, who helps guide Ciri to her intended destination. One of Nimue's lovers is the Fisher King, another direct nod to Arthurian legend.

The short stories 'A Little Sacrifice' and 'A Shard of Ice' reference tales by Hans Christian Andersen ('The Little Mermaid' and 'The Snow Queen' respectively), which would have also been familiar to Sapkowski's Polish readers. In 'A Shard of Ice,' Yennefer explains the etymology of the eponymous Elvish town's name as related to an Elvish legend concerning "a Winter Queen who travels the land during snow-storms in a sleigh drawn by white horses. As she rides, she casts hard, sharp, tiny shards of ice around her, and woe betide anyone whose eye or heart is pierced by one of them. That person is lost" (Sapkowski, *Sword of Destiny* 91). 'A Little Sacrifice' is Sapkowski's take on the tale of the Little Mermaid. Unlike Hans Christian Anderson's timid and lovestruck maiden (who falls in love with a prince and decides to take on human form to win his love and thereby obtain a soul), Sh'eenaz is gusty, brash and independent. It is she who is pursued by Duke Agloval, and she counters his demand that she give up her tail for him with her own suggestion that he sacrifice his legs in order to live in her world. In a sinister side plot, Geralt and Dandelion investigate the area near the continental shelf during low tide and discover that there is an entire underwater civilization, which Dandelion refers to as "the legendary Ys [...] the city of the chasm" (Sapkowski, *Sword of Destiny* 221). His exclamation refers to the Breton tradition of Keris/Ker-Is/Ys, a city that is submerged beneath the waves as punishment for the wicked behavior of its residents, especially the King's daughter, Dahut (Doan 77). Interestingly, in some versions of the tale, Dahut is compared to a mermaid (Doan, 78). In the end, Sh'eenaz makes a grand entrance, on human legs, with Dandelion pronouncing "She has gained legs for him, but has lost her voice" (*Sword of Destiny* 240). This is a nod to the original tale, in which the mermaid gives up not only her tail and her family, but her voice as well, being unable to talk or sing after her tongue is cut out as payment to the sea witch.[5]

Most importantly, three of Sapkowski's short stories – 'The Witcher,' 'The Bounds of Reason,' and 'Eternal Flame' – directly reference the very Slavic folklore that he had disparaged. The first centers on the Balkan strzyga/striga (vampire), the second the tale of Queen Wanda, and the third the Dragon of Kraków and the Bulgarian *zmey* (a shape-shifting dragon). 'The Witcher' is not only broadly based on the Slavic legend of the vampiric strzyga, but more specifically draws

---

5 For a longer analysis, see Larsen (2016).

from Romantic Era Polish poet and folklorist Roman Zmorski (1822-1867) and his work in the "black romanticism" style, which is "characterized by romantic frenzy, madness, fatalism, and despair" (Michułka 95). The titular character of his tale *Strzyga* is a princess born from the incestuous relationship between King Goździk and his sister. Despite his monstrous daughter's transformation into a vampire every full moon, Goździk will not kill her, and instead offers half his kingdom and his daughter's hand in marriage to anyone who can reverse the curse. A "poor orphan named Martin" succeeds, and is well rewarded (Michułka 95). In Sapkowski's version King Folest of Temeria's daughter with his sister Princess Adda is cursed and becomes one of these horrific creatures. Geralt the professional monster killer arrives at court instead of a would-be suitor, and accepts the job simply for the financial reward. But Sapkowski's ending is more melancholy, as the princess (whose transformation, Geralt reveals, was not related to the parents' incest) "changes into a mentally ill teen girl who acts like a child, not a pretty woman" (Michułka 95).

In 'The Bounds of Reason' Geralt meets a mysterious stranger named Borch who prevents the local townspeople from robbing Geralt's personal effects while he is fighting a basilisk (also a creature known in Polish legend). A local cobbler named Sheepbagger had tricked a nuisance dragon into eating a dead sheep that had been stuffed with poisons, "brimstone and cobbler's tar" (Sapkowski, *Sword of Destiny* 17). The poisoned dragon had weakly flown back to its lair, pursued by a circus of would-be dragonslayers. Geralt is surprised to see his sometime lover, Yennifer, among the assembled herd. The throng's nefarious intentions are thwarted by a magnificent golden dragon (Borch's true form), who is protecting hatchling of the poisoned dragon. Yennifer urges Geralt to kill Borch, as a favor to her, as she needs the golden dragon's valuable corpse to pay for an operation to reverse her infertility, something Geralt's personal code of conduct will not allow him to do.

There are multiple versions of the source material for Sapkowski's short story, the tale of the dragon of Wawel Hill. In each version of this creation myth of the city of Kraków, a dragon terrorizes the local village, carrying off livestock and children. A wise man (sometimes the king or the king's son) named Krak/Krakus devises a ruse to slay the dragon through deception, by smearing a sheep (in some versions both inside and out) with a sulfurous paste. The dragon devours the sheep and in order to quench the resulting indigestion drinks uncontrollably from the local river until he explodes (Uminski 37-42; Waszkelewicz-Clowes 135-36). In another version, it is a shoemaker or his apprentice who hatches the plot, using his skills to construct a fake sulfur-filled sheep (Seidler 10). Michułka (95) explores Sapkowski's "playful" use of the story, from first suggesting that the dragon is "just a figment of their imagination" to the final reversal of roles; in Sapkowski's version, it is the dragon who is the wise heroic figure while the cobbler is evil and gluttonous (in terms of his greed). Sapkowski explains his reworking of the tale as a necessary one to make the story "real," because cobblers "don't kill monsters. Soldiers and knights? They are idiots generally. And priests want only the money [...]. So who's killing monsters? *Professionals.* You don't call poor cobblers' apprentices: you call for professionals. So then I invented the professional" (Purchese).

Finally, the shape-shifting ability of the golden dragon in the short story is a nod to the Bulgarian zmey, who is "part snake, part bird, and part human. Usually portrayed as a benign creature, it guarded the fertility of the land and had the ability to change into human form. As a human the zmey could walk among people unrecognized, except by the pure of heart" (Sherman 522). We see here that Sapkowski utilizes the Slavic folklore in creative ways, not only by referencing issues of fertility (specifically the lack thereof), but highlighting the dragon's ability to fool everyone in his human form, thus demonstrating the largely depraved nature of humanity in the Witcher universe.

A third Slavic folktale referenced (albeit in passing) in Sapkowski's short stories is the patriotic tale about Princess Wanda, the daughter of the aforementioned King Krakus. According to a tale attributed to Bishop Vincent Kadlubek in 1206 (Waszkelewicz-Clowes 142), Wanda kills herself rather than marry the German Prince Rytgier, because he demands her nation as a dowry. Specifically, in the folktale Wanda drowns herself in the River Vistula rather than she (and her people) becoming German (Uminski 43-47; Waszkelewicz-Clowes 139-42). In Sapkowski's tale 'Eternal Flame,' the bard Dandelion is supposed to have written a song "About Princess Vanda, who drowned in the River Duppie, because no one wanted her. And about the kingfisher that fell into a privy

[…]" (*Sword of Destiny* 162). It should be noted that the word *dupa* is Polish for "arse," so the river's name and the kingfisher's fate here form a clever pun only discernable by Polish speakers.

A final example of Sapkowski's use of Slavic myth (although in a metaphorical as well as literal sense) is noted by Aleksandra Mucha in the context of translation concerns. A *rusałka* or dead girl's soul is depicted in Byelorussia and Ukraine as "a beautiful and usually naked girl wearing only a flower wreath and dancing under the moon" (66). They lure human victims and tickle them to death. Sapkowski uses the term in several instances in *The Last Wish* and *Blood of Elves*, and Mucha notes that the translator leaves the term in Polish when included in lists of harmful creatures, but changes it to *water nymph* when used to describe a woman's slender body, apparently in an effort to make the reference clearer to English-speaking audiences (Mucha 66).

But while Sapkowski's creative reworking of Slavic mythology and folklore undoubtedly speaks to his successful creation of a uniquely Polish fantasy, it is perhaps in his ecological themes that he most clearly resonates with the concerns of modern Polish society. Having environmental themes within a work or series certainly does not make a subcreation inherently Polish. For example, numerous authors have described at length the important environmental themes within Tolkien's legendarium (Campbell; Curry; Dickerson and Evans; Jeffers; Light). In the case of Sapkowski, however, he specifically draws upon the Polish experience with environmentalism in the second half of the 20th century.

4 Sapkowski and Polish Environmental Concerns

Historically, there have been four main sources of pollution in modern Poland – industry, mining operations (especially coal), chemical runoff from farms, and a lack of modern sewage treatment (Cole 14). The response of the Communist government to these issues was not only slow, but in many ways exacerbated the problem. For example in the 1960s and 1970s

> the Polish government attempted to reduce the surface run-off [of agricultural chemicals] by burying pesticide wastes in concrete containers at special burial sites called *mogilniki*. More than 100,000 metric tons of pesticides, including more than 50,000 metric tons of highly toxic organochlorides,

were buried in *mogilniki* around the country, with little to no regard for long-term environmental threats, including soil and groundwater contamination. (Cole 16)

The result was that in 1983 the Polish government designated twenty-seven official "ecological danger zones," comprising more than 10% of the country's area and more than a third of its population (Cole 13). The air pollution levels in Kraków were so high by the fall of Communism that residents with respiratory issues could only find relief in underground salt mines, and "whenever the rains fell in Southern Poland, everything literally turned to black – the sky, the streets, even the people" (Cole 21).

But water pollution has been the main concern of the population. With no sewage treatment plants until the fall of Communism, Warsaw routinely "dumped 1 million cubic metres of untreated sewage directly into the Wisła" per day (Cole 16), while coal mining in the Silesia region led to the Odra and Vistula rivers being so polluted that billions of dollars were lost due to contaminated farms and the corrosion of industrial machinery (Jasinski 23). By 1989 70% of the available water supply in Poland "posed an immediate threat to human health" with 40% of river water "too polluted for any use," including industry (Cole 19). As a result "60 percent of all food produced in the Kraków region was considered unfit for human consumption because of massive concentrations of metals that contaminated the soil," and horrifically "in the industrial region of Katowice, 40 miles to the west of Kraków, two-thirds of all 10 year olds suffered from mental and physical disabilities as a result of pollution […]" (Cole 2). It is no wonder, then, that polls taken in 1992 and 1993 showed that up to 80% of the Polish population is "seriously or very seriously concerned about the state of the environment" (Jasinski 9).

Thus as a Polish native, Sapkowski has witnessed a serious degradation of his environment over his lifetime. The problem has continued to accelerate, with Poland not only considered the overall most polluted country in Europe, but home to six of the top ten most polluted European cities (Boren). Sapkowski poignantly mourns the fate of his homeland in the voice of an unnamed druid character in *Blood of Elves*: "Instead of living according to Nature we have begun to destroy it. And what have we got for it? The air is poisoned by the stink of smelting furnaces, the rivers and brooks are tainted by slaughter houses and tanneries, forests are being cut down without a thought" (Sapkowski, *Blood of Elves* 21-22). This certainly describes the predicament of modern Poland, albeit couched in medieval examples.

As expected, such largescale pollution of the environment has led to the destruction of Polish ecosystems. Cole reports that "of 714 registered mammal, bird, reptile, amphibian and fish species in Poland, 15 became extinct, 41 were 'dying out' and 174 were threatened" (21). As a result, "only 10 per cent of Poland's 430 native (and non-migrating) vertebrate species were *not* endangered" (Cole 21). We see parallels to this Primary World catastrophe showcased in Sapkowski's subcreation. For example, in *Blood of Elves*, Geralt debates with academic Linus Pitt about which species still exist in the waterway they are sailing over. Pitt bemoans the "Degradation of the environment" in that region, noting that "of more than two thousand species of fish living in this river only fifty years ago, not more than nine hundred remain. Truly sad" (221). When Pitt argues with Geralt as to whether one of Sapkowski's original creatures, the aeschna, is the cause of disappearances and deaths on the river, Pitt opines that the creature no longer exists in that region, having been "wiped out a good half-century ago, due – incidentally – to the activity of individuals such as yourself who are prepared to kill anything that does not instantly look right, without forethought, tests, observation or considering its ecological niche" (223-24).

Linus Pitt also rattles off a list of fish that have become extinct in the Pontar Delta, what appears to be a mixture of names of actual fish (some native to Poland, other not) and creatures from Sapkowski's imagination (*Blood of Elves* 222). This passage not only blends the Primary and Secondary worlds, but drives home a particularly disturbing point: to the Polish children of today, the once common sturgeon (last seen in the wild in Poland in 1967) has become an almost mythical beast, having disappeared within the memory of their parents' parents (Oleksyn and Reich 956). Not surprisingly, when asked if the Witcher series can be thought of as "an elegy," Sapkowski replies

> Absolutely. Perhaps my case is not so extreme as that of Tolkien. He suffered a hecatomb from his youth, and he spoke of pollution and poisoned rivers; I now am 60 years old, many of the living things which I have known have disappeared, animals, plants, insects, crustaceans…from what there was when I was 10 years old, already not remaining, it is a disaster. And all that has occurred in the course of one man's lifetime. What can happen here in 50 years?

Perhaps all will disappear and the world will be reduced to ashes. Thinking of it terrifies me. (Nolen, 'Part II')

Sapkowski's concerns here echo those of Polish society at large. Sapkowski's Secondary World is therefore certainly one that the Polish reader can immerse himself or herself into and feel a particularly Polish sense of melancholy, because this environmental tragedy is all too real and hits far too close to home. Sapkowski's Polish fantasy therefore draws deeply from the everyday struggles and sorrows of both its Polish author and its Polish readers.

5 Conclusion: A Mythology for Poland?

Mark Wolf notes that "all cultures create fictional, imagined worlds. We humans find these imagined worlds intrinsically interesting" (4). As demonstrated in this essay, Andrzej Sapkowski's Witcher series is not only a fictional world, but a true Secondary World, in the Tolkienian sense. But more specifically, it is an inherently *Polish* Secondary World, written with the Polish reader in mind. It is certainly a Polish fantasy as well as a fantasy written *for* Poland; but is it a *mythology* for Poland? To answer this, it is necessary to contemplate just exactly what it means to construct a mythology for a country or a culture. The prime example is, of course, the Kalevala. As Verlyn Flieger reflects, in assembling these folktales into one coherent collection, Elias Lönnrot "in effect gave Finland its own myth and mythic identity equal to that of Greece or Scandinavia. He gave it its own prehistory and its own cultural individuality apart from the overlordship of Russia and Sweden, both of which had annexed Finland at one time or another" (279). As Tolkien realized, in contrast with Lönnrot's work, his subcreation was not a true mythology for England. Stenström (313) argues that what Tolkien accomplished was to use his invented languages as an impetus to write stories, a "body of legend" rather than a true mythology, and while, as previously noted, there are certainly aspects of the legendarium that draw from English culture, in Flieger's words "neither *The Silmarillion* nor its offshoot, *The Lord of the Rings*, will ever inspire patriotic emotion in the English breast, or culturally distinguish any English person from the rest of the world" (283). But can the same be said for Sapkowski's series?

Certainly Sapkowski's work draws upon far more than Polish culture, and in this respect can be seen to parallel C.S. Lewis's *Chronicles of Narnia*. Wolf (191) describes how Narnia's mythology – complete with "dwarves, dragons and giants of Northern mythology; Bacchus, Silenus, fauns, and centaurs from Greek and Roman mythology; talking beavers; and Father Christmas" – violates Tolkien's "purist" view on subcreating a consistent mythology. This is reflected in a November 1964 letter in which Tolkien offers that "'Narnia' and all that part of C.S.L.'s work should remain outside the range of my sympathy" (*Letters* 352). Given that Sapkowski's mythology contains many of these same elements and, in addition, characters from Hans Christian Andersen and the Brothers Grimm, Arthurian legend, Elves, Slavic monsters, unicorns, and creatures of his own design, one can only imagine how much Tolkien's nose would have wrinkled in disapproval. But Drenda (186) argues that "Geralt's connection to his Anglo-American predecessors does not strip him from his Polish literary heritage. On the contrary, it is that heritage that makes him simultaneously Old and New, a distinctly Polish fantasy hero." In this way, Sapkowski not only parallels Tolkien's integration of distinctive aspects of 20th century England within a medieval framework, but furthers Tolkien's mission to create a legendarium that uniquely reflects the author's homeland in the late 20th and early 21st centuries.

I therefore argue that while Sapkowski's subcreation does not, in practice, fulfill the role of a mythology for Poland (in the same sense as the Kalevala does), it appears to have, in Flieger's words, the ability to "inspire patriotic emotion." It is also the archetype for a fantasy for Poland, accomplished by embracing Polish culture and its already existing legends and myths, which Sapkowski, ironically, simultaneously disparaged in interviews and literary criticism. The ultimate result is a celebration and perhaps resurrection of the already existent Polish mythology, and its reintroduction to a new generation of modern Poles who may have forgotten their own mythological heritage. This uniquely Polish subcreation has now been shared with the world, but the non-Polish reader will always be at a disadvantage; for while we are all invited to enter Sapkowski's Polish faerie realm, only those who understand the nuances of the history, politics, environment, and culture of Poland can truly experience its deepest secrets and piercing sorrows.

About the Author

Dr. KRISTINE LARSEN is Professor of Astronomy at Central Connecticut State University. She is the author of *Cosmology 101, Stephen Hawking: A Biography*, and *The Women Who Popularized Geology in the 19th Century*, as well as co-editor of *The Mythological Dimensions of Doctor Who* and *The Mythological Dimensions of Neil Gaiman*. Her research interests include the intersections between science, society, and popular culture. She has written and presented on myriad Secondary Worlds, including those of J.R.R. Tolkien, C.S. Lewis, Phillip Pullman, Neil Gaiman, George R.R. Martin, and Andrzej Sapkowski.

Abbreviations

Letters   TOLKIEN, J.R.R. *The Letters of J.R.R. Tolkien*. Ed. Humphrey Carpenter, with the assistance of Christopher Tolkien. Boston: Houghton Mifflin, 2000.

MR   TOLKIEN, J.R.R. *Morgoth's Ring*. The History of Middle-earth, Vol. X. London: HarperCollins, 1994.

TOFS   TOLKIEN, J.R.R. *Tolkien On Fairy-stories*. Expanded edition, with commentary and notes. Ed. Verlyn Flieger & Douglas A. Anderson. London: HarperCollins, 2008.

Bibliography

BOREN, Zachary Davies. 'Poland: Europe's Most Polluted Country in Trouble with the EU but Still Won't Clean Up Coal.' *Greenpeace*. 25 June 2015. 1 Nov. 2017 <http://energydesk.greenpeace.org/2015/06/25/polands-smog-crisis-europes-most-polluted-country-in-trouble-with-the-eu-but-wont-cut-coal-emissions/>.

CAMPBELL, Liam. *The Ecological Augury in the Works of J.R.R. Tolkien*. Zurich and Jena: Walking Tree Publishers, 2011.

CARPENTER, Humphrey. *Tolkien: A Biography*. New York: Ballantine Books, 1977.

COLE, Daniel H. *Instituting Environmental Protection: From Red to Green in Poland*. New York: St. Martin's Press, 1998.

CURRY, Patrick. *Defending Middle-earth: Tolkien, Myth, and Modernity*. Boston: Houghton Mifflin, 2004.

CUTALI, Daniele. 'Interview with Andrzej Sapkowski.' *Sugarpulp*. 15 July 2015. 1 Nov. 2017 <http://sugarpulp.it/en/26893>.

DICKERSON, Matthew and Jonathan EVANS. *Ents, Elves, and Eriador: The Environmental Vision of J.R.R. Tolkien.* Lexington: University Press of Kentucky, 2006.

DOAN, James. 'The Legend of the Sunken City in Welsh and Breton Tradition.' *Folklore* 92 (1981): 77-83.

DRENDA, A.J. 'Geralt of Rivia: The Old and New Hero in Andrzej Sapkowski's *The Witcher* Cycle.' *New Directions in the European Fantastic.* Ed. Sabine Coelsch-Foisner. Heidelberg: Universitätsverlag, 2012. 179-86.

FLIEGER, Verlyn. 'A Mythology for Finland: Tolkien and Lönnrot as Mythmakers.' *Tolkien and the Invention of Myth.* Ed. Jane Chance. Lexington: University Press of Kentucky, 2004. 277-83.

GUTTFELD, Dorota. *English-Polish Translations of Science Fiction and Fantasy.* Torún: Wydawnictwo Naukowe GRADO, 2008.

HONEGGER, Thomas. 'A Mythology for England – the Question of National Identity in Tolkien's Legendarium.' *Hither Shore* 3 (2006): 13-26.

HOSTETTER, Carl F. and Arden R. SMITH. 'A Mythology for England.' *Proceedings of the J.R.R. Tolkien Centenary Conference.* Ed. Patricia Reynolds and Glen H. GoodKnight. Milton Keynes: Tolkien Society, 1995. 281-90.

JASINSKI, Piotr. 'Introduction: Environmental Regulation in the Process of Systematic Transformation.' *Environmental Regulation in Transforming Economies: The Case of Poland.* Ed. Piotr Jasinski and Helen Lawton Smith. Aldershot: Ashgate, 1999. 3-30.

JEFFERS, Susan. *Arda Inhabited: Environmental Relationships in* The Lord of the Rings. Kent: The Kent State University Press, 2014.

KETTLEY, Sebastian. 'When is The Witcher out on Netflix?' *Daily Express.* 25 Oct. 2017. 1 Nov. 2017 <http://www.express.co.uk/showbiz/tv-radio/805954/The-Witcher-Netflix-release-date-latest-news-Geralt-Rivia-Andrzej-Sapkowski-trailer-cast>.

KOWALIK, Barbara. 'Introduction - Tolkien in Poland: a Medievalist Liason.' *"O, What a Tangled Web": Tolkien and Medieval Literature. A View from Poland.* Ed. Barbara Kowalik. Zurich and Jena: Walking Tree Publishers, 2013. 1-8.

LARSEN, Kristine 'Red Comets and Red Stars: Tolkien, Martin, and the Use of Astronomy in Fantasy Series.' *Proceedings of the 2nd Mythgard Institute Mythmoot.* Ed. Kris Swank. Mythgard Institute, 2014. 1 Nov. 2017 <http://www.mythgard.org/wp-content/uploads/sites/15/2014/07/Mythmoot2_Larsen_Astronomy-in-Fantasy1.pdf>.

LARSEN, Kristine. '"Mutant, Monster, Freak": The Mythological World of Andrzej Sapkowski's Witcher series.' *Fastitocalon* 6 (2016): 65-77.

LIGHT, Andrew. 'Tolkien's Green Time: Environmental Themes in *The Lord of the Rings*.' The Lord of the Rings *and Philosophy: One Book to Rule Them All*. Ed. Gregory Bassham and Eric Bronson. Chicago, IL: Open Court, 2003. 150-63.

MUCHA, Aleksandra. 'Translating Polish Fantasy – translational challenges and problems concerning culture-rooted elements.' *Między Oryginałem a Przekładem* 28 (2015): 55-71.

MICHUŁKA, Dorota. 'Looking for Identity: Polish Children's Fantasy Then and Now.' *Filoteknos* 5 (2015): 84-105.

NOLEN, Larry. 'Part I of the June 2008 Fantasymundo interview with Andrzej Sapkowski.' *The OF Blog*. 27 July 2008. 1 Nov. 2017 <http://ofblog.blogspot.com/2008/07/part-i-of-june-2008-fantasymundo.html>.

'Part II of the June 2008 Fantasymundo interview with Andrzej Sapkowski.' *The OF Blog*. 27 July 2008. 1 Nov. 2017 <http://ofblog.blogspot.com/2008/07/part-ii-of-june-2008-fantasymundo.html>.

OLEKSYN, Jacek and Peter B. REICH. 'Pollution, Habitat Destruction, and Biodiversity in Poland.' *Conservation Biology* 8 (1994): 943-60.

PURCHESE, Robert. 'Meeting Andrzej Sapkowski, the writer who created *The Witcher*.' *Eurogamer*. 24 Mar. 2017. 1 Nov. 2017 <http://www.eurogamer.net/articles/2017-03-24-meeting-andrzej-sapkowski-the-writer-who-created-the-witcher>.

ROGERS, Stephen D. *A Dictionary of Made-up Languages*. Avon: Adams Media, 2011.

SAJ, Macief. *The Amateur Translation of Humour on the Basis of* The Witcher *by Andrzej Sapkowski*. BA Thesis. Kraków: Tischner European University, 2013.

SAPKOWSKI, Andrzej. *Baptism of Fire*. Trans. David French. New York: Orbit, 2014.

Blood of Elves. Trans. Danuta Stok. New York: Orbit, 2002.

The Lady of the Lake. Trans. David French. New York: Orbit, 2017.

The Last Wish. Trans. Danuta Stok. New York: Orbit, 2007.

Sword of Destiny. Trans. David French. New York: Orbit, 2015.

SEIDLER, Barbara. *The Wawel Dragon and Queen Wanda*. Warsaw: Sport i Turystyka, 1973.

SHERMAN, Josepha. *Storytelling: An Encyclopedia of Mythology and Folklore*. New York: Routledge, 2015.

SHIPPEY, Tom A. *Roots and Branches*. Zurich and Berne: Walking Tree Publishers, 2007.

Sims, Harley J. 'A Polish Tolkien? The Fantasy World of Andrzej Sapkowski.' *MercatorNet*. 13 Dec. 2016. 1 Nov. 2017 <https://www.mercatornet.com/features/view/a-polish-tolkien-the-fantasy-world-of-andrzej-sapkowski/19137>.

Stenström, Anders. 'A Mythology? For England?' *Proceedings of the J.R.R. Tolkien Centenary Conference*. Ed. Patricia Reynolds and Glen H. GoodKnight. Milton Keynes: Tolkien Society, 1995. 310-14.

Tighe, Carl. 'Poland Translated: the Post-Communist Generation of Writers.' *Studies in East European Thought* 62 (2010): 169-95.

Tolkien, J.R.R. *The Letters of J.R.R. Tolkien*. Ed. Humphrey Carpenter, with the assistance of Christopher Tolkien. Boston: Houghton Mifflin, 2000.

Morgoth's Ring. Ed. Christopher Tolkien. Boston: Houghton Mifflin, 1993.

Tolkien On Fairy-Stories. Ed. Verlyn Flieger and Douglas A. Anderson. London: HarperCollins, 2008.

Uminski, Sigmund H. *Tales of Early Poland*. Detroit: Endurance Press, 1969.

Waszkelewicz-Clowes, Florence (ed.). *Polish Folk Tales*. Rev. ed. Vero Beach: Palmetto Press, 2004.

Whitbrook, James. 'How to Get Into the *Witcher* Novels.' *Io9*. 21 May 2015. 1 Nov. 2017 <https://io9.gizmodo.com/how-to-get-into-the-witcher-novels-1706064080>.

Wolf, Mark J.P. *Building Imaginary Worlds: The Theory and History of Subcreation*. New York: Routledge, 2012.

Andrew Higgins

More than Narrative: The Role of Paratexts in the World-building of Austin Tappan Wright, J.R.R. Tolkien and Ursula K. Le Guin

Abstract

In his work *Paratexts: Thresholds of Interpretation*, Gerard Genette defined paratexts as any thing external to the text itself that influences the way a reader interacts with it. Genette called this 'a transaction'. In his monograph *Building Imaginary Worlds* (2012), Mark J.P. Wolf explored several types of invented paratexts, including maps, timelines, genealogies, invented artifacts and lexicons and grammars of invented languages, which authors utilize in their world-building to both imbue their diegetic world with a greater sense of reality, while also creating a point of interaction and 'transaction' between the author and the reader. This paper will explore these two aspects of paratexts in three related narratives. In the 1930's the American legal author and philosopher Austin Tappan Wright utilized a combination of narrative and paratexts to privately invent a world which, after his tragic death, his wife would publish in the novel *Islandia* (1940). At roughly the same time, J.R.R. Tolkien was using a similar process to continue building his world of Arda, which readers would first experience in his masterworks *The Hobbit* (1937) and *The Lord of the Rings* (1954-55). Then in the 1980's the science fiction and fantasy writer Ursula K. Le Guin would build upon both the tradition of Tappan Wright and Tolkien to invent a world for the Kesh people in her unique novel *Always Coming Home* (1985). This paper will investigate how each of these authors invented and used paratexts as part of the gestalt of their world-building. It will explore how each author used similar paratextual elements, including maps, charts, genealogies and both lexicons and grammars of invented languages, to both construct their diegetic worlds and also encourage Genette's process of interaction and transaction between the author and reader.

Introducion

The *Oxford Dictionary of Literary Terms* defines a *paratext* as a textual item that serves some supplementary function in relation to a principle text that it describes, introduces, justifies or explains (42). Mak has linked the development of the literary paratext with the rise of universities in the 12th century. She suggests that before this time reading, understood as a spiritual exercise, emphasized the slow and steady contemplation of a single text. With this approach, readers were less likely to be in need of reminders of their location in the larger context of the book. With the development of the university these academic environments fostered analytical modes of engagement with text encouraging the development of paratextual fostering of the reading process, helping scholars in their studies and fabricating both visually and verbally a context for reading (43-44). The earliest of these types of paratexts were functional in nature with the addition of elements like chapter headings, indexes and introductory pages to the main body of the text. These soon expanded to more illustrative and imaginative paratextual elements which not only supported the readers study of the main text but also sought to illustrate and add to the experience of reading and exploring the environment the narrative was set in.

One key early genre that started to imaginatively utilize these types of illustrative paratexts were the traveler's tale topos which became popular in the late Middle Ages and early Renaissance. These travelogues merged elements of non-fictional experiences and observations primarily in the East with fictional accounts of travels to distant lands and encounters with strange peoples. Two contrasting early examples of this mix of factual and fictional traveler's tales is Marco Polo's account of his real journey to the East in his *Travels* (c. 1298) and the fictional account of a crusader knight's supposed travels and adventures in the East in *The Book of Sir John Mandeville* (c. 1357) which actually imitated Polo's chronicle and included paratextual illustrations of some of the strange peoples and creatures encountered on these feigned travels (Wolf 72-77). This practice was soon taken up by authors of purely fictional works who used the traveler's tale to introduce their readers to strange new lands and, eventually, fantastic worlds. One of the earliest adapters of this structure was Thomas More's socio-satirical novel *Utopia* (1516); which depicted a journey by the fictional explorer, Raphael Hythlodaeus, to a strange new land and included, outside of the main narrative, an engraved map of the land of Utopia, a fragment of poetry written in More's invented Utopian language and an attendant graphically designed writing system to express the words of Utopian in (Conley and Cain 202).

The paratextual elements of the map, information on invented languages and writing systems would become the hallmark of fictional world-building used in varying degrees by such authors as Jonathan Swift in *Gulliver's Travels* (1726), Edward Bulwer-Lytton in *Vril: The Power of the Coming Race* (1871) and Percy Greg in the early Science Fiction work *Across the Zodiac: The Story of a Wrecked Record* (1880). These, and other paratextual elements, would became a key element of what Michael Saler has called The "New Romance" movement among late Victorian and Edwardian authors who sought to use scientific and empirical methodologies to give adventure, fiction and fantasy stories a stronger sense of realism (Saler 57-104).

Moreover, the addition of these highly detailed paratextual elements not only added to the readers exploration of the narrative but also encouraged readers to move from just passively reading the text to actively engaging with the elements of the world the authors developed through paratextual elements. In his 1987 work *Seuils*, the French literary theorist Gerard Genettte explored the role of paratextual elements. This work, which was subsequently published in 1997 as *Paratexts: Thresholds of Interpretation*, suggested that paratextual elements establish a complex mediation between book, author, publisher and reader. Paratextual elements like maps and information on invented languages gave readers an opportunity to create and explore this mediation with an author's creative work. A good early example of this complex mediation and active interaction between author and reader occurred in 1891 when a group of fans of Bulwer-Lytton's *Vril: The Power of the Coming Race* organized a fundraising bazaar at the Royal Albert Hall in London which they converted to a cavern of the Vril-ya and participants were encouraged to speak in Vril-ya aided by printed brochures containing a glossary and elements of the grammar of Bulwer-Lytton's Vrill language which was outlined in the book.[1]

Wolf brings these two key roles of paratexts in fictional works together; suggesting their importance as world-building elements by authors used to both imbue their worlds with a greater sense of reality, while also giving readers paratextual elements to use and build upon the creative work of the author, thus creating a powerful mediation between between the author and reader.

---

1 https://observationdeck.kinja.com/was-this-ill-fated-victorian-festival-the-first-sf-them-1632616198

Wolf characterizes these paratexts as elements of the overall make up, or *gestalt*, of invented worlds; suggesting that they are in themselves dynamic entities that are compelling objects of inquiry that invite speculation and exploration through imaginative means (51-57).

Three authors who imaginatively composed paratextual elements that accomplished Wolf's two key roles for literary paratexts outlined above were Austin Tappan Wright, in his private invention of the land of Islandia; J.R.R. Tolkien, in his literary world-building of the world of Arda from which his masterwork *The Lord of the Rings* emerged, and Ursula K. Le Guin in her unique novel *Always Coming Home*. In each case these authors put as much, if not arguably more, focus on the invention and incorporation of paratextual elements which introduced, supported and extended the narrative of their worlds. This chapter will investigate several key paratextual elements that these authors used to build their worlds and also explore how these paratexts offer the opportunity for Genette's complex mediation between author and reader.

Austin Tappan Wright and his *Islandia*

Since childhood and throughout his tragically short life the American legal author and philosopher Austin Tappan Wright (1883-1931) privately constructed the imaginary country of Islandia; located on the southern tip of the equally imagined Karain subcontinent in the southern hemisphere of the real or primary world. According to his daughter and posthumous editor Sylvia Wright (1917-81), Tappan Wright originated Islandia as "my island" when he was a child and continued to work on building it when he was a law student at Harvard University and into the 1920's. He achieved this through composing an extended narrative and inventing a substantial collection of paratexts. After his death in an automobile accident in September 1931, several large and complete Islandia related manuscripts were discovered, including a novel of over six hundred thousand words and a volume of appendices nearly as long, as well as nineteen hand-drawn and finely detailed maps, some colored. Tappan Wright's six hundred thousand word novel was edited down by over a third by Sylvia Wright and seen through publication by Farrar & Rinehart publisher Mark Saxton. The novel *Islandia* was published on April 9, 1942. This large text of close to a thousand pages of narrative contained several paratextual elements including a map in the frontispiece that immediately introduced the reader to the land of Islandia.

In Tappan Wright's conception, Islandia is an isolationist agricultural country with hardly any technological development. In the novel, Tappan Wright employs the traveler's tale framework to introduce the reader to the world of Islandia. He creates the primary world character John Lang an American student at Harvard University (just as Tappan Wright had been) who meets a student from Islandia, Dorn, and through him learns the strange Islandian language which Lang describes in the novel as "without declensions, conjugations, moods or tenses, or genders except where sex required them." (9) This makes Lang qualified when he leaves Harvard in 1910 to become the first American consul to Islandia which had recently begun to consider opening their borders to limited foreign interaction and investment. The reader encounters the people, cultures and language of Islandia through the eyes of John Lang who becomes the transmitter of knowledge of this strange culture to the West. This suggests a similar narrative framework that J.R.R. Tolkien used in the earliest versions of his legendarium when he created in his *The Book of Lost Tales* the characters of Eriol and Aelfwine; mariners who sailed into the West and encountered the exiled Elves on the Lonely Island, Tol-Eressëa from whom he would learn, record and transmit their lost tales. Within the land of Islandia, John Lang would become the author of many of the paratextual elements Tappan Wright invented in his world-building. For example, as part of the publicity campaign for the promotion of the novel *Islandia* a separate pamphlet in a limited edition was printed primarily for reviewers and booksellers; although some copies were also sold to the public and the pamphlet survives as a rare book today. The literary critic and academic Basil Davenport (1905-66) was commissioned to write an essay for this booklet and *Islandia*'s publisher Mark Saxton selected hitherto unpublished paratextual material from Tappan Wright's vast world-building work to comprise the second half of the pamphlet. These extracts included photographs of three Islandian maps; a section on the population of Islandia by area; notes on the climate of Islandia and its calendars as well as some specimens of Islandian literature and a selection of Tappan Wright's invented Islandian language expressed in glossaries. This booklet was called

An Introduction to Islandia: Its History, Custom, Laws, Language and Geography as prepared by Basil Davenport from 'Islandia: History and Description' by John Perrier, First French Consul to Islandia and Translated by John Lang, First American Consul with Maps drawn by John Lang.[2] The publishing of this pamphlet made more of the paratextual information that Tappan Wright had created for his authorial world-building of Islandia available.[3]

The Paratexts that built Middle-earth

Some of the first evidence of J.R.R. Tolkien's use of paratexts in his literary world-building was seen by readers of *The Hobbit* when it was published in 1937. Before the main narrative readers would have seen Tolkien's use of the paratextual element of Thror's Map which both established the spatial nature of part of the world of the narrative and also introduced some key elements, such as the hidden moon runes, which would be explored in the narrative to follow. Tolkien greatly expanded his use of paratexts in *The Lord of the Rings* which, in addition to maps, also introduced and offered other paratextual elements to the reader such as glossaries of Tolkien's invented languages, chronologies, family trees and calendars. The majority of this paratextual information which appeared in the appendices of the last volume of *The Lord of the Rings* was based on information readers had asked Tolkien to expand on from the main narrative of the first two volumes. In a letter to Rayner Unwin, Tolkien lamented that no matter how much paratextual information he put in to appendices their appearance in truncated and compressed form will satisfy nobody: "certainly not me; clearly from the (appalling mass of) letters I receive not those people who like that kind of thing – astonishingly many" (*Letters* 210). As is now known through the publishing of much of Tolkien's mythological and linguistic material around his world building of Arda, the invention of paratextual elements goes back to some of Tolkien's earliest work on his mythology; starting with

---

2 According to Douglas A. Anderson, in May 1942 the original holograph manuscripts of the novel, the history, the appendices, and the maps were lost in transit on return from a successful exhibition at the Philadelphia Ledger Book Fair. Rewards were offered for their return, but nothing ever surfaced and some of these important items – in particular the volume of appendices and the nineteen maps – were lost forever. The typescript manuscripts and seven of the maps survive as photostats or photographs.
3 Tappan Wright's Islandian papers are currently kept at The Houghton Library, Harvard Library, Harvard University - http://oasis.lib.harvard.edu/oasis/deliver/~hou01122

drawings and illustrations around some of the earliest poetry and then with the first series of maps Tolkien composed for his *The Book of Lost Tales* as well as other paratextual elements; such as *The Heraldic Devices of Tol Erethrin* (*Parma Eldalamberon* 13, 93-96) which not only established key places in Tolkien's earliest world-building but also incorporated Tolkien's emerging Elvish language invention in the naming of these places within this world.

Go to "The Back of the Book": The Paratexts of Ursula K. Le Guin's *Always Coming Home*

Ursula K. Le Guin's novel *Always Coming Home* (1985) is about a future cultural group of humans called the Kesh. It is part novel, part text book and part anthropological report of a post-apocalyptic California.

> THE PEOPLE in this book might be going to have lived a long, long time from now in Northern California. The main part of the book is their voices speaking for themselves in stories and life-stories, plays, poems and songs. If the reader will bear with some unfamiliar terms they will be all made clear at last. Coming at my work as a novelist, I thought it best to put many of the explanatory descriptive pieces into a section called "The Back of the Book" where those who want narrative can ignore them and those who enjoy explanation can find them. (xi)

Le Guin also characterizes the paratextual information in her "Back of the Book" as things from here on will be just as fictional, but more factual, although equally true (408). In this statement Le Guin suggests that the material that is to follow, while drawn from the fictional world of the Kesh, is actually closer to fact as it reports on the more realistic elements of the world. There is an interesting resonance with how Le Guin presents her paratextual "Back of the Book" and a statement Tolkien made in one of his letters about his work on his appendices to *The Lord of the Rings* stating that those who enjoy the book as an "heroic romance" only and find "unexplained vistas" part of the literary effect, will neglect the appendices, very properly (*Letters* 210).

Like *Islandia* and the various frame narratives of Tolkien's legendarium, Le Guin's *Always Coming Home* is, in a sense, a traveler's tale to an imagined future. Le Guin suggests to the reader that the way to achieve this trip to the future to hear the voices of the Kesh people is to take your child or grandchild in your arms and stand quietly. Perhaps the baby will see something, or hear a voice, or speak to somebody there, somebody from home (5). Interestingly one of the voices we hear in the narrative has an autobiographical resonance through the name Little Bear Woman which is what the name Ursula means in Latin.

Maps – Defining the Spatial Environment of These Worlds

As introduced above, one key foundational paratextual element that each of these three authors utilize in their world-building is a detailed series of maps. Wolf characterizes the role of the map in the creation and structuring of fictional worlds as serving two key roles. First, maps relate a series of locations to each other, visually unifying them into a world. Secondly, they provide a concrete image of a world and fill in many of the gaps not covered in the main narrative, such as gaps in between locations those at the world's edges and places not otherwise mentioned or visited by the characters (156). Moreover, Pavlick characterizes maps as often leaving blank spaces, unfinished roads and paths or differing perspectives. The visual nature of the space of a map draws attention to these absences and oddities, and these blank spaces and perspective shifts encourage a greater interaction with the map because, in one sense, this strangeness and openness engenders a projection of the reader's self into the map (39). These blank spaces and unknown places on a map of invented worlds engage the reader in a sub-creative process through interaction with this paratextual element; suggesting Genette's definition of the paratext above as encouraging an active mediation between author and reader. For example, the frontispiece map at the start of the novel *Islandia* immediately draws the reader into the traveler's tale framework. Tappan Wright's paratextual map is said to be from the maps in John Lang's notebook (i-ii). Tappan Wright's focus on the details of the paratexts through which he built his world is exemplified by the fact that in developing his maps he enlisted the help of his brother Dr. John K Wright who was the former head of the American Geographical Society, thus giving his world-building cartography a sense of realism. This is evident in the two page map called 'The Country of Islandia'; a reproduction of an original map from John Lang's notebook which was included in the promotional pamphlet and shows in great detail very specific mountain ranges, rivers, and key places that Lang visits on his travels around Islandia.[4]

In describing his own world-building, J.R.R. Tolkien stated that he wisely started with a map, and made the story fit (*Letters* 144). Tom Shippey in *J.R.R. Tolkien: Author of the Century* argues that Tolkien's maps are larger than the plot of his stories; as opposed to merely illustrating the layout of the fictional setting. When Tolkien drew his maps and covered them with names, he felt no need to bring all the names into the story. They did their work by suggesting that there is a world outside the story, that the story is only a selection (68). It is not only the defined places on Tolkien's maps that support his sub-creation but also those blank spaces and unknown places that engage the reader in a sub-creative process through the active mediation with this paratextual element as again Genette suggested. At every period in the development of his legendarium, Tolkien used maps to visualize his world and track in great detail the people and places of his world-building. This visualization started with the earliest sketch of a map Tolkien made for his emerging world which Christopher Tolkien reproduces in the the first volume of *The Book of Lost Tales*. This pencil sketch demarcates Tolkien's earliest vision for one specific area of his world of Arda and to support the narrative of the Valar's first attempt to light the world by setting up two lamps in the North and South (marked on the map) only to be thwarted by the evil Melko who constructed the pillars to hold these lamps out of ice which subsequently melted and cause these great lights to fall and burn the earth (*LT I* 69). Another early map Tolkien drew is a conceptual view of his world rendered in the shape of a Viking ship; called "I Vene Kemen" which is Qenya for "The Shape of the World" (*LT I* 83). Other maps would follow including the first 'Silmarillion' map and the aforementioned Thror's treasure map of *The Hobbit* and the well-known maps 'A Part of The Shire' and 'The West of Middle-earth' which the reader encounters at the start of *The Lord of the Rings*. In each case Tolkien used these maps as a paratextual authorial tool in his world-building. For example, in writing *The Lord of the Rings*, Tolkien carefully coordinated the story timelines with distances and positions on his working sketch map by overlaying *The Lord of the Rings* map

---

[4] The author of this paper is indebted to Douglas A. Anderson for showing me his copy of this rare promotional pamphlet.

with a one-hundred-mile square grid to aid in calculating distances for each daily journey of ten to seventeen miles (*TI* 300).

In *Always Coming Home*, Le Guin also establishes the importance of maps to the Kesh people. She states that the Kesh drew maps mostly of the Valley. They evidently enjoyed laying out and looking at the spatial relationships of places and objects they knew well. The better they knew them, the better they liked to draw and map them (450). This was apparently an early learned trait among the Kesh children whom Le Guin describes as drawing maps of the fields and hills about their home town often in incredible detail – "a dot for every rock, a mark for every tree" (450). Le Guin also states that the larger maps were remarkably accurate, considering that the function was mostly aesthetic or poetic; but then accuracy was considered a fundamental element of a quality of poetry (450). Like Tolkien, Le Guin's maps also incorporated her language invention and Kesh writing system. On one map all the locations are rendered in the invented Kesh Alphabet (451). Map place names are also constructed from invented words that are found in the glossary Le Guin provides in 'The Back of the Book'. Many of these place names use an element of the key Keshian word "heyiya" which signifies an sense of the holy and sacred (515).

Paratexts and Invented Languages – Giving Voice to these Worlds

As indicated above all three authors also included elements of invented languages in their narrative which are supported, explained and expanded through such paratexts as glossaries and grammars for the reader to both review, interact and transact with.

As already indicated in *Islandia*, John Lang's learning of the foreign Islandian language through his friend Dorn is the way he ultimately becomes the first American consul to Islandia. One of the key elements of the Islandian language Lang encounters are the different words to express concepts of love which parallels Lang's own experiences in the novel and his struggle to comprehend these different types of love he encounters among the Islandian people. These invented words are *Apia, Alia*, and *Ania* (corresponding roughly to Eros, love of place, and the mature love that comprises the closest marriage). In the course of the novel, Lang loves three different women and is tested by the experiences, although he ultimately finds contentment and a kind of acceptance for each form of love. Therefore, the paratextual elements of invented language frame the story of Lang's encounter and understanding of Islandian culture. The lexicon included in the paratextual pamphlet expanded on the Islandian words John Lang learned in his time on Islandia with a glossary that included words for people, place and items including the different versions of love outlined above and a complex numbering system. In the afterword to the novel, Sylvia Wright also mentions that there was evidence of an Islandian writing system which was inspired by Christian travelers to the court of the King Alwin XI although Islandian is not a European language and its origins remain obscure (1023).

For J.R.R. Tolkien the act of making stories and inventing languages started out as separate boyhood pursuits but quickly become intermingled and intertwined together in his creative thought and method. As he expressed in his November 1931 talk on language invention 'A Secret Vice' Tolkien felt invented languages for fiction should have four key characteristics: the creation of word forms that sound aesthetically pleasing, a sense of fitness between symbol (the word-form and its sound) and sense (its meaning), the construction of an elaborate and ingenious grammar and the composition of a fictional historic background for the invented language including a sense of its (hypothetical) change over time (*ASV* xv-xvi). Tolkien invented paratextual elements to create this sense of philological depth in his languages. For example, he composed several lexicons, word lists and grammars which explored in great detail the historical development and growth and nature of his nexus of languages for Arda. These paratexts created an illusion of historicity and also, for the interested student, a chance to learn these languages at their various stages of development. The first arguably major point of interaction between Tolkien and his readers in terms of paratextual elements came when the last volume of *The Lord of the Rings* was published in 1955 in which Tolkien included in the appendices several sections on the invented languages; Appendix E 'Writing and Spelling' and Appendix F 'The Languages and Peoples of the Third Age' which outlined for readers the morphology, grammar and writing systems of Elvish and other languages of Middle-earth. These paratexts were not only informative but also created active mediation between author and reader as evidenced by many interested readers attempt to understand Tolkien's language and, as soon became evident by the number of fan magazines and later online websites, active use of the languages to communicate and actively interact and immerse themselves in Tolkien's world (*ASV* 126-29).

Le Guin also peppers her various *Always Coming Home* narratives with words in the Kesh language which she then expands, like Tolkien, in great detail in the glossary of the Kesh language. Interestingly, in constructing these paratextual elements Le Guin pays homage to both the language invention of Tappan Wright and Tolkien. The compiler of the Kesh glossary, Pandora, in a section specifically on words to signify different types of love states that at first she thought the Kesh distinctions were similar to the Islandian "the subtle and useful trilogy of ania, apia, alia but the overlap of meaning is only partial" (493). Also at the start of the glossary, Le Guin herself tells the reader that a number of other words were included for the pleasure of my fellow dictionary-readers and adepts of what an illustrious predecessor referred to as the 'Secret Vice' (509). Le Guin here is deliberately referring to Tolkien's talk. In another paratextual piece Le Guin includes called 'Long Names of Houses' she explores the understanding of old forgotten names.

> Need every word be translated? Sometimes the untranslated word might serve to remind us that language is not meaning, that intelligibility is an element of it only, a function. The untranslated word or name is not functional. It sits there. Written, it is a row of letters, which spoken with a more or less wild guess at the pronunciation produces a complex of phonemes, a more or less musical and interested sound, a noise, a thing. (413)

Here Le Guin seems to be suggesting some of the phono-aesthetic ideas that Tolkien felt words inherently contain and the contemplation of the sound of words without meaning (*ASV* 16). There are also some interesting parallels between the process Tappan Wright, Tolkien and Le Guin used in their word-building for their invented languages. Although there is not a great amount of it published, the evidence of words in Tappan Wright's narrative and glossary indicate that he put focus on creating consistency in his word-building. For example, it seems that the suffix *-ta* was always used to create a diminutive; so that a romantic crush is made up of the word for love *apia* and the suffix *-ta*. Also Tappan Wright used prefixes attached to roots to create related words. For example, the root win (river) is used in the narrative and the maps of Islandia in such descriptive names as *matwin* (broad-river) and *alwin* (swan-river).

At roughly the same time on the other side of the Atlantic, Tolkien's earliest word-building process for his first version of Elvish, Qenya, also involved inventing a root that had a certain phono-aesthetic sense to it and to use this form to construct a series of related consistent and coherent words. An example of this can be seen in the Qenya root Moro, which itself through primary world word association suggests a feeling of literal or metaphorical darkness. Tolkien used this root to construct a series of words directly and indirectly related to concepts of darkness and, by extension, the night and hidden things.

> Mori – night
> morinda – of the night, nightly
> morina – nocturnal
> morna, morqa – black
> moru – hide, conceal
> morwa – unclear, secret
> (*Parma Eldalamberon* 12, 62)

In a similar way Le Guin's Kesh language is also clearly agglutinative, building words and grammatical forms from base roots, prefixes and suffixes (Higley 94). For example from the Kesh word *HWA* "sun" Le Guin invents a series of words that, like in Tolkien's process, are all related in some manner to the sun:

> hwadihua – south
> hwaha – southwest
> hwai – time (time of day at which event occurs)
> hwan – yellow, golden
> hwapeweyo – the dry season (approx May-October)
> hwavgediu – morning
> hwavgodiu – noon
> hwavgemalo – afternoon
> hwavgomalo – evening
> (Le Guin, *Always Coming Home* 516)

Unique Paratexts

In addition to sharing some common foundational paratexts, each of these authors also invented elements outside of the main narrative based on their specific interests which both added to their authorial world-building and created opportunities for mediation between author and reader.

For Tolkien, as already explored, many of the paratextual elements that he invented was clearly around his focused interest in the invention of languages that possessed a historic and linguistic depth and could show change over feigned time. However, with his interest in art and illustration Tolkien also created such visual paratexts as his illustrations of 'The Doors of Durin' and his facsimile of 'The Book of Mazarbul' which he burned and distressed to make it look like the war torn chronicle found by the fellowship in Moria (Hammond & Scull 66-71; 77-87)

Throughout the narrative of *Islandia*, Tappan Wright, through the character of John Lang, shows an interest in the facts and figures of the different provinces of Islandia. A paratext that Tappan Wright creates to support and expand on this interest appeared in the promotional pamphlet as a page titled 'Population' outlining the detailed census figures of each area of Islandia. By engaging with this paratext the reader learns how many farms there were on Islandia and a detailed listing of who lived in them by area. This not only provides the reader with additional paratextual information but also both helps create a sense of scope and depth to this land; supporting Tappan Wright's emphasis on the agrarian nature of Islandia as it opens up to the interest and investment of the West. Through this paratext the reader learns that the twenty-one provinces of Islandia contained 146,266 farms and 1,979,860 farmers, their families and dependents. Tappan Wright also uses his language invention in this chart by designating farmers and their families with the Islandian word *tanar* and the dependents with the word *denrir*.

In the case of *Always Coming Home*, Le Guin's focus is very much on composing paratexts that reflect the anthropological and sociological elements of the Kesh people; suggesting Le Guin's own anthropological interests from her father's work. According to Erlich, Le Guin's *Always Coming Home* is a fictional retelling of much of Le Guin's father, A.L. Kroeber's anthropological study *Handbook of the Indians of California* (67).

Therefore, many of the paratextual elements Le Guin offers the reader focus on the anthropology of the Kesh people. For example, the reader is given reports on the animal life of the Valley, kinship rituals, clothing, food and the musical instruments of the Kesh people. Readers are also given opportunities to interact with the Kesh people by preparing such recipes as Pragasiv Fas which is a Keshian summer soup and FatFat Clown Clown which is a sweet dessert (440-42).

Given their similarities in the invention and use of paratexts in their world-building it is astounding that Tolkien was not aware of Tappan Wright's work. According to Douglas A. Anderson, Tolkien appears never to have read Wright's novel, for in a 1957 letter he answered a correspondent's question by saying that he had never before heard of *Islandia*. (Anderson 455). Le Guin, on the other hand, clearly knew both Tappan Wright's and Tolkien's works and, as explored above, made several inter-textual references to both of them in her own world-building of the land of the Kesh. Indeed, Le Guin seems to be slightly subverting the more traditional use of the literary paratext which seeks to orient and support the reader in the narrative of the world by disorienting the reader through a series of texts that are only supported and explained when the reader gets to the paratextual information in 'The Back of the Book'.

Conclusion: Not Just Narrative – The Integral Role of Paratexts in Authorial World-Building

In his seminal talk 'On Fairy-stories', Tolkien stated that to make a Secondary World that is credible and commanding will require labor and thought and will certainly demand a special skill, a kind of Elvish Craft (*TOFS* 61). Given the incredible achievement in their authorial world-building Tappan Wright, Tolkien and Le Guin each possessed this skill and they achieved this by not just using descriptive narrative but by laboring over the invention of a series of well crafted and integrated paratextual elements which were a key part of their authorial world-building. The gestalt of their worlds was made up of these layers of paratextual elements that not only added to, but expanded on, the narrative of their stories and are in themselves important elements in understanding these worlds. The results were 'worlds' that readers wanted to both visit and explore in varying degrees through Genette's concept of paratexts as inviting a complex mediation between author and reader. In the case of Tappan Wright's sprawling building of Islandia many readers having read the published novel wanted to engage with the world in more depth. In the afterword to *Islandia*, Sylvia Wright reports that in 1943 the news reporter Elmer Davis wrote an entry for the *Britannia Year Book* in which he depicted Islandia as being opened up to foreign trade including coffee (1015). The original publisher of *Islandia* Mark Saxton went on to write several books set in the land of Islandia at different historical times.[5] There is no question that Tolkien's world-building has become the source of much interest in all aspects of Middle-earth and from its first readers to today there is a hunger to explore the cultures and languages of the world which Tolkien's paratextual elements introduced and invited readers to explore and transact with. In the case of Le Guin, her paratextual elements of the Kesh people added to the reality she was looking to create. As Le Guin said in a talk she gave

> the story of *Always Coming Home* is set in a Californian valley that I have known all my life and love dearly, the earthquake shaken, immovable center of my world. I strove to be absolutely faithful to the nature of that place in the sense of the actual geology, flora and fauna, also to my understanding of its nature and as holding the potentially of sacredness. (More 163-64)

The rich and complex work of Tappan Wright, Le Guin and of course Tolkien underscores the importance of paratextual elements in authorial world-building. The maps, reports of invented languages, charts and graphs that the reader encounters in the works explored above clearly imbue these worlds with a greater sense of depth and reality while also creating the opportunity for a complex mediation between author and reader. When this invitation is taken up by the

---

5 These novels are: *The Islar, Islandia Today – A Narrative of Lang III*. Published 1969, this book is set in the then-present day. The plot concerns a coup attempt in Islandia that occurs while the national government is debating whether to join the U.N.. The protagonist, as indicated in the title, is John Lang's grandson. *The Two Kingdoms*, published 1979, is a prequel set in the 14th century. The plot concerns the events surrounding the reign of the only female ruler in Islandian history, and the dynastic change that ensued from this. *Havoc in Islandia*, published 1982, is yet another prequel, set in the 12th century. The Roman Catholic church attempts to overthrow the government of Islandia, and, having failed, is itself expelled from the country.

reader for further exploration and discovery the result is another layer of creative world-building that serves to make up the overall gestalt of the world. The reader becomes the author who themselves have the potential to create new related paratextual elements which, in turn, creates more avenues of reader speculation and exploration through imaginative means – an 'Elvish craft' indeed.

About the Author

DR ANDREW HIGGINS is a Tolkien scholar who specializes in the role of language invention in Tolkien and in other fiction. His PhD thesis *The Genesis of Tolkien's Mythology* explored the interrelated nature of myth and language in Tolkien's earliest work on his legendarium. Co-edited with Dr. Dimitra Fimi *A Secret Vice: J.R.R. Tolkien on Language Invention* – a new edition of Tolkien's 1931 talk published by HarperCollins in April 2016. Andrew also taught a 13-week online course for Signum University/Mythgard Institute on 'Language Invention through Tolkien'. He has also given Tolkien related papers at The International Medieval Congress at Kalamazoo, Michigan and Leeds as well as for The Tolkien and Mythopoeic Societies. He is currently working on turning his PhD thesis into a book for publication. Andrew is also the Director of Development at Glyndebourne Opera in East Sussex, England.

Abbreviations

ASV   TOLKIEN, J.R.R. *A Secret Vice: Tolkien on Language Invention.* Ed. Dimitra Fimi and Andrew Higgins. London: HarperCollins, 2016.

Letters   TOLKIEN, J.R.R. *The Letters of J.R.R. Tolkien.* Ed. Humphrey Carpenter, with the assistance of Christopher Tolkien. London: George Allen & Unwin, Boston: Houghton Mifflin, 1981.

LT I   TOLKIEN, J.R.R. *The Book of Lost Tales I.* Ed. Christopher Tolkien. London: George Allen & Unwin, 1983.

TI   TOLKIEN, J.R.R. *The Treason of Isengard.* Ed. Christopher Tolkien. London: Unwin Hyman, 1989.

TOFS   TOLKIEN, J.R.R. *Tolkien On Fairy-stories.* Expanded edition, with commentary and notes. Ed. Verlyn Flieger & Douglas A. Anderson. London: HarperCollins, 2008.

Bibliography

ANDERSON, Douglas A. (ed.). *Tales Before Tolkien: The Roots of Modern Fantasy.* New York: Ballentine Books, 2002. (Kindle Edition)

BALDICK, Chris. *The Oxford Dictionary of Literary Terms.* 4th edition. Oxford: Oxford University Press, 2015.

CONLEY, T. and S. CAIN (eds). *Encyclopedia of Fictional and Fantastic Languages.* London: Greenwood Press, 2006

EHRLICH, Richard D. *'Always Coming Home.' Coyote's Song: The Teaching Stories of Ursula K. Le Guin.* New York: Wildside Press, 1997. 232-303.

GENETTE, Gerard. *Paratexts: Thresholds of Interpretation.* Cambridge: Cambridge University Press, 1997.

HAMMOND, Wayne G. & Christine SCULL. (eds.). *The Art of the Lord of the Rings.* 60th anniversary edition. London: HarperCollins, 2015.

HIGLEY, Sarah. *Hildegard von Bingen's Unknown Language. An Edition, Translation, and Discussion.* London: Palgrave Macmillian, 2007.

LE GUIN, Ursula K. *Always Coming Home.* New York: Harper and Row, 1985

'A Non-Euclidean View of California as a Cold Place to Be.' *Utopia.* London: Verso, 2016. 163-94.

MAK, Bonnie. *How the Page Matters.* Toronto: University of Toronto Press, 2011.

MORE, Thomas. *Utopia.* London: Penguin Books, 2000.

PAVLICK, Anthony. 'A Special Kind of Reading Game: Maps in Children's Literature.' *International Research in Children's Literature* 3 (2010): 28-43.

SALER, Michael. *As If: Modern Enchantment and the Literary Prehistory of Virtual Reality.* Oxford: Oxford University Press, 2012.

SHIPPEY, Tom A. *J.R.R. Tolkien: Author of the Century.* London: HarperCollins, 2001.

TAPPAN WRIGHT, Austin. *Islandia.* New York: The Overlook Press, 1942.

TOLKIEN, J.R.R. *The Letters of J.R.R. Tolkien.* Ed. Humphrey Carpenter, with the assistance of Christopher Tolkien. London: George Allen & Unwin, Boston: Houghton Mifflin, 1981.

The Book of Lost Tales I. Ed. Christopher Tolkien. London: George Allen & Unwin, 1983.

The Treason of Isengard. Ed. Christopher Tolkien. London: Unwin Hyman, 1989.

'Qenyaqetsa: The Qenya Phonology and Lexicon: Together with the Poetic and Mythological Words of Eldarissa.' Ed. Christopher Gilson, Carl F. Hostetter, Patrick Wynne, and Arden R. Smith. *Parma Eldalamberon* 12 (1998): 1-121.

'Heraldic Devices of Tol Erethrin.' Ed. Christoper Gilson, Bill Welden, Carl F. Hostetter, and Patrick Wynne. *Parma Eldalamberon* 13 (2001): 93-96.

Tolkien On Fairy-stories. Ed. Verlyn Flieger and Douglas A. Anderson. London: HarperCollins, 2008.

A Secret Vice: Tolkien on Language Invention. Ed. Dimitra Fimi and Andrew Higgins. London: HarperCollins, 2016.

WOLF, Mark J.P. *Building Imaginary Worlds: The Theory and History of Subcreation*. London: Routledge, 2012.

Tom Shippey

The Faërie World of Michael Swanwick

Abstract

This paper suggests that Michael Swanwick's 'Industrialised Faerie' fantasies perhaps use *The Denham Tracts*, a set of folklore pamphlets which are also a putative source for Tolkien's hobbits. It argues further that Swanwick combines 'immersive' and 'portal' strategies in creating his imagined world, centering his works on 'changeling' characters who belong in a sense to both the real and the faerie worlds, while also exploiting reader-awareness of traditional folklore motifs.

'Industrialised Faërie' is a term sometimes applied to Michael Swanwick's two novels, *The Iron Dragon's Daughter* (1993) and *The Dragons of Babel* (2007), together with a handful of associated stories.[1] Nothing could appear less Tolkienian: Tolkien might well have been appalled by the very idea. The novels have also been repeatedly described as 'anti-fantasy', and as 'subversive' of the genre.[2] Such claims need not be taken seriously. Declaring that works of fantasy, or science fiction, are too good to be considered fantasy or science fiction is part of the rhetoric of modern criticism, so often genre-biased, and claims of "subversion" are often no more than a critical pose. Swanwick himself has given a more nuanced and respectful explanation of his intentions.[3] Nevertheless I hope to make clear in this paper that in one way at least Swanwick is much

---

1 Several sections of both novels appeared originally as novellas or short stories, usually in *Asimov's Science Fiction Magazine*. One related story not so far taken into a longer work is 'The Bordello in Faërie', reprinted in the Swanwick collection, *The Dog Said Bow-Wow* (2007). It is discussed in note 9 below. Two other elvish but unrelated tales are 'The Changeling's Tale', reprinted in *Tales of Old Earth* (2000), and 'The Armies of Elfland', with Eileen Gunn (2014), available at http://www.lightspeedmagazine.com/fiction, accessed 13th November 2017. A third novel in the series, *The Iron Dragon's Mother*, is said to be in preparation.
2 For the 'anti-fantasy' claim, see the entry on Swanwick in John Clute and John Grant, *The Encyclopaedia of Fantasy* (1997), p. 914. For subversion, see the Wikipedia entry on *The Iron Dragon's Daughter*, accessed 13th November 2017. Both claims have been repeated, usually more summarily than in the references given.
3 In 'The Literary Alchemist', an interview with Nick Gevers, see http://www.infinityplus.co.uk/nonfiction/intms.htm, accessed November 13th 2017. Swanwick makes it clear that he was reacting not against Tolkien but against derivative successors of Tolkien.

closer to Tolkien, and to the roots of Tolkien, than any other fantasy author; and moreover that the originality of his work needs a much more thoughtful response than claims of subversion.

To begin with one strange Tolkien/Swanwick connection: it is well-known now that the only occurrence of the word 'hobbits' prior to Tolkien comes in *The Denham Tracts*, a series of pamphlets on folklore published in North Yorkshire in the mid-nineteenth century by an enthusiast called Michael Aislabie Denham, and little-known till they were reprinted in 1895 by the Folklore Society.[4] There they appear as 154th in a list of 196 kinds of strange creatures. Denham's list was highly eclectic – he included creatures from Classical mythology like satyrs, fauns, nymphs and cenaturs, and from Celtic and Scandinavian mythology like korigans, leprechauns and nisses. It was also rather repetitive, with bugbears, boggiboes, buggaboos and boggleboes all listed separately. Nevertheless, after making all appropriate deductions, what is left is a very impressive list of supernatural creatures once familiar but now, in most cases, no longer known at all.

Except, that is, by Michael Swanwick. An immediately striking aspect of his image of Faërie is the number of denizens it contains. From the start we come across knockers and hogmen, spriggans, pillywiggins, kobolds and korrigans, a dunter, a spunky, gwarchells and orends, and many other creatures as well as the more normal kinds of non-human (elves, dwarves, trolls, etc.) and mythical animal (manticores, basilisks, wyverns, cockatrices and of course dragons). By my count, which is surely an underestimate, Swanwick's world has more than seventy types of supernatural creature, and that excludes the extensive but extremely eclectic fifteen-line list given near the end of *The Dragons of Babel*. The overlap with the Denham list is quite considerable, and the more marked if one lists only the least familiar ones: knockers, hobthrushes, shellycoats, cluricauns, spunks or spunkies, chittifaces. Billy Bugaboo is a named character, and one of the casualties of the Teind is 'the Cauld-Lad', another of Denham's species.

---

4 See *The Denham Tracts*, ed. James Hardy (London: Folklore Society, 1895). Since the list is not easy to access, I reprinted it in full in my article 'The Ancestors of the Hobbits: Strange Creatures in English Folklore', in *Lembas-extra* 2011, 97-106, which is readily available under my name on the academia. edu website.

Guessing at an author's sources is a risky business – especially when the author is alive to contradict the critic – but it is possible that Swanwick went back to one of Tolkien's possible sources in Denham; and certain that both authors are drawing on a whole 'lost world' of early English folklore, sometimes surviving as names alone. One of the charms of 'Industrialised Faërie' is its copiousness, its sense of an entire world, like Middle-earth, with its own inhabitants, largely unexplained and unexplored.

That world is moreover ruled by several of the most familiar folklore motifs. The very basis of it is the 'changeling' idea: that human children may be stolen away by the elves for their own purposes, leaving a simulacrum behind. Why? Swanwick's explanation is to use another familiar motif. Elves and fairies are often said to be unable to bear the touch of cold iron, and so changelings are vital to them for certain tasks. The third element making up Swanwick's initial scenario is not part of folklore at all, but a matter of simple observation. The traditional dragon, like the fire-breather in *Beowulf* who swoops down 'to burn the bright halls' – repeated, of course, by Tolkien's Smaug swooping down on Laketown – can hardly avoid the modern parallel with warplanes, fighter-bombers or ground-attack aircraft. It became overt in the Vietnam War, when the Gatling gun on the American A-10 warplane was jokingly dubbed 'Puff the Magic Dragon'. Swanwick's dragons are iron dragons. Like warplanes, they need pilots. These must be able to endure the iron that surrounds them. That's why elves need changelings.

Jane, the heroine of *The Iron Dragon's Daughter*, is accordingly a mortal child, snatched from her home in contemporary America, and employed in a dragon-factory. That is, however, only a temporary role for her. The elves do not intend her to be a dragon-pilot, for she could not be trusted. Once she reaches puberty she will become a breeder, to produce half-human half-elvish children: it is they who will become dragon-pilots. Meanwhile (though this is never made entirely clear), her connection with the human world is not totally severed. There can be no physical transfer between the two worlds. In some way, then, it is her 'subtle body' – soul or intelligence or personality – which has been harvested and used to inform a new body. One may deduce that a husk of some kind has been left behind, as in some versions of the changeling legend.

Jane, however, in the long novella which opens *The Iron Dragon's Daughter*, knows nothing of this. She knows only her immediate surroundings, which are a kind of Victorian sweat-shop for child-labour. She and her mixed crew of non-human children – some of them tailed or feathered – work in the dragon-factory, wiping grease off cogwheels, swabbing out tunnels too small for adult workers, ill-fed, unschooled, repeatedly beaten. The novella opens with them making a plan to kill their ram-horned supervisor Blugg, by the method, again traditional, of the 'gooly-doll' – an image of him containing some part of him, which they will throw into a fire, so that (according to the Law of Contagion) he will be destroyed along with his nail-parings.

That plan does not work (though another plan does). But my point here is merely to show how familiar much of this is to any regular reader of fantasy. What we recognise is that we are in a 'world where magic works'. And the basic idea of that – which goes back at least to Lyon Sprague de Camp and Fletcher Pratt's 'Incomplete Enchanter' stories of the 1940s and later[5] – is to take up the even earlier parallel drawn by Sir James Frazer in *The Golden Bough*, which explained magic as a kind of science, with underlying laws akin to the Newtonian ones.[6]

None of the above is intended to cast doubt on Swanwick's originality. What makes his work so unusual, and so challenging, is that in it the familiar folk-loristic background is repeatedly brought into jarring contact with a real-world and even mundane foreground. Jane is working for elves in a dragon-factory, but at lunch-time she is fed from a lunch-cart – brought round, it's true, by "an old lake hag" – and what she is given is "a plastic-wrapped sandwich and a cup of lukewarm grapefruit juice", a meal normal enough for many low-grade real-world workers. When she suddenly begins to menstruate she is sent off to the factory nurse, "a sour old creature with piggy eyes, a pointed nose, and two donkey's ears", but what this not-quite-human creature hands out is a sanitary napkin, two aspirins, and "a memorized lecture on personal hygiene", all of it far more industrial than Faërian.

---

5 I discuss the way in which Frazer was used in fantasy and science fiction in 'The Golden Bough and the Incorporation of Magic', reprinted in my collection *Hard Reading*, 162-81.
6 Other famous examples of Frazerian fantasy include Robert Heinlein's *Magic Inc.* (1940), and Randall Garrett's 'Lord Darcy' stories (from 1964 onwards).

In the same way, when an elf-lord turns up to inspect a prototype dragon-leg assembly, he is not marked out, as in fantasy convention, by sword or armour or jewellery, but by "an Italian suit and tufted silk tie", while he is trailed not by henchmen but by clipboard-carriers and an (admittedly "vulture-headed") "cost accountant from Accounting". In fact he looks like a CEO rather than a lord. More generally, while Jane's companions may have tails and feathers, they quarrel and bicker and bully for dominance in a manner familiar from any schoolyard, or if one prefers a literary parallel, from *Lord of the Flies* (1954). What marks Swanwick out from other fantasy authors is that in his work such clashes between the mundane and the fantastic occur again and again.[7] They suggest that while Faërie has its own rules, their rules parallel ours in areas other than magic / science.

One important and early example of this kind of double vision is the Time Clock. Time clocks (without capital letters) used to be and perhaps still are normal in some kinds of industrial or institutional environments. The worker arrives at work, takes his or her card from its rack, puts it into a slot and pulls a handle, the card then being stamped with time of arrival or departure, so that late arrival or poor time-keeping can then be penalised. 'Clocking-on' and 'clocking-off' were entirely real-world forms of low-status servitude.

The Time Clock in Jane's factory is, of course, different. One of the most familiar assertions about folklore fairies is that they can control time. Someone who spends a night in a fairy hill may come out to find that centuries have passed in the world outside. This happens (in a way) to one of Jane's fellow-slaves, Stilt, a 'shifter' said to be of low intelligence. He like Jane is approaching puberty, signalled in his case by developing feathers. But he will not be marked for breeding but for castration. Frightened, Stilt tries to escape, runs

---

7 We need a word for the discrete details which create these clashes and collectively build up a world-picture. Darko Suvin has suggested that in science fiction the critical element is the *novum*, the detail which tells you that you are not in the real world. I have suggested that recognising the *novum* is not entirely different from the process of recognising a datum in fiction more generally – something one is told, by the author, for a reason which one has to work out for oneself, see my article 'Learning to Read Science Fiction', reprinted in *Hard Reading*, 6-23. What should one call the fantasy-analogue of the single, discrete *novum* or *datum*? I can only suggest, the *nunquam*, from the Latin word for "never": it tells the reader, so to speak, that we are now in 'Never-Never Land'. I count about a dozen such in the first two pages of *The Iron Dragon's Daughter*, but there are as many examples there of a real-world detail, or *datum*.

past the Time Clock and immediately starts to age, first becoming adult and beginning to fly, then aging, moulting, crashing to his death. The Time Clock stores time but seemingly releases it for those who cross its guard-line without having punched their card and been granted permission.

These constant clashes of awareness serve as preparation and background for the most important clash, which is over the nature of dragons: are they animals, or intelligent animals, or war-machines, or (which seems to be the right answer) sentient war-machines, not born but manufactured? In favour of the idea that they are machines are the facts, dropped in from time to time, that they burn gasoline, have fuel tanks, have jets and afterburners, drop napalm and launch missiles, have instrument panels and need pilots. On the other hand, they have intelligence: a very Smaugian intelligence, cruel, calculating, treacherous. Jane's dragon is thought to be a wreck and looks like one, ruined, rusted, broken. 'Stealth technology', explains the dragon. She finds out about the dragon only because, while trying to steal Blugg's nail-parings – a job she has been given by the other children because as a human wards and hexes do not work on her – she comes upon a "grimoire". Grimoires are normally books of magic spells, but this one might better be called a manual for dragon-operation. The details it gives are not magical but technical: compression ratios, calibration settings, symbols for "capacitors and potentiometers and resistors and grounds". But – and this does not happen with vehicle manuals – as she reads it the dragon begins to talk to her, and form a plan for them both to escape.

As with Jane's companions, Rooster and Dimity and Thistle and the others, the Jane / dragon relationship becomes an issue of dominance. Jane needs the dragon to get her out and past the Time Clock. The dragon needs Jane as a pilot, and also to obtain two missing components, a "ruby" which is also a kind of data-storage microchip needed to "enable [the dragon's] laser guidance system;" and a "hex-nut" which contains part of the dragon's memory. Jane has already found the ruby while harvesting "toad-eggs". The hex-nut comes her way more strangely, and in a way which begins to even the power-balance between her and the much older, wiser and more powerful dragon.

Jane — in another literary parallel, this time with Pip in Dickens's *Great Expectations* (1861) — has been drafted to go and play, to amuse an old elf-lord who appears to be all but senile. The hex-nut is in the toy-box she is given to play with. But contact with the powerful Greenleaf family — while unsuccessful and even disappointing for supervisor Blugg — seems to develop Jane's own independence. At the end of the initial novella she forces the dragon to divulge his true name. In another conventional fantasy / folklore motif, knowledge of the true name gives one power over the named. "Melanchthon", then, no longer just "7332", has to do her bidding as they break out of their factory / scrapyard / jail.

One further factor is that contact with the human world has not entirely been lost. Jane herself has an early vision of "Home", a place of "green lawns" and "Bland white houses" where she is well-fed, well-clothed, cared for: "She owned toys." Her quest is simply to get back to home and mother. The other children also seem to have memories or awarenesses, though less comforting ones. Jane's semi-friend Rooster, injured in the attempt to steal Blugg's nail-parings, comes out in delirium with advertising slogans, "Fly the friendly skies … Join the Pepsi generation", and the scene is repeated later. He and Jane also share a vision which is quite clearly of shops prepared for Christmas. One might adapt her conclusion and suggest that Swanwick's Faërie is not so much an Other World as a Congruent World, marked simultaneously by similarity / difference.

Both *The Iron Dragon's Daughter* and *The Dragons of Babel* are structured by repeated changes of place and setting, in each of which the reader has to adjust to different expectations, and which also record a process of growing-up and developing independence for Jane and her successor Will, in the second novel. Jane, escaped from the factory, lives to begin with in the pilot's cabin of what appears to be (stealth technology again) a wrecked dragon. Nevertheless, her environment is now much more American-suburban, with her time divided between those two real-world teenage foci, high school and the mall. High school in Faërie is (realistically) once again a place of contests for dominance, but (fantastically) discipline is far stricter: being "sent to the Principal" involves an encounter with his basilisk, whose shrieks daunt the boldest. It is in the mall that Jane develops her talents for shoplifting, assisted by her humanity, which nullifies many wards and hexes. Once again, though, the Faërie penalty for shoplifting is harsh: "Flogging, public humiliation, possible loss of a hand". It is a security operative who points out that the penalty for burglary is no worse, and sets Jane on a new course: for burgling apartments of the rich brings her into contact with elf-lords, who can arrange a scholarship for her, to study alchemy.

In what follows, a repeated pattern is to centre sections on a familiar folkloristic motif, which is nevertheless buttressed by realistic elements and presented as normal within the fantasy world. One of Jane's acquaintances, Gwen, becomes the "wicker queen" – an idea now familiar from the 1973 movie *Wicker Man* – which means she will be burned alive as a sacrifice: Jane manages to save Gwen's consort from the same fate. One question never quite answered is, to whom is the sacrifice made? To Cernunos, the Celtic god, whose name is sometimes mentioned? To "the Seven", whoever they may be? Or "the Goddess", who lives in "Spiral Castle", clearly a version of Robert Graves's 'White Goddess'?[8] More threatening, but equally unexplained, is the sequence centred on "the Teind" (as Swanwick spells the word). This derives from a line in the ballad of 'Tam Lin', in which Tam, a human trapped in Fairyland, explains that, "pleasant if the fairy land, / But an eerie tale to tell, / Ay at the end of seven years, / we pay a tiend to hell. / I am sae fair and fu o flesh / I'm fear'd it be masel."[9] Tam assumes that the sacrifice will be picked for beauty, but in Jane's world the sacrifice is not a single person but literally a "tiend", a tenth of goods and population. She is told that she has been marked out as expendable, but is saved once again by her upper-class connections.

Other motifs used include "fairy gold", the well-established idea that payments given by the fairies will turn in the morning to dead leaves or trash; and the mortal who loves a fairy, only to be abandoned and left desolate, as

---

8 Graves, *The White Goddess: a historical grammar of poetic myth* (New York, 1948).
9 For the text of the traditional ballad of "Tam Lin", see http://tam-lin.org/versions/39A.html, accessed 13th November, 2017.

in Keats's poem 'La Belle Dame Sans Merci'.[10] These however are continually balanced, or set against, more normal aspects of teenage growth. Jane experiments with sex, though she does it in order to gain control over sex magic, and eventually to accumulate the true names of her lovers, which she passes on to the dragon, who has his own project of flying through the Dream Gate to attack the Goddess and destroy Spiral Castle. In the end they make the attack together. Jane dies – in Faërie; finds herself in Spiral Castle; and is sent on to Home, where no-one appears to have noticed her absence, and she resumes a normal life. It is doubtful whether any reader can quite make sense of this, but exposure to the science fiction idea of alternate universes, at different energy levels, perhaps provides an avenue for acceptance.

The Dragons of Babel, in brief, follows a similar course. Will, another half-mortal in Faërie, lives in a village which is taken over by a crashed war-dragon, becoming its lieutenant and executive agent. He manages to escape its domination and kill it by using a "name-stone", taken from a sergeant recruiting for the Faërie wars. Exiled from his village, he becomes a Displaced Person in a camp, and is moved on to the great city of Babel, where he becomes in effect a "ward heeler", working for the corrupt alderman Salem Toussaint. As a mortal, he is useful to Toussaint, whose constituents, especially the haints, like to see a mortal running errands for non-human voters. There is a very strong analogy with early twentieth-century New York, with the different species of non-human replacing the immigrants of different origins. At one point an ogre mentions a character called "Deianira the Diener" and adds, "That's a new one on me. I thought I knew all the ethnics, but I ain't never heard of a diener before."

Ethnics and displaced persons are creatures of the real or human world. At the same time, *The Dragons of Babel* is even more packed with non-human varieties than its predecessor. Will is accompanied by a strange child who proves to be – as he is warned by a centaur sergeant – a luck-eater. In the

---

10 These are major aspects of a Swanwick story not subsumed into his two 'dragon' novels, 'The Bordello in Faërie', referenced in note 1 above. Here a human boy visits an elvish brothel, only to find that he becomes not a customer but a sex-worker. He is paid in fairy gold, but it turns into trash. The experience of sex with the brothel clients makes human females uninteresting to him. Keats's poem about a deserted human lover is quoted in one scene in *The Iron Dragon's Daughter*.

underground world of "Lord Weary's Empire" Will duels a wodewose, and inherits the wodewose's consort, who is a hulder, in Swanwick's world a kind of bovine female. Wodewoses were brought back into general knowledge by Tolkien, in *The Lord of the Rings*, but hulders are a much less familiar import from Scandinavian folklore.

Another short story subsumed into *The Dragons of Babel*, 'A Small Room in Koboldtown',[11] is a classic locked-room murder mystery, in which a boggart is found dead with his heart torn out. It seems the murder can only have been committed by a haint, who can pass through walls, but Will succeeds, much to the relief of Toussaint's haint community, in showing that the haint has been framed: the story turns on the unknown properties of boggarts. All through, the controlling character of the novel, rather like Jane's dragon, is Will's mentor the con-man Nat Whilk. His name is a transliteration of the Anglo-Saxon phrase found in *Beowulf*, *nat hwylc*, literally, 'I don't know which', and that is the overall impression of Swanwick's fantasy world – kept up with a range of detail and of imagination to which no paraphrase can do justice. Should our expectations be those of the real world or the fantasy world? One never knows which.

One can see, then, why some have described 'Industrialised Faërie' as 'anti-fantasy'. It never settles down to the increasingly conventional set of fantasy tropes given new life and made hegemonic by Tolkien, and all too readily imitable. Nevertheless it is also in many respects squarely in the tradition of twentieth-century fantasy. A simple pro/con opposition is in no way satisfactory as a description.

I would suggest that a better way of considering its methods and effects is to note that in all fantasy there is a potential three-way relationship. On the one hand there is the reader, with expectations formed by the real world, allusions to which can readily be recognised (malls, shoplifters, DP camps, ambitious politicians etc.). All fantasies meanwhile must create a fantasy world, each one in its way original – if tending increasingly to share features, and indeed to

---

11 Also reprinted in *The Dog Said Bow-Wow*.

become conventional, just because of the shared experience in fantasy of readers and writers.

The two worlds, however, inevitably create a running process of comparison in the mind of the reader, who has to understand what is strange and fantastic, but also has to be persuaded that the fantastic has some kind of rationality, or plausibility, a reality of its own. A vital third factor, accordingly, in many if not all fantasies (and especially 'worlds where magic works'), is what one might call the 'focus character', through whom understanding is mediated, and who acts, in one way or another, as a kind of prompt for the reader engaged in the vital task of comparing and contrasting real and fantasy worlds.

The simplest strategy – which also offers least in the way of helpful prompting, and relies most on the reader's awareness – is to tell the story from the viewpoint of an inhabitant of the fantasy world. (In Farah Mendlesohn's terms, these are 'immersive fantasies'.)[12] A good example is Poul Anderson's story sequence *Operation Chaos* (1971). Here the focus character is also the I-narrator, and is a werewolf. He is telling the story of a military campaign, in a straightforward 'this is what happened to me' fashion. But in this campaign air cover is provided by broomsticks, the cavalry ride unicorns (the riders being necessarily virgins), the armoured corps consists of dragons, and as a werewolf the role of the narrator is to act as scout. The underlying parallel, confirmed by many further details, is magic = science, and the explanation for the re-appearance of magic in a modern world is the discovery of a process for "degauss[ing] cold iron" – degaussing being a genuine technique developed in World War II to shield iron ships from the threat of magnetic mines. Anderson relies on the reader being able to pick out the fantasy details set into an apparently real-world frame, and assemble them (largely unconsciously) into a logical and rule-bound scenario. This, one may say, is the characteristic activity of the reader of modern fantasy, and even more so of the reader of its sister-genre, modern science fiction.

Nevertheless the Anderson or 'immersive' strategy demands quite a lot of the reader. A popular and alternative strategy is accordingly to make the 'focus

---

12 See Farah Mendlesohn, *Rhetorics of Fantasy* (2008).

character', not an inhabitant of the fantasy world, but a normal human being transported *into* the fantasy world, and learning its rules and its nature as he or she goes along – taking the reader's understanding with them, and counterfeiting the reader's surprise. In Mendlesohn's terms again, these are 'portal-quest' fantasies, an extreme example being C.S. Lewis's *The Lion, the Witch and the Wardrobe*, in which the children go through the wardrobe into a world which is strange and marvellous. This is also the method of de Camp and Pratt's influential 'Incomplete Enchanter' sequence, in which the focus character is trying to understand 'how magic works' in the light of the rational or scientific knowledge shared by focus character and reader: in this sequence the reader is led on a kind of voyage of discovery. More modern examples would include Stephen Donaldson's 'Chronicles of Thomas Covenant' sequence, in which the focus character's misunderstanding of the nature of the fantasy world becomes a major part of the story; as also J.K. Rowling's 'Harry Potter' stories, in which Harry of course ought to have been an inhabitant of the magical world (and takes to it as to the manner born), but has nevertheless to begin with been trapped among the 'muggles'.

Both 'immersive' and 'portal' fantasies nevertheless share a problem, for which writers of science fiction (many of them also writers of fantasy) have developed several strategies. This is simply the problem of conveying information without delaying narrative. One solution in fantasy is to have a focus character who is a denizen of the fantasy world, but who (on one pretext or another) takes on the role of instructing the reader overtly in the nature of that world: in Randall Garrett's 'Lord Darcy' sequence the role is given to Master Sean, the Irish sorcerer, who explains his magical procedures as he goes along to other less-knowledgeable characters in the fantasy world. In the case of *The Hobbit*, Bilbo is again a denizen of the fantasy world, but one who knows almost nothing about it, apart from his highly English-normal environment of the Shire. *The Hobbit*, one might say, is an 'immersive' fantasy to its readers, but something like a 'portal-quest' to its hero. Bilbo is instructed by the dwarves and by Gandalf, growing in knowledge (and moral stature) as he too goes along: the gap between Bilbo's knowledge, the reader's knowledge, and the world Bilbo lives in is comically exposed by Tolkien's off-hand remark, "for trolls, as you probably know, must be underground before dawn", or they turn back to the stone they are made of.[13]

Swanwick's case is interestingly different. In essence he uses a variant of the immersive strategy, plunging the reader into the fantasy world and relying on the reader to see both the real-world similarities (factory workers, supervisors, lunch carts, storemen, yellow order-slips, etc.) and the many differences (such as the Time Clock). The reader is moreover plunged into the fantasy world much sooner and much deeper than is the case with Bilbo, or Frodo, who start from the relatively normal world of the Shire, or de Camp and Pratt's very American focus characters entering the fantasy world through their portal. Swanwick's focus characters, Jane and Will, are in tune with their world from the beginning and the reader follows the story through their understanding.

Nevertheless, Jane is a changeling, at some point in her past brought into Faërie through a portal which still exists and through which she will eventually return. Will too is a half-human. While both, then, are denizens of the fantasy world, Jane in particular, as Mendlesohn (162) says, "acts simultaneously as a knowing and as an ignorant protagonist". Her flashes of vision or memory sharpen the contrast with the real world from which she has been abducted, and increase the sense of dismay and deprivation: Swanwick's is a much darker and less comic scenario than Anderson's, or even Rowling's. Moreover the reader is not entirely without guidance or prompting, for Swanwick makes heavy use of folklore motifs which (at least for readers of fantasy) are fairly common knowledge – cold iron, true names, time stasis, elvish glamour, wicker queens, fairy gold, etc. – as well as the entire *dramatis personae* of folklore, listed and used by many authors including the encyclopaedic Michael Denham.

There is then a constant negotiation between real-world background, understood by the reader; folklore background, also quite likely understood by the reader; the fantasy world as understood and explored by the focus characters; and even the real world as glimpsed, occasionally and in vision, by the focus char-

---

13 Swanwick remembered Tolkien's trolls. In one scene in *The Dragons of Babel* a character repeats Strider's words in *The Lord of the Rings*, "Get up, old stone", and breaks a stick on a stone, which then stirs to life.

acters. Many details, like the ruby needed for laser guidance (is it a microchip?), or the clean-up squad "in orange environmental suits" after the accident that kills Rooster (are they checking for radioactivity?), bring the two worlds into close contact – of course, in the reader's mind alone.

Reading Swanwick, then, is an experience of continuous and unpredictable contrasts and comparisons, not at all different in nature from the experience of reading modern fantasy and science fiction,[14] but certainly different in both quantity of detail and quality of unexpectedness.

Darko Suvin famously declared that science fiction was the literature of "cognitive estrangement"[15] – understanding that matters in science fiction are not as you have always understood them in fact – and it is this technique which Michael Swanwick has imported and raised to a higher power than any other author of fantasy. It is this which makes reading him such a uniquely rewarding experience.

About the Author

TOM SHIPPEY is Professor Emeritus of Saint Louis University, Missouri. His books include *J.R.R. Tolkien: Author of the Century* (2001), *The Road to Middle-earth* (4th revised edition 2004), *Roots and Branches: Selected Papers on Tolkien* (2007), *Hard Reading: Learning from Science Fiction* (2016), and *Laughing Shall I Die: Lives and Deaths fo the Great Vikings* (2018).

Bibliography

ANONYMOUS. 'Tam Lin.' (ballad) http://tam-lin.org/versions/39A.html (accessed 13th November, 2017).

CLUTE, John, and John GRANT (eds.). *The Encyclopaedia of Fantasy*. London: Orbit, 1997.

GRAVES, Robert. *The White Goddess: a Historical Grammar of Poetic Myth*. London: Faber and Faber, 1948.

HARDY, James (ed.). *The Denham Tracts*. London: Folklore Society, 1895.

---

14 Which thus negates the rather simplistic 'anti-fantasy' claim.
15 Darko Suvin, *Metamorphoses of Science Fiction*, 7-8.

MENDELSOHN, Farah. *Rhetorics of Fantasy*. Middletown, CT: Wesleyan University Press, 2008.

SHIPPEY, Tom. 'The Ancestors of the Hobbits: Strange Creatures in English Folklore.' *Lembas-extra* 2011. Ed. Cecile van Zon (Tolkien Genootschap Unquendor), 97-106. See also academia.edu.

'Learning to Read Science Fiction.' *Hard Reading*. Liverpool: Liverpool University Press, 2016. 1-23.

'The Golden Bough and the Incorporation of Magic.' *Hard Reading*. Liverpool: Liverpool University Press, 2016. 162-81.

SUVIN, Darko. *Metamorphoses of Science Fiction: On the Poetics and History of a Literary Genre*. New Haven, CT: Yale University Press, 1979.

SWANWICK, Michael. *The Iron Dragon's Daughter*. London: Millennium, 1993.

The Dragons of Babel. New York: TOR, 2007.

'The Bordello in Faërie.' *The Dog Said Bow-Wow*. San Francisco: Tachyon, 2007. 179-200.

'A Small Room in Koboldtown.' *The Dog Said Bow-Wow*. San Francisco: Tachyon, 2007. 249-62.

'The Changeling's Tale.' *Tales of Old Earth*. Berkeley, CA: Frog Ltd., 2000. 218-35.

'The Armies of Elfland.' With Eileen GUNN (2014). http://www.lightspeed-magazine.com/fiction (accessed 13th November 2017).

'The Literary Alchemist.' An interview with Nick GEVERS. http://www.infinity-plus.co.uk/nonfiction/intms.htm (accessed 13th November 2017).

Łukasz Neubauer

Absence of gods vs. Absence of God: The Spiritual Landscapes of J.R.R. Tolkien's Middle-earth and George R.R. Martin's Westeros

Abstract

At first glance, the worlds (sub)created by Tolkien and Martin may seem to have a number of crucial features in common. Both are meticulously crafted, with various, often deeply incompatible, layers of cultural identity and ethics (Gondor vs Mordor, Starks vs Lannisters etc.). Likewise, despite sometimes markedly different approaches in their worldbuilding strategies, the writers' indebtedness to medieval literature, history and values has been repeatedly examined by many a scholar, providing fertile grounds for cross-cultural explorations and evaluations. There are, however, certain vital, perhaps even fundamental, issues where the worlds of *The Lord of the Rings* and *A Song of Ice and Fire* are as distinct from one another as the proverbial chalk and cheese. One such issue – clearly discernible to every Christian (or, at least, Christian-raised) reader of Tolkien – is the intriguing spiritual disparity between the characters living in Middle-earth and those that inhabit Martin's Westeros. The world of the former is almost practically devoid of any explicit manifestations of the divine (at the time of its first publication the readers were not yet aware of the (pre) existence of Eru Illúvatar), yet, at the same time, it is suffused with numerous Christian values and underpinnings which cannot be ignored if one seeks to get a fuller (and thus more meaningful) picture of Tolkien's fiction. The latter, on the other hand, appears to be resplendent with all sorts of gods – greater and lesser, "real" and imaginary, more or less merciful and forgiving – yet in the long run it fails (in most cases it seems to fail all along the line) to even partly comply with the Christian (or, as for that matter, any religion-based) ethics, perhaps in some ways implying that all religions (or theologically-based systems of beliefs) are equal, and therefore equally false (or, at least, uncertain) in their nature and moral direction. The following paper seeks to examine some of these differences, juxtaposing Tolkien's Catholic worldview with that of evidently agnostic (or even atheist) Martin.

Despite the fact that, over the past two decades or so, the genre of fantasy has enjoyed a substantial resurgence of interest amongst the readers,[1] and, consequently, captured the critical attention of literary scholars, thus leading

---

[1] Here, the word 'readers' encompasses, by extension, both the people who read fantasy novels and short stories and those who come into contact with the genre by means their various cinematic and televisual adaptations (as well as, less frequently, the original productions in the fantasy field).

to its more systematic study as an autonomous branch of speculative fiction, it seems that – with all due respect to the writers like J.K. Rowling, Andrzej Sapkowski and the late Ursula K. Le Guin – there are nowadays primarily two names that electrify the visitors of subcreated realities all over the world to a far greater extent than those of other writers in the fantasy field. These are obviously the names of John Ronald Reuel Tolkien (1892-1973) and George Raymond Richard Martin (b. 1948), the creators of fictional worlds of, respectively, Middle-earth and Westeros.[2] Needless to say, each has his own dedicated groups of enthusiasts, some of them enjoying the works of both writers, some preferring the books of either one or the other. Finally, there are also those who only read the narratives penned by Tolkien and, on various grounds, reject (or at least disregard) the stories written by Martin (and the other way round).

Be it as it may, it cannot obviously be denied that the author of *A Song of Ice and Fire* series is, in some ways at least, noticeably indebted to his English counterpart (and, perhaps indirectly, any contemporary writer that is believed to have inspired Tolkien in his literary endeavours).[3] Indeed, it appears that, to a certain degree, in the wake of the first wave of popularity that *The Lord of the Rings* enjoyed in the late 1950s and in the 1960s, an overwhelming majority of modern fantasy writers born in the second half of the twentieth century (or somewhere around that time) are Tolkien's literary heirs. Sure enough, he might not always be their foremost source of inspiration – Martin, for instance, regularly alludes to the French novelist Maurice Druon and his book series *Les Rois maudits* "The Accursed Kings" (1955-77) as a highly significant afflatus for his own writings (Johnston and Battis 5)[4] – nevertheless, Tolkien's impact upon the fantasy genre is enormous (even when it cannot always be objectively assessed with any quantifiable accuracy), from C.S. Lewis's *The Chronicles of Narnia* to George R.R. Martin's *A Song of Ice and Fire* (and its televisual adaptation).

---

2 Although the plot of Martin's *A Song of Ice and Fire* and, consequently, HBO's *Game of Thrones* is actually set in two fictional continents of Westeros and Essos, it is the former that is in fact the focus of most of the action in the series.
3 Some of the most notable non-medieval writers whose works in some way inspired the author of *The Lord of the Rings* include, amongst others, William Morris, Lord Dunsany and George MacDonald.
4 Not without reasons, factual as well as commercial, are the latest paperback French editions of Druon's novels published with the following incentive from George R.R. Martin on the cover: "Si vous aimez *Game of Thrones*, vous adorerez *Les Rois maudits*". Not surprisingly, analogous encouragements may also be found on the novels' translations into other languages.

That there are certain similarities between, say, *The Lord of the Rings* and *A Song of Ice and Fire* is, of course, self-evident and does not call for much further elaboration. Suffice it to say, with some level of terminological flexibility, both Tolkien and Martin could be classified as writers of high fantasy (regardless of whatever this now well-worn term actually means). Both happen to be authors of immense creativity, each of them having published (in the case of the former, also posthumously) a substantial body of work. Tolkien's writings thus include: academic papers, scholarly editions, translations and adaptations of various medieval texts, original mythological narratives, short stories and novellas (some of them initially written with the writer's own children in mind), poems (both lyric and narrative), novels, book illustrations and maps as well as personal correspondence. When it comes to Martin, the list comprises: novels, novellas, novelettes and short story collections in the numerous subgenres of speculative fiction, film and television scripts, companion books (*The World of Ice and Fire* and forthcoming *Fire and Blood*) as well as blog entries. Worth noting are also the truly epic proportions of their best known publications, respectively, *The Lord of the Rings* and *A Song of Ice and Fire*,[5] and the fact that in their writing both authors are well known to have drawn extensively upon the cultural and historical heritage of the Middle Ages. Perhaps just as complex and multi-faceted (but not quite similar in their literary execution) are also their approaches to character- and, in particular, world-building (whither we shall soon turn our attention).

It appears, however, that at least some of these similarities are in reality no more than purely superficial resemblances. Their respective 'high fantasies' of Middle-earth and Westeros are almost entirely different. The works of Tolkien are invariably characterised by Christian-inspired idealism and morality, while those of Martin may be described as 'grimdark', and thus considerably more

---

5 Depending on the font style and size, the former, is normally more than a thousand pages long (1,031 in the standard, three-volume hardback HarperCollins edition, 1,178 with the appendices and indices). The latter currently spans over five full-length novels (two more books are yet to be published), in which the total amount of pages well exceeds 4,500 (4,671 in the popular paperback editions from HarperVoyager; likewise, without the appendices). Given such proportions, it is no surprise that it took Tolkien as many as twelve years (from 1937 until 1949) to write his masterpiece and six more to have it published. In the case of Martin's series, the matter is a bit more complicated. To begin with, it took him about five years to write the first novel, *A Game of Thrones* (1996). Since then, his writing pace has been rather uneven. All in all, up till now, more than two decades have elapsed and there are still two more books in the series to be published.

violent and, for the most part, amoral in their ethical stance. Notably dissimilar seems also their above-mentioned indebtedness to the historical tradition. In the case of Tolkien, it is more (but not solely) the literary legacy of the Middle Ages.[6] Martin, on the other hand, appears to be more inspired by some specific historical events and their often complex political implications.[7] Moreover, both writers clearly elaborate, albeit in a different way, upon certain general notions traditionally associated with the medieval period (heroism, chivalry, courtly love etc.). Last but not least, quite contrasting are also their world-building techniques and resources, with Tolkien's Middle-earth narratives being evidently much more *logos*-centred and those of Martin sometimes image-inspired.[8]

One of the biggest differences in their creative efforts, one that stems not only from their almost totally dissimilar approaches to religion and world-building techniques, is the spiritual landscape of Tolkien's Middle-earth and Martin's Westeros. Tolkien was of course a practising and deeply committed Catholic, while the author of *A Song of Ice and Fire*, despite his upbringing and early education,[9] could perhaps, at best, be described, in his own words, as a "lapsed"[10] one. For Tolkien, the Christian faith permeated practically all the spheres of his life, familial, professional as well as social. For Martin, it appears to be fascinating solely in the cultural sense, i.e. when Martin decides to creatively exploit some of its components in order to somehow 'authenticate' his vision of the spiritual practices in Westeros. Consequently, *The Lord of the Rings*, Tolkien's greatest and best-known book, is, as the author himself described it in a letter to Father Robert Murray SJ, "a fundamentally religious and Catholic work; unconsciously so at first, but consciously in the revision" (*Letters* 172), whereas Martin's still-ongoing masterpiece, *A Song of Ice and Fire*, is not only a work

---

6   Well known is Tolkien's indebtedness to such works as *Beowulf*, the *Eddas*, some Arthurian romances, the *Kalevala* etc.
7   Arguably, his best acknowledged source of historical inspiration is the series of fifteenth-century English civil wars, commonly known as the War of the Roses, between the two branches of the Plantagenet dynasty, the House of Lancaster and the House of York.
8   In his 2014 interview for the Rolling Stone magazine, Martin claims that the landmark scene in which the direwolf pups are found in the snow (*A Game of Thrones* 14-18) came to him when he was working on a science-fiction novel called *Avalon*. The vision was so "strong and vivid" that he instantly knew he "had to write it" (https://www.rollingstone.com/tv/news/george-r-r-martin-the-rolling-stone-interview-20140423).
9   http://www.georgerrmartin.com/about-george/life-and-times/bayonne/
10 http://www.ew.com/article/2011/07/12/george-martin-talks-a-dance-with-dragons/

of a self-proclaimed atheist (or agnostic),[11] but also, despite the rather clear-cut contrast between the ultimate evil (in the form of the demonic Others) and those who wish to restore the pre-brumal order, a rather dispiriting vision of the world in which nihilism, Machiavellian cynicism, scepticism and the feelings of irreparable decay seem to walk hand in hand.

Paradoxically, given, on the one hand, the evident, if not always immediately perceptible, Christian substratum of *The Lord of the Rings*[12] and, on the other, the often skin-deep religiosity and misuse of religious symbolism in *A Song of Ice and Fire*, there are noticeably more explicit references to all sorts of spiritual and cultic practices in Martin's series than there are in all the literary works ever penned by Tolkien combined. In fact, while there are innumerable allusions to the so-called "old gods" or "the Seven Who are One" in the novels of Martin – in some cases replete with much revealing details concerning the complexities of their ceremonial traditions, including a wedding (e.g. in *A Storm of Swords* 382-94, where Tyrion Lannister espouses Sansa Stark), a funeral (likewise in *A Storm of Swords* 474-77, where the body of Lord Hoster Tully is sent down the Red Fork river in a funeral boat) and an individual prayer (e.g. in *A Clash of Kings* 449-52, where we see Catelyn Stark pray to the Seven in an abandoned village sept) – there is, surprisingly or not, very little on the subjects of faith and some forms of institutionalised worship to be found in *The Lord of the Rings* (or, as a matter of fact, any literary composition that emerged from Tolkien's pen). The reason for this is, however, quite plainly explicated in the above-mentioned letter to Father Robert Murray SJ. In Tolkien's own words, "I have not put in, or have cut out, practically all references to anything like 'religion', to cults or practices, in the imaginary world. For the religious element is absorbed into the story and the symbolism" (*Letters* 172). That is to say, Tolkien felt no need to duplicate the spiritual landscape of our own world and translate the particulars of our Salvation onto the subcreated reality of his Middle-earth, where it would obviously have no historical justification. Not

---

11 http://www.ew.com/article/2011/07/12/george-martin-talks-a-dance-with-dragons/
12 Since the publication of *The Lord of the Rings* in 1954-55 much has been written about its numerous Christian undercurrents and subtleties. A good and detailed, if not always entirely convincing, examination of the Christian substratum in Tolkien's best-known work may be found in Fleming Rutledge's book *The Battle for Middle-earth. Tolkien's Divine Design in The Lord of the Rings*.

surprisingly, as an atheist (or agnostic), the author of *A Song of Ice and Fire* would not be bothered by any such considerations.

Monotheism, henotheism or polytheism?

Naturally, no examination of the spiritual fabrics that have been so dexterously woven into the subcreated canvases of Middle-earth and Westeros would ever be complete without a prior attempt to determine which models of theism are to be found in the respective worlds. Are the numerous peoples populating Tolkien's and Martin's books monotheistic or polytheistic? Or, perhaps, some form of henotheism[13] should be taken into consideration, especially in the case of the colourful spiritual mosaic of *A Song of Ice and Fire*? Is the existence of two entirely different (and mutually hostile) ethical perspectives in the world of *The Lord of the Rings* a valid piece of evidence for Tolkien's novel to be examined as being duotheistic? And, finally, does the spiritual landscape of Martin's Westeros in any way resemble that of (early) medieval Europe, where, up to a point (i.e. until the advent of Christianity), numerous peoples lived side-by-side, worshipping different (but not always entirely dissimilar) deities?[14] Or is it, perhaps, in any way comparable to that of Ancient Greece, where, despite the fact that the majority of people believed (or not) in the existence of several gods and goddesses, some monotheistic tendencies could already be sensed in the teachings of certain notable philosophers, including Thales of Miletus, Socrates, Plato and Aristotle.

There could be no doubt whatsoever that the worlds of Tolkien's imagination, whether that be *The Lord of the Rings* or any other, not necessarily Middle-earth-based, narrative, are essentially monotheistic, even if the Supreme Being is not always as indisputably identified as in *The Silmarillion* or the oft-quoted letter to Father Robert Murray SJ (both obviously unpublished before Tolkien's death, and thus unknown to the readers prior to, respectively,

---

13 Henotheism means the devotion to and worship of only one god, without, however, rejecting a possibility of the existence of other deities.
14 Some reverberations of that may be seen in the way that the Faith of the Seven gradually expanded its territorial reach in Westeros.

1977 and 1981).[15] Of course, leaving aside some thinly disguised allusions to a divine scheme that happens to cohere with the ways of God, there is absolutely no mention of Eru Ilúvatar in the story of the One Ring.[16] However, it is rather clearly visible in *The Lord of the Rings* that, notwithstanding the indubitable differences which inevitably exist between the numerous peoples of Middle-earth (ethnic, cultural, linguistic or other), the ethical principles they seem to hold, particularly in the face of the common danger, are practically unanimous. Consequently, it may be inferred that the notion of some universal and morally approvable conduct, stemming, perhaps, from some Higher Being (as yet unidentified by the reader), was not in the least unknown to the Elves, Ents, Dwarves, Hobbits and Men.

As for the possible duotheistic interpretations of the spiritual landscape of Tolkien's Middle-earth,[17] there is very little evidence to posit that, regardless of his undiminished spirit[18] and supernatural powers, the Dark Lord should be interpreted as a fallen, but nonetheless authentic, deity. True enough, the practically blind obedience to the malevolent authority of Sauron (and, before him, that of his predecessor Morgoth) might seem to bear certain features of, on the one hand, mind-control and, on the other, well-nigh cultic practices.[19] Moreover, the Dark Lord has, of course, an enormous, supernatural, potential to do evil; a potential he incessantly exercises in a frantic effort to recover his lost Ring. However, at the same time, he has a limited ability to

---

15 In it, the author of *The Lord of the Rings* explicitly states, "There is only one 'god': God, *Eru Ilúvatar*" (*Letters* 205).
16 At the time of the original publication of *The Lord of the Rings*, the character of Eru Ilúvatar, whose names in Quenya quite appropriately translate as "The One", "He that is Alone" (*Silmarillion* 303) and "Father of All" (310), was not yet known to the general public. However, by 1956, i.e. within a year of the publication of *The Return of the King*, Tolkien had already referred to Him in his letters (or existing letter drafts) to Milton Waldman (*Letters* 131), Father Robert Murray SJ (156), Michael Straight (181) and W.H. Auden (183).
17 The terms "Ilúvatarism" and "Sauronism" may sometimes be spotted in the various forums of internet discourse. It appears, though, that they are, in fact, no more than just terms of convenience which should not be used in any serious academic discussion concerning the spiritual landscape of Tolkien's subcreated world.
18 Once the Ring of Power had been taken from him by Isildur, Sauron's physical body vanished "and his spirit fled far away and hid in waste places; and he took no visible shape again for many long years" (*Silmarillion* 272).
19 The Black Númenóreans, for instance, are said to have "worshipped [Sauron], being enamoured of evil knowledge" (*LotR* 888). The actual nature of this worship is not specified in *The Lord of the Rings*, nevertheless the evident fanaticism exemplified by, for instance, the so-called Mouth of Sauron seems to point to their excessive adoration, bordering on genuine idolatry of the Dark Lord.

conceive entirely new forms,[20] the majority of his 'creations' being merely perversions and deformations of the already existing creatures and things. Consequently, remaining, in fact, subject to the laws of Ilúvatar, the Supreme Being of Tolkien's subcreated world, Sauron is certainly not a god, but, rather, a Satan-like figure whose ultimate fall, as in Christian theology, is, fortunately, only a question of time.[21]

In contrast to Tolkien's Middle-earth, the world portrayed in Martin's *A Song of Ice and Fire* could only be described as being polytheistic, although its polytheism certainly begs a number of vital questions that need to be answered prior to any further examination of the belief systems in Westeros. On the whole, the term 'polytheism' refers to the belief in and worship of multiple gods and/or goddesses. This means that a certain group of people could venerate a number of deities, some of whom, like Dagon, Marduk, Zeus or Odin, are likely to enjoy a noticeably higher status than the other gods in their respective cultures. Consequently, a tenth-century inhabitant of, say, Norway, Sweden or Iceland could consider the last of the aforementioned deities to be the supreme god of the local pantheon, but this would not in any way prevent him/her from invoking the aid of other divinities (such as Thor or Freya) if such were his/her immediate need. 'Polytheistic' (although in a much broader sense of that word) could also be the worlds in which various peoples of different faiths and denominations – mono- as well as polytheistic – live side by side, much as was the case with the early civilisations of the Fertile Crescent or the pre-Christian inhabitants of the Mediterranean.

In Martin's novels, the colourful amalgamation of various religious systems, those in which venerated are, in particular, the nameless old gods of the North, the "Seven Who Are One" of the Seven Kingdoms, the primarily Essosian Lord of

---

20 The last of the Rings of Power, the Ruling Ring he secretly forged in the fires of Mount Doom, can, of course, be hardly referred to as a 'new form'. It is, after all, but the last, albeit the most powerful one, of the rings which, it appears, Sauron could not have created (or caused to be created) without the assistance of the Elvish smiths from Eregion.

21 Tolkien does admit, in the published draft of his letter to Father Robert Murray SJ, that Sauron is "of course a 'divine' person" (*Letters* 205), but he then immediately clarifies his meaning by explaining that in this particular case the word 'divine' should be understood in a purely mythological sense. The Dark Lord was, after all, "a lesser member of the race of Valar" (205).

Light and the Drowned god[22] of the Iron Islands, provides a good example of numerous mono- and polytheistic cultures living side-by-side. Sometimes tolerant and sometimes noticeably unreceptive to any form of spiritual competition, they regularly clash with the adherents of the other faiths (although these do not always seem to be too zealous about their own religious convictions). Yet, while there are not any serious international or intertribal conflicts over the matters of faith (most of the discords that arise in Martin's novels are brought about by the unceasing lust for political power, the titular "Game of Thrones"), there are at least a few passages where the question of one's spiritual identity, even indirectly, appears to be of major concern to the conflicted sides, particularly when religion is embraced as "a source of legitimacy to gain power and to support [political and territorial] claims" (de Ramón Ruiz 41).[23]

The distinguishing characteristics of Westerosian religions, their dogmatic conceptions and ritual observances, are not, unfortunately, outlined in any greater detail in the five novels that have been published to date. There are, of course, some scattered references and allusions to certain historical events that helped to shape the religious landscape of Westeros in the series' companion book *The World of Ice & Fire*,[24] It is, however, often by means of his point-of-view narration that Martin provides the reader with good, if not always exhaustive, images that illustrate some of the ritual particulars of the individual faiths, with such characters as Eddard Stark, his wife Catelyn, Melisandre and Balon Greyjoy, frequently (in some cases, up to the point of their death) acting as some sort of paragons of their respective religions.

---

[22] Throughout the series, Martin is somewhat inconsistent in his use of the capital (e.g. the Drowned God) and small case letters (e.g. the old gods) with regard to the deities mentioned in *A Song of Ice and Fire*. Perhaps contrary to his intentions (but in compliance with my own faith), I have decided not to capitalise the word *god* (hence, for instance, "the Drowned god") unless it is used in connection with the Christian/Hebrew God.

[23] One such example may be Stannis Baratheon's embracement of the Lord of Light, a clever political move (or so it initially seems) which comes to legitimise (at least in the pretender's own eyes) all his subsequent moves, including the military conquests, various court intrigues and outright assassinations he is known to have instigated.

[24] From the chapter on 'Ancient History', we learn, for instance, of the coming of the Andals, an ancient people who, under the leadership of one Hugor of the Hill, came to Westeros from northern Essos, having been erstwhile given a vision of a promised land by the Seven (*The World of Ice & Fire* 17).

The ultimate result of this – the depictions of particular faiths from various, often subjective points of view, the disturbing illustrations of certain dubious policies (e.g. the followers of the High Sparrow) and forbidding rituals (the Lord of Light and the Drowned god) etc. – is what, for the sake of terminological clarity, may be described as spiritual relativism, so increasingly common these days in the largely post-Christian world of, particularly but not exclusively, Western Europe and North America. In other words, with regard to the matters of faith, *A Song of Ice and Fire* appears to be characterised by the evidently postmodern (and, it should be added, not quite logical) assumption that one religion could be true for one inhabitant of Westeros, but does not necessarily have to be so for another. Consequently, the spiritual convictions in Martin's series often take the form of a solely cultural phenomenon by dint of which the reader may sometimes be led to believe that the religious practices and institutions of the Westerosian people have only been devised (perhaps by some power-seeking sages of old) and sustained (by the successive rulers who wished to maintain the religio-political status quo in their kingdoms) to somehow coordinate the lives of those who live in the Seven Kingdoms.

Despite the existence of some indefinable providential power that upholds at least some things in Westeros,[25] there seems to be no common ground, ethical or not, for Martin's gods, each deity (or group of deities) affecting the course of events for his/their own sake. In this, they are, therefore, more like the Greek gods in, for instance, Hesiod's *Theogony* and Homer's Trojan epics, where they are usually seen competing with one another, both for their Olympian supremacy and, perhaps most importantly, to have their anthropomorphic vanities satisfied with their worshippers' ritual sacrifices and offerings. Likewise, their Westerosian priests and priestesses as well as other adherents and devotees of the respective faiths often seem to believe only in

---

25 Perhaps the most apparent (and best remembered) example of some form of divine intervention (or so it seems) in Westeros is the aforementioned passage where, on the way back from the execution of Gared of the Night's Watch, Robb Stark comes across a body of a direwolf that must have been killed by a stag (*A Game of Thrones* 14-18). This, it appears, serves as a grim premonition foreshadowing the eventual fall of Houses Stark and Baratheon (the animals happen to be their sigils). However, whether this should actually be identified as the workings of the gods – old, new or other – is not yet known and, it seems, given the ambiguity of Martin's books, that the issue may never be unequivocally resolved.

the righteousness (but not necessarily the exclusive existence)²⁶ of their own god(s). Hence, they are sometimes rather negatively disposed towards the practitioners of other religions and, for that reason, may wish to have them eliminated or otherwise removed from the competitive range.²⁷ All in all, much as in real life, in Martin's novels faith could sometimes be the cause of some serious friction, particularly when the notions of the divine blessing, guidance and protection, notions that not only define the very essence of Christianity, but also seem to underlie the deep structure of *The Lord of the Rings*, are replaced by the somewhat anthropomorphised (and thus evidently un-deified) vision of covetous and cruel beings that, regardless of their actual existence, the people of Westeros choose to call their 'gods'.

The Nameless One vs. the named ones

Whether it be the monotheistic Judeo-Christian conception of God or the polytheistic heathen religions of the Mediterranean or Celto-Germano-Slavic Europe, there has always been in man a deep-seated yearning to name the One/ones that he believed in. This, of course, is the reason why, despite His definite declaration, הְיֶהָא רֶשָׁא הְיֶהָא "I am who I am" (Exodus 3:14), the God of Abraham, Isaak and Jacob ultimately came to be referred to by a great number of names and titles (as many as seven in Rabbinic Judaism;²⁸ even more, of course, in the Christian tradition),²⁹ including יְהֹוָה (Yahwe), םיהלא (Elohim) and יָנֹדְא (Adonai). Likewise, in the primitive beliefs of, say, early Germanic peoples, Óðinn (Odin), the principal god of the Norse pantheon came to be known under a great variety of names and descriptive titles (some of which

---

26 Cf., for instance, the not infrequent Westerosian oaths sworn "by the old gods and the new". Samwell Tarly also famously remarks, "The Seven have never answered my prayers. Perhaps the old gods will" (*A Game of Thrones* 499).
27 Of all the Westerosian belief systems only those who worship the old gods seem to be relatively tolerant towards the practitioners of other religions. All the others are, at least on certain occasions, known to sacrifice or otherwise supress their enemies, however, not necessarily upon strictly speaking religious grounds.
28 Seven is obviously the number of spiritual perfection, applicable only to God, both in Judaism and in Christianity.
29 It ought to be remembered, though, that, despite the fact that God's name is to be praised throughout the world (as it is professed in, for instance, Psalm 8:1), it must not be misused, which would be, of course, against the second commandment of the Decalogue (Exodus 20:7).

he was even believed to have used himself), such as, for instance, *Alfǫðr* "All-father", *Gangleri* "Wanderer" or *Hávi* "High one".

Naturally, in human affairs, first names, patronymics, family names, bynames, pseudonyms, titles etc. are used for a wide range of communicative functions, ranging from various interpersonal relationships (formal as well as informal) to certain referential purposes (all sorts of academic publications, indices etc.). By the same token, in the early beliefs of various polytheistic cultures different theonyms were used not only in connection with one specific deity (e.g. Odin), but also, understandably, with regard to the various gods and goddesses believed to have been connected with a multiplicity of aspects of life and death, and thus worshipped for different reasons and, quite often, in different places. These names (sometimes in varying forms) would then regularly appear in all sorts of works of mythological character, in verse as well as in prose,[30] where they could be used in various verbal interactions between the divine and human participants (interpersonal function) and to distinguish between these characters in the narrative passages (referential function). In other words, when it comes to the very onomastic layer of the World's numerous mythologies, the anthropomorphised gods and goddesses of pre-Christian beliefs and traditions are perhaps just as human as are the inhabitants of our own world, bearing idiosyncratic names (sometimes, in fact, defining the very scope of their territorial authority), identifying themselves with these appellations and using them in different interpersonal communications.

In contrast, notwithstanding the numerous theonyms by means of which the God of Abraham, Isaak and Jacob is referred to in the Judeo-Christian tradition, there is obviously no need for Him to be called by name. After all, no word in any human language or dialect – be it the Latin *Deus*, Greek Θεός, Hebrew םיהלא or English *God* (each or which happens to have undisputable pre-Christian or even pre-Judaic etymological roots) – could ever express, with any degree of accuracy, the genuine extent of the Lord's might and love for

---

[30] In skaldic poetry, for example, a substantial number of the so-called kennings (figurative compounds consisting of two or more words) relied heavily upon the poets' knowledge of the divine matter.

mankind.³¹ Consequently, it is perhaps fair to conclude that, both in in Judaism and in Christianity, God does not actually have what we could call a wholly idiosyncratic theonym.³² His 'name', Franz Rosenzweig argues, is therefore "utterly vocative [and] frees God from being a thing, or from needing to be called by another [name]" (Young 38).

Prior to the publication of *The Silmarillion* (1977), the Supreme Being of Tolkien's subcreated universe was, of course, neither named, nor even explicitly referred to.³³ The reason for this is rather obvious – the author of *The Lord of the Rings* did not really want to replicate the historically-determined roots and culturally embedded heritage of the Christian Faith, with all of its impact upon our identity. Unlike C.S. Lewis, who did not hesitate to portray the Messiah in his leonine Aslan, Tolkien chose not to allegorise, emblematise or otherwise turn into some functional reality, the accounts of Christ's nativity, crucifixion or resurrection. True enough, there are certain notable episodes in his narrative which evidently echo those of the Scripture. Nevertheless, rather than downright allegory, they should all be explored in the light of their evangelical applicability, evoking analogical (or, at least, roughly similar) emotions to those that might be felt during the reading of the Gospels.

This does not obviously mean that there is no God in Middle-earth. In the 1940s and early 1950s, i.e. when he was still in the process of writing or correcting of what would become his magnum opus, Tolkien was perfectly aware of the fact that his mythology, modelled, of course, predominantly upon the Judeo-Christian vision of the world, was not yet fully developed and, at least at that time, would not yet be of much relevance to the readers of *The Lord of the Rings*. Hence, no matter what the circumstances, none of its characters, from the High Elves of Lothlórien to the most common Hobbits of the Shire, ever speaks of or otherwise unequivocally refers to, Eru, the One, and His

---

31 See, for instance, The Book of Revelation, where, regardless of the authorship question, John the Apostle clearly finds no words good enough to describe the One he sees sitting on the throne (4:2-3).
32 Nor does He ever use one, the אֱלֹהִים (*Elohim*) of Genesis (1:1), אֵל שַׁדַּי (*El Shaddai*) of Genesis (17:1) or Α και Ω "Alpha and Omega" of the Book of Revelation (1:8 ff.) being, in fact, no more than descriptive bynames which God decides to use in order to describe Himself to man.
33 See, however, the aforementioned letters to Milton Waldman, Father Robert Murray SJ, Michael Straight and W.H. Auden.

numerous creations. Nor is there in Tolkien's book even the slightest explicit mention of the ultimate purpose of Ilúvatar's divine design for the peoples of Middle-earth.

In fact, in Middle-earth the One is never even referred to as a personified entity (and so, of course, cannot be named), embodied in some anthropomorphised form, incarnate in the flesh of elvish, human or other frame. On the contrary, as Tolkien himself explains in a letter to his son Christopher, regardless of what we do and where we are, God is always "behind us, supporting, nourishing us" (*Letters* 66), even at times when we cannot tangibly sense His actual presence. No doubt, the same rule applies to the world of *The Lord of the Rings*, where His not infrequent interferences and blessings are always so subtle and indirect that they may sometimes be easily overlooked, ignored or even taken – by the characters as well as the readers – for no more than just pure 'chance'.[34]

Tolkien may have disliked allegory (though he sometimes used it in his academic publications),[35] but even more, it seems, he disliked all explicitness in the use of Christian themes, symbols and motifs.[36] The religious element, be it the beliefs or practices of the characters that appear in *The Lord of the Rings*, is, he argues in the aforementioned correspondence with Father Robert Murray SJ, thoroughly "absorbed into the story and [its] symbolism" (*Letters* 172). It is but a natural consequence, then, that there are to be found in his Middle-earth neither images (or, alternatively, other representations) of a personified God-figure (*sensu stricto*), nor, for the most part, some anthropomorphised

---

34 Cf., especially, the words of Tom Bombadil and Elrond, for whom the common noun 'chance' evidently broadens its semantic horizons. The former famously remarks, once he has rescued the hobbits caught by the spell of Old Man Willow, "Just chance brought me then, if chance you call it. It was no plan of mine, though I was waiting for you" (*LotR* 126). The latter just as famously addresses the council assembled at Rivendell, saying "You have come and are here met, in this very nick of time, by chance as it may seem. Yet it is not so." (242). In each case, of course, both Tom Bombadil and Elrond (as well as, indirectly, Tolkien himself) clearly wink at their respective audiences (and, metatextually, the readers of *The Lord of the Rings*), clearly implying that the said "chance" is but a cleaver terminological disguise for the workings of God.
35 Cf., in particular, his correspondence with Milton Waldman, where Tolkien, nonetheless admits that "any attempt to explain the purport of myth or fairytale must use allegorical language" (*Letters* 145). After 1955, the author of *The Lord of the Rings* often had to deny any allegorical – moral, political, or contemporary (232) – intent and meaning behind his work.
36 He sometimes criticised C.S. Lewis for his direct – too direct, in Tolkien's view – references to the Christian faith in *The Chronicles of Narnia*.

god-like figures (*sensu lato*) in the mould of Homeric, Hesiodic or other mythological beings of divine status and aspirations.[37] Scattered throughout the three volumes of Tolkien's masterpiece, we find imprecise colourings and half-hinted subtleties that point to the existence of some roughly defined celestial scheme. They are, no doubt, what the author expected to be entirely sufficient for the reader to realise that, even if unnamed, there must be more than meets the eye in his subcreated world and that there is, in effect, some greater Force in operation behind the mundane reality of Middle-earth.[38]

Here again, the question of theonymy (i.e. gods' names) is where Martin's narratives differ on quite a number of issues from Tolkien's *The Lord of the Rings*. As has been observed, in *A Song of Ice and Fire* the gods are usually referred to not only by means of their personal names (e.g. R'hllor, Mother Rhoyne), but also by (in some cases more than one) descriptive bynames (the "Lord of Light", "He Who Dwells Beneath the Waves", the "Seven Who Are One").[39] It is not, unfortunately, possible to say anything about the former group of theonyms,[40] the latter, however, notwithstanding the author's actual intentions, offers us a truly valuable insight into the character of Martin's deities.

Being, at least in some way, onomastically or connotatively, restricted to the confines of their territorial and/or elemental authority (water and fire, north and south), the gods of Westeros appear to be more like the primeval spirits of "forest, stream and stone" (*A Game of Thrones* 713), particularly the so-called 'old gods' who have been venerated for thousands of years in the sacred weirwoods of the North and beyond the Wall or, at best, the essentially place-bound

---

37 There are, of course, certain rare instances when the attentive reader may get a feeling that there are to be found in Tolkien's universe some greater and more powerful beings (such as Elbereth/Gilthoniel/Varda). It must be observed, though, that the identity of these remote figures could only be more or less clear to those who have previously read *The Silmarillion* (1977), and so their divine origin was not common knowledge for at least the first two decades after the original publication of *The Lord of the Rings* (1954-55).
38 For a detailed examination of the 'greater Force' in Tolkien's fiction, see, in particular, the two books which came out in 2003: Stratford Caldecott's *Secret Fire: The Spiritual Vision of J.R.R. Tolkien* and Matthew Dickerson's *Following Gandalf: Epic Battles and Moral Victory in The Lord of the Rings*. Some interesting thoughts on the matter of providence may also be found in Tom Shippey's *The Road to Middle-earth* (2005, 172-74, 426-68).
39 In numerous instances, of course, the gods are known by both, their personal and descriptive names, as in the case of R'hllor, the Lord of Light.
40 Unlike Tolkien, Martin does not seem to attach any greater significance to the actual meaning of names.

deities of pre-Christian Europe, such as, for instance, Poseidon/Neptune, the Greek/Roman god of the sea, usually imagined as living in a palace on the ocean floor, or Helios/Sol, the Greek/Roman personification of the Sun (here the Drowned god of the Iron Islands and the Lord of Light, worshipped in Essos and in some parts of the Seven Kingdoms, both of whom are limited in their divine activity to their 'natural habitats', should inevitably spring to mind). Even the Seven (or the 'new gods', as they may sometimes be referred to), a single deity with seven aspects – the Father, the Mother, the Warrior, the Smith, the Maid, the Crone and the Stranger[41] – who may, perhaps at first sight, give the appearance of being rather universal in his/her/their divine design, is/are in fact hard to conceptualise in terms of the quasi-Biblical monotheistic paradigm. Instead, unlike the three hypostases of the Holy Trinity, whose support and guidance could be invoked at practically anytime, by anyone and with any good intention in mind, a particular 'face' of the Seven (e.g. the Warrior) is not usually approached when some form of assistance is sought with regard to other aspects of life (e.g. farming, happiness in love, successful childbirth etc.) that are markedly different from the field in which this very 'face' operates or where he or she appears to be divinely competent.

To illustrate, when she is distressed over the safety of her sons, Robb, Bran and Rickon, Catelyn Stark resolves to plead the Mother to "spare them if [she] can" (*A Clash of Kings* 449-50).[42] Fearing for the safety and honour of her daughters, Sansa and Arya, however, she turns to the Maiden, imploring her to "lend [them] courage [and] guard them in their innocence" (451-52). Following that, Catelyn prays to the Father, "for justice, the strength to seek it and the wisdom to know it" (452), to the Warrior, "to keep Robb strong and shield him in his battles" (452) and, finally, to the Crone, so that she could "guide [her and] show [her] the path she must walk [...] in the dark

---

41 Carolyne Larrington correctly observes that, in terms of its aspect-wise distribution, the Westerosian faith of the Seven seems heavily indebted, at least in its conceptual dimensions, to the tripartite nature of the Holy Trinity (2016, 132-33). To this, one could also add some polycephalic gods of pre-Christian Europe (Janus, Triglav, Svantevit) and the trifunctional hypothesis of Georges Dumézil, which he first outlined in his book *Flamen-Brahman*, with the figures of the Father and, perhaps to some extent, the Crone roughly reflecting certain facets of the sovereign (*souveraine*) function, the Warrior standing for the martial (*guerrière*) one and the Smith being a representative of the economic (*productrice*) role.

42 It is quite intriguing that, at this point, Catelyn uses the conditional, as if expressing her budding disbelief in the Mother's omnipotence (or even existence).

places that lie ahead" (452). By contrast, she would not, of course, request the Maiden to, say, help Robb unite the northern lords against their common enemy, the Lannisters, or ask the Smith to make sure that Sansa should marry a handsome and courageous knight.

Martin's gods are therefore just 'gods' and they have their roughly discernible limitations, clearly accentuated in the onomastic layer of Westerosian theology. Powerful as they may seem to be to the inhabitants of the Seven Kingdoms, they could, in reality, hardly be described as being omnipotent (let alone their alleged omnipresence, omniscience and omnibenevolence). Unlike Tolkien's 'chance' (if 'chance' we should call it, of course), they are both named and, in some cases, even quite graphically described (at least as far as their iconography and cultic practices are concerned), not infrequently with some historical background to them, yet they are not, it seems, by any means almighty. Consequently, their divinity, particularly in comparison with the mystic substratum of *The Lord of the Rings*, is significantly deficient. Finally, it appears that the spiritual foundations of Tolkien's Middle-earth prove to be not only more solid (in the Christian theological sense, that is), but also, paradoxically (given the scope of Tolkien's literary interests and inspirations), less medieval-like (at least when it comes to the inevitable conflict between the pre-Christian beliefs of early medieval Europe and the then New Faith from Rome).

The old and the new faiths

The history of mankind is a very complex and multi-facetted process, one in which religious beliefs and practices have always played a highly significant role. Since the very dawn of our flourishing consciousness of the transcendental structures of this world, man has evolved to the heights of intellectual (philosophical, cultural, technological etc.) glory that the early humans could never have even dreamt of. Similar, though not essentially identical, has also been the development of the Christian understanding of God, not merely as the Prime Cause of all being (which was not, it seems, so difficult to grasp, even for the naturally pre-Christian peoples of first pre-Bronze Age civilisations), but also as a just but merciful Judge of mankind (a concept that came to be more fully comprehended in the wake of the teachings, death and resurrection of Christ).

There were (and, obviously, still are) some areas of this world where the local people have not come in contact with Christianity. Nevertheless, even there, the inhabitants of, say, north-western Europe or South America, gradually developed their own, often highly distinctive, yet in some ways comparable or even analogous, ideas of the Absolute, usually polytheistic, but very often with a figure of one supreme god (Zeus, Jupiter, Odin, Dagda etc.) presiding over the worlds of mortals and of the other deities. Quite distinctive (and colourful) were also their conceptions of the world's origins, obviously modelled upon their idiosyncratic perception of the surrounding reality. The natural consequence of this was, for instance, their ability to perceive the divine spark in practically every aspect of life (not so un-Christian-like, of course) and the often highly captivating interpretations of some natural (but at that time not easily explicable) phenomena – usually of general cosmological or weather-related character – regularly sifted through the sieve of their mythologically-conditioned minds.[43]

As has been observed, these vastly idiosyncratic visions of the world which, ages ago, sprang up like mushrooms in every corner of the pre-Christian world were, at the same time, astonishingly universal, with numerous easily definable patterns of mythopoeic thought (personification, animism, euhemerism etc.) present in practically every belief system on every continent of our globe. Over the centuries (in some cases even millennia) of systematic contacts between the neighbouring peoples, these 'doctrinal' developments came to affect each other (much as the languages they spoke), often resulting in some truly fascinating narratives that many a modern scholar, not only in the fields of comparative mythology and philology, has tried to dissect in search of some shared roots and branches. The ultimate effect of all these interactional processes is what in figurative language may be called 'multicoloured threads of mythological lore', a rich tapestry of past and present

---

[43] Some of them were later adopted and reinterpreted – obviously on the linguistic and symbolic levels – in the light of Christian theology and doctrines.

images, beliefs and attitudes in which certain motifs join and break off to form a usually (but not always) predictable pattern.

But how do these threads and patterns translate onto the spiritual landscape of Tolkien's Middle-earth? Unfortunately, there is not enough evidence to assume that there were once some earlier forms of worship practised by its numerous peoples with not much revealed history of their own (such as the Drúedain, the Wild Men of the Woods). Somewhat enigmatic hints of ancient beliefs (or, at least, ways of living) may be heard from the lips of Denethor and Gandalf. Fallen into boundless despair over the seemingly mortal wounds of his son Faramir, the Steward of Gondor decides that they both should be placed upon a funeral pyre with the intention of being burnt "like heathen kings before ever a ship sailed hither from the West" (*LotR* 825). Having thwarted his plans, the wizard rebukes him for this clear outburst of madness, this time using the word 'heathen' in a strictly derogatory sense: "only the heathen kings, under the domination of the Dark Power, did thus, slaying themselves in pride and despair, murdering their kin to ease their own death" (*LotR* 853). The problem with both Denethor and Gandalf is that it is not quite clear whether in these particular situations, the aforesaid adjective was actually meant to be given the meaning of 'non-Christian' (or, rather, 'non-Ilúvatarian') or, simply, 'uncivilised', 'uncouth' and 'lacking moral principles'.[44] In fact, it is not even known who these heathens really were, although it appears that, in both cases, the subject might be the rebellious Númenóreans who, having been corrupted by Sauron (*LotR* 1084), abandoned their faith in Eru Ilúvatar in favour of the worship of the Dark Lord.

It is not a secret that the Númenóreans have not always been faithful to the One. Some instances of their disregard for Ilúvatar's authority, strongly reminiscent of the Israelites' defiance of God's commandments, in for instance, Exodus (32:1-35), are outlined in *The Silmarillion* ('Akallabêth') and *The Unfinished Tales* ('The Line of Elros: Kings of Númenor'). There is, however, no evidence of their spiritual practices ever having any sizeable

---

44 The etymology is, unfortunately, of little assistance here, as the oldest attested uses of the Old English adjective *hæþen* (as well as its numerous cognates in other Germanic languages) is already synonymous with the Modern English word 'pagan', i.e. 'not adhering to the Christian faith'. For a more detailed discussion of the pagan and Christian elements in *The Lord of the Rings*, see Claudio Antonio Testi's book *Pagan Saints in Middle-earth* (2018).

influence upon one another or their faiths being in any way similar, apart, of course, from the fact that in both instances, the Númenóreans appear to be solely monotheistic, first worshipping Eru Ilúvatar, and then, deceived by Sauron, re-directing their veneration to the Dark Lord. In other words, those 'multi-coloured threads' of religious (or, in the case of their new 'god', quasi-religious) experience, which, in our reality, are usually to some degree interwoven with those of other peoples, thus constituting rather firm evidence of their comparable or even analogous efforts to rationalise certain natural phenomena etc., are in Middle-earth not known to have ever been in any way conflated or even remotely associated.

Had the author of *The Lord of the Rings* ever meant such subtleties to be uncovered, he would have probably given more attention to the way that various peoples of Middle-earth interacted with one another with regard to their respective faiths. His foremost interest was, however, in their languages. Hence, even though these issues are often related (particularly at the earlier stages of human civilisational development), driven by the wish to exclude "practically all references to anything like 'religion'" (*Letters* 172), Tolkien chose not to reproduce these rudimentary components of our cultural heritage in what is, after all, a complex but, unavoidably, incomplete subcreation.[45] Incomplete, of course, in the sense of its not being an entirely faithful reflection of our reality.

Unlike Tolkien, Martin tries in his Westerosian novels, at least in some way, to emulate the spiritual landscapes of Europe and the Middle East in the period between the roughly defined Late Antiquity and the fourteenth and fifteenth centuries. There are in his world the old beliefs (the so-called 'old gods' of the North or the Drowned god of the Iron Islands) enduring in the considerably more 'heathen' (both in the sense of being 'uncivilised' and, as seen from the point of view of the inhabitants of the southern kingdoms, 'not adhering to the only 'true' faith', i.e. the faith of the Seven) regions of Westeros and, of course, beyond the Wall. There are also the new ones, such as, in particular, the dominant and, in fact, now semi-official religion of the

---

45 Even if his intentions had been different, it is really hard to imagine how he could have actually managed to successfully reflect such religious nuances without seriously disturbing the narrative flow.

majority of realms within the Seven Kingdoms, the belief in the seven-faced god, the 'Seven Who Are One'.

In relative terms, of course, it is hard to avoid some sort of comparison between these two and, on the one hand, the indigenous beliefs of, for instance, north-western Europe and the Christian Faith, whose gradual expansion was a long but steady process in consequence of which the Word of God could reach, following some fourteen centuries of various missionary efforts, practically every corner of the European continent.[46] In fact, some such efforts are likely to have inspired, albeit only superficially, the author of *A Song of Ice and Fire*, as the advocates of the new faith, the faith of the Seven, appear to be continuously expanding their spiritual and territorial reach, so that by the time of the events outlined in *A Game of Thrones* (and the subsequent four novels in the series), most of Westeros (minus, of course, the area around Winterfell, the Iron Islands and the lands beyond the Wall) has been, at least nominally, 'converted'.[47]

It must be observed, though, that, regardless of his evident determination to render realistic the spiritual landscape of Westeros, much as in the case of Tolkien, Martin's depiction of the interrelationships that, in our world, develop quite naturally between the peoples, clearly lacks in two major elements. The first of them is the lack of any common roots of at least some of their religious beliefs and cultic practices. The second evinces itself in the apparent absence of mutual influences; influences that, under normal circumstances are simply bound to come into being between the cultures of two (or more) neighbouring peoples. In the case of the former, a good case in point – in our own world, of course – might be the numerous similarities between the pre-Christian beliefs of some Indo-European groups, such as the enormous popularity of all sorts of thunder gods – Zeus/Jupiter, Perun(as), Thor or Ukko – in the areas of, respectively, Greek/Roman, Balto-Slavic, Germanic and Finnish dominance. The latter could be illustrated by the unmistakable borrowings quite regu-

---

46 The last to be converted were the inhabitants of the Grand Dutchy of Lithuania, whose rulers officially adopted Christianity only in the last decades of the fourteenth century.
47 The effects of these 'missionary' efforts, however, leave a lot to be desired, with several characters still praying to and swearing by the "old gods and the new". Perhaps in this way Martin wishes to reflect some features of the religious syncretism that characterised numerous newly converted peoples in the Middle Ages (and beyond), not only on the Old Continent.

larly identified not only in the world's countless mythologies,[48] but also in the Judeo-Christian traditions, particularly within the lexical and symbolic layers of the Hebrew Bible, where some reminiscences of the mythical beliefs originating in Assyria or Babylonia may often be identified.[49]

There are, it seems, no signs of any such developments in any of the five volumes of *A Song of Ice and Fire* that have been published so far. Nor are they to be found in Martin's two other books, *The World of Ice & Fire* and *A Knight of the Seven Kingdoms*. In fact, it is as if the main religions of Westeros, along with their rites, traditions, dogmas and values came to be developed in complete isolation, with no consequences whatsoever of the contacts, direct or indirect, between the worshipers of, say, on the one hand, the Drowned god of the ironborn and, on the other, those who profess to the faith of the Seven. Naturally, with the four major belief systems in the Seven Kingdoms having their own, ostensibly unrelated histories,[50] it is indeed no surprise that there are no great similarities between them, at least in the earliest stages of their dogmatic development (apart, of course, from the rather universal need to find some spiritual purpose in life). Yet, even if we disregard the temporal, geographical and cultural discrepancies that must have affected their very foundations, it is quite surprising that there appear to be no similarities at all between the four religions of Westeros, not even after the long centuries of coexistence (barring, obviously, the most recent religious trend, namely

---

48 Some such borrowings (in this case from the Christian tradition) are, for instance, usually identified in the mythical poems of the *Elder Edda*, including *Vǫluspá* (with the prophecy of the second coming of Baldr) and *Hávamál* (where Odin's self-sacrifice upon the world-tree Yggdrasill almost certainly echoes the crucifixion of Christ).
49 For more information on the non-Hebraic imagery in the Bible, see, for instance, Norman Cohn's book *Cosmos, Chaos and the World to Come: The Ancient Roots of Apocalyptic Faith* (2001).
50 The old gods were originally worshipped by the children of the forest, known to have inhabited Westeros at least since the days of the Dawn Age, i.e. prior to the coming of the First Men, some twelve thousand years before the events outlined in *A Song of Ice and Fire* (*A Game of Thrones* 713). Considerably younger, though still relatively old in comparison with, for instance, the veneration of the Seven, is the belief in the Drowned god, which in several aspects of its observance evidently replicates the maritime culture of the ironborn. It appears to be an indigenous religion of the Iron Islands, practised since at least some years prior to the Andal Invasion. The faith of the Seven, which originated in the north-western parts of Essos, in the hills of Andalos (*The World of Ice & Fire* 17), was brought to Westeros by the Andals. In order to distinguish the 'Seven Who Are One' from the older deities, the Andal god(s) is/are also sometimes referred to as 'new'. Likewise, the last of the four main religions of Westeros, the mysterious cult of R'hllor, the Lord of Light, which is by far the most recent addition to the spiritual landscape of Martin's novels, also originates in the continent of Essos, not too far, in fact, from where the Andals are believed to have met their Seven.

the belief in the Lord of Light); centuries which, it appears, must have seen both military conflicts and peaceful interactions.

Much as with Tolkien, the reason why Martin chose not to embrace such peculiarities in his vision of Westeros is that the author of *A Song of Ice and Fire* appears not to be much interested in the evolutionary aspects of his subcreated world (a fairly common mark in all fantasy literature, where things like technological progress are often either entirely disregarded or so downgraded as to seem almost practically irrelevant). Unlike his English counterpart, however, whose strong Catholic convictions prevented him from replicating the historical context of Christianity (its ethical framework, nevertheless, remaining for the most part intact), Martin is not in any way hindered by any religious scruples. In fact, he treats his numerous gods as no more than intriguing cultural developments (with no real transcendental foundations and authority) that perfectly integrate with his vision of the world as a brutal arena of continuous struggle between often similarly self-important and covetous people. Being, therefore, no expert on either historical linguistics or the history of the world's religions and mythologies (here, of course, Tolkien was by far more knowledgeable than Martin), he evidently sees no reason why the four main belief systems of Westeros should be, in the first place, related or why they should in any way affect one another in the subsequent stages of their territorial expansion. After all, the world might seem perhaps even more colourful when there is more variety in it, both in terms of the novels' numerous plotlines and in their author's attempts to refabricate the spiritual realism of the Middle Ages.

Yet another reason for his disregard of these natural components of our own world's spiritual history (and this is where Martin seems to be just as much impeded as Tolkien) is, of course, the literary conventions that would not allow his novels to become too detailed and nuanced for the average reader with not much specific interest in (and knowledge of) the worldbuilding techniques in speculative fiction. It would not be entirely inconceivable, though, for some such subtleties to be included, even in a brief and tangential way, in the series' companion books, such as, for instance, *The World of Ice & Fire*. A glimpse, even if rare, of such spiritual realism would not, of course, do them any harm. Unfortunately, here again, Martin's narrative inventiveness does not seem to go far beyond his otherwise exceptional ability to illustrate the complex world of political machinations and martial carnage that Westeros certainly is.

Institutionalised worship

Practically every belief system, be it the most primitive cultic practices of some nameless Stone Age peoples or the current groups and denominations of the Christian faith, has been in regular need of some form of mediation between the advocates of a given religion and the Supreme Absolute that they happen to hold in reverence. In various pre-Christian societies these were usually all sorts of shamans, prophets and sages who could, for instance, get into an extrasensory interaction with a particular deity (or their tribe's dead ancestors), often by way of putting themselves into a state of narcotically-induced trance. In some parts of Europe, some such practices could prevail, wholly or in part, even as late as the fourteenth and fifteenth centuries (sometimes even later, in the form of no longer comprehensible customs and traditions), i.e. until the ultimate advent of Christianity.[51]

In Christianity, the role of mediators between man and God is, of course, performed by the members of the clergy, from the humblest priest to, in Roman Catholicism, the Bishop of Rome, Christ's vicar and His highest representative on Earth. Through the Word of God and the Holy Sacraments, the role of the Church is then to continue the presence of the Messiah in preparation for the Parousia, i.e. the Second Coming of Christ. A priest therefore acts *in persona Christi* while administering the Sacraments, e.g. hearing the confession or offering the Holy Sacrifice. This is not, of course, in any way induced, enhanced and sustained through the priest's own state of mind, trance or other means of mental alteration, but by the sole aid of the Holy Spirit, the παρακλητος (*Paraclete*) "advocate, comforter" of John 14:16.

There is, it seems, no divine worship, institutionalised or not, in the subcreated world of *The Lord of the Rings*. Consequently, then, there are to be found in it

---

51 This obviously does not apply to the so-called modern pagan movements (such as Wicca, Ásatrú etc.), which are, in reality (but not in the eyes of the practitioners), little more than just forms, albeit sometimes very active ones, of historical re-enactment.

neither churches, nor chapels, nor monasteries, nor any traces whatsoever of some ecclesiastical organisation whose aim would be to preserve the faith and foster some form of religious practices amongst the local people. There could, of course, be heard in Minas Tirith "a clear sweet bell ringing in a tower of the citadel" (*LotR* 760). Several times of the day, or so it appears, the inhabitants of the "Guarded City" may hear the sounds of the bells – the "bells of the day" (*LotR* 818), the "noon-bells" (*LotR* 767) and the "sundown-bells" (*LotR* 771). It is, regrettably, not known whether they were actually meant to have any ecclesiastical objective or whether their chimes are to be understood as no more than the sounds that could normally be heard from the town hall tower in well-nigh every European town. Likewise, the word "temple", used in the novel only once (*LotR* 795), with regard to the enigmatic Hold of Dunharrow, a prehistoric fortified refuge in the White Mountains, some ten miles to the south of Edoras, is at no time unequivocally acknowledged to be a place of worship, apparently the word itself being used there only in the conjectural sense: "For what purpose they had made this place, as a town or secret temple or a tomb of kings, none could say" (*LotR* 795).[52]

Naturally, there are in *The Lord of the Rings* some veiled references to the major components of the eucharistic liturgy. Both Aragorn and Gandalf often seem to have some sort of a priestly (or even Christ-like) air around them, the former, for instance, hearing Boromir's heart-rending confession (*LotR* 414) and reviving the wounded in the Houses of Healing (*LotR* 963),[53] the latter partaking in the doubtlessly Eru-instigated mission to save the world and being himself resurrected (following his fatal fall in the mines of Moria)[54] and transfigured

---

[52] Some sense could, nevertheless, be made from toponomastic evidence. According to Christina Scull and Wayne G. Hammond, Rohirric (or, in fact, Old Mercian) *Dunhærg* should actually be translated as "the heathen fane on the hillside" (2014, 769), thus naturally strengthening its interpretation as a place of worship, in all likelihood that of the Númenórean cult of Melkor. In addition to this, in his posthumously published writings, Tolkien refers by name to only three other locations in which some forms of veneration were at some point regularly practised. Two of them may be found in Númenor: the Holy Mountain of Meneltarma (dedicated to Eru) and the Temple in Armenelos (where human sacrifices were carried out in connection with the worship of Melkor). The third one, Mindolluin, is the easternmost peak of the White Mountains, between Gondor and Rohan, where Aragorn finds a sapling of the White Tree.

[53] The very institution of the Houses of Healing could be, of course, an indirect allusion to the healing power of the Church. See also Gisbert Kranz's essay on Aragorn as healer (1984, 11-24).

[54] In his letter to Father Robert Murray SJ, Tolkien claims that "Gandalf really 'died', and was changed" (*Letters* 201).

(in front the three of his companions Aragorn, Legolas and Gimli).[55] There are also striking analogies between Lembas, the waybread given to the members of the Fellowship by the Elves of Lothlórien, and the transubstantiated Eucharist which satisfies our spiritual hunger for God.[56] Last, but certainly not least, and particularly in the moments of greatest danger, some of the characters' emotional invocations (*A Elbereth Gilthoniel* evidently being the most eminent example) sound very much as if they were meant to be genuine prayers, desperate supplications by dint of which they could hope to be delivered from the Dark Lord and his evil servants and allies. As such, however, there are absolutely no signs, explicit or not, that any forms of organised, institutionalised religion could be found in the world of *The Lord of the Rings*.

The reason for this is, once again, as plain as the hair on the hobbit feet. There is no need for any form of meditation or acting *in persona Dei*, when the sheer existence of any specific deity (or other God-/god-like entity) is never, in a plain and unambiguous way, communicated to the reader. Besides, as has already been observed, under such completely different circumstances, features cultural as well as historical, the veneration (or, in fact, even merest mention) of Christ or the supplications to the Virgin Mary would simply not make any sense. Indeed, even allowing for its evident Christian substratum (both in terms of the ethical foundations of Tolkien's world and the not infrequent biblical *topoi* and *mythoi* that may be identified in *The Lord of the Rings*), it would be an altogether artificial creation, devoid of any historical justification of its existence in Middle-earth.

One may argue, of course, that Tolkien did, as a matter of fact, create some sort of a religion, an ingenious faith of the peoples of Middle-earth, the

---

[55] It is not, perhaps, a proper transfiguration in the sense of unveiling of Gandalf's divine glory, although his glory and might may (and should) seem to be divinely orchestrated. After all, he is now, in his own words, much as Saruman, "Saruman as he should have been" (*LotR* 495). Nevertheless, at least its visual (and in some degree spiritual) resemblance to what must have been experienced by Peter, James and John upon the top of Mount Tabor/Hermon (Mt 17:1-8; Mk 9:2-8; Lk 9:28-36) is hard to be denied. For a more in-depth analysis of the transfiguration analogies in *The Lord of the Rings*, see Milbank (2007, 50-51).
[56] In a letter to Forrest J. Ackerman, Tolkien admits that, apart from being a "device for making credible the long marches with little provision" (*Letters* 275), lembas "also has a much larger significance, of what one might hesitatingly call a 'religious' kind" (275). Some interesting views on the eucharistic properties of the elvish waybread may be found in Birzer (2002, 63-64), Holmes (2011, 134) as well as Gilliver, Marshall and Weiner (2009, 208).

above-mentioned 'Ilúvatarism'. This would, however, be a serious contradiction in terms. What Tolkien designed in *The Silmarillion* is not a religion but mythology, the book itself being, much as the *Poetic Edda*, a collection of mythopoeic tales and heroic legends in which the questions of religious affiliation and worship (to say nothing of any forms of organised cultic practices) are, at best, only tacitly implied. As has been observed, in 1954-55, at the time of the original publication of *The Lord of the Rings*, these narratives were not yet known to the general public (and would remain so until 1977). Consequently, throughout the course of at least the following two and a half decades, any allusions to the One and His divine plan for the peoples of Middle-earth and, accordingly, their attempts to praise and give thanks to their Maker would not only be quite unintelligible to the readers but, given the manifestly Christian ethics of Tolkien's world, would also constitute a rather superfluous addition to the main narrative which, judging by the number of readers and devoted fans all over the world, clearly defends itself, also in terms of its numerous spiritual concerns.

Martin's approach to the issue of institutionalised worship in his Westeros is, of course, diametrically different, since he is not in any way constrained by the ethical principles of his personal faith (or, as a matter of fact, the aforementioned lack of it). As a result, the author of *A Song of Ice and Fire* evidently feels quite free to explore some of the areas that, doubtlessly on account of his strong religious convictions, Tolkien almost certainly considered to be of lesser significance in his own world of Middle-earth.

One such area is, no doubt, his vivid, if at times somewhat sketchy, depiction of the faith of the Seven, the most dominant of the belief systems that the peoples of Westeros either hold to be true or feel they are in some way connected with. More often than not, it appears, Martin tries to sidetrack from the actual question of faith and its moral implications in order to direct the readers' attention to the remarkably high level of political involvement which the clerical advocates of 'the Seven Who Are One' (as well as those who ally with them for mutual gain) evidently consider to be their absolute right and duty. In this, he seems to believe, the consecutive High Septons and their entourage bear some resemblance to the way that various ecclesiastical leaders in Europe, both in the Middle Ages and beyond, sometimes used the authority of the Faith for their own political purposes and against their own enemies.

Some such machinations are obviously regularly seen in the generally very instrumental relationships between the consecutive Lannister monarchs (or their often highly independent Hands, the chief advisors to the Lord of the Seven Kingdoms) and the High Septons of King's Landing. There are as many as three of them mentioned in the five novels that have been published so far. The first one meets his death in a riot (*A Clash of Kings* 542; accidentally, of course, but it would not have happened if it were not for the general discontent with King Joffrey's reign), the second is murdered in his own bed (*A Feast for Crows* 272; officially of old age, but the true reason is to be found in the secrets confined to him by Ser Lancel Lannister) and the third, the self-dubbed High Sparrow, dies (so far only in the television series) in the fatal explosion in the Sept of Baelor. Their deaths might not always be directly linked with any particular political actions, but they are certainly indicative of the role they actually play in the administrative life of the realm. They carry on with their regular duties for as long as their services are needed by the ruling monarch and once they have become dispensable, they are simply 'removed' from their offices. Seen in the light of relentless brutality which characterises life in Westeros, it should come as no surprise that such cruel practices (or, at least, some form of cold-blooded political pragmatics) are to be recurrently found on practically every level of ecclesiastical jurisdiction and in almost every corner of Westeros where the Seven are worshipped. With such instrumental treatment of faith and abuse of ecclesiastical power, it is therefore little wonder that the 'new gods' so often turn their eyes away from the inhabitants of the Seven Kingdoms.

On the other side of the scale, it should be admitted that, as far as the cultic practices are concerned, Martin's idea of the old 'heathen' beliefs in the North is a relatively faithful literary reflection of the spiritual reality in early medieval Europe, particularly with regard to the indigenous pagan religions of Northern Europe. We may often take it for granted, reading, for instance, the mythical accounts of the two *Eddas*, that the beliefs of the pre-Christian inhabitants of Scandinavia (as well as Iceland, Faroe Islands or anywhere else that Odin, Thor, Frey and other gods and goddesses came to be venerated) were in some way codified. In reality, though, the Norsemen had neither their own 'bibles', nor 'catechisms', nor 'prayer books', nor, it appears, anything we could now refer to as some kind of 'dogmas' or other 'doctrinal' statements in the mould of our Judeo-Christian Decalogue.[57] Instead, the early Germanic peoples are known to have worshipped wooden idols in all sorts of sacred groves and other natural locations, where, it appears, they were more inclined to sense the 'presence' of their deities.[58] Even much later, when at least some of their cultic practices eventually came to be performed inside more architecturally advanced temples (such as the one at Gamla Uppsala),[59] the actual 'dogmatic' depth of their templar routines appears not to have gone far beyond the mere ritual frame of mind.

Likewise, in *A Song of Ice and Fire*, those who, despite the pressure from the south, still pray to the 'old gods' (the northmen, the crannogmen and the so-called free folk) are not known to have ever been in the possession of any holy texts, chanted songs of worship or performed some specific rites. Nor is there any mention, in Martin's novels, of some priests or priest-like figures. The advocates of the 'old gods' come to pray in the godswoods, sacred groves or other wooded areas, typically contained within the castle walls, as is, for instance, the case with Winterfell, the capital of the north, where, we are told, there are always "deep silence and brooding shadows" (*A Game of Thrones* 19). Indeed, sitting there with Eddard Stark, it is really hard not to think of the Norsemen and their gigantic Yggdrasill or the continental Saxons praying in front of their Irminsul, the *axes mundi* of their respective realities.[60] Sure enough, the weirwood heart trees with carved faces, in front of which the people of

---

57 Some such functions may be noticed in, particularly, the eddic poem *Hávamál*. However, sometimes interpreted as some sort of an ethical decalogue of early Germanic beliefs, it is, in all likelihood, a late compilation of several shorter poems of gnomic and sententious character.
58 Such practices are quite vividly described especially in the ninth chapter of *Germania*, a valuable, if somewhat biased, ethnographic work written by the Roman historian Tacitus in the last decade of the first century AD.
59 A vivid description of the impressive *templum* [...] *quod Ubsola dicitur* [*et*] *quod totum ex auro paratum est* (ch. 26) "temple which is called Uppsala and which is entirely decked out in gold" may be found in the eleventh-century *Gesta Hammaburgensis ecclesiae pontificum* by the German chronicler Adam of Bremen.
60 In Norse cosmology, Yggdrasill might be described as a world tree, a gigantic ash connecting all the nine worlds inhabited by gods, men and giants. In the beliefs of continental Saxons, Irminsul was a sacred tree (or wooden pillar) around which the people gathered and prayed. Despite some superficial similarities, their names are not etymologically related. Nevertheless, both are usually linked (the former with far greater certainty, of course) with the supreme god Odin.

the North may sometimes be seen at silent prayer, are not in any way central to the world of Westeros. It seems, however, that they are somehow central to the northerners' ethical conception of the world,[61] the world in which honesty and loyalty often prove to be fine but ultimately empty words.

All in all, the sole mention of various cultic practices and organisational structures of 'ecclesiastical' power (as is certainly the case with Martin's faith of the Seven) does not guarantee any genuine spiritual experience. Nor is it to be found in the sacred groves of the North, where, it seems, the old gods remain invariably silent. Here again, despite some evident (but often superficial) analogies between the belief systems in *A Song of Ice and Fire* and those of, particularly but not exclusively, early medieval Europe (some of which are lacking in *The Lord of the Rings*), Tolkien emerges as the more theologically accurate of the two writers. In his novel, the noticeable absence of any 'ecclesiastical' organisation in Middle-earth should not pose an obstacle to seeing it as "a fundamentally religious and Catholic work" (*Letters* 172). After all, to use the well-known words of the little fox in Antoine de Saint-Exupéry's *The Little Prince*, *"L'essentiel est invisible pour les yeux"* (76) "What is most important is invisible to the eye". In this case, the invisible being what should constitute the very foundation and essence, the *sine qua non*, of all religious practices, both as part of a larger congregation and in one's solitude, namely, the actual presence of God, even in some of His most covert and least likely appearances.[62]

Conclusions

The above examination of the often utterly dissimilar approaches to the spiritual dimensions of worldbuilding in J.R.R. Tolkien's *The Lord of the Rings* and George R.R. Martin's *A Song of Ice and Fire* is, of course, but a brief, and thus necessarily sketchy, overview of some of the most essential religious (or, in the case of the latter writer, quasi-religious) features of, respectively, Middle-earth

---

61 It is said, for instance, that "no man could tell a lie in front of a heart tree [for the] old gods know when men are lying" (*A Clash of Kings* 185). Seen in the light of northern honesty, the centrality of, in this case, weirwood trees clearly acquires a new, ethical, dimension.
62 In our own world, it could be the new-born Child in Bethlehem while, in Tolkien's subcreated universe, His presence may be sensed in the mysterious 'chance' in Tom Bombadil's and Elrond's explanations of how certain things come to pass within the boundaries of Middle-earth.

and Westeros. The epic dimensions (in the sense of their narrative scale) and proportions (particularly in the case of Martin's still unfinished series) of both works make practically any attempt to produce a more systematic analysis of these issues in the form of an individual academic paper a truly difficult, if not utterly impossible, effort. As a result, the present study could only offer a cursory glimpse into such fundamental religious matters as the concepts of fate and providence or the question of hope, faith and trust in God/god.[63] Moreover, it evidently lacks in a more complex investigation into the various moral dilemmas that are inevitably faced by the characters created by both Tolkien and Martin.

Nevertheless, it is hoped that, at least with regard to the above-delineated issues of, roughly speaking, 'divine' ('Monotheism, henotheism or polytheism?'; 'The Nameless One vs. the named ones') and 'ecclesiastical' ('The old and the new faiths'; 'Institutionalised worship') nature, the present examination will turn out to be of some interest to those who would wish to see the worlds of Tolkien's and Martin's imagination in a broader perspective of theological anthropology, particularly in connection with their numerous characters' understanding of and relationship with God[64]/gods. This should not only facilitate our perception of the intricate spiritual landscapes that might be found in *The Lord of the Rings* and *A Song of Ice and Fire*, but also, most importantly, allow us to see that, in the sometimes complex world of fantasy, the titular absence of gods (as is invariably the case in Tolkien's fiction) does not in the least rule out the possibility of there being a more profound substratum of religious (in this case obviously Christian) imagery and meaning. On the other side of the coin, the notable abundance of all sorts of deities, larger and small (as in the works of Martin) is not a prerequisite to the same feelings about the world of Westeros. There, the recurrent supplications to 'the old gods and the new' should, for the most part, be treated as no more than rather shallow, if often attractively depicted, attempts of a 'lapsed Catholic' to re-visualise the intricate spiritual mosaics of, principally but not exclusively, the European Middle Ages. After all, even in the Scripture, the

---

63 Needless to say, all of them have already been discussed by a number of scholars (e.g. Caldecott, Dickerson, Rutledge, Shippey and others), particularly with regard to the works of Tolkien.
64 As has been observed several times in this paper, in the case of Tolkien, the idea of God is obviously contained within the general ethical framework of *The Lord of the Rings*.

hand of God is not always perfectly visible (and/or comprehensible) to the readers, both clerical and lay. However, to once again quote from the letter Tolkien wrote in 1944 to his son Christopher, in such instances He is always "behind us, supporting [and] nourishing us" (*Letters* 66). Not a mere god (old, new, seven-faced, drowned, burnt or other), lurking in various parts of Westeros, but the real, if permanently concealed, *Creator Spiritus*, "Eru, the One, who in Arda is called Ilúvatar" (*Silmarillion* 3).

About the Author

ŁUKASZ NEUBAUER received his PhD in English philology from the University of Łódź. He is a researcher and lecturer at the University of Koszalin, Poland, where he teaches courses on Tolkien, Old English literature and Arthurian romances. Apart from his publications dealing with various medieval as well as Christian influences and resonances in *The Lord of the Rings*, he has also written papers on *The Battle of Maldon*, *Beowulf*, *Héliand*, Icelandic sagas and the so-called 'beasts of battle' trope in, particularly but not exclusively, Old Germanic poetry. He is a member of the British branch of the International Arthurian Society and a conceptual coordinator of the annual Medieval Fantasy Symposium in Mielno-Unieście, Poland.

Abbreviations

Letters TOLKIEN, John Ronald Reuel. *The Letters of J.R.R. Tolkien*. Ed. Humphrey Carpenter with the assistance of Christopher Tolkien. London: George Allen and Unwin, 1981.

LotR TOLKIEN, John Ronald Reuel. *The Lord of the Rings*. London: HarperCollins, 2005.

Bibliography

ADAM OF BREMEN. *Gesta Hammaburgensis ecclesiae pontificum*. In: *Quellen des 9. und 11. Jahrhunderts zur Geschichte der Hamburgischen Kirche und des Reiches*. Ed. Werner Trillmich and Rudolf Buchner. Darmstadt: Wissenschaftliche Buchgesellschaft, 2000. 137-499.

BIRZER, Bradley. *J.R.R. Tolkien's Sanctifying Myth: Understanding Middle-earth*. Wilmington: ISI Books, 2002.

CALDECOTT, Stratford. *Secret Fire: The Spiritual Vision of J.R.R. Tolkien*. London: Darton, Longman and Todd, 2003.

The Catholic Bible: *Revised Standard Version*. San Francisco: Ignatius Press, 2006.

COHN, Norman. *Cosmos, Chaos and the World to Come: The Ancient Roots of Apocalyptic Faith*. New Haven: Yale University Press, 2001.

DICKERSON, Matthew. *Following Gandalf: Epic Battles and Moral Victory in The Lord of the Rings*. Grand Rapids MI: Brazos Press, 2003.

DUMÉZIL, Georges. *Flamen-Brahman*. Paris: P. Geuthner, 1935.

GILLIVER, Peter, Jeremy MARSHALL and Edmund WEINER. *The Ring of Words: Tolkien and the Oxford English Dictionary*. Oxford: Oxford University Press, 2009.

GROSSMAN, Lev. 'The American Tolkien.' *TIME*, 13 November 2005, vol. 166, issue 21, 139.

HOLMES, John R. "Like Heathen Kings': Religion as Palimpsest in Tolkien's Fiction.' *The Ring and the Cross: Christianity and The Lord of the Rings*. Ed. Paul E. Kerry. Madison and Teaneck: Fairleigh University Press, 2011. 119-44.

JOHNSTON, Susan and Jes BATTIS. 'Introduction: On Knowing Nothing.' *Mastering the Game of Thrones: Essays on George R.R. Martin's A Song of Ice and Fire*. Ed. Jes Battis and Susan Johnston. Jefferson NC: McFarland, 2015. 1-14.

KRANZ, Gisbert. 'Der heilende Aragorn.' *Inklings – Jahrbuch für Literatur und Ästhetik* 2 (1984): 11-24.

LARRINGTON, Carolyne. *Winter Is Coming: The Medieval World of Game of Thrones*. London & New York: I.B. Tauris, 2016.

MARTIN, George R.R. *A Clash of Kings*. London: HarperVoyager, 2011.

A Dance with Dragons. London: HarperVoyager, 2011.

A Feast for Crows. London: HarperVoyager, 2011.

A Game of Thrones. London: HarperVoyager, 2011.

A Storm of Swords. London: HarperVoyager, 2011.

MARTIN, George R.R., Elio M. GARCÍA Jr. and Linda ANTONSSON. *The World of Ice & Fire. The Untold History of Westeros and The Game of Thrones*. London: HarperVoyager, 2014.

MILBANK, Alison. *Chesterton and Tolkien as Theologians*. London: T&T Clark, 2007.

DE RAMÓN RUIZ, José Luis. 'The Favor of the Gods: Religion and Power in George R.R. Martin's *A Song of Ice and Fire*.' *Fafnir – Nordic Journal of Science Fiction and Fantasy Research* 3.3 (2016): 41-50.

RUTLEDGE, Fleming. *The Battle for Middle-earth. Tolkien's Divine Design in The Lord of the Rings*. Grand Rapids and Cambridge: Wm. B. Eerdmans Publishing Company, 2004.

SAINT-EXUPÉRY, Antoine de. *Le Petit Prince*. Paris: Gallimard, 1999.

SCULL, Christina and Wayne G. HAMMOND. *The Lord of the Rings: A Reader's Companion*. London: HarperCollins, 2014.

SHIPPEY, Tom. *The Road to Middle-earth*. London: HarperCollins, 2005.

TACITUS, Publius Cornelius. *Germania*. Ed. Tomasz Płóciennik. Poznań: Wydawnictwo Naukowe UAM, 2008.

TESTI, Claudio Antonio. *Pagan Saints in Middle-earth*. Zurich and Jena: Walking Tree Publishers, 2018.

TOLKIEN, J.R.R. *The Letters of J.R.R. Tolkien*. Ed. Humphrey Carpenter with the assistance of Christopher Tolkien. London: George Allen and Unwin, 1981.

The Silmarillion. Ed. Christopher Tolkien. London: HarperCollins, 2006.

The Lord of the Rings. London: HarperCollins, 2005.

YOUNG, William. *Uncommon Friendships: An Amicable History of Modern Religious Thought*. Eugene: Cascade Books, 2009.

Internet Resources

http://www.georgerrmartin.com/about-george/life-and-times/bayonne/

http://www.ew.com/article/2011/07/12/george-martin-talks-a-dance-with-dragons/

https://www.rollingstone.com/tv/news/george-r-r-martin-the-rolling-stone-interview-20140423

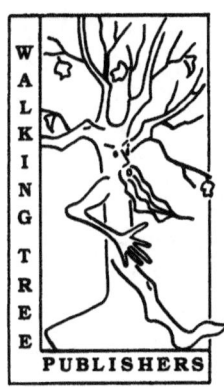

Walking Tree Publishers
Zurich and Jena

Walking Tree Publishers was founded in 1997 as a forum for publication of material related to Tolkien and Middle-earth studies.

http://www.walking-tree.org

Cormarë Series

The *Cormarë Series* collects papers and studies dedicated exclusively to the exploration of Tolkien's work. It comprises monographs, thematic collections of essays, conference volumes, and reprints of important yet no longer (easily) accessible papers by leading scholars in the field. Manuscripts and project proposals are evaluated by members of an independent board of advisors who support the series editors in their endeavour to provide the readers with qualitatively superior yet accessible studies on Tolkien and his work.

News from the Shire and Beyond. Studies on Tolkien
Peter Buchs & Thomas Honegger (eds.), Zurich and Berne 2004, Reprint, First edition 1997 (Cormarë Series 1), ISBN 978-3-9521424-5-5

Root and Branch. Approaches Towards Understanding Tolkien
Thomas Honegger (ed.), Zurich and Berne 2005, Reprint, First edition 1999 (Cormarë Series 2), ISBN 978-3-905703-01-6

Richard Sturch, *Four Christian Fantasists. A Study of the Fantastic Writings of George MacDonald, Charles Williams, C.S. Lewis and J.R.R. Tolkien*
Zurich and Berne 2007, Reprint, First edition 2001 (Cormarë Series 3), ISBN 978-3-905703-04-7

Tolkien in Translation
Thomas Honegger (ed.), Zurich and Jena 2011, Reprint, First edition 2003 (Cormarë Series 4), ISBN 978-3-905703-15-3

Mark T. Hooker, *Tolkien Through Russian Eyes*
Zurich and Berne 2003 (Cormarë Series 5), ISBN 978-3-9521424-7-9

Translating Tolkien: Text and Film
Thomas Honegger (ed.), Zurich and Jena 2011, Reprint, First edition 2004 (Cormarë Series 6), ISBN 978-3-905703-16-0

Christopher Garbowski, *Recovery and Transcendence for the Contemporary Mythmaker. The Spiritual Dimension in the Works of J.R.R. Tolkien*
Zurich and Berne 2004, Reprint, First Edition by Marie Curie Sklodowska, University Press, Lublin 2000, (Cormarë Series 7), ISBN 978-3-9521424-8-6

Reconsidering Tolkien
Thomas Honegger (ed.), Zurich and Berne 2005 (Cormarë Series 8), ISBN 978-3-905703-00-9

Tolkien and Modernity 1
Frank Weinreich & Thomas Honegger (eds.), Zurich and Berne 2006
(Cormarë Series 9), ISBN 978-3-905703-02-3

Tolkien and Modernity 2
Thomas Honegger & Frank Weinreich (eds.), Zurich and Berne 2006
(Cormarë Series 10), ISBN 978-3-905703-03-0

Tom Shippey, *Roots and Branches. Selected Papers on Tolkien by Tom Shippey*
Zurich and Berne 2007 (Cormarë Series 11), ISBN 978-3-905703-05-4

Ross Smith, *Inside Language. Linguistic and Aesthetic Theory in Tolkien*
Zurich and Jena 2011, Reprint, First edition 2007 (Cormarë Series 12),
ISBN 978-3-905703-20-7

How We Became Middle-earth. A Collection of Essays on The Lord of the Rings
Adam Lam & Nataliya Oryshchuk (eds.), Zurich and Berne 2007
(Cormarë Series 13), ISBN 978-3-905703-07-8

Myth and Magic. Art According to the Inklings
Eduardo Segura & Thomas Honegger (eds.), Zurich and Berne 2007
(Cormarë Series 14), ISBN 978-3-905703-08-5

The Silmarillion – Thirty Years On
Allan Turner (ed.), Zurich and Berne 2007 (Cormarë Series 15),
ISBN 978-3-905703-10-8

Martin Simonson, *The Lord of the Rings and the Western Narrative Tradition*
Zurich and Jena 2008 (Cormarë Series 16), ISBN 978-3-905703-09-2

Tolkien's Shorter Works. Proceedings of the 4th Seminar of the Deutsche Tolkien Gesellschaft & Walking Tree Publishers Decennial Conference
Margaret Hiley & Frank Weinreich (eds.), Zurich and Jena 2008
(Cormarë Series 17), ISBN 978-3-905703-11-5

Tolkien's The Lord of the Rings: Sources of Inspiration
Stratford Caldecott & Thomas Honegger (eds.), Zurich and Jena 2008
(Cormarë Series 18), ISBN 978-3-905703-12-2

J.S. Ryan, *Tolkien's View: Windows into his World*
Zurich and Jena 2009 (Cormarë Series 19), ISBN 978-3-905703-13-9

Music in Middle-earth
Heidi Steimel & Friedhelm Schneidewind (eds.), Zurich and Jena 2010
(Cormarë Series 20), ISBN 978-3-905703-14-6

Liam Campbell, *The Ecological Augury in the Works of JRR Tolkien*
Zurich and Jena 2011 (Cormarë Series 21), ISBN 978-3-905703-18-4

Margaret Hiley, *The Loss and the Silence. Aspects of Modernism in the Works of C.S. Lewis, J.R.R. Tolkien and Charles Williams*
Zurich and Jena 2011 (Cormarë Series 22), ISBN 978-3-905703-19-1

Rainer Nagel, *Hobbit Place-names. A Linguistic Excursion through the Shire*
Zurich and Jena 2012 (Cormarë Series 23), ISBN 978-3-905703-22-1

Christopher MacLachlan, *Tolkien and Wagner: The Ring and Der Ring*
Zurich and Jena 2012 (Cormarë Series 24), ISBN 978-3-905703-21-4

Renée Vink, *Wagner and Tolkien: Mythmakers*
Zurich and Jena 2012 (Cormarë Series 25), ISBN 978-3-905703-25-2

The Broken Scythe. Death and Immortality in the Works of J.R.R. Tolkien
Roberto Arduini & Claudio Antonio Testi (eds.), Zurich and Jena 2012
(Cormarë Series 26), ISBN 978-3-905703-26-9

Sub-creating Middle-earth: Constructions of Authorship and the Works of J.R.R. Tolkien
Judith Klinger (ed.), Zurich and Jena 2012 (Cormarë Series 27),
ISBN 978-3-905703-27-6

Tolkien's Poetry
Julian Eilmann & Allan Turner (eds.), Zurich and Jena 2013
(Cormarë Series 28), ISBN 978-3-905703-28-3

O, What a Tangled Web. Tolkien and Medieval Literature. A View from Poland
Barbara Kowalik (ed.), Zurich and Jena 2013 (Cormarë Series 29),
ISBN 978-3-905703-29-0

J.S. Ryan, *In the Nameless Wood*
Zurich and Jena 2013 (Cormarë Series 30), ISBN 978-3-905703-30-6

From Peterborough to Faëry; The Poetics and Mechanics of Secondary Worlds
Thomas Honegger & Dirk Vanderbeke (eds.), Zurich and Jena 2014
(Cormarë Series 31), ISBN 978-3-905703-31-3

Tolkien and Philosophy
Roberto Arduini & Claudio R. Testi (eds.), Zurich and Jena 2014
(Cormarë Series 32), ISBN 978-3-905703-32-0

Patrick Curry, *Deep Roots in a Time of Frost. Essays on Tolkien*
Zurich and Jena 2014 (Cormarë Series 33), ISBN 978-3-905703-33-7

Representations of Nature in Middle-earth
Martin Simonson (ed.), Zurich and Jena 2015, (Cormarë Series 34),
ISBN 978-3-905703-34-4

Laughter in Middle-earth
Thomas Honegger & Maureen F. Mann (eds.), Zurich and Jena 2016
(Cormarë Series 35), ISBN 978-3-905703-35-1

Julian Eilmann, *J.R.R. Tolkien – Romanticist and Poet*
Zurich and Jena 2017 (Cormarë Series 36), ISBN 978-3-905703-36-8

Binding Them All. Interdisciplinary Perspectives on J.R.R. Tolkien and His Works
Monika Kirner-Ludwig, Stephan Köser, Sebastian Streitberger, Zurich and Jena
2017 (Cormarë Series 37), ISBN 978-3-905703-37-5

Claudio Testi, *Pagan Saints in Middle-earth*
Zurich and Jena 2018 (Cormarë Series 38), ISBN 978-3-905703-38-2

Music in Tolkien's Work and Beyond
Julian Eilmann & Friedhelm Schneidewind (eds.), Zurich and Jena 2019
(Cormarë Series 39), ISBN 978-3-905703-39-9, forthcoming

Sub-creating Arda: World-building in J.R.R. Tolkien's Work, its Precursors and its Legacies
Dimitra Fimi & Thomas Honegger (eds.), Zurich and Jena 2019
(Cormarë Series 40), ISBN 978-3-905703-40-5

Middle-earth, or There and Back Again
Łukasz Neubauer (ed.), forthcoming

"Something has gone crack": New Perspectives on J.R.R. Tolkien and the Great War
Janet Brennan Croft and Annika Röttinger (eds.), forthcoming

Beowulf and the Dragon

The original Old English text of the 'Dragon Episode' of Beowulf is set in an authentic font and bound in hardback as a high quality art book. Illustrated by Anke Eissmann and accompanied by John Porter's translation. Introduction by Tom Shippey. Limited first edition of 500 copies. 84 pages.

Selected pages can be previewed on:
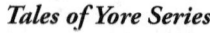
http://www.walking-tree.org/beowulf

Beowulf and the Dragon
Zurich and Jena 2009 , ISBN 978-3-905703-17-7

Tales of Yore Series

The *Tales of Yore Series* provides a platform for qualitatively superior fiction that will appeal to readers familiar with Tolkien's world:

The Monster Specialist

Sir Severus le Brewse, among the least known of King Arthur's Round Table knights, is preferred by nature, disposition, and training to fight against monsters rather than other knights. After youthful adventures of errantry with dragons, trolls, vampires, and assorted beasts, Severus joins the brilliant sorceress Lilava to face the Chimaera in The Greatest Monster Battle of All Time to free her folk from an age-old curse. But their adventures don't end there; together they meet elves and magicians, friends and foes; they join in the fight to save Camelot and even walk the Grey Paths of the Dead. With a mix of Malory, a touch of Tolkien, and a hint of humor, The Monster Specialist chronicles a tale of courage, tenacity, honor, and love.

The Monster Specialist is illustrated by Anke Eissmann.

Edward S. Louis, *The Monster Specialist*
Zurich and Jena 2014 (Tales of Yore Series No. 3), ISBN 978-3-905703-23-8

Tales of Yore Series (earlier books)

Kay Woollard, *The Terror of Tatty Walk. A Frightener*
CD and Booklet, Zurich and Berne 2000, ISBN 978-3-9521424-2-4

Kay Woollard, *Wilmot's Very Strange Stone or What came of building "snobbits"*
CD and booklet, Zurich and Berne 2001, ISBN 978-3-9521424-4-8

Information for authors

Authors interested in contributing to our publications can learn more about the services we offer on the "services for authors" section of our web pages.

http://www.walking-tree.org/authors

Manuscripts and project proposals can be submitted to the board of editors (please include an SAE):

Walking Tree Publishers
CH-3052 Zollikofen
Switzerland

e-mail: info@walking-tree.org

Walking Tree Publishers, Zurich and Jena, 2019

www.ingramcontent.com/pod-product-compliance
Lightning Source LLC
Chambersburg PA
CBHW050829230426
43667CB00012B/1927